SAYAJIRAO GAEKWAD III

Uma Balasubramaniam is a graduate in history from the Faculty of Arts of the M.S. University of Baroda. Brought up in the cosmopolitan environment of Bombay and schooled in the convent school tradition, her broadminded views are evident in her writings, particularly in her debut novel *Beyond The Horizon,* published in 2015.

Uma began her writing career in 2002 contributing to various publications like *The Hindu, The Indian Express* and the *Deccan Chronicle.*

Uma lives in Chennai with her husband and they are parents to three children settled in the United States. Uma's interest in history takes the Balasubramaniams travelling around the world and writing about the places they have visited.

SAYAJIRAO GAEKWAD III
The Maharaja of Baroda

Uma Balasubramaniam

Published by
Rupa Publications India Pvt. Ltd 2019
7/16, Ansari Road, Daryaganj
New Delhi 110002

Sales Centres:
Allahabad Bengaluru Chennai
Hyderabad Jaipur Kathmandu
Kolkata Mumbai

Copyright © Uma Balasubramaniam 2019

Photograph copyright © Royal Gaekwad Collection, Baroda. The photo captions have been provided by the Royal Gaekwad Collection, Baroda. The spellings in the captions might differ from those mentioned elsewhere in the book.

The views and opinions expressed in this book are the author's own and the facts are as reported by her which have been verified to the extent possible, and the publishers are not in any way liable for the same.

All rights reserved.
No part of this publication may be reproduced, transmitted, or stored in a retrieval system, in any form or by any means, electronic, mechanical, photocopying, recording or otherwise, without the prior permission of the publisher.

ISBN: 978-93-5333-792-6

First impression 2019

10 9 8 7 6 5 4 3 2 1

Printed at Parksons Graphics Pvt. Ltd., Mumbai

The moral right of the author has been asserted.

This book is sold subject to the condition that it shall not, by way of trade or otherwise, be lent, resold, hired out, or otherwise circulated, without the publisher's prior consent, in any form of binding or cover other than that in which it is published.

*This book is dedicated to His Highness,
the late Maharaja Sayajirao Gaekwad III,
and to the wonderful people of Baroda*

Contents

Foreword — xi
Preface — xiii
Map of the Erstwhile Baroda State — xvi-xvii
Royal Baroda Family: Family Tree — xviii

PART 1

1. Early History of the Gaekwad Royal Family — 3
2. Tussle with the Peshwas — 13
3. Internal Disputes and Conflicts — 17
4. Over to the British — 21
5. First Anglo-Maratha War (1775–82) — 28
6. Govindrao's Reign and the Emergence of British Dominance — 32
7. Factors Leading to the Third Maratha War (1817–18) — 43
8. Sayajirao Gaekwad II — 51
9. Ganpatrao Gaekwad — 67
10. Khanderao Gaekwad — 70
11. The Bahandari System — 80
12. Plots and Intrigues to Depose Malharrao Gaekwad — 86
13. Back to Kavlana — 104

PART 2

14. Maharaja Sayajirao Gaekwad III — 109
15. Education of the Young Sayajirao III — 115
16. Baroda Acquires a Queen — 124
17. Investiture and Handing over the Reins — 126
18. Durbar Etiquette and British Protocol — 133
19. Sayajirao III Establishing His Powers as a Ruler — 137

20.	Off with the Old and On with the New!	142
21.	Tour of the Province	145
22.	Another Tragedy and a Wedding	153
23.	Playing Professor Higgins to Chimnabai II	156
24.	Early Reforms	159
25.	Sayajirao III's First European Tour	160
26.	Administration of the State from Abroad	166
27.	Some Flak, Reynolds and Administration	172
28.	A Battle of Wits	180
29.	Colonel John Biddulph: A Resident in Phayre's Garb	185
30.	Leaving Troubled Waters for Distant Lands	195
31.	A Difficult Phase	202
32.	A European Trip	209
33.	Widow Remarriage Gets a Boost	220
34.	Purposeful Speeches and Land Reforms	222
35.	The Silver Jubilee	233
36.	Sedition in the Air	243
37.	The Coronation Durbar Incident	250
38.	The Truth about Sedition	269
39.	Chimnabai II Steps In	288
40.	Over to Scotland Yard	294
41.	Sayajirao III: A Patron of Arts	306
42.	Abandonment of the Purdah and a Royal Escape	309
43.	Farzand-i-Khas-i-Inglish-Daulatia	313
44.	Sayajirao III: A Patron of Music	317
45.	Aftermath of the First World War	319
46.	Okhamandal's History	327
47.	The Villiers Debacle	335
48.	Sayajirao III as an Administrator	338
49.	Declining Health of Sayajirao III	345

50. The Golden Jubilee of Sayajirao III's Rule	351
51. Visit of Their Excellencies, the Readings	354
52. Port Rights in Okhamandal	359
53. Busy Days	362
54. Sayajirao III's 'Split Personality'	367
55. Sayajirao III's Address to Professors and Students	372
56. Sayajirao III: The Reformer	374
57. Establishing the Library System in Baroda	379
58. Social Reforms and General Administration	382
59. A Portrait of Chimnabai II	390
60. Transforming Baroda	393
61. Revamping the Judiciary and Other Systems	405
62. Family Affairs	426
63. Rebellion in the Air	451
64. Birthday Celebrations	459
65. Niggling Doubts and Anxieties	466
66. The Diamond Jubilee and Thereafter	469
Epilogue	491
Acknowledgements	496
Endnotes	498
Bibliography	510

Foreword

It is a matter of delight for me to write this foreword for Uma Balasubramaniam's well-researched book depicting the many-splendoured personality of H.H. Maharaja Sayajirao Gaekwad III. While a good number of writings on the illustrious Maharaja do exist, a lot still remains to be written, particularly because a significant body of the archives of Baroda state has not yet been investigated by scholars and historians.

Balasubramaniam's book is distinguished from other writings on the subject by its emphasis on moving beyond the known facts relating to the life of Maharaja Sayajirao III. In fact, the book is not just a biographical sketch of his life and contributions; it also tells the story of the whole Gaekwad dynasty, beginning with Pilajirao Gaekwad.

Maharaja Sayajirao III, who ruled for more than six decades, ranks among the most visionary and progressive princely rulers of modern India. In the late nineteenth century, when the movement for social reforms was at an incipient stage in India and innovative approaches to governance were not heard of much, he promoted such policies and reforms that made Baroda state one of the most progressive and vibrant places at that time. He prohibited the evil practices of untouchability and child marriage in his state. He also supported several bright young people, including the great Dr Babasaheb Ambedkar, to receive high-quality education abroad. The imprint of his reformist, progressive and innovative approach could be found in several spheres: higher education institutions, provision of free and compulsory education for all, encouragement of education of the backward classes, establishment of libraries across towns and villages in his state, judiciary and legislations of Baroda state, agricultural reforms, panchayat system, construction of water reservoirs and roads, development of railways and so on. Indeed, there are several lessons to be learnt for today's policymakers and administrators from the philosophy and welfare-oriented system of governance implemented successfully by Maharaja Sayajirao Gaekwad III.

Balasubramaniam's book is rich in terms of historical facts, analysis and style of writing. Being an alumnus of the Maharaja Sayajirao University of Baroda, she lends a personal touch to the analysis in her book. There is no doubt that it would interest and appeal to scholars and laypersons alike. It would help them appreciate the leadership prowess and administrative acumen of the great Maharaja Sayajirao Gaekwad III.

Rajmata Shubhanginiraje Gaekwad
Chancellor, the Maharaja Sayajirao University of Baroda
June 2019

Preface

I have been asked by quite a few people in Baroda why I chose to write about Maharaja Sayajirao Gaekwad III, the erstwhile ruler of Baroda state. My answer is this—there comes a time in one's life when one has mellowed with age and the tendency to look back is far more attractive than looking forward. The truth is that there is really nothing to look forward to when one becomes decrepit at the age of seventy-three!

Baroda did a lot for us as a family and I look back upon those years as the best time of my life. The opportunity that presented itself to study in the most prestigious university of India at that point of time was a golden one. I was a student in the Faculty of Arts (Baroda College), and the experience was richly rewarding as it helped me to evolve as a human being with a broad outlook without losing sight of the fundamental values so essential in our life's journey. It is time now to pay back what was given to me unstintingly by the founder of the university, the faculty of the university and the people of Baroda.

This book is a tribute to the phenomenal human being and the righteous ruler—Maharaja Sayajirao III—who left his mark as a leader of the people. It is written with the intent to offer my gratitude in a small, humble way to the great king of Baroda. I hope that the royal family of the Gaekwads in Baroda will accept this tribute for its sincerity with which it has been written.

A historian tries his best to reconstruct the past and bring it to life, to weave a rich tapestry filled with facts, figures and places coloured with not only landscapes, but also events. It has not been an easy task, but nevertheless a fascinating one. I have tried my best to marshal all the facts impartially and bring to readers the events that took place more than a century ago. It is indeed the historian's chief concern to conjure up the atmosphere of the past, to see things in the light in which they were seen centuries ago when circumstances of time, place and people were different from what they are now.

With most writers, imagination is synonymous with the invention of characters, places, events and other factors but for a historian, it is recreative and reconstructive. It becomes the medium of making that which was once dead alive—or one might say a triumphant walk with the spirits of the dead over an empty grave.

History is a science but it is also an art like the great historians Thomas Babington Macaulay, Charles Downer Hazen and S. P. Verma have observed. To hold the attention of a reader while enumerating facts and figures is not an ordinary task and demands the consummate artistry of the writer.

I am not a historian but I have donned the mantle of one for the purpose of writing this book.

Sayajirao Gaekwad III: The Maharaja of Baroda retells the history of the Gaekwad royal family of Baroda. It traces the ancestry of the family and recounts past events to explain their ultimate supremacy as Marathas over a Gujarat province and the establishment of their sovereignty in Gujarat. The focus in the story is on Maharaja Sayajirao Gaekwad III, his ascendancy to the throne, his relationship with the British government in India, his remarkable administration and his outstanding reforms, which were a result of his several trips abroad where he observed the systems of Western countries and studied their infrastructure. Some facts about his family life are mentioned as well, which explain the regimental discipline he enforced upon his grandchildren.

There are several books written about the Gaekwads of Baroda and there are many volumes on Maharaja Sayajirao Gaekwad III in Marathi and Gujarati but as far as I know not many are available in English. Most importantly, there are many people of the present generation in Baroda, particularly students in the Faculty of Arts who claim ignorance of the identity of the founder of their university. Another fact that has shocked me to the core is that the majority of Indians, particularly in the south of our country, are not even aware that there was once a great ruler by the name of Sayajirao Gaekwad III who was responsible for contributing to obtaining freedom from the British for India. He funded the Indian national movement till he went to his grave. But surprisingly, there is not one statue of the Maharaja in any of the major cities of India. I fondly hope that my book will do its job of dispelling this ignorance from the minds of all people and enlighten them with knowledge.

The fact that his true identity lay in being a farmer's son was never obscured by the grandeur of the palace and the immense riches of the Gaekwads. He was perpetually worried about the hardships that villagers faced in times of adversity in the villages of Gujarat. The chief among these adverse factors were the scarcity of water and the lack of education of the villagers, which acted as impediments to raise their standards of living. These two main factors drove him relentlessly to secure both, not only for the villagers but also for the people of Baroda. He was also aware that many of the problems arose from the social taboos and superstitions that governed the actions of the people and set about to remove these prejudices through reforms. He achieved all this in spite of the hostile environment created by priggish British aristocrats and also by those who ran the machinery of the British government in India.

On a deeper analysis, one fact emerges from the history of Maharaja Sayajirao Gaekwad III—he was born to rule! Lord Brahma, the creator of our destinies, had a great hand in it. The first step had been taken by his adoptive father Maharaja Khanderao Gaekwad who had secured adoption rights from the British government for his timely help in the Sepoy Mutiny. The second step was taken by Queen Jamnabai whose connivance with Colonel Robert Phayre, British Resident in Baroda, had Maharaja Malharrao deposed from the throne of Baroda after which she exercised her right to adopt an heir. Third, the propitious words that fate had prompted Maharaja Sayajirao Gaekwad III to utter secured him the throne. But, it did not stop with Maharaja Sayajirao Gaekwad sitting on the throne; the divine hand of fate continued to guide the ruler till the end of his life. It is now up to the reader to find out how destiny's favoured child matched wits with and won over a battle with the supreme power that was wielding its baton over India, more than a century ago.

No doubt great leaders of the Indian national movement and various governments after India attained her independence did constructive work and laid the foundation for our success today as one of the most progressive nations of the world. No doubt the present government too is doing its best to keep up the glorious tradition of the past in the country.

However, we also need to remember the great ruler of Baroda who unstintingly funded the freedom movement and devoted his entire life for the cause of humanity. I fondly hope this book will be able to discard the ignorance from the minds of those who are unaware of this fact and would request the government of India to commemorate this noble ruler by erecting statues of him in all the important cities of India as the late Maharaja Sayajirao Gaekwad III of Baroda richly deserves.

MAP OF THE ERSTWHILE BARODA STATE

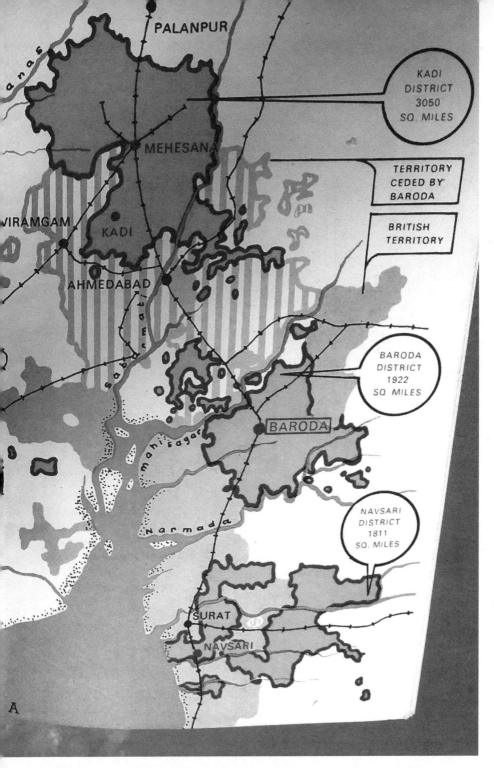

Photograph courtesy: Maharaja Fatehsingh Museum, courtesy Manda Hingurao, the curator of the museum.

Royal Baroda Family: Family Tree

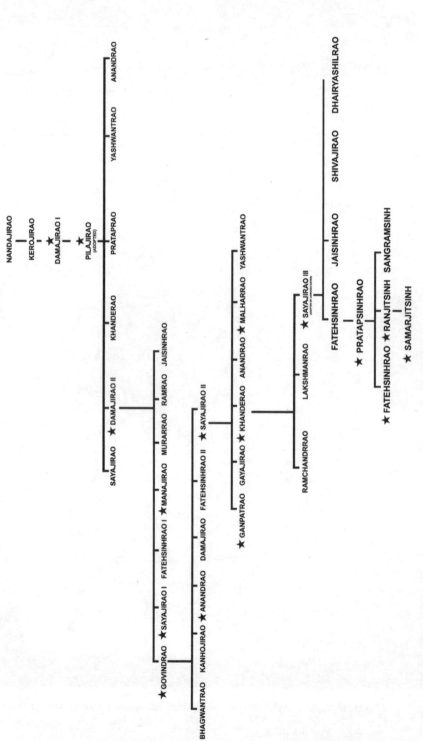

Source: *Sayajirao of Baroda: The Prince and the Man* by Fatehsinghrao Gaekwad, 1989.

PART 1

1
Early History of the Gaekwad Royal Family

The story of Gopalrao Gaekwad, whose ancestry can be traced to Pilajirao Gaekwad, begins like a fairy tale.

Once upon a time, there lived a boy named Gopalrao in the small village of Kavlana in Nasik district. He had a fairly happy and carefree childhood which he spent playing with his brothers in the vast fields belonging to his father. One fine morning, when he was thirteen years old, some people from Baroda arrived in his village and took him, his brother and his cousins to the royal palace as Jamnabai, queen of Baroda, had expressed a desire to meet them. The palace was beautiful, the queen gracious and they were very well looked after.

One morning, Jamnabai sat the boys down and asked each one in turn, 'Why do you think you have been brought here?'

Some replied, 'to see the city', others answered, 'for a holiday'.

Then, it was the turn of the thirteen-year-old boy to answer. The queen duly asked him, 'Gopal, why do *you* think *you* have been brought here?'

Looking her straight in the eye the lad replied, smiling, 'Why? To rule Baroda of course!'

The beautiful queen drew the child near her and whispered into his ear, 'And so you shall, my boy, so you shall!'

True to the words of the queen, Gopalrao came, saw and conquered Baroda with the same astuteness that is inherent among the truly great who are destined to rule, since they are chosen by the divine hand of fate.

Gopalrao Gaekwad was renamed Sayajirao Gaekwad III at the adoption ceremony—and the day he sat on the gaddi (throne) was the dawn of a new era, an era of happiness and contentment for the people of the state of Baroda. The wisdom, greatness and magnanimity of the king of Baroda, Maharaja Sayajirao Gaekwad III who administered the state of Gujarat from

1878 to 1939, not only brought prosperity in terms of material gains but something far more precious—he raised awareness in the people of the importance of education and the power of possessing knowledge.

To unravel the fascinating history of the Gaekwads we must travel far back in time to a place called Bhare in Haveli taluka, a subdistrict of Poona (modern-day Pune), for it was there that it all began.

The ancestry of the Gaekwads can be traced to Nandaji Matre, a prosperous farmer credited with the ownership of more than one village. Perhaps it was because he was the headman of these villages and oversaw their administration that he came to be addressed as Mantri, which, plainly put, means 'minister' and from Nandaji Matre, he became Nandaji Mantri. The story, of course, does not stop here. His act of saving a cow from a Muslim butcher's knife was applauded by the Hindus of that district. This act earned him the reputation of a 'cow protector' and the name Mantri radically transformed to Gaekwad, which means 'protector of cows'. It is further believed that the Gaekwads of Dwarka are descendants of Lord Krishna. The legend of Krishna portrays him as an ancestor of the Gaekwads, which fits with his avatar of being a cowherd as well as firmly establishes his royal Kshatriya lineage.

Returning to the story of Nandaji Gaekwad, his son Keroji had four sons, out of whom only two are worthy of attention—Damaji and Jhingoji Gaekwad. However, before we get into the history of these two, we need to digress a bit and talk about the Dabhades who in a way laid the first stone of the Gaekwad Empire.

Right after the Kurukshetra war in 3132 BCE, there were different dynasties that took over India; noteworthy among them were the Chavada dynasty, the Solanki dynasty and the Vaghela dynasty which ended in AD 1299 when the last Vaghela ruler Karna was defeated by Alauddin Khilji. This brought about theMuslim power in India beginning with the Khiljis.

For a little over a century, Gujarat formed a part of the Delhi Empire which, during the reigns of both the Khiljis and Muhammad bin Tughlaq, reached incredible heights of prosperity, only to collapse later due to the quixotic administration of Muhammad bin Tughlaq. Subsequently, at the commencement of the fifteenth century, the house of the Ahmedabad kings was founded under a very capable ruler, Ahmed Shah, who was able to assert his independence. As a result of his efforts and those of some of his able successors, the province of Gujarat became extremely prosperous and the most important state outside the Delhi Empire. It is not surprising then that it soon became the bone of contention between different factions of Maratha clansmen comprising the Peshwas, Holkars, Scindias and Gaekwads.

The Mughal and Maratha wars were fought between 1680 and 1707. When Emperor Aurangzeb died, the Muslim edifice built by Emperor Akbar crumbled and the Maratha confederacy was established by Chhatrapati Shivaji Bhonsle. The Marathas were ably aided by tribesmen from the hilly areas, including the Bhils and the Kolis. They were anxious to free themselves from Muslim domination, as were the Rajput rulers who had established themselves in the distant mountainous peninsula. All of them hailed the Marathas as the saviours of independence from Muslim persecution. Hindu landowners in Gujarat felt the same way and, thus, amidst this cry for freedom against Muslim tyranny, the Marathas entered Gujarat and gained a strong foothold there.

The Marathas had no administrative experience—they were strong, able-bodied men who used their physical prowess on the battlefield rather than in administrative affairs, they were better at working out military strategies than solving issues in the administration, whereas the Peshwas, a prime ministerial position created by Shivaji's grandson Prince Shahu, were Brahmins and had the brains, ability *and* the experience to do so and were also capable enough to command an army. Shahu was also indolent and couldn't exert himself much. After Shivaji's death in 1680, the Peshwas gained in power and influence under Prince Shahu. Balaji Vishwanath, who was Prince Shahu's counsellor, friend and revenue officer, introduced a new revenue policy which was designed to consolidate the state and to render Brahmin assistance indispensable to Prince Shahu, by which, he made a complex division of the revenues between Prince Shahu and his sardars (chieftains) in 1719. Broadly speaking, his system implied placing the entire responsibility for the collection of chauth (one-fourth part of the sale of the land revenue) and sardeshmukhi (an additional 10 per cent levy on top of the chauth) on the Maratha sardars. Out of these collections, a fixed share was to be paid to the king—sardeshmukhi plus 34 per cent of the chauth. The king thus became heavily dependent on his sardars for finances. Care was taken to divide this responsibility of collecting chauth and sardeshmukhi in such a way that no individual Maratha sardar could easily dominate over large areas, as these were controlled by the Peshwa via a centralized system of administration. Since the administration was still in the hands of the Peshwa, over a period of time this gave him absolute control over the dominions of Gujarat. The Maratha sardars were given an added incentive like estates for their plundering and overrunning of Mughal territory which made them practically independent of the king. However, by the time Sayajirao II ascended the gaddi, the sardars had been reduced to nothing, a reason for their apathy towards defence.

The Dabhades, a faction of the Maratha clan, came into prominence during Prince Shahu's reign. The Dabhade's ancestry can be traced to Bajajirao Dabhade whose son Yeshwant Rao Dabhade had been a personal bodyguard to Shivaji and probably this fact drew the attention of the Peshwa to his son Khanderao Dabhade who became a military leader. The family rose to prominence when he was conferred the title of Sarsenapati (commander-in-chief) on 11 January 1717 by Prince Shahu of Satara.

Now, it is time to return to Keroji Gaekwad and his four sons who were farming in the village of Bhare. One of them had an adventurous spirit and decided to not follow in his father's footsteps. Equipped with a horse and a sword, he left the village and rode on to enlist himself in the army commanded by Khanderao Dabhade. The man was no other than Damajirao Gaekwad who rose to be the deputy commander of the Maratha army under Khanderao Dabhade. Damajirao I, making his saddle his home and throne, set out on a number of military exploits, never leaving the saddle till he had achieved his goal. He rose to the rank of deputy commander-in-chief and was conferred the title of Shamsher Bahadur. However, shortly after, he died in battle in 1721 and was succeeded by his nephew Pilajirao Gaekwad, who had accompanied his uncle on his campaigns and had seen a good deal of military planning and strategies. He was adopted by Damajirao I since Damajirao I had no sons of his own. Pilajirao was Damajirao I's brother Jhingoji's son. Khanderao Dabhade too died shortly after a battle against Shahu's opposers and was succeeded by his son Trimbak Rao Dabhade.

Pilajirao was no milk- and water- soldier but a hard-headed professional and, like his uncle, he was a dynamic, adventurous and ambitious person striving hard to attain his goal. Very early in his career, he became an important field commander in his own right. On account of his discipline as head of a squadron of forty horses, he was promoted to the command of three hundred in 1718. Heady with his newfound success, he dashed off on a campaign of revenue expedition in Gujarat which was an unqualified success in spite of stiff resistance from the Mughal soldiers installed in Surat. As a result, he was rewarded with a promotion as the independent commander of a wing of cavalry and was given Navapur as an independent station to be used as his own headquarters. The place was ideally suited for carrying on further raids in Gujarat. However, he found to his dismay that a small Maratha outpost had already been established there and the place was under the jurisdiction of Kanthaji Kadam Bande. Kanthaji held the same status in rank and position as Pilajirao, but Pilajirao and his uncle had held Kanthaji in high regard earlier as his rank and position had come directly from the king. Apart from that, he had been on the Gujarat scene much before the Gaekwads and as such was very *au fait* with the thinking of the local people living there. Needless to say, Pilajirao was well aware of the situation and decided to hold his horses and cooperate; he even went as far as carrying out a few joint expeditions along with him and his men.

Pilajirao, on his earlier expeditions, had set his eyes on the fort of Songadh, standing on the hilly terrain of Gujarat and inhabited by the Mewasi Bhils, as being ideally suited to carry out his operations in Gujarat. From the fort, he had the vantage position of spotting the enemy before they could spot him. Pilajirao, along with his men, captured the fort, then set about strengthening its fortifications. It was a step in the right direction because soon a strong Mughal army was dispatched from Surat to dislodge him from his stronghold, but the attack was repelled and the attackers fled. Pilajirao was left free to ensconce himself and his battalion in Songadh which became the family's bastion for half a century or more. Thus, Pilajirao laid the foundation for Gaekwad rule in Baroda.

Pilajirao's meteoric rise to power, from commanding forty horses to a thousand within a short time of two years, during which he also won a major battle and repulsed another, aroused resentment and envy among his colleagues, especially when he inherited the position and title of Shamsher Bahadur from his uncle. When he increased the strength of his contingent to three pagas (wings of the cavalry), rivalries between him and his colleagues reached out of proportion and had far-reaching consequences for the country as a whole.

Things were happening in the Peshwa court too. Balaji Vishwanath, who was the Peshwa of the Maratha confederacy in Poona, died in 1720. Balaji Vishwanath's tenure of office is significant because it was after he captured most of the Konkan coast that he rose from the rank of a revenue officer to become the Peshwa on 16 November 1713. His son Bajirao succeeded him as the Peshwa, as the rank was made hereditary by Prince Shahu. Bajirao I was perhaps the most daunting figure amongst all the Peshwas. Possessed with a brilliant, conniving brain, indefatigable energy and ambition, it is said that he fought forty-one battles without losing a single one! He is noted for his rapid tactical movements in battle, using his cavalry.

After Khanderao Dabhade's death in 1721, the office of senapati passed on to his son Trimbakrao Dabhade though unlike earlier, the senapati was now a nominal head, with the real power resting with Peshwa Bajirao I. Gujarat, over which the senapati had exercised control earlier, was now no longer his 'exclusive preserve' and Bajirao exercised his power there through his deputy Udaji Powar. He was to collect the revenue for the Marathas from certain territories in Gujarat. Thus, there were four different commanders who were allotted the task of collecting tribute from Gujarat—Kanthaji who acted as the king's deputy, Udaji Powar who took orders from Peshwa Bajirao I, Trimbakrao Dabhade who was only exercising his right inherited from his father Khanderao Dabhade, and lastly, Pilajirao who was the deputy commander of the senapati, his 'authorized agent'.

☆

Gujarat was regarded as a Mughal province and it was accepted as such even by the Marathas who, however, had been given the right to levy chauth (tribute) in Gujarat by the Mughal emperor Muhammad Shah in 1719. The Maratha confederacy, including the Gaekwads, affirmed from that date that only they had the exclusive right to do so.

The four appointed agents of their respective masters had their task cut out for them—the extraction of chauth—for which they made annual expeditions to Gujarat, sometimes using strongarm tactics for the purpose, so much so that they began to be looked upon as terrorists, no better than their Muslim overlords. Pilajirao, realizing that it was futile to arouse the hatred and animosity of the people of Gujarat, set out to wrest large tracts of territory from the Mughal commanders and bring in a more benevolent way of acquiring the revenue from the land so as to not antagonize the people of Gujarat. Pilajirao, in the role of a knight in shining armour, engaged himself in rescuing pretty maidens from lecherous Mughal officers and won the confidence of the locals and many tribal chiefs. His rule was seen as a relief from Mughal tyranny. With the increase in Pilajirao's domination over the people of Gujarat, the Muslim control over the province weakened and was doomed to perish. The hilly, forested area beyond Songadh was inhabited by the Bhils and Kolis whose chiefs willingly cooperated with Pilajirao and enabled him to take over most of Gujarat.

Pilajirao's hold over Gujarat kindled resentment in his fellow commanders; they thought Pilajirao had set himself up as the ruler of Gujarat when his sole responsibility had been to collect chauth from the province, and, therefore, he had no right to conquer and occupy territory. This breach in Pilaji's conduct was considered reason enough to open hostilities. Kanthaji Bande marched with a column against Pilajirao, but he was intercepted by the Nizam of Hyderabad who wanted both of them as his allies. The Mughal Empire was disintegrating under petty skirmishes and hedonistic rulers. The Nizam after resigning from his post as the vizier in the court of Muhammad Shah, the emperor of Delhi, set off for the Deccan to resume the viceroyalty there. He vanquished Mubariz Khan who had been installed there nine years earlier and set up his own government. Afterwards, he was formally declared, 'Asif Jah', the highest tribute paid to a minister by the emperor of Delhi. He was now anxious to set up his own rule in Gujarat and administer the province through a deputy appointed by him. The appointed deputy governor was Hameed Khan who had the wily mind of a fox. The Nizam reached Gujarat at the head of a force and persuaded Pilajirao and Kanthaji to support his cause and for their help he promised them equal share in the right to collect chauth in Gujarat. Pilajirao was given the area south of the Mahi River and Kanthaji was given the area north of the river. Thus the Nizam succeeded in patching up their differences and enlisting both of them as his supporters. By 1725, Pilajirao had thrown out most of the Mughal satraps in the area of Baroda but could only collect chauth in the area south of the Mahi River and beyond.

However, the patch-up between Kanthaji and Pilajirao caused feuds to flare up between the other two contenders—Senapati Trimbakrao Dabhade and Bajirao I.

The franchise for collecting chauth was nothing short of a licence to raid the territory and enrich oneself. By the mid-eighteenth century many of them began to conquer territories within their sphere of operations and even set themselves up as rulers, though not independently but as feudal lords answerable only to the king. As a result of this, franchise for a traditionally rich land like Gujarat drew many contenders. In 1720, Prince Shahu had passed on the entire responsibility of collecting chauth in Gujarat to his senapati Dabhade; likewise, he had allotted Malwa to Bajirao I. The Maratha generals, taking full advantage of this given responsibility, had begun to acquire territories in their field of operations. In view of this, Bajirao I suggested to Trimbakrao Dabhade that he should part with half his conquests in Gujarat to him and in a reciprocal gesture, he would do the same with his conquests in Malwa.

Trimbakrao turned down the proposal, but in doing so he incurred the wrath of the most powerful man in the Maratha kingdom.

Earlier also, Pilajirao had crossed swords with Trimbakrao over his Gujarat conquests and Trimbakrao had considered Pilajirao an interloper in Gujarat.

Gujarat was perhaps the richest province in India at that time, not only because of its crops and cotton, but its opium exports to China had brought in a lot of revenue into the state. It must be remembered that the British had already established themselves in most parts of India a century earlier and the East India Company was becoming a powerful influence. The British too had their eyes on Gujarat as with her ports in Cambay, Daman, Diu, Surat, Okhamandal and Broach; the province opened out to the Arabian Sea, making overseas trade possible. This led to a dispute between the senapati who had Pilajirao and Kanthaji on his side and Bajirao I had Udaji Powar on his.

The peshwa, roused to a pitch at the turn of events, decided to force the issue and with a strong army under his brother's command, he attacked Ahmedabad and coerced the Mughal governor to give the Peshwas the exclusive right to collect chauth in Gujarat or face battle. The governor Sarbuland Khan faced with a Hobson's choice, meekly submitted and made sure of the Peshwa's support for the future. The Peshwa also guaranteed protection of Gujarat from marauders and freebooters like the Gaekwad, Kanthaji and others. The arrangement was regardless of the fact that the senapati had an exclusive right to collect chauth in Gujarat.

This is considered a senseless dispute among the Maratha clan governed by greed and egotism that outlived the chief players in the drama for gain and was passed down to their descendants who in the years to come were forced to seek an alliance with the British. It brought an increase in British power and interference from the East India Company—with disastrous results!

Six long years went by before the issue was resolved during which time Gujarat underwent another change of governors and was 'ravaged by a plundering expedition of such rapacity that it made the Maratha raids look like tame affairs.'[1]

Emperor Muhammad Shah of Delhi was so infuriated with Sarbuland Khan for ceding revenue rights to the Marathas that he sent an army under Abhai Singh, ruler of Marwar (Jodhpur), to severely reprimand him and replace him as the governor. In 1730, Sarbuland Khan was defeated and imprisoned in Delhi and Abhai Singh lost no time in enriching his coffers with the spoils. Meanwhile, Pilajirao unaware of these happenings continued to consolidate his position in Gujarat and extract chauth from the areas within his dominion. Bajirao, a seething spectator to these acquisitions, set out with a formidable army in 1730 to vanquish Gaekwad and subordinate him. Trimbakrao, who had earlier incurred the Peshwa's displeasure by turning down his proposal, now found himself on the brink of war with him. Quickly putting aside his animosity over acquisitions with Pilaji he enlisted his help. Pilajirao and Senapati Trimbakrao joined forces and prepared for battle. The new governor of Gujarat, Abhai Singh, instead of allying with Gaekwad, invited the Peshwa to a wheel and deal meeting where he offered him the same terms that had been offered to the Peshwa earlier by Sarbuland Khan, in return for 'protection'. The Peshwa, after this agreeable turn of affairs, swooped down on the combined forces of the senapati and Gaekwad on 1 April 1731. The battle took place in Dabhoi, a place near Baroda, ending in a victory for Bajirao I. Trimbakrao, it is said, behaved with exemplary courage on the battlefield but was slain along with Pilajirao's eldest son

Sayajirao I. Pilajirao was badly wounded. Dismayed at the thought of the consequences of killing a senapati, and anxious to get back to his hometown as the weather conditions were not conducive for delays, he did not press his advantage. Instead, he tried to resolve his differences with his adversaries in a battlefield settlement. Bajirao, as a conciliatory step, made Trimbakrao's younger brother Yeshwantrao the senapati with the stipulation that half of the revenue of Gujarat should be handed over to Prince Shahu's treasury and that additional conquests of tributary states should be accounted for. As Yeshwantrao was underage, Pilajirao was appointed as his mutalik or regent by Bajirao I. Pilajirao had now the resources of the senapati at his disposal, was the master of Songadh, Baroda and Dabhoi, an ally of the Bhils and Kolis and a friend of the zamindars. The people of Gujarat were now friendly with him whereas earlier they had viewed him with suspicion. Handicapped as he had been earlier with his credentials being suspect, now he was considered altogether impeccable. The interloper had become the official entrusted with the affairs of Gujarat. Impervious to the Mughal governor's hatred, he went about on his mulukgiri expeditions (excursions to extract tributes from the local people) with the same zest as before. Thus all of Abhai Singh's attempts to subdue him proved futile.

Ultimately, resorting to treachery, Abhai Singh had Pilajirao assassinated by a Marwari in his tent at Dakor in 1732. Taking advantage of the situation, he hurried with his troops, who under Dhokal Singh took the fort of Baroda and handed it over to Sher Khan Babi.

Pilajirao's eldest living son Damajirao Gaekwad II became the worthy successor to his father's position and title of Shamsher Bahadur. Damajirao II was as enterprising, ambitious and as adventurous as his father was and his tenure was marked with territorial achievements. If the foundation of the Gaekwad sovereignty was laid by his father Pilajirao, who, interestingly, was also responsible for bringing the gaddi from Songadh, Damajirao II consolidated the Gaekwad sovereignty in Gujarat most successfully.

2

Tussle with the Peshwas

The mourning period in Pilajirao's family was not quite over when Abhai Singh attacked Baroda again and drove the family to their stronghold, Songadh.

Damajirao II had two younger brothers named Prataprao and Khanderao. Damajirao II, after a brief period of inactivity for the time that he had needed to put his resources together and seething with fury over his father's murder, set out to avenge it. He hit back at Abhai Singh in 1734 with such verocity that Abhai Singh was hard put to defend himself. Damajirao II retook Baroda from its Mughal commander Sher khan Babi and it has been in the Gaekwads' possession ever since. He then ravaged the territory around Jodhpur, placing Abhai Singh's personal domain in such jeopardy that the latter had to rush there from Baroda, leaving Gujarat to fend for itself under the crafty Ratansingh.

Apart from the Mughal power, Damajirao II had to contend with the Powars, Bandes and Holkars who knew it was a now- or never- situation for them to stake a claim in the Gujarat revenue, which they did venture to do but failed. While Damajirao II was driving out the Marvadis, his agent (deputy) Ranghoji Bhonsle (Ranghoji Bhonsle and Rangoji was the same person. Ranghoji Bhonsle was a Maratha general from Nagpur during the reign of Prince Shahu.) met Kanthaji Kadam Bande in the battlefield at Anand-Mogri and defeated him there. Then, he obtained from Momin Khan who had been made governor of Gujarat in 1737 after Abhay Singh had been removed from that post, the chauth of the revenues north of the Mahi River. He was soon joined by Damajirao II who entered Viramgam after expelling the kasbalis (small-town dwellers) of that town. Ranghoji had to further contend with an attack from Ratan Singh who defeated him near Viramgam. Meanwhile, Kanthaji, ambitious as ever, sided with the Peshwa and invaded northern Gujarat with Malharrao Holkar. Their ambitious venture however stopped with pillaging Vadnagar and Palanpur as they feared a head-on collision with Damajirao's brother Prataprao Gaekwad's powerful army. Udaji Powar too made an attempt to seize the Gujarat spoils but was defeated in a battle and lost his life. Momin Khan realized he could not expel the Marvadis without Damajirao II's help and, at the same time, he was also anxious to establish himself as an independent ruler. Thus, he purchased the alliance of the Marathas by the cession of one-half of the produce of Gujarat with the exception of Ahmedabad, some lands in the neighbourhood and the port of Cambay. To these cessions, he subsequently added half the city of Ahmedabad and the entire district of Viramgam. The alliance made in good faith was kept till Momin Khan's death in 1743. Ranghoji was placed in charge of half of Ahmedabad as allotted to Damajirao II and to him by Governor Momin Khan and the two allies soon besieged Ahmedabad and got rid of Ratan Singh. Ranghoji was placed in charge of Ahmedabad city. Damajirao II, after his conquest of Ahmedabad, centred his attention on increasing his hold on Surat and was able to suppress the Kolis around Viramgam by capturing Bansda. He attempted a conquest on Broach (modern-day Bharuch) too but did not succeed though he managed to acquire a part of its revenues. After that he began assiduously to extend his domain and by 1740 Damajirao II became virtually the ruler of Gujarat.

There had been a tacit understanding between Damajirao II and Prataprao that whatever territorial conquests that either of them made—Damajirao II in Gujarat and Prataprao in Maharashtra, where he had opted to reside to look after the forty-six villages that had come to him as his share from his father Pilajirao—they would share it equally. But he was deprived of these villages when the Peshwa exchanged some of his own territory in Gujarat for them. So, while Damajirao II acquired more territory, Prataprao lost his forty-six villages and was forced to retire to Kavlana, a small village in the district of Nasik. Hence, his descendants came to be known as Kavlana Gaekwads.

Damaji II's other brother, Khanderao, used to accompany their father Pilajirao on his expeditions in Gujarat and was apportioned a part of Gujarat territory—Kadi—as fief; thus, that branch of the family came to be known as Kadi Gaekwads. Khanderao had no conscience whatsoever and became a thorn in Damajirao II's life from then on. First, he joined with Damajirao II's enemies to further his own interest and later even played Damaji II's one son against the other. He sided with Damajirao when it suited his own interests and betrayed him by siding with Damajirao II's enemy if it was more profitable to do so.

On the whole, Damajirao II paid little attention to his acquisitions in Gujarat and left the maintenance to his general Ranghoji Bhonsle. He waited anxiously in his mountain fortress in Songadh for the time when he would cross swords with the Peshwa. Damajirao II was no insignificant opponent who could be dismissed nonchalantly; rather he was the master of a large territory and was also the real chief of the party as Senapati Yeshwantrao Dabhade didn't possess any leadership qualities requisite in a leader. He had an ally in Ranghoji Bhonsle, the deadliest rival of Bajirao I. The Peshwa's own powers had increased to an incredible degree. At the head of the armies of the Peshwa, Scindia and Holkar, Bajirao had reached the gates of Delhi when Nadir Shah's invasion halted him in his tracks and checked his victorious career for some time. However, when the Peshwa was at the pinnacle of success, he suddenly died in April 1740 and Damajirao II believed that the moment he had been longing for had finally come.

Balaji Bajirao also known as Nana Saheb succeeded his father as the Peshwa and Damajirao II, hiding his disappointment, forged ahead and conquered Malwa.

Meanwhile, Bapuji Naik, a rich banker and a disappointed creditor of the Peshwas, had also vied for the peshwaship after Balaji Bajirao's death. However, he came to terms with Balaji Bajirao and invaded Gujarat. He even burnt Songadh but was forced to retire on the approach of Damajirao II's general Ranghoji's troops. Fida-ud-din, the acting viceroy after Momin Khan's death in 1743, summoned Muftakhir Khan and Sher Khan Babi to his assistance and after defeating Ranghoji forced him to surrender Borsad and Viramgam. However, soon after, Fida-ud-din fled the country, Ranghoji captured Petlad and Khanderao Gaekwad established his brother Damaji's rights over the city of Ahmedabad. By this gesture, he thought he stood to gain sometime in the future, as his brother was more occupied in fighting battles. Who knew what might happen on the battlefield? Damajirao II and Balaji Bajirao were too preoccupied with their own problems to really come to grips with one another. But the enmity created during the lifetime of Pilaji had been duly handed down to his son along with titles, privileges and responsibilities.

Meanwhile Prince Shahu's death triggered a succession scandal that rocked the Poona court.

The widowed queen Tarabai, queen of Chhatrapati Rajaram I of Satara, had many axes to grind with the Peshwa and was also fighting for succession to the throne for her grandson Rajaram II. She called on Damajirao II to rescue the young raja of Satara from the Peshwa's tentacles and the whole Maratha nation from the domination of the Brahmin party. Damajirao II answered the call and Umabai Dabhade, mother of Trimbakrao Dabhade, sent him as the head of an army of 15,000 men which he brought down from Songadh through the Salpi pass. The Peshwa's officers drew back before the onslaught of Damajirao II's forces which attacked and defeated them, and the pratinidi (representative) was won over to their cause. Soon after, the Peshwa's army was reorganized and attacked Damajirao II and his men encamping on the banks of the Venna River and defeated them. Damajirao II was forced to retreat with heavy losses. Meanwhile, Balaji Bajirao returned from the frontiers and learning of the situation, demanded as war indemnity half of the Gujarat conquests in addition to two and a half million rupees as arrears of tribute. Damajirao II pleaded that he was only a mutalik (regent) and had no right to cede territory. On the face of it this reasoning was rationally sound as Yeshwantrao Dabhade, though weak, considered himself the officially designated custodian of Gujarat. He also claimed to have used all his resources to pay Dabhade's creditors. Unfortunately for Damajirao II, Balaji Bajirao turned a deaf ear to this reasoning. He stalled for time, then after a few days, in a surprise attack on the Gaekwad encampment, took him and his immediate fellow advisers as prisoners. Later he had them sent to the fort of Lohgarh near Poona where they were confined within the four walls of the fort.

Damajirao II remained in the Peshwa's captivity for two years till March 1753. The Dabhades were deprived of their jagirs as well as their hereditary title of Senapati. Damajirao II, realizing it was better to make peace with the enemy, abandoned the services of the Dabhades which anyway ended with Yeshwantrao Dabhade who was unfit to be senapati. With this break, the significance of the Dabhades ends and the reign of the Gaekwads' dynasty as the Maratha chiefs of Gujarat begins.

3
Internal Disputes and Conflicts

Damajirao II was restless and very perturbed at the happenings in Gujarat and longed to be free. He realized that caught as he was in captivity, Balaji Bajirao, his arch-enemy, could make his own position in Gujarat stronger. Khanderao was unreliable and could easily be bought by the Peshwa, who anyway was sending out columns under his most trusted commanders to bring Gujarat under his control from the Mughals. But the attempt made by him was a resounding failure and the Peshwa realized he needed the Gaekwad's support if he was to control Gujarat. This induced him to negotiate with his prisoner. Thus, the two of them made an agreement which influenced the future of the whole of Gujarat.

Since earlier Pilajirao's debts had been paid erratically, his son Damajirao II was called upon to do so. He was instructed to pay a sum amounting to nearly Rs 8,00,000, maintain a troop of 10,000, always answer the Peshwa's call for aid, pay the Peshwa an annual tribute of Rs 5,25,000, part with half of his dominions and all his future conquests in land had to be accounted to him, besides paying a sum for maintaining the Dabhade family who had been politically removed from the scene. In return, Balaji Bajirao promised to assist him to capture Ahmedabad and rid Gujarat completely of Mughal domination. However, all was not lost for Gaekwad because of his conquests in Gujarat; his gains exceeded those of the Peshwa who did not know the territories of Gujarat as well as Gaekwad.

But Balaji Bajirao kept a close account of the debts that were owed by Gaekwad, thus affirming the subordination of one over the other. Though the Gaekwads were forced by circumstances to be subordinate to the Poona durbar, they were never servile. They must be applauded for their resoluteness because even when hit hard, they gathered fresh energy to combat their foes. The Gaekwads never heartily entered into the Maratha confederacy, of which Poona was the centre and was ruled arbitrarily by the Peshwa. They also never reconciled with the Peshwas. Damajirao II and Fatehsinghrao

Gaekwad I, as will be seen later, sided with Raghoba, the Peshwa's brother, in his war with the Poona ministry and Fatehsinghrao I with the English when they entered into rivalry with the Peshwa. Govindrao, Damajirao II's son, was saved by the British government from political annihilation and the administration of his successor delivered itself into the hands of the British government, rather than fall under Scindia, Holkar or the Peshwa. From this, we can gather how difficult and bitter the struggle was and how great the consequences.

The settlement with Balaji Bajirao had been distasteful to Damajirao II, but he did not allow it to deter him from his purpose nor hamper his stride. He knew he stood to gain by making peace with Balaji Bajirao who could be counted upon to make vast contributions to his campaigns in Gujarat, much more than the senapati had ever done. As if to prove this, Raghoba was gathering his forces to enter Gujarat at the head of a strong army. The partition of Gujarat took place in 1753 after Damajirao II was released from prison by Balaji Bajirao. He, along with the combined Maratha armies comprising Holkar, Raghoba, Scindia and others, undertook the siege of Ahmedabad. After a long struggle, with one side attempting to penetrate and the other staunchly defending, Jawan Mard Khan Babi finally surrendered to the Marathas due to starvation. The portion of the country that fell to Damajirao II was valued at approximately Rs 25,00,000 besides land acquisitions valued at approximately Rs 3,00,000 and half the revenue from Kathiawad. After the conquest of Ahmedabad had been concluded, Raghoba set off on another campaign, leaving Ahmedabad in the hands of an agent named Shripatrao, who was in charge of all except one gate which Damajirao II retained.

A sudden turn of events caused a second siege on Cambay-occupied Ahmedabad necessary but Momin Khan II could be bought with an adequate bribe. He departed for good. The Muslim power in Gujarat became weak as they had no wish to cross swords with the Marathas. Damajirao II's general Ranghoji Bhonsle died in 1755.

The next five years were spent in resettling the Ahmedabad territory, bringing order in the areas that resisted the change in rule and also family disputes called for his attention. In spite of the settlement with Balaji Bajirao that had been most draining on the Gaekwads' financial resources, the accord with the Peshwa brought its own share of commitments. In 1761, the threat of invasion from Ahmed Shah Abdali of Afghanistan threatened the peace of the country. In answer to Balaji Bajirao's call, Damajirao II took his contingent to amplify the Maratha armies and was swept into the cataclysm of Panipat.

In the disastrous battle of Panipat, he like Casabianca remained bravely on the field 'whence all but he had fled' (the quote is from the poem 'Casabianca' by Felicia Hemans). It was only when he had slain 8,000 of the Rohillas from Afghanisthan, who had formed the right wing of Ahmed Shah's army, did he leave the battlefield. Damajirao II returned to Gujarat with renewed energy and zest and was engaged in a series of conquests which resulted in the expulsion of the Babi family who along with others had risen against the Marathas. The Babi family was stripped off all their possessions except their ancestral property of Sami Radhanpur and Momin Khan was punished. Damajirao II made Vishalnagar his headquarters and took Kheda after which he moved to Patan from where he turned out Jawan Mard Khan and made Patan his capital instead of Songadh. Between the years 1763 and 1776, Damajirao II acquired Patan, Vishalnagar, Vadnagar, Kheralu, Raozanpur, Bijapur, Dhamni, Maujpur and Vijapur from the Babi family. Out of all these conquests, five were given as saranjam (reward) to Damajirao II while Balaji Bajirao retained four. With these additions, some of the finest districts were added to the Gaekwad territories.

Balaji Bajirao did not live long after the Panipat disaster and though he did some constructive work—such as transforming the village of Poona into a city, building temples and reservoirs to provide drinking water to the people of that city and bringing the Maratha power to its peak—he did nothing to bridge the yawning gap between the Maratha confederacy and the Gaekwads. He died in 1761, and his son Madhavrao succeeded him to the title of Peshwa along with its powers. Raghoba who had set his covetous eyes on the position was distressed over this, but there was nothing that he could really do as the Poona durbar supported the newly elected Peshwa.

Madhavrao, a mere boy of seventeen, did not relish having Raghoba as his regent and wished to shake off the yoke of being too young for administration. The resentment grew and festered till it ultimately broke the Maratha confederacy and brought it to ruin. However, for a time, they collaborated to oppose the invasions of the Muslims in Gujarat. In one of these battles against the Nizam, who was ultimately defeated at Tandulza on the Godavari River, Damajirao II distinguished himself when one of his men killed the Nizam's prime minister and was awarded the title of Sena Khas Khel by the king of Satara. Since the title was hereditary, it has been passed down in the Gaekwad's line of succession.

The gulf between Madhavrao and his uncle grew wider with each day. Damajirao II, who had formed an alliance with Raghoba since the Ahmedabad siege, strongly supported him against the reigning Peshwa, a fact that was not lost on Madhavrao who brought on his wrath on Damajirao II who had to pay dearly for it. On the grounds that the partition of Gujarat had been too favourable for Damajirao II, the six mahals (districts) were confiscated from him. This unfair confiscation of the territories that he had earned weighed heavily with Damajirao II and tilted the balance in Raghoba's favour when he made a final bid to break away from the Peshwa.

In 1768, the open hostility between Madhavrao and his uncle culminated in a war which was fought in a place near Dhodap on 10 June. Since Damajirao II was on the side of the uncle, he sent a cavalry under his eldest son Govindrao to Raghoba's aid. Both Govindrao and Raghoba suffered a crushing defeat at the hands of the Peshwa and were taken as prisoners to Poona. This was the final defeat that Gaekwad was inflicted with by the Peshwa and the war indemnities were severe. He was fined Rs 23,25,000 and the tribute for three years preceding was fixed at Rs 75,000. The six mahals taken from him was restored, but for the future the tribute on these was raised from Rs 5,25,000 to Rs 7,79,000 taking the value of the mahals into account. Damajirao II died soon after this in 1768 and the state and family lost a capable, ambitious and a most eminent ruler, in whose long and active career of nearly forty years the whole of Gujarat was wrested from the Mughals. His death was the signal for family's dissension which eventually brought the East India Company to play a vital role in the politics of Gujarat.

4

Over to the British

Damajirao II had three wives and a son from each. His first wife's son, Govindrao, was born later than the first son, Sayajirao I, of the second wife; therefore, a dispute arose between Govindrao and Sayajirao I regarding the succession. Fatehsinghrao I was Sayajirao I's younger brother and could hence not contest the line of succession but as Sayajirao I was a weak-minded person, Fatehsinghrao I saw himself as the prince regent ready to administer the affairs of the state of Baroda. Huge sums of money were paid by both the parties (Govindrao and Fatehsinghrao I) to the Poona government, but Fatehsinghrao I proved himself the most capable and energetic of the three, a person with remarkable ambition, astuteness and daring, a prince who could carry out a campaign with as much ability as he could hold his own in a political contest. He obtained a sanction from the Poona durbar to seat Sayajirao I on the gaddi while he himself acted as the deputy chief or regent. Govindrao was still a prisoner in Poona. (He had been sent by Damaji to fight along with Raghoba against Madhavrao in 1768 and had been taken prisoner along with Raghoba.) Madhavrao got Govindrao to agree with his terms. Govindrao was to pay a fixed annual tribute to Madhavrao and maintain a contingent of 3,000 horses, which were to be at Madhavrao's disposal apart from an indemnity of Rs 6,00,000. Govindrao, anxious to claim the gaddi, agreed and was released from prison. Owing to his proximity with the Poona durbar he was able to obtain the succession for himself for a fine of Rs 50,00,000. In 1771, Fatehsinghrao I, who had fortified himself with troops in Baroda, came to Poona and obtained a reversal of this decision. While Sayajirao I was declared as Shamsher Bahadur Sena Khas Khel, he himself took the title of Mutalik after paying practically the same amount paid by Govindrao earlier. Thus, the Peshwa's coffers were now richer by Rs 1,00,00,000.

The hard fact of the matter was that neither of the brothers had the resources to pay such a heavy amount and could pay only in instalments which would take years for them to fulfil. The fault lay not with them but with Madhavrao for asking far too much. Ultimately, this harsh severity imposed on them by Madhavrao drove the Gaekwads to seek an alliance with the East India Company.

The brothers, henceforth, became bitter enemies; to add fuel to the fire, Khanderao, who had caused enough trouble for his brother Damajirao II earlier by proving to be a traitor to the cause, had been awarded the title of Himmat Bahadur by Madhavrao who was perpetually ready to play the cat-and-mouse game with the Gaekwads. Khanderao who had by his intrigues acquired the districts of Nadiad and Borsad from Damajirao II, resolved to side with either of the two brothers as best as might suit his interests.

In 1772, Fatehsinghrao I, before leaving Poona, made an agreement with Madhavrao which absolved him from sending troops every year to Poona, but he was to pay a sum of Rs 6,70,000 if his troops were not called out for foreign service, which was later increased to an annual tribute of Rs 14,54,000 for remission of services.

Fatehsinghrao I did not trust the Brahmin party in Poona and to consolidate his position against Madhavrao and his brother Govindrao, he made overtures to the East India Company in Bombay in 1772, soliciting their support in the matter. However, the Company, preferring to bide their time, did not respond to his call.

On 18 November of the same year, the British captured the fort of Broach and the Nawab was driven out of the city. Now, the possession of Broach had long been the desire and ambition of the Gaekwads, particularly Fatehsinghrao I who wanted to use it as his headquarters in Gujarat. Earlier, Pilajirao had ceded some of his districts to get two-fifths of Broach customs; even Damajirao II had ventured to wrest it from the Nizam but was unsuccessful because of the stoic defence put up by the faujdar of Broach (his real name was Abdullah Beg, but when appointed by the Nizam was named Nek Alam Khan) and also by the floods in the Narmada River which had brought the siege to an end. He would have renewed his attempts, but he was bought off by a grant. Three-fifths of the customs, the revenue of Broach and half of the revenue from Jambusar and Ahmod, and finally after the partition of Gujarat, Broach and Koral had come under the rule of the Gaekwads.

Hence, Fatehsinghrao I was anxious to keep it at all costs and offered the British Rs 6,00,000 a year for Broach and Rs 60,000 a year out of his share of revenues in Surat. The British naturally refused and referred to a treaty made earlier on 12 January 1773, according to which the Gaekwads were allowed to retain Rs 6,00,000–Rs 9,00,000 a year of the gross revenue and the rest was supposed to be transferred to the British.

Meanwhile, the years 1772–73 were spent in a tussle between the brothers for the gaddi, unaided either by the British or Madhavrao. Khanderao, Fatehsinghrao I's uncle, and jagirdar of Kadi, who had earlier espoused his cause, deserted him to support Govindrao. While all this was happening in one part of the country, in Poona a major catastrophe occurred. Madhavrao, the most wise and efficient of the Peshwas, died of tuberculosis. He was acclaimed for his victory over the Nizam in the battle of Rakshasbhuvan and for keeping a tight curb on his rebellious uncle Raghoba by defeating him and placing him under house arrest in 1768. He was admired and feared by his ministers and the Maratha clan of the Maratha confederacy. He was succeeded by his son Narayanrao in 1772, who, shortly after his succession, was murdered by Raghoba's bodyguard in 1773. If Raghoba had thought that the line was now clear for him to step into the murdered man's shoes, he was doomed for disappointment since Narayanrao's son Madhavrao II was born in 1774 and was strongly supported by the ministers of the Poona court.

In Poona, all was not well as a civil war had broken out. There was bitter enmity among the peshwas and Raghoba fled to Gujarat with a coalition of ministers headed by the chief minister, Nana Phadnavis, in close pursuit of him. On 3 January 1775, Raghoba reached Baroda with a small army as he had been deserted by the two Maratha chiefs, Scindia and Holkar. He allied himself with Govindrao who was engaged in a dispute with his brother Fatehsinghrao I; Raghoba had earlier been his ally in the battle of Dhodap and had also recognized Govindrao as Sena Khas Khel when, for a brief while, the latter had been the undisputed Peshwa after Madhavrao's death in 1772. Raghoba was disliked by the ministers of the Poona court and had been overthrown by Chief Minister Nana Phadnavis and eleven other ministers in what was known as the 'Baarbhai Conspiracy'. He had sought help from the British and the Portuguese, but his claim had been ignored. It was not until 6 March 1775 that the East India Company agreed to come to terms with Raghoba and the Treaty of Surat was signed whereby they agreed to assist Raghoba in his cause, and he, in return, agreed to cede Bassein, Salsette and the districts around Surat. He also promised to obtain the Gaekwad's share of Broach from Govindrao. The offer was a tempting one for the British and they did not stop to consider whether the person granting it had any right to do so and because of it they would be committed to take part in a civil war which was no concern of theirs. The ethics of their action simply did not occur to them. But only after the Treaty of Surat was signed did the British start the campaign for what is known in history as the First Maratha War.

Strangely, neither the Peshwas nor the Gaekwads realized the value of the seaports in Gujarat which, opening out to the Arabian Sea, were viable for overseas trade. Though they did attach great importance to the ports of Cambay, Surat and Broach, it was more for prizing the revenue from the customs rather than a policy dictated by knowledge of commerce. On the other hand, the Europeans had a very clear idea of the value of seaports and the growth of their power in India was based on the acquisition of ports along the coastline of India. Now, as the prize of a share in Broach dangled before them, offered by Raghoba, they got entangled in a senseless war which was brought to an abrupt end with no possible advantage to anyone as the British, the Peshwas and the Gaekwads fought each other with no clear idea of what they were fighting for and only ended in being in the bad books of the council at Calcutta and Warren Hastings, the governor of Bengal. However, it is important to know about the active part the Gaekwad brothers took in the campaign. The Poona army, under Haripant Phadke, together with the troops of Scindia and Holkar forced Raghoba and Govindrao to raise the siege of Baroda. Then, Phadke and Fatehsinghrao I followed the retreating army and attacked them when they were camping in Vasad on the plains of Aras, quite close to the Mahi River. They crossed the river simultaneously at three points and fell suddenly on the flank as well as in front of Raghoba's camp and routed his army with severe losses. The victory was mainly due to Fatehsinghrao I's excellent generalship and knowledge of the territory, causing his reputation to grow along with his prospects.

Raghoba never recovered from the defeat during the whole campaign; in fact, the leader himself fled to Cambay and joined the British in Surat. Govindrao and Khanderao retreated in haste to Khanderao's stronghold at Kapadvanj where they were able to ward off the blows that were following in quick succession from Fatehsinghrao I. With the astuteness that one could credit Napoleon with, Fatehsinghrao I reduced his uncle's districts around

Nadiad—the possessions he had always coveted —while he behaved in a judicious way with the British hinting that he was open to being their ally in the near future.

Colonel Keating with a small army joined Raghoba's disorderly forces near Cambay on 19 April 1775 and Govindrao too joined his forces with them. But Fatehsinghrao I forced Khanderao to join forces with him and the cavalry of Haripant Phadke. The hostile armies of Fatehsinghrao I's, Holkar's and Scindia's on one side against the British force under Colonel Keating dispatched by the Bombay government, together with the forces of Raghoba and Govindrao on the other side, met about thirty miles from Cambay. A series of combats followed on the Sabarmati and Vatrak rivers and another as Raghoba and his British allies entered Kheda. The ministerial army was no match for the disciplined British forces and, thus, had to retreat rapidly. On 8 June, Colonel Keating attempted to surprise the ministerial army by crossing the Narmada at the Bavapierah pass, in the neighbourhood where the enemy was camped. The surprise attack did not take place as Raghoba's disorderly troops impeded his movements, but the ministerial troops of Haripant were forced to leave Gujarat for good. The early monsoons made Colonel Keating's further advance impossible, but the British troops managed to win their way to Dabhoi while the Maratha allies settled down at Bhilupur near Baroda.

Govindrao urged his allies to seize Baroda in the absence of the ministerial army, but Fatehsinghrao I, well aware of this danger, decided it was better to join the enemy than fight them and resolved to change sides. He persuaded Colonel Keating to ignore Govindrao's interests 'in the most barefaced manner'.[1] By managing to maintain armed neutrality, a treaty was entered into between Fatehsinghrao I and Colonel Keating on 8 July by which the former agreed to furnish a troop of 3,000 horses for the service of Raghoba and to pay him the arrears due to the Poona durbar as well as an indemnity of Rs 8,00,000 and cede to the English the parganas of Broach, Chikhli, Variav and Koral, provided Govindrao made no claims. To Govindrao, Raghoba promised a jagir of Rs 10, 00,000 in addition to other promises, and Fatehsinghrao I pledged an amount of Rs 26,00,000 to Raghoba payable within sixty days. But Colonel Keating, who from experience had learnt to distrust Raghoba, extorted from him a sum of Rs 10,00,000 as payment for servicing him with his troops and this came mostly in the form of jewels, elephants and other commodities. Raghoba, on the other hand, had to provide Govindrao the jagir of the Deccan. Meanwhile, orders were issued to Colonel Keating by Warren Hastings, the governor of Bengal, to stop all hostilities and to bring an immediate end to an 'impolitic, dangerous, unauthorized and unjust war.'[2] and break off all connections with Fatehsinghrao I. Colonel Keating was also told to surrender all the territory acquired during war. Fatehsinghrao I, of course, was quite ignorant of this fact and that Colonel Keating and Raghoba had decided to pull out of the war, but it gave Colonel Keating the opportunity to milk the Gaekwad as much as he could. Colonel Keating prevailed upon Fatehsinghrao I to sign a treaty of alliance on 8 July 1775, agreeing to give up all claims to Broach as well as to a good bit of the surrounding territory, a treaty the Gaekwads were to rue later! Perhaps even though aware of signing a treaty which was more in the nature of a death warrant for the Gaekwads' possessions, Fatehsinghrao I did so in the desperate hope of isolating Govindrao from his powerful allies. The treaty made Fatehsinghrao I an ally of the British. The struggle between the Marathas and the English did not end here but only got deferred and though the Gaekwad brothers were left to fight their own battles, the English knew they had a valuable ally in Fatehsinghrao I—Fatehsinghrao I knew this too, and waited to take advantage of it.

In 1778, the Poona court recognized Fatehsinghrao I as Sena Khas Khel and he was persuaded by Nana Phadnavis, the de facto minister in the Poona court, to side with them against the Bombay government and Fatehsinghrao I willingly conceded. The title, of course, came at a price as it was with the Peshwas and similarly with the British and a total sum of Rs 10, 00,000 together with arrears was paid to the Peshwa. The unfortunate Govindrao had retired to Poona where he did receive the Rs 2,00,000 promised to him by Fatehsinghrao I in 1778 but the jagirdar, Khanderao, did not pay him anything.

By the Treaty of Purandar in March 1776, which ratified the cessation of hostilities, the East India Company obtained the whole of the Maratha share in the city and pargana of Broach and territory worth Rs 3,00,000 in its neighbourhood, but they retained the parganas of Chikhli and Koral and the town of Variav. In all fairness to the East India Company, they stipulated that if Fatehsinghrao I could prove that he had no authority to cede any of the territories without prior permission from the Peshwa, they would restore all the territories ceded by Sayajirao I or Fatehsinghrao I, but Fatehsinghrao I was far too shrewd and far-sighted to make use of this opportunity to regain lost territory since he was still skating on thin ice with the Poona durbar. He did try to get back the money that had been extorted by Colonel Keating, but the appeal was rejected. He got back Savli and as for the rest of his territories, neither he nor the other Gaekwads were successful in getting them back. In fact, the battle continued till the Peshwa's downfall forty years later.

Warren Hastings had abruptly called off the war midway for the sole reason that it was not going the way it should have and not because of any scruples or dictates of his conscience; he was merely buying time because at the end of 1778 the Company was once again at war with the Marathas supporting the cause of Raghoba against the Poona court. Hastings soon realized that the Marathas collectively were very powerful; therefore, he adopted a strategy of siding with different factions of the confederacy in their internecine disputes and this became the bedrock of the British regime till they had subjugated India under their rule. The Peshwa was the head of the Maratha confederacy and it was decided that as a first step in their strategy he should be isolated from factions that were pro-Peshwa like the Holkars and the Scindias. The Gaekwads' age-old animosity towards the Poona durbar was well known to the British. Geographically too they were some distance away from the Poona court, therefore, the Gaekwad was the ideal candidate among the Marathas to be won over first. Fatehsinghrao I on his part saw this as an opportunity to relieve the Gaekwads from the chains of the confederacy in Poona. Half of the Gaekwad's territory was claimed by the Gaekwad's legitimate enemy, the Peshwa, and now it was decided that the territory could be retained only by the person who defeated him.

5

First Anglo-Maratha War (1775–82)

On 30 March 1779, the East India Company and Madhavrao II engaged in the First Anglo-Maratha War in which the East India Company suffered defeat. Governor Hornby proposed to make use of Gujarat in the campaign because it was accessible from the sea for British vessels, unlike the Deccan which was divided by precipitous ghats. The British relied on Fatehsinghrao I as an ally and a reliable one at that; he was a cut above the rest, they thought, and if the Peshwa was beaten, there could be a partition of the country—the Peshwa's districts north of the Mahi River would go to the Gaekwads who would then be free of the Peshwa's domination and those south of the Tapti River would go to the British. In the middle of December 1779, with the approval of Warren Hastings, Colonel Goddard who was a different kettle of fish from his predecessor Colonel Keating, crossed the Tapti and took Dabhoi from Madhavrao II in January 1780. Fatehsinghrao I, caught between Nana Phadnavis on one side and the British on the other, signed an offensive and defensive treaty at Kandila (Dabhoi). The treaty made the Gaekwad independent of the Peshwa; he also had to aid the British with 3,000 cavalry, divide Gujarat with the the East India company and cede some territory. Ahmedabad was taken on 15 February 1780 and handed over to Fatehsinghrao I who in return ceded certain territories of the Surat athivasi (large areas) with the exception of Songadh. The Maratha War continued between Goddard and Holkar's and Scindia's troops which had crossed the Narmada River towards the end of February, threatening to take over Dabhoi. Attacks and counterattacks followed one after another, with the Marathas proving that they were no mean adversaries, forcing Goddard to resort to night attacks, which were unsuccessful with the Maratha leaders retiring to the Pavgadh Hill near Baroda. After a brief lull, hostilities resumed and Fatehsinghrao I proved himself a willing and efficient ally in the defence of Gujarat. At the end of the campaign, he placed at the disposal of the British a force of 5,000 cavalry, commanded by his brother Manaji Gaekwad.

While the Anglo-Maratha War was occupying the time, energy and lives of the British and the Marathas, another threat to the British supremacy in India loomed on the horizon. Hyder Ali, the sultan and de facto ruler of Mysore, who was proving to be a formidable enemy of the British with his victory over a British detachment, the Nizam and all the Maratha chiefs were planning to join his forces in ousting the British from Indian soil. The British were no fools and saw that it was imperative to disassociate the Maratha confederacy from Hyder Ali and decided to make peace with the current enemy. For some time, they hoped to arrive at a favourable agreement with Nana Phadnavis, who still ruled the roost in the Poona durbar, by negotiating terms through Colonel Goddard whose position had strengthened, as it was, by Fatehsinghrao I and Raghoba. The defeat of Scindia's army made negotiations with the confederacy easier and got Mahadji Scindia to make separate terms for himself with the British government. Mahadji Scindia volunteered to mediate between his late foes and the Poona court, for he saw the importance of acquiring a position equal or superior to that of the central authority of the Marathas. Then, negotiated on behalf of the British with the Poona durbar, resulting in the Treaty of Salbai on 17 May 1782. The Peshwas were given the city of Ahmedabad and the upshot of the treaty was that Fatehsinghrao I was to be left in full possession of all the territories he had possessed at the commencement of the five-year Anglo-Maratha War and the territories ceded by the Treaty of Purandar. Above all, he was absolved of all the arrears due to the Peshwa, but the Peshwa had a right to expect the usual service from him. Fatehsinghrao I was saved from this commitment due to the fierce fighting that had broken out among the principal noblemen and courtiers at Poona, which put an end to the Peshwa sending out his army on campaigns.

For a few years, Fatehsinghrao I was left undisturbed to enjoy the fruits of his labour and the possession of his territories. Parsimonious by nature, his administration was marked with no lavish expenditures. He made one grave error in allowing the Arab mercenaries to enter Gujarat. They had been brought in to render assistance with the troops and the horses in case of trouble from outside the country or within, and were to be maintained at the expense of the Baroda state. The Arabs, however, were unscruplous to the extreme and caused a lot of trouble in Gujarat in the years to come.

Fatehsinghrao I is to be admired for his tenacity and resourcefulness;

he was one of the rulers to whom the House of Gaekwads owes its wealth, prosperity and its continued life 'for he deftly steered the bark of the state through a time of great danger and extricated it from difficulties with trifling loss.'[1] A tragedy occurred on 21 December 1789 when Fatehsinghrao I died from an accidental fall from the upper storey of his palace. (It is unclear whether it was an accident or murder.) He would have been succeeded by his brother Govindrao, but the Poona durbar favoured his stepbrother Manajirao Gaekwad; not without a price though, they received approximately Rs 33,13,000. His reign, however, was of no consequence and he died on 1 August 1793. Govindrao's succession to the gaddi was not without controversies. First, the Poona durbar did not recognize his succession until he had paid a heavy price in terms of cash and jewels amounting to nearly Rs 44,00,000 and worse, he had to cede all the Gaekwads' territories south of the Tapti River along with their share of the customs duty of Surat.

It is here that we need to understand the Gaekwad's relationship with the British which really began with Fatehsinghrao I who walked the tightrope between the British and the Peshwas. While trying to be on the side of the Peshwas, he had really sided with the British in the wars against the Marathas, which not only stood the Gaekwads in good stead but saved Gujarat from falling completely under British domination. Now, the British stepped in, remembering their old ally Fatehsinghrao I, and peremptorily informed the Poona durbar that as per the Treaty of Salbai, the possessions of Govindrao were to be left intact and all thoughts of annexing any part of his territory must be abandoned, thus putting an end to Nana Phadnavis who had been bent on ruining the Gaekwads and causing the dismemberment of the Baroda state. The Peshwa never again got an opportunity for causing an injury to his long-standing enemy and the families of the Gaekwads as well as the people of Baroda have much to thank Fatehsinghrao I for his far-sightedness and prudence in his approach towards the British. He laid the foundation for diplomatic ties with the British and later on, Khanderao cemented it for Sayajirao Gaekwad III, so he could rule and administer the state effectively.

It must be mentioned here that the authority of the Peshwas as the de facto rulers of the Maratha confederacy weakened after the First Maratha War against the East India Company during 1775–82. The Maratha losses after the first battle of Panipat had already halted the expansion of their empire and reduced their power. After 1782, the empire became a loser confederacy with political power resting in a pentarchy of five Maratha dynasties—the Peshwas of Poona, the Scindias of Malwa and Gwalior, the Holkars of Indore, the Bhonsles of Nagpur and the Gaekwads of Baroda.

During this time, a lot of wars were being waged in India in which the British were engaged. The Anglo-Mysore wars between 1760 and 1799 ended in victory for the British against Tipu Sultan who died on the battlefield. The Anglo-French wars in the latter part of the eighteenth century that ended with the British driving the French out of Indian soil also indirectly influenced the fortunes of the Gaekwads. The war with Mysore alone enabled the government to fight the Peshwa with success, and establish British power in Gujarat. In Poona, there was rivalry between Mahadji Scindia and Nana Phadnavis, as their policies were at variance—while Scindia's policy was one of self-aggrandizement at the cost of the Maratha confederacy, the other's was to keep the Brahmin authority supreme in Poona. However, Mahadji died in 1794 and Phadnavis, undeterred, continued to carry on his policy of making the Poona durbar strong.

Madhavrao II's death in 1795 left the position to his cousin Bajirao II whose hatred for Nana Phadnavis led him to lease a large tract of territory to Gaekwad. The entire conflict among the different parties was for sovereignty over Gujarat and the Gaekwads, resulting in complete independence of the Gaekwads from Poona dominance.

6

Govindrao's Reign and the Emergence of British Dominance

Govindrao at last realized his long-cherished ambition and was invested with the title of Sena Khas Khel on 19 December 1793. It had taken him twenty-five years to succeed to what had been rightly his.

Unfortunately for him, his reign was anything but peaceful beset as it was by multitudinous problems. The first set of trouble came from Kanoji, his illegitimate son from the Rajput princess of Dharampur, who attacked Baroda with the help of a troop of Arab men and horses. However, as the Arabs knew no loyalty at first opportunity they handed over their leader to Govindrao who threw him into prison. He managed to escape to the hills disguised as a woman and was joined by the Bhils. Then Kanoji and the Bhils wreaked havoc in the villages of Sankheda and Bhadarpur. Later, Malharrao, son of the late jagirdar Khanderao, rallied to his support and together they planned for the future.

The next lot of trouble came from the Arabs who were threatening to take over Gujarat and proving formidable even to the British. The Arabs' rampage and pillaging in Gujarat, his family dissensions and open defiance by feudatories and dependants were proving too much for Govindrao to handle.

During Govindrao's time, the Baroda state became more amenable to the dictates of Bajirao II since Govindrao owed him huge sums of money which the Peshwa had demanded for his succession to the gaddi. This is the main reason that drove the Gaekwads to seek an alliance with the British for they soon realized that to be a part of the Maratha confederacy was to keep paying the Peshwas huge sums of money with no return. Every time a Gaekwad was to be recognized as a successor to the gaddi he had to pay a large sum to the Peshwa. Manaji, Fatehsinghrao I, Govindrao had all paid, incurring debts in arrears as the sums demanded were huge, crippling the resources of the Gaekwads.

Malharrao, the new jagirdar of Kadi (a position he had inherited from his father after the latter's death in 1785), thought that the yearly peshkash (tribute) due from him to Gaekwad could be written off since his father Khanderao had supported Govindrao against his brother; but, his crude way of asking for the remission of this sum was so distasteful to Govindrao[1] that he refused to grant it. Thus, in retaliation the jagirdar joined forces with Kanoji, who also had an axe to grind with Govindrao, and a battle ensued in which Govindrao's men were driven back by the powerful forces of Kanoji. Meanwhile, there sprung a rivalry between the two allies. Kanoji's fiery prowess and success in the campaign made him lose favour with his relation (and ally) and Govindrao capitalized on this by dropping a forged letter into the jagirdar's hands which stated that the other was planning treachery. This open rupture caused Kanoji to escape to the Satpura Hills in fear for his life where he was caught and imprisoned. In 1794, the jagirdar of Kadi sought peace with Govindrao by agreeing to pay the stipulated peshkash of Rs 5,50,00. The terms of the agreement were for a time faithfully kept for he even cooperated by taking an active part in the campaign against Aba Shelukar in the fight for Ahmedabad.

Meanwhile, the hatred between Bajirao II and Nana Phadnavis had reached a pitch with the latter being arrested in the Scindia camp. With his arrest, Aba Shelukar, the acting nominee for Appasaheb of the Poona durbar (his name was Chimnaji Pant, the nominee of Bajirao II, as suba [officer-in-charge] of the Peshwa's possessions in Ahmedabad) who looked after the Peshwa's possessions in Ahmedabad, met with the same fate and Govindrao was given the charge of Ahmedabad. His vassals, Raoji Appaji, the dewan from the Prabhu family, and his brother Babaji (who later became the commander of the state army), were well disposed towards Aba Shelukar and got him released on a fine of Rs 10,00,000 with Petlad as collateral till the sum was repaid to them. But this only led to disputes as Aba Shelukar was unscrupulous and attacked the Gaekwad garrison in Ahmedabad. Govindrao immediately prepared for war and deputed messengers to inform the Peshwa of the incident. Just as the Peshwa received the news, Nana Phadnavis breathed his last and the Peshwa felt free to take his revenge on Nana Phadnavis's supporters. He directed Govindrao to oust Aba Shelukar from the farms in Ahmedabad and take over the city. The fight for Ahmedabad continued between Aba Shelukar and Babaji, who suddenly attacked Aba Shelukar's army and routed it. Aba Shelukar attempted a siege on Ahmedabad the second time, but was defeated and, four months later, his Arab mercenaries, in keeping with their character, handed him over to Babaji. Babaji handed him over to Govindrao, who imprisoned him in Baroda. Later, he was transferred to Borsad where he lived in a prison for many years till the British had him released, when he could no longer cause anyone any anxiety.

The Ahmedabad districts were given for farming for a period of five years to Bhagvantrao, who was another illegitimate son of Govindrao, at Rs 5,00,000 a year, but the proceeds of the first two years that amounted to Rs 10, 00,000 were pledged to Scindia by Bajirao II's orders. Considering that the farm fetched only around Rs 3,50,000, the deal at Rs 5,00,000 was still considered worth it as it removed, with one stroke, the problems which arose from having two governments (Gaekwad and the Peshwa) whose boundaries were not accurately fixed and, at many points, interlaced with one another.

The anxiety of Govindrao to retain the farm, the interest on the part of the East India Company in maintaining Govindrao's hold on it and the policy of Bajirao II to gain a hold in Baroda by resuming his administration in Ahmedabad—all of this eventually led to the rupture which ended in the fall of Bajirao II, resulting in the complete independence of Govindaro.

Govindrao died on 19 September 1800. His reign was uneventful as far as his achievements are concerned with the exception of his one victory gained over the Nizam at Kurdia, and his attempt, though unsuccessful, to seize the port of Cambay in Gujarat.

Accordingly, his eldest son Anandrao Gaekwad was placed undisputed on the gaddi along with the title of Sena Khas Khel. Raoji was Anandrao's regent as he was too timid and mentally incapable of administration with a mind rendered infirm from addiction to opium. Besides the Gujarat province was also going through turbulent times. It was impoverished and its treasury was almost empty due to the Rs 60,00,000 that had to be paid to the Peshwa two years earlier. In this penurious condition, almost all the districts were pledged to creditors and the few remaining ones were farmed out to unscrupulous men who were only interested in extorting money. The tributary states were tardy in their payment of tributes and only paid when they were forced to. The maintenance of the army alone exceeded the revenues of the state. Administration was virtually non-existent, in fact, there was no government at all and the real power was with the despicable Arabs who, in simple language, could be termed as thugs.

The early years of Anandrao's reign witnessed a fierce squabble among the coterie, not for the gaddi, but for ministerial power and administrative control of the Gaekwad's dominions. The reigning sovereign's rule was nominal because infelicitous circumstances had made Anandrao a mere figurehead, capitalising on whose weakness, ambitious politicians and political hangers-on tried to further the cause of their own personal ends.

The dramatis personae that figured in the faction's struggle for power and position were five parties—Raoji who was Anandrao's minister, Kanojirao his stepbrother, Malharrao, the Arab soldiers in Baroda and the East India Company.

A few days later, Kanojirao corrupted his guards in prison, regained his liberty and coerced Anandrao to surrender to him the seals of the state, which he did; but Raoji who had served the late Govindrao and was a faithful subject, had him arrested and thrown into prison again. The aged widow of Govindrao and Anandrao's mother Rani Gahenabai somehow did not relish the idea of her son being a mere puppet in the hands of Raoji. She invited Malharrao to take up the regency in Baroda; he responded with alacrity by taking up arms. Kanojirao, who had escaped yet again from his confined space, ingratiated himself with Anandrao and secured a place for himself in the palace where he went about trying to deprive Raoji of his authority. Kanojirao, however headstrong, was unable to bend the Arab troops to his will. He became unbearable, ill-treating the women in the palace and trying to squeeze money out of relatives to satisfy the Arabs. Raoji along with the Arabs rid the palace of Kanoji's obnoxious presence—Raoji's terms were fair, so one night they surrounded Kanoji's house and arrested him. They then delivered him to Anandrao who had him imprisoned in the fort of Ranpur. The situation was getting out of hand for even the capable minister Raoji—the city was beset with external troubles from the Arabs who were on a rampage in the province of Gujarat. Wanting to extricate his master from all the perils surrounding them, he made overtures to the British, chiefly, the East India Company in Bombay presidency to intervene with armed assistance, which they agreed to give. However, on Raoji's return from the Bombay office, his palanquin was fired upon by the Arabs, wounding most of his palki-bearers. The Arabs were afraid of the British forces as they knew that the British could surely turn them out of the state.

Besides the Arabs, Raoji also had to deal with unscrupulous family members. Malharrao, who saw himself as the regent in Raoji's place, set Kanoji free from his confinement and gave Anandrao his freedom to administer the state without Raoji. Matters were brought to Jonathan Duncan, the governor of Bombay, by Raoji for arbitration but Duncan did not immediately intervene, preferring to weigh the pros and cons of doing so, for he knew that his intrusion could result in a possible confrontation with Bajirao II while Anandraowould most likely be a possible ally. The Bombay government was viewing the affairs in Baroda with anxiety, but finally decided to send Major Alexander Walker to Baroda to arbitrate between Raoji and Malharrao according to the apparent justice of their views and the wishes of Anandrao. To support Major Walker's decision, a small and as it turned out, an inadequate force of 2,000, troops was sent to Cambay. Finally, Major Walker's troops and the troops of Sir William Clarke carried out an assault on 30 April on the enemy's camp and Malharrao surrendered to Major Walker. He was later allowed to live in Nadiad on an allowance of Rs 1,25,000 a year, but he was not content with this generosity and ran away to begin fresh insurrections. However, his uprisings were quickly suppressed and his territory was annexed to the Baroda state. With the addition of Kadi, Anandrao'slandholdings increased by districts worth Rs 5,00,000, but more importantly, they were rid of the existence of a chief who for years had wrought havoc in Baroda with his duplicity and mischief.

The East India Company had demanded a heavy price, either in cash or kind, for the supply of their troops against Malharrao, which suited Anandrao as he, by then, had a lot of territory, which he could afford to cede but hardly anything in cash. It was decided that in case any financial assistance was required from the British, it should be paid from Gaekwad's portion of the chauth of Surat and the Chaurasi pargana; also, the expenses of the campaign were to be borne by Anandrao. The Surat aththavasi, a part of which belonged to Anandrao, was to be mortgaged as security for the sum due. Apart from this, on 4 June, the pargana of Chikhli was gifted to the

British on 3 May 1803, the fort and jagir of Kheda were added as well. The British also took the responsibility of paying the Arab mercenaries their dues in arrears, expecting to be reimbursed by Anandrao before June 1805; till then, they were already pledged the revenues of Baroda, Koral, Sinor, Petlad and the Ahmedabad parganas. All these terms were settled and put down in writing in a treaty signed between the two parties—the East India Company and Anandrao on 6 June 1802.

Finally, after the Kadi War (24 April 1802- 3 May 1802), and after the Arabs were disbanded, a force of 2,000 British sepoys with a battery of European artillery was to be subsidized by Anandrao. The monthly cost of these troops was estimated at Rs 65,000, and cessions in jaidad (property or territory) were to be made at that value.

More importantly, Anandrao officially gave all rights of interference to Major Walker in case of trouble from outsiders. Major Walker, Captain John Carnac and Sir William Clarke had upright motives and were assisted by the wise and honest Gangadhar Shastri, well known to Raoji and was appointed mediating officer by Raoji before he died; he had been nominated as a confidential medium between the Resident and the durbar on a salary of Rs 100. Besides, it was tacitly understood that all interference would cease once the state was free of all troubles and debts and could operate independently.

Subsequently, there were a few treaties which were neither abrogated, nor were there any specific references that the fundamental terms of the original treaty had been annulled. Therefore, it is not clear to what extent the treaties made the Gaekwads subservient to the British. This was something that worked to the advantage of the future rulers who came to sit on the gaddi.

For some time, things moved along smoothly till the state got out of its debts and was rendered solvent; but slowly resentment began to creep in which led to plots, insurrections and wars that culminated in the murder of Gangadhar Shastri and to many other tragic events, the effects of which were felt for a long time.

In the Poona durbar, Daulatrao Scindia and Yashwantrao Holkar (Daulatrao Scindia was the Maharaja of Gwalior. His reign coincided with the struggles for supremacy within the Maratha confederacy. Yeshwantrao Holkar was the Maharaja of Indore. They were subordinate feudatory kings of the Maratha Empire of which the Peshwa was the de facto ruler.) were engaged in a squabble for supremacy and for the custody of the Peshwa, which made Bajirao II seek help from the British in 1802 to put these rivals down. The result was the Treaty of Bassein signed on 31 December 1802, which had its own consequence on the state of Baroda. As Mountstuart Elphinstone, lieutenant governor of Bombay, said, 'The Peshwa realized the situation that had been brought about by Raoji's convention at Cambay and the Treaty of Baroda signed on 29 July 1802, by which were fixed the establishment of British instead of the Peshwa ascendancy at Baroda; British protection of the Gaekwad, and interposition in the negotiations with Poona; British guarantee to the succession to the gaddi.' A careful analysis of these words will convey that in 1802 the British deprived the Peshwa of all but nominal suzerainty over the Gaekwad that gave power to the British and established their supremacy in Baroda while dwindling the hold the Peshwa had on the state earlier.[2] (It will be remembered that Raoji had sought British intervention by meeting the British governor in Cambay when on his return his palki had been nearly shot at.) The Treaty of Baroda of 29 July 1802 was signed between Major Walker and Anandrao, the sum and substance of which gave the British the right to intervene in all matters that threatened the safety of the state of Baroda and its welfare. F.A.H. Elliot in his book *Rulers of Baroda,* mentions that Anandrao in approving the Treaty of Baroda wrote officially 'that in consequence of there being many evil disposed persons among the Arabs who have plotted against my liberty and even my life, I desire that my subjects will pay no attention to my orders in this situation, but hear what Major Walker has to say. In the event of any evil-disposed persons attempting anything unfair or unreasonable against my person, my dewan, or his relations, or even if I myself or my successors should commit anything improper or unjust the English government shall interfere'. Such was the ill-defined powers given to the British by Anandrao which brought in scrutiny and high criticism from the British on the administration of Baroda accompanied by a strict control over its finances.

Bajirao II who had been watching the affairs of Baroda from a distance and recognized the fact that with British protection and the Britishers' right of interference in its affairs, Anandrao had signed off the Peshwa's suzerainty over the state. There were, of course, outstanding debts, tributes and claims on the side of Gaekwad to the Peshwa to be paid but the arbitration for these was now left to the British. No interference from anyone within the country or outside was allowed in the matters of the Baroda state, except the

British—this was now evident to Bajirao II. But, the Peshwa did not take it lying low and for twelve years he laboured to regain control by undoing the effects of the treaties with plots and counterplots but he laboured in vain, for the task was beyond his powers, as will be seen later.

The British were keen to reduce or dismiss the Arab sibandi (contingent) from the state as the cost of maintaining them was very high. The sibandi absorbed a sum that was totally disproportionate to the revenue of the state. Major Walker returned to Baroda as Resident after the Kadi campaign on 11 July 1802 and he set about his plans for reducing the Arab troops who initially had been brought in by Fatehsingh for trade. Raoji agreed with Major Walker on the expediency of this step.

The Arabs were on the brink of a mutiny and they held all the gates of the state, with Anandrao as a prisoner in his own palace. Matters were brought to a crisis when Anandrao demanded the surrender of Kanoji who was imprisoned in Ranpur with an Arab guard to guard him. Kanoji was to be handed over to certain parties who were to take him to Bombay, and Anandrao demanded that he should surrender to them and leave since he wanted him to leave Baroda state for good. The messenger who conveyed the order was a nephew of Sultan Jafar of the Arab jamadars who urged the jailors to disobey, and he was abetted by two of the Arab chiefs in Baroda—Zehya and Abud the Lame. Sultan Jafar, as he had not been consulted in the plan, disapproved of the step and a sharp quarrel sprung up between the two parties, Sultan Jafar and his Arab jamadars, which developed into a fierce fight.

During this time, Kanoji absconded and those who had caused the fight (the nephew of Sultan Jafar, Zehya and Abud the Lame) also escaped and fled from the city. On 18 December, the Ranpur fort was guarded by British troops. The Lehripura gate was held by Ben Haider, the Champaner gate by Jafar, the water gate by Zehya and the Barhanpur gate by several jamadars, including Abud. It was a fight to the finish between the Arabs and the British troops till the Arabs evacuated the fort on their terms—their arrears would be paid and they would be allowed to leave Gujarat unharmed.

Kanoji, after his escape from Ranpur, fled to Rajpipla where he gathered a force comprising the Kolis; he was later joined by the Arabs and Sindhis, and in no time, he raised a small army. Major William Holmes succeeded in driving him out of Gujarat in a combat in Vazira on 11 January 1803 and pursued him till he finally escaped and took refuge in Ujjain. Finally, realizing that they were up against the powerful British force the Arabs agreed to come to terms. The British promised them full settlement of the arrears due to them if they consented to their dismissal from Baroda service. Even though the British with their powerful army could have brought the Arabs to their knees, they preferred discretion to valour because they feared that the Arabs would not hesitate in killing their princely hostage, Anandrao, as vengeance against their foe. And, as far as the British were concerned, the reigning Gaekwad was worth his weight in gold since he completely identified himself and his state with the East India Company and its interests—territorial, financial and commercial. The Gaekwad state had every reason to be thankful to the British for ridding it of the Arab mercenaries who would have taken over as overlords and subjected the people of the state to a rule of tyranny. After the disbandment of the Arabs and the Kadi War (waged earlier against Malharrao of Kadi in which Major Walker won), a force of 2,000 British sepoys, loaded with European artillery, was kept in the state of Baroda at a cost of Rs 65,000 along with the cession of jaidad of equal value—thus proving the old adage that everything comes at a price.

While Major Walker was kept busy in trying to keep off the Arab forces from Baroda and dealing with Kanoji's nuisances in the years 1802 and 1803, there were other events taking place which were to prove inimical to the Baroda state. As mentioned earlier, Yeshwantrao Holkar and Daulatrao Scindia were squabbling for supremacy and taking over the Peshwa. Both of them had their sights set on Gujarat; Yeshwantrao with his army made an abortive entry into the Surat aththavasi, while Daulatrao, on the other hand, was more devious, as he had a claim of Rs 10,00,000 due to him on the Ahmedabad farm. He hoped that by attacking Ahmedabad and driving out Anandrao, Bajirao II would give him the farm and he would gain control of the Ahmedabad districts. However, Major Walker, anticipating something of this sort, got Prabhudas, an agent of the Scindias who had lent the Baroda state Rs 20,00,000 of which Rs 5,00, 000 was still due to him from the Baroda state, Major Walker got the Bombay government to persuade Prabhudas to pay Daulatrao, under guarantee that the debt would be discharged. This way Baroda was saved from getting involved in a war it could ill afford at that point of time.

Thus, with order restored in Baroda and all over Gujarat, the British set about claiming the territories ceded to them by Anandrao. By this time, the East India Company was beginning to emerge as a dominant power in India with its officers working hard to consolidate its position in the country. Even with the Gaekwads, they shifted gradually from their stance of an ally to that of being their masters and overlords. However, in spite of the loss of some territory to the Company, Anandrao had managed to preserve a good portion of it. Above all, he was free from all the obligations in the form of arrears, past and present, to Bajirao II.

When Raoji died in July 1803 Anandrao lost a faithful servant. The British government in Bombay owed Raoji a great deal and thus made the dewanship hereditary. They approved of his nephew, Sitaram, succeeding to the high post of dewan. However, Sitaram, whom Raoji adopted before his death, had none of his uncle's qualities and proved unworthy of the dewanship.

Kanoji was permitted to return to Baroda in 1812 and to live in Padra, a small village near Baroda. But not one to live in peace and let sleeping dogs lie, he tried once more to disrupt the government abetted by Rani Takhatbai, one of the favourite wives of Anandrao. A few others too were a part of the plot: Kanoji was to seize the capital with troops purchased with the money provided by one Jam Jesaji of Navanagar who had got into trouble with the British and wished to divert their attention by creating a disturbance in Gujarat. As the Resident was in Kathiawad and the capital denuded of its troops, the Kolis were to attack the minister's house, the Arabs the Residency and the neighbouring house of Gangadhar Shastri, Rani Takhatbai was to open a wicket gate which would give admittance into the citadel to Kanoji and his followers. The details of the plot were made known to the Residency in no time and a few days prior to the attack on the capital, Captain Ballantine, with a small force surrounded Padra and Kanoji was once again arrested. This was his last attempt to regain a foothold in Baroda; after his arrest, he was transported to Surat as a prisoner, from where he was sent to Bombay and finally to the Madras prison from where he never returned. Rani Takhatbai henceforth came under the strict British vigilance at the Residency, but she was spared because of Anandrao. In spite of being let off lightly, she continued to plot and this time with Sitaram against Gangadhar Shastri; Sitaram met her halfway hoping to regain his old post as dewan, a position he had lost through his own conduct. In the matter of any reform, particularly in expenditure, Major Walker as Resident found himself thwarted by Sitaram. This displeased the Bombay government who deprived Sitaram of his position. Sitaram ventured to crush the British party in Baroda through the aid of Bajirao II who also had an axe to grind with the British.

In August 1806 Fatehsinghrao II, Govindrao's younger son who had been offered to the service of the family god Khandoba and sent to reside in the neighbourhood of Poona, had returned to Baroda and was back in the palace to reside permanently. He was purchased back on 3 April 1806 from their family deity Khandoba by a Tula ceremony where he was weighed on one side of the scale with gold, silver and jewellery on the other, which were distributed among the Brahmins. Fatehsinghrao II was made the regent. Collecting tribute from the Baroda state was no easy task for anyone no matter what his abilityor efficiency amounted to. Many refused to pay and those who paid, did so at the point of the sword. Political disturbances were welcomed as they served as delaying tactics for paying the revenue, which in arrears amounted to nearly Rs 50,00,000. Major Walker did not approve of the moribund method of collecting revenue and decided to appoint a British officer for the purpose. The Mewasis and the Kathiawad chieftains were the main offenders and they were the supporters of Malharrao. However, Major Walker tried to reorganize the system of revenue collection by appealing to the goodwill of the various tributaries of the state and hoped to arrive at an amicable understanding with them.

7

Factors Leading to the Third Maratha War (1817–18)

Bajirao II, who by the Treaty of Bassein had lost the power the Peshwas had once enjoyed but had enriched their coffers with most of the revenues from the surrounding districts as well as from Gujarat, was no longer in a position to dictate terms to the Gaekwads in Baroda. Though he still held Ahmedabad under his control and the right to lease the Ahmedabad farmland to whomsoever he wished, it was not enough. His rights in Kathiawad had been seriously reduced to his disadvantage, arousing his hatred for the British and the desire to avenge this insult.

We need to digress here and trace the history back to the mulukgiri days to explain the Maratha wars and the ultimate supremacy of the British in Gujarat.

Major Walker was aware of the pressing urgency to reduce the expenses of maintaining the army in order to relieve the state of its pecuniary situation. He needed and expected large revenue from the district of Kathiawad to maintain an army there for some time which brings us to the mulukgiri system in Kathiawad.

The peninsula was divided and subdivided into numerous areas and inhabited by different tribes, including the Rajputs. Okhamandal, a valuable port in Kathiawad district was practically given to pirates. The inhabitants of Kathiawad were a passive lot and never got together to fight invaders; it was also perhaps due to its geographical position that they were unable to fight subjugation by rulers of other provinces.

Earlier, this peninsula was under Muslim domination and was invaded by Muslims repeatedly to extract tributes from the local people—these excursions came to be known as mulukgiri. According to Major Walker, this term simply signified 'systematized' raids to collect tributes. In Gujarat, it was an exercise of lawful sovereignty enforced by the principle that 'might is right' or, in other words, the law was in the hands of the powerful. The tribute varied according to the resistance or power of coercion which the collector of tribute possessed and exercised. As the army approached the territory from which a tribute was due from its chieftain, a vakil (mediator) ensured a settlement to be effected at the earliest. A bond called hat zalamanee (agreement) was executed—if a settlement was intended by the vakil, the chief was obligated to comply with every reasonable demand and that secured his territory. For this protection, the villages were supplied bandars or protectors, but it literally meant 'rocket bearers' who were men with horses. The number of such bandars varied according to the size of the village. However, the villagers could have done well without these 'rocket bearers', as they were a burden on the economy of the village chieftains who had to feed not only the men but also their horses and provide whatever they asked for. The villagers, being a sturdy lot, could have defended their villages well without this unnecessary appendage.

Under the Maratha government, this settlement ceased and the villagers and their chiefs were rid of oppression. Mulukgiri under the Marathas, particularly the Gaekwads, was conducted on very reasonable and lenient lines which left the people of the peninsula happy and even eager to pay their tribute to the Marathas. This attitude enabled the Marathas to establish their sovereignty in Kathiawad and also greatly enhanced the treasury of the Baroda state.

The year after Gujarat had been partitioned between the Peshwa and Damajirao II, the divisions of Kathiawad took place which entitled the Peshwa to draw revenues from a major portion of the peninsula. After the battle with Abu Shelukar over Ahmedabad, the entire share of the Ahmedabad subedari (jurisdiction), including the Peshwa's share of Kathiawad fell to Gaekwad, which should have brought the subjugation of the entire peninsula under Gaekwad. But Govindrao's death was followed by a period of chaos so much so that for five years no mulukgiri was conducted in Kathiawad. After Major Walker brought order into the affairs of Baroda, Raoji, to relieve the state from its dire straits, sent a powerful mulukgiri expedition to Kathiawad under his brother Babaji. With repeated expeditions of this kind, he restored a sum of Rs 51,03,063, thus rendering the state of Baroda solvent.

In August 1807, the combined forces of Major Walker and the Gaekwads along with Babaji's men encamped in Morvi taluka and invited all the chieftains of the villages of Kathiawad for a discussion on the terms for a permanent settlement of the Gaekwad's mulukgiri claims; once settled, they would inform the Bombay government about it. In these discussions, a lot of excesses of the past were moderated and proper protection for the villages was offered. However, there was one big flaw in the settlement which had grave consequences in the future—Gaekwad was not the principal owner of nearly one-half of Gujarat, but only an official exercising the Peshwa's rights. Therefore, he had no right to draw up a settlement without the approval or prior sanction of the Peshwa. When this fact was known to Bajirao II, he refused to renew the lease of the Ahmedabad farm to the Gaekwads once it expired.

Major Walker extracted revenue from Morvi and from other talukas as past arrears. The Gaekwad's requisition on Malia amounted to Rs 3,00,000 but the amount was reduced by the Residentto Rs 1,00,000 and the tribute due from Bhavnagar to the Gaekwad was transferred to the British as part of the territories ceded in jaidad for the services of the subsidiary force on 24 October 1808. The tribute which had been paid by the Rawal to the Peshwa was also made over to the British as stipulated in the Treaty of Bassein. Porbandar also came to terms without any difficulty. Thus, with one stroke the Resident put an end to the mulukgiri system that had been the cause of a lot of friction, wars, bloodshed and lawlessness. He also conferred upon Baroda as well as on its tributaries the means of enjoying certain revenues that would increase prosperity in the peaceful years to come. The revenue was fixed permanently at an approximate figure of Rs 9,50,000. One battalion, as subsidiary, together with horses was to remain in the Baroda state to ensure peace.

From 1814 to 1816, Mountstuart Elphinstone urged Bajirao II to allow the Company to collect the revenue on his behalf, to which the Peshwa demanded that the entire revenue should be handed over to him without any deductions for services rendered. Bajirao II drove a hard bargain but in order to keep up the relationship with the Peshwa, the Bombay government acquiesced and the Peshwa on his part also agreed to not upset the decennial system of revenue. In June 1816, Bajirao II reiterated his displeasure at being excluded from the Kathiawad settlement, but was abruptly told off by the Bombay government that according to the arrangement, he could not demand or increase the tribute due to him from the Kathiawad peninsula. The Peshwa not used to having his wishes met with a peremptory dismissal bristled with anger, resulting in widening the crack in the relations between the two. The Peshwa's rights in Kathiawad, which earlier formed a portion of the Ahmedabad farm territory, were now assigned to the East India Company, which put an end to the Peshwa's right to interference in that peninsula. This action resulted in only two factions playing a significant part in the affairs of Kathiawad—the British government and the Baroda government. Earlier, the Bombay government had secured Fatehsingh's II portion of the Kathiawad revenue as part payment for the subsidiary forces kept in the state for its protection from invaders. Negotiations in this matter, however, were met with a firm refusal from Fatehsingh II, and it was not much later, until his brother Sayajirao II ascended the gaddi, that the entire management of the country along with the collection of tribute was entrusted to the British by an agreement dated 3 April 1820. By this agreement, Gaekwad was to get a fixed sum from the tributary chiefs of Kathiawad and was denied any control over the territory with the exception of the districts of Amreli and Okhamandal. The British government in Bombay was henceforth solely responsible for the collection of tributes from the Kathiawad chieftains and maintaining relations with them. At the same time, they promised, while negotiating during the convention, to uphold all the legitimate claims of the Baroda government. Meanwhile, the Baroda government under Anandrao was divided into two factions—one headed by Gangadhar Shastri relying on the British and the other headed by Sitaram and Rani Takhatbai. The queen wished to side with Bajirao II who was voluble in stating that the British had unjustifiably deprived Anandrao of his powers because they wanted to run the administrative affairs of the state. Bajirao II's motive, of course, was to instigate an uprising in Gujarat against the British which would reinstall the Peshwas as the ultimate suzerains of the province. This brings us to the Third Maratha War (1817-18) that crushed Bajirao II completely. But, before that, the intrigues and plots being hatched in the palace must be exposed.

Earlier, in 1805, the British Resident in Baroda, Major Walker, had wanted to reform the state army but had postponed it and given priority to the Kathiawad affairs that had been settled when the convention with the chieftains had taken place; it had ensured a good source of revenue for the state. Now, in the matter of army reforms and all other reforms regarding expenditures, he found himself being thwarted by Sitaram who had given, by his dishonesty, such displeasure to the Bombay government that they decided to get rid of him by depriving him of his post. The first step in this direction had been to appoint Fatehsinghrao II as the regent. Next, was recalling Babaji from Kathiawad and entrusting him with executive powers while simultaneously depriving Sitaram of all his ministerial powers.

Army reform measures were taken up by which the maintenance cost was reduced to Rs 24,00,000. It was also decided to pay the army regularly, twice a year, and gradually to resume the landed jaidad, worth Rs 5,50,000, assigned to the principal officers. Sitaram's downfall was certain when it was discovered during the administration of Babaji that he had embezzled to the tune of Rs 30,00,000, a fact revealed through his correspondence with Hafiz Gulam Hassan, his partner in crime.

Fatehsinghrao II's appointment as the regent did not seem to augur well for the administration in Baroda as he was proving a dead weight with his hedonistic habits alarming the Resident as the state coffers did not allow for such extravagance. He cautioned the Bombay government to continue its vigil on Baroda's affairs.

Another plot was being hatched by Sitaram in connivance with Rani Takhatbai and Trimbakji Danglia (a Maratha Brahmin minister in the Peshwa court) vying for the Ahmedabad farm. Bajirao II too, for reasons of his own, was in the plot to assassinate Gangadhar Shastri who had been made head of the party attached to the British, in other words, as amutalik of the Resident, Walker. He was sent to persuade Bajirao II to withdraw his claims of nearly Rs 4,00,00,000 from Gaekwad, settle for a sum of Rs 50,00,000 and renew the lease of the Ahmedabad farm for an annual payment of Rs 8,00,000. However, the wily Peshwa had already leased the farm to Trimbakji Danglia, but preferring to play a cat- and- mouse game, he led Shastri along, pretending to consider his offer and playing on his vanity with flattery. He even suggested that his son marry the Peshwa's wife's sister and that Shastri take up the dewanship in Poona, lulling the poor Shastri into a false sense of well-being. On 14 July, while returning from a temple in Pandharpur, Shastri was attacked and murdered by Sitaram's agent Bandoji and his men. Fatehsinghrao II, when he learnt of the vile act, was beside himself with rage and to appease the Shastri family, he appointed his son Bhima Shanker as a minister.

Needless to say, the culprits were brought to justice. On 20 September, the ex-minister Sitaram was put under house arrest and in April 1816, he was deported to Bombay and was not seen for some years. Trimbakji was imprisoned in Thane, but escaped on 12 September 1816. It also became known to the British that Bajirao II had been assisting him with money to levy troops but was also conniving with Holkar, Scindia and the Raja of Nagpur to overthrow the British. The Resident demanded that Trimbakji be delivered to them along with the surrender of three hill forts. By 10 May 1817, Bajirao II who had up to that time kept his preparations for war at bay, agreed to do so. On 13 May, a treaty was drawn up by which the Peshwa was to surrender all future claims on Gaekwad. He was also to accept a sum of Rs 4,00, 000 a year for all the past claims and cede his tributes in Kathiawad to the British, renew the lease of the Ahmedabad farm to Gaekwad for a sum of Rs 4,00,000 a year and finally give up all rights in Gujarat, except over Ahmedabad and Ulpad. Also, the annual dues from Gaekwad were ceded to the British. This comprised the cession of Jambusar, Amod, Desbora, Dabhoi, Bahadarpur and Savli. Gaekwad was once and for all recognized as an independent prince who was no longer subordinate to the Peshwa and was free of paying him any nazrana (tribute). Thus, Anandrao gained enormously as compensation, as Elphinstone puts it, 'for the murder of his prime minister'.

On 25 June 1817, the sanad or a document of importance for the perpetual lease of Ahmedabad was drawn up and put into effect within a month.

Fatehsinghrao II was called upon to increase the numbers of the subsidiary army, but not at the cost of his Kathiawad revenues. The farm of Ahmedabad district was made over to the British for the maintenance of the increased subsidy and Anandrao had to pay Bajirao II Rs 4,00,000 a year as earlier agreed upon. Some territories in the villages were also exchanged with the British who presented him Okhamandal and Beyt as gifts since they were prominent places of worship for the Hindus.

Fatehsinghrao II died on 23 June 1818 at the age of twenty-six under mysterious circumstances. The demise of the prince regent marked a new beginning in the history of the Baroda state.

Relentless interference on the part of the British in the affairs of the Peshwa, considerably weakening of the Maratha confederacy and the humiliating terms of the last treaty served to increase the jealousy and anger of Bajirao II. This fury culminated with an attack on Resident Elphinstone by the Peshwa's army which led to the Third Anglo-Maratha War, resulting in a crushing defeat for Peshwa Bajirao II. The war began with an invasion of the Maratha territory by the British forces under the command of Governor General Hastings (no relation of Warren Hastings) supported by a force under Thomas Hislop. British victories were swift, resulting in the breakup of the Maratha Empire. The Peshwa was defeated in the battles of Khadki and Koregaon. Several minor battles were fought by the Peshwa's forces which included the armies of the Holkars, Scindias, Bhonsles and the Raja of Satarato prevent the Peshwa's capture, but he was ultimately caught and placed on a small estate in Bithur near Kanpur. Here it must be stated that Fatehsinghrao II before his death assisted the British and proved himself a staunch ally. He spared neither men nor money in aiding Sir W. Keir's army with 2,000 horses under the command of a very able commander, Kehmal-ud-din, who unfortunately died in the campaign. This support from the Gaekwads to the British went a long way in cementing their cordial relationship with the paramount power and augured well for the future generation.

Most of the territories belonging to the Maratha confederacy were annexed to the Bombay presidency. Much later in 1848, Satara was annexed by the policy of Lord Dalhousie's Doctrine of Lapse. The northern portion of Bhonsle's dominion; the Peshwa's territories in Bundlekhand; Nagpur, Indore and Gwalior from Shinde; and Jhansi from the Peshwa were annexed to the British, whose proficiency in warfare was aptly demonstrated through their rapid victories in Khadki, Sitapur, Mahidpur, Koregaon and Satara. The mighty Maratha confederacy, so carefully built by Chhatrapati Shivaji, crumbled and disintegrated with the Third Anglo-Maratha War. Even though the British had generally become the masters of the Maratha confederates which included the Gaekwads, but on paper, Gaekwad was a little more independent than the others. In 1819, the British had not only the territory ceded to them by Anandrao, but also those possessed by the Poona durbar, making them owners of practically three-quarters of Gujarat. But they discovered to their consternation that the bits and pieces of their territory interlaced with that of the Gaekwads had no clear boundary to demarcate the possessions of each. They got Anandrao to exchange some of these bits and pieces to gain a comprehensive layout of the part yielded to them. Thus, in 1819, the domain of the Gaekwads of Baroda received a more concrete geographical shape that satisfied both parties.

From past events, one can comprehend the significance of two proceedings—one, the manner in which the British were able to establish themselves as the paramount power in Gujarat in cessions leading to the expansion of their territories; and two, the reasons for Gaekwad support in their battles, which in turn ensured the British support of the Gaekwads on the gaddi, by which Gujarat did not fall completely under British domination.

8
Sayajirao Gaekwad II

Anandrao died on 2 October 1819. He was succeeded by his younger brother Sayajirao II who had earlier, for a brief period, been acknowledged as the regent in 1806 since Anandrao had been too weak-minded to rule. Now, after the death of Anandrao, Sayajirao II formally ascended the gaddi and was in control of the internal affairs of his state. He was to take administrative decisions after seeking the advice of the British whenever there was an urgent need to do so, in short, whenever there was an emergency. His reign was beset with family dissension over jewellery. All eyes were centred on the family jewels; it is said that even Anandrao had died with 'his head resting on a stone…with his eyes fixed on the treasure room'.[1]

Immediately after his death, a petty family quarrel started. Rani Takhatbai, who was planning all kinds of intrigues for gaining the gaddi for her sons and acquiring the contents of the treasure room, claimed that it was the property of the deceased Anandrao. Sayajirao II, who was no milksop, told her in no uncertain terms that the treasure belonged to the state. He kept the room locked for months under the guard of a British soldier although there was a back entrance to it which was used secretly by the sovereign. However, the governor of Bombay, Sir John Malcolm, was obliged to intervene to settle the claim and other disputes. Under the British guarantee, a nemnuk (allowance) was settled on the queen and her sons who separated after the death of their mother. Fatehsinghrao II's widow, Radhabai, who had been prevented from committing sati by her well-wishers, also put forward a claim for the gaddi for her adopted son Govindrao. However, it was pointed out to her that the proviso made when granting her the right for adoption did not allow her adopted son the right to succession. The matter should have ended there, but Radhabai did not accept this proviso. As a result, the British guarantee was withdrawn and Sayajirao II withheld their nemnuk. It was not until 1826 that Radhabai and her adopted son withdrew their claim and got their allowance. But Sayajirao II refused to fulfil his promises and arrested a number of Govindrao's dependants. A bitter fight ensued between the two and ultimately, Govindrao was completely suppressed and taken away to Surat in 1830 on Sir John Malcolm's orders. Later, he was shifted to Ahmedabad where he languished in prison. Sayajirao II secured the properties of both Fatehsinghrao II's widows.

Once that had been settled, Sayajirao II tried to shake off the dictates of the Company's officials. It was fortunate for him that the governor of Bombay, who had decided to be heavy-handed with him, was recalled from office before his term ended. Sayajirao II was a callow youth when he ascended the gaddi and needed an adviser. Unfortunately, he selected one of the worst scoundrels in India—Dakji Dadaji whose rascalism totally overshadowed the great merits of his predecessor, Gangadhar Shastri. Sayajirao II chose Dadaji as he was aware that the man had considerable influence over the Resident.

Dadaji was Major Carnac's pet. He had first appeared in Baroda in 1816 during the reign of Fatehsinghrao II who, to his credit, had mistrusted the man and disliked him intensely. Dadaji's family was well thought of by Captain Major Carnac's father, whose firm was in Bombay; hence, the Resident appointed him to be the native agent in the murdered Shastri's place in 1816. Soon, he became an influential person in the durbar due to the Resident's support. The clever man used this to create misunderstandings between Sayaji II and the British government, tricking both to fill his own coffers. Earlier, in 1816, he had turned the potadari system (loans raised by the state to pay off the debts of the previous year and meet the expenses of the coming year) in his own favour by persuading the Resident to make him a potadar (one who arranges the loans) and then he forced Hari Bhakti and Marial Narayan, both bankers, to charge 9 per cent interest instead of the usual 12 per cent, by threatening to get the money from abroad, and to give him an equal share in the business. Since Dadaji did not have the capital to start with, the two bankers put in Rs 8,50,000 each while he put in nothing. He took up the Kathiawad potadari in the same way with Ratanji Khandas, a moneylender, and also undertook a valuable contract for supplying cash to the contingent force in Malwa. The state gained by 3 per cent by way of interest, but Dadaji got rich by robbing people—he took commissions from the farmers for guaranteeing the payment of their revenue at the right time; he cheated the state by transferring public money into his private accounts, charging a high commission for cashing the durbar accounts and so on. This was the man whom Sayajirao II wished to appoint as his adviser and in 1819 he became the dewan of the state. Dadaji did not intend to remain long in service; he planned to stay only till his purpose of enriching himself had been achieved. However, Sayajirao II soon got suspicious of him and since his influence with the Resident had not benefited the ruler in any special way, he was happy to dispense with his services when it was suggested by the Bombay government.

The state of Baroda was in debt to the tune of over Rs 1,00,00,000. Loans were raised to repay debts and reduce expenditure. Sayajirao II proposed to cut down the allowances of his ministers by one-third and also bring down other expenses. To introduce and maintain a healthy system of expenditure, it was advisable to bring in a good minister to render the job effectively. Vithalrao Bhau, who was Babaji's son, was appointed as minister but he did not meet the desired expectations and was soon replaced by Divanji who had rendered the state brilliant services during the Kadi War as well as in Kathiawad, as Babaji's lieutenant, when he had captured Malharrao Gaekwad of Kadi and had him imprisoned. During his time, he had increased both the revenues and the territories of the state. At first, Sayajirao II was very pleased with his minister but as time went on he began to suspect that he had leanings towards the Resident and was listening to his suggestions—this turned his affection for the man to bitter hatred. Sayaji II's problem lay in his policy. He refused to accept the British as his overlords and wanted the administration to lie chiefly in his own hands—this attitude drove a deep cleft in his relationship with the British.

Here we need to understand the bahandari system in order to comprehend and link the turn of events that followed over the years. The bahandari system was a guarantee given during the reign of Anandrao by the Arabs for protection against foreign invaders or invaders from other states. Eventually expelled by the British, the Arabs had agreed to disband their troops; however they did so on the condition that the guarantee should be extended to the Gaekwad state as well. Before the expulsion, a few guarantees had already been given to Desai of Navsari in 1793; second one to the deserving Raoji by the agreement of 29 July 1802; and the third one to Malharrao, the jagirdar of Kadi, which, however, lapsed when he was proved to be a traitor, and was imprisoned and exiled.

Raoji's guarantee is of significance as it was hereditary as far as the emoluments were concerned, but the office of the dewan was not. Thus, his adopted son Sitaram continued to receive the pension and after his death in 1823, his son Narayanrao continued to hold the nemnuk of Rs 60,000, but this was withdrawn when his guardians tried to pass off a forged version of the treaty of 1802 on the Resident. Once the Arabs had been disbanded and the guarantees had been taken on by the British giving them enormous power to interfere in the administration and finance, payments such as grants, pensions and loans had to be first authorized by them. 'This power established a connection with the moneyed men from which the company reaped much benefit; and for a time Gaekwad did not mind it, for the step, as the Resident wrote, deprived the sardars of a powerful means of controlling the government.'² The Arab guarantees were of two kinds—one for the due payment of money and the other for personal security. The breach of an engagement made by the sarkar was held to absolve the giver of the guarantee from 'his duty as a subject'.³ The Arabs presented many instances when to enforce guarantees they filled the durbars of the raja and minister, to hold their persons in rigorous confinement. The Arabs had maintained a force in Baroda for service to the Gaekwads, the expenses of which had been maintained by the Gaekwads to the extent of reducing the state to insolvency. The British, by taking over the guarantee, kept a force for the state's protection which was maintained by the Baroda state at a reduced expense.

In return for the aid given to the British in accomplishing their views in Baroda these people were given British guarantee like in the case of Raoji, but making the emoluments received by them as hereditary was proving deleterious to the state's finances. This proved quite deleterious to the state's finances as it has been rightly said that 'no guarantees were so calculated to make mischief as the hereditary ones, which not only extended to persons and property, but guaranteed the continuance of office to particular families'.⁴ Gradually, the number of guarantees was reduced and the Bombay government set down, as an established policy, to clear itself of all the guaranteed loans and to 'contract no more pledges in the future'.⁵ In 1849, Captain French, the officiating Resident, strongly recommended that many of the bahandari engagements should be held to have lapsed and was successful in the case of the Shastris (Gangadhar's family) and of the moneylender Manekchand Rupchand who also had British guarantee. In

1853, the Court of Directors determined that the 'guarantees granted by the officers of Arab troops were in their nature temporary' and hence Colonel Outram brought many of the temporary engagements to an abrupt end, using the word 'chalu' meaning 'temporary' and therefore, not hereditary; and the Court of Directors accepted his version in 1856. But the British contingent in Baroda as a guarantee continued to remain there and at the expense of the Gaekwads till some years after Sayajirao Gaekwad III ascended the gaddi.

In all fairness, Mountstuart Elphinstone had shared with Sayajirao II that the commission that had been installed earlier because of Anandrao's infirmity and had now been withdrawn and in future the Maharaja would conduct the affairs of his government himself. He also said that Maharaja Sayajirao II would be solely responsible for the debts, and he should deal openly with the British government and abstain from any dealings with other states. The payments referred to were with the guaranteed ministers, bankers and tributary states. There was less risk of Sayajirao II breaking his engagements with the tributary states as Gaekwad's troops had been withdrawn from Kathiawad and Mahikantha and all political connections with these districts had been severed; the British government bore the onus of collecting the revenues. The Maharaja could now independently govern the affairs of the state of Baroda. Sayajirao II's reign began well even though there were debts and engagements with ministers and bankers but still they were not so onerous as to cow him down. These could have been cleared with careful manipulation of finances and Maharaja Sayajirao II, in time, could have settled down to a comfortable existence. The Resident's position at this time was more in the nature of a persona non grata, though he was to be acquainted with all financial matters with regard to the state and at times render advice on behalf of the Bombay government.

The refusal on the part of the Bombay government to recognize any claims of Gaekwad to certain portions of Kathiawad district, in the Kheda collectorate, in the districts which were a part of Ahmedabad and in the dominions of the Nawab of Cambay caused Gaekwad to seethe with fury. Apart from this, certain reductions in his revenue added to his resentment and anger. We need to understand how the establishment of British power in western India had a twofold effect on the state of Baroda. As seen earlier, the encroachments of Bajirao II had come to an end in 1818 and Sayajirao, though seated firmly on the gaddi, was prevented from extending his influence in Kathiawad, Mahi, Rewa Kantha and also in the neighbouring tributary states. British political agents were appointed for Palanpur and Radhanpur and also for the small states bordering on the Rann of Kutch, Sind and Marwar. In 1825, a series of smaller states were placed under a political agent who had the power to mediate between Gaekwad and his Mewasi subjects. Before the British stepped in and took control over these tributary states, there had been constant gains and losses, disputes over tributes and so on but with the advent of the British, all claims were settled once and for all after thorough investigation and all 'that was in a state of transition was rigidly crystallized.'[6]

Sayajirao II did not keep his promise of settling debts and fulfilling his engagements with bankers. With the influence of Rani Gahenabai, Sayajirao III directed his attentions towards hoarding his private treasury, in other words, he indulged in corruption. In spite of the fact that he had amassed wealth into his private treasury, he did not pay off his debts to the bankers and others. While his private treasury was filling in, the financial condition of the state was deplorable. Most of Sayajirao II's reign was marked with intrigues and plots guaranteed to bring about the downfall of one minister or another, and several temporary sequestrations of Baroda territories by the Bombay hierarchy. Vithalrao Divanji, an efficient and able minister, was dismissed from his post on the grounds that he was in conspiracy with the Resident Mr Willoughby. Veniram Aditram and Prabhakar Dixit were appointed as Sayajirao II's advisers in 1828. He consulted them and the counsel of these two men led him away from the agreements he had entered into and persuaded him to persecute those of his own subjects who looked for protection to the British guarantees made in their favour. These men did their best to incite Sayajirao's II rancour against the Bombay government, particularly Veniram who was very active in this matter and did his best to drive both the governments further apart. Gopal Atmaram who was appointed as the joint minister in 1829 was ousted from his post in 1833 by the manipulations of Veniram and such manipulations went on for some more years.

A lot of constructive suggestions for clearing the debts were given to Sayajirao II by Mountstuart Elphinstone who was the governor of Bombay till 28 November 1827; he always treated the suspicious Sayajirao II with courtesy and consideration. His successors Sir John Malcolm and Lord Clare tried with gentle persuasion to bring the young Maharaja to see reason and resolve his problems concerning his huge debts, but it took Sir James Carnac to bring this long struggle to a close. On 28 March 1828, Sir John Malcolm issued a proclamation—'The temporary sequestration of certain resources and territories of the Gaekwad state till the fulfillment of the pecuniary engagements made with the bankers under the guarantee of the British government; but, when that object shall have been attained, it will remain to consider of the reparation which may be due to itself for expenses, and to take ample security against any future violation either of the term of treaties, or of the pledges and guarantee given to individuals.'[7] The list of mahals sequestrated were Petlad, Bahiyal, Kadi, Dabhoi, Bahadarpur, Sinor, Amreli, Sainagar and the tributes were from Kathiawad, Mahikantha, Rewa Kantha and other sources. A peculiar step was taken by Governor Lord Clare. He ordered creditors who were holders of septennial leases to give up their leases assuring them that their losses therefrom would be refunded to them. The onus for this was put on Sayajirao II to pay them Rs 7,00,000 as reimbursement; this way the debt was reduced to a certain degree. For reforming the contingent of horses, a few more districts were sequestrated in order to pay the force and maintain them from the proceeds of those districts.

Meanwhile, as the gulf between Sayajirao II and the Bombay government widened considerably and James Williams was posted in Ahmedabad as political commissioner of Gujarat. He was to reside in Ahmedabad and exercise all the powers of a Resident and to 'superintend the strict fulfillment of the treaties of subsidy and alliance.'[8] Simultaneously, the subsidiary force was incorporated with the subdivision of the Bombay army, with headquarters in Ahmedabad. When Williams left for Ahmedabad, he carried with him the guaranteed bankers who were Sayajirao II's creditors as they feared for their safety.

After his dismissal from service, Vithalrao, the old minister, was given protection by the Bombay government. He was granted a pension, made manager of the confiscated mahals and given certain other privileges which also included the adoption of a son named Krishnarao. However, Sayajirao II refused to recognize the adoption and hence no nazrana was paid.

Meanwhile, Sayajirao II's antipathy towards the Bombay government and his obstinate refusal to meet their demands created such alarm in the minds of those in the Baroda durbar that some of his wives, together with his relatives, conspired to seize his person and punish his favourites and advisers, and, if he still proved obstinate, to proclaim his son, Ganpatrao, sovereign instead.

The conspiracy failed and the chief conspirators were executed. Sir John Malcolm left India in 1831 and was succeeded by Lord Clare who decided to deal with Sayajirao II with a firm hand.

Lord Clare made a couple of visits to Baroda to forge a better understanding between the two governments wherein he treated Sayajirao II with the utmost consideration and respect. During his second visit, a settlement was arrived at by which he agreed to Sayajirao II's suggestion of paying off his creditors in one lump sum instead of in instalments. Lord Clare, in conjunction with the Bombay government, agreed to it provided the state was not plunged further into debt and if the creditors were satisfied with the payment in one instalment. Subsequently, the deeds or promissory notes with the creditors were destroyed. The governor was in the dark as to the actual amount paid to the creditors, though the sum owed to them stood at Rs 39,00,000. One fact emerged from the supposed transaction that Sayajirao II had paid Rs 2,00,000 from his private treasury. A couple of years later, Colonel Outram exposed the settlement to be fictitious, but as far as the Bombay government was concerned, they were done with the matter and had freed themselves of their obligations to the creditors who had preferred to put their faith in the native prince rather than in them. Some of the sequestrated districts were restored to their rightful owners. However, there were still vast sums owed to others who had no guarantors and the debt owed to them amounted to Rs 60,00,000. Lord Clare extracted a promise from Sayajirao II that he would settle this amount within a year. The cost of maintaining a force in the sequestrated districts was proving to be costly and Sayajirao II deposited Rs 10,00,000 in a British treasury which the government was at liberty to expend if the contingent force was not paid on time. Lord Clare accepted the payment without interest and extracted a promise from Sayajirao II that he would maintain the contingent force in a healthier way after which he restored the remaining sequestrated districts to him. This dealing was approved by the Bombay government and they even suggested that the Rs 10,00,000 should be returned to Sayajirao II, but this did not happen till the year 1841. The British government detached itself from the financial affairs of the Gaekwad government and people who were looking for redressal of their grievances of the British government had to look for it elsewhere as it was not extended to them.

Mr Williams returned to Baroda as a political commissioner towards the end of 1835 and resided at Sayajirao II's durbar; the Bombay government insisted on 'frequent personal communications between him and the Gaekwad prince'.[9]

Between Lord Clare's visit in 1832 and James Carnac's visit in 1841 was the time when Gaekwads came mostly into conflict with the British authorities till they decided to change their attitude from indifference to synergy due to the state of affairs in Gujarat. Sayajirao II failed to keep his promise of paying his debtors which led to fresh sequestrations. Negligence of the district of Kathiawad had given rise to piracy by the Waghers of Okhamandal. In 1833, an opium broker, who was a British subject, complained to the Resident that sixteen of his relatives had been imprisoned because a friend of the minister Veniram had instituted judicial proceedings against his brother. The governor general ordered Sayajirao II to release them, but Sayaji II refused to comply, and this resulted in the death of the petitioner who committed suicide, unable to bear the misfortune thrust upon him. There were quite a number of similar cases with tragic ends due to Sayajirao II listening to the advice of his unscrupulous ministers of which Veniram was the chief one. In 1837, the Bombay government demanded the dismissal of Veniram, who was a British subject. Sayajirao II pleaded that he had been a resident of Baroda for twenty-five years, out of which he had spent ten in Sayajirao II's employment with the high-sounding title of Vakil Himmat Bahadur. Eight months before this demand from the Bombay government, Veniram had disappeared from the scene for a short while. Later on, he declared that he had made a trip to Benares as he had feared for his life and even cited some names in that context. He later contradicted his earlier statement by which it was learnt that his trip to Benares was a fictitious one; he had remained in the state 'because the people of Baroda had begged him to stay'.[10] While he was pleading his case, the Bombay government received an anonymous letter which clearly stated that Veniram was so hated by the people of Baroda that he had thought it safer to run away. He was robbed on his journey and Sayajirao II, in order to justify his return, had forcibly wrangled from the leading people of Baroda the petition which Veniram had boasted of earlier. The petition was a contrived one obtained through violence and bribes. The victims were Parbhuda, Lala Mangal Parekh, the sardars and the agent of

Gopalrao, Mairal. Later, Gopalrao and Hari Bhakti had purchased Veniram's support, as had the Nawab of Baroda, who obtained from him the suba of Kathiawad, where he made a large fortune by oppression. The other ministers who were a little better were allowed to be kept on by the government but were to have no say in any of the matters in which the British government or any of its guarantees were involved. Subsequently, when in 1841 Sir James Carnac visited Baroda and expressed his wish that Sayajirao should under no circumstances have any contact with Veniram, Sayajirao II acquiesced, declaring that he now hated him, and in the future he wished to run the administration without a minister. James Carnac granted this request 'so long as His Highness should continue on good terms with the Resident and listen to his advice and avoid all breach of engagements'.[11]

The famous 'twenty-eight demands' were made on Sayajirao II by the Bombay government, out of which the first was to render justice to the unjustifiable act of imprisoning the opium broker's relations; second, the dismissal of Veniram; third, to restore order in the district of Okhamandal and many more. He was to cooperate with the police and rectify the past gross acts of carelessness on the part of Sayajirao II's officers. Measures were adopted to prevent offenders, who were subjects of the British government, from being given refuge within the boundaries of the Baroda state—this problem occurred due to there being no clear boundaries between the Baroda state and British-owned territories. This problem was carried over till India got its independence. These were some of the many demands that testify to the awful state of insecurity to life and property which existed during those years within and along the boundaries of the Baroda state.

Sayajirao II was also to recognize and confirm all the guarantees of the British government, including those made to Gangadhar Shastri, Dakji Dadaji and others, and he had to assent to all the measures the British government had taken to satisfy all those individuals of their claims.

Such was the state of Baroda's affairs after Lord Clare's settlement. What had not been achieved by gentle persuasion was to be achieved by harsh measures. Sayajirao II's personal finances from the account given by the assistant Resident, J. Ogilvie, in 1845 presents a picture of affluence, a very different one from the state of Baroda's financial situation. According to his report, even after the sequestrations, Sayajirao II was getting Rs 2,00,000 a year and before the septennial leases about Rs 4,00,000–5,00,000; he was getting much more by way of nazranas from farmers and bribes. His private villages, grasslands, taxes from firewood and other sundry items went into his private treasury which could have well brought the state out of its Rs 60,00,000 debt. Besides, Sayajirao II was a great banker. The Central Bank of Ganesh Ishwar in Baroda was founded in 1829. He had two banks in his palace which yielded money and another bank in the city with branches in Sadra, Kadi, Petlad and Rajkot each yielding around Rs 5,000. This way his private fortunes increased by Rs 5,00,000 a year and what he did not save was spent in disbursements to relations and dependants, sports activities, shows and, regretfully, even in bribes and secret service employment.

On 6 August 1838, the government of Bombay decided to confiscate Petlad, a drastic measure to bring Sayajirao II to his senses as till then no effort had been made regarding their demands. It was also decided that if this measure also proved futile, then Sayajirao II would be deposed and his son would be elevated to the throne instead. Petlad was sequestrated from Sayajirao II on 1 November 1838 and the proclamation of 5 November stated, 'After many years of useless discussion His Highness had been granted one month, within which period he was to satisfy certain demands. The demands had not been satisfied, and as the district had been sequestrated: if in two months more, compliance had not been made, the district would be wholly forfeited.'[12] On 12 February 1839, the British Crown notified that with regard to Sayajirao II, 'Petlad had been absolutely and entirely forfeited.'[13] Sayajirao II soon came to his senses, realizing he would be the loser in the long run and expressing his determination to the Resident to meet all the demands of the government. He set about suiting action to words and in the years 1840-41, nearly all the twenty-eight demands were met to the satisfaction of the Bombay government.

Petlad and Navsari were restored to Sayajirao II along with his tributes from Mahi, Kathiawad and the Rewa Kantha. James Carnac also restored to Sayajirao II his Rs 10,00,000 deposited in 1832 in a British security for the punctual payment of the contingent to Sayajirao II. The irregular horse (a British contingent kept as protection against disturbance but maintained by Sayajirao II) raised in March 1839 was not disbanded and as Petlad had been restored to him, Sayajirao II agreed to pay Rs 3,00,000 for its maintenance. Ideally, he would have liked to be done with this payment altogether but his entreaties were of no avail and the payment continued till Khanderao,

Sayajirao II's second son, ascended the gaddi.

A radical change was also brought about in the customs prevalent in the state. It had been the tradition for the British authorities and the British troops at Baroda to take part in the Ganpati and Dusshera festivals, but it was resolved henceforth that British officers and soldiers would not do so as it was 'ill-suited' to them. The procession was to draw up at a selected spot and give its salute only to Sayajirao II. The Resident was also barred from accepting gifts or dresses of honour from Sayajirao II or honour the prince with a reciprocal gesture. Sayajirao II was thus put in his place, much to his annoyance and disgust.

Certain barbaric customs were put to an end by the British government—sati was made punishable by law; the prohibition on selling Hindu children to Muslims was enforced in 1847; and a check was kept on the practice of slavery.

For a proper analysis of the acrimony between the two governments, we need to dwell on the point which was the source of irritation to both parties. The British government strongly disapproved of Sayajirao II's harsh treatment of his subjects who held the British guarantee of protection from the tyranny of the Maharaja. Sayajirao II's resentment stemmed from the fact that his own people sought protection from the British and Sayajirao II was, therefore, eager to set about bringing the British authority to nought. The twenty-fifth demand of the twenty-eight demands stipulated that 'persons holding the guarantee should be strictly ordered to obey the commands of the Sarkar (British officer) and to perform their duties'. When James Carnac pointed out to Sayajirao II that he should respect the guarantees given by the British, he retorted with the request that 'these men should be enjoined to treat him with respect and not to forget that, after all, he was *their* sovereign'.[14] Over a period of time, it was seen that possessors of the guarantee were making a thorough nuisance of themselves claiming British involvement in matters that did not concern them. They were also found wanting in *that* respect and obedience which they were bound to pay Sayajirao II who was their sovereign.

He felt the British had initially come to trade and they should have remained as traders. They had no right to exert control over a country that did not belong to them. This being the underlying reason for his uncompromising attitude, he waited to show them the door one day.

Even after the long-drawn-out battle between the two governments had come to an end, the hatred that Sayajirao II harboured in his mind towards the British did not diminish and he continued to have his spies inform him of the goings-on in the Bombay government's office; also, he resorted to bribery, ever recognized as a weapon in politics, to unearth important documents and secrets of the Company in Bombay. Intrigue reigned supreme in the Baroda durbar, till at last, all Gujarat believed that every Englishman had his price. Top officials with good reputations were at the mercy of the meanest rogues and tricksters. By now the Gaekwads had realized they were no better off under the British rule than they had earlier been under the Peshwas. Sayajirao II's reign had been wholly taken up with the struggle for independent rule sans British interference while the British officials were equally determined to demonstrate that they were the real masters and rulers of the land. The moves and countermoves made by both parties in this contest would make all those stories of espionage and the improbable stories of the Arabian nights seem pale and colourless in comparison. They included blackmail, forgery, slander, mysterious deaths, bribery and corruption and black magic. This went on regardless of British official's watchful eyes inside the four walls of the palace and in the Company too. On the Company's side, the weapon used was power, bolstered by the belief that a native, whether prince or pauper, was a dishonest man. Sayajirao II on the other hand had wealth which he used freely to get what he wanted in the firm belief that every Englishman was susceptible to bribes—it just depended on the price. Sir James Outram who had succeeded Mr Andrews as Resident in May 1847 stayed on in Baroda till 1849. He was mostly occupied in resolving cases of fraud and treachery which took a toll on his health, forcing him to leave Baroda to recoup his shattered health.

Throughout his reign, Sayajirao II was treated by the British government with consideration and respect. Even when he deliberately flouted their wishes, he was treated with leniency; it was only after he did not respond to their 'twenty-eight demands' that they took stringent measures against him. Severity on their part got the desired result and the battle of wits drew to a close.

This unwarranted exercise of power by the East India Company was brought about by Anandrao, when he had allowed the Company to involve itself in the affairs of the Baroda state. The East India Company had decided to help Anandrao as he was the rightful heir to the throne of Baroda, but Anandrao at that time did not realize that the invitation to the foreign power would constitute the greatest danger to the state in times to come as he was anxious to maintain his position as ruler at any cost. This was the beginning of the expansion of the paramount power and it began to slowly exert its influence over the state. The treaty that had been signed in 1802 and subsequently signed in June and July of the same year were consolidated in 1805 in a definite treaty which was supplemented by the treaty of 1817 which bound the Company to support Maharaja Gaekwad II. An offensive and defensive alliance was entered into by which the state agreed to receive from the Company a subsidiary force for which, as payment, the state ceded territory and gave over the direction of its foreign policy to the East India Company. By the treaties of 1802, 1805 and 1817, the independence of Baroda was recognized and because of these far-reaching changes Anandrao's reign is very important in the annals of Baroda history.

The treaty of 1802 dated 6 June stated: 'There shall be a true friendship and good understanding between the Honourable English East India Company and the State of Anandrao Gaekwad in pursuance of which the Company will grant the said Chief its countenance and protection in all his public concerns according to justice and as may appear to before the good of the country. Respecting which he is also to listen to advice.'

The concluding part of the treaty reads: 'There should be continous mutual friendship between the Gaekwad Sena Khaskhel Shamsher Bahadur and the Company *Ingrez* Bahadur and assistance should be rendered by the Company's government according as may appear proper. They will do what may be good for the Sena Khas Khel.' This became a major point of dispute between the Company and the Baroda government; however, the definite treaty of 1817 reiterated that the friendly alliance between the two governments be maintained. The basic terms of the treaty were first, a subsidiary force to be kept for the protection of the ruler's person; second, for the security of the state, third, for the security of British Indian districts bordering those of the Baroda state and lastly for the purpose of opposing the common enemy in India.

On 1 October 1830, all British troops in Gujarat were combined in the Northern Army and the subsidiary as a separate command was abolished. Later, the force was completely merged in the British Indian army, and no separate force was maintained in Baroda, except a battalion of eight hundred from the Indian infantry that was stationed in the cantonement which was a piece of ground about a mile away from the city of Baroda.

On Sayajirao II ascending the throne, the East India Company government ceased its interference in the internal affairs of the state which they were exercising while Anandrao was alive. At this time the control of the tributaries paying revenue to Baroda was retained by the Company. This was another milestone in the history of Baroda which was gradually losing its sovereign rights resulting in Sayajirao II's reign being marked by differences arising between the Baroda government and the Company, which continued for nearly twenty years till they were finally calmed by Sir James Rivett-Carnac the governor of Bombay in 1841. In fact it was due to him that Sayajirao II was not deposed from the throne of Baroda. Sayajirao II however was able to see the intention of the East India Company of gaining complete control over the state though, not by deposing him but by binding him to their will in bringing the whole of India under their suzerain authority. Sayajirao II was thus unable to check the gradual passing of their sovereignty from Maharaja's hands as it was beyond his capacity to rise against the Company militarily. His brother had bound his hands and feet and rendered him impotent against the Company's devious aims.

On 28 December 1847, Maharaja Sayajirao Gaekwad II breathed his last, leaving the throne vacant for his successor. In all the events that have been narrated so far regarding Sayajirao II, he comes across as an enfant terrible, with his rebellious attitude and reluctance to accept authority even to the extent of refusing to accept the British government as the master who must be obeyed. Even though Sayajirao II has been severely criticized for his reign of the Gujarat province, he can be considered as one of the most remarkable of all the Gaekwads. First, he did more than anyone to increase the power of his throne and he was respected and truly loved by his people. If he was parsimonious, it was to render the state solvent; if he was obstinate, it was because he saw the British as greedy and grasping interlopers. He proved it through his actions successfully. In spite of several sequestrations and agreements, he got back his entire country for his people. Though he had to pay Rs 3,00,000 for the maintenance of Roberts Horse (nickname for the British contingent), the amount for him was a trifle and he must have laughed up his sleeve while putting on a show of being overcome with shame at the disgrace. In actual fact, he had his hold over his army, his sardars, the moneyed men, the ministers and every party in the palace, while he drove the British to relinquish by degrees all interference in the state. The negative side to his reign was that it had damaged the goodwill and cordiality, carefully built by Fatehsinghrao I and Fatehsinghrao II.

Sayajirao II had five legitimate sons—the four older ones were born from his first wife Chimnabai, thus, by the order of primogeniture, Ganpatrao, being the eldest, succeeded to the gaddi at the age of thirty. Khanderao, the second son and younger by ten years, was to succeed some years later.

9

Ganpatrao Gaekwad

Though not fortunate enough to receive a formal education, Ganpatrao Gaekwad was receptive to good advice. During his reign, some useful reforms were introduced and public welfare work was carried out. Ganpatrao did not have the shrewdness and the wisdom needed to check intrigues that were being carried out under his nose; as a result, the nine years of his reign were taken up in a relentless struggle to be independent of British dominance, which was a futile effort as the British were equally determined to subordinate the Gaekwads to their rule. The goings-on talked about earlier continued regardless.

During the year Colonel James Outram was away from Baroda, Captain French was Resident from October 1848 to May 1850. In May 1850, Colonel Outram returned to Baroda, and with his usual zest reasserted his opinions concerning the men of Baroda and the prevalence of intrigue. He sent in his khatpat report to the Bombay government on 31 April 1851, in which he blamed the government for not taking more stringent measures to overcome bribery and corruption which were rampant and destroying the state of Baroda. This led the governor of Bombay, Lord Falkland, and Messrs Blane and Bell under Sir Richmond Campbell, to advise Colonel Outram to leave the Baroda state. Accordingly, he left on a month's leave on 21 December 1851 and on 20 January 1852, he was replaced with J.M. Davies. In July of the same year, the Court of Directors passed in review the whole of Colonel Outram's career as Resident and 'even while noticing a certain lack of respect in the khatpat report', they concluded their review by praising the 'zeal, energy, ability and success with which enquiries had been prosecuted and attended with great difficulty. But, they hoped Colonel Outram would be once more trusted with high employment.'[1]

During the period 1851 to 1852, Colonel Outram, who was still the political officer in Baroda, stopped certain letters from being delivered from the post office and the people to whom the letters were addressed were kept away from him. The letters revealed that the old practice of buying confidential documents of the Bombay council was being vigorously continued by the officials of the Baroda durbar. He had also received a letter in September 1851 sent to him anonymously, and the letter had a message for Ganpatrao's younger brother and heir apparent, Khanderao. The message had these alarming words: 'Arrangements are being made to carry out what occurred to Fatehsingh Maharaj; you wait a little.' The exact origin of this letter was not known. These instances prove that intrigue was still teeming in the Baroda durbar as well as in the Bombay government.[2]

J.M. Davies had been Resident for a year and a half when he fell ill. He left in June 1853; after his departure, the work was carried on from June 1853 till March 1854 by the officiating Resident, G.B. Seton Karr. Regarding the khatpat report about the intrigue in Baroda, which was still rife, it was resolved that stringent measures should be taken to rectify the impression created by it. Meanwhile, Colonel Outam had managed to clear his name sullied by a person who had falsified the khatpat report sent to top officials in England and as a result, Lord Dalhousie, the governor general, was entrusted to carry out the wishes of the Court of Directors by reappointing Colonel Outram as the Resident in the Baroda state on 24 February 1854. He joined duty in March toweed out the office of the Residency and abolish the post of native agents. It was decided that Baba Fadke, who managed the sequestrated district of Petlad, would not be re-employed.

Lord Dalhousie had been directed to take charge of the relations between the British government and the Baroda state. When the difficulties of such a charge were pointed out to him by the Bombay government, he retorted, 'Nearly the whole business which is transacted between the two governments arises more or less directly out of the peculiar position of those subjects of Gaekwad who hold the guarantee of the British government, and it is out of this class of business that those abuses and attempts to carry on a system of corruption have sprung.'[3]

The power of khatpat was great, but greater was the power of Colonel Outram who slashed it with the shining weapon of truth at the risk to his own life and in the face of opposition from his fellows and superiors who could not see the extent of the evil. As far as the British officials serving in the Raj were concerned they were never in the wrong, they were the masters and hence always right. It is probably from them that the phrase 'the boss is always right' was coined and is used in corporate houses today.

Ganpatrao had appointed Bhau Tambekar as his minister. He had a good reputation but he had incurred the displeasure of the British government because he was supposed to be the author of the kharita (anonymous letter) suggesting that there was a plot to depose him and place his brother Khanderao on the gaddi; the kharita also mentioned that Resident Colonel Outram should be deprived of his Residentship and another person be appointed instead. This resulted in the governor general demanding that the Resident should dismiss Bhau Tambekar without further ado.

Ganpatrao was fond of his minister and took it as a personal affront but as his interview with the Resident did not produce the desired result, he parted with him most reluctantly. This was just one of the many scenes that had been enacted in the past by his predecessors and were to be repeated by his descendants. Against all odds, Ganpatrao refused to nominate a new minister and retained Tambekar as his confidential adviser. This blatant flouting of the Resident's wishes angered the English gentleman and he broke all communication with Ganpatrao. Later, on learning that Bhau Tambekar and his partisans had really been dismissed, he consented to renew cordial relations with Ganpatrao. As a matter of fact from the time, the treaties were entered into, the Baroda state remained a faithful ally of the East India Company and later of the British government by not showing open hostility towards the Company or the Crown. The cessions in territory made to the East India Company for the maintenance of a subsidiary force was a calculated demand by the British to give them political ascendancy in Gujarat and since then the British government's stance from being only one of the several powers in India gradually acquired supremacy over the others and their natural tendency was to regard all the states in India as being in subordinate union irrespective of the period and the express provisions of their individual treaty relations. This came about in spite of the Proclamation of Queen Victoria in 1858.

Colonel Outram's fame as a soldier, his astuteness in all matters, adherence to truth no matter what the cost and his zest for work as a political officer distinguished him from his contemporaries.

10

Khanderao Gaekwad

Ganpatrao died in 1856 and since his three sons had died before him, his brother Khanderao Gaekwad ascended the gaddi. Ganpatrao is mainly remembered for founding the first railway connection in Gujarat. The thought was triggered by the acting Resident Mr French who encouraged Ganpatrao to read, and after returning from one of his trips to London, presented Ganpatrao with a steam engine toy. The gesture probably sowed the germ of an idea and in 1853 work commenced with a view to laying a railroad. This work began in Surat and necessitated laying a line through Baroda territory. When they discussed this matter with Ganpatrao in 1856, he surrendered the land that was required for the construction of the railroad with the stipulation that compensation should be paid to the owners of private land and for protection against any loss in Baroda's revenue due to transit duties. However, it was not until 1860 that the first train departed from Baroda.

With his flamboyant good looks and cavalier manner, Khanderao soon became the darling of the people while also endearing him to the British. All the goodwill from the British that Fatehsinghrao I had secured, and which had been undone by Sayajirao II and Ganpatrao, was again secured. Khanderao established good diplomatic ties with the Company, which were to augur well for the Gaekwads in the future. Khanderao was a sportsman at heart and had no patience with paperwork. He spent his time employing his great physical strength and boundless energy in outdoor sports of which hunting and riding formed a major part. He was an accomplished wrestler, a crackshot with a pistol, a hard rider after pigs and above all, an impeccable host with a boisterous, hearty manner. Soon after his accession to the gaddi, the Great Mutiny of 1857 took place; for a time, it seemed that the very existence of British power would be in peril. Unexpectedly, Khanderao sent his troops to the Britishers' aid, enabling them to put down the rebellion. Out of all the princes in the land, none showed his allegiance to the paramount power except Khanderao. Perhaps it was divine intervention that had put this thought into the prince's mind as this incident paved the way to seat one of the greatest rulers in the Gaekwad family, who was unrivalled and unparalleled in world history on the gaddi, albeit much later.

The most significant impact of the Mutiny, one can say, was the dissolution of the East India Company by Queen Victoria who became the empress of British India and remained so till her death on 22 January 1901.

When in 1857, the British troops were withdrawn from Gujarat there was great disturbance in Mahi and Rewa Kantha. Khanderao indefatigably set about to preserve order. Afterwards, Khanderao became the blue-eyed boy of the British and in their eyes, he could do no wrong. The British were so impressed with him that Brigadier General Richmond Shakespeare (an Indian born British officer who was appointed Resident in 1857) wrote in his report, 'The contingent was kept up in a state of thorough efficiency, they have had an extraordinary amount of work, attended with much fatigue, exposure and expense to themselves all of which they have cheerfully done.'[1] (It was part of a Resident's duty to send in regular reports to the government of India in England on Baroda affairs.)

Khanderao was amply rewarded in 1858 for his services and a resolution was passed by the British government of India stating: 'In consideration of the unswerving attachment and active assistance of His Highness the Maharaja Khanderao, without which our hold on the whole of western India would have been most seriously compromised, the exaction of the annual sum of Rs 3 lakh for the maintenance of the Gujarat Irregular Horse [a regiment of irregular cavalry was raised by the order of the British Crown in 1839 designated "Gujarat Irregular Horse" consisting of 812 men under a British commandment], a fine imposed on Khanderao's father in 1839 and considered in the light of public disgrace, was remitted with retrospective effect from the date of His Highness's ascension.'[2] In addition to this material benefit, Khanderao was, at his own request, presented with morchals or fans made of peacock feathers, and in a sanad (licence) dated 11 March 1862, conferred the right of adoption on him.

To some, his help to the British might have seemed as treachery to his own country, but it should not be viewed in that light as his object was to keep Gujarat, chiefly Baroda, safe from complete British domination and he was successful in that.

In 1858, disturbances were created by the Rajputs and some of the Wagher tribes who had resorted to piracy in Okhamandal, which had its consequences in Queen Victoria's declaration of 1858.

In order to understand the perennial problems arising in Okhamandal, one needs to understand its geographical situation and its history. F.A.H. Elliot in his book *Rulers of Baroda* has given a comprehensive account of it: 'At the western end of Kathiawad, bounded on the south and west by the Indian ocean, on the north and east by the Gulf of Kutch and on the lower half of the east side by the Rann of Kutch, lies the lonely little province of Okhamandal. This strip of country is indented with bays, creeks and caves. Dense forests had obscured the place and with its healthy invigorating climate, it became the home to bold, hardy people who took to piracy for their living as the rocky soil offered little scope for agriculture.'[3]

These inhabitants were the Waghers, tribal Rajputs, who were actually the original fishermen and ferrymen of Okhamandal who rose in the world by marriage. This was what happened—earlier, the land was held by the Hadad and the Chavada Rajputs, who fell out with each other and called in Rathod Vader, a tribal chief, to settle their dispute. Rathod in settling their differences took all the country for himself and his brother-in-law Jadeja who had married a Wagher girlfrom an inferior Wagher caste. This union gave rise to a new breed of Manek Waghers who called themselves Rajputs.

Okhamandal was conquered by Muslims in 1446. They destroyed the temple of Jagat and built a mosque there. After the Muslim rule, Rathod was back in power, but was driven back to a place behind Ran by Meru Khavas who was the Jam of Nawanagar who had earlier helped a certain Babaji to take the fort of Positra. This Babaji had also taken over Beyt from his nephew an infant and his brother's son. His brother was the chief of Aramada and from his hands it had passed into the hands of the priests of the temple. In 1807, there were six chiefs in Okhamandal—the Vader chief of Aramada, the Positra chief, the chiefs of Beyt and Dhinge, the Bayad of Mula Manek who possessed Dwarka and the Rao of Kutch who had a small fort. These chiefs had annoyed the British government with their piracy, but in 1807 the chief of Beyt promised to mend his ways.

By 1809, all the chiefs promised to give up their nefarious trade and compensate for it, but they went back to their old profession later and even though they did pay a part of their compensation, they also continued to cause trouble. A series of attempts were made by the British government to put piracy in Okhamandal down but it resurfaced after a temporary respite. In 1817, Colonel East with a small force succeeded in crushing the pirates with some help from Anandrao's troops and Okhamandal was bestowed to Anandrao as a gift, one he was most happy to receive as it was one of the most treasured shrines in India. However, as even gifts come with a price, he had to pay the balance compensation owed by the pirate chiefs to the British government. The trouble with these chiefs of Okhamandal did not end there and a series of risings took place in the following years and troops after troops under different heads were sent by the British to subdue them. In 1857, the chiefs complained that their pensions were not being paid regularly by the Gaekwad government and though some settlement was made by Lieutenant Barton, they rose again in a place called Vasai, a part of Okhamandal, in February 1858 and seized Beyt without opposition because the sibandi were on their side. Barton returned to Okhamandal and after occupying Beyt, handed it over to Gaekwad and left him to settle matters with the Waghers. The Gaekwad's troops were held at bay by the Waghers from behind the dense forests of Vasai. When they heard of the 1857 mutiny and that the sepoys of Bengal had overpowered the British, they rose against Gaekwad and promptly took away Beyt and Dwarka and drove Anandrao's s troops to Kathiawad.

    Khanderao wisely placed the affairs of Okhamandal in the hands of the British and a tedious campaign ensued. Beyt was evacuated on 6 October. After a siege for several days, Dwarka was abandoned on 31 October. The Waghers took up a strong position on the Abhapura Hill of the Barda range in Kathiawad. They were dislodged by Colonel Horner on 18 December 1859 and the war finally came to an end. The British guarded the place with a battalion under a commander and kept a strict watch over the Wagher population. The collection of revenue and the administration of the place were left to Khanderao. Some prisoners from the Wagher state escaped in 1862 and again started causing trouble which was finally crushed on 29 December 1867. The Waghers were able to put up stiff resistance against the British forces for the simple reason that the territory, with its rocky terrain, caves, bays and jungles, was well known to them and they were supported by the outlaws of Kathiawad. As time went by, the Waghers slowly reduced in numbers and some of them took to cultivation for their livelihood. The Waghers were actually not only brave and physically strong but also capable people gifted with many fine qualities[4] and had resorted to piracy as a desperate means for survival.

After the help rendered by Khanderao to the British in the sepoy mutiny, the ties with the British were strengthened further when in 1858 Queen Victoria, shocked by the hatred the East India Company had generated among Indians, guaranteed that there would be no further territorial conquests on the domains of the Indian princes and that their 'right, dignity and honour would be respected as our own'.[4]

After this declaration, the East India Company's board of directors was replaced by the British government. The arbitrary manner of the officials in India was now replaced with caution and tact and even though they were seething inside because of the halt on empire-building, they adopted the new policy laid out for them and tried to make friends with the Indian rulers. Needless to say, Lord Dalhousie's Doctrine of Lapse did much in tempering this declaration for it allowed annexation of a state held by a native prince only if there was misrule and if he did not produce an heir apparent.

A man and ruler like Khanderao with his hearty, sporty manner and love for outdoor games was easy to like. He was looked upon by the British as a friend and not just an ally and they accompanied him on his hunting expeditions, of which pig-sticking was a popular one, and participated in festivities as well. He built the fabulous Makarpura Palace in 1870 standing on acres of land with a Japanese-style 130-acre garden designed by William Goldring with a swimming pool and a lake with swans. There was also a huge deer reserve for hunting, which was Khanderao's favourite sport, along with fountains in the centre, which were activated to welcome Khanderao whenever he entered the garden.

Khanderao was at heart a soldier and he made a good attempt to create an army that would obey the orders of its officers. He also took the bold step of obtaining the services of British or Anglo-Indian officers who were free to issue such commands that the military service might require. Unfortunately, his attempt at reforming the army was not very effective and for this reason we need to look back at the time when Damajirao I joined forces with Khanderao Dabhade as his lieutenant. After that there was no looking back for Damajirao I as he went on his conquests and his mulukgiri expeditions on behalf of the Peshwas; these conquests which brought territorial gain for the Gaekwads were successful due to the sardars. Since the Gaekwad Empire had been consolidated and established in Baroda, nothing had been done for these men, monetarily or by the way of estates. Gradually, these sardars were pushed more and more into the background, reducing the military class to practically nothing. Due to this lapse in building their defence, Fatehsinghrao I had to call in the mercenary Arabs and we have already seen what that led to.

Later, the necessity of maintaining British subsidiary troops to safeguard the state from other invasions caused an inordinate pressure on the state's finances. A brief account of the manner in which the army was organized during the days of Damajirao I offers a comprehensive view of the situation.

The state cavalry had the paga swars (cavalry chiefs) at the head of the Gaekwad's army. The Ain Huzarat Paga were the corps entitled to bear all the royal symbols bestowed on them by Prince Shahu. They were under the direct command of the Gaekwads. This was followed by the cavalry of the sardars. In the front rank of this cavalry were shiledars who rode their own horses and accompanied the Gaekwads from the Deccan. Those descendants of aristocrats like Ghorpade Raje, Mir Saheb and Narayanji Pandhare kept their own pagas, were treated with high honour and were paid accordingly.

Then there were the foreign troops. Later, foreigners were even employed to assist them which gradually grew in numbers. Initially, the foreign troops were employed mainly to guard the gates of conquered towns, forts and thanas, but gradually, they were used in every other way possible.

Before Khanderao's time, the Gaekwads used only the cavalry for their military purposes and the infantry was used to guard the garrisons and comprised mainly foreigners. Since the Marathas were incapable of conducting a siege effectively, the Arab mercenaries became politically powerful through their possession of all the military posts in the state.

Finally, there were those men with horses who were independently engaged, known as ekondies who had no leader; also, there were the bargirs, men when needed acted as soldiers for a small payment; they were a humble lot and were the most useful of all Gaekwad's troops.

Right from the beginning, the military class was compensated with well-paid military posts which were made hereditary, but very little land was bestowed on them. This system worked to Gaekwad's advantage, and also to that of Major Walker as the ruling Gaekwad agreed to disband his own military troops and subsidize British troops for protection. This understanding with the British virtually brought the military class to their knees and Sayajirao II could with perfect impunity break any sardar who he suspected of obeying the British rather than himself.[5] With his suspicious mind, he did this too often, bringing the attention of the British on his policy.

If the truth must be known, the military class dwindled with the sardars being reduced to a state of insignificance during the reign of Sayajirao II. When the days of conquests drew to a close, their work also came to a halt as scientific warfare replaced desultory marauding expeditions. They could be paid by some other authority using their services, but for regular work against artillery, regular infantry and in successful sieges of forts and towns which were considered impregnable, these irregular cavalry leaders were useless. Thus, the sardar was limited to being a trooper.

Damajirao II had the Peshwa Balaji Bajirao troops at his command but from the revenue he derived from his mulukgiris, five-sixths went to the Poona durbar and towards the maintenance of the military class. Up to the end of his reign, wars and battles occupied Damaji II's mind, but they were conducive to an increase of his territories along with his stature.

Fatehsinghrao I had got rid of Govindrao, reduced the numbers in his army and took the disastrous step of calling the Arabs to guard the Baroda state. Anandrao and his minister added to the Arab numbers and relied on them completely for aid. These Arabs exercised complete control over the administration of the Baroda state. This was how low the military class had fallen. Internal dissensions in the Poona durbars as well as in the house of the Gaekwads did not encourage any military enterprise or mulukgiri. Even though mulukgiri was not the beginning or the end for which the Maratha class lived, undoubtedly it was the means by which it survived. Another fact that caused military power to dwindle was that the Maratha invaders of Gujarat were few in number and they came from the Deccan; as long as the tide was high for conquests, they could procure more men, but in time there was a decrease in Maratha adventurers and the Gujaratis were a passive lot, not warlike by nature, thus, the Gaekwads had no choice but to take recourse to foreign mercenaries for support. The tribal people of Gujarat—the Bhils and the Kolis—were another matter. They had aided the Gaekwads in ousting the Mughals but after that, particularly after the Kathiawad debacle, they became the Gaekwads' enemies.

The subsidizing of the British force was, as seen earlier, the result of anarchy, military as well as civil. During the reigns of Govindrao and Anandrao, a large portion of the revenues was swallowed up by the military class. In Anandrao's time, the Arabs' cost of maintenance was around Rs 36,00,000 a year, Babaji's (Ravji Appaji's brother) sibandi for the mulukgiri expeditions to Ahmedabad cost Rs 12,00,000 the siledars and pagas Rs 20,00,000 and around another Rs 15,00,000 was supposed to have been spent on fortifications. The nominal cost of the army exceeded the total revenues of the state. In order to pay the arrears, over Rs 19,00,000 was raised by a British loan and over Rs 21,50,000 was borrowed from bankers in Baroda with British guarantees. Over the years, the debts increased which led to British confiscations and interference and Sayajirao II had to maintain a British contingent of 3,000 men as per the treaty signed on the 6 November 1817. The Gaekwad government bound itself to maintain, hold, and at the disposal of the company, act with the subsidiary force wherever it may be employed, and to be subject to the general command of the officer commanding the British troops.

This agreement, of course, was never fulfilled for the simple reason that the contingent between the years 1821 and 1823 was drafted off to Kathiawad and Mahikantha after they returned from participating in the Malwa War, and Sayajirao II could not get them back to serve in the Baroda state. The contingent was to act with the subsidiary force and had to be efficient. But the Maratha irregular cavalry could never reach the expected British standards. By force, regular payment of dues to the soldiers could be expected, but the military discipline in conforming to British standards left a lot to be desired; further, equipment, arms and accoutrements could not accord with 'the custom of the Gaekwad government.'[6] Apart from all this, the Gaekwad contingent could do the general body work of the police, revenue and escort duties as well as act as couriers for messages and parcels, but when it came to acting as efficient cavalry they fell short of expectations. The contingent was 'never raised to the level of a military body fit to face an enemy or to quell the rising of a petty hill tribe' and just could not manage both types of work.[7]

This inefficiency is not relegated to any one period in history or any one ruler and has existed from the early years and in the entire Gaekwad army. It became the aim of the sardar to get as much pay as possible for doing practically no work. His paga was a long way off and he lived a life of ease in Baroda. Besides, as the post was hereditary, no attention was paid to physical fitness and the quality of the men degenerated to insignificance.

During the reign of Ganpatrao, the contingent force gave the British inspecting officers less to complain about, and in 1861, when Khanderao ascended the gaddi, he put hundred of each of the three quotas on an effective footing; in 1863–64, the force relapsed badly and when disturbances occurred in Kathiawad and Okhamandal, the men were found to be unfit for military as well as police duties. Till the end of his reign, Khanderao kept remonstrating with the British that the army should not be employed for any work other than military warfare and defence, but the Bombay government wanted a reduction to five hundred efficient troopers. Khanderao protested that a reduction in numbers would be fatal to the prospects of the military class. The matter was not resolved, neither in his time nor during his successor Malharrao's reign. However, there was a significant addition to the contingent force due to the manoeuvres of Colonel Outram who was successful in raising a local corps of Kolis in Mahikantha in 1858 and of Waghers in February 1861. The Okhamandal force was enrolled in the regiment as a way out of their illicit trade in piracy. But since they were used to their adventurous evil ways, they could not succumb to discipline and after a short time returned to their homes. Sindhis and Baluchis were brought in their place in December 1862. Later in 1865, Rajputs and Maratha settlers entered the force and thus, it came to be known as the Okhamandal force. A similar force was created in Amreli and both these corps were under European command and took their orders from the Resident in Baroda.

Colonel C. Davidson, the Resident in Baroda, had this to say about Khanderao in his report: 'A man of bodily and mental energy, sometimes self-willed, was very shrewd and observant and took a large share in the administration. He had a mind open to kindly impressions and was actuated by generous impulses.'[8]

His florid, robust, flamboyant appearance was a manifestion of his extravagant mind. The Makarpura Palace built by him for his seventeen-year-old bride testifies to it. At the same time, he was shrewd and observant and had a retentive memory. It must also be remembered that his predecessors had not set up examples for an efficient administration for Khanderao to follow. His intentions to remodel the army, to reform the revenue and judicial system, to start constructive public works and so on remained intentions only. To be fair to him, the intentions were thwarted by incompetent ministers whose sole aim was to further their gains at Khanderao's expense.

Later, Resident Colonel J.T. Barr spoke of his rule as being one of reform and real progress.

Brigadier General R. Shakespeare, Resident in Baroda, in a letter dated 30 March 1859 remarks on Khanderao's government as being 'very popular with his people though that is not a yardstick for assessment. But, the two years I worked as Resident, life and property are generally secure in Gaekwad's districts and highway robbery is so very rare an occurrence that, in except a few cases from the Ahmedabad collectorate, no complaints have reached me during my tenure of office there. In conclusion I beg to say that I think the administration of the Gaekwads' territories is highly creditable to the present ministers and to His Highness Maharaja Khanderao Gaekwar.'

Political Agent R. Wallace also stated that the Khanderao administration on the whole was favourable.

11

The Bahandari System

In order to understand the indifference and apathy of the Gaekwads when it came to developing their contingent against invaders, it is necessary to explain the bahandari system that existed in that era. The system was a guarantee for protection to the Baroda state and was first introduced by Anandrao who sought protection from Arab mercenaries. Once the Arab troops had been dispensed with, the guarantee was handed over to the British who, in turn, supplied troops for the protection of the Gaekwad state, but the cost of maintenance of the troops had to be borne by the Gaekwads. This bahandari system was also extended to individuals who sought protection from injustice, as was in the case of Dewan Raoji Appaji by the agreement of 29 July 1802. After the Kadi War, a guarantee had also been given to Malharrao which lapsed when he escaped to Kathiawad, rebelled, was made a prisoner and ultimately exiled. As mentioned before, the office of dewan was not hereditary but the emoluments were. After Raoji's death, his allowance was passed down to his adopted son Sitaram even after his fractious behaviour in 1808. After Sitaram's death in 1823, his son Narayanrao held the guarantee that a nemnuk of Rs 60,000 should be paid to him. The guardians of Sitaram forfeited all protection when they resorted to a fraudulent method of passing a treaty of 1802 on to the Resident. Even after 1842 (the guarantee was withdrawn), James Ogilvie and Sir R. Arbuthnot endeavoured to preserve some villages that were erroneously believed to be the private property of the Prabhu family, from which Raoji hailed), but Colonel Outram dissuaded the government from doing anything further for the house of Sitaram was responsible for embezzling money.

The Arabs, and those whom they had protected, had stipulated that the guarantees should be taken up by the British, which gave the Company enormous powers of interference; it also 'established a connection with the rich from whom the company had reaped benefits. For a time, Sayajirao II accepted it since it reduced the powers of the sardars as military men controlling the government.'[1]

As mentioned earlier, there were two types of guarantees handed down by the Arabs—one was for due payment of money and the other was for personal security. Any breach of engagement made by the government absolved the giver of the guarantee from 'his duty as a subject, the Arabs presenting many instances when to enforce the guarantees; they filled the durbars of the king and the ministers and held their persons in rigorous confinement.'[2]

However, the British confined their guarantees to loans to save the Baroda government from embarrassment. These guarantees were hereditary and, therefore, it has been aptly remarked 'that no guarantees were so calculated to make mischief as the hereditary ones, which not only extended to persons and property, but guaranteed the continuance of office to particular families.'[3]

During the early years of Sayajirao II, there was a tendency among the British officers to consider the guarantees as hereditary, which incited Sayajirao II to treat those, who were under British protection with extreme harshness. In 1828, the British Crown decided that these guarantees or the 'bahandari engagements were no less objectionable in principle than embarrassing in practice and that they were glad to learn that the government of Bombay had laid it down as an established principle to clear itself, as soon as possible, of the guarantees to existing loans, and to contract no more pledges of such nature in future.'[4]

However, the general opinion shared was that Sayajirao II's good intentions and plans were hampered largely by incompetent ministers and advisers of whom a few were really the 'bad ones'. He made attempts to reform the iniquitous revenue farming system but was unable to fully implement his schemes due to the lack of cooperation and the inefficiency of his ministers; it was also probably due to his dislike for dealing with administerial work and other paperwork involved. However, in spite of it, he made a good attempt at reforming the administrative system of justice. To understand this reform, we need to look at the way justice was administered right from the time the Gaekwads came to stay in Baroda.

As we have seen in earlier chapters, the conquest of the Gaekwads gave them dominance only over those portions which they had conquered. There were, of course, those districts where they only had the right to levy tribute which was collected whenever an armed force could be dispatched to collect it. Therefore, it is not surprising that their control over the unconquered wild territory was much lighter than on those in the plains and chief towns. They could, thus, administer the kind of justice they wished with more weight in the latter (that is, plains and towns) than in the former. During the time of the earlier Gaekwads, the chief aim had been to collect tribute and their passion continued to be the acquisition of either taxes or tributes. There were no written laws and justice administered was of a simple nature with the penalty for crime being confined to fines. The dispensation of justice was held by those who dispensed as an excellent remunerative business, and the dispensers of justice were those very people who had bought the privilege of extracting from the Rayats (a tribe) the revenue of the land. No wonder the Gaekwads, until the time of Sayajirao III, brought little progress in the administration of justice.

Earlier, the Marathas had divided the country into two classes—the Rasti and the Mewasi. The former were a passive and peaceful lot while the latter were wild and troublesome. Thus, it was easier to dispense justice to the Rasti. The Rasti mahals occupied moderate extension of areas which, at intervals, increased and also gained stability. The Marathas could exercise their will in these Rasti mahals, and there was some semblance of law and order as justice could be administered.

When the Mughal government was unleashing its authority in Gujarat, the entire province was criss-crossed by territories originally owned by Rajas, Rajputs, Kolis and Girasias who were known as zamindars. These people did not lose their independence under the Marathas and as the Mughal dominance began to weaken, they became more powerful and rebellious than ever. It was only in the face of new conquerors (the British) that they gradually sank under the exacting influence of their masters.

According to Mr Diggle, assistant to the first Resident, the Rayats of Rastibut (also referred as Rayats) were a peaceful, tractable community of people who acquiesced quietly to all judicial processes. The main trouble came from the wild tribes of the hilly areas, such as the Bhils. These tribals were scattered all over, in different villages, sometimes even living in walled places or areas of their own and sometimes intermixed with the rest of the inhabitants. They considered it their privilege to tote guns for offence or defence, whatever the case may be, as they determined the points of justice as they thought fit. Justice was given as per the will of the head of the Garasias (like the Bhils and Kolis, they were a tribe but they all bore the name of zamindars) whose decisions were based on customs and rules, which were not guided by any standardized system. For example, when a murder was committed, it frequently led to another murder being committed in retaliation. Murders were committed galore and the criminal just threw himself under the protection of the chief. The penalty, if it was at all exacted from the criminal, was normally took shape in the form of an inadequate fine. On the whole, this system of justice was of no consequence to the Mewasis.

It must be remembered that the Gaekwad government was not restricted by positive law but was influenced by the customs of the country which it was obliged to respect. In Major Walker's words, 'Justice in Gujarat is not administered according to the written law of the several castes, but depends on the will of the person in whose hands the local authority may be placed.'[5] In civil cases, the decision was directed in accordance with the Hindu or the Muslim law, according to the faith of the disputing parties, and in criminal cases, the order of the government determined the punishment. It must be supposed that in those cases where the faiths of the two disputing parties differed, the judgement depended entirely on the will of the person in charge.

Then, there were those districts where the law rested with the farmer or agriculturist of the land he farmed. After paying the stipulated amount to the government, they were allowed plenary power in the district. Since the farmer's object was mercenary, he paid little attention to the wants of his people which rendered them restless and dissatisfied. Khanderao tried to bring about a radical change in the proper administration of justice with little effect.

The kamavisdar (judge or mediator) as he was called, demanded one-fourth of the sum that was paid to the arbitrator by the disputing parties and the cost of which was borne by the parties. The gumastha or accountant recorded the payment but not the procedure undertaken to settle the dispute. This haphazard manner of dealing with civil matters resulted in people running to arbitrators to settle disputes out of court without the kamavisdar (during Sayajirao II's as well as Khanderao's reign).

In criminal cases, the kamavisdar was a judge but with limited powers as he could not pronounce capital punishment. The usual punishments given to criminals were banishment, imprisonment, mutilation and, in some exceptional cases, death. Fines were commonly inflicted and were considered as a regular branch of revenue. Land was also extracted from guilty people as security and was classified under six different kinds—chalu zamin, security for good behaviour; hazir zamin, security for personal appearance; mahal zamin, security for money, property for revenue, permanent security for good behaviour considered more binding than that first mentioned; the fifth being ad zamin, additional security; and the sixth, when a person of the Bhat caste was required to guarantee the performance of an engagement, the conduct of the offender, or the observance of other securities.

At the head of this ineffectual judiciary system was the king or the sovereign to whom cases involving capital punishment were referred; also, any kind of appeals could be made to him. The fate of the criminal was left to the discretion of the king and his body of advisers. This is amply testified during the reign of Sayajirao III when matters came to a head and he ordered the death sentence for murder, which resulted in the erstwhile statesman, Sir T. Madhavrao, resigning from his post of dewan.

However, it was during the reign of Sayajirao III that significant changes were brought about in the administration of justice by which the people of Baroda benefitted enormously.

As mentioned in an earlier chapter, Khanderao's passion for sports, among which hunting topped the list, led him to build the Makarpura palace. Since this was an expensive venture, vast sums were acquired from the state treasury that were originally supposed to be spent on building a huge reservoir to supply water to Baroda. Instead, this money was spent on this lavish palace for his young bride Jamnabai. Among other things, he had qualities that endeared him to the people, followed a style of living that matched his flamboyant good looks and was marked with lavish generosity. He was also an expert judge of precious stones and had one of the most renowned collections of jewels in the world. He astutely bought the 'Star of the South' a diamond larger than the Kohinoor weighing 125 carats. 'It was found in Brazil, in the state of Minas Gerais and the place where it was found has since been called Estelle-do Sol. At one time, it was a part of the crown jewels of France. Khanderao purchased it in 1867. He also had another necklace—a resplendent piece made up of 288 graduated pearls of the best quality and the finest water, interspersed with 168 diamonds.'[6]

The man, though loved by all, was not without his share of eccentricities. He got a carpet woven entirely of pearls and gifted it to a mosque because he venerated holy men and places and made no distinction between a Hindu and a Muslim. As far as he was concerned, a fakir was to be treated with the same veneration as a sadhu. He had his own battalions dressed in kilts with pink tights to make them resemble the Scottish Highlanders. He had a cannon cast out of pure gold though the money should have been spent on supplying water to the people of Baroda.

Despite his eccentricities, Khanderao, was an easy man to like and the British addressed him as 'Eastern king Hal.'[7]

12

Plots and Intrigues to Depose Malharrao Gaekwad

Khanderao's brother Malharrao, jealous of his position and popularity, plotted to have Khanderao overthrown and seize the throne by leading an expedition to plunder the British district of Ahmedabad. To his good fortune, the British Resident took a lenient stand on his offences and let him off the hook by putting his behaviour down to juvenile delinquency. Another time, he arranged to have Khanderao shot by hiring a British sergeant, but the plot was discovered in time and Khanderao had Malharrao imprisoned in a village called Padra, seven miles from Baroda. Malharrao was kept in a dark, narrow cell in solitary confinement; his wife wanted to share his life in captivity but was not allowed to do so. He was given all he wanted for his basic needs except money. He nurtured his hatred against those who had caused his imprisonment, and waited for the day when Khanderao would breathe his last and leave no heir to the throne as both of Khanderao's wives were dead with no children, which meant he was still next in line to succeed to the throne of Baroda. But Khanderao was only in his late-thirties and in robust health therefore the likelihood of Malharrao stepping into his brother's shoes was a remote possibility. Seven years spent in a dark, narrow cell must have warped his thinking and crippled his reasoning abilities. As fate has its own way of moving the pawns on the chessboard of life, Khanderao, who was only in his late thirties, married again in the summer of 1866, and put a stop to Malharrao's aspirations to sit on the throne of Baroda. Now all that was needed to put the last nail in the coffin of his ambitions was for the new young queen to give birth to a son. In her, Malharrao found a new object of hatred.

On 28 November 1870, Maharaja Khanderao died. He was only forty-two years old. Political Commissioner J.T. Barr rode over to the village where Malharrao was imprisoned to invite him to the capital to take over as regent, since Jamnabai was expecting a child. Malharrao was released with the words, 'Malharrao! You will now rejoice to learn that we hold thee no longer a prisoner. It is as well, we should now ungrudgingly cheer you to the throne of one with whom we lived on the best possible terms is no more. Take up this authority and let the relations be continued as before. We do not touch the durbar, we give it to you as it was. You are at full liberty to make full use of your own party. You are left in free and undisputed possession of all the wealth and property of the state. You will now see that from a pining beggar we have made you an all powerful and opulent king! Prize well the best grace we can show you!'[1]

On hearing this news, Malharrao, who would have gone on his knees for his liberty, must have felt a joy that knew no bounds as just moments ago he would have gladly endured any restriction imposed for simple liberty granted to him and now he was getting it at no cost. He was jubilant over his freedom but the news about Jamnabai's pregnancy was a blow to his aspirations as the decision regarding succession to the throne would now be delayed. However, swallowing his disappointment and rage at being outdone by a child that was yet to make its appearance, he decided to take advantage as regent and gather the weapons that would be needed for the battle for the throne.

He needed to play his cards well because Jamnabai, in spite of her youth and appearance of unworldliness, proved to be a formidable adversary. Every effort was made by the scheming Malharrao to rid himself of his adversary, but all his efforts proved futile as she outsmarted him at every step in moves and countermoves. Her pregnancy, which he tried to disprove, was medically confirmed. Accusations of adultery too were scotched as soon as they were made. He then resorted to attempting murder by poison and also witchcraft but to no avail. It seemed that Jamnabai had her planetary positions leaning favourably on her side. She refused food that was brought to her and cooked her own meals. She stayed within her apartment and refused to step out. Moreover, she slept with a dagger under her pillow and had a ferocious dog tied to her bedpost for protection. Malharrao was beset by a new fear—if the child turned out to be a girl, the queen might substitute her with a male child. He expressed his doubts to the Resident J.T. Barr. Since Jamnabai had expressed her fear of someone threatening her life, she was shifted to the Resident's bungalow in the Residency where she had the security of the

British guards commanded by Major Coles while his wife attended on her till her confinement was over.

On a hot day in July, Jamnabai delivered a daughter and Malharrao demonstrated his jubilance by setting out in a procession through the town and distributing gold mohurs. In the ordinary course of events, the loser should have gracefully bowed out to make place for the winner, but the rivalry which had taken the shape of a deadly duel continued, though this time from afar. Haughtily spurning the Maharaja's olive branch in the shape of an amicable settlement, she left for Poona to bide her time. 'Convinced that the fates had played her false,'[2] she sat in her modest establishment and planned her revenge. She was a very determined young woman who had her whole life before her and she intended to use it to secure the gaddi rights through adoption. Being the recipient of the affection and care showered on her by her late doting husband, she was now a wealthy woman. She had in her possession a tidy fortune in jewellery which her besotted husband had given her and she put some of it to use. By selling some of her jewellery she was able to fund the expenses required to maintain a network of spies. These agents were to fill Resident Phayre's ears with complaints about the misrule of Malharrao who was now the Maharaja. Contrived instances of tyranny corroborated by bribed witnesses did the work of causing a violent dislike of Malharrao who was a man of no scruples whatsoever. Indian clerks and secretaries of the Residency were bribed by Jamnabai's agents to espouse her cause in deposing Malharrao. The viceroy, the governor of Bombay and other high-ranking officials familiar with India and native skirmishes would have treated the matter lightly, but it assumed serious proportions as Robert Phayre strongly disapproved of Malharrao, and made no bones about his dislike of him.' If Malharrao was in official eyes, the archetype of the spoilt, ignorant, oriental despot, Robert Phayre was equally typical of the overbearing, irrascible British official of caricatures, dreaded and detested by all Indians who came into contact with him.'[3] Jamnabai had a valuable ally in her scheme of things and she used him to the utmost to bring Malharrao down.

This act would have, in all probability, been ignored as malicious spite regarded as a part of the way of life by courtiers and servants in the palace who thrived on intrigues. The servants in the Residency too were not above bribery and corruption, interchange of gossip and money changing hands resulted in filling the too-willing ears of Phayre, who had replaced J.T. Barr, Phayre's dislike of Malharrao served Jamnabai's purpose and all the complaints against Malharrao served like an incendiary spark that would flare into a raging fire at the least provocation. The Resident's dictatorial manner and Malharrao's protests caused a growing hostility between the two which was taken full advantage of—people seeking special favours had only to go to the Resident's officials and seek redress.

After six months, Phayre set up a commission to investigate Malharrao's misrule in Baroda. The report read, 'The misgovernment is stated injuriously to affect British interests'—this was not true as in spite of the misrule, there had been no danger to life and property of the British officials. Anyway, a commission was set up with Sir Richard Meade as its president and two other officials, the third being the Indian dewan of Jaipur. After two months, the verdict was that there was no actual danger to the British subjects in Baroda and that Phayre's impressions had been too insignificant to warrant any action. The commission recommended to the viceroy that Malharrao should be given eighteen months to improve his administration. Thus, the matter was settled with a rap on the knuckles to both Malharrao and Phayre, but only superficially. Phayre, with his ego dented, was seething with anger and when Malharrao got Dadabhai Naoroji as his dewan to bring the administration under order, Phayre did his best to object to his appointment and even wrote to the Bombay government about it, but his objections were overruled and Dadabhai Naoroji was appointed. Dadabhai Naoroji was extremely capable and one of the most brilliant Indians of that time who was bound to set the administration right and would brook no interference from the British Resident. This was galling to the Resident and he furiously sent an ultimatum to the state officials to choose between him and the dewan. The new dewan realized that this was a vicious political battle where he would not be able to work progressively as long as Phayre was there, acting as an impediment to all the measures taken by him. The only way out of this deadlock situation was to get the viceroy to have Phayre recalled to England, or simply have him removed from Baroda. It was also apparent that it was a no-win situation since Jamnabai was hand in glove with Phayre and could wreak havoc on Malharrao's attempts in administration by playing the invisible enemy. Servants in both camps of the palace and the Residency were also susceptible to bribes and would swear to anything, even murder, if the price was worth it. Malharrao, now desperate as he had only a short time to bring the administration to a desirable level, appealed to the viceroy to recall Phayre from Baroda so that they could carry on their work in the administration in peace. The remedy worked. It worked simply because the viceroy and the India Office were thoroughly displeased with the way Phayre had flouted their orders and the Bombay government's attempts to shield him. The viceroy, Lord Northbrook, who had already found Phayre 'unequal to the demands of his charge'[4] appointed Sir Lewis Pelly as the agent to the governor general (AGG), which was henceforth to be the new designation of the office of a Resident. After this, Lord Northbrook brought the Baroda administration under his control. Sir Lewis Pelly arrived on 4 December 1874 and took over charge from Phayre. But the rebuke administered to Phayre and the change in command that implied a slur on the efficiency of the governor of Bombay came in too late as Phayre, anticipating the change and his removal from office, had already aimed one last blow which was to damn Malharrao forever. Determined as he was to come out a winner in the vendetta game against the Gaekwad, Phayre made an 'attempt to murder' charge on poor Malharrao. Phayre who had earlier in his report to the Bombay government hinted of threats to the safety of British subjects that the Meade Commission had found to be absolutely baseless, now gave validity to that complaint by sending them a wire which said that Malharrao had attempted to murder him.

On 9 November after complaining that he had been feeling seedy for some time, Phayre claimed that he had noticed 'strange dark sediments' at the bottom of his glass of sherbet which he was in the habit of drinking every morning and which he suspected was poisoned. He claimed to have summoned Dr Seward to examine the contents and the verdict had been 'a compound of arsenic and diamond dust'. Phayre immediately sent a telegram to the Bombay government and Lord Northbrook, accusing Malharrao of the crime. The Bombay government still smarting after the viceroy's censure delivered earlier, sent a police officer named F.H. Soutar to investigate. Soutar reported to Sir Lewis Pelly that he had signed confessions from two of Phayre's servants that they had been bribed by Malharrao to poison their master. Lewis recommended to Lord Northbrook that Malharrao should be dethroned, the British should take over the administration and a minor should be chosen to succeed Malharrao. The actual truth of the plot, if at all there had ever been one, was never known but common sense dictates that Malharao could not have been so stupid as to attempt murder by poison and that too of a British official. He was fully aware of the consequences of such an act.

Lord Northbrook's confidential report dated 8 April 1875 finally sealed the fate of the unfortunate ruler. It summed up the case based on which the verdict of imprisonment was given. The report said: 'It may be desirable that I should put down shortly, without entering into detail, my view of the transacions [sic] relating to the State of Baroda during the last two years. Malharrao the reigning Gaekwar, succeeded his brother, Khanderao, in 1870. His antecedents were not favourable. He had been accused of being concerned in a conspiracy to murder his brother by poison or other means in 1863, and had, in consequence, been kept in confinement as a State prisoner during his brother's lifetime. He was then described in the Residency records as being 'intellectually feeble' and apparently irresponsible for his actions.

'On 18th March 1873, Colonel Phayre was appointed British Resident. Very soon after his appointment he brought to notice the serious maladministration of the State by the Gaekwar. In the course of the year much correspondence took place between the government of Bombay and the government of India with reference both to general maladministration and to particular cases. Among these cases, there was the death, in prison, of Bhau Scindia, the minister of the late Gaekwar, who was supposed to have been poisoned, and investigation was rendered impossible by the immediate burning of his body. There was also a case in which a person died in consequence of flogging administered to him in the streets of Baroda. Complaints were made by the widow of the late Gaekwar that she was in personal danger owing to ill-treatment by Malharrao, and on enquiry, her statements seemed to the Government of India to be sufficiently substantiated to render it necessary to address Malharrao, in very strong terms, placing upon him, personally, the responsibility for her safety.

'The general complaints and the refusal of Malharrao to listen to the remonstrances and advice addressed to him by Colonel Phayre, together with his pertinacious opposition to the proposals of the Government of Bombay in regard to the organization of the Contingent, were represented by that Government to the Government of India with a strong opinion that some further measures were necessary. Accordingly in the winter of 1873, a Commission was appointed for the purpose of investigating and reporting upon the general condition of the State.

'Sir Richard Meade, whose character for calmness of judgement is well known, who is second to no officer in India in knowledge of the general condition of the Native States, - and who, throughout his whole career has shown that he is ready to make every allowance in their favour, and that he has no wish to enforce a standard which would be unreasonable to expect in their administration, was appointed to be Chairman of the Commission. Nawab Faiz Ali Khan, who had been the prime minister of the state of Jeypore, and in whose character and ability great confidence was placed by the Maharaja of Jeypore, as well as by the British Government, was appointed to be a member of the Commission. The other two members—Mr Ravenscroft and Colonel Etherridge—were appointed by the Bombay Government and are men of high-standing and character.

'The report of the commission substantiated, to a very considerable extent, the charges made by Colonel Phayre against the Gaekwar; although, the manner in which they were brought forward and pressed by Colonel Phayre showed in some cases, more zeal than discretion. Taking the report of the Commission as a whole, it showed a condition of things highly discreditable to the Gaekwar, and which contained the elements of serious disturbance, which might at any time, owing to the manner in which the Gaekwar's and British territory are interlaced, have been greatly prejudicial to the peace and order of Her Majesty's dominions. The Commission established so serious an amount of general misgovernment as to necessitate decided intervention on the part of the British Government.

'The details of this maladministration are amply given in the report of the Commission, or in its appendices.

''Among the complaints established against the Gaekwar's government were—the arbitrary and unjust treatment of bankers and traders; arbitrary and sudden reductions made among the military class; the practice of barbarous processes in realizing revenue; the levy of nazrana on appointments; the practice of torture on the part of subordinate officials; scandalously excessive punishment for crimes; abduction of women for forced labour in the palace, thereby bringing a most serious scandal on the personal character of the chief himself; the personal illtreatment and corporal punishment of women; the vindictive treatment of the relatives and dependents of the late Chief. There is no doubt as to the right which the British Government possesses both under treaty and by frequent practice to interpose in the internal affairs of the Baroda state. The provisions of the Treaty of 1802 are clear, and the letter fom Mountstuart Elphinstone then Governor of Bombay to the ruling Gaekwar in 1820, lays down in the plainest possible terms the rights of the British Government. Accordingly authoritative advice given by the Government of India to the Gaekwar for the remedy of the principal evils disclosed by the report of the Commission; and, while he, could select his own minister he was required to dismiss those of his former ministers whose malpractices had been pointed out by the Commission.

'A period of eighteen months was allowed to the Gaekwar for effecting the necessary reforms, and every assistance was offered to him for the purpose. The Government of India considered whether it would be desirable to replace Colonel Phayre with another officer while making these communications to the Gaekwar. Although we were not satisfied with with the judgement shown by Colonel Phayre in some of his proceedings, his representations of the misgovernment of the Baroda state had proved to be correct in the main, and we thought it would weaken the position taken with the Gaekwar to show any want of confidence in Colonel Phayre, while we were trusted that the instructions given to him would be sufficiently precise to prevent him from acting injudiciously in future.

'Accordingly in a letter to the Gaekwar, the government expressed their full confidence in Colonel Phayre.

'The expectations which we entertained were not realized. Colonel Phayre- in his communications with the Gaekwar and with the Minister, whom the Gaekwar had selected Dadabhoy Naoroji was wanting in consideration, and in some respects he misunderstood and indeed acted contrary to his instructions. Colonel Phayre's proceedings were unfortunately not reported to the Government of India until long after they had taken place, or a change would have been made sooner than it actually occurred. Just at the time when we received full information of his proceedings, we also received the representation from the Gaekwar of November 2nd, 1874, asking for his removal. An option was given to him to retire, of which he declined to avail himself, and he was therefore removed and replaced by Sir Lewis Pelly. While these arrangements were in progress, information was received of the attempt to poison Colonel Phayre.

'The Government of India did not consider that this attempt ought to alter the conclusion at which [h]e had previously arrived. In consequence of the serious inconvenience which had occurred owing to Baroda affairs passing through the Government of Bombay, it was determined that Sir Lewis Pelly should have the position of Agent to the Governor-General at Baroda, and that all communications relating to reforms in the Baroda State, depending upon the report of the Commission should be made direct to the Government of India.

'Sir Lewis Pelly found the affairs in Baroda in a very critical condition although assurances had been given from time to time by the Gaekwar that he would carry out the reforms which he had been required by the Government of India to undertake, no substantial progress had been made.

'The Gaekwar had married a person of low rank, whose antecedents were doubtful. She had borne a son five months after marriage (the child was conceived before marriage).

'The condition of the cultivating classes was represented as desperate, owing to the overassessment of the land revenue, while the difference between the Sardars and the Gaekwar threatened a serious disturbance of peace. Gaekwad gave assurances to Sir Lewis Pelly that remedies would be applied to this condition of affairs, and the Government of India entertained some hope that, although no confidence could be placed in the personal character of Malharrao, yet he might be induced by the serious position in which he was placed to allow the administration of the state to be effectually reformed.

'Immediately after the attempt to poison Colonel Phayre, Sir Lewis Pelly instituted an enquiry and examined the servants at the Residency. No evidence of any value was procured but Colonel Phayre entertained and expressed a confident opinion that the attempt was instigated by the Gaekwar. It was impossible without any evidence to accept Colonel Phayre's conclusions and the enquiry was for the time being closed.

'Sir Lewis Pelly was instructed to take measures to investigate the case and for that purpose he obtained the assistance of a senior police officer. Mr F.H. Soutar and the police officers of Bombay. For sometime, they could obtain no evidence of importance but, in the middle of December they discovered a clue which resulted in strong evidence to the effect that the Gaekwar had been in the habit of holding secret communications with the

Residency servants, and two of those servants—Raoji and Narsu—confessed that they had committed the offence, and alleged that they had done so at the personal instigation of Malharrao Gaekwar. Raoji made his confession on receiving the promise of a pardon but, Narsu was distinctly told by Sir Lewis Pelly that he must not expect a pardon. Sir Lewis Pelly was instructed to communicate the evidence to the Advocate - General of Bombay, who reported that if it stood the test of cross-examination, it would be sufficient to convict the Gaekwar of the offence in a Court of Law. Mr Souter [sic] was immediately dispatched to Calcutta with the evidence and the opinion of the Advocate - General. When the papers were received in Calcutta, they were referred for the opinion of the acting Advocate General and the Standing Counsel to the Government at Calcutta, who expressed their opinion that the evidence was sufficient to commit the Gaekwar to trial, but stated their doubts with regard to the position and credibility of the witnesses and also indicated the possibility of there being a conspiracy against Gaekwad. The case was then considered with great care and attention by the government of India.

'We examined Souter most carefully with respect to the nature of the police investigation, and were assured by him that greatest precautions had been taken to prevent the evidence being concocted by the subordinate police officials. We discussed the probability of their being a conspiracy against Gaekwad [Malharrao], and we could find no reasonable ground for such a supposition. We considered, therefore, that there was a strong *prima facie* reason to believe that the attempt had been instigated by the Gaekwar. The question then arose, how we were to deal with this condition of things? It was impossible to pass over an attempt on the life of a British Resident at the Court of a Native Prince. The sanctity attached to the lives of Ambassadors extends in our opinion, if possible, in a greater degree to British Residents at the Courts of Native States, and no offence could be greater than that an attempt upon the life of a British Resident should be instigated by the Ruler of a Native State.

'At the same time, the evidence was far from being sufficient to enable us to condemn Gaekwad. He had no opportunity of making his defense and the witnesses had not been subjected to cross-examination. Some enquiry, therefore, was essential and we had to consider the form which the enquiry should take. Having regard to the antecedents of Gaekwad, and to the strong prima facie case against him, it appeared to us that there was no probability of a fair enquiry being made so long as he remained in the position of the ruler of Baroda, and, moreover, with such a strong prima facie against him, it would have been highly improper for us to have continued friendly communications with him pending the investigation. We, therefore, were determined to arrest Gaekwad and to assume, on behalf of the queen, the administration of the state of Baroda pending the result of the enquiry. This action on our part was an act of State, or, in other words, an act of war, carried out by superior force and based upon no legal grounds. Troops were sent to Baroda, and the arrest of Gaekwad and the assumption of the administration of the state were affected with promptness and success by Sir Lewis Pelly. We had then to determine what form the enquiry should take. Notwithstanding the obvious objections to which a public enquiry was open, in our opinion a public inquiry was more advisable than a private one,which would undoubtedly have given occasion for suspicion and mistrust. The composition of the commission was next considered. Our desire was that it should be thoroughly independent, and we, therefore secured the services of Sir Richard Couch, the chief justice of Bengal and the highest judicial authority in India, as the president [sic] We joined with him Sir Richard Meade, whose character I have already described, and being unable to obtain the services of Mr Justice West of Bombay, whom we desired to appoint, we selected Phillip Melville, officer who had been the Judicial Commissioner of the central provinces and acted as the judge of the chief court of Lahore,who had no connection whatever with Baroda affairs, and whose character for independence and ability was well known in the service. We considered it was desirable to obtain the assistance of natives of high rank and position on the commission. Sir Dinkur Rao was summoned to Calcutta and consented to serve. I wrote to request Maharaja Scindia, Maharaja Holkar and the Maharaja of Jeypore to join the commission. Maharaja Holkar, while giving his complete adherence to the course taken by the government, excused himself from serving, but the other two princes consented to serve the commission.

'In making public the course taken by the government in deposing Gaekwad, we determined to announce that it was our intention, whatever the results of the inquiry might be, to re-establish a native administration at Baroda. We were aware that some distrust prevailed of the motives of the British government in dealing with the case, and that notwithstanding, the solemn announcements that had been made from time to time that there had been no desire to extend the British possessions in India, all our proceedings with respect to the native states were watched with jealousy which indicated that those declarations were hardly yet accepted as expressing the real intentions of the British government. It was therefore our view that, while it was essential to deal strongly with the attempt to poison the British Resident, it was equally essential to announce that, in doing so, we had no intention of annexing the territory of Baroda. It will be obvious that there were several alternatives to the course which we were determined to adopt in each of the particulars which I have recounted. Those alternatives were considered by us. None of them appeared to us to be preferable.

'The matter was surrounded by the gravest difficulties. Action had to be sharp and decisive. For my own part, on looking back at what has been done, I do not think any other course would have been better. It is to be noted that the deposition of the ruler of one of the principal native states in India, the assumption for a time of the administration of his dominions and the enquiry into his conduct by means of a commission appointed by the British government, involved the exercise of an authority of the paramount power in India of the widest possible nature; it cannot but be regarded with satisfaction that the course which was taken received the concurrence of the Maharajas Scindia, Holkar and Jeypore. The action of the government having been taken upon no legal grounds, the commission was not constituted as a judicial tribunal. Its function was to report its opinion to the Government of India, with whom the decision must ultimately rest.

'The commission commenced their proceedings upon the 23 February and concluded them upon the 31 March.

'Almost at the same time, the evidence against Gaekwad was received, but before the government had determined upon the course which should be taken, Dadabhai Naoroji resigned office and the State of Baroda was left without a minister. It therefore rested with Sir Lewis Pelly to conduct the whole administration of affairs, and, in doing so, it was necessary for him, in consequence of the critical position of the country to which I have alluded, to carry out certain reforms, more especially with respect to the collection of the land revenue and the grievances of the sardars. These reforms had been promised by Gaekwad previous to his arrest, and Sir Lewis Pelly carefully conformed to the instructions given to him by the government of India, not to introduce, during his temporary tenure of authority, any other changes of importance in the government of the state, but to confine himself to carrying gradually into effect the advice which had been given to the Gaekwad and had been accepted by him.

'Up to the appointment of the commission the proceedings of the Government of India appear, so far I can judge, to have met with the general approval of independent and well educated Natives, and they certainly were approved by those princes of India with whom I then happened to come into contact. I may mention that Sir Madhav Rao, Holkar's minister, expressed his entire concurrence with the course we adopted.

'But, as the proceedings before the commission went on, there can be no doubt that there was a great change of feeling upon the subject, and that the general confidence that was entertained first in the motives of the Government was altered into a feeling of mistrust. I have taken every means in my power to ascertain the reason for this change. I attribute it in some degree, to the injudicious writings of the English Press, both in India and at home. Annexation was openly advocated, and there were several articles written in the *Times* which were circulated in India about that time, and which were calculated to create great apprehensions in the minds of the Native Princes of India, who are apt to associate the utterances of that journal with the opinions entertained by the Government in England. Next, I believe that the general feeling of the natives in India is that of pity for a person under trial, however grave his offence may be. That feeling in the case of Gaekwar was greatly increased by the humiliating position in which he was put by being confronted in a court of justice with witnesses of low position, and thereby put in some degree on an equal level with them. The publicity of the enquiry doubtless added strength to this feeling, which I know was entertained very keenly by Maharaja Scindia, so much so, that he pressed upon me to be allowed whilst the enquiry was proceeding, to communicate with Gaekwar, and to arrange that he should abdicate in order to avoid the continuance of so painful a procedure. I need hardly say that I was obliged to tell the Maharaja that this was a course to which I could not be a party, and that it would place His Highness as a member of the Commission in a very false position. Besides the feelings of mistrust of the intentions of Government, and of sympathy with the position of the Gaekwar, I have no hesitation in expressing my belief that a considerable amount of money has been used by the adherents of Gaekwar for the purpose of influencing public opinion in his favour. There can be no doubt, however, that there is a strong feeling of nationality among the Maratha population, and that the more able and better educated of them had all their sympathies enlisted in favour of Gaekwar and against the British government. It is remarkable how soon the gravity of the offence which had been committed, and into which the enquiry was being made, appears to have been entirely forgotten amid the other circumstances which surround it. There is still another point which tended to enlist the sympathies of the native princes of India in favour of Gaekwar. It was indispensable, in order to investigate the case, that the commission should be instructed to enquire not only into the connection of Gaekwar with the poisoning of Colonel Phayre, but into the alleged practice of Gaekwar of holding secret communications with the Residency servants, and of giving them money for the purpose of obtaining information as to the business conducted at the Residency. We had best reason to believe that systematic attempts of the kind had been habitually made by Gaekwar and it was necessary, for the purpose of clearing the way to the examination of his connection with the poisoning, that the truth of his secret communications with the Residency servants, who were also supposed to be agents in the crime, should be established. If the evidence with respect to those communications had broken down, it would have been a strong argument in favor of the innocence of Gaekwar. If, on the other hand, the secret interviews were established, the antecedent improbability that Gaekwar should have been in personal communication with persons of that class would be removed.

'I have said this in order to explain the necessity under which we were placed in directing the commission to enquire into the communications between Gaekwar and the Residency servants apart from the poisoning case. This enquiry, however, excited considerable alarm at other native courts, where, I believe, the practice of paying money for the sake of obtaining information is by no means unknown if indeed it is not common. This of itself will account to a considerable extent for the desire generally felt among native princes that Gaekwar should be cleared from the charges brought against him.

'It would be premature for me, while the government of India is judicially examining the reports of the commissioners and the evidence which has been given before them, to add any more than that we have been actuated throughout solely by the determination of supporting the honour of the Crown in the case of one of the greatest insults which could be offered in the person of a British Resident at a native court, while showing every consideration that was proper and possible to Gaekwar, and dealing with him in a spirit of perfect impartiality. Looking not only to the poisoning case, but to the antecedents of Gaekwar, to the maladministration of the state of Baroda and to the measures taken in consequence, I can confidently assert that he has been treated with utmost forbearance that was compatible with the duty of the British government to insist that a state enjoying British protection, the peace of which we are bound to maintain by Her Majesty's forces, should be so administered as to secure the people from grievous abuses. If the same course be pursued to the end, if we fearlessly act towards the Gaekwar in such a manner as we believe in our conscience to be just and right,having regard to his own conduct and to the interests of his subjects; and if at the same time we show by our action that no self-interest whatever influences the British Government in the course that is taken, I am confident that the princes of India will soon recognize the justice and moderation which has been shown,and that any misrepresentations to which we may be subjected from ill-informed or reckless writing in the English or native press will do the British government in India no serious or permanent injury.' [5]

This report from Lord Northbrook, one might say was the last nail in Malharrao's coffin; it justified the action taken by the British government and prevented the press from criticism and the public from a demonstration of their belligerence. Poor Malharrao was arrested presumably on a false charge and British Resident Sir Lewis Pelly took charge of Baroda till a minor prince could be found.

Sir Lewis Pelly, after the second commission, had conducted an enquiry and had pronounced Malharrao as guilty of attempted murder. However, he had to give up office due to ill health and Sir Richard Meade was appointed to take his place in Baroda.

Malharrao was formally deposed on 10 April 1877, and hustled off to Madras where he lived in obscurity for seven years. His reign in Baroda had run to four.

The Press reported the arrest:

This morning, His Highness Malharrao Gaekwad was pale, most plainly dressed, and scarcely had an ornament about him. Perhaps he knew what was coming and had not sufficient vanity to go into captivity with his state jewels on. One of the first questions asked when he arrived at his temporary prison was whether the water was good and how many attendants he was to have. A list of the number allowed was made out and given to him. Several 'table' companions have been allowed and a modest household establishment of some 20-30 servants. The gates leading to the bungalow compound are barred and no one is admitted without a pass from the Resident.

From *The Times* correspondent: 'The fallen prince has accepted his fate with quiet dignity, which, however bad the man may be morally, one cannot but admire. Judging from the expression used by him to Sir Lewis when he knew what was to follow, "that the very ground cried, cried out against him." He is not willing to acknowledge his sins which have at length surely found him out.'

It is to be doubted whether the real truth of the matter was ever made public.

Disarmament of the Gaekwads' force was completed the following day. Steps were taken to protect the palace and the palace jewels were kept in a safe place till the crisis was over.

In accordance with their express desire, five of the sardars had been allowed to go to the palace for the purpose of mounting guard over the gaddi. This was a curious custom of the state and at first Sir Lewis Pelly could not comprehend why the sardars were so anxious to guard the gaddi, but he subsequently permitted them and immediately after Malharrao's arrest, five of them faithfully watched the throne vacated by Malharrao. By the time Sir Lewis Pelly's letter conveying the news to the viceroy was published, it would be known all over the world. It was without doubt the most important political *coup d'etat* that the government had affected in a very long time. It owed its success to the really masterly manner in which it was carried out. Sir Lewis Pelly's personal influence over Malharrao had a large share in the success. Certainly Malharrao, as soon as he saw that his game was up, became very docile. Had he chosen not to do so, he might have given a great deal of trouble.

It yet remained to be seen how the Marathas of the presidency would view the matter, but Malharrao had few friends and many enemies so no one really regretted very much that he had been deposed. The sardars, in fact, seemed rather pleased than otherwise.

Several of the sardars said through an interpreter, 'The words used by Your Honour are very good and we are satisfied with them. Our prayer has reference to the protection of the state and we are confident that the government will deal out justice to Malharrao.'

Sir Lewis Pelly said, 'What am I to understand by your reference to Malharrao? Do you mean to say you consider His Highness guilty of crimes or mismanagement?'

The sardars said, 'We cannot say. It's for the government to decide!'[6]

Strangely, the phrase 'to protect the gaddi' conveys the mystery or the caprices of fate. But the gaddi was definitely protected for the greatest of rulers to occupy it and change the face of the history of Baroda in the years to come.

Ironically, Dr Seward, Malharrao's guardian and personal physician, was with him at the time of his death in 1884. He confessed to the dying man that he had been threatened and bribed by Phayre to write a false report regarding the poison in the glass of sherbet. There had been no traces of poison in the glass containing the sherbet. It is doubtful if poor Malharrao in his dying state could comprehend what was being said to him and his death must have weighed on the consciences of Phayre and Dr Seward.

Malharrao was made out to be a villain in the medieval drama played out by the Resident with Jamnabai probably peering from the wings, but Malharrao was sincere in his efforts to do good for the state of Baroda, and had the Resident allowed it, the administration would have been remarkably efficient. His reign is significant for building a high school and a number of other vernacular medium schools, but it is most fondly remembered for his construction of the Sur Sagar tank in the heart of the city that still provides water to the Residents living there. Between the years 1870 and 1874, he established four banks—Lakshmidas Narsidas and Malhareshwar in Baroda, and again Malhareshwar in Navsari and Lakshmidas Narsidas in Bombay. In 1871-72 he established the banks of Lakshmidas Narsidas and Mhalsakant in Surat. In 1873-74, he established the Parvatikant bank in Bombay. His object was to remove as much capital as possible out of the Baroda state, in order to have the command of it if his actions were hampered by the British government, or if he himself was deprived of power. In order to move the money safely and secretly it was necessary to have fresh establishments in

Baroda as well as Bombay, so that the transfer might not be known to the old bankers. In this manner he transferred Rs 57,00,000 in cash balances and bullion. When he was confirmed on the gaddi he took back the bulk of this money, closed the first bank he had opened in Baroda and transferred the funds to the Malhareshwar bank. He then openly declared the existence of the Lakshmidas Narsidas bank in Surat with the intent that this bank and that in Navsari might, when he chose, transit sums to Bombay. So in 1873-74 when he was on the brink of being deposed, he transferred Rs 30,00,000 to Surat. This sum formed the bulk of the Rs 40,00,000 found in the palace when he was deposed. The other intent with which the banks were set up was to abolish the potedari system which had given rise to unscrupulous moneylenders.

His rule is not marked by any spectacular achievements but had he been allowed to rule longer, he would have achieved a lot more. But fate has its own way of moving the pawns on the chessboard of life and for a very significant reason as we shall see.

13

Back to Kavlana

The stage was now set for Jamnabai to enact the last piece of the sordid drama, which she did, and how. Barely ten days after Malharrao had been sent by a special escort to Madras, Jamnabai arrived in Baroda by a special train and was given a queen's welcome—she was received by Sir Richard Meade, guards of honour and a gun salute.

Jamnabai had exercised her right to adopt an heir to the throne of Baroda, a right that had been granted to her late husband as one of the rewards for helping the British in the mutiny of 1857 and she chose to adopt a young person who could be moulded by her. The British too wanted the same. Malharrao had a son but that complication was resolved by debarring him from the line of succession on grounds of illegitimacy, as he was conceived out of wedlock. The British, of course, quietly offered to guide her in the choice of an heir to the throne.

Here, we need to go back to the time when Fatehsinghrao I died in 1818 and his widow Radhabai was dissuaded from committing sati by her courtiers on the plea that all her jewellery would pass on to her relatives and it would be better if she could ensure that it remained in her line. So Radhabai had adopted a son from Wadi, a place in Baroda, but had signed an undertaking that he would never, at any time, have a claim to the Baroda throne.

Now, with Jamnabai's plans for adoption, there rose a clamour from the Wadiwala Gaekwads that if she could do so then they too were perfectly eligible for adoption as the earlier stipulation was only valid if there was a direct line in the order of succession; since there wasn't, the earlier condition was invalid and could not be cited to bar them from the claim to the throne. Out of the Wadiwala progeny, there were four who could have made it to the throne based on this argument but since they were all older than Jamnabai, she being only twenty-two at that point of time, their claims were passed over and the fact that they had supported Malharrao in her feud with him too went against them. Jamnabai's motives were slightly different from the

British Raj, she probably wanted someone who could be guided by her while the British wanted to have absolute control of the ruler and prevent him from doing anything that was detrimental to their interests. Their claims were rejected by the British and Jamnabai was allowed to adopt someone of her choice to rule the state of Baroda.

Here we need to traverse all the way back to a village called Kavlana in Nasik district. Apart from Damajirao II, Pilajirao's other two sons were Prataprao and Khanderao. Khanderao who had accompanied his father on his campaigns in Gujarat had been well provided for by Pilajirao who apportioned the Kadi territory in Gujarat as his fief. He took up his residence there as the jagirdar and hence his descendants came to be known as Kadi Gaekwads. Prataprao chose to remain in Maharashtra to look after the family's considerable holdings there comprising forty-six villages in Nasik district. There had been tacit understanding between them that whatever conquests each made in his territory it would be shared equally between them. Unfortunately for Prataprao he lost these to Bajirao I who exchanged some of his own territory in Gujarat for these forty-six villages. While Damajirao II gained in Gujarat, Prataprao's family were left with hardly anything and were forced to fall back on farming as a means of their livelihood. Sometime later they moved on to Kavlana and settled down there as farmers and gradually bought a share of the hereditary rights of the headmanship of that village. Prataprao's descendants are known as Kavlana Gaekwads. Sayajirao III was a Kavlana Gaekwad.

They lived the simple life of farmers, getting up at dawn and going to bed at sunset. They kept cows for their milk supply and grew crops for their food. Their social life in the villages began and ended with attending betrothals, weddings, births and funerals at regular intervals. In time, they virtually lost all contact with the Baroda Gaekwads and had in their possession a few family relics to testify to their common origins.

The direct descendants of Prataprao were five brothers out of whom only Ukhajirao and Kashirao had sons. When a commission was appointed by Jamnabai and the British officials to look into the bona fides of the Kavlana Gaekwads, Kashirao's two sons, Gopalrao and Sampatrao, were aged thirteen and nine respectively. And Ukhajirao's son Dadasaheb was ten years old. Once it was established that Ukhaji's son and Kashirao's sons were in the direct line of descendants, the three boys were taken to Baroda for the final selection for adoption by Jamnabai.

Now, we go back to the fairy tale beginning of 'once upon a time' when a beautiful queen asks the boys, 'Why do you think you have been brought here?' The younger two gave the usual answers which were labelled 'unsatisfactory' but the oldest of the three replied with the assurance of one born to the throne as he said, 'To be made the Maharaja and rule of course!' The beautiful queen completely bowled over by the boy's panache and confidence replied, 'And, so you shall!'

That day heralded the dawn in Baroda. The decision, of course, was not made by a single throw of the dice; the children were closely observed by the dewan and others in the palace before the final call was taken.

Interestingly, the palace astrologer who had been given all three boys' horoscopes to study had pronounced Gopalrao's to be the most favourable. He revealed that 'the horoscope presaged a powerful sovereignty, extension of territories, ever increasing riches and a rule unhampered by foes!' Jamnabai had been very cautious to make the right choice and had all the boys under close observation by her courtiers and also by Sir Richard Meade and the unanimous choice had been Gopalrao.

After the formalities for adoption were over, an official notification was put out by Richard Meade on 25 May 1875 that Gopalrao, son of Kashirao Gaekwad, had been chosen as the next Maharaja and called upon all the well-wishers of the state of Baroda to 'unite in invoking the blessings of Providence on their future chief and in wishing him a long life and prosperity as the ruler of the country.'[1]

PART 2

14

Maharaja Sayajirao Gaekwad III

In 1875, the lad from the district of Kavlana became the focal point of interest for Jamnabai and Sir Richard Meade as they had the difficult task of transforming an unlettered rustic lad into a thoroughly accomplished aristocrat. Though it must be said that there were ulterior motives at play on the part of the British Resident and other British officials; they wanted to bring a reign in Baroda which would be dictated by the British sovereign powers and seated on the throne would be a king who would be loyal, dutiful and subservient to his British overlords. He would be a role model for other Indian princes to follow. In spite of these murky intentions, the British officials set out with exemplary zeal and tenacity of purpose to play 'Professor Higgins' in the young ruler's transformation. Sir Richard Meade set out a rigorous routine in education that the boy was compelled to follow.

The astrologers had said that the auspicious date for the young prince's coronation was 27 May 1875. The adoption ceremony, purely a private one, had been completed two days earlier. Gopalrao's parents and relatives had been invited and the young prince's name, Gopalrao, had been cast aside and a new, more appropriate one replaced it. The name given to him was Sayajirao, the most favoured name of the family of Gaekwads. The adoption ceremony was followed by his coronation performed in the palace. The crown was placed on his head with a lot of ceremony and the head priest pronounced him Maharaja Sayajirao Gaekwad III, ruler of Baroda. Afterwards, a British party of seventeen officials headed by Sir Richard Meade and his assistant J.R. Richey with quite a few interpreters arrived on the scene. Sir Richard Meade then led the young Maharaja to the gaddi, which was a huge stuffed brocade-covered cushion, embellished with precious stones, lifted the new Maharaja and placed him on the gaddi. 'A salute of a 122 guns was fired by the Baroda artillery and twenty-one guns, the highest for any Maharaja in India by the British artillery.'[1]

Gifts were exchanged between prominent members of the royal family and British officials. The young Maharaja was hailed by the subjects of Baroda, and cries of 'Long live Maharaja Sayajirao Gaekwad' filled the air. Sweets were distributed, the poor fed and prisoners freed. The new Maharaja, who was still a raw, callow youth who could hardly write his own name in English, thanked Viceroy L. Northbrook in a letter written probably by Sir Richard Meade himself or the newly appointed dewan, Sir T. Madhavrao who was well aware of the sort of language pleasing to a viceroy when addressed by his Indian subjects. Sayajirao Gaekwad III thanked the viceroy for the possession of the kingly seat which without his kindness he could never have obtained and for which he would 'eternally be grateful'.

In a reciprocal letter, the viceroy addressed him as 'my honoured friend'.[2] However, this boy from Kavlana became used to being addressed as 'His Royal Highness Maharaja Sayajirao Gaekwad Shamsher Bahadur Sena Khas Khel'. In the years to follow, he proved more than a match for his British superiors and was the recipient of several more titles, but for the moment those titles acquired hereditarily were heady enough!

The British had thought it imperative to instal a new dewan or chief minister in Baroda to put the state's affairs, which had become chaotic during and immediately after Malharrao's dethronement, and their choice had fallen on Madhavrao, a scholar with vast experience in Indian administration, who had worked in the same capacity in two other princely domains, Travancore and Indore. As he was a man who was well-educated with a good knowledge of Western culture, he was relied upon to influence his pupil, Sayajirao III. In the eyes of the British officials, Madhavrao represented the highest ideal of an Indian administrator. In spite of his education and exposure to Western ideas of the times, he was shrewd enough to avoid applying these if they conflicted with the ideas of the paramount power; he was tactful in voicing his opinions if they were contrary to the opinions of those in power and never stepped out of line in protocol or rules laid down by the British. For example, he would never have done anything so undiplomatic like Dadabhai Naoriji did in writing to the viceroy requesting the removal of a Resident. He worked with diligence and if the proposals made by the reigning power were based on their policies contrary to his, he accepted it as part of the realities of political life and did not contradict or resist them. In short, he was what Baroda needed at that time—an honest minister who would set about applying himself to the task of improving the Baroda state.

Madhavrao was given limited powers; it was the AGG who was in real overall control. The advice given by the AGG could never be ignored and had to be heeded but Madhavrao was so efficient that the AGG rarely felt called upon to render advice. Sir Richard Meade who continued as the AGG after Malharrao was deposed was not the only person who drew on the dewan's diplomatic resources—there was also the stong-willed Jamnabai who was used to getting her own way and extremely lavish in her expenditures. Jamnabai was arrogant and with her haughty demeanour was even more difficult to handle, especially now that she had to budget her expenses. She was told that she could neither indulge in her passion for jewellery, nor bestow expensive gifts on her favourites as she was inclined to do. This stricture must have been extremely galling on one who had fought tooth and nail for just such privileges. One can imagine the plight of a dewan who had to walk the tightrope between two tough masters. His dexterity is certainly commendable and in the fact that he remained in office for six years and during his tenure managed to maintain amicable relations with both.

Sayajirao III began his educational journey with two tutors—Keshav Rao Pandit who remained his tutor all through his adolescent years and Venkatesh Joshi, also known as 'Bhau Master' who tutored the Maharaja in Marathi. A month later, a Gujarati tutor was also brought in to help the young Maharaja learn Gujarati so that he could administer his state effectively.

Sayajirao III lived in the Sarkarwada Palace, which we now know as the Central Library, with Jamnabai. He was given a room on the uppermost floor of the palace for his studies. The winding staircase with trapdoors at alternate levels in keeping with the dangerous times, while the gaddi was kept on the first floor, which also housed the shrine in which pictures and bronze statues of Hindu gods and goddesses were kept for worship. The palace, though large, was not well ventilated and to a boy who was used to open spaces that verdant fields offered, it must have felt claustrophobic.

Sayajirao III adjusted to his new surroundings without a word of complaint and with the same sagacity that had prompted him to utter those words that had won him the gaddi. He seemed confident, an assurance that perhaps sprang from his intuition that the divine hand that had guided his destiny so far would continue to do so.

On 26 August, Sir Richard Meade reported that the young Maharaja's progress was not progressing the way it should have been, so he recommended that Sayajirao III be removed from the environment of palace females and menials as they could hamper the young Maharaja's education and outlook, and impressed upon the British government the importance of a male-dominated estate for the boy. He also suggested setting up a special 'Rajas' school' for aristocrats where English teachers could teach. However, this plan had to be shelved for the moment as the Prince of Wales, the future king of England—Edward VII—chose to visit India in November 1875. His impending visit was, of course, thought of as the most appropriate occasion to have the young Maharaja, who was to be the future ruler of Baroda, meet the future heir to the imperial throne of Britian.

On 25 October, the young Sayajirao III accompanied by Jamnabai and Sir Richard Meade, along with a large retinue of officials, left for Bombay (now Mumbai). After being received at the station to a salute of booming guns and a deputation of government officials headed by the governor, Sir Philip Wodehouse, they were escorted to a bungalow in Lal Bagh, which had been done up to be fit for the young king's residence. After his formal visit to Governor Sir Philip Wodehouse, Sayajirao III was at leisure to see, for the first time in his life, the sights of Bombay. Later, he was taken to the queen of all railway stations—Victoria Railway Station (now Chhatrapati Shivaji Maharaj Terminus)—to receive Viceroy L. Northbrook who arrived in Bombay on 2 November. At the station, where all the native princes were gathered to receive him, Sayajirao III made the acquaintance of Maharaja Chamarajendra Wadiyar of Mysore, who was about the same age as him and a quick friendship sprang up between the two which grew and strengthened in the years to come.

An exchange of ceremonial calls followed.

The strangest part of all these meetings between the British royals and the aristocracy was that since Sayajirao III was not conversant with the English language, communication took place by signs, a sort of 'dumb charades' conversation, but was conducted with impeccable propriety for that was the standard by which the British ran their empire, marked with ritual and strict protocol.

Six days later, the Prince of Wales arrived at the Bombay harbour on *HMS Serapis* and the viceroy went on board to conduct him ashore while the governor and the commander-in-chief, along with a large number of European officials and Indian princes were there to receive him. The following day, at the reception given in his honour at the Government House, the Prince of Wales in his conversation with Sayajirao III urged upon him the necessity for continuing his education in English and also spoke about sharpening his horsemanship skills. The following day, Sayajirao III was presented with a whip, a sword, a jewelled snuffbox, a ring and two albums as gifts from the Prince of Wales.

Ten days later, the Prince of Wales announced his decision to visit Baroda and Sayajirao III with his retinue—the dewan as well as Jamnabai—left for Baroda to make the necessary arrangements in honour of the Prince's visit to their state.

When the Prince of Wales arrived in Baroda on 19 November he was given a grand reception. He rode with Sayajirao III in a golden palanquin placed on a royal elephant decked in finery for the occasion. At the Residency, the Prince of Wales was greeted in the traditional Indian manner with a sprinkling of rose water on his person and a shower of flowers. Many sports activities was organized for the prince, who seemed to have a peculiar penchant for sathmari (a sport similar to Spanish bull fights, only in this case, elephants were used instead of bulls) followed by cheetah fights which involved years of hard work and rigorous training of the cheetahs to run behind blackbucks and kill them. The cheetahs had to be very skilfully manoeuvred to ignore the does in the herd and chase only grown males. The handler's skill lay in deftly manipulating the chase in such a way that the cheetah would be in the right position to make the kill, which required split-second timing. The cheetah had to be let loose at the precise moment the blackbuck was running within a hundred yards or so for the kill. The spectators rode on horseback following the cheetahs to be in at the kill. Pig-sticking was a similar sport in which the hunters chased and killed wild boars with spears. Both sports brought danger to the hunters as the cheetah and the wild boar could turn around and attack the hunters instead and accidents were quite frequent. Pig-sticking at Dabka, which was Maharaja Khanderao's hunting box eighteen miles west of Baroda city, was included in the sports events as were rhinoceros and ram fights.

At night, the city and the palace were illuminated.

At the banquet hosted in honour of the Prince of Wales, Madhavrao spoke of the pleasure his visit to Baroda had given him and predicted that Sayajirao Gaekwad III had a great career before him and would devote himself to promoting the welfare of his people and developing the resources of his country. A prophecy was singularly fulfilled! The speech concluded with the prince raising a toast to Sayajirao III and Jamnabai, after which the evening closed with music and fireworks.

It must be said here that since Sayajirao III was not familiar with British etiquette and was also unfamiliar with the English language, he remained a passive onlooker while his dewan did the honours in English.

Life returned to normal after the prince left on 23 November. Jamnabai and Madhavrao realized that it was to educate the young Sayajirao III in English. The new AGG, P.S. Melville, who had earlier sat on the Meade Commission to enquire into the subject of Malharrao's guilt also realized this and got the desired approbation from the Bombay government. After some debate, the district judge, H.M. Birdwood, appointed F.A.H. Elliot (son of a former acting governor of Madras and holding the post of director of public instruction in Berar; incidentally, he was married to Judge Birdwood's sister-in-law) as Sayajirao III's instructor. Elliot arrived in Baroda in December 1875 to take up his new assignment.

15

Education of the Young Sayajirao III

Within a short time, a school in a small bungalow was set up in the Moti Baug building in the present grounds on which the Laxmi Vilas Palace stands. A new building which was to be a permanent one that could accommodate a fairly large number of pupils was built for the purpose.

Elliot lost no time in drawing up a rigorous academic timetable for the young Sayajirao III. Apart from the English language, the boy was to be taught Marathi, Gujarati and Urdu. He also had to master the Modi script in Marathi, a tough exercise for a boy who was just getting used to the alphabets of the languages. His curriculum included mathematics, history and geography too.

Under Elliot's direction, studies began in real earnest. Sayajirao III had his brother Sampatrao, his cousin Dadasaheb and a few other boys from the elite families in Baroda as his schoolmates. They had classes from 10 in the morning till sunset. This assignment was a tough one, both for the instructor as well as the royal pupil; in Elliot's own words, 'The beginning was an absolute beginning.' The very foundation was proving an arduous task which prompted Elliot to remark that the lad was 'apparently and actually dull'[1] and Elliot spent considerable effort in the enlightenment of his student's mind. Fortunately for Sayajirao III, it dawned on his tutor that it was his regimental schedule and the sheer torrent of instruction[2] that was at fault and must have been enough to arouse apathy in the brightest. So Elliot set about to remedy the matter without delay. He rescheduled his hours of study and eased the pressure put by his curriculum and found, to his delight, that his young pupil who was king responded to it most favourably. Elliot now had nothing but praise for the diligence and intelligence of his pupil.

The new schedule, however, came to a temporary halt when it was decided that Sayajirao III should travel on an extensive tour of 3,500 miles and attend the great durbar in Delhi at the invitation of the viceroy where

Queen Victoria was to be proclaimed as the Empress of India.

On 7 December 1876, Sayajirao III, his retinue along with Jamnabai, her daughter Tarabai, Melville and, of course, Elliot, who in the years to come proved to be a valuable friend and counsellor to Sayajirao III, travelled all the way to Delhi by a special train and reached on 14 December.

The day after Christmas, the new viceroy, Lord Lytton, received Sayajirao III in the durbar pavilion and presented him with a special banner of the Baroda colours and an imperial gold medal engraved with Queen Victoria's face. On 29 December, the young Maharaja was informed by the viceroy that the queen was pleased to bestow on him the title of Farzand-i-Khas-i-Inglish-Daulatia, which meant favoured son of the British Empire. The following month, the newspapers, after the Imperial Assemblage, recorded the event describing 'how the young Gaekwad, resplendent in velvet and diamonds' was led across the arena by Melville. A public announcement of his new title was also made that day.

Sayajirao III's return journey to Baroda, which was interspersed with halts at various places of interest and baths in holy waters of the five rivers, brought home to his mind what progress meant in terms of travel. Perhaps, it was then that the germ of an idea to widen his horizons by travel was sown in his mind.

The Maharaja's return and the title conferred upon him were celebrated enthusiastically with a round of festivities which included a durbar at the Nazar Baug Palace, a review of the British troops at the camp and some sporting activities followed by a dinner and a ball at the Makarpura Palace as the grand finale to the celebrations.

Elliot had four other masters to assist him in the education of his pupils which was conducted in the conventional British public school discipline. Physical exercise was not given much importance, though exercises and sports in the open air on the palace grounds were conducted (by the time the new school had been built about two miles from the old palace) included Indian games like hututu, kho kho and atyapatya, as cricket, football and hockey were not introduced in India. Squadron drill, sword fencing and swimming were also taught and practised after school. The school also boasted of a billiards table and Sayajirao III 'laid the foundations for his future proficiency in the game.'[3] Fortnightly hunting excursions too were included among their sporting activities.

Regarding education, much was crammed into the heads of the students, but the young Maharaja was able to cope with it and his steady progress was received with delight and admiration by his tutors, particularly Elliot. A strict watch was kept on him both at home by Jamnabai and at school by Elliot; however, it did not irk him since tact was employed in their method of surveillance.

Sayajirao III's daily routine began thus—he was woken up at six in the morning and after his morning ablutions, an hour would be spent in the wrestling pit of the palace, training under a well-known professional, Dudhia Pehelwan. A bath and light refreshments followed after which he took lessons in riding under a riding master named Rahim Mia in a paddock near Nazar Bagh Palace, the construction of which had commenced during Malharrao's reign and was not yet finished. Homework followed for an hour after which he sat down with Jamnabai to partake a rich meal. The food made him and his friends so drowsy during class hours that Elliot began to suspect that it was laced with opium.

The year 1877 was significant for one event—a brief visit by Sir Richard Temple, the governor of Bombay—and one tragedy—the death of Sayajirao III's father Shrimant Kashirao Babasaheb on 26 July. This was young Sayajirao's first brush with death and personal loss, but it prepared him for many more in the years to come. Kashirao had come to live in Baroda; considering he was the father of the Maharaja of Baroda. Kashirao for some inexplicable reason did not live in the palace and the meetings of father and son were restricted. 'I remembered him often and felt lost without him', Sayajirao III was to write many years later. 'My father was a shy man, but with a real nobility of mind and we had been very close. But I could not see him as often as I would have liked to. From the balcony of my apartment, I would sometimes wave to him and make signs.' [4]

The school curriculum advanced to a higher standard and chemistry and many other subjects like political science, administration and governance were introduced and formed the principal part of Sayajirao III's education. English, Marathi and Gujarati were the main languages for study and Sayajirao III devoted special attention to history and English. English essays too formed an integral part of his studies to improve his language skills as well as spellings and handwriting. However, the Maharaja took it all in his stride and progressed sufficiently well for Elliot to remark at the end of an association of four years that the young Maharaja had a remarkable memory and 'he refused to forget much of anything which he has once learnt'. He also asserted, 'I have not had any occasion to find fault with him. A better or more affectionate pupil could not be found'.[5]

Along with six years of rigorous mental exercise, there was also a hard physical training course for which he had various veterans in their respective fields as his masters. For Indian farigad (sword play), he had Kamal Khan to train him; his fencing master was Sergeant Griffith; and there were other professionals for malkhamb (greased wrestling pole) and jodi, another typical Maratha sport. After the sessions, the boys returned sore in their limbs for another hour of homework after which it was time for dinner and bed.

Sayajirao III slept like the proverbial king in a gold-plated bed with servants in permanent attendance to swish away mosquitoes or massage his aching limbs. He was conscious of the fact that he was someone very special with the attention showered upon him at school, by companions who gushed over him and servants who ran to do his bidding; there was a hush whenever he approached and 'the grandest of courtiers bowed low to him'. There was glamour, glitter, excitement and unimaginable wealth that one could ever dream of, but strangely enough, it did not turn his head and make him arrogant. On the contrary, he became more cautious, reserved and wary of people. For one who had just lost his 'milk teeth', he developed discernment and perceptiveness that was to stand him in good stead later on when the reins of the kingdom of Baroda fell into his capable hands.

The impartial and regimental discipline of Madhavrao must have put an end to any impulsiveness or impetuosity on the part of Sayajirao III as he began to comprehend British phrases, figures of speech and their metaphors, and understood the common message that both Melville and Madhav Rao instilled in him—the British Raj was God's gift to mankind, with infinite powers, and its wrath should never be incited as it was most destructive. Its goodwill was a blessing and, most important of all, the Raj was always right and therefore unquestionable.

Sayajirao III did well under the tutelage of Madhavrao, Melville and Elliot. The first two were good, diligent men who were part of a pattern of authority, of discipline, but neither was sensitive to the young Maharaja's need for companionship and for this he turned to Elliot who had grown genuinely fond of the boy. From Elliot, he got the warmth and a father's affection that he craved for and in him, Sayajirao III saw someone he could respect and look up to, as Elliot was not only one of the finest officers of the Indian Civil Service, but also possessed all the qualities to endear him to people. He was good-looking, kind and well-bred, a scholar and a sportsman with a keen sense of humour who was able to laugh at Hindu customs as well as British snobbery. Young Sayajirao III found it easy to confide in him. Elliot played games with him and even joined his pupils in raucous sing-song ditties which endeared him to his students, Sayajirao III in particular, who was going through acute pangs of homesickness and missed his parents, farmlife and the rustic environment dreadfully. (In *Sayajirao of Baroda*, Fatehsinghrao Gaekwad writes about the homesickness pangs, 'when he had not quite made the incalculable adjustment between his old life and new, that he was often racked by a vague sense of guilt at having been torn away from his roots and particularly from his father...'). No amount of riches can compensate for parental love and Sayajirao III was finding it hard, even though Jamnabai did her best to make him comfortable and lavished care on him. Yet, it was not the same as sitting down to a simple meal of bajra roti served by a loving mother's hand. Elliot understood all this and that was what was so special about him, as he understood without being told and gave the young king the companionship and the affection that he was craving for. Sayajirao III also turned to him more and more for almost everything as the days went by.

In 1880, it was decided by Jamnabai that it was time for the young Maharaja to get married and the onus for scouting for a suitable bride fell on Madhavrao. Soon detailed letters with photographs of young girls from elite families along with their horoscopes poured in. Astrologers were consulted to predict the mystic influences of the zodiac signs, special prayers in the Hindu ritualistic way with priests were offered to invoke the blessings of the gods and goddesses, but Jamnabai, for whom pragmatism prevailed above impulsiveness, decided to obtain the approbation of Madhavrao before deciding. Needless to say, the field was limited to Maharashtrians only. After a lot of hoopla, 'the predestined sharer of the young Gaekwad's fortunes was at last found on the banks of the river Cauvery'.[6]

She was Princess Laxmibai of the Mohite clan of the Marathas, the daughter of Haibatrao Mohite and the niece of the maharani of Tanjore. She was only sixteen years old, which made her a year younger than Sayajirao

III. The Tanjore family was well known and fit the bill to form a matrimonial alliance with the royal Gaekwads of Baroda. The Bombay government too gave its approval. Simultaneously, Jamnabai's daughter Tarabai's betrothal to Raja Saheb Raghunath Rao of Sawantvadi was also arranged, but that did not go the way it was contemplated, as we shall see.

The year 1880 was also crucial for young Sayajirao III as the reins of the administration of Baroda were to be handed over to him, with of course, the British government having a final say in all important matters. What this really meant was that no decision made by the Gaekwad ruler was in any way to be a threat to the British sovereignty in Gujarat or go against their imperialistic policies.

Both Madhavrao and Melville felt that it was a little too early in the boy's education to let Sayajirao III rule. The main reason could have been, and probably was, that they were reluctant to let go of such unfettered power that had been their prerogative till then. Sayajirao III himself regretted that the decision had come too early as he would have preferred another three years in which he could travel across the country and interact more with the people of his state and the country.

Madhavrao had brought about an effective and efficient administration when seen through a broad spectrum, though many local people of importance accused the dewan of being pro-British and newspapers like the *Kesari* and *Maratha* made no bones of their opinion and were quite blatant about it in the Poona press. Probably this was another reason for the government to release the dewan from his administrative duties and let him remain in the capacity of adviser, which also was a proof of their own integrity of purpose.

A realistic picture of the dewan had been drawn by the author of Sayajirao III enabling us to visualize the Brahmin in his pattu (silk) dhoti tied round the waist and flowing to his ankles, a silk turban wound round his head, diamonds sparkling in his ears and fingers, quite a striking figure even for the British officials. He was regarded as a 'typical courtier and a man of the world'. Prodigious to the extent of being a workaholic, Madhavrao was highly educated, could speak six languages and was an excellent administrator. At the beginning of his dewanship in Baroda, he had set himself a formidable list of duties which included radical changes in the administration that were both beneficial to the ruler and the ruled. He went about it with dogged determination to bring the state of Baroda on par with any British district in Britian. The infrastructure of the city was improved along with improvements in education, sanitation and medical facilities for the public.

Reduction in taxes was, of course, a welcome measure and in spite of all the funding spent for public works, Madhavrao was able to balance the budget and the state treasury showed a surplus instead of a deficit—such was the man's brilliance. Needless to say, in the fashion of a true Brahmin, he had blown his own trumpet claiming that his administration with its substantial advantages was the state on which the Maharaja would 'shortly be exercising his power'. His critics have called him a sop to the sensibilities of the British sovereign power. Some accused Madhavrao of filling the offices with south Indian Brahmins for which his sense of discernment, probably, was responsible as Brahmins were well-educated and dexterous in handling accounts.

However, there were two major defects in Madhavrao's administration— the first was his tendency to side with the Raj so much so that he surrendered the state of Baroda's right to manufacture its own arms and ammunition or buy them from whomsoever it chose. It was the state's sole prerogative which had now been handed over to the British. The British agreed to offer arms and ammunition to Baroda at cost price and also waive the customary excise duty, making the state more dependent on them. It was a blow to the prestige of the ruler and the state as an independent state. The other defect was the disbandment of the Baroda contingent. The Baroda contingent belonged primarily to the Gaekwads and had been used earlier, in 1800, for their mulukgiri expeditions; then they had been asked to offer the contingent to aid the East India Company whenever needed by it, and in return 'Gaekwad would benefit by any future territory acquired by war'.[7] However, when Anandrao had asked the Company's help to put down a rival for the gaddi, the company had responded with troops but had demanded a sum of Rs 8,00,000 as annual payment for their maintenance which by the year 1817 had increased to a sum of approximately Rs 25,00, 000.

Now, in 1878, the subsidiary force had been abolished and the Company's troops in Baroda had been reduced to eight hundred men who were there more to keep a check on the Gaekwads stepped out of line rather than for their protection. The Baroda contingent maintained law and order in the surrounding districts of Kathiawad and Gujarat. These principalities paid a tribute to the Gaekwads for their protection and were known as tributary mahals. Once the company took control over these, acting as agents to collect tribute, the existence of the contingent had no purpose and hence, when the British suggested its disbandment, Madhavrao agreed to it. The British then argued that since the collection of tribute had been delegated to them, half of the expenses saved by disbanding the contingent should be paid to them and Madhavrao, without the slightest compunction, also agreed to this irrational logic and committed to pay the Company an annual sum of Rs 3,75,000 for performing the work of the contingent. It must also be said that he hardly had a choice, considering the Company was the master of the land and wielded real power behind the throne.

There were other minor offences in the administration of the dewan; the two that affected the economy of the state were the ban on the production of salt and the manufacture and sale of opium. For the latter, however, Madhavrao should be lauded rather than criticized for agreeing to limit the production of opium in Gujarat and its sale overseas.

The opium that made its way into the history of that time was known as Bengal opium and Malwa opium over which the East India Company had the sole monopoly; they got richer by the day with the sale of the drug to China.

Another kind that made its way into the politics of that time was Baroda opium from the carefully cultivated poppy flowers. As huge quantities were produced, it posed a threat to the Company which immediately pressurized the state to limit its production of opium and forbid its sale outside its boundaries. However, with Gujarat possessing four ports, the drug found its way to China, seriously cutting down on the Company's profits. In the year 1877, the British government got Madhavrao to agree to limit the production of the drug and forbid its export unless this was done through British agencies. The motive here was no doubt profit on the side of the British but to give the dewan the benefit of the doubt, he was probably motivated on humanitarian grounds.

The salt industry too was arbitrarily treated with a ban on production of salt in Gujarat, with the exception of Okhamandal. The people of the state had to buy salt imported from British India at a much higher price. Okhamandal salt could not be sold to other parts of the state even after paying duty, thus ensuring a limit to salt production there too. The merchants in Gujarat did not take the embargo in their stride but before they could vociferously protest against it, Madhavrao 'threw in the towel' and signed a document agreeing that the Gaekwad government did not possess the right to either produce salt by their own manufacturers or others, except Okhamandal; however, they could not buy salt from that district nor allow trade of salt from there and any breach or violation of this law would be severely punished. It must be supposed that Madhavrao, though a brilliant administrator, lacked the guile and dexterity in handling the British government and preferred to follow the policy of 'better safe than sorry'. After all, with the paramount power resting with the British, it was the only way to adopt to avoid a major confrontation with them.

16

Baroda Acquires a Queen

The auspicious date fixed for the wedding of Sayajirao III was 6 January 1881 after a lot of verbal warfare and a tussle of wills between the parties concerned, with each trying to get the better of the other and a primary clash of egos between the astrologers on both sides. However, after allowing the combatants fair play of their talent, a date was agreed upon and everyone breathed a sigh of relief. Preparations began in earnest for the 'Great Day' and everyone who was anyone was involved. The women of the palace were prodigiously active in preparations for the trousseau while the wedding celebrations, which were to be on a very grand scale, were left to the administrative departments where Madhavrao wielded the baton, having complete say in the entire arrangements.

The wedding was celebrated in a lavish style befitting a Maharaja with all the trimmings to enhance the grandeur of the occasion. The festivities began three weeks prior to the wedding and went on till mid-January. There was entertainment galore for invitees and the public saw the city illuminated to resemble a fairy tale wedding. Fireworks sparkled every night and dazzled the eyes of the citizens of Baroda. The city was decorated with triumphal arches and the streets thronged with processions of elephants, camels and horses. Music filled the air throughout the day and heralded the dawn. The palace hummed with the chanting of sacred texts as one after another various rituals were performed and offerings made to gods and goddesses for blessings to be showered on the bridal couple—all this started days prior to the wedding. On the actual day, the couple went through the motions of solemnizing the marriage while the priests recited the appropriate mantras. After the saat pheras (seven rounds), the bride was made to stand on a flat stone, used for grinding spices, and vows of fidelity were exchanged. The ceremony ended with the groom showering his blessings and good wishes on the bride. Plenty more ceremonies were conducted in the palace after which, to quote Elliot's remark, 'The earth has changed, races have altered in their distribution and destinies, empires have risen and fallen, yet our rituals remain the same.'

According to custom, the bride's name was changed from Laxmi to Chimnabai.

17

Investiture and Handing over the Reins

The wedding ceremonies were over but the festivities continued for another week and coincided with the foundation being laid for a palace to accommodate the young couple on 12 January 1881 by P.S. Melville. The palace was named Laxmi Vilas after the 'goddess of wealth' and seemed appropriate as the queen's maiden name too was Laxmi. Richard Temple arrived from Bombay along with the commander-in-chief, General Warren to grace the occasion with their presence. Speeches suitable to the occasion were made in the august presence of the royal couple and their guests. The Laxmi Vilas Palace took a decade to complete and by the time it was finished, both the architect, Major Charles Mant, an officer of the Royal Engineers, and Maharani Chimnabai had bowed out of this world.

The palace unmistakably bears the stamp of the architect and is a blend of Mughal and Hindu styles of architecture in its façade with Italian Gothic influence in the interiors. The marble floor and pillars were the handiwork of craftsmen brought from Florence. On the whole the palace, with its 720 acres of parkland with exotic trees, lakes and manicured lawns, was and still is a splendid architectural feat. It stands testimony to the Gaekwads' rich historical past.

Sayajirao III's schooling had proceeded at a galloping pace even during his wedding festivities and he had shown an amazing capacity to learn and absorb all that he had been taught. With indefatigable zeal, as shown by his ancestors, he displayed his enthusiasm for learning from his tutors so much so that his companions and other children of the Baroda courtiers found it difficult to keep pace with him. Other bright, boys were taken in to inculcate a competitive spirit in Sayajirao III but since the boys were in awe of their ruler, even though he was just a boy like them, it did not work out according to their expectations.

Early in 1881 (6 January), when Sayajirao III was a married man, it was decided to make his education more intensive and the date for handing over his responsibilities as a ruler was fixed by Lord Rippon for 28 December 1881 when he would be well over eighteen years of age.

Madhavrao, who believed in the personal character and capacity of the ruler, was keen to accelerate his education especially in the areas where he felt he had much to learn. In keeping with his intentions and suiting action to words, he drew up a long memorandum on the principles on which the young Maharaja should govern—his policy on administration should be based on the principle that a ruler was made for the people and not they for him and every action or decision should revolve around the welfare of the people of Baroda. The course of intensive study devised by Madhavrao was, for obvious reasons, meant solely for Sayajirao III.

The original curriculum that had involved a time frame of three years was cut short and reduced to nine months, a tough assignment for the royal student and even tougher for his educators. It was also decided that the extensive tour of the state's public offices and institutions and of the surrounding districts of the country should be postponed till later, after the assumption of power.

Subjects that could be dealt with later were dropped, but Gujarati, Urdu and arithmetic were retained. A lot was expected to be imbibed from lectures on the principles of general government and circumspective behaviour on the part of a ruler. The next nine months would have had any other ruler pulling his hair if he had been subjected to the gruelling task of sitting through 150 lectures the way Sayajirao III was! The lessons taught were on the principles and practice of good governance both in the palace as well as outside it and particular emphasis was made by Madhavrao on Sayajirao III's deportment with the officials of the Raj. Kazi Shahbuddin in his capacity as the revenue commissioner of the state came up with different systems of assessing land revenue and of recovering it. The chief justice explained law procedures and the function of law courts while other luminaries like J.S. Gadgil shared their knowledge on Hindu law; Assistant Dewan Kirtane spelled out the workings of the police department; the workings of the defence were explained by Pestonji Jehangir (a settlement officer as well as the military secretary) who also spoke about the structure and functions of the army of the Baroda state; and A.H. Tamhane, the chief accountant, explained the intricacies of the book-keeping procedures to the best of their abilities but none, according to Elliot, matched the brilliance and charm of the dewan. A born orator, he gained expertise from his years spent in Indian courts which gave him the power of holding the attention of his listeners. Madhavrao's lectures were published as a book meant 'for private circulation only'. Carried away with his task of educating the Maharaja through his lectures, he seems to have fancied himself in the role of Francoise Fenlon whose royal pupil were Louis XIV's grandson during the illustrious reign of the emperor and citations are from Louis XIV, Manu, Dalhousie and Edmund Burke to instil their guiding principles. Along with these, a host of advice followed on good judgement, recognizing genuine well-wishers, to rule with a gentle but firm hand and to curb incessant benevolence in charity and religious matters as well as the extravagance of the royal household The chief instruction that he imparted to his pupil was his constant reminder to be subservient to the paramount power. The pupil sat through it all like a solitary reaper and was expected to give all his attention to the lectures in order to ask intelligent questions later. Books on the subjects were given to him to provide him with the background and he was expected to read and assimilate as best he could. Sayajirao III was only a boy of eighteen and as yet not quite *au fait* with the English language, but he possessed those two rare qualities—patience and the willingness to learn—and above all the wisdom to concentrate on the more important subjects connected with the art of governance. Endowed with a logical and argumentative mind, he was able to grasp the fundamentals and, even more, thrash them out with his ministers.

If Sayajirao III was being smothered underneath an avalanche of scholarly instructions, he still had the time to enjoy domestic bliss with a wife with whom he was deeply and irrevocably in love. Perhaps the vacuum left in his emotions by a premature separation from parents had now been filled by the woman who was now his wife and there was no dearth of affection there for her. The swift transition from being a farmer's son to becoming a king and all the ramifications that came with it, not to mention being uprooted from the familiar, must have been traumatic, but with the resilience of youth, he took it all in his stride. This included Jamnabai, who fussed over his food, clothes and education; but even though she was sincere, she was still a poor substitute for parental love and affection. It must have been particularly hard for him to wave out to his father in a crowd when he must have longed to rush out and enfold him in an embrace. Before his wedding, this distance from his parents had made him withdrawn, moody, a little too fond of studies for his own good and inclined to keep to himself, which Elliot had been quick to notice. However, once he was married, he had someone with whom he could be himself and share his thoughts and feelings; there was a marked difference in his demeanour. His marriage restored a sense of having a home which had been denied to him for six long years.

The royal couple continued to live in Sarkarwada in the heart of the old city along with Jamnabai and a couple of dowagers, waited upon by hundreds of servants. On 14 July 1881, Sayajirao III's first daughter, Bajubai, was born prematurely.

The investiture of Sayajirao III with the full powers of a ruler took place in December 1881. The celebrations lasted for a week and the investiture ceremonies took place in a shamiana on the grounds of the Nazar Bagh Palace. Madhavrao once again surpassed himself with his organizing abilities and like the wedding earlier, the investiture was a spectacular affair. All princes of neighbouring states, officials and scholars from all parts of India were invited to witness the coronation.

The viceroy of India, Lord Rippon, unable to come himself, sent his representative Sir James Fergusson, the governor of Bombay, to do the honours. Presenting the Maharaja with the robes of the state, he placed him on the gaddi and after an appropriate speech befitting the occasion, declared Sayajirao Gaekwad III as the ruler of Baroda and a ruler in his own right. 'A salute of twenty-one guns was fired and the British regiment and the Baroda troops fired a *feudejoie*.'[1]

In continuation of the fable, the boy from the village of Kavlana who had been brought to the palace at the tender age of thirteen but had answered the million-dollar question with an adroitness far beyond his years became, in his eighteenth year, a full-fledged ruler to be henceforward known by his full title—His Highness Sayajirao Gaekwad III, Sena Khas Khel, Shamsher Bahadur, Farzand-i-Khas-i-Inglish-Daulatia, Maharaja of Baroda.

A most outstanding achievement in world history is that a foreigner, an Englishman at that, had crowned a native of the country he had acquired, placed him on the throne and declared him the ruler. Even Napoleon had to grab the crown at Notre Dame, place it on his own head and declare himself the 'Emperor of France'.[2]

The demeanour of the young Maharaja in perhaps the greatest moment of his life has been described by his great-grandson, Fatehsinghrao IV: 'A photograph of Sayajirao in his investiture attire shows a trim young man with cool, dark eyes and a confident expression, sporting a moustache and side burns that look oddly contemporary. He wears a somewhat severe dark velvet suit with gold cuffs and collar almost like the uniform of a cavalry regiment, but over the collar are draped rows upon rows of implausibly large diamonds. On the pagree, or the turban, there is a jewelled turban-clasp called the shirpech which the Marathas traditionally regard as a symbol of loyalty.'[3] Dressed as such, he had been placed on the gaddi and had made his own speech of thanks, written no doubt by the dewan as a reciprocal gesture to the viceroy's message of good wishes.

The British government was probably even then a little apprehensive about an eighteen-year-old wielding the despotic baton over a population of nearly two million subjects, even though the chosen ruler had been their choice and carefully trained by them. Therefore, like a codicil inserted in an agreement, the government decided to impose curbs so that the young ruler did not have the reins entirely in his hands for a probationary period of two years. Of course, Sayajirao III was not even aware of the precise significance of these restrictions and even if he had been, there was nothing he could have done at that stage. One major proviso was that death sentences were to be carried out only by hanging and 'in no other way'. This was supposed to be an improvement on the earlier more barbaric method of killing the criminal by getting his head trampled by an elephant. Of course, they let slide the fact that they had thought nothing of their more barbaric method of blowing the heads off of their victims from the barrels of their cannons. Next was the institution of an advisory council being set up to 'help' the boy in his 'self-rule'. Another condition laid down by them was that Sayajirao III was in no way to strengthen his forces and increase the number of arms, a stipulation that was not relaxed even after the probationary period of two years was over. This order for what it really was, was further emphasized by Madhavrao, 'Your Highness will do well to resist the temptation to raise the efficiency of your regular forces to British standards'. [4] This must have gone against the grain of good ethics in Sayajirao III's mind, but keeping his thoughts to himself, he must have taken the advice of the older man at its face value as not to be considered seriously.

The new Resident, Colonel Waterfield, was deputized to issue the dos and don'ts to Sayajirao III and it was done in such a manner as to drive home the fact that they, the British, were the real masters of the soil and Indian princes would do well to remember that.' It was also like a scene, enacted with meticulous attention to detail, and perhaps even its lines rehearsed in advance.'[5] By this time, the British had been a paramount power for over a century and knew how to handle Indian kings with a dexterity born out of long practice; their official rudeness was well cultivated—while it gave offence, it did not warrant retaliation.

As far as most of the native kings were concerned, they accepted the slights as part of their subordination to their masters and also the price for staying on the throne. They lost no sleep over it, or spend time brooding. The king, who met the Resident in the morning in his study, probably played polo, or tennis with him and exchanged polite pleasantries in the evening over a sundowner and life continued as before. As mentioned earlier, if Khanderao had established a strong bond of friendship between the royal Gaekwads of Baroda and the British, Malharrao had done everything in his power to undo the goodwill created by his predecessors. Sayajirao III was as yet too inexperienced in the ways of the British and his brief period of training and education did not provide him with the tools necessary for handling the paramount sovereignty in India. The British Residents, who came and left, were quite different from one another—some like Phayre were unreasonable and flouted their authority unreasonably, while there were some who were quite embarrassed at their own position and went about their business as something that had to be got over with for the day and were more relaxed in the evenings. Sayajirao III, still a little wet behind the ears, had a while to go before he realized that these better representatives of the British had two sides to them as well—one reserved for official purposes, which was intimidating and quite often uncompromising, while the other was more humane and relaxed. Sayajirao III decided that he would abide by the book of rules, if that was to govern his relationship with them. Perhaps his path might have been smoother if he had taken a leaf from his adoptive father's book and had charmed the officials with sports during the day and invited them frequently to the palace for cocktails and dinner in the evenings, but Sayajirao III preferred a more quiet, unobtrusive manner in dealing with them. The result was that in spite of the title of Farzand-i-Khas-i-Inglish-Daulatia, relations between the Gaekwads and the Residents remained formal and never really thawed.

The protocol was strictly observed and even when they met formerly at the Golf Club, greetings were 'cool and perfunctory' after which they returned to their own places and forgot the other's existence till it was time to leave.

Sayajirao III had an onerous task before him—his predecessor had left the province in a deplorable state and some earnest attempts had been made by Madhavrao to bring about radical changes in administration by way of reforms. Even though he was quite successful in certain areas like education, sanitation and construction of road, it was only a small fraction of the work that had to be done to bring the state to the desired level for habitation. However, Madhavrao's assiduousness and zest earned him the title of Raja conferred on him at the imperial assemblage of January 1877.

18

Durbar Etiquette and British Protocol

Whenever the Resident and other British officials were invited to attend the annual durbars or special durbars in the palace, proper etiquette was observed by Sayajirao III and his dewan. On special days like Vasant Panchami, Rang Panchami, Sayajirao III's birthday, the Dusshera procession and special durbars like the Barsa ceremony or the birth of children, grandchildren were held in the palace. The dewan would go to the Residency to personally invite the Resident to the durbar on behalf of the king. The same courtesy was extended to the political agent of the Rewa Kantha (a political agency managing the relations [indirect rule] of the British government's Bombay presidency with a collection of princely states) whose headquarters were then in Baroda, and to the colonel commanding the troops.

The Resident would be received by the dewan as he alighted from his carriage and escorted to the entrance of the Durbar Hall where the king would receive him. He along with the other British officials would be led to chairs placed on the left side of the gaddi. The king took his seat on the gaddi while his sons, relations, the dewan, sardars, bhagdharakdars, pagedars (those in charge of stables) and bankers sat on the floor according to their status and rank. The dewan sat between the Resident and the king. After greetings were exchanged by the Resident and the king, paan supari (betel leaves and betel nuts) would be brought and offered to the king; then, the sarkari poshak, a garland of flowers, rose water, attar and paan would be offered to him which he, in turn, would offer to his guest, the Resident, while being seated on the gaddi. The Resident would receive the same, standing in front of the king. The same items of welcome were offered to the British officials, the commissioner and the political agent.

After the durbar, the Resident and his officers took leave of the king at the entrance and were sent off by the dewan in their carriages. A guard of honour by the state's troops in all their regimental colours and with the band assembled in front of the palace to present arms to the Resident; guns were placed at strategic points in the city to fire salutes on the arrival as well as departure of the Resident.

During the reigns of Sayajirao II and Ganpatrao sixteen shots were fired in the air, while Khanderao and Malharrao were honoured with a 21-gun salute from the Indian artillery, but only a salute of thirteen shots were fired from the British artillery. Further to these elaborate formalities, there was also a dress code that had to be adhered to for the durbar—officers in full dress, police officers in uniforms (with helmets which they had to wear while saluting and take off when seated), educational officers in their academic gowns, European civil officers in their frock suits or morning coats and Indian officers in white muslin *angrakhas*, patent leather shoes, black socks and shelas (end part of the turban that flows along the neck on to the back). For afternoon parties, European officers wore lounge suits in dark colours, mostly dark blue. For evening parties, balls or banquets, it was mess dress for those officers in uniform and long evening suits for civil officers. While European wives of officers had to wear ball gowns, Indian ladies had to wear saris while attending these functions. The officers were obliged to wear their medals and other decorations on their uniform to display their rank and status at the durbar as well as at banquets.

Among Indian festivals, Dusshera was very elaborately celebrated and the Resident and some senior British officials also participated. The procession would commence from the palace and the king would be accompanied by the Resident and his coterie mounted on separate elephants, suitably decorated for the occasion. While the king rode in the centre, the Resident rode on his left and the dewan and the other officers of the durbar rode a little behind on the right side. A detachment of artillery and subsidiary forces would be drawn up outside the town, a little distance away from where the worship of the Shami tree was to take place. On the king's arrival with his party, the commissioner officer advanced and saluted the king and the troops fired the three *feudejoie;* then, they presented the arms while the artillery fired a salute of twenty-one guns in honour of the king. After the formalities were over, the Resident and the officials partook of the refreshments provided in the tent set-up. Their departure too followed the same ritual which was followed upon their arrival. The colourfully decorated streets were crowded with people who stood for hours on end to watch the procession and the air was filled with cries of '*Maharaja ki jai* (long live the Maharaja)'.

There was strict protocol to be followed whenever a newly appointed Resident arrived to take up his duties in Baroda. In the absence of a proper railway service in Gujarat, the Resident travelled by boat on the Mahi River right up to Cambay or Tankari Bundar and then proceed to Baroda by road. Needless to say, the king deputized the durbar vakil (lawyer) and the dewan to proceed in advance to receive the Resident and accompany him to Baroda. Later, when the railway line was extended, the Resident was cordially received at the Baroda station by the dewan and some seniors from the durbar along with a salute of thirteen guns by the Indian artillery, standing a few yards from the railway station at a convenient place. He was then escorted to the Residency in a carriage.

On arrival, the Resident first paid the king a visit and presented his credentials to him and also a kharita (letter) addressed by the governor of Bombay to the king wherein he introduced the Resident as a man in whom he had full confidence and that it would be his principal object to cultivate and improve relations between the state of Baroda and the British government. The kharita was read out to a full durbar. A few days later, the king reciprocated the visit in full state dress accompanied by his state durbaris. The Resident received the king as he alighted from his elephant and escorted him indoors. The king sat on the right side of the Resident while the European officers of the cantonment sat on the left. A 21-gun salute was fired on the king's arrival and departure. The right side of the seat was always reserved for the king whenever British dignitaries like the viceroy, the governor general of India and others arrived in Baroda till April 1872 when it was taken exception to by the government of Bombay. The government declared that no such custom was prevalent in any other premier state of the native rulers and hence the right-hand seat should be allotted only to the British Resident who was the representative of Her Majesty, the queen. A lot of protests over this seating arrangement had earlier been made by Malharrao to the government of India and to the secretary of state but to no avail; till 1874, however, the Resident sat on the left side of the king at durbars held in the palace and it was only after 1875 that the right-hand seat was given to the Resident and the durbaris were provided with chairs instead of the floor to sit on.

In 1876, it was ruled by the government of India that the Resident and British officials would not attend Indian festivities nor participate in festival celebrations. The exception to this rule was the king's investiture and anniversary.

If any festival clashed with the date of the king's investiture or anniversary, then the festival celebrations were postponed to another date to allow the attendance of British officers and troops.

19

Sayajirao III Establishing His Powers as a Ruler

Sayajirao III was sorely in need of sympathetic advice. Elliot, who over the years had become his guide, mentor and friend, was to be dispensed with as the imperial masters thought that his job as a tutor for the king had ended and thus, he had no need to remain in Baroda any more. Sayajirao III didn't want to be separated from his only friend, so quickly found a place for him as the head of the settlements department, which required Elliot to probe into the ownership of land and accordingly assess the revenue needed to be paid to the state. Elliot was obtained as a 'loan' for further services from the East India Company in Bombay and, to Maharaja's relief he continued to live in close proximity in Baroda. Sayajirao III had won the first round in the battle of wits against the paramount power, but this was only the beginning. There was a lot more to come.

Melville, who had been responsible for bringing Elliot to Baroda was against his close proximity to Sayajirao III as he thought that it would weaken the influence of the Residency. Fortunately, Melville's term as Resident ended and the new Resident, Major General J. Watson saw no objection to Elliot staying on and obtained the necessary permission from the Bombay government.

Elliot's influence over Sayajirao III incurred a good deal of disapprobation, not only from certain British officials but also from the denizens of Baroda who were apprehensive that the Maharaja might be influenced into Western ways and become a nonconformist as opposed to following Hindu beliefs and traditions as Elliot, in the capacity of a personal adviser to the Maharaja, wielded great power. On the other hand, British officials felt that Elliot, who owed his first allegiance to the British, seemed to be turning more towards the side of the Maharaja. Poor Elliot was in a no-win situation. A gentleman to the core, Elliot refrained from interfering in the administrative affairs of the state; he did offer solicited advice to the king, but it was more as a friend rather than an official, so much so that when he was asked by the people of Poona to urge the ruler to bring about more effective administrative reforms in the state of Baroda, he replied that it was not his position to do so and those who were in the position would definitely prevail upon the Maharaja for the required amendments in the reforms.

Elliot was too passive and tolerant of another person's point of view to render efficiency in his administration. Elliot's forte was in teaching, not in administration, but for someone who badly needed a friend and a counsellor while taking his first steps as a ruler, Elliot's support was indispensable. At the beginning of his reign, he was expected to deal with all issues—trivial as well as the major ones with more pressing matters.

Madhavrao tendered his resignation immediately after the investiture, but it is presumed that on the advice of Elliot, Sayajirao III retained his services as it would have caused a stir among the British officials for dismissing a man they had planted as a restraining hand in case Sayajirao III stepped out of line. After all, Elliot had earlier been witness to the farce played out by Malharrao in his choice of a dewan and its consequences.

Madhavrao continued as dewan but was no longer vested with the sole authority in governance. Sayajirao III made it clear from the beginning of his reign that he would scrutinize all matters concerning the administration of his state. He might have been a man of few words, but he was certainly a man of action and to testify to this fact he spent most of his time in office work. As mentioned earlier, Khanderao had minimal interest in administrative work and preferred to spend time in outdoor sports, while Malharrao's brief reign had been spent in outwitting Jamnabai and Resident Phayre, leaving him barely any time for administrative work. Now, for the first time in the history of the royal family of Gaekwads, the state had a ruler who plunged into work and was more interested in occupying himself with official work rather than the usual activities his predecessors had indulged in. He kept late hours and got up at dawn to tackle whatever had been left undone At the beginning of his rule, he was expected to deal with and decide all matters, no matter how trivial, to the extent of deciding on the purchase of candles and gunnysacks and the transfer of one acre of waste to arable land. Some years later, he noted that he had expended considerable effort in disposing of requests for sanction of door handles and mats. However, it must be said that beginning his career with trivialities gave him a thorough grounding in the practical aspects of administration, which stood him in good stead all his life. Sayajirao III, speedily convinced of the importance of reorganizing the powers of departmental heads and the functions of their subordinates, set about patiently—patience being his greatest virtue—in revamping the administration by clearly defining the duties of the officials and their subordinates. It was an uphill task, especially for one so young and one who had yet to come to grips with the immense responsibilities set before him. The old hands at the subordinate level of clerks, village officers and others were kept on even though dismissing them would have been the best thing to do, but Sayajirao III was aware that their families depended on them. However, he was anxious that they should learn the work properly and even let an official carry on till his retirement before he recruited a well-qualified person for the job. He believed that reforms could not be carried out in a hurry and could not be pushed.

Sayajirao III believed in decentralizing powers and advocated the system to his ministers and mostly to the dewan. 'Power,' he advised, 'should not be concentrated on departmental heads alone, but should be divided among the subordinates allowing them to assume responsibility with regard to those powers.'[1]

The Maharaja's energy was spent in learning his business. 'His day,' said his tutor, 'was regulated by the clock.'[2] He was up at sunrise and after some light refreshments went for a walk or rode, then he came back to his desk and worked till lunchtime; a brief rest was in the schedule after lunch and then it was back to work till a tea break. After an evening stroll, he would read until it was time for dinner and then again followed it up with reading until eleven o'clock when he would retire to bed.

As the days went by, Sayajirao III found that as a ruler, he had even less time for leisure than he had earlier as Elliot's pupil. The office routine devoured all his time, leaving him hardly any for recreation; still, whenever he had time to spare, he rode at dawn, indulged in a game of billiards and other sports, ending up with a book till bedtime.

Gradually, with experience and observation, he began to delegate authority and reduce his workload, which probably meant leaving the decision on door handles and mats to officials while he focued on the more important ones. This way his administrative staff were encouraged to take decisions on their own and work independently. In his resolve to bring his administrative methods into a more comprehensive and practicable manner, he dealt with them personally. He dealt with them personally, setting aside one day of the week for each of the principal ones. In the end, he had all the essential details on his fingertips.

Sayajirao III was now the ruler of a vast and prosperous state, but he was ruling without any idea of the conditions existing outside the state. Realizing that it was imperative that he travel across Gujarat to assess the conditions prevailing there, he organized a tour. Sayajirao III had expressed his intentions of scrutinizing all administrative matters concerning the running of the government. And hence the tour was postponed. He decided to utilize the time when he was not desk-bound to get his personal life in order. He shifted his residence from the cloistering city to the Makarpura Palace, which he refurbished according to his taste; the landscaping around it was redone too. On 4 June 1882, his second daughter Putlabai was born in the Makarpura Palace.

Sayajirao III, who was prudent by nature, was shocked at the extravagance that went into the running the palace. The palace workers outnumbered the family, which comprised Jamnabai, the king, his consort and his daughters, but to look after their wants, there were at least a hundred servants, yet if he wanted something, it took hours before someone could be found to do so. Most of the servants were actually mankaris (family retainers) drawn from the children of the hereditary dependants of the Gaekwads.[3]

Wherever the king went, whether it was for a walk in the garden or from a room in the palace to his private chambers, he had a retinue of staff following him, wasting their time in such a profitless activity when they could have been put to better use. Now that he was in a position to do so, he decided to allot specific duties to his staff and the servants were placed under a strict disciplinary routine. The mankaris were mainly from the upper class of courtiers who had no specific portfolios except to be the companions of the Maharaja. They lived in the palace and dined with the king, walked or rode with him, played tennis and other sports. Whenever Sayajirao III needed recreation, they provided conversation punched with humour to amuse him. These mankaris had not received formal education and had no knowledge of the English language which was so vital to enable them to attend to the needs of the English guests whenever they visited the palace, which was frequently. There were too many of them lobbying in the corridors of the palace, prompting Sayajirao III to select just ten of them. These ten were allotted duties; of course, their training would have taken some years but at least he had got rid of his 'swarming corridors', leaving the way clear and passable. If the palace was overstaffed, the household department presented an even more appalling problem in wastage. There was gross mismanagement in the purchase of food and beverages, such as the cook ordering ten dozen apples to prepare a dessert for eight people! Sayajirao III took over the household department which had been the sole prerogative of Jamnabai and placed it in the hands of a full-time comptroller.

20

Off with the Old and On with the New!

A clash of egos, between people where there is a generation gap or between a tutor and a pupil, brings with it a conflict of wills.

Madhavrao had ruled de facto for seven years, being answerable only to the paramount power, but with Sayajirao III on the gaddi, it must have been, and understandably so, a little trying to cater to the opinions of, and justify his actions to an inexperienced youth whose training for the supreme role was still incomplete. Moreover, Sayajirao III was proving adequate to the responsibilities thrust upon him. He asked searching questions to make sure that the decision he was required to concur with as a matter of form was something he would have made himself. In other words, he wanted to make sure that the pros and cons of a situation had been weighed and the right decision had been made. Therein laid the crux of the matter. This must have caused a dent in the dewan's ego and he must have thought, *How quickly horns grow on the foreheads of lambs*. No doubt if Madhavrao had stayed on Sayajirao III would have benefited enormously from the older man's experience, intelligence, knowledge and training, though the minds of the tutor and the student were as different as chalk and cheese (in relation to pandering to the Britishers), but still it would have speedily aided the young ruler's grooming for the exalted position he now occupied.

The debate in the minds of Sayajirao III and Madhavrao must have worked this way—'To stay or not to stay' for Madhavrao, and in Sayajirao III's case, 'To keep him on or not'. However, this dilemma was resolved one late summer in 1882 when a man named Pathaji Lalji murdered a boy for the jewellery that he was wearing. When Lalji was tried for murder he was found guilty of the charge and sentenced to death penalty, but the higher court took a lenient stand and recommended life imprisonment instead. Madhavrao nodded his assent to this recommendation, but Sayajirao III, after a thorough study of the case, judged that the way to deal with a murderer was death penalty. Disregarding the dewan's wishes, he ordered that the lower court sentence should be carried out. Here it must be clearly understood that it was not due to the fact that the king lacked the 'milk of human kindness' nor was he by any standard a harsh man, but he believed in justice and in his young mind, murder was an unforgivable offence and had to be dealt with accordingly. Besides, he was only nineteen years old and wanting to prove himself a just ruler, he passed a judgement without seeing the necessity of tempering it with mercy. However, it resolved the dilemma. Madhavrao went on a long leave of absence which Sayajirao III granted with alacrity and Kazi Shahbuddin, the revenue minister and a more amenable man, was installed in his place.

Though Madhavrao left under a cloud, it is important to remember that he left with a good record of work accomplished. Madhavrao did for Baroda what he had done for the debt-burdened state of Travancore during his tenure there, and in doing so, laid the foundation on which the modern progressive Baroda has been built.

Even Madhavrao's harshest critics have acknowledged his abilities as a great orator, an erudite scholar and a knowledgeable administrator. The only real criticism that can be offered in this context was that he got his priorities wrong in pandering to the ego and dictates of the British. But at the same time it must be remembered that Madhavrao was a thorough realist. The British were the paramount power and obedience to their policies was called for, so it was better to swim with the tide rather than against it and by doing so, save one's skin. After all it must not be forgotten that some years earlier when he had been in Holkar's court as a minister, he had concurred with the Meade Commission's decision over the deposition of Malharrao. He believed strongly on the 'irresistible' might of the paramount power and the only way to deal with such a force was to go along with them in a spirit of conciliation. 'Conciliation being an absolute and unavoidable necessity,' he would advise his pupil Sayajirao III, 'always give in'. He might as well have added, 'for that is the best way to stay out of trouble!' Too much efficiency in the administration that overshadowed British efforts in that direction was to be avoided. Stepping up the defence was to be avoided at all costs since it was a very sensitive issue for the British who had conveyed this stipulation through Madhavrao to Sayajirao III. The Maharaja was not to introduce any changes in the number and equipment of his army. 'Your Highness will do well to resist the temptation to raise the efficiency of your regular forces to

British standards,' Madhavrao warned Sayajirao III.[1] The Maharaja listened, but for all his youth and unworldliness it is doubtful if he agreed. Madhavrao never failed to remind Sayajirao III of the correct stance that Indian princes should adopt in dealing with the masters of the British Empire. A tutor who believed in absolute subservience to the paramount power and a student who did not believe in subservience, not even to the Peshwas who were his own countrymen, not aliens like the British—that was the dividing line between him and the youth from Kavlana who was now the ruler.

21

Tour of the Province

With a more amiable minister at the helm of affairs in Baroda, Sayajirao III ventured to tour across Gujarat.

The Baroda state as inherited by him was not a unified area of land but comprised bits and pieces and islands, lost in the vast ocean of British India as described in *Sayajirao of Baroda: The Prince and the Man*, 'wedged deep inside other princely domains, others as large as fair-sized English counties. The pieces of land were peppered all over the map of Gujarat and Kathiawad in a seemingly meaningless fashion, and stretched for more than 300 miles from west to east and for 250 miles from north to south.'[1]

However, Barodawas divided into five groups called subas or districts—three in Gujarat and two in Kathiawad. Those belonging to the Gujarat province were Kadi, Baroda and Naosari and those of Kathiawad were Amreli and Okhamandal. To the amazement of his dewan and other officers, Sayajirao III chose to tour the district in a bullock cart as he was a simple man at heart, disliked ostentation which would be displayed in a grand horse-driven carriage, and second, the slow-moving bullock cart would him the opportunity to view the countryside and enjoy the fresh air as against a closed carriage, and it also afforded the freedom to stop and mingle with the villagers, converse with them and understand their needs. The proximity to the people would provide an insight into their lifestyle.

Sayajirao III with his entire paraphernalia of what he might need for the trip was to be burdened with a very large tent and thousands of pairs of shoes, a decision made by the palace household and staff, along with a 'bustling township with a population numbering 2,637, to say nothing of 910 animals.'[2]

The bullock cart left Baroda city in advance and Sayajirao III followed by train a week later, stopping first in Ahmedabad where he spent a whole week. The Maharaja had a busy and interesting time as there was much to absorb his attention. He had a look at the territory that had once belonged to the Gaekwads and was now British India territory. Not letting that aspect disturb his mind in any way, he toured around the city spotted with famous mosques, tombs and gardens as well as the schools and public institutions to observe and learn how the British administered India. It was also at the Ahmedabad railway station that he got his first taste of European food, which is not surprising, considering it was a British territory and the standard of hygiene would have been in accordance with British standards. But whoever heard of a Maharaja having lunches at a railway station? Apparently this Maharaja did. As it has been said, 'Simplicity is a sign of true greatness.' Jamnabai had chosen well!

The roads in Gujarat were conducive for experimenting with different modes of transport—part of Sayajirao III's journey was done in a bullock cart, on horseback, on an elephant and sometimes in a carriage. At every halt, a durbar was held in the village for the villagers who could meet him and express their wants in person. Needless to say, he was buried under an avalanche of fruits, flowers, savouries and sweets from the adoring village folk. All edible gifts that they brought were farm produced or homemade. He was overwhelmed by the genuine affection displayed by the humble villagers and a bond was quickly established between him and them. Perhaps for the first time in history, there was a direct contact between the ruler and his subjects, unhampered by the dewan, or by ministers or their subordinates, carrying messages back and forth, which were very often misrepresented or misconstrued. The Maharaja got to listen straight from the villagers' mouths what their problems were, which were chiefly scarcity of water and lack of education.

Sayajirao III's youth combined with robust health lent enjoyment to the trip and the time spent outdoors in the fresh country air elated Sayajirao III. Being young, he revelled in the fanfare and adulation he received from his people without letting it go to his head. Perhaps mingling with villagers reminded him of his Kavlana days and dispelled some of the pangs of homesickness that he was often subject to. Sayajirao III was a loyal friend to his childhood playmates of Kavlana, who had enriched his childhood with fun and laughter. This can be amply testified by this story: After Sayajirao III became the ruler of Baroda, one of his playmates, Chunder from Kavlana visited him in the palace where he was holding a durbar. Even though

Chunder had received rigorous training on the etiquette to be followed in the august presence of the Maharaja, as soon as he walked in and saw his old friend seated high on the gaddi, he exclaimed, '*Arre Gopal, tum vahan kya kar rahe ho?*'(Gopal, what on earth are you doing there?). [3] The king's joy knew no bounds on seeing his childhood friend and being addressed as in the old days. He laughed and drew Chunder close; then he got him seated beside him on the gaddi and chatted away nineteen to the dozen, hungry for news of his home town. He was distressed to learn of the drought in the village and that the pond they used to bathe in as children had run dry. The villagers were in dire straits and had to sell their cows and buffaloes for survival. He resolved to take steps towards improving the water situation in all the villages in the districts.

Another instance of the king's simplicity was when on one of his tours around Gujarat, he stopped in a farmer's house in a village where a lavish meal was prepared for him. When Sayajirao III looked at the spread which the farmer and his wife had gone to great lengths to prepare, he turned to his host and asked for a bajra roti and a glass of chaas (buttermilk) saying, 'I have been dreaming of it ever since I started out on this tour.' The poor host had to send one of his servants to buy flour as there was none in the house and only after the flour was bought and the bajra rotis made did the king sit down to the meal, enjoying it thoroughly. After complimenting his host on the meal, he left. Despite his vast wealth, he continued to remain the simple farmer's boy at heart.

Sayajirao III's tour lasted for two months during which he visited every town and every village of his kingdom, and got acquainted with all the available details concerning it.

This paternalistic, direct approach towards his subjects was not unusual on the part of a benevolent ruler. Much earlier, Emperor Akbar had walked around incognito on the streets at night to see for himself the plight of his subjects and assess the conditions in which they lived. He also mingled with the people to find out their grievances as this was most effective in getting first-hand information. Though Sayajirao III was quick to realize the responsibilities that came with the adulation. He must have, several times a day, agreed with the hackneyed axiom, 'Uneasy lies the head that wears the crown. His notebooks were crammed with notes that he had jotted down as a result of his observations and conversations with people.

Sayajirao III extended his district tours to Naosari in 1883-84; to Baroda district in 1884-85; and to Amreli, the Kathiawad section of his state in 1886-87, which gave him first-hand knowledge of his realm. He visited every taluka of every prant (district), examined the local records and inspected offices, schools and other buildings and also reviewed the police.

In spite of his innumerable trips to Europe later, he never stopped his district tours.

Soon after his tour of Kadi, Sayajirao III was invited by Viceroy Lord Rippon to visit Calcutta in January 1883. Such invitations were more in the nature of summons; any delay or refusal on the part of an Indian ruler was interpreted as a deliberate act of disrespect. Sayajirao III, who was eager to get the viceroy's approval for appointing Shahbuddin as his dewan since Madhavrao's leave was due to end in March, accepted the viceroy's invitation and left for Calcutta. The matter could have been brought up in a letter, but as the Gaekwads' prerogative of appointing whomsoever they liked as their dewan would have been in jeopardy, he thought it more prudent to bring the matter up in conversation. It must also be remembered that the British regarded Madhavrao as a very highly rated British protégé. Sayajirao III did not want to give the impression that he had disregarded that fact by offering the job to someone else. Apparently, Sayajirao III had kept up his study of the English language and was now capable of handling a conversation with the viceroy without assistance.

Sayajirao III, who journeyed to Calcutta by train, was escorted by a coterie that numbered anywhere between 700 and 800 people. The size of his entourage, a relic of a bygone era, was mainly regarded as a status symbol. However, years later, after he became a much-travelled man, he cut down drastically on his camp followers on his journeys.

On meeting the viceroy, Sayajirao III 'casually' brought up the subject of appointing Shahbuddin as his dewan. The viceroy 'no doubt, equally casually, gave his assent'. With the object of his visit achieved, Sayajirao III who was visiting the city for the first time made haste to see something of the city built by the British. Calcutta, a city testifying to the British paramount power in India. It was fascinating to the young man whose eyes took in everything from gleaming palaces and monuments to the tall white statues of the builders of the empire vying for attention across the vastness of the maidan—it must have been a cruel reminder of the blunders and shortcomings of his ancestors. 'However, the circular road now marked as the Maratha Ditch, a canal dug by the British to defend themselves against the attack of the Maratha armies led by the Gaekwads, would have been a moment of pride to the awestruck prince standing there.'[4]

On his way back to Baroda, Sayajirao III paid visits to Benares, Allahabad and Agra where he saw the Taj Mahal and other Mughal monuments. He spent four days with the Maharaja of Gwalior Maharaja Jayajirao Scindia with whom he had formed a steady and close friendship. Interestingly, Jayajirao had earlier served on the commission when Malharrao had been tried for murder and by influencing the other two Indian members of the commission had obtained the verdict of 'not guilty'. Jayajirao was reputed to be shrewd enough to match wits with the British and Sayajirao III set great value on his advice on governing the affairs of kingdom and the firmly established bonds of friendship remained strong. In fact, Sayajirao III, years later, wanted to strengthen it further by a marriage between his daughter Indira Raje and the son of his old friend, the then Maharaja of Scindia in 1912 but the princess chose otherwise and became the maharani of Cooch Behar instead.

By the time Sayajirao III returned to Baroda in March, the complex problem of replacing Madhavrao had resolved itself in an amicable manner, achieving something of the 'old world flourish'. Madhavrao submitted his resignation while still on leave, probably realizing what had taken place with Sayajirao III's visit to Calcutta. Thus, relying on his intuition that he was now dispensable, he did the obvious thing with good grace. Sayajirao III responded equally gracefully by paying him a sum of Rs 3,00,000 as gratuity to keep him in comfort for the rest of his days. Cordial relations between them continued as both were endowed with compassion and a sense of fair play. They corresponded frequently and the ex-dewan was even invited over as a house guest by the Maharaja. Madhavrao too, not one to let bitterness dominate sensible thinking, learnt to appreciate the other's good qualities and even extolled his virtues in prose and Marathi poetry to such a level as to cause embarrassment to the one extolled.

These early years of Sayajirao III's rule charted the course for his administration in the years to come. He loved his people and his world did not extend beyond the borders of his state. Anxious for good governance, he spent hours tirelessly to deal with the day-to-day problems of administration. It was much later that he learnt to delegate responsibility and authority to his subordinates but still, work was the driving force and the pivot of his existence. His turning himself into a workaholic was perhaps due to the fact that his mentors, Melville and Madhavrao, had repeatedly said that 'native' princes were born lazy and cared little for work. Perhaps wanting to disprove them, he immersed himself in not only the major bulk of the administrative work, but also in the nitty-gritty issues that he was plagued with. Years later, he is said to have expressed his regret over this obsession, with the words, 'There has never been room in my life for relaxation, that is a mistake I would rectify if I could live my life over again!'[5]

However, his work-filled hours did not come in the way of his daily exercise. He enjoyed sports and participated with gusto. He exercised in the gym, played games and rode twenty miles every day, riding being his favourite sport. He also went pig-sticking once a week in the hunting preserve of Dabka when he was not too tied down with administrative work.

In 1883, Sayajirao III was only twenty years old with a robust family life. He had a devoted wife and two lovely daughters; Chimnabai was on her way to deliver the third. His cup of joy overflowed when tidings were brought to him of the birth of a son. Jamnabai was so ecstatic that she impulsively took off her necklace and gave it to the harbinger of the good news. Her adopted son, with no such tendencies for extravagant impulses, rejoiced quietly. Sugar and sweets were distributed in the palace and to the people on the streets by courtiers riding on elephants. Saris were distributed to women. The festivities to celebrate the event went on for a month—after all, the newborn was the first direct heir to the throne of the Gaekwad in four generations. He was named Fatehsinghrao III.

Not one to sit back and allow a dent in his governance or in the work that he had set for himself, Sayajirao III began to implement the schemes he had in mind. His tours of the districts had given him a deep insight into the lives of the people; he realized that provisions should be made for a better supply of water to the people of Baroda. He set about to work on it. Earlier, his adoptive father, Khanderao's efforts in this direction had proved futile (the cost of the scheme of course being prohibitive), but Sayajirao III wasted no time worrying about the cost. He called in an engineer, Jagannath Sadashiv, and adopted his scheme to dam the Surya River, a tributary of the Vishwamitri and a neighbouring watercourse, to form a lake from which water could be led through settling tanks, filter beds and a service reservoir to Baroda city. The first cut was made on the ground on 8 January 1885. The work was completed five years later when the Sayaji Sarovar (also known as Ajwa Lake) began to supply the residents of the city of Baroda with clean water. The lake when full could supply 10,50,00,000 gallons of water. This supply compensated for the time when there was scanty or no rainfall. This boon to Baroda was priceless.

Never one to take credit for himself, at the inauguration of the lake Sayajirao III said in his speech:

> I am well contented with your suggestion that the artificial lake should be named 'Sayaji Sarovar' and so let it be. But, in my mind, I shall associate with this work the names of Playford Reynolds and Jagannath Sadashivji who have been responsible for the success of this venture. It is the co-operation of my people which I require to gain for them the advantages of physical health. Some simple book learning therefore, I wish the masses to acquire that I may take them into my confidence and partnership. I am as you know, all for publishing the laws, the regulations, the acts, the appointments of government, but will the masses learn to avail themselves of the information? I entertain the hope that they will do so however chimerical it may appear...physical improvement, mental development, the independence of self-help cannot, I am aware, be expected so long as the state lays upon its subjects a crushing taxation. It has therefore, been my task to reduce the aggregate government demand while equalizing it as far as possible, spreading its burden over many shoulders and at the same time simplifying the demand so that both the government and the taxpayer may know what each man pays and why! I repeat that it is my desire to take my people into confidence by publishing the Acts of Government so that all those who wish to, may read and criticize.[6]

Greatly encouraged by the success of this scheme, in 1900, 1901 and again in 1906, he went on to develop irrigation schemes for all districts in need of water.

Sayajirao III, as mentioned earlier, paid a visit to Naosari in 1883 as his principal object was to familiarize himself with his state by touring the districts. As he had nearly five times as much territory to cover as compared to his earlier trip in 1883, and his districts were widely separated from one another, he decided to start straight away on 28 March, the beginning of the summer season. It was a time when most of the affluent people and the British would have opted to stay in their residences or travelled to cooler hills, yet Sayajirao embarked on his journey.

The Kaliparaj are the aborigines of Naosari district. These primitive people ran away in fear whenever Sayajirao III approached them for a chat and had to be patiently cajoled to shed their inhibitions and talk to him. Their lack of education made a lasting impression on his mind and brought home the two basic shortcomings—lack of education on their part and travel on his.

In spite of the heat, Sayajirao III enjoyed his tour. He ordered the building of a large house for himself at a seaside village called Umtah about twenty miles from the Naosari railway station, where he hoped to get away for the summer. He had the house suitably furnished.

He followed this up in several other places in the districts to avoid having to put up tents for lodging.

He returned to Baroda in the blazing heat of the summer in May to tackle the arduous tasks in administration. Conscious of the gap in his education, which had been left incomplete by hastening his investiture, it now acted as an incentive to keep up his studies. 'The ruler must have more knowledge than the ruled' were his oft-spoken words. Mere education was not enough to broaden one's horizon, he soon realized that it was important to travel abroad to learn from the advanced methods in industry and science in the West. This was something that could not be remedied immediately as he was still a newly installed Maharaja feeling his way around; besides there was a taboo on crossing the seas, considered 'black waters' which if crossed meant a person would lose his caste, the religious penance for which was drinking cow's urine, but even that did not completely absolve you of the 'sin'. He did the next best thing and sent his younger brother Sampatrao to England as a proxy for studies. He sent a couple of boys of the same age and a couple of elders from the family to dispel any pangs of homesickness that Sampatrao may feel. After that he resumed his tour of the districts for a couple of months till the middle of February of the following year when he was to have his first brush with personal tragedy that was to be the start of many more to follow and undermine his health for the rest of his life.

22

Another Tragedy and a Wedding

The month of harvest, that is, January, is the best time of the year in Indian villages. The mood is festive, the skies clear, the nights starry, the earth a shimmering gold, the landscape a motley of colour under benevolent skies, the heady scent from mango blossoms intoxicates the senses and there is music and dance to celebrate the rich produce that is brought in.

Tragedy struck Baroda just when the harvest festivities got over. The pole of the palanquin carrying Sayajirao III's second daughter, Putlabai, snapped and the toddler fell to the ground, suffered serious injuries and died a few days later. This was followed soon by another resounding blow when Chimnabai died of tuberculosis on 7 May 1884. Sayajirao III grieved in silence which worsened his insomnia that had become chronic with time and remained with him for the rest of his life. The loss of his wife affected him deeply and he retreated further into his world. The depth of his feelings could be well understood when he was laying the foundation stone of the 'Chimnabai' market, a vast shopping complex for the public. On 28 May, he said, 'I wish to commemorate the virtues of her late Highness, and the admiration I entertained for her—the mild, charitable, amiable woman, the devoted mother and the loving wife.'[1] These words were carved on a marble slab and the stone work of the entrance hall above a life-size statue of the Chimnabai. The building was completed five years later and proved to be too large to house Baroda's market; therefore, the building was converted into Nyaya Mandir (temple of justice or law court), sans the stone slab with those emotional words. Only the marble statue stands in the central hall today, a hazy reminder of the queen who had been such an integral part of the great ruler's life.

Four months later, in response to a long-standing invitation, he left for Poona where the public gave him a warm and enthusiastic reception. In Poona, the Gaekwads' homeland as it were, he familiarized himself with the people, particularly the intelligentsia, who had earlier predicted a collision between Madhavrao and the British would come to naught, being the cautious man that he was.

Sayajirao III's insomnia continued to plague him and it was thought by his family and advisers in the court that a second marriage would be the answer to this problem that was deleterious to his health. Under pressure, Sayajirao III relented, but with the stipulation that he would first meet the selected girls and his choice would be the deciding factor. The search by the courtiers narrowed down to two girls from highly respected families—one was from Tanjore and the other was from Dewas. Both girls were uneducated.

After a quick peek from behind a reed curtain, Sayajirao III chose the girl from Dewas who was fourteen years old, probably with the idea that the younger the girl would be, the easier to mould and educating her would be. The prospective bride whose name was Gajrabai was the daughter of Bajirao Amritrao Ghatge Sarjerao, with the sobriquet of Mamasaheb and a member of a well-known Maratha family of the Dewas state. According to the Marathi *Life* magazine, Bajirao's sister was married to Bapusaheb Maharaj, who belonged to the Dewas junior branch of the Ghatges, which is why Bajirao stayed in Dewas, leaving his ancestral property in the Deccan. Probably it was this background that had prompted Sayajirao III to choose Gajrabai over her rival. The wedding took place on 28 December 1885. The bride's name was changed to Chimnabai, a clear manifestation of Sayajirao III's love for the late queen who in a most unobtrusive way had contributed so much to his happiness. There was a grand wedding where British dignitaries and the people of Baroda were invitees to an elaborate wedding procession in the afternoon, illumination of the city at night and fireworks too. There were school children's fetes at the Warasha parade ground, balls and banquets for the honoured guests, sports in the arena, military sports at Warasha, a special dinner for the British troops and a grand state banquet at the Nazar Baug Palace. After all the fuss was over, Sayajirao III took his bride with him to the Makarpura Palace to live 'happily ever after'.

Young as he was, it would have been natural for him to enjoy the revelry, the grand display of fireworks and all the elaborate arrangements made in his guests' honour, but Sayajirao III had by then dug in his heels into the responsibilities that came with his position and was conscious of the expense that the ostentatious wedding would have brought with it. Jaysing

Angre, the chief secretary, in his enthusiasm had organized the wedding with great zest, going overboard with the arrangements. After the wedding, he brought the expense sheet to the king for his scrutiny. Sayajirao III noticed that a sum of Rs 25,000 had been incurred for travel expenses of those girls who had been rejected; the cost of their stay in Baroda with their relatives and servants had also been added. Sardar Angre had treated them as royal guests by showering lavish hospitality and farewell gifts when they left Baroda. The Maharaja felt that this was something uncalled for and said, 'You have incurred these unnecessary expenditures without my approval, therefore, I will not bear these expenses!' Angre answered, 'For the sake of the state's good name and prestige, I did what was right. I know you will not understand these formalities and besides I am the organizer and treasurer of the Khangi Kharbari and I know what I am doing and on the contrary, I should be thanked for it!' His Highness said, 'Because of the extravagance of the Khangi Kharbari, this expense is not going to be borne by me!' Angre asked, 'Then who will pay for it?'[2]

According to historian G.S. Sardesai, the argument went on for quite some time and the angry, protesting tones of the chief secretary reverberated in the corridors of the palace with little effect as Sayajirao III was adamant and stood his ground. Always conscious of unnecessary wastage of money, the king sought to keep expenses to the barest minimum. It is not clear how the matter was resolved; perhaps the dewan and Angre together resolved it some other way between themselves.

23

Playing Professor Higgins to Chimnabai II

Sayajirao III, anxious that his new wife should understand and share in the progress of reforms, took the first step in this direction by drawing up a plan for her studies and engaged two tutors to teach her English, Marathi and the vernacular as she probably needed to be literate to converse with the locals. He then set himself to instil in Maharani Chimnabai II his views on the purdah system. Sayajirao III's first wife had never appeared in public. His own views on the system as expressed in his words were, 'The custom of seclusion is bad...but no one in India, not even myself...can at the present time, lift up the veil...(it is the men), of whom the greater part are uneducated, who do not favour female freedom or female education.'[1]

The disapproval from relatives and the more orthodox sect of his courtiers had to be faced, but Sayajirao III did not waver as he knew this was an important aspect of her education. However, it required several trips abroad and exposure to Western culture to complete the process. It was not until after the tenth foreign trip, at a prize distribution ceremony in Nyaya Mandir in 1914 that the royal couple, with the maharani occupying the same sofa as the Maharaja, gave the sign that the era of the purdah system was over. Despite best efforts, Sayajirao III was unable to remove the demand that he should maintain his royal rank in his intimate family circle. With great misgiving, he is said to have expressed his regret saying, 'I never had any family life, no casual physical contact, no familiarity, but all salaams! This was so when I was a boy. When I married and had children of my own, I did not know how to be anything else other than a Maharaja. I have never ceased to look after them but, there has been no intimacy. My children have said to me, "You are always the Maharaja".'[2] He further added that he would have given a lot to have been able to cut his life into two, to retire, when he pleased, from palace to 'home'. He faulted his initial training to be the cause for it.

This confession coming from a man of his stature is not surprising but quite comprehensible. It was the same with many great men of the soil who could stoically stick to their guns and break barriers undeterred by opposition, but when it came to action in the personal element, their will got paralysed!

Soon, Lord Reay, the governor of Bombay, made a three-day visit to Baroda and finally left for Delhi. Later in the year, the first viceroy to favour Baroda with a visit was Viceroy Dufferin, who, but for his son's illness, would have been accompanied by his wife. The usual respect and honour due to a viceroy was given to him—he was duly entertained with fireworks at night while the day was declared a public holiday. The most important aspect of the meeting between Sayajirao III and the viceroy was that the latter advanced to the edge of the carpet to meet him when the Maharaja paid his call! It was an honour accorded only to a few of the truly great princes of India.

The most important ceremony was kept for 9 November. The opening of the just completed hospital designed by the late Major C. Mant, and erected at a cost of Rs 3,50,000. The hospital stood on the right-hand side of the road leading to the western gate of Baroda city. It was named 'Countess of Dufferin Hospital'. The Maharaja in his formal opening address said, 'It would bear the honoured name of Her Excellency, in order that this auspicious visit may forever be recorded, and that Lady Dufferin's exertions in the cause of the women of India may be gratefully remembered in Baroda.'[3] The viceroy in his turn paid a tribute to the great progress which Baroda, 'Thanks to the intelligent energy of its ruler' had made in everything to ameliorate the social conditions of the inhabitants. The hospital was thus officially opened after which the Maharaja along with his guest drove to see the Baroda jewels, and after that to a review the state army. The viceroy was very impressed with the way the Gaekwad army had been reorganized. In place of a large inefficient force, it had been reduced to a small, compact number of men with strict discipline being the order of the day.

In the evening, a banquet was held in the viceroy's honour. The Maharaja while proposing a toast to the viceroy's health expressed his joy at the viceroy's first visit to Baroda. He then alluded to the forthcoming jubilee celebrations of Queen Victoria whom he called 'one of the most fortunately glorious and beneficent rulers the world has ever seen'. He then asked Viceroy Dufferin to present his respects to the Prince of Wales whom he had met as a child. Viceroy Dufferin in response praised the administration which had brought prosperity, happiness and contentment to the people of Baroda. 'The marks of a conscientious and intelligent administration,' he said. 'This was the hallmark of a good administrator and confirmed his opinion that Gaekwad was one of the most promising high-minded and wise rulers with whom India had ever been blessed with, and that in him the Queen-Empress possessed a noble *Arkan-i-daulat* (pillar of the state)'. [4] The banquet closed with another display of fireworks and the following day Viceroy Dufferin left Baroda for Bombay with the relationship of utmost cordiality firmly established between Baroda and the paramount power. This happy state of affairs was no doubt due to the bestowal of the GCSI (Grand Commander of the Order of the Star of India) upon Sayajirao III.

The honour was not gazetted till 15 February 1887, but in a letter to Viceroy Dufferin on 16 January. Sayajirao III 'spoke' (used metaphorically) of Queen Victoria's extreme kindness in honouring him with the insignia of the Order.

As Chimnabai II found the rigorous coaching to be arduous, her tutors were dispensed with. The tutors were taken away, but not the teaching which went on for many years till she had become a well-educated young woman capable of holding her own in conversations with any of the British dignitaries who visited the state. Possessed with arresting good looks and the poise and confidence that comes with knowledge, she could be quite peremptory and imperious in her manner and was quite ready to occupy an equal place along the side of her husband at home and abroad. She was a courageous lady with a broad vision and did the Maharaja proud in her comprehension of his immense responsibilities as a ruler.

24

Early Reforms

The early years of his reign saw Sayajirao III's reforms well under way and quite a few of them were accomplished as well such as the provision of drinking water for the city by the installation of the Ajwa Lake, the completion of the Laxmi Vilas Palace, the construction of the Baroda college, a public park, government offices, schools, dispensaries and other ventures. In the districts too, progress had been made with regard to public works with special focus on the development of a railway line in Kadi which was extended to many other branches later on. In 1885, he had given orders that steps should be taken with regard to the land settlement of his state. Elliot was commissioned to deal with the annoying question of Barkhali lands, a legacy handed down from the ancestors of the Baroda sovereigns. The complexities of these Barkhali lands which even Madhavrao's fertile brain had been unable to resolve kept cropping up every now and then like a blot on the landscape refusing to be erased. The problem had been created by the past rulers of the state by presenting, rather recklessly, tracts of land for various purposes to favourites and courtiers or as a reward for some imaginary service rendered or for pious reasons like constructing temples, mosques and other religious institutions. This was also done by officials who had no right to do so and without even checking to whom these pieces of land actually belonged. Malharrao had, in gratitude for recovery from an illness, granted land to priests and soothsayers. As a result, these lands were exempt from taxation. The Barkhali lands took up nearly one-tenth of the entire area of the state. Sayajirao II and Anandrao had attempted to stop further alienation of these lands; Khanderao had gone further by demanding quit-rent from genuinely alienated land, while refusing to recognize recent sales or mortgages of such lands. Sayajirao III took eight years to bring these lands into a uniform system of tenure, thereby restoring the most challenging and complicated problem of the time pertaining to land settlements. Elliot's Herculean efforts ultimately bore fruit in 1889, when legislation was introduced on the subject.

25

Sayajirao III's First European Tour

The year 1887 was the most significant period of Sayajirao III's reign. It was the start of a series of tours and travels abroad while making significant changes in the administration of his state and matching wits with British peers. His health at the beginning of the year left much to be desired and in his letter to Viceroy Dufferin dated 16 January, he complains of 'feeling seedy and unwell' and of contemplating a trip to Ceylon (modern-day Sri Lanka). 'I hate the idea of an absent Maharaja,' he states in the letter.' I love my people and I would not have chosen to be away had it not been imperatively necessary…I will make the best possible arrangements under the circumstances for the safe going of my state.'[1]

Sixteen days later, his uneasiness is conveyed in a letter to his friend Elliot, 'The truth is that people do not like to see me run about so much… They do not know the reasons that compelled me to go. Still, taking all in all, I cannot say they are wrong.'[2]

His three-week stay in Ceylon did not do much either to cure his insomnia or make him feel physically better. In his letter, dated 11 April, to his brother Sampatrao in England, he mentions that he 'suffers from loss of weight and sleepless nights'[3] and that probably six months of rest would be the cure. From Colombo, he went to Mahabaleshwar, hoping to feel better in the cool hills but, even there he was no worse nor better.

When Sayajirao III consulted Sir William Moore, the head of the Bombay Medical Service, about his insomnia and nerve trouble, the doctor recommended a trip to Europe; proverbially, it was 'the doctor ordered just what the patient hoped for'. It answered his longing to see the world! The significance of his determination is evident from the subsequent history of his administration of Baroda. Thus in May 1887, he handed over the reins of governance to his dewan, Laxman Jagannath, who had replaced Shahbuddin the previous year, and set sail for the distant shores of Europe. He was accompanied by his wife and a large retinue of fifty-five people to cater to all his needs. This, of course, was reduced to a handful in the years to come. He could not immediately dispense with the ceremonies as his policy was to be slow but sure; old customs and traditions could not be 'shattered with one blow'. The sentiments of his people in the palace and the state were at total variance with his eagerness to see the world. He was seen off by them with tears in their eyes and was implored by his adoptive mother and relatives to only take care of his health and forget about everything else. However, their real dread lay in their Maharaja converting to Christianity. This fear arose from the fact that Rajaram, a Maratha prince from Kolhapur, had broken the taboo of crossing the 'black waters' by visiting England seventeen years ago and had returned converted to the Christian faith. Even the public strongly suspected that it was some trick on the part of the crafty British to entice him abroad. As far as Sayajirao III was concerned, none of the disapprobation from his family and his people could dim his enthusiasm for seeing the world that he had heard and read so much about.

Sayajirao III imparted careful instructions to his dewan to forward only those matters that needed his decisions and were urgent and not to run to the Resident unless it was a matter of urgency. The Maharaja was accompanied by Elliot, his wife and an Englishwoman named Mrs Taylor who was a companion to the maharani. His entourage included a barber, a tailor, two cooks (as the ship food could be contaminated) and a family priest (to perform the last rites in the event of a tragic occurrence). Elliot, as a matter of course, dashed off to Bombay to book a passage for fifty-five people during the height of the season when every Englishman living in India was dying to return home.

Needless to say that impeccable propriety with regard to the custom had to be observed. Therefore, separate cabins were arranged for the maharani and her coterie to be able to maintain purdah. Storage for all the groceries needed to feed the party was arranged. ayurvedic medicines were carried, as the English ones might contain alcohol. Two cows also accompanied the illustrious travellers on the voyage to ensure a fresh supply of milk. The two English companions went on a shopping expedition to Bombay for socks, shoes, petticoats and other sundry items needed to combat the cold weather abroad. These items must have thrown the maharani and her coterie into a dither. As part of purdah, the use of these items was not explained openly, but perhaps to each in private. The bills too were taken care of in a most confidential manner. As the time for the voyage drew nearer, a few people from the group of fifty-five developed 'mysterious ailments' and dropped out and had to be replaced by the more adventurous ones. On 31 May, the royal couple, along with their band of fifty-five and two cows, sailed in the P&O liner from Bombay with the Maharaja soon after falling sick with influenza and the ladies all down with bouts of seasickness. However, they reached the shores of Aden intact but for the two cows which had died en route.

Sayajirao III's love affair with the Western world had begun and was neither dimmed nor satiated with time. In fact, if anything at all, it grew more passionate with repeated trips over the years. He was happiest when visiting Europe and looking at the sights.

In Europe, they were objects of amusement, especially for the hotel staff who charged them exorbitant prices, something like 30,000 francs extra in Paris, and to passers-by who probably mistook them for a travelling circus. All these were slight pinpricks to the man who had turned into a schoolboy at a fair. Sayajirao III visited every place, institution, industry, museum, art gallery, even the most obscure ones in wayside hamlets and lazy old towns. He studied the churches, tombs, historical buildings and monuments that evoked interest in engineering and technology and even had his companions take notes of his observations. His focal point of interest was schools, libraries, hospitals and every other conceivable element that went to make a well-organized and efficient city. Schools for the blind and even culinary schools were not left out from his itinerary. His obsession with education and anything that meant an enhancement in knowledge was looked at and studied with avid interest. By the time he returned to Baroda, he had suitcases filled with notebooks crammed with notes of his observations. It was a manifestation of what was to follow in the administration after his return.

This is not to say that Baroda was still in its primitive stage of development when he left for his tour—the state had progressed by leaps and bounds since the reins of governance had been given to him. After Sayajirao III had improved the water situation in Baroda by constructing the Ajwa Lake, other improvements had followed one after the other. A committee had been appointed to codify laws in the state and the work had been completed. A high court had been set up and several lower courts had been established in the important urban sectors. A police force had been organized and a prison house was built. A separate criminal investigation department was established to look into crimes with a discerning eye. The army too was revamped, reorganized and trained under British instructors. Those who had been retrenched as unfit for the army were absorbed in the police force and the rest were granted gratuities or pensions. Cultivable land lying fallow was given to them for cultivation, which was further made easy with loans on easy terms. Wells and canals were dug for irrigation purposes. Public sanitation now came under a separate department to ensure better hygiene. Medical facilities were provided by opening dispensaries and hospitals with proper qualified staff to cater to the sick. All lands with dubious holdings were now absorbed into a standardized system of tenure patterned on the British system followed in the advanced British provinces. An annual budget was initiated for all the departments. With regard to education, Sayajirao III left no stone unturned. Between the years 1891 and 1893, 632 new schools were established in the state, that is, twenty schools in each taluka, which greatly contributed towards establishing primary education in the state. It had been Sayajirao III's idea that a schoolmaster should be added to the body of village servants and that one should be provided in every village that had no regular schools, but could produce sixteen students of either sex for attendance. Between the years 1883 and 1884, a cotton weaving and spinning mill was set up with a capital expenditure of Rs 6,35,000. This investment from the king was with a view to encourage local manufacture of cloth and bring about an awareness of the importance of the mill industry. Once Sayajirao III took this first step towards privatization, quite a few cotton and spinning mills mushroomed in the state.

The main railway line between Baroda and three districts of Gujarat that was laid earlier was further connected to other districts. Roads connecting major towns were widened and rest houses were built along the way. In short, by 1887, when Sayajirao III left for his first trip to Europe, Baroda was developing into a handsome city with its tall, imposing buildings, parks and broad roads. With these achievements, none among the British hierarchy could fault his administration or doubt his sincerity as a ruler.

While travelling across Europe, he soaked in the sights that the cities offered. He keenly observed the infrastructure built by the Europeans, particularly the British, which enabled their administration to run smoothly. He was determined to incorporate these into the buildings of his state.

His first visit was to Venice. He spent three days in the city of canals and cathedrals and from there he, along with his family and companions, proceeded to Aix-les-Bains. He remained in the French town till the end of September and then proceeded to carry out his long-cherished wish of seeing England. In England, he was able to gratify his desire to visit Oxford where Sampatrao and his cousin Ganpatrao were residing. He spent a part of October and November in the university town and promised himself that one day he would come here for a year to complete his education that had been left incomplete by his investiture. The end of November saw him in London where he resided in apartments booked for him on Victoria Street. Here, he was visited by the secretary of state for India, Viscount Cross, to arrange the details of a call at Windsor Castle for the purpose of being invested with the insignia of the GCSI. On 2 December, with due regard and respect to 'native' customs, no males, except the officials on duty, were allowed on the Windsor platform. The maharani, studiously avoiding public attention, walked to the closed carriage waiting for her outside the station with a lady on either side of her, and drove to the castle behind her husband's open carriage. Surely an ordeal for a queen in those days.

Sayajirao III enjoyed the drive through Windsor Park with Lord Cross after lunch and was ready well before time for the investiture ceremony, which was scheduled for six o'clock that evening.

The same evening, after the ceremony, he got to meet Queen Victoria for the first time. The meeting set the tone for mutual affection, regard and respect which lasted till the end of Queen Victoria's life.

Sayajirao III took some time off to spend in Brighton, with the fond hope that its therapeutic waters would improve his health. He remained there until February 1888 when he returned to Baroda after a stay of nine months abroad. One cannot proceed further in this history of the Gaekwads without making an allusion to the strength of character, grit and determination displayed by Sayajirao III during his foreign tours. Europe, with its innumerable distractions—the extravagant life of 'high society', gambling, racing and restaurants—held no charm for him and left him unmoved. He was there for a specific purpose, which was to learn. He implemented the knowledge that he derived into his administration to make it more effective, which remained the sole interest for the rest of his life. Of course, his health needed attention; he found the clear, cool air of the Swiss mountains invigorating, the verdant meadows of England abounding with flowers soothing and the quietness was a welcome change, and he revelled in it. What Europe held for him as a ruler, whose ambition lay in making his state the most progressive and prosperous state in India, were the railways, industries, the educational system, libraries, art and architecture. He cared for neither their ways, nor their society.

26

Administration of the State from Abroad

Sayajirao III's frequent absence from Baroda, beginning with his trip to Ceylon, did in no way impair the administration of the state, which continued like a well-oiled machine. 'His methods of governing and the sheer volume of work he had put in, to institute them, had shown splendid results,'[1] a fact that must have put the AGG's nose out of joint. For, it would not have escaped the eagle eye of the British that no emergency had arisen which would have required the interference of a British official.

The progressive West as seen by Sayajirao III had made a tremendous impact on his mind and he was anxious to adopt some of its methods in his own state and even inside the palace. Earlier, to procure a glass of water for the Maharaja, the request would pass through several attendants and by the time it was procured a good forty-five minutes would have passed. Now he had an electric calling bell installed in every room and also instructed his chief engineer to install lifts. During his sojourn abroad, there had been frequent and rapid communication between him and his ministers, suggesting improvements in roads, the kind he had seen in Europe. He asked for proposals to be submitted for the extension of railways, and providing the city with gas and electricity. He also ordered that the *Cassell's Dictionary of Cookery* be translated into Marathi'[2] presumably for the use of the cooks in the palace who would be able to provide the table with European fare when British dignitaries were invited to dine. Above all, topping the list of 'improvements', was his desire to enhance the city's library for public use and for that reason he supplied his staff with a long list of books to be procured. He also had plans for starting a museum in Baroda and collecting rare Sanskrit manuscripts. It should be noted that Sayajirao III was not obsessed with the English language; his regard and esteem for the languages of India remained deeply entrenched in his heart. There are also clear instructions in his letters to the ministers for improving the performance of the sugar factory and cotton mills, and for introducing methods and tools for printing on calico.

Whatever had been hoped for with regard to his health was not achieved by this trip to Europe. Sayajirao III was still ailing; he still suffered from insomnia which had probably got worse with his mind bursting with ideas and in his eagerness to implement them, sleep must have eluded him, forcing him to spend the night pacing in his room till dawn. Perhaps overwork coupled with insomnia had undermined his health and brought on attacks of gout from which he had been ailing for quite some time. After his return, Sayajirao III left soon for Ootacamund, also known as Ooty, hoping the hill station with its greenery, pure air and silence might help him. His health got better and in a letter to Viceroy Dufferin he was able to say with confidence that he was sleeping soundly and his digestion had improved considerably. However, the main purpose of the letter was to let Viceroy Dufferin know that he had received a congratulatory letter from Queen Victoria on the birth of his second son Jaisinghrao. For after all, it augured well for the British higher-ups in India to know that Indian princes had bonded well with the crown. Madhavrao would certainly have approved.

A month after his return from Ooty, Sayajirao III, again on medical advice, left on a short visit for Switzerland, where he made St Moritz his headquarters and benefited enormously from his two and a half months' stay there.

Looking at his itinerary, his British superiors must have been frustrated to find that this Indian prince had opted to stay at a remote health resort in the Swiss Alps. Here was no feudal despot seeking the carnal pleasures found in night clubs and casinos abroad. Besides, as witnessed earlier, the administration ran smoothly without a hitch in his absence. This time, since the maharani could not accompany him, the number of his attendants was drastically cut down by him from fifty-five to just fourteen. Elliot was to accompany him as a political officer but the British AGG Oliver St John came down on him in a letter, while he was still in Ooty, stating that since he was only going to be residing in health resorts, it did not warrant the presence of a political officer accompanying him on the trip. It must be remembered that Elliot still belonged to the Indian Civil Service of British India and was on loan to the Baroda state. Sayajirao III, never one to say die, asked Elliot to apply for leave and accompany him to Europe as his friend. The government of India had no real reason for turning down Elliot's request for leave to go abroad in his private capacity.' Sayajirao III had managed to circumvent a departmental prohibition'[3] and, throwing caution to the winds, they sailed from Bombay on *SS Clyde* on 26 June 1888. Sayajirao III had got away with it but not without ruffling some feathers in the British hierarchy. En route, they made brief stops at Naples, Rome and Florence to see the sights, but the zing had gone out of the trip because Elliot, who was uneasy and understandably so, knew that his English brethren would wait for an opportunity to hit back.

Sayajirao III made St Moritz his headquarters and enjoyed the fresh, cool and crisp mountain air and the silence. His health improved substantially, enabling him to go on long treks into the mountains every day from which he derived considerable benefit.

He and his party were back in Baroda on 9 October 1888.

It must be clearly understood that Sayajirao III was not a hypochondriac suffering from imaginary ailments. He was a sick man who suffered from fatigue and other health problems due to lack of sleep brought on by an overactive mind and a rich diet. Brought up on the farm on a simple but healthy diet of bajra roti and buttermilk, he found the food in the palace too rich for him.

In spite of his long spells of illness, he never slackened his governance nor did he allow progress to slow down. Deeply impressed with the art galleries of Europe, he hired the services of an Italian landscape painter named Gironi to paint the Baroda landscape, street scenes where the more imposing buildings stood and the façades of the palaces, such as Moti Bagh, Makarpura and Laxmi Vilas. He also commissioned his manager, Abbas Tyabji, to employ a doctor from England as his personal physician, for after all, an English doctor's diagnosis and treatment could not be brushed away by the Resident or those higher up in the British government, especially if he recommended a voyage abroad as a tonic for the king's poor health and jaded spirits. Abbas Tyabji was also given the task of buying a yacht which was safe to sail on the seas. After a lot of scouring around in England, he managed to source a doctor named Nevins, who fit the bill of being a physician as well as a companion, who could ride and shoot, perfectly. However, he was not so lucky with the yacht. He did find one for less than the stipulated price of £10,000, but after repairs and extra fittings as the king's tastes now ran along European lines, the cost ran into another Rs 3,000. After a trial run on the Arabian Sea, *Zingara* (as the vessel was named) crashed at the entrance to

Alibag, which is 20 miles from Bombay. 'Luckily, no lives were lost', records historian, G.S. Sardesai who was enrolled into Sayajirao III's services about this time.

In the spring of 1889, just as Baroda was getting hot, Sayajirao III left for Mahabaleshwar. From there, he wrote to Elliot in May that he was much better, had taken to working again and was enjoying it. He did not return to Baroda until 22 October of the same year. By now, the people of Baroda had begun to frown upon his frequent absences from the state. News of the Maharaja riding and hunting outside the state reached their ears and they began to view his 'poor health' with scepticism.

'It was probably a ruse to get away from work and enjoy himself', they said to one another. If his absence called for speculation among his own people, one can imagine what the British officials thought of it. In a period of six years and three months, he was absent from his domain for nearly four years. Admittedly, there was nothing in the treaties that prohibited a native ruler from seeking the coolness of hill stations or travelling to Europe in the summer months if he so desired, so long as the administration ran smoothly. Besides, if the climate was proving deleterious to his health he had every right to seek a cure wherever it was available. This was Sayajirao III's own justification; but the Residency unfortunately took a different view. They professed that a ruler's domain run in absentia would inevitably be detrimental to the welfare of a state and that Sayajirao III spent two-thirds of his time away from it. Something had to be done. Considering the fact that in absentia alone could not be made to look like a major fault unless there were proofs of misrule, they decided to bide their time till enough ammunition had been secured to be used against him to prevent him travelling. The Residency had been neatly put in its place over its efforts to prevent Elliot from accompanying Sayajirao III to Europe—considerably miffed over this slight the Resident now retaliated by getting Elliot's promotion withheld. It was his way of punishing him for accompanying Sayajirao III to Europe even when he had objected to it. Sayajirao III was considerably upset over this, but there was nothing he could do.

In Mahabaleshwar, he wrote a letter to Laxman Jagannath to send him more work to do. He began to receive papers on a regular basis and with his improved health in the cool climate of the hill station, he worked with renewed vigour.

Contrary to the opinions of those who thought him a ruler neglectful of his duties, Sayajirao III spent most of his time working out schemes for improving the drainage system, the settlement of the Bharkali lands and other vexing matters that were impediments to the administration. There were those people who thronged the hill station in summer who had ample evidence that the Maharaja put in as much deskwork in Mahabaleshwar as he put in Baroda. Sayajirao III's time was not spent in pursuit of pleasure but devoted to work. He preferred working away from the Baroda state where he was bothered with the petty details of administration. Here he was free from the tale-telling and scrimmage of courtiers filling his ears and could concentrate fully on weightier issues that had been left unresolved for decades and needed to be addressed without further delay.

While in Mahabaleshwar, Sayajirao III had let it be known that he wanted to appoint a reader. One day, a man who was called for an interview for the post and had to wait a considerable while as the king was occupied in a discussion with his chief engineer, Elliot and a few others on the more pressing matter of the Bharkali lands. After the meeting ended, the man was called in for a dictation that went on for hours, past lunch time. It was half past four in the afternoon when the private secretary came in and very hesitatingly, revealed that the man who was typing had not had his lunch. Sayajirao III released the man from his work with the admonition, 'Why didn't you tell me that you hadn't eaten?' Needless to say, the man got the job for after all, a man who could work continuously forgoing his meal proved that he was a diligent worker.

The man referred to here was none other than the reputed historian Govind Sakharam Sardesai. Being a man who placed the value of education above everything else, Sayajirao III encouraged Sardesai in his passion for writing and editing. Under the great man's patronage, Sardesai went on to become a historian too. He became a close friend of the family as the years flew by and travelled with them on their trips abroad. During Sayajirao III's stay in Mahabaleshwar, he was visited by some of the great think tanks of that time. One of them was Mahadev Govind Ranade, who was said to have inspired the king to break away from customs that fettered him from taking progressive steps towards betterment. For Sayajirao III, caution was the watchword and he exercised it in matters of reform that had the risk of offending the sensibilities of diehard conventionalists.'In removing one evil, we must take care to see that another does not crop up,' he would often remark. ⁴

Sayajirao III shifted his residence in 1890 from the Makarpura Palace to the newly constructed Laxmi Vilas Palace, which was built mostly in the Indo-Saracenic style. It had taken ten years to build the palace during a period in which the Maharaja's tastes had undergone a drastic change with his visits to Europe. Major Charles Mant had designed some of the famous palaces in India, but 'barely had the foundation stone been laid when he lost control of his senses convinced that the structures would collapse, he died but the palaces continue to remain.'⁵ The construction of the Laxmi Vilas Palace was completed by the architect Robert Chisholm. The palace accommodates several of the earlier summer palaces and a couple of monuments; the landscaping of the garden does full justice to the vast imposing structure standing on it. Surrounded by verdant lawns, artificial pools and enclosed by a fence, which would take a day to walk around, the palace has exotic trees and plants imported from abroad which add to the landscape's lush beauty. William Goldring was given the assignment of landscaping and lived up to the Maharaja's expectations with his work. One could get lost in the gardens of the palace just looking around or while wandering on miles of footpath; it's easier to enjoy a drive on the motor roads provided for the purpose. 'There is also a tan ride for the use of the household that is more than a mile and a half in length.'⁶ The façade of the palace which is a confluence of Hindu and Mughal architecture resembles most of the monuments in India, though when Chisholm took it up, there was an attempt to bring in the Gothic influence. The palace, a symbol of prosperity and grandeur, lives up to its name with its marble floors, ornate work on the pillars and its lavish interiors for which Florentine craftsmen were imported from Italy, who were probably responsible for the strong Italian overtones in the ambience.

The Durbar Hall is ninety-three feet long and fifty-four feet wide, intended to seat a thousand courtiers and the private rooms are more or less similar in size. The stone it was built of was quarried from the vicinity of the Songadh fort, which was a place Pilajirao had first occupied to gain a foothold into Gujarat and which ultimately became the family bastion for his descendants. 'That chiselled pile' Sayajirao III refers to later seems to be caught in a time warp and has weathered well over a century.

27

Some Flak, Reynolds and Administration

Colonel Reynolds had replaced AGG Oliver St John a year ago in 1888 and John had given a scathing report of the Baroda administration in which Elliot was portrayed as the chief villain. This was a way of hitting back at Elliot, who had been the most sincere employee appointed by the British, as he had flouted John's wishes when he had accompanied Sayajirao III abroad even after being denied explicit permission. Elliot's uneasiness on the trip, it will be recalled, had not been unfounded. John's report tore the management of the administration to pieces, particularly the Barkhali department. He stated that nothing had been done in that regard as Elliot was not qualified for the job and had him replaced with a trained settlement officer named Jenkins, after which there was some progress.

Apart from inefficiency, Elliot's friendship with Sayajirao III was misinterpreted as disloyalty, bordering on treason to the Crown, and John advised his immediate removal on the grounds that his stay in the state was detrimental to the paramount power's interest. Not content with this direct criticism against Elliot, John launched a tirade on Dewan Laxman Jagannath as well. The dewan's rise from a clerk, on a salary of Rs 8 per month, to that of a dewan, on a salary of Rs 5,000 per month, had been through diligence, sincerity and hard work. But John's opinion was to the contrary: 'his transfer to Baroda service has been on his interest alone and not for public service.'[1] Jagannath had been loaned as an assistant collector to the Baroda administrative department. '[Had he remained in British service, the highest salary he would have reached would have been Rs 800.'[2] This allusion to his remuneration shows that it was just a point for criticism since he had nothing adverse to say about the man, certainly not about his work which had been more than satisfactory. The same criticism followed with regard to Naib Dewan Manubhai. John's report accused both Elliot and Manubhai of disloyalty to the British government by favouring the Maharaja. As one gathers from the report, the gist of his grievance seemed to have been the remuneration of these people. He stated that the salaries received by the dewan and his deputy far exceeded the normal pay and was very censorious about it. The report was sent to the higher officials in Calcutta with a copy to his successor, Colonel Reynolds, who accepted it, like the Bible. Later, Reynold's successor Colonel Biddulph used it to his own advantage in his tirade against Sayajirao III and Elliot.

Two very important goals achieved by Sayajirao III before he left for Europe for his third trip must be noted here. With regard to public health, a sanitary department under a commissioner was set up in 1891 for the benefit of the whole state. The department took over the work which had hitherto been performed by bhangis, that is, sweepers. Second, on 29 March 1892, the work of the Ajwa Waterworks or Sayaji Sarovar, as it had been named, was resumed (the work had begun in 1885), in order to supply clean drinking water to the people of Baroda, and completed in 1890. This was the greatest gift from Sayajirao III to his subjects.

Sayajirao III decided to leave for Europe in early May1892. In the interim two years that he was in Baroda he received distinguished visitors; fortunately, he was well enough to entertain them. At the end of 1889, Lord Reay accompanied by his wife paid his second visit to Baroda. His term as the governor of Bombay was drawing to an end and he wished to visit the state and meet his good friend Sayajirao III with whom a firm and steady friendship had been formed over the years. The letters that they exchanged testify to that. The other visitor was Prince Albert Victor, Prince of Wales, who was on a sporting tour of India and arrived in Baroda on 13 March from Terai, Nepal. As the Laxmi Vilas Palace had been completed and 'finished' to European standards, he was entertained in royal splendour, and after a three-day visit he left for Kathiawad in search of lions. Sayajirao III left for Umrath during the hot summer months where he worked quietly most of the day. He was a voracious reader and a bibliophile. He also spent time playing the same rustic games on the seashore that he had played in his boyhood. He returned to Baroda for the monsoon spell when Gujarat's weather changed from dry heat to warm humidity, which added to his unhealthy condition. His two sons, Fatehsinghrao III who was now seven years old and Jaisinghrao, were sent off to Deolali, a quiet place near Kavlana, in the care of Dr Nevins and Sardesai in the role of tutor.

The monsoon brought with it an epidemic of fever, that, fortunately, neither Sayajirao III, nor his queen caught. During this time, they were gifted with a son, Shivajirao, who too survived the epidemic. But in early December, the Maharaja caught double pneumonia and had to be confined to bed for two months under Dr Nevins's care. While in bed, he answered all the letters and cables of 'get well soon' messages from home and abroad that had been piling up. One of the first to be answered was that of Lady Reay. Sayajirao III thanked her for her good wishes and kind enquiries pertaining to his health and also for recommending Lord Houghton's *Life and Smalling's London Letters* for him to read. Again, just as soon as he began to recover, an onset of boils on his neck prevented him from carrying out his normal routine. After a treatment of 'native remedies', he was back to normal to brave the summer but longing for the cool hills, he once again set out for Mahabaleshwar for the summer. He enjoyed there for three months, from where he wrote letters one to Elliot, lamenting the government of India's decision to withhold Elliot's promotion and the other to his dewan to send him more work because he was on the 'high road to recovery'. The Maharaja was back in Baroda in September.

He saw that the city had a copious water supply owing to a heavy rainfall in the monsoons, filling the Ajwa reservoir to the brim, and was overjoyed at the sight. He immediately made plans for a grand opening ceremony but was taken ill with a severe attack of dysentery, common in India as an aftermath of the monsoons. After a week's treatment in Baroda under Dr Nevins's watchful care, he was sent to Bombay to be treated by a specialist. This time too his recovery was disturbingly slow and he was in Bombay for two months until he was well enough to travel. He was also advised, on medical grounds, an ocean voyage to Europe; even though the recommendation was tempting to him, he wanted to be back in Baroda for the opening of the reservoir, which was scheduled for 29 March, and put off the trip. Besides, in accordance with Indian orthodox tradition and perhaps Victorian too, he did not want to go on the voyage without Chimnabai II who was expecting a child again. So, he returned to Baroda. On 19 February 1892, Chimnabai II delivered a girl who was named Indira who grew up to be a beautiful woman with a mind of her own and an avant-garde outlook.

At the opening of the reservoir, the author of *Sayajirao of Baroda* writes, 'The public of Baroda rejoiced to see a unique phenomenon...the first shoot of clean, sweet water in plenty...' In his speech at the inauguration of the

Ajwa Waterworks, Sayajirao III drew a picture of the state as it was before and after his rule. Eleven years of his rule reflected his dedication to his subjects' welfare in the state of Baroda. The years 1889 to1892 saw a good number of his reforms underway and some completed.

Sayajirao III's speech reflected some of his hopes and ideas for the welfare of his subjects, exhorted them to grab opportunities and give him their best assistance. His inaugural speech began with the words:

> Though Mr Lynn rightly places this scheme among the earliest I considered, I must allow that chronologically, it was the railways that first occupied my thoughts. I am mighty glad that I have seen 118 miles of railway constructed and can look forward to further progress. It is not only that the public convenience has been consulted but my scattered dominions are now linked together by iron roads to the improvement of the administration of the headquarters of my talukas.
>
> Those are now tied together—Patan, Sidhpur, Kheralu, Vadnagar, Visnagar, Mehsana, Karjan, Naosari and Gandevi—and in the near future, I hope many other places will also be connected. But today, I put the thoughts of railways aside and joyfully confess that I look upon the Ajwa Reservoir and this water scheme as the most important single public work brought to completion since my accession to power. I am well content with your suggestion that the artificial lake should be called Sayaji Sarovar and so let it be. But, in my mind, I shall associate with this work, the names of Playford Reynolds and Jagannath Sadashivji. The Laxmi Vilas Palace has perhaps cost more, but I cannot strictly place among works of public utility the construction of that richly chiselled pile and of the costly Makarpura Palace now encircled by tasteful gardens we owe to Goldring. No! It is this gift of pure filtered water that I am most pleased to have bestowed upon the capital. The great domed college, the Countess of Dufferin hospital, the school's tower that we can discern from here on the banks of the reservoir which my predecessor gave to Baroda during his reign.

Here he made a graceful reference to Malharrao, 'The Chimnabai Market, which will cover all the space on which we stand, the museum in the public park, the vast public offices which are in contemplation, all these monuments of my friend Chisholm's skill are works of utility and adornment to Baroda. They will be revealed to us as one harmonious whole, when after solving our next great difficulty—the proper conservancy of the city—we shall rapidly widen and readjust our main streets and communications according to the plans I have long since matured. But, all this to my mind are nought, compared with this blessing of pure water, the first requisite of sanitary well being. Abundance of water, sanitary reform, these are the good things I wish to give to my people in profusion. This water scheme is but the foremost instance of what I am doing or hope to do for all 3,500 towns and villages of the state. Good wells are being provided for all villages which have not yet got them. Except the areas where water is quite close to the surface or where the river flows past the village site, means have been provided, from Rs 6 to Rs 8, for the drawing of water from the wells. As for sanitation, a great army of scavengers will soon, I trust, be called into existence, to be disciplined by special officers. Approx. Rs 8 per 100 of the population are to be devoted to the purpose in all villages, while in the market towns I have just doubled the conservancy funds and I look to the panches, my civil surgeons and the newly created sanitary commissioner to see that these funds are turned to good use under the clear and simple rules which I hope my people will study...It is the cooperation of my people which I require, to gain for them the advantages of physical health and some simple book-learning, which I wish the masses to acquire so that I may take them into my confidence and partnership. I am as you know, all for publishing laws, the regulations, the acts, the appointments of government; but will the masses learn to avail themselves of the information?

'I entertain the hope that they may do so, however chimerical it may appear. In this city, and in most of the big towns, there are now many schools, some of them advanced. Our Baroda College now teaches up to the second year BA and BSc; institutions have been called into existence for the study of handicrafts, for agriculture, for law, and even for music. Books are being compiled and books are being translated.

'That, we do not think of expansion alone, we are in the habit of occasionally sending a few select pupils to Europe to receive higher education is proof of it. But, I will say that, after a multiplication of girls' schools, there is no measure I have more at heart than the dissemination of primary education among bonafide cultivators and more especially by inducements of gifts and other things among the depressed classes of my subjects. I have of late promised to subsidize a schoolmaster and to aid the schools with books, slates and other necessities for any village which will supply a regular attendance of at least sixteen pupils. Let my people take advantage of this offer of assistance. I note that within the last two months, 128 villages have opened its [sic] own little school. This movement is in its infancy. Requests for schools are pouring in. I want to and expect to see hundreds of villages develop themselves in an intelligent manner.

'It is in order to encourage self-help that I have issued orders intended to give fresh life to the village community headed by the patels, assisted by the panch (a member of the panchayat-arbitrator). The salaries for patels throughout the state are being uniformly raised, and for the village, a police guard has now been appointed who would receive 4 percent of the entire revenue paid by the village to the government. I trust that these and some other similar measures such as setting up a Devasthan Fund for each community will lead to good governance, security and helpful activity. Remember, that the government aid cannot go very far, it depends mainly upon you to turn its assistance to good account.

'Physical improvement, mental development and the independence that self-help gives, cannot, I am aware, be expected, so long, as the state lays its crushing taxation upon its subjects. It has therefore been my task to reduce the aggregate government demand, while equalizing it as far as possible, spreading its burden over many shoulders and, at the same time, simplifying the demand so that both government and taxpayer may know what each man pays and why. That is why I have reduced the tax on government lands from 10 per cent to 50 per cent and more in the great majority of villages now surveyed and settled. That is why I have called on alienated lands to contribute a share of the revenue, granting sanads at the same time to their landlords, which makes their position more secure than it has hitherto been. That is why I propose to regulate the dues from the non-agricultural community. That is the reason, why, with a single stroke of the pen, I wrote off Rs 23,00,000 of arrears due to the state from cultivators, and the reason I have patiently heard and brought to a close once and for all, the thousands of disputes which have been left to simmer for a quarter of a century between the government and my subjects, regarding rates and tenure of certain lands.

'We start afresh, my people and I. Each man will now be called upon to pay in accordance with a simple demand based on clear grounds, publicly set forth. Here let me thank heartily Mr Elliot for the assistance he has given me in carrying out these measures taken by me.

'I repeat that it is my desire to take my people into my confidence by publishing the Acts of Government so that all who wish to read may do so and criticize. I own that recent changes have produced a momentary sense of confusion and disturbance which, I trust, will subside as the years go by giving way to a general feeling of contentment. I own that in many directions the government is still groping for a way to rule wisely.

'Have patience! Let time show the real value of what is now being done.

'I assure you that all my energies are being directed to free my people and enrich them and to improve the machinery of my administration.

'You are aware how within the last year export dues have been entirely swept away and the range of import duties is shortly to be restricted, and small imports dues have been abolished. Some of you may also be aware of what I propose to do, to relieve inamdars (those who have acquired land on lease and are unable to pay) and others, of their burden of debts. The measure has been lately published. Others may have noticed the tentative efforts of the State Bank and the freer hand with which taccavi (lump sum) advances are made. This and other measures are being undertaken to free you, while to benefit you, I have caused and am causing, a great drainage work to be made.

'I am making an effort to conserve our forests, to push on agricultural experiments to discover what riches, if any, the earth holds for us in her bosom; in short, to utilize within the state, the savings from my revenues. As for the machinery of the government, I own that in some fear and trembling, I am attempting to decentralize and at the same time to supervise the new small cause court system and the bench system for civil and criminal cases. The separation of the judicial from the executive branch and the panchayat system are among the efforts I am making to improve and simplify our administration. We stand at the very threshold of reform. The basis of a tolerable administration is the business like keeping of accounts.... To do better in future, we must aim high, very high. We must use more despatch, summon up more courage, enforce and submit to more discipline, cherish more public spirit. Then, will the stream of our progress flow smoothly and pure, and reach our homes, as does this water from Ajwa which cleanses our lips, fortifies our bodies and bids our spirits rejoice!'[3]

His audience listened with rapt attention and admiration for their ruler, who went to such lengths to procure a comfortable living for his subjects no matter what the sacrifice was with regard to his own health or money, and went home deeply gratified.

28

A Battle of Wits

Now that Sayajirao III had completed what he had set out to do, he was free to travel and go on the ocean voyage that the specialist from Bombay had recommended.

Since his daughter, Indira, was born in February 1892, the Maharaja postponed his voyage to 9 April and made a brief halt at Lonavla, a hill station near Bombay, to rest till his travel arrangements were through. The Maharaja was to be accompanied by his queen and their two older sons aged eight and six respectively. Baby Indira and Shivajirao, who must have been barely two, were left behind in the care of the elders in the family.

All was not smooth sailing for Sayajirao III. Reynolds demanded to know whether adequate arrangements had been made with regard to the administration in Sayajirao III's absence. He was also keen to know who would be travelling with him and wanted a list of the party members who were to accompany the king on the trip. To avoid any confrontation with the Residency, Elliot had been excluded from the trip and was to remain in Baroda fulfilling his duties in the capacity of the head of the land settlement department and sit on its administrative council. With regard to the political officer, Manubhai Jassabhai, the dewan who had replaced Laxman Jagannath, informed the Resident that since Sayajirao III was only going abroad for his rest, it did not warrant a political officer to be present. Three years earlier, this same argument had been put forth by the political department to sabotage Elliot accompanying Sayajirao III on his trip to Europe, but now, for an ulterior motive things had changed. Thus, when Reynolds was told that Dr Nevins would be one of the party, he immediately insisted on a political officer accompanying the entourage, which anyway had been reduced considerably; also, the Resident brushing away Dr Nevins' capabilities as a political officer escalated the matter to the government of India. Meanwhile, the voyage was put off and the bookings cancelled in view of the fact that approval had to come from the high and mighty in the British hierarchy.

Reynolds must have exaggerated the case because the government now insisted that the administrative council must be invested with full powers and Elliot was not to be a member of it. Reynolds gleefully informed Sayajirao III in a letter that he, Reynolds, had been told by the government to act as political officer on the voyage. He also added, though in a less severe manner, that his wife too might be included in the voyage as she could be of great help to the maharani. Now it was clear not only to Sayajirao III but also to the government that the real reason for the fuss had been that Reynolds wanted to go on a leave and was seeking a free passage for himself and his wife and a holiday cruise in the bargain.

A fuming Sayajirao III wrote to the foreign secretary to the government of India, Sir Mortimer Durand, about the matter, explaining the facts of the case and stating that he was going abroad for health reasons only and he would be leaving on 7 May on medical advice, presumably with or without the government's blessings. He also mentioned in his letter that it was not necessary to invest the council with full powers in his absence. Sir Mortimer Durand broke the golden rule that one must never let one's own countrymen down. He agreed in his reply to Sayajirao III's argument that it was not necessary to invest the council with 'full powers' but ruled out Elliot as a council member because he was the employee of the government of British India. Contrary to the Maharaja's wishes, he confirmed that Reynolds would accompany him on the voyage as political officer thus salvaging departmental propriety and keeping his pride intact.

With the matter settled, on 7 May 1892, Sayajirao III left for Europe. The presence of Reynolds and his wife must have been irksome, but they had little to do on the voyage and by dodging the attentions of the two by a quick change of plans, he managed to shake them off after they had passed the Suez Canal after which one can safely say that the rest cure had begun!

As soon as the party reached Europe, the Reynolds left the party and later in London, another political officer was foisted on them. Colonel Fitzgerald was a welcome change from his predecessor as he was amiable and it was with genuine regret that Sayajirao III saw him off when the tour came to its end.

In Paris, the Maharaja was advised to try the waters of Vichy as the minerals in the waters of the baths were said to be beneficial for health. But he opted for London where he took his family on a whirlwind tour of sightseeing. Conscious of his own shortcomings in education, Sayajirao III tried to soak up the environment as much as he could from his visits to art galleries, universities, libraries, industries, spinning and cotton mills, sewage farms, prisons and other institutions, wherever and whatever he felt would be useful for him to learn from. He urged his children along the same lines, hoping they too would learn from the exposure and be encouraged to steer their own paths towards self-improvement.

Sayajirao III was conscious that courtesy demanded that he call on the queen and the dignitaries who ran the empire. Thus, 'he embarked on a dizzy round of making friends and influencing the people who ran the Empire from the queen downwards'.[1]

At a time when the thought of constitutional emancipation from external control would have only occurred to a few, the Maharaja intrepidly voiced this thought in reply to the toast of 'Our Indian and colonial visitors' at Lord Mayor's banquet at the Guildhall, London, on 10 November 1892. The speech reflects how much he had evolved from the time of his investiture. He began his speech by lauding the people of England on the country's progress:

'I have enjoyed myself thoroughly during this short trip to the industrial towns of this country. The resources and wealth of it impressed me very much. The people of England have not only not remained satisfied with discovering the means of wealth which they possess, but they have, with their usual sagacity and intelligence, made admirable use of their opportunities. This banquet is quite a fitting termination in one way of my short and hurried trip.

'The city of London is the heart of this vast country, not only on account of its vast population and its noble institutions, but because it has been the stronghold of commerce and enterprising men—men who have added to their wealth by subjugating and conquering vast territories...'

Here, the subtle inference that England had gained from snatching what belonged to others would not have been lost on the white coloured race as well as the guests at the banquet.

'The possession of which has made the government of England very difficult, arduous and responsible, and I wish the ministers of Her Majesty, some of whom we see here this evening, every success in their undertaking. The various interests involved and the problems which arise in the government of England are so great, engaging and serious, that men saddled with the cares of office must find little time to watch closely the rapid and gigantic changes that are going on in the different parts of this Empire—an Empire unique in its extent, population and civilization.'

Was this a warning?

'The government of this Empire is rendered very difficult owing to the many nationalities, and men of different faiths and creeds, of which it consists. To understand all their wants, and to administer to their aspirations, is a task which is not very easy. I think it would be well to allow the generous and liberalizing instincts of the British nation full play by conferring on its colonies and dependencies the blessings of reasonably representative self-governing institutions. The introduction of such measures will not only lighten the cares of government but it will also be a powerful means of fulfilling the noble wish of securing the contentment and happiness of Her Majesty's subjects, and will also draw together several parts of the Empire together to strengthen it by consolidation.

'The reference you have made to me is indeed very kind. In opening banks, in extending railways, in building and funding hospitals, in constructing rest houses, bridges, public offices and schools. In encouraging literature by opening libraries, in introducing elective municipalities in my territories, in creating village councils, in securing supply of potable water and so on, I have made use of the opportunities at my disposal.'

He introduced a placatory note in conclusion, 'The little that I have been able to achieve is due to the kind sympathy and assistance of the government of India. In all my actions, I am moved with feelings of staunchest loyalty to Her Majesty, and with the desire of co-operating with the British government in India to the best of my ability in the work of introducing progressive government. We are no longer moved by the desire of pageantry and show, but by the principles of good and sound government. As far as I and others in my position are concerned, all that we desire is that our field of usefulness may not suffer curtailment, and that we may be allowed increased freedom to make use of the opportunities offered to us, not in gratifying our personal ambitions and desires, but in fulfilling our noble duties.'

The reference to how well his state had progressed under him and the request to not 'curtail' must have caused a certain amount of alarm in the minds of the top officials at the banquet.

Soon after, Sayajirao III left London for Norway where he found nothing to stimulate his mind nor was he charmed by the people whose intelligence and manners were nothing to rave about. From Norway, he went to Dresden and Berlin where he found much to appreciate and admire, and finally to 'my tried friend St Moritz'[2] as mentioned in one of his letters. Here, he engaged an English tutor for his children, by now convinced of the importance of the language, to 'widen one's horizons'. However, anxious that the Western culture they were being exposed to should not influence them adversely, he asked Sardesai to join him in St Moritz and continue tuitions in Marathi.

The Maharaja spent a few weeks trekking to the less frequented parts of the Alps, keeping St Moritz as his base for residing. Camping in wayside inns, the pristine and pure mountain air and the exercise did him a world of good, so much so that Dr Charcot, who he consulted in Paris, recommended another three months' stay in the Alps, while the specialist Dr Hunter in London advised a whole year. But, even in the snowy Alps of Switzerland, his heart and spirit were in Baroda.

Following his own instincts, he ignored the advice of the doctors and returned to India on New Year's day in 1893.

29

Colonel John Biddulph: A Resident in Phayre's Garb

The British officials in India must have been baffled, for here was a 'native prince' who did not seek the pleasures denied to him in his home town and instead of frequenting the casinos, nightclubs, bars, he emerged as a 'devoted Victorian paterfamilias', escorting his family to educational institutions and industries, and spending time with them in the quietest of resorts.

The ruler of Baroda was certainly giving them no grounds for complaints. While abroad, Sayajirao III continued with a good deal of administrative work too. All administrative matters that required his attention were mailed to him weekly in sealed boxes and he dealt with them in a thorough manner, allowing work in the affairs of governance to run smoothly. It has been rightly said that 'though he was on the other side of the earth, his mind and heart were in India and Baroda.' Anything that could be adopted for the betterment of his state and people, he incorporated it into his notes and accordingly instructions were mailed to his ministers. With a ruler such as this, the highest in the British hierarchy could not have faulted him for negligence or indifference to his own responsibilities as a ruler, and they were at a loss to find some point of criticism to disfavour him and bring about his downfall. However, they could and they did cavil about his frequent trips abroad, saying that the state was being run by an 'absentee ruler', yet they could not criticize the way it was run as it was being governed most efficiently and there were reports from the political officer that the Maharaja worked just as hard at his desk in St Moritz as he did in Baroda. There was enough correspondence between Sayajirao III and his ministers that testified to that fact. The truth of the matter was, with a well-administered state, the AGG and others in the Residency were mere onlookers and were prevented from intervention and direct control. This was unpalatable as it defeated their purpose. They had come to this country to rule.

The administration could not be faulted, but at the same time there was a growing suspicion that the Maharaja was secretly in league with those favouring home rule in India. However, there was no concrete evidence to support this suspicion and the seed of doubt was probably sown when he began associating with the Poona intellectuals who were part of the Indian National Congress. Ironically, this movement was founded by an Englishman, A.O. Hume, who also shortened the party's name to Congress. Hume was an English liberalist who, along with other English liberals, encouraged Indian officers to ask for favours from the higher British officials in the hierarchy.

Many of the British were a discontented lot and missed the shores of England where the weather and the infrastructure afforded them a far more comfortable life. Besides, being away from their families must have been irksome to them. It was no skin off their noses if Indians wanted home rule, they would have been happy to hand over the country to the rightful owners and rush home to the cool climate of England where the roses always bloomed. They had a lot to lose and nothing to gain by remaining in the hot climate and putting up with the 'natives' for company.

Sayajirao Gaekwad III was at this point of time only in his mid-twenties with no definite political ideals, in fact, politics was of little interest to him. His mind was completely taken up with administrative matters of Baroda that had to be resolved, before worrying about the country's politics. But this is not to say that he ostracized himself from those involved in the Indian national movement, for they formed the crème de la crème of India's erudite scholars and intellectuals. Whenever he chanced a meeting, he exchanged a few words with them, a fact that was not lost on the watchdogs of the British Empire who drew the conclusion that he must be 'one of them'. Interestingly, Shirish Kumar has said that the confidential letters of Aurobindo Ghosh (Sri Aurobind) published in the *Vasumati* magazine give evidence of Aurobindo Ghosh's involvement in the freedom movement of India and the Maharaja silently supporting it. Any such support given by native princes or citizens of the country was termed as sedition.

Reynolds was replaced by Colonel John Biddulph as the new AGG, who happened to be cast in the same mould as Robert Phayre. Biddulph was a well-read scholar and the author of several books on India. He was no mean opponent to match wits with. A superficial diplomat with a diabolical mind, he set about, in the summer of 1888, to bring about Sayajirao III's downfall, while the king was away in the quiet coolness of the Niligris. A summary of contrived events to throw poor light on Sayajirao III's administration formed the major content of his report. The report was kept as a secret document for obvious reasons, and Sayajirao III himself was not aware that such a report with a concoction of lies even existed.[1] If there was one thing that the British could find fault with it was that the king didn't grovel before the top British officials. Sayajirao III adhered strictly to the terms and obligations set in the treaty at the time of his investiture. On his return from Niligris, he was met with hostile looks from the British officials and he sensed the widening gap between him and the Residency, with no way to counteract it. Thus, he went on about his work, providing more fuel for vilification from the ruthless Biddulph whose term too was to end shortly. The AGG spent considerable time trying to gather material that could end the rule of Sayajirao III and if it did not happen during his tenure of office, he left behind enough in the report for his successor to take up the cause.

Nothing untoward happened in the running of the administration of Baroda, a state that had come to be regarded as a model state for other princes. Sayajirao III was considered a highly cultured and well-travelled man with a head full of progressive ideas, which other rulers could emulate. In spite of his popularity with his people who were more than satisfied with his rule, Sayajirao III did not escape the 'initial blast which came in the form of an ultimatum from the viceroy',[2] put plainly either he should step down and hand over the reins of government to the British or be deposed like his predecessor. This ultimatum came on the basis of a cooked-up report which proves that Malharrao had been falsely accused of murder and been done away with by the unscrupulous Resident Phayre. However, the divine hand that had brought Sayajirao III to rule Baroda showed up once more in the form of the First World War that was hovering on the horizon of Europe. With this to occupy their minds and in the atmosphere of awakening Indian nationalism, the British authorities could hardly bother about deposing an Indian ruler. Besides, they dared not depose one who was India's most popular ruler and incite a cause for rebellion. Apart from that, they needed the Indian army to fight on the side of the Allies in order to win the war against Germany. Thus, they could not affect Indian sensibilities now of all times, and so the charges made against him fizzled out.

Coming back to Biddulph's report, it spoke disparagingly of the king's background and stated that he acquired the throne through serendipity. There were also charges against Elliot who had set himself to be indispensable to the young Gaekwad with the intention of ruling the state himself. Elliot who had been employed purely in the role of a tutor was a fair-minded man—a fact that irked the British officials. Thus, whenever Elliot, out of a deep sense of justice, was forced to take the side of the young Sayajirao III in any controversy with British officials, he was seen as being a traitor to the paramount power in whose service he had been employed. 'Who does he think he's working for—the British or for that native upstart, the prince?' they must have asked each other, turning up their supercilious noses. Point no. 4 of the report referred to the period when 'Sir Madhavrao was practically allowed a free hand in the administration' and implied that as Elliot wanted to exercise his influence on the Maharaja, he caused the dewan to resign from his post. 'From an early date, the young chief was prejudiced against Madhavrao so that shortly before the minority came to an end, a pamphlet called "The Groans of Baroda" was published anonymously in Bombay and disseminated through the Bombay Presidency.' In it, the whole administration of Baroda was vilified and Madhavrao was accused of various heinous and disgraceful acts.

The five authors of the offensive pamphlet were V. Sammarth, employed as a subha in Baroda; Vasudev Sadashiv Bhat, the late Naib dewan; and G.V. Athalye who had been brought to the Baroda administration by Elliot and were considered his protégés enjoying, according to the report, special favours from Sayajirao III and Elliot. The other two authors were Mr Ranade, a judge of the Bombay High Court, and Bal Gangadhar Tilak who as the notorious editor of the newspaper *Maratha* had criticized Madhavrao's administration as being pro-British. But, at the time of publishing the pamphlet, Athalye was practising as a lawyer in the Bombay High Court. Tilak accused Elliot of bringing these people to the state who were anti-British, which was as good as accusing him of treason. The report exaggerated the not-so-cordial relationship between Sayajirao III and Madhavrao, which ended in the latter's resignation since 'the constant troubles given to Sir Madhav Rao made his position untenable... He resigned after eight months, followed by Kazi Shahbuddin, who was dewan for three years, then by Laxman Jagannath, who was forced to resign after three years...The incumbencies of these ministers have been described to me as periods of quarrels with Mr. Elliot...' and here with relish he draws attention to the fact mentioned in the Residency records in a note made by Melville against the retention of Elliot in the Baroda service. Here it must be recalled that Melville had not been in favour of retaining Elliot once the Maharaja had been given the reins of governance of the state of Baroda, perhaps the reason being that Elliot had not sided with the Resident in extracting a larger concession from the Maharaja after the investiture, causing their relationship to sour a little. Ironically, it must be remembered it was Melville who had been responsible for appointing Elliot as the tutor for Sayajirao III and had brought him to Baroda for this very purpose. Melville had probably planned a 'yes man' role for the tutor who could be manipulated to delay the handing over of the controls of the state to the young Gaekwad so that the Resident could hold on to the reins a little longer, on the plea that Sayajirao III's education was still incomplete and he could not be allowed to rule for a few years more. But Elliot being Elliot had not cooperated with the scheme as desired by Melville. Well, whatever the reason, Melville too seemed anxious that Elliot's tenure of office in the Baroda service should end as expressed in the note and Biddulph felt himself justified.

Then there was an oxymoron type of criticism on the administration which, while sounding positive, had negative overtones. Biddulph after his slanderous campaign against Elliot trained his guns on Sayajirao III to a blast intended to scorch him and reduce him to ashes. 'The feverish zeal with which he works has had a serious effect on Gaekwad's health...in view of his very limited capacity...he is incapable of taking broad, comprehensive views and fusses over detail. He is a man of poor physique and very moderate mental capacity. I have failed to discover in him any real ability...Overtaxing his powers... has so affected his nervous system as to inflict permanent injury on him....' and so on implying that the Maharaja was neurotic and could not be depended upon to rule efficiently

According to Biddulph, 'The first six or seven years after the Gaekwad's accession to full authority were years of feverish activity, spent in what has been called carrying out reforms, which really consisted of pulling the whole administration to pieces and building up in its place an unworkable system that the Gaekwad has been taught to believe is superior to anything in British India. The Maharaja when first invested with full powers seems to have been taught that everything in the state, as it then existed was wrong, and that it was the simplest thing in the world to put it right.' Here Biddulph allows himself to tone down the acerbicity of his criticism. 'It may at once be admitted that many of the changes were beneficial. Proper salaries were assigned to officials. A public works department was formed, with an adequate expenditure proportionate to the means of the state, and a large educational system founded.' Biddulph as though tired of his grudging praise reverts to his former caustic criticism of the administration, 'Other changes, made apparently only for the sake of change have not been so successful while the rapidity with which one change after another was introduced have given a serious shock to the administration, from which it will take years to recover. The evils of many of these changes are only now beginning to be felt, and the next few years promise to be years of great difficulty in Baroda.' He then mentions in his report that Sayajirao III has committed the grievous sin of increasing the strength of his army, and a list with meticulous details incorporating facts and figures to corroborate his statement is given. It will be remembered that Madhavrao's cautionary words had been, 'Your Highness will do well to resist the temptation to raise the efficiency of your regular forces to British standards.' It had been the standing rule laid down by the British and Biddulph capitalized on it to show up Sayajirao III in the light of a law-breaker. Biddulph's attack alternates between Elliot and Sayajirao III. Elliot comes under his volley of fire as he blames him for the resignation of Madhavrao who 'after eight months of mortification at last retired to Tanjore, and from there tendered his resignation. His successor Kazi Shahbuddin who underwent the same experience, and in three years was obliged to resign. To him succeeded Laxman Jagannath as minister, who in turn was forced to resign in less than four years', thus implying that Elliot's treatment of them had forced them to resign from office.

Regarding Sayajirao III, it was obvious that since he had no real ground for criticism either in his decorum as a ruler nor in the way his administration was being run, the AGG pounced upon his health and his zest for work as negative factors for making him incapable of ruling. The report must have taxed Biddulph's thinking prowess a lot for how can one build up a case against someone when there were no grounds for it? But Biddulph waited and probably had his watchdogs lurking around the dark corridors and corners of the domed palace, waiting to report on some misdeed for the AGG to come down heavily on the ruler and have him deposed. He also stated his opinion of what should be done with the administration of Baroda, 'It appears to me that, as a matter of general policy, it is desirable that all first-class states should be directly under the government of India, rather than under a provincial government; unless there are very strong reasons to the contrary. I wish in the last fifty years, the government of India had found itself obliged to take the direct supervision of Baroda state from Bombay government...'[3]

Further, there was very adverse criticism of Elliot's handling of the Barkhali land department. Originally, it was intended to properly devise a system that would clearly indicate the ownership of these lands by delving into the records of alienated lands and bringing some sort of order in their tenure. As mentioned before, in the past, rulers had indiscriminately gifted lands for some favour done or to their favourites in a generous mood. During Sayajirao III's rule, attempts were being made to scrutinize title deeds so as to assess their validity, which was bound to cause hostility arising out of discontent among the landowners, particularly among those whose claims to the lands were invalid. It was not the aim of the department to expropriate such lands, but to make the owners pay their dues to the government. The owners, as a reaction to the measure taken by the department, complained to the Residency against it. Biddulph tried to make capital out of the situation that would show the administration of Sayajirao III's in a poor light and thought to recommend to his superiors that they should call for a report on the aims and methods of the Barkhali department. Elliot, not one to sidestep issues, compiled a long exhaustive report on what had been asked. After reading it, the Indian government came to the conclusion that Baroda's policy, in respect of its alienated lands, was far more lenient than their own.

The administrative procedures introduced by Sayajirao III were so strong and efficient that Biddulph had to wait for five years before an opportunity presented itself to show up the administration of Baroda in a poor light and get him deposed.

Sayajirao III's mind was full of his schemes for introducing compulsory education in the state, though his ill health kept acting as an impediment to putting thoughts into action. He was advised to try a cure at Carlsbad and he left in April 1893 unaccompanied by his wife, who was in the last stages of her pregnancy, travelling to Triest by *Austrian Lloyd*. This time

Biddulph for reasons of his own did not object to the trip but insisted that a political officer should go along. Sayajirao III was pleased to find that he had a small staff to cater to his needs. He expresses to his minister in one of his letters from Vienna in May 1893, that it was satisfying to have a small number of well-trained assistants who knew their job rather than 'a large number which mostly consists of useless idle men'. While holidaying in the quiet resorts of the Swiss Alps, he met Edward St Clair Weeden, a young man from Oxford and a protégé of Elliot's who later joined the Maharaja's staff as a reader. Sayajirao III's other reader, Sardesai, filled the post adequately but was handicapped by his ignorance of English literature. With Weeden, the Maharaja was able to scale new heights in the field of English literature. He delighted in the *Adventures of Alice in Wonderland*, was rewarded a rich and thrilling reading experience in the *Decline and Fall of the Roman Empire* and together they even tried to produce an abridged version of Gibbon's work under the title *From Caeser to Sultan*. Weeden soon became a friend of the family and is said to have become infatuated with Maharaja's daughter Indira.

Meanwhile, while Sayajirao III was in Europe Chimnabai II was not having it easy, being within reach of government irritations. Mr French, who had been engaged as the children's tutor, had attended a Government House reception where 'he was told by the Governor Harris that Maharani Chimnabai had shown discourtesy to his wife by failing to pay a call on her'. He added, 'Her Majesty the Queen was sure to be annoyed if she were to know of this lapse'. [4] Chimnabai II, who was hardly in a condition to pay formal calls on governors' wives, packed her bags and left Poona for Baroda. It was there that on 31 August her son Dhairyashilrao was born.

In Carlsbad, Sayajirao III met Viceroy Lansdowne and probably conscious that his absence from the state might meet with the viceroy's disapproval explained, it is to be presumed, before the man could ask the reason that had prompted the trip. No one regretted the Maharaja's absences from the state more than the Maharaja himself as is testified to in his letter to Lord Reay in July declaring that 'he felt more than anyone else the evils of his absence'. He went back to Baroda in October only to return seven weeks later to spend the winter months in the Riviera and complete his cure as advised by his doctors. His departure this time met with high disapprobation from Viceroy Lansdowne. The reason, or rather the excuse, to exert his authority and prevent Sayajirao III from embarking on another voyage was provided by the disturbance that had taken place recently in the state of Baroda. When Sayajirao III had returned in October, the capital had been in the grip of a 'particularly obnoxious bout of khatpat'. There had been resentment among the Gujaratis against the Marathas considering them as usurpers who had no right to own land in their province much less rule them. They had conveniently forgotten that if not for the Gaekwads, they would still have been subjected to Muslim domination or worse, the British would have subjected them to their particular brand of tyranny. It was because of the Gaekwads' relationship with the Crown and the paramount power in England that allowed a Gaekwad supremo to rule without undue interference. Biddulph, of course, seized the opportunity to create a disturbance that would end in Sayajirao III's deposition and sided with one faction of the opposing parties, namely, the Gujaratis, and also craftily won over Manibhai Jassabhai, who had been appointed as the dewan in 1891. Instead of putting down the strife, Biddulph abetted the Gujaratis to incite trouble so that it could be linked to Sayajirao III's absence from his state and brand him as an irresponsible ruler who neglected his administration. Biddulph had his knife ready to plunge into Elliot's back too. Elliot had decided to continue working in the service of the Baroda state, instead of reverting to his original post of an ICS officer. Elliot's decision to serve Baroda had already lost him the chance of a place in the hierarchy of the Indian Civil Service. Perhaps he enjoyed his work in Baroda service or perhaps it was his fondness for his old pupil with whom he shared a rare camaraderie—whatever it was, it had made him an enemy of Resident Biddulph.

Lord Lansdowne was quick to remark with belligerence that the 'native prince' had got quite above himself and should be put down. He issued an ultimatum that he should hand over the administration of the state to the administrative council with 'substantial authority' to govern in his absence. It was only a ruse to get Biddulph what he wanted, which was unfettered authority to interfere in the administration of Baroda. In the end, Sayajirao III thinking that it would be better for him to be far away from an atmosphere that was bristling with hostility signed an agreement with the AGG along with his dewan Manibhai acting as a witness. The terms of the agreement were altered by Biddulph to suit his purpose and Sayajirao III trusting his dewan signed it without further ado, an impulse that he was to regret later. In his letter dated 24 September 1895 to Dr Nevins, he alluded to the powers of the Resident Agent and said, 'The effects of my absence are determined very much by the personal characteristics of this officer; but it may be generally stated that the result of my being away is to make his intervention more frequent and more felt. The result of this is external and I might add, needless intervention is that it multiplies and accentuates the slight inconveniences of my absence into serious difficulties.'

30

Leaving Troubled Waters for Distant Lands

Thus, in the middle of December 1893, Sayajirao III left Baroda for Europe. This was to be his longest absence from the state and the system that he had organized earlier of keeping in touch with the administrative affairs of the state continued as before and with more promptness and alacrity.

Copies of all political correspondence were sent to him with a précis of the history of each case. Reports from his ministers and the heads of all departments were sent to him for approval or any changes to be made, or for incorporating some new methods in the departments of agriculture, education and others which he had seen abroad and had proved effective. Weekly reports from ministers and monthly reports from the heads of subhas as well as heads of departments also had to be sent to him. Even the agenda for all council meetings were forwarded to him. Cables flew back and forth on matters of urgency that needed his decision. This way he made himself cognizant of all the functions of all departments, holding the reins of his government firmly in his hands.

On this trip, he visited Constantinople in addition to all the other places he had visited earlier. Chimnabai II accompanied him after delivering their son Dhairyashilrao earlier in August that year. Their children were left behind with their tutors Thomas Harvey French and Mrs French. However, Sayajirao III had little respite from his ailments on the voyage. Dr Hojel, who had been appointed as his personal physician a few months earlier, also accompanied him on the voyage and advised a month's stay in the south of France, from where he remarked in one of his letters home that the carnival in Nice reminded him of 'our Holi' and lamented that 'western education and its influence had deprived the life and vitality of our Indian festivals'.

In France, Sayajirao III showed a marked improvement in his health and spirits and immediately penned a letter to Elliot that at least hundred villages must have elective village councils before he left India next. 'I am deeply interested in that measure and wish to extend it to all my state. It will be the keynote of what I wish to develop...the policy of the curtailment of people's rights is ...weakening the Rajas.'[1]

Before he left Baroda, there had been some friction with the AGG. Sayajirao III complained, some time after his return, that he had been forced to delegate practically all his powers to the council and to the AGG.

Like an actor waiting in the wings for his cue, Aurobindo Ghosh entered the services of Baroda in the capacity of a subordinate officer in the revenue department. Sayajirao III returned to Baroda in January 1895 after an absence of nearly a year, only to find the state in chaos. There were sporadic disturbances erupting in some parts of the city. Discontentment seemed to prevail in Baroda and Sayajirao III blamed his absence for it.

The truth of the matter was that two plotters—Biddulph and Manibhai—had been busy stirring discontentment wherever they could.

'I am astonished,' Sayajirao III expressed in one of his letters to Colonel N. C. Martinelli, the officiating AGG, soon after his return, 'at the change wrought in the people during the last twelve months...Khatpat is very rampant. How one is forcibly reminded of old khatpati Baroda.... Without a great change, which I am afraid cannot safely be postponed too long, I cannot expect thorough sympathy and honest help. I don't think I am faithfully and rightly served by those from whom I have a right to expect it.'

The allusion to 'old khatpati Baroda' is to the days of Sayajirao II and Ganpatrao, and to the famous report of Colonel J. Outram of 30 April 1851, which led to his temporary removal from Baroda by the Bombay government, stung by his criticisms of their neglect in dealing with the situation. They later relented and sent Outram back to the Residency in spite of Ganpatrao's protests.

Sayajirao III remained in Baroda for the next five years—except for leaving for the hills in the summer and one brief visit to Egypt, he remained in the state to put things back in order.

Elliot left for England leaving behind his deputy Vasudev Sadashiv Bapat in charge. Now Bapat was known for his irascible temperament and already with the accusation of being one of the authors of *The Groans of Baroda* hanging over his head, he soon made enemies—his chief one being Manibhai. Soon, there were corruption charges against him and the case was brought to court. Instead of putting the complaints down to the daily petty feuds between Gujaratis and Maharashtrians, they were blown out of proportion with Manibhai siding with the Gujaratis. Bapat had displeased the dewan with his cocksure attitude and his irascible temperament. As soon as Bapat got to know that E. Maconochie from the Indian Civil Service, and who was another Phayre in the making, had been promoted in his place and given the powers of a special magistrate to try the charges against him, and, unable to bear the cold, disapproving stares he was subjected to from the officials in Baroda as well as the locals, he decided to sprint across to the railway station on the pretext of seeing a friend off, jumped into a moving train while the startled policemen sent to keep a watch on him looked on and escaped to Poona. Manibhai's reaction to this was that Bapat's escape was an admission of his guilt and announced that a commission should be set up to try the case in his absence. Bapat upon hearing that Maconochie would not be the judge, sent word that he would present himself before the commission. In Poona, the most eminent lawyers rallied to his support, thus drawing attention to the dissension between the two factions of the people of Baroda—the Maharashtrians against the Gujaratis providing a *cause célèbre*. Newspaper editors of both the factions had a field day playing up the 'contest' to the hilt with wild accusations against their respective opponents. The Maharashtrian press criticized Manibhai and the Gujarati press criticized Bapat. The Bombay English papers were severe on the Maharaja and Elliot, while rending solid support to the AGG and the dewan. Biddulph, of course, with this event had hit the jackpot. Though both factions were equally loyal to Gaekwad, the fact that the Gaekwads chose to marry only within their clan must have seemed like they were a sort of colonizers. When Sayajirao III was in Baroda, his presence acted like a douse on the flaring hostilities on both sides but in his absence, an incident like this made the discord flare up. But at that moment the contest had become Maharashtrians versus Gujaratis in Sayajirao III's absence.

The prosecution too had engaged some lawyers of repute headed by Ferozeshah Mehta of Bombay. Ferozeshah on analysing the case found a lot of the charges against the accused baseless as most of the evidence brought forward had been fabricated by the Baroda officials under strict instructions from the two principal antagonists of Bapat—Manibhai and Maconochie. Ferozeshah, well known for his integrity, decided to abandon the case. With Ferozeshah abandoning the case midway, his place was taken by another barrister from Bombay whose name was Branson. The commission sat on the case for four months during which Bapat and his lawyers from Poona were able to expose the bribery and corruption that was resorted to by Manibhai and the Resident to get their own way with the officials. Witnesses were called in to testify to this. One reported that he was instructed by the dewan to follow the police inspector's instructions verbatim. The police inspector whose name was Chhotumia told the witness to swear in court that he had bribed Bapat for favours. The witness had done so under threat of imprisonment.

Another witness said he too was made to sign a confession but in a fit of remorse had stated below his signature 'who denies what is stated above' this was written in the Marathi Modi script (a type of script written in longhand), which the police officer being a Gujarati could not read. The case was dissolved but the war of words between the two factions remained unabated and also minor incidents of violence in the state were reported through the press. Manibhai and the Resident were lending their strong support to the Gujaratis, so that ultimately they could be made to turn on Sayajirao III. The Maharaja being a Maratha did not escape from the crossfire, with the Gujaratis hinting that he was partial to the Maharashtrians residing in Gujarat. Sayajirao III was advised to return by relatives and Lord Reay who reminded him that an absentee ruler was always in the wrong. But Sayajirao III, mindful of the probability that his return might cause more damage than good, as the two scheming villains would have pointed out that he had rushed back to save his underlings from just punishment, opted to stay on. He was also aware that a Resident's tenure of office was five years and Biddulph's had already run to four.

In the final analysis of the case Bapat was able to prove his innocence. He also proved that the charges had been cooked up against him, yet he was not acquitted. The members of the commission recommended that Bapat be sent to prison for six months and asked to pay a fine of Rs 10,000. The members of the commission were Baroda officials and could not risk the displeasure of the AGG and the dewan. The final verdict was left to the Maharaja, who passed on the case to three judges of the high court and when they too found the accused not guilty, Bapat was acquitted but removed from Baroda service as the Maharaja felt that the place was still bristling with hostility towards him.

Biddulph, who had been aiming for the deposition of the Maharaja and Elliot being sent back in disgrace, had to swallow his disappointment and anger and resorted to slandering of names of those two to the peers in the hierarchy.

A flurry of correspondence were exchanged between the Resident and the viceroy where his criticism of Sayajirao III was so contradictory as to verge on the ridiculous; in fact, it did trigger quite a few titters among those who were privy to it. For example, in a letter he criticizes the Maharaja, charging him of disloyalty to the Britsh government. 'His attitude is most unsatisfactory. He has been taught to believe that the Baroda state is practically equal to the British Government. It has no more right to interfere in the affairs of Baroda than...in the affairs of Denmark or Portugual. This is his perpetual grievance that is conspicuous in all official dealings and manifests itself in ill will towards Englishmen constantly shown in small matters.' The above paragraph roused a titter in the viceroy's secretariat for someone who had read the report had marked on the side 'but see overleaf' where Biddulph had assailed the Maharaja for his marked preference for European society.[2] Such contradictory remarks of no other but one who was still the undoubted favourite of the British Empire would certainly have raised the eyebrows of those highbrow officials in England. The Resident's vitriolic pen didn't spare Elliot either. He was supposed to have poisoned the ruler's mind against British authority in India and at the same time aspired to complete domination over the ruler's mind and rule as a regent. According to Biddulph, the people of the Baroda state were unhappy and the sardars deeply discontented. He blamed the Maharaja's long absences from the state for its deplorable administration and recounted with facts and figures his period of absences from the Baroda state.

Nothing of his carefully aimed darts had any effect in deposing the Maharaja but it did succeed in bringing coolness into the relations between the Gaekwad royal family and the British officials. Poor Elliot did not fare as well for he was sent to Bijapur as its collector and asked to sever all connection with Baroda, which must have caused him a great deal of pain because in the twenty years of service there, the people had grown to like and trust him. Bijapur was something like a punishment station. He was, however, recalled to England a few months later without being given a reason, where he lived quietly in retirement. The exact reason was never known but he had, according to English standards, broken the golden rule—an ICS officer employed by the British must not show loyalty to a native prince. As per Biddulph's reports, he had 'gone against the grain of racial and service loyalties'. Moreover, his wife had served Chimnabai II as a companion on a salary basis—the propriety or impropriety of it being a debatable point. However, earlier, Mrs Reynolds had also worked as a companion in the same capacity, so why was it wrong for Mrs Elliot to do so too? Apparently it was in the eyes of those wanting to get rid of Elliot as speedily as possible.

Sayajirao III, unhappy over the manner of his friend's dismissal, asked whether Elliot could serve in Baroda after his retirement but that query was never answered, and the Maharaja thought it wiser to not press the matter. In his letter to his friend Lord Reay, he complained that 'you could no longer get people to work with honest and unflinching courage...'

Biddulph had served his term and was recalled to England. He left with the small satisfaction that at least his hatred of Elliot had succeeded in getting him removed from Baroda.

Sayajirao IIII replaced Manibhai in November 1895 with a man who did not belong to either of the two warring factions of Baroda—V.R. Iyengar, a native of Madras (now Chennai). He was the new dewan of Baroda.

Explaining his dismissal of Manibhai and other officials to V. Samarth, one of the authors of the pamphlet *The Groans of Baroda*, who had been employed as a revenue officer in Baroda and had left to pursue his revolutionary activities, in a letter, Sayajirao III wrote that from the confusion arising from the mismanagement during his absence from Baroda, 'the machinery of government had been thrown out of gear'. He had been kept in the dark about all the corruption that had taken place in the settlement department, the administration of justice had been slack and there had been a total disregard of his instructions in the accounts department with the result that progress had been thrown out of the window and confusion remained. To Dr Nevins, he wrote that 'had not the Residency forced my hand to delegate all my powers to the council and the AGG, all the mischief could have been avoided'. It was evident that Sayajirao III felt a distinct grievance against the Residency, or at least, against some person or people in it, whom he suspected of being behind the troubles in his state. He wrote particularly of a certain assistant in a sarcastic manner to Manibhai in August 1895, 'He thought I am told that he was an able police officer, having learnt that useful art in the malicious districts of Burma.'³ Echoes of the storm of 1895 continued to be heard through the Maharaja's correspondence for a considerable time. To Lord Reay, he complained in January 1897 that the AGG did not have the independence of character to fight for the views of Baroda against the surrounding political officers and others, and suggested that this was one of the reasons which had resulted in the Residency being reduced to a lower status. Whether this was considered as gross impertinence on the part of a native king is not known but this subtle criticism definitely bore fruit. In April 1899, the designation of the Resident was restored (earlier the political officer was designated Resident then was replaced with AGG, Colonel Martelli being the first to bear it).

Sayajirao III had much to say to Lord Northbrook a few weeks later about the removal of Elliot from his service. The officials who wanted to get rid of Elliot had talked of him as his old tutor exercising absolute influence over him. He reiterated his opinion with a profound remark, 'This sort of report, especially when first started by Residents and other European officers, will always serve to blind people.' Former Residents', he added, 'are said to have recorded unfavourable opinions of Elliot; but the truth is that they, and still more the native officials, were jealous of the trust imposed in him. The manner of his departure and the circumstances under which it was brought about here had a very demoralizing effect on the administration. You can no longer get people to do progressive work, which goes against the grain of the people with an honest and unflinching courage!'⁴ Elliot retired from work in India in May 1896, but the Maharaja's affectionate regard for his old friend and tutor was unabated until his death in London on 18 March 1910. Sayajirao III must have silently grieved for him and felt the loss of his companionship deeply.

31

A Difficult Phase

The new AGG, Colonel N.C. Martelli arrived to take up the Residency in Baroda.

Sayajirao III, for his part, had not allowed these turbulent times to disrupt the smooth tempo of his life and work. He and the new AGG got along well, as is evident in his letter to Lord Northbrook referring to Martelli's 'kindness and sympathy'. As long as the Residency did not create undue trouble, he could handle all the problems and getting along with the Resident was half the battle won! Martelli was an amiable person, which made things easy. The Maharaja, who was probably carrying a hangover from the behaviour of the previous two Residents, was inclined, at times, to be short with him, but the other man did not take offence. With nothing disrupting the smooth tenor of their daily routine, life continued. At a banquet given in honour of the new viceroy, Lord Elgin, and Lady Elgin at the Laxmi Vilas Palace in 1896, Sayajirao III in proposing a toast to his distinguished guests said, 'Ten years have rolled by since I had the pleasure of welcoming Your Excellency's distinguished predecessor, the Marquis of Dufferin, who was the first viceroy to visit this city. Whatever changes may have taken place in the country during this period, the Baroda Raj in its loyalty and friendship to the British Throne is as firm and unflinching now as it ever was, indeed our affection for and veneration of the Sovereign Lady are growing deeper and deeper daily!' These words were spoken with such sincerity that when broadcasted all over London would have helped to smooth ruffled feathers.

Apart from the confusion and chaos that had arisen in the long absence of the Maharaja, the financial department gave cause for worry. Sayajirao III was astonished to find that Baroda had been spending, on an average, over Rs 4,00,000 more than its income since Manibhai had not been able to keep within the limits of the budget and had also delayed to present a new one. This state of affairs had to be brought to an end.

With Sayajirao III's personal supervision and control, the political and financial problems took a turn for the better, but two domestic afflictions in successive years caused him grief. In June 1897, he lost his adoptive sister Princess Tarabai who succumbed to liver cirrhosis in her twenty-sixth year. It brought a curtailment of the public ceremonies, including the celebration of Queen Victoria's diamond jubilee in Baroda. The Maharaja, however, in commemoration of that auspicious occasion ordered the building of a ward with fifteen beds in Dufferin Hospital and named it 'Victoria Ward'.

In the autumn of 1897, Sayajirao III was sufficiently recovered and the stability of the state satisfactorily restored to allow him to visit Egypt. He planned to be away for two months. He sailed up the Nile to Cairo and through the region of the pyramids to Thebes. The irrigation works in Egypt by Sir William Willcocks, a student of the Roorkee College in India, aroused his deep interest as did the progress on the Assuan Dam. He was always conscious of the importance of water for health and sanitation. Two months later when he returned to India, he found affairs anything but peaceful.

The second bereavement was more close to his heart when Jamnabai passed away on 29 November 1898. Thus, the two kinswomen with whom he could attach his boyhood days in Baroda were snuffed out from his life and only the memories remained.

Son after there was an outbreak of plague and the measures taken to cope with it aroused a lot of opposition. In his letter to Elliot in May 1898, Sayajirao IIII wrote about the troubles that he was facing in dealing with the Resident and other British officers who constantly came in to inspect the arrangements, 'These well-meant inspections have a very tangible result on native states.'

Relations with the Residency became more strained. As if this was not enough, there was a storm brewing in Kadi district. The ambitious 'Thakores', who were the hereditary revenue collectors of Kadi (Mehsana) district, refused to allow Baroda officials to carry out a survey of the entire territory of the state as they were defrauding the cultivators and along with the government were collecting far more revenue than they were entitled to. They convinced the ignorant cultivators to do the same as it was inimical to their interests as well. Together, they barred the officials from entering their properties. Matters came to a head, resulting in a massive showdown in the village of Pilwai, which necessitated calling out the troops to crush the insurgents, which they did, and the ringleaders were punished and sentenced to severe imprisonment.

Troubles don't come in singles is a clichéd axiom and well justified in this case as a famine followed close on the heels of khatphat. In the monsoon of 1899, there was no rainfall in Gujarat as well as Kathiawad, and as a result, all the crops were ruined. People were faced with death and devastation, and prices of food commodities increased by a 100 per cent. Large amounts of rice were imported from Rangoon. Sayajirao III visited the famine struck areas and relief work commenced with 55,000 workers being employed for it. Earlier, before the tragic onslaught of the plague and famine, another disaster had struck the state when Lord Elgin paid a visit to Baroda in November 1896. The usual celebrations to mark the visit of a high dignitary of the British hierarchy were on in full swing. A display of fireworks was another aspect of the variety entertainment put together for the visit and was held in the public park. People thronged to the park to view the fireworks and also to get a glimpse of the viceroy. The railings of the bridge, on which hundreds of onlookers had climbed to get a better view, collapsed due to the weight—many were killed and quite a few injured.

Coming on top of this tragedy was an epidemic of the bubonic plague which ravaged many lives in early 1897 and lasted till the summer of that year. The drastic measures taken to deal with the epidemic were severe that the people dreaded the measures more than the disease itself. People were evacuated from their homes and shifted to camps. All the clothes and other utensils of houses that were suspected to have come in contact with the disease were burnt. It must be remembered here that most of the inhabitants of Gujarat and Kathiawad were uneducated and saw these measures only as a means on the part of the British officers to tyrannize them, which resulted in hatred of the authorities and culminated in the murder of a plague officer of Poona. On top of this came the famine of 1899, as mentioned before, resulting in the loss of more lives in Gujarat and Kathiawad. Hitherto, eastern Baroda had been considered practically immune from famine, though the western section of the state, like the rest of Kathiawad had suffered severely in 1877–78. But now in the monsoon of 1899, there had been complete failure of rain in Gujarat as well as Kathiawad. Lack of rainfall caused crops to wither and the farmers were plunged into penury and starvation for the rest of the people.

In 1891, the census record showed the population to be at 2,415,396. The census of 1901 showed it at 1,952,692. A reflection of the effect of the calamities. Sayajirao III, not one to sit quiet in the event of such tragedies affecting his people, set up an efficient system for relief work, which could be put into operation the moment it was required. Wells were sunk, tanks built for storage of water, drainages constructed and new railway embankments were built. Loans were advanced to farmers on easy terms to enable them to sink private wells, buy seeds and so on, and all those afflicted by the famine were given loans and state grants. The Maharaja also ordered the construction of the Orsang irrigation waterworks as part of the relief measures taken.

At its opening, Sayajirao III, amid cheers of those assembled, said, 'Gentlemen, my first duty before opening this work today is a very pleasant one. It is to thank the officers to whose exertions and intelligence the institution of this work is mainly due. At first, I have to thank Mr Khaserao Jadhav for his suggestion of this idea...the acuteness and intelligence which made him perceive the possibilities of the site deserve every single praise.'

There were loud cheers from his listeners.

'I have also to thank the engineers for the zeal and energy with which they have arranged the details of the scheme. Their professional ability has given a working shape to an excellent and highly practical idea. Their example is worthy of imitation, both the mental activity and shrewdness that suggested as well as the professional talent and energy which worked out the scheme. I trust that execution will be as sound and thorough as its development so far, and I may again have the occasion to thank them for completing ably what they have so ably initiated.'

Again there were cheers from the people.

'The relief work I am opening today is of some magnitude. Beneficial results beyond mere temporary relief are expected from it. Such an undertaking is eminently suited to the needs and warnings of the terrible visitation under which the country is suffering...'

After the Maharaja had spoken about the relief measures being undertaken for the victims, he asked the people gathered there at the site, 'Today is the opening of a work which will be of permanent agricultural benefit to the district...learn from this terrible experience, for relief measures may merely palliate the evil but not for a moment strike at its roots. If the evil is allowed to grow, eventually the resources, even of the richest government, will be baffled by it...The educated class must break through the bonds of apathy and dependence...'

The speech ended with loud cheers of appreciation from the people assembled there. Then, Sayajirao III proceeded to the site where arrangements had been made for laying the first stone of the works. Copies of the local papers—*Shri Sayaji Vijaya* and *Baroda Watsal*—with a few current coins of the Raj were placed by the Maharaja in the small pit prepared for receiving the first stone. After the stone was put into position, the Maharaja touched it with a silver hammer with an ivory handle, saying the words, 'I declare this stone well and truly laid.' He then ordered that the labourers should be fed with sweets and kansar at the expense of the state.[1]

Sayajirao III had sanctioned the building of a club where people could meet socially in a relaxed, friendly atmosphere and exchange views. The building took some time and when it was completed, the Maharaja was asked to formally open the club and address its members.

At the opening of the Sayaji Vihar Club on 10 April 1899, Sayajirao III addressed the gathering formally, 'Gentlemen, it was at your request some time ago that I laid the foundation stone of this building. It is again at your request that I am here to open your club. I congratulate you on your final completion of the building and on the inauguration of a laudable social undertaking, which I sincerely hope will bear all the wholesome fruits which such an institution is meant to produce. Some years have elapsed since the building was commenced, but let us hope that the proverb "Rome was not built in a day" will apply here in the best sense that even if its completion has been a little tardy, its career will be fortunate and lasting.

'A club is the expression of the most natural and universal impulse of gregarious mankind. Man's impulse is to seek the society of his fellows, which is his most essential happiness. Once conscious of it, he is always trying to find the best means of satisfying this instinct.In olden times, it found its outlet chiefly in family and village life, but formal institutions to bring together those who are connected not merely by the accident of birth or residence but by similar culture, objects or pursuits, come with a more complex civilization.We naturally feel the want of such institutions when we pass outside the limits of family circles, the more varied our lives and the more our interests are multiplied and differentiated, the more numerous and diverse in kind clubs become.

'Nowadays, even women need clubs! In the present age "the new woman" has appeared seeming to aspire not only to rival man, but if possible to bring about a reversal of the present mutual relation. In Europe, women have their own exclusive clubs, and even our ladies are fast copying their sisters of the West. It is hoped that our society, in attempting to assimilate this change, will not suffer from severe fatal indigestion!'

There was a ripple of laughter in the audience.

'Though in olden times clubs did not exist under the present name or in a formal manner, the concept itself has always been with us. Men always congregated under canvas roofs, under banyan trees, under an open roof with the Heaven above, often even in cellars, and in secret places of the earth. Now, with peace and an increase in material wealth and security, they meet in splendid ornamental buildings furnished with all the comforts and appliances representing a luxurious and finished civilization.

'The objects of such institutions remain after all essentially the same, however much the form, manner and the place may vary. Those objects are as various as the activities of civic society—literary society, sporting, medical, religious and political clubs are only a few of the multifarious varieties. We all know what potent dynamic forces the last two kinds have been in the history of human society, and what sinister forms one of them has taken when repressed by superior authority, or when struggling against the sympathies of the major part of the community. The club, as we now have it, is an institution on the western model. In our country, we had our castes and met under the roofs of influential men. Europe had its castes in the shape of guilds, but while there the institution liquefied and disappeared, with us, it has solidified perhaps beyond what is quite compatible with the laws of nature and the needs of humanity. But today, under the impact of western ideas, our form of social unions is weakened and crumbling; therefore, the need for an increase of clubs arises, so that these may replace where we cannot save those elements of the old society which met an imperative social want.

'Purely social clubs such as this one that we are opening, though the merits are not so obvious or striking, have effects which are pervasive, if more subtle and have the advantage of being almost always peaceful and beneficent (neighbourly, public-spirited). Their effect is to humanize and harmonize society by that free and kindly intercourse and interchange of thought which civilized and enlightened society demands, and for the sake of which it encourages such institutions. They help to remove sharp angles men present to each other and make comrades of them or at least good companions.

'Let me express hope that the present institution will work towards this goal. There are clubs which deserve to be named as "scandal clubs" into which the enemy, backbiting, too common in the outer world has been brought.

'This institution will, I am sure, be a very different one. Its members will abandon their rancour if it exists when they enter, and when they leave they will carry with them all good feelings of friendship to the outer world promoting peace, amity and concord.

'I gladly observe that you have recognized the liberal support given to you by the government in allowing you the land free of cost and also by meeting half the cost of the building. I also appreciate its desire to not merely employ you on a pay but to promote your health and happiness!'[2]

The club was opened before the Orsang irrigation works opened.

32

A European Trip

Sayajirao III's troubles were not over; Chimnabai II had been ailing for some time and a lady specialist was summoned from Bombay to diagnose the cause. After a brief examination, she advised immediate surgery and for that it was imperative for her to go to England for it.

This, coming at a time when it was more important to stand by his subjects in their hour of need and show a selfless devotion to duty, must have left the Maharaja in a quandary. To leave or not to leave that is the question! He must have debated within himself. A ruler going off, as was presumed by the people, on a pleasure trip was unavoidable, but the queen could not be sent alone for a major operation; besides, he too needed a change of climate and some air as he was being incessantly troubled with sleeplessness and stomach cramps. Also, his three sons were now ready for education abroad—Fatehsinghrao III was to be enrolled in a good university and Jaisinghrao and Shivajirao in some good public schools there.

Here, in Baroda, there was an able dewan and ministers to look after the administration. Relief work continued unabated, and there was really nothing more for him to do regarding the famine relief work by staying on. Thus, considering the matter in a more pragmatic light, he decided to leave for England in the spring of the year 1900. There was strong disapproval among the officials as well as the public at large who thought that the Maharaja was not acting in accordance with his image—an assiduous and benevolent ruler, devoted to the cause of his people—providing grounds for the officials of the Raj to raise their eyebrows and point a finger at him. Sayajirao III, not one to let himself be governed by the minds of others, one who knew his business, and who knew that his treaty rights allowed him to be an all but absolute ruler, felt he did not have to justify to anyone how many trips he made abroad and was free to come and go as he chose. The viceroy and the British officials in order to drive home the point that 'all Indian potentates were alike' set a fine example by touring all the famine-affected areas of the districts.

However, in spite of all his problems, Sayajirao III was never distracted from his schemes of general improvement in the state. Letters flew, back and forth from wherever he was, on questions of water supply, new methods for irrigation, the drainage system, a contract act for the state on the lines of the British act, the assimilation of the state currency to the British which would be a great boon for commerce at large. His preoccupied mind, which never had a moment's respite, was also occupied with his children's education. He wanted Prince Fatehsinghrao III to go to Eton or Harrow in 1895 but had to abandon the idea as it might prove too strenuous to gain admission by passing the entrance exams (he wrote in a letter to Dr Nevins dated 24 September). He then resolved to send him to Oxford instead and have him prepare for the entrance exams in Baroda to gain admission into the university. Sayajirao III entrusted the job of tutoring Fatehsinghrao III as well as Jaisinghrao and Shivajirao to Thomas Harvey French. In a letter to Dr Nevins in 1898, he stated that the prince had not done as well in the examination as he had been led to expect. 'Rich children have their own dangers.'[1] In a letter dated 2 May 1898 to French, who accompanied the prince on a trip to Japan after the examination, Sayajirao III expressed his opinion on Fatehsinghrao III learning to dance, with the comment, 'I do not wish him to be initiated into the art of cutting capers yet. Good manners may be taught without bringing youngsters into close contact with girls and young ladies.'[2]

As the world got ready to herald in the new century, there was a change in Baroda too with the arrival of the new viceroy, Lord Curzon, a year before. Lord Curzon who hailed from Keddleston was reputed to be 'more imperious than the Empress herself'.[3]

He was capable and very conscious of the fact that he was an Englishman—one of a race that was destined to become masters of the world. 'A dyed-in-the-wool Tory', he had no patience for those who had inherited wealth, titles or authority. Viceroy Curzon's particular brand of *de haut en bas* attitude towards native princes was far more offensive than Biddulph's antagonism or Phayre's venom. The year 1900 also brought a new AGG to Baroda—Colonel C.W. Ravenshaw, who had been an assistant to

Colonel Martelli. After the state of Baroda had been through a tumultuous phase with one calamity after another, not to mention the Pilwai rebellion which came on top of it, there was one silver lining in that dark phase that had served to make the situation bearable—the amicable relationship that Sayajirao III had with the Residency. Had Martelli been anything like his predecessor, things might have been very trying for the Maharaja to handle. Martelli just happened to be different. Unlike many of the arrogant British officials, he was blessed with an amiable, understanding nature and preferred to resort to diplomacy rather than enforce his will. Aware of the special sensitivities of Indian rulers, he made it a point to 'avoid misunderstandings and abrasive incidents in dealing with them.'[4] Indeed, he went out of his way in not retaliating even when provoked; for instance, when the Resident expressed his opinion to the official in charge that the arrangements made for shifting affected patients with plague was unsatisfactory, the Maharaja retorted with 'these remarks ought to be communicated to the dewan and not subordinate officials.'[5] A trivial matter such as this could have well been ignored, especially in the face of the fact that Martelli and the Maharaja had become such firm friends. In another instance, when Martelli within a few weeks of his arrival asked to see the Bapat commission report, he was royally snubbed by the Maharaja who waspishly reminded him, 'In the interest of the state, no such demands should be made, as such inquiries always do harm.'[6] A rebuff of this kind would never have been taken lightly by any other Resident, but not a frown marred Martelli's brow. It was his restraint and his amiable disposition that made him and Sayajirao III close friends. Both instances cited here were trivial matters and could have well been ignored, which would have been more in the spirit of their amicable relations. Perhaps the angst at the Raj and the unfair occupation of a country over which the British had no right whatsoever was beginning to be felt more and more as the days went by and was also starting to manifest itself in that he chose to take an official stand, and is a pointer to his stiffening attitude towards the Raj in general; it also explains the Maharaja's involvement in the Indian national movement in the years to come.

Among his numerous, multifarious concerns over public affairs, Sayajirao III found time in the summer of 1899 to respond to Viceroy Curzon's invitation to visit him in Simla (now Shimla). The Maharaja seemed to form an impression that the viceroy was very clever and businesslike, while 'other aspects of the man were to strike him later'.[7]

Famine was still prevailing in Baroda and Sayajirao III, with grave concern over the situation as well as over Chimnabai II's health, reluctantly boarded the P&O *S. S. Caledonia* for Europe in May 1900, with the maharani and his five children in tow. Always maintaining that travel was the best way to broaden one's views and implement reforms, the Maharaja advocated travel to youngsters as an integral part of their education. This thinking manifested itself in the number of scholarships that the Maharaja Sayajirao University of Baroda has given to young professors and students to enable them to enrol for higher studies in universities abroad.

The twenty-people party that accompanied the royal couple included a secretary, a companion, two tutors, maids, valets and a chef. After a brief halt of ten days in Paris, the entourage spent most of the first three months of the trip in London. Sayajirao III had rented Bushey Hall as his residence.

The royal entourage's departure from Baroda was noted and frowned upon by none other than Viceroy Curzon, who was relaxing in the cool hills of Simla. Viceroy Curzon also pointed out to his officials that the native princes had duties and obligations towards their subjects as well as towards their masters, and should 'devote their best energies not to the pursuit of pleasure, nor to the cultivation of absentee interests and amusements'.[8]

The Times in an editorial on 27 August also endorsed this criticism. 'The Curzon Circular' was circulated which stated that any native prince who chose to go abroad should have a valid reason endorsed by the Resident for doing so and could leave only after getting prior sanction from the viceroy. Plainly put, meant that any Resident could object and the prince's permission to leave would be withheld!

Needless to say, Sayajirao III was unduly disturbed by the circular which was grossly unfair.

Being summer, Sayajirao III found the climate in London neither bracing nor very salubrious; also, he was racked with worry by the issue of the famous or rather infamous Curzon Circular that was doing the rounds. He had also just been through a bout of anxiety over the maharani's operation which had been performed by Dr Mary Scharlieb, who was well known to the royal couple through her medical work in India.

The circular was not actually made public until late August 1900. Lovat Fraser, in his book *India Under Curzon and After*, writes, 'It obtained a publicity which I believe was never intended, and was the object of a good deal of criticism arising partly from lack of knowledge of the facts and partly from the indiscreetly literal manner in which the letter was interpreted by some political officers.'

The Times of 25 August published, from its Simla correspondent, the gist of the circular, which was stated to have been issued to all local administrations, directing that all appeals for leave to visit Europe by native chiefs shall be submitted to the government of India, that would exercise unfettered discretion whether to allow or refuse them. The government, it was pointed out, in return for its protection of the ruling families, was 'entitled to claim that the ruler shall devote his best energies, not to the pursuit of pleasure nor to the cultivation of an absentee interest in amusements, but to the welfare of his own subjects and the administration.'

The Times correspondent added that the letter should have a good effect on chiefs such as the Gaekwad of Baroda and the Maharaja of Kapurthala, who were the habit of constantly visiting Europe and leaving their states in the hands of their dewans. But, didn't the British officials themselves escape to cooler climates in India and abroad leaving much of their work to their subordinates? This was just one of their ways to bring an Indian ruler to subservience. In Sayajirao III's letter dated 8 August to Dewan Iyengar, he said, 'Allow me to remark, without wishing to injure the feelings of anybody, that our health and our interests are treated as nothing when a decision is being arrived at, as to our trip to Europe. Had I the experience and assurance that we can always arrange our journey to Europe, and be also sure that during our absence the state affairs would be carried on smoothly, I should never have allowed Her Highness to suffer as much as she has done.'

Viceroy Curzon had passed through Baroda a week before this letter was written and had asked to be received by Sayajirao III in person in the following November. But that had not been possible as the Maharaja had been obliged to stay on abroad due to health reasons concerning not only himself but his wife as well. On this pretext, Viceroy Curzon refused a state reception. Sayajirao III went to Scotland where he was the guest of Mr and Mrs Kent at Lochindorb; Chimnabai II and he then travelled to Germany so that she could benefit from the waters at Schalbad; from there, they went to attend a Paris exhibition and finally to Brighton to test its therapeutic waters. They were not back in Baroda until January 1901.

Most of his letters to his dewan during this phase are full of his views of the high-handedness of the British government in India towards Indian kings and princes and his opinion of the circular.

'I do not think the Rajas are well treated,' he stated, 'we are supposed to be chiefs, but are treated worse than paid servants.'[9] Nevertheless, this was his sixth trip to Europe and he made the most of it. He renewed his acquaintance with Lord Northbrook, Lord and Lady Reay, Sir John Watson and a host of other dignitaries but was especially gratified by an invitation from Queen Victoria to stay at Windsor. On this occasion, Sayajirao III introduced his three sons to the queen and told her of his intention of giving them an English education. The dowager queen heartily approved. It proved to be his last and final meeting with the gracious queen, who had been genuinely fond of him.

Sayajirao III was back in Baroda on 12 January 1901. Ten days later, Queen Victoria died. With her passing away, the curtain finally came down on an era of gentility and graciousness, and a new one began. Public offices and schools were closed on orders from the Maharaja as a mark of sorrow and respect. He also donated Rs 1,00,000 to the Victoria Memorial Fund.

Sayajirao III had taken his three sons to England with the sole purpose of getting them into Oxford. While Fatehsinghrao III was preparing for the entrance to Balliol College, princes Jaisinghrao and Shivajirao attended the preparatory school run by C. C. Lynham, who was popularly known as 'the skipper' as he was fond of yachting. Nevertheless, the Maharaja had some misgivings about sending Fatehsinghrao III to Europe for education as is evident in his letter to French after his return to India. 'It is a very bold experiment to send Fatehsinghrao III to Europe for education. It will depend upon him to make a success of this experiment. Kindly impress upon him the seriousness of the step.'[10] His anxiety over the matter was not groundless because Fatehsinghrao III failed in the entrance exams at Oxford and Sayajirao III was prompted to take all his sons back to India with him. The Maharaja like any other anxious parent, had wanted to do his best for them. He hated being parted from them and was fearful that with the circular posing a threat to his foreign trips, he might not be able to see them for several years. However, he soon sent Fatehsinghrao III back to Oxford for another attempt with French. In July 1901, he received the glad tidings that Fatehsinghrao III had passed the entrance for Oxford. Rejoicing over this news, he wrote to Lord Reay with whom he had kept up a steady friendship, 'As soon as he finishes his studies, I shall systematically initiate him in the workings of all the departments.'

The other tiding was that Colonel C.W. Ravenshaw was transferred and replaced by A.J. Meade of the Indian Civil Service, who was the son of Sir Charles Meade, the Resident at the time of Sayajirao III's adoption. The Maharaja wrote to him on 5 March 1902 and expressed his wish that as Viceroy Curzon would be visiting Hyderabad the following month, he would be glad 'to welcome him to Baroda during the course of his trip'. But Viceroy Curzon was still smarting from the slight he had received from the king who had refused to return to the capital at the time of the viceroy's visit in November 1900 and did not respond to the invitation. Sayajirao III's strong disapprobation of the Curzon Circular had made its way in letters to several friends both British and Indian. One of his letters to Sir John Puleston expressed his hurt and anger in the most forthright manner, 'It is a cruel and humiliating treatment we Indian Rajas are put to...to make the Rajas dependent on British officials saps their very position as ruling chiefs, and renders them quite unfit to protect their own interests and those of their states and subjects.'[11] He also expressed his views strongly on the circular to an ex-AGG in Baroda, General Watson, which undoubtedly must have reached the ears of the viceroy. Meanwhile, forty-eight hours after Queen Victoria's death, the viceroy arranged for a durbar to be held in Delhi in honour of the new Emperor Edward VII and publicly proclaim him as the emperor of India. In the ordinary course of things, the word durbar means holding court, but it gained monumental significance during the days of the Raj and was held with a lot of extravagant display of grandeur, 'An extravaganza of oriental splendor organized with occidental meticulousness of detail.'[12]

Lord Curzon, as the monarch's representative, would receive his share of homage from the Indian rulers and important subjects on the occasion and was eagerly looking forward to it. He saw himself leading the elephant procession followed by all the princes and kings of India seated on their state elephants, according to rank. The respective princes and kings were asked to get ready for the great day and get their elephants trained appropriately for the procession.

Sayajirao III, still annoyed with the circular, was most reluctant to fall in with the instructions issued from the high command regarding the durbar and dashed off a reply to the Resident saying that it would seriously inconvenience him to take part in the procession. If it hadn't been for the circular, perhaps he would have been more prudent and cautious but understandably the circular had provoked him beyond measure. Unfortunately, without Madhavrao and his good friend Elliot to restrain him, the letter was sent without any fear of dire consequences. Madhavrao, of course, would have been shocked to the core.

Now, King Edward, who had met Sayajirao III several times and knew him to be a responsible, progressive and popular ruler, dismissed the circular as of no consequence as long as the length of absenteeism of the rulers was not detrimental to the affairs of their respective states. Viceroy Curzon refrained from pursuing this line of thought and decided to get even with the Maharaja by insisting that the uniforms of the personal servants of the ruler be changed from the traditional red to something else so as to not clash with those of the viceregal bodyguards who also wore red. Viceroy Curzon also insisted that the elephant procession would be led by him and the princes and kings were to follow him, a sign that he was master and the rulers his subordinates. He derived immense satisfaction from the knowledge that he would, as the representative of the emperor, sit on the throne in the durbar and would receive all the homage that would be paid to him as the highest-ranking personage in the land. Regarding uniforms, Sayajirao III had no choice but to comply besides it was a trivial matter; regarding the procession, he demurred at first, but since it was construed as a sign of disrespect to the emperor, he complied. However, he let his opinion be known through his secretary.

'His Highness,' wrote his secretary, 'is ready to withdraw his refusal... but it seems to him very hard that he should pretend to do so willingly, spontaneously, as if it were of his own accord, what is only forced upon him under the threat of an insult... As regards the plea that His Highness is now in the good grace of the government of India or of Anglo-Indian society, His Highness is aware that argument will always be brought forward when his hands are to be forced and he is to be coerced into a certain line of action.'[13]

He sent a second letter dated 27 August 1902 through his dewan R.V.

Damnaskar, 'It is more than needless,' he protested, 'to bring in the person of His Majesty, the Emperor into this question, as it would be folly, to say the least, to entertain the notion of any disrespect towards him. It is most inconvenient that such official matters should be so mixed up with questions of one's feelings towards high personages...I may suggest that I am more in favour of the ceremonies [that were] observed when Lord Lytton arrived in Delhi at the time of the Imperial Durbar of 1877 than the present procedure, which, it seems to me, is lacking in respect towards the native princes.'[14] Curiously, it had been Viceroy Curzon who had said in the year 1877 that 'he was most anxious to provide that the Indian princes should not be mere spectators at the *durbar* as they were in 1877, but actors in it'.[15] Viceroy Curzon had probably wanted an exaggerated display of obsequiousness from the native princes and kings. Ultimately, Sayajirao III did not take part in the procession but let it be known that he would attend the coronation durbar in Delhi, and the newspapers accordingly reported the information. Viceroy Curzon had no choice but to accept, as the matter could not be forced in view of the fact that King Edward himself would not be present and the viceroy was only acting as the king's representative. The durbar was to be held in Delhi on 1 January 1903.

Sayajirao III did attend the durbar but very subtly let it be known to all the spectators and chiefly to the representative of His Imperial Majesty that he was paying homage to the king only, not to his local representative. When it was his turn, which was second after the Nizam of Hyderabad, he turned and made a short speech in which he asked the viceroy to convey 'to His Majesty the King-Emperor, my hearty and loyal congratulations on his Coronation'.[16] Thus, in a coup de grâce masterstroke, he reduced the viceroy to the level of a messenger boy.

Poor Lord Curzon who was thus neatly put in his place by a native king must have been seething like a bull that has just been shown a red flag, but with no tangible cause for complaint, he had to resort to silence.

The incident illustrates the marked characteristic of the man who believed above everything else in the correctness of things. Riding in a procession alongside the highest representative of the emperor was one thing but for the Indian princes and kings to follow behind was another, and a direct insult to the dignity and status of the highest position in the country.

Moreover, it was in no way inconsistent to the complete loyalty to the paramount power. Unfortunately, Curzon being Curzon apparently thought otherwise; under his regime, there was a tendency to misinterpret this attitude, thus a series of pinpricks followed, which produced some resentment.

The other principal ceremony in which the Indian princes and kings took part at Delhi was the investiture of the Orders of the Star of India and the Indian Empire on the evening of 3 January of the same year. It was held in the public hall of the old Mughal emperors, an ornate structure and very large. The function was a grand affair and the Maharaja was the cynosure of all eyes, resplendent as he was, wearing the famous necklace, 'worth a quarter of a million with the historic Star of the South as a pendant', remarked *The Times* in its 5 January 1903 edition.

The coronation durbar had passed off without a ripple but Sayajirao III was still disturbed by the restrictions placed on foreign travel and generally the treatment meted out to Indian princes by the representatives of the paramount power in India; his correspondence in 1903 is full of it. The demand for a fixed itinerary whenever a trip to Europe was contemplated and the insistence on a political officer accompanying the royal couple was annoying and irksome to the Maharaja and in his letter to the dewan he complained about it. Before he left for Kashmir, Sayajirao III wrote a long letter to Resident Meade in which he spoke of 'ignorant and irresponsible persons and newspaper editors' who had, on pure, malicious conjecture,[17] attributed his trips abroad to hedonistic reasons. He logically pointed out that one need not necessarily travel to foreign countries for their pleasures which could be derived here as well. He also added that in India, people's image of a raja was one who lived in grandeur, wore rich clothes and jewellery and enjoyed a life of comfort. All work and no play would seriously dent their image. This line of argument was only to gain a point as it was well known that with the Maharaja, ever since his investiture, it had been only work, work and more work which was responsible for his insomnia and other health problems. Meade suggested a meeting with Lord Curzon when Sayajirao III asked him to forward his letter of complaints to him. The Maharaja did not demur but said it would not serve any purpose, 'I should certainly not mind a friendly talk with the viceroy; but I have no confidence that the government will change their views on any important subject. The misfortune is that greatness or apparent greatness is severely dealt with in India. The wretched princes have not even the right of a common Indian merchant.'[18] Relations between the Gaekwads and Viceroy Curzon were not exactly what one would wish for, but before it became a running feud, Lord Curzon in April 1904 proposed changes in the Imperial Service System. The Curzon Circular had, by this time, died a natural death and was heard of no more, with only the originator mourning in private over it. The proposed changes suggested by the viceroy included that the Indian rulers should feel obliged to assist the British government with money and troops in times of war, not to defend the Indian dominions of only the Crown, but of all foreign interests of the empire.

Sayajirao III's response to the letter concerning the changes was a long and well-thought-out and well-reasoned memorandum. In the memorandum he pointed out that the origin of the Imperial Service in India had been a spontaneous gesture on the part of various princes in 1889 as a result of the Russian scare in the year 1885. Russia was gaining great influence in the Balkans and Great Britain recognized this as a threat to her interests. 'The Great Game' played by both the nations marked a strategic conflict between the British and Russian empires for supremacy in Central Asia. War seemed inevitable to both London and St Petersburg when it was learned that Russian troops had occupied Panjdeh after driving out a body of Afghan troops. A large Russian force, under General Komaroff, attacked the Afghan troops at Panjdeh on 30 March 1885 and occupied the town. This gave the Russian army a splendid base for preparing their future operations, being close to Herat and, more importantly, to the gates of India—a most frightening prospect for the British!

'The creation of the new obligation proposed,' continued the memorandum, 'would seem to demand the concession of a corresponding privilege, a recognized voice in the councils of the Empire. The privilege is the natural corollary of any general military federation, and would alone justify the creation of new burdens.'[19] The suggestion of a conference of princes was welcomed, and eventually became the Council of Princes with Sayajirao III as a strong and consistent supporter.

33

Widow Remarriage Gets a Boost

The attention Sayajirao III had paid to external matters during this time did not, in any way, divert him from his zest for reforms in the state. In 1902, the Maharaja had put into operation the law permitting Hindu widows to remarry. His opinion on widow remarriage was not accepted by the orthodox Hindus who had expressed shock and disbelief, so it could not be made compulsory. However, after the dust had settled, he demonstrated his broad-mindedness in the case of Ganesh. The following instance proves that the Maharaja put into practice what he advocated.

In Baroda, there lived a man named Sri Sadashiv Bhat of the Rudichusth family, whose young son Ganesh was returning to India in 1908 after completing his education in England. Ganesh got deeply involved in Baroda's reform work; it must be noted that the Maharaja always stipulated that those who went abroad on scholarships funded by him should return and serve the country first. Thus, young Ganesh was working in accordance with the Maharaja's wishes by carrying out reform measures in the state. Ganesh had recently lost his wife and his parents wished that he should marry again. Ganesh had no objections to marriage but he wanted to marry a widow as he was a champion of widow remarriage and wanted to support the cause by setting an example. His parents, being orthodox, strongly objected to this and threatened to disown him. The matter was brought to G.S. Sardesai who was not only a close confidant of Sayajirao III but also to Ganesh's family. Sardesai was also involved in the reform work in the state and in one of his conversations with the Maharaja, he blurted out that Ganesh wanted to marry a widow against his parents' wishes. Rumours about his intentions were rife in the state and all diehard conventionalists had put their foot down and objected to the marriage. No pandit was willing to perform the marriage rites. At this juncture, the Maharaja lent his support to the marriage, silencing all the conventionalists in Baroda.

Sayajirao III had a mandap erected, and invited the press as well as other important dignitaries from Bombay and Poona to the wedding. He worked round the clock to make the wedding celebrations a success. Bombay's famous social reformer who was a barrister by the name of Mukundrao Jadhav also cooperated in the matter and a lecture was delivered on the subject of widow remarriage in the wedding hall. Sri Jayakar Dulhe Bhate (a very well-known social worker) also propounded his views on the subject in support of the Maharaja. A grand dinner as part of the wedding celebrations was given in the Laxmi Vilas Palace for about three hundred guests. The Bhats, who had objected to the marriage, had sent a reply in response to the Maharaja's invitation that they would not be able to attend the dinner. Sayajirao III sent a message to the Bhats stating, 'It's quite all right if you do not want to participate in the dinner but surely you cannot object to be seated next to me for a chat?' Bhat was left no alternative but to comply. The Maharaja had a plate full of sweets placed before him and as he saw others at the dinner table eat, Bhat too began eating and it slowly dawned on him that the first step towards the removal of the stigma attached to widow remarriage had been taken by him!

This reform measure was followed up two years later with the Infant Marriage Prevention Act along with a legislation on primary education as well as a penal code and criminal procedures.

34

Purposeful Speeches and Land Reforms

It was not only the caste system that Sayajirao III disapproved of; fanatics who committed crimes in the name of religion were also utterly abhorrent to him. He advised religious tolerance to his people. For instance, while in Kashmir in the summer of 1903, the Maharaja took advantage of a number of opportunities for showing his great interest in education and his keen sympathy for all serious efforts to promote it in any part of India regardless of the community. As he had visited a Hindu school a few days earlier, on 30 May, he made it a point to visit the madrasa Nusrat-ul-Islam where he met the students and questioned the boys on various topics paying special attention to their knowledge of religious subjects. The Maharaja then gave a short speech in Urdu, expressing pleasure at visiting a madrasa. He expressed his intention of encouraging the work of the madrasa by sending it a liberal donation, hoping that it would be well spent. In the course of his remarks, the Maharaja observed that poor people required liberal support in their endeavours. He believed that Hindus and Muslims should cooperate with each other, especially in the field of education. He added that in his own state there existed Hindu and Muslim schools, and the people had an equal share in the services of the state. The art work of pashima was a good example of the skill set of the people and he hoped that higher education would enable the Kashmiris to rise higher. He recognized that it was necessary to educate girls and women. Finally he observed that English education needed to be raised to a level so it became a means for earning.

The Maharaja's remarks in the book of visitors ran thus:

> I was glad to visit the madrasa on 30 May 1903. The attendance was very large. I was not able to see much here, but from the little that I saw, it struck me that the school is managed on a very elementary scale for want of funds. This of course must seriously affect the staff as well. Without good pay, you cannot get good and efficient teachers.

I may remind my Muslim friends of many of the sentiments that I expressed to them in my speech. The Hindus and Muslims must go on progressing side by side like two brothers, for the interests of the two are closely interwoven and the rise and fall of one must affect, to some extent, the other as well. Judging from the manners and intelligence of some of the Muslims, I have casually come across here, I am inclined to think that with good education, they will be able to hold their own with their brethren in the plains. I know, as I have said some where else, that there are a few authors who have spoken favourably of the Kashmiris; though Sir Walter Lawrence has found excuses for their shortcomings. The Kashmiris must do their utmost to rid themselves of their defects and weaknesses. Without character, they cannot expect to rise, and education without character is worthless. I hope the present and future students of this and similar institutions will prove by their careers that men improve in favourable circumstances, the seeds of goodness being common to all mankind, though it is checked or encouraged by outward forces. Once the forces are favourable, let us hope that the Kashmiri will show himself to be a bold, courageous and a straightforward man.

On Sayajirao's III's forty-first birth anniversary, which fell on 11 March 1903, students of the local vernacular schools assembled in the Durbar Hall of the Laxmi Vilas Palace to honour him as well as Thakor Saheb of Gondal, who was on a visit to Baroda.

The proceedings opened with a programme of songs, recitations, garba and dialogues in Gujarati, Marathi, Urdu and Sanskrit. There was also a drill by girls. The Maharaja gave a short speech and distributed prizes to children who had done exceptionally well.

Sayajirao III dwelt upon the reforms Thakor Saheb had made in his state, mentioning among others, the inauguration of a splendid institution of the Girasis College—a unique and splendid institution tending to ameliorate the condition of the fallen race of the Girasis of Kathiawad. His example was offered for emulation to the ruling princes and kings of India, 'If adopted by the majority of them, it would go far towards removing the grounds for blame commonly thrown upon them by administrators.'[1]

Among the various means for the attainment of this laudable object, the Maharaja alluded to the quality of education which should be bestowed upon the 'young princes'.

He was determined that religious conflicts between the Hindus and Muslims in his state should end peacefully and thus made it a point to visit Muslim institutions whenever an opportunity arose. On 26 September, on an invitation from the principal, he visited the Islamia College in Lahore. His visit was much appreciated by the Muslims as a sign of goodwill towards them.

Besides the staff and the students, there were leading members of the Anjuman Charitable Trust and other important people. In his reply, the Maharaja said, 'It is a singular pleasure to be able to pay a visit to this institution. When Mr Mahbub Alam asked me yesterday to visit this college if I had the time and inclination, I agreed to do so as it was an invitation which I thought would be a mistake to decline, as it would give me an opportunity of seeing the progress that our Muslim brethren are making in Punjab. The progress of the whole community must depend on the advancement of all sections of the community and therefore the advancement of any one section must interest all. Division must lead to ruin and union to strength. It is incumbent upon us leaders and persons of influence in society to promote unity and not division. Hindus and Muslims must work hand in hand. A few moments ago, I was conversing with Mr Mahbub Alam on this subject, and he pointed out several matters in which there existed differences in principles and actions between Hindus and Muslims. Not being acquainted with the details of local circumstances, I am not in a position to suggest remedies to minimize points of differences and promote unanimity, but I am sure, men of experience and men versed in local affairs must know the means to bridge over the difficulties. Even where Muslims may be a minority, some reasonable compromise must be found such that the interest of the minority may not suffer. This may not be the popular view, but it is surely the right view.

'If one propounds an opinion divergent from that held by the majority, one will meet with opposition; but if one continues to advocate the right view, it will be accepted in the long run. For instance, Galileo proved certain laws concerning the earth. People in his time were against his theory, but after his death, his scientific theories came to be recognized. However, in practical politics, we have to give some consideration even to popular prejudices. Granting that we differ as to certain lines of action, it is still incumbent upon us to consider whether it is not in our ultimate interest to try to secure the advancement, not of one community only, but of the whole of India.

'Division has ruined India and must ruin it as long as it exists—I do not mean politically, but socially and materially.'

Sayajirao III then expressed the pleasure he had derived from the visit and his desire to revisit the college to check the progress it had made.

'One thing more, it is incumbent on me to reply to the kind words in which this gentleman (Shaikh Abdul Quadir, leader of the Muslim community) has alluded to me personally and my interest in the movements for the good of the country. My interests are not limited to one province or one community. I do not consider provinces or communities separately. I regard them as parts of one whole. If the parts improve and become perfect, the whole is bound to be complete. I wish therefore to encourage every good movement and every good institution.

'In Kashmir, I paid several visits to Hindu and Muslim schools, since diversity of religion makes no difference to me, when considering the encouragement of useful objects...Muslims, in general, in Baroda are perhaps more advanced than those in similar social positions in Punjab and even more than some of their Hindu fellow-subjects. We have schools here where Urdu and Persian are taught, though many Muslims, being aware that Gujarati is the prevalent language, have learnt the language and are quite fluent in it. Moreover, there are religious institutions where charity and kindness are shown to Muslims. In my service, there are many professing Islam who have distinguished themselves as civil servants. There have also been Muslims who have fought battles and have shed their blood for the House of Baroda. We have paid them not just in words but by granting positions of dignity and trust and giving them emoluments.

'It is not only in 1903 that the principle of unity between Hindus and Muslims has been recognized, it has been in existence for a long time.

'Look at Muslim states and those who have risen to eminence in them, as for instance Hyderabad at the present day, and the kingdom of Bijapur and Golkonda in olden times. Such being the case, there is ample reason for us to be united. Upon due consideration, I am convinced that our interests lie in acting in unison.

'You are part and parcel—an inseparable part and parcel—of this vast country. In religion we may differ, but within the world, advancing in the knowledge of scientific truths and progressing materially, it is strange that we should depend only on religion for agreement or differences, when so many other points of contact are offered. Because we differ in religion, it does not follow we oppose one another from birth to death. We are destined towards the same goal. As human beings gifted with the faculty of reasoning, we should be able to rise above petty prejudices.

'We are children of the same God and should live as brethren.

'I thank you, and assure you, your interests will always have a place in my heart!'[2]

If the Maharaja were standing for elections, his speech would have certainly garnered him all the Muslim votes, for when he had finished there was a moving response from the audience.

There is an interesting story which speaks of Sayajirao III's ability to handle sensitive issues pertaining to the Muslim community.

Sayajirao III was getting the roads widened to allow for traffic and so on. Most of the Muslims lived in the main part of the town and it was known as the Muslim area. The Muslims venerated a holy fakir called Baba whose cemetery with its huge stone slab lay at the edge of the main road which needed to be widened. The engineer was aware that disturbing the cemetery would lead to a violent protest from the Muslim community, so he called a halt to the work and sought to seek an audience with the king to relate the problem to him. The king asked him whether there was any other spot further down away from the road and the engineer, after a moment spent in thought, confirmed that there was indeed. Sayajirao III then asked him to summon the artisans and masons and construct a similar cemetery in a place away from the road. The workers worked all night and the cemetery was completed by dawn. The road too was widened and finished for the morning traffic of bullock carts and carriages. In the morning, when the people went to pay their customary homage at the cemetery, they found that it was in the place away from the road. They were stunned and news spread like wildfire in the Muslim neighbourhood, 'Our Baba has walked, with his cemetery, in the middle of the night to the other side, in order to make place for His Highness's road to be widened!' The simple folk actually believed that was what had happened. The incident speaks volumes for Sayajirao III's presence of mind and his ability to have his cake and eat it too!

In 1904, Sayajirao III was still dissatisfied with the land and revenue questions and settlements; therefore, he appointed an amatya or a revenue minister by the name of Romesh Chandra Dutt. Earlier, when Dutt had been commissioner of Burdwan in 1895, he had been offered the job but he had wanted to wait till he had retired from the service of the government of India. In 1904, at the age of fifty-six, he arrived in Baroda to reorganize, revamp and reform the revenue department, confident that his financial theories would be accepted and implemented. A letter to this effect sent to his brother dated 18 October of the same year mentioned that the Maharaja had agreed to all his suggestions about income tax, customs duties and so on, 'but the greater land question looms ahead; all western India is watching my land measures in Baroda to see if I have the courage to practise what I have preached to the British government all these years'. In July 1907, he ceased to work with the revenue department as he was appointed by the government of India to serve on the royal commission on decentralization. Again, in 1909, he returned to Baroda to take up his responsibilities as the dewan, a post he agreed to hold for one year only. However, he did not have the stamina for the rigorous work, a fact that he expressed in his letter to B.L. Gupta (minister of justice in Baroda) in 1906, 'Baroda is not like any other native state in India where you can take things easy. It is hard grind here, and the hard-worked administrator is not his own master.' He died of heart failure in 1909 while still on duty. However, his service in Baroda 'does not do only him an honour but also to the ruler who brought him there.'[3] Sayajirao III, on one occasion, mentioned Dutt as 'an instance of India's ability to produce statesmen, though so often they are swallowed up by the machinery of the British government and condemned only to rise to positions of minor eminence'.[4]

To revert to 1904, at the end of which Sayajirao III accepted an invitation to preside at the Social Conference of the Indian National Congress in Bombay where he was asked to deliver the inaugural address. He spoke at length on the two most dominant issues acting as impediments to India's progress: caste prejudices and the status of women.

He said that his ultimate aim was to do away with the caste system and if it could not be removed immediately at least an awareness could be created to reduce prejudices and increase tolerance. In 1902, while on a visit to Madras, the Gujarati community presented an address to which his response was, 'It is a matter of great gratification to me to learn that the

Gujarati community has been able to get along so well in Madras among people who are so intelligent and whose manners and customs, as far as my experience goes, are not very different from our own. It is a matter of great pleasure to hear it from the lips of my own people and this fact that is seldom told to rulers and princes as they are often accustomed to hear complaints... The trading classes have to bring to bear upon their countrymen the truth that the quality of honesty is the best policy in all their dealings!'[5]

With regard to Indian women, he stated that they were handicapped by convention, of which three were most deleterious to their progress—early marriage, the purdah system, and denial of education.

'What is it we seek?' he asked.'It is nothing new or revolutionary. Our real aims are the true and noble ideals of our forefathers, ideals eternally beautiful, eternally worthy of the search of men.'[6]

This speech at the Indian National Congress is a clear indication of his progressive thoughts and aims and also spells out the steps required for the well-being of India and her people. The audiences at societies and associations were generally made up of people well past their prime and steeped in tradition and conservatism, hence Sayajirao III felt the need to speak to students who were the future of the country and nurture their young, receptive minds with progressive thoughts to build a better future for themselves and the country. In view of this, he accepted the invitation to visit the college in Madras.

At his formal address to students at Pachaiyappa's College in Madras in 1902, he said, 'Stages of life have been divided by Shakespeare into seven and yours is the most important for if it is fulfilled to the best of your ability you may be rest assured of your success thereafter...Whatever you are taught whether trivial or important, pay your utmost attention to it. Whatever appears trivial now may one day be of great benefit and of interest to you.'[7]

At the opening of the Industrial Exhibition in Ahmedabad in December of the same year, after lavishly praising the exhibition in Paris, which he had recently attended, for its efficiency and extraordinary ingenuity in the appliances displayed, he said:

> But beyond all this triumph of Man over Nature and her powers, one fact struck me with curious emphasis—the enormous gulf which separates the European and the native of India in their ideas of comfort...There rose before me, the interior of a typical Indian

home and as I contrasted it with the truly surprising inventions around me, all devoted to that one object—refinement—our much boasted simplicity seemed bare and meagre beyond description. I do not mean that we should dispense with simplicity but let it be a wise moderation in the midst of plenty, not the fatalistic acceptance of poverty as a virtue itself... If we realize the progress of science and mechanical inventions and resolutely part with old antiquated methods of work, if we liberate ourselves from hampering customs and traditions, none of which are an essential part of religion; if, instead of being dazed by the magnificent progress of Europe and meet it with our own progress, there will be no reason for us to despair but if we fail in this we must not expect to occupy a place in the civilized and progressive world... Experience is the only path to knowledge, comparison perfects it. Knowledge is the dominant factor in the spirit of the age and the basis of all reforms...But there is another aspect to this apparent incompetence. We have to learn trustworthiness, a capacity for obedience, the art of management, accuracy, punctuality, method and a sense of justice and the only school that will teach this is a position that will call out for its use... Government, like the climate and geographical conditions of a country, has a peculiar force of its own and must leave an indelible impress on the mould of the destinies of nations. It may powerfully hamper as promote the moral and material development of the people entrusted to its care. If the government were supported by a more informed and intelligent public opinion and if the people awakened to a sense of national life, were allowed and induced to take a livelier interest in their own concerns and if they worked in unison, they would conduce to mutual strength. Government is a matter of commonsense and compromise and its aim should be to secure the legitimate interests of the people governed.[8]

Though his speeches at inaugurations and functions smacked of ultra-seriousness, Sayajirao III was not devoid of a sense of humour and had his moments of fun in schoolboyish escapades. Once while spending the summer in the cool climate of Kashmir, as was his habit, he went for a walk taking his ADC with him. As they walked along in companionable silence, admiring the beautiful landscape, the Maharaja spied a cornfield on the banks of a river where the corn was ripe and ready for harvest. In the mood for a little fun and also wanting to satiate his taste for corn, he entered the field taking his ADC with him. The cornfield obviously belonged to someone else and they had no right to trespass on it, but in their eagerness to pluck corn, they entirely forgot that they were trespassing and began to devour what they had managed to pluck. Suddenly, they heard a loud shout from a farmer and incidentally the owner of the field was sitting close by. It had not escaped the farmer's notice that these two men were stealing his corn. He ran towards them with a stick reserved for such occasions and started angrily berating them for stealing his corn that was ready for harvest. The Maharaja, to wriggle out of an uncomfortable situation that was getting to be embarrassing, silenced him with the words, 'You know, we are senior officers from the Gaekwad government.' The farmer replied, 'I simply do not believe you can be so because the Gaekwad government is fair and just. It holds moral uprightness above everything else and would never tolerate a person infringing on another person's property or rights. Therefore, you could never belong to the government of His Highness Maharaja Sayajirao Gaekwad!'[9]

Needless to say, the farmer's listeners were stunned to hear him extol the virtues of the administration and of course were secretly pleased with the farmer's words. Apologizing profusely, they paid him generously for the corn and gladly made their escape!

The year 1904–05 may be considered as the beginning of a new period of Sayajirao III's reign where his administrative measures for improving the state bore fruit. Three important acts concerning cooperative credit societies, religious endowments and the customs marked the year with significance. With this on the agenda, the Maharaja left with his family in tow, on his seventh European trip, in the spring of 1905. On 30 June, he was among the distinguished guests at Harrow School when England's royal couple came for the inauguration of the new sports field. In London, he found himself in a whirl of social activities which also included His Highness addressing the members of the Society of Arts on the relations of Indian princes and British political officers, and visits to the Horticultural College for Women at Swanley, the Leicester Galleries and to a working men's club at Lambeth. Towards the end of July, he left London for Dublin where he made the acquaintance of Lord and Lady Aberdeen. He was in Paris on 12 August. After that, the rest of the year, he spent in the continent, and in the spring of 1906, the Maharaja and the maharani left for Territet in Switzerland and then Geneva. Determined to enhance his knowledge and broaden his views with further travel to countries not visited so far, he left from London on 5 May with the maharani and his brother Sampatrao for the United States. The country interested him and he was perpetually on the lookout for new, constructive ideas that could be adapted and implemented in Baroda. He was particularly interested in the American system of education and invited Dr Cuthbert Hall, an expert in the field, to visit India, inspect the schools there and offer his expertize for improvements in the infrastructure and curriculum. Always aware of his own shortcomings in that aspect, he gave education all the impetus that he could muster and command from his resources. In connection with education, he studied the system of circulating libraries with absorbing interest.

There was also the need to look into industrial development and agriculture and study the farming methods adopted in America. Labour unions and child-rearing too interested him. While in America, he asked a lot of questions and compared its systems with those in India. His visits to horticultural gardens resulted in him sending packets of seeds to Baroda for experimenting, and after he had visited Colorado Springs, he conceptualized the idea of starting a paper-making industry in Baroda.

On the whole, Sayajirao III was most satisfied with his trip to the United States as it was most educative. He kept busy with numerous visits to universities and in observing and learning their farming methods, which led to a host of new schemes that the Maharaja later introduced in Baroda. However, a couple of things marred his enjoyment of the country and tempered his admiration for it. The American people's naïve disappointment at an Indian king not appearing in his traditional bejewelled attire and other embellishments amused him greatly, while he was irritated by the attention foisted on him by the American press.

August saw him back in England, and in September, John Morley, who was the secretary of state for India received a letter from Sayajirao III expressing his desire for greater autonomy for Indian states. 'A greater degree of autonomy is needed to secure the natural and healthy development of the native states…It is the right of man to have good government; and in the present day, the people themselves demand it.'[10] This was sent along with some notes which Sayajirao III had drawn up on the subject.

After his return to Baroda on 19 November after an absence of a year and seven months, Sayajirao III also sent his notes to Lord Minto (the new viceroy) with a covering letter similar in trend to Morley, adding that 'it could not have been intended by the British government to crush out all initiative and originality from these states and destroy their distinctive features altogether.'[11] He was also careful to express approval of the idea of a Council of Princes, thereby smoothening ruffled feathers. The Council of Princes was under discussion during this time.

35

The Silver Jubilee

Sayajirao III's investiture had taken place twenty-five years ago and the state was gearing up to celebrate the silver jubilee on a grand scale. The Maharaja, however, had promised to deliver the inaugural address at the opening of the Industrial Exhibition Conference in Calcutta in December; hence, it was thought to postpone the event till the following year on 5 March 1907.

In the inaugural address at the second Indian Industrial Conference delivered by Sayajirao III in Calcutta, he warned,

> The danger of extinction which our industries are threatened [with] is therefore imminent. Keep to your conservative methods, cling to your orthodox ways of work and your industries must perish! Such is the inexorable law of the survival of the fittest and such an admonition which a true swadesi should give you. I would warn you against some false methods of encouraging industry, such as the 'movement' to use no cloth not produced in the country. The idea is quite unsound so far as any economic results go and the true remedy for any industry which needs support is to study the market, find out what is wanted and improve the finish of the work and design until an increasing demand shows that the right direction has been found...I would however direct your attention to the establishment of larger industries involving an extensive use of machinery, for it is upon this that our economic future and any increase of our wealth depends... England's Free Trade Policy crushed our manufactures and trade inducing profound dejection, hopelessness and inertia. Unable to react against that dominating force, we came to believe that the inability was constitutional and inherent in ourselves...that Indians as a race are lacking in enterprise, deficient in business faculties and barren in organizing power. There is another fault which is nearly

as fatal to any system of industry and that is our lack of confidence in ourselves and in one another. Without self-confidence, you can never do anything; you will never find an industry or build up a trade, for you have nothing to carry you through the first anxious years when the only dividend is hope, and the best assets are unfaltering courage and faith in oneself. Moreover, without confidence in one another, you will never have a credit system and without a credit system, no modern commerce can exist. It is this want of cooperation, this mutual distrust which paralyses Indian industry, ruins the statesman and discredits the individual even in his own household...Failures and defalcations are as common in Europe as among ourselves, yet we allow ourselves to be too easily discouraged by such incidents. Hence, arises the habit of censorious judgment, a disposition to put the worst construction on the conduct of our friends and relatives without trying to find out the truth, which destroys all trust and tolerance. Our view on the conduct of friends, of the policies of administration, of the success and integrity of commercial undertakings, are all vitiated by a readiness to believe the worst. It is only when we learn to suspend judgment and know the man and the motive before we criticize that we shall be able to repose trust where trust is due. [1]

The speech ended with a thundering applause.

The silver jubilee functions were celebrated on a lavish scale in the city of Baroda as befitting a King worthy of his throne. The photo of Sayajirao III taken at the time of his silver jubilee contrasts from that taken at his investiture. The years sit well upon him in spite of insomnia. He has matured with age—one sees a face yet unlined, with ears held back, a short, straight nose above a firm well-rounded chin, eyes that at eighteen had been bright with curiosity, now are pensive and alive, striking a predominant note below a wide forehead marked distinctly with two bushy eyebrows. Even in the photo he makes one aware of his earnest scrutiny of what was happening around him.

The following five days were to be jubilee holidays.

At the birthday durbar, it was announced that many concessions were to be made in honour of the event—arrears in taxation were remitted to the extent of over Rs 5,00,000, vernacular education was made free, new hostels for students from the depressed classes were to be opened at Patan and Amreli, free primary education, five scholarships for students in Europe were founded. A new market—the Khanderao Market near the gates of the Laxmi Vilas Palace—was presented to the Baroda municipality along with four new hospitals to serve the outlying districts of the state, an orphanage, more public parks in the capital and other towns for the benefit of the public as the Maharaja himself advocated exercise and fresh air to remain healthy. The Jubilee Gardens were also opened in the northeast area near the Sur Sagar Tank. A huge sum of Rs 5,55,000 was to be spent to provide public wells. As always, the subject of water dominated his thoughts.

The most gratifying part of the silver jubilee celebrations was that they were not confined to his state alone but brought spontaneous reactions from people outside the city and other parts of the country as well. Meetings were held in almost all of India's major cities to felicitate the Maharaja.

The same year saw the work of the settlement department being submitted to a joint commission, appointed by the Baroda state, and the formation of a legislative council, which took concrete form in the following year.

All these steps taken to ensure progress in the state of Baroda and the fact that the state had progressed by leaps and bounds under Sayajirao III's rule had not escaped the eagle-eyed British hierarchy in England. On 31 March 1908, in a session in the House of Commons, James O'Grady, who was a member of the Independent Labour Party and a member of Parliament, asked the secretary of state for India, John Morley, whether he was aware that the Maharaja of Baroda had separated the judicial from the executive functions, had restored local self-government, had instituted primary education in his entire state, and further instituted popularly elected members in the legislative council; and if so, would the Council of India consider the application of such reforms to other native states and to India as a whole. Morley's answer was tempered with caution as he said that the results of these measures taken by the ruler would be watched with keen interest but was diffident on recommending the same for the entire British India as he could not interfere with the discretion of rulers of other states.

The other most significant step taken by the Maharaja during his reign is the establishment of the Bank of Baroda in 1908, under the management of C.E. Randle which has been a remarkable success and has drastically revolutionized the financial situation in Baroda. In 1910, the Maharaja transferred the state treasury work to the bank on the understanding that the state should keep a minimum balance of Rs 550, 000 without interest.

Sayajirao III's eldest son Fatehsinghrao III was married at the age of twenty-five to Padmavati, princess of Phaltan, on 4 February 1904. Fatehsinghrao III had studied at Balliol College whereas his bride was an uneducated thirteen-year-old.

If the period 1904 to 1908 saw significant achievement, it also brought great grief to the Maharaja when he lost his eldest son and heir. Fatehsinghrao III died unexpectedly in 1908. He was an alcoholic; he was not strong and had missed out on the care and affection that a mother would have given him. The loss of a mother had left a permanent scar in his mind and he was prone to depression, which was not helped by his stepmother's hatred of him and was noticed not only by Sayajirao III but also by the courtiers in the palace, which gave rise to rumours regarding his sudden death. He left behind an infant son, Pratapsinghrao Gaekwad, who was destined to rule the state of Baroda years later. Overcome with grief at the loss of his son, Sayajirao III already taciturn by nature, became silent and withdrawn.

Colonel Meade, who had been the Resident in Baroda since 1901, retired from his post in February 1909. Sayajirao III gave a banquet in his honour and in his speech he alluded to the fact that Colonel Meade had, among his illustrious predecessors at the Residency, his grandfather Major D. Malcolm and his father Sir Richard Meade. The speech was complimentary as the Maharaja had shared cordial relations during his tenure as the Resident.

The sun seemed to be shining on the political climate of the state of Baroda, and the cloudless sky showed no hint of the storm that was to come.

Ever since the mutiny of 1857, many Indians were under a cloud of suspicion. The worst years after the mutiny made many Hindus suspect in British eyes and the abler they were, the more dangerous. If the storm centre of western India was the chief stronghold of the Marathas, it was natural that suspicion should alight upon a state ruled by a Maratha king who had never made a secret of his progressive views and who was applauded by the nationalist press.

One can safely say that to some extent the suspicion had some grounds and was not entirely baseless. Aurobindo Ghosh had been employed by Sayajirao III in the service of the Baroda state and was also serving in the Bombay presidency to keep his revolutionary activities strong and effective. Aurobindo was a staunch nationalist, deeply involved in revolutionary activities. He got Jitendra Upadhya, another revolutionist, into the cavalry regiment in Baroda who, after he had been trained, continued to serve in the army. In 1902, Aurobindo sent him to Bengal to organize revolutionary activities against the British there. He was brought under the suspicious eyes of the British who realized that if Aurobindo was to remain in Baroda, it would be dangerous for them. Hence, they prevailed upon the Maharaja to have him dismissed on some pretext or the other. Meanwhile, Aurobindo was responsible for some anti-British articles published in the newspaper *Yugantar*, which upset the British officials, and the press persons of the newspaper were arrested. Aurobindo, uneasy over this turn of events, returned to Bengal taking a long sabbatical from his work in Baroda. Sayajirao III, loath to let him leave, ordered his dewan by cable that on no account should Aurobindo be allowed to resign from his administrative work in Baroda or from the faculty where he had been employed as a professor.

There is a curious incident relating to the working of the minds of both these extraordinary men. One day, Sayajirao III was taking his morning walk as usual. As he walked briskly ahead, Aurobindo followed behind. After a few minutes, the Maharaja came across an old woman with a heavy pot on her head. She had stopped on the banks of a stream reluctant to proceed because the weight she was carrying on her head was too heavy for her to wade through a stream that had slippery rocks underneath. The Maharaja, sensing her discomfiture, lifted the pot from her head and offered to carry it for her till they had crossed the stream together. After they reached the other side of the stream safely, he took the pot and placed it on her head and bade her goodbye. The woman in turn thanked him and blessed him as she left. The Maharaja was astonished to hear unsuppressed laughter from someone nearby; turning around, he saw Aurobindo laughing at him. Sayajirao III asked him, 'Aurobindo, what amuses you so much? Is there something wrong with my appearance that makes you laugh so?' Aurobindo, after controlling his laughter, replied, 'No, Your Highness, there is nothing wrong with your appearance but when you lifted that pot from that old lady's head, I said to myself, *The Raja certainly knows how to relieve a person of their burden and when you replaced it on her head after crossing the stream, I said to myself, he also knows how to burden people with responsibilities.*

Sayajirao III's connection with revolutionaries naturally brought him under strong disapprobation from the British hierarchy and they frowned upon his associations. In August 1909, the viceroy, Lord Minto addressed the princes and kings of India on the burning question of sedition.

The first sign of trouble came in the form of a warning letter from the viceroy about the danger of sedition that was rife in different parts of British India. The letter was sent to all the ruling princes and kings of India.

The one addressed to Sayajirao III stated:

My Honoured and Valued Friend,

There is no longer any doubt that seditious people are endeavouring to establish their evil doctrines and practices in the native states of India. At this juncture, I naturally turn to the ruling princes of India to warn them of their danger and to seek their counsel as to how we can best assist one another to stamp out the common enemy. For the interests of the ruling princes and the paramount power are the same. A new element has been introduced into the country which not only aims at the embarrassment of the British administration, but works openly or covertly against the constitutional order of society. I trust Your Highness will agree with me that much good may result from a full, frank and friendly discussion between us at this juncture on the question of how best to keep sedition out of native states. I shall greatly value the opinion of Your Highness and I shall be glad to know of any way I can assist you. It is far from my wish to interfere in the internal administration of native states, but it seems to me to be an occasion for close consultation and a clear understanding of common interests.

    I desire to express the high consideration which I entertain for Your Highness, and to subscribe myself,

Your Highness's sincere friend,

Minto
Viceroy, Governor General of India.[2]

Sayajirao III in his reply dated 19 November 1909 assured cooperation in the matter. Four days prior to the letter, the Maharaja had given a banquet in Baroda in honour of Lord Minto and in proposing a toast to his honoured guest, he had said, 'The friendly relations of my state with the British government remain unchanged, and the firm unalterable loyalty of my house to the British Throne remains unshaken... We are inspired by the same object, which is the preservation of peace and public tranquillity, and we are animated by the same wish, which is the promotion of the progress, the prosperity and the happiness of the people.'[3]

After referring to the Morley-Minto reforms of 1909 (Also known as the Indian Councils Act wherein membership of the central and provincial legislative councils was enlarged. Communal electorates introduced as part of these reforms were meant to create disunity between Hindus and Muslims.), the Maharaja alluded to the fact that the people should have a large and proper share in the administration of the country. This, of course, was relished by the nationalist newspapers for its own ends for he had made a significant allusion to sedition, 'Those who confound liberty with license and seek to undermine authority must be repressed with a firm hand, and not allowed to endanger the public tranquility or general progress... I cordially acknowledge the ready assistance which my administration receives from Your Excellency's government, and as cordially I assure Your Excellency of my readiness to respond, within my power, to any call for cooperation with the government of India.'[4]

This placatory toast was enough to annul any suspicion of Sayajirao III's involvement in sedition.

There is an interesting story which dates as far back as 1908 which indicates the thinking of Sayajirao III, which is contradictory. In 1908, Sayajirao III and Sir Aga Khan III who was the founding member of the All India Muslim League were the guests of the governor George Clarke, and were staying in Poona's Governor House. After dinner and when all the guests had left for their homes, the Maharaja and Aga Khan III took a stroll in the garden. After a while, they sat down to indulge in desultory conversation. The conversation gradually led to India's independence from British rule. Sir Aga Khan III asked the Maharaja, 'Are you also of the opinion that the country can be freed of British domination?'

Sayajirao III replied, 'This is possible, even if India does not get independence in the near future, the people of India will become aware of the need to rid themselves of British rule. The germ of this idea will be sown into their minds before long and the world will be aware of this need and that Indians are willing to fight for it.'

Aga Khan III said, 'Can the Indians match against someone whose military strength is incomparable?'

The Maharaja answered, 'The reign of the British will not end just with a rebellion, but in the coming years, there will be such a situation that nobody will be able to stop India from gaining her freedom!'

Aga Khan III said, 'How do you visualize India's future?'

The Maharaja replied, 'After the British leave India, the country will have to be freed from all the petty, useless rulers and become an absolute free nation. That will be the beginning of a truly liberated nation!'

Aga Khan III said, 'What? Will you also give up your rule in the state?'

The Maharaja replied, 'Why not? For the sake of the country, every individual will have to make the sacrifice which is not too great for the good cause of the country!'

Then he, according to Aga Khan III, made a very profound remark, 'The first thing you'll have to do when the English are gone is to get rid of all these rubbishy states. There will never be an Indian nation until this so-called Princely order disappears. Its disappearance will be the best thing that can happen to India—the best possible thing.'[5]

Some years later, Sayajirao III spoke to the great independence fighter and reformer Lokmanya Tilak about it. He was willing to abdicate the throne and openly fight for India's independence but Tilak cautioned him against such open defiance. He said, 'Continue the good work you are doing now; with you largely funding the independence movement is of great help to us, and besides, you are our eyes and ears in the British hierarchy, what more do we need? If you expose yourself now we will all be arrested and all will be lost!'[6]

That Sayajirao III cared more for his country than anything else is well demonstrated by his offer.

Perhaps it was because of this letter from Lord Minto that the Maharaja in his speech in early September made in Baroda dealt with the view that education was partly responsible for the prevailing political unrest as it broadened views and enabled people to rationalize their aspirations.

Discontent, he maintained, was not necessarily an evil. But the recent crimes in England had aroused belligerence and it was the duty of the government to stamp out sedition.

'Fortunately in Baroda there was no trouble' and he hoped that the good sense of the people would render repression unnecessary.[7] The recent crimes which the king referred to in his speech alluded to the assassination at the Imperial Institute in England on the night of 1 July. Sir Curzon Wyllie, a British Indian army officer and a noted friend of Indian students, had been attacked by M.L. Dhingra, a Punjabi student in London. Dr C. Lalcaca, a Parsi physician, had bravely tried to step in between, interposing himself to ward off the attack and had got himself killed instead along with Sir Curzon Wyllie. It was a gruesome senseless murder and the assassin paid the due penalty of the law.

The other unfortunate incident that took place was in Baroda. The viceroy, Lord Minto, was on his autumn leave and had Baroda on his itinerary. In Ahmedabad, as he was driving from the railway station, a bomb was thrown at his carriage, which fortunately missed and the intended victim escaped. These two incidents involving Indians gave food for thought and caused grave concern not only among the British but also among the Indian princes and kings who feared that the paramount powers would subject them to unnecessary vigil and suspicion.

Perhaps Sayajirao III thought so too, for he went overboard in the arrangements for the reception given in honour of the visit of Lord Minto and his family when they arrived in his state on 13 November. The grandeur of the reception was such that it was meant to placate the indignant officials in the British hierarchy and allay their suspicions over the unfortunate incidents.

On the day he arrived, Lord Minto was cheered warmly by the citizens of Baroda as he rode through the city escorted by 'Inniskilling Dragoons (a cavalry regiment in the British army) and the Royal Horse Artillery' amid dense crowds that had thronged the streets to welcome him. At the state banquet given in honour of the viceroy, Lady Minto and their daughter, in the Laxmi Vilas Palace, Sayajirao III proposed a toast to the Mintos wherein he expressed his horror at the attempt made by an Indian to harm a representative of the Crown of England. He reassured the viceroy of his unwaveringloyalty to the British Crown, 'Loyalty has always been considered in the East as one of the first virtues in people; but loyalty, when merely sentimental, is of small value. It should be real, genuine and active...' Here, he quietly put his oar in, 'To secure such loyalty, there should be a community of interests between the subjects and the ruling power. The former should have a proper share in the administration of the country, and should feel that the government is their own.'[8] Having achieved his objective, he proceeded to squash any misgivings that may have clouded the minds of his honoured guests, and concluded his speech by alluding to the Morley–Minto reforms, 'It is for this reason that I hail with pleasure those great measures of reforms which Your Excellency initiated and His Majesty's government has accepted. These reforms will open out to the people of India a larger field of activity, and inspire them with a greater sense of responsibility in the performance of their civic duties; and future generations will recognize in these statesman-like measures a forward step in the progress of the country under the enlightened rule of Great Britain.'[9]

The viceroy must have been swept off his feet with such placatory words that eulogized his work, at the same time giving credit to Great Britain. Lord Minto, not to be outdone, reciprocated in a similar manner and praised the Maharaja for his administrative efficiency in his own state. He also gave him special credit 'for his bold attempt to separate the judicial functions from the executive, which had elicited the warm interest of the government of India.'[10] With the success of this visit, the sun was shining once more on the House of the Gaekwads and the path seemed clear for a peaceful reign for the ruler.

36

Sedition in the Air

A tsunami of hatred churned between 1907 and 1911, which unleashed the terrible rancour brought on by resentment and anger against the paramount power. During that phase, the national press made the stream of abuses that poured out from its editorial offices against the British public; all those who hurled bombs or aimed pistols at the white race were hailed as martyrs in the 'holy' cause of freedom for their motherland—Bharat Mata. The platform was as busy as the press. Men of intellect and force delivered speeches or had their thoughts translated into books in the vernacular and distributed throughout the country, which did the work that it was meant to do. Murder and violence were rampant—two ladies, mistaken in the dark for an obnoxious magistrate, were shot and Mr Jackson, the collector of Nasik, a scholar and a friend of India, was shot in a railway carriage.

The paramount power of course, needless to say, was not a passive onlooker to this open display of hatred against its rule and a very strict vigil was enforced on all with no exception to the 'native princes'.

On 19 November 1910, Sayajirao III wrote to Lord Minto in reply to the warning that he had received that seditious people were spreading their evil doctrines in native states; he claimed ignorance of the extent of the damage, but had enquiries made and a note prepared by his ministers. The note had all the information regarding those involved in sedition but was not revealed in the correspondence with Lord Minto Yet, a couple of months later, many were surprised to see the Maharaja being singled out from among other native princes for attacks by the British government. He was accused of lacking in response to the requirements of the government of India. However, he let the matter ride, absorbed as he was in the codification of the rules of departmental work, particularly that of the khangi or the palace's household department.

The year ended well for him personally as both his children, Indira and

Shivajirao, passed their respective examinations. He agreed to let Shivajirao study in Oxford while Indira went to Baroda College.

In 1910, the storm that had been looming on the horizon intensified, needing just a whiff of air before it could blow over with such ferocity as to wipe out every vestige of the fine fabric of a progressive rule so carefully woven and interwoven by Sayajirao III. *The Times*, in its Calcutta edition, dated 27 January, mentioned that 'the opinions of the ruling chiefs, on the measures required for suppressing sedition in India, was proving effective, and that the chiefs, with one "prominent exception" had declared that they would adopt any measure recommended'. Here the message suggested that Gaekwad of Baroda had denied the knowledge of the spread of sedition in the native states and had only given a 'qualified assurance' of his willingness to respond to any reasonable call for assistance against sedition. However, it also admitted that as demanded by the Residency, strict surveillance was being kept on itinerant Indian preachers and offending newspaper editors were being reprimanded. The implied criticism of the Maharaja was not lost on the well-wishers of the Baroda state and they were shocked enough to ask each other what had happened since Lord Minto's visit two months earlier. There had been cordiality and the viceroy had been more than satisfied with the reception, especially with the toast that Sayajirao III had raised to the viceroy with the words, 'The friendly relations of my state with the British government remain unchanged, and the firm and unalterable loyalty of my House to the British throne remains unshaken...We are inspired by the same object, which is a preservation of peace and public tranquility, and we are animated by the same wish, which is the promotion of progress, prosperity and the happiness of the people.'[1] The Maharaja had also made a significant allusion to sedition in his toast. Lord Minto must have been overwhelmed with this assurance and any niggling doubt in his mind must have been obliterated with the sincerity of the words uttered in the speech at the banquet, given in his honour.[2] Even *The Times* correspondent had described it as a splendid success! Then, what had gone wrong?

A clue to this mystery was in the article appearing in the *Amrita Bazar Patrika* praising Sayajirao III for what it assumed to be his attitude towards the government's request. As seen later, this was not the only instance of deliberate misinterpretation of his views which was to cause him trouble and unnecessary anxiety. Much later, in 1926, he admitted, with regret, that his troubles during that seditious phase were due to his excessive popularity in India, owing to his zest for reforms. At a guess, there may have been rumours that if and when India became a republic, Sayajirao III would be India's first president. Not that Sayajirao III paid any attention to it but it may have influenced negatively on the Anglo-Indian officialdom at that time. The golden rule was—'A native prince must not become too popular, even when he does not court popularity.'³

These were, at best, minor pinpricks but presage what was to come later.

However, throwing caution to the winds, Sayajirao III left Baroda for the Far East, stopping briefly at Hong Kong and Shanghai, and spent a month in Japan. During his stay there, the Indo-Japanese Association presented the Maharaja with an address which said:

> We have watched with deep interest, the moral and material progress made by Your Highness' subjects under your wise and beneficent rule. The rapid development of Your Highness' territories, the increased attention paid to sanitation and public works, wonderful strides made in primary as well as secondary education have made Baroda a model state in India. Your Highness' liberal, sympathetic and enlightened administration conducted with rare ability and devotion to duty, and Your Highness' sincere and earnest desire to promote the welfare of your subjects have elicited our respect and admiration. We most humbly and respectfully beg to congratulate Your Highness on the highly successful results of your benign and progressive rule.⁴

This must have acted like a balm to Sayajirao III's sore sentiments after all the pinpricks that he had constantly been made victim of. Afterwards, he sailed for San Francisco on 1 July. After a brief stay there and a short trip to Canada, he arrived with his family in London on 19 July. Here, he took the opportunity to call on Lord Morley and spent nearly an hour in discussions, closeted with him in the India Office. In early August, he hopped over to Oxford as a visitor of Dean Strong at Christ Church to discuss the possibility of his son, Shivajirao's admission to the college. On 25 August, he was in Scotland as a guest of Lord Middleton's shooting party. The maharani was away on the continent for a cure and returned to England in October and the family were all together spending their time between Bushey Hall and a London Hotel. The Maharaja had consented to deliver an address at the Indian Union Society, where he spoke of the Indian progress and emphasized the need for knowledge in science of different kinds, proper organization and tolerance of views on political matters. The royal couple returned to Baroda on 16 December. Jaisinghrao had proceeded to America to continue his education after leaving Harrow, while Shivajirao and his younger brother Dhairyashilrao remained in England.

Four months later, the royal couple made their way to Europe as the maharani needed a cure for her indifferent health, which could be obtained at Bad Nauheim. Apart from that, she wished to see the realization of a literary project on which she had been engaged. The Maharaja's motive was to be present at the coronation of King George at Westminster Abbey. Edward VII died in 1910 and his son George V became the emperor.

In India, Viceroy Hardinge was busy trying to organize for the grand coronation durbar which was to take place in Delhi. Hardinge was aware that Sayajirao III had violated the precision of the ritual at Lord Curzon's durbar and anticipated something like that would happen again.

Sir Charles Cleveland, head of India's Criminal Intelligence Department had asked the Scotland Yard to keep a watch on the Maharaja's activities in Europe and send him periodic reports. Watch was kept but when the report came it was obvious that the arrangements for the watch had not been adequate as it contained only information about tips given to servants and the handing of drinks when neighbours called.

On 1 March 1911, Sir Herbert Risley of the India Office in London asked to see the report and it was sent to him the same day. The report came with a disclaimer that the information should not be taken as first-hand and that 'it would be difficult to prove the incidents so long after they had actually occurred'. The report divulged, 'In August 1910, the Maharani of Baroda was taking the cure at Vichy... at this time, Madam Cama was also at Vichy, and received numerous calls from Indians there.' Then, there was a list of all the people the Maharaja was mixing with when he was in Paris towards the end of December 1910 (the list contained names of those Indian nationalists living in Europe) and had attended a soiree given by Divachand Harirama Varma, at his villa ten miles from Paris. The list had the names of Mr and Mrs Rana, V. Chattopadhyaya, Mrs Cama, Govind Amin, H.B. Godrej, P. Nowrojee, Miss G. Nowrojee and Banker. The soiree was kept very quiet...

what actually happened is not known, but Gaekwad is supposed to have said that he had no intention of being in India when King George V went there, as he did not intend to pay his customary servile homage.'

Then it also mentioned the Oxford University Indian Club incident and Shivajirao's remark on Western civilization. (Shivajirao had been the host at a meeting in the Oxford University Indian Club where he had opined on the evils of the Western civilization, which had gone down in official records.)

It also stated that Madam Cama spoke of Sayajirao III disparagingly but had a high opinion of the maharani. This is significant and worthy of consideration. (Madam R.D. Cama was the wife of a prominent Parsi solicitor of Bombay, K.E. Cama. She was a well educated lady and a linguist. She was a nationalist operating from Paris, convinced as she was that if she returned to India she would be arrested. The other names mentioned were also like-minded nationalists who met regularly in her house.)

It was not only the political department of the British government that had its spies planted in the palaces of princes and kings who shared with them bits of gossip and information which could be used against a prince or a king, but the princes and the kings too were adept at the spying game and had their informers among the household servants of the Residents and among the clerks in the government's secretariat. Thus, the worsening relationship between Sayajirao III and the viceroy had become common knowledge. One can gather from this the nature of the evidence that was slowly piling up in the government's secret dossiers to support a charge of sedition against Sayajirao III.

The Maharaja duly attended the coronation on 22 June 1911 which took place at Westminster Abbey. After the coronation, he asked for an audience with Lord Crewe, the secretary of state for India, as he had heard from two Indian princes—Aga Khan and the Raja of Bikaner—who had also come for the coronation that his own reputation was under a cloud linked as it was with sedition. When he finally met Lord Crewe in the latter's house he had a frank talk with him. Lord Crewe acknowledged the rumours and that the king too had been made aware of it. He then proceeded to tell the Maharaja that it was said that he had shown 'special sympathy with the India House Gang (a hostel for Indian students in London), of whom Krishna Varma was the leader, and also that he had helped Bipin Chandra Pal.'[5] The stigma of being dangerous extremists had been attached with both these names and to be associated with them or even acknowledge them as acquaintances was to sign your name off as an extremist too. Shyamji Krishna Varma, an Indian patriot and 'one of the leading lights' of the band of Indian enthusiasts who were passionate about India's freedom from the white-skinned race, was living in exile in Europe. He was the proprietor of India House. He was also the editor of the weekly paper *The Indian Sociologist*, which was responsible for fervently propagating nationalistic views. Bipin Chandra Pal shared the same views and was also a close friend of Aurobindo Ghosh. Bipin ran the English weekly *Bande Mataram* and Aurobindo had regularly contributed to it with his fiery articles.

Sayajirao III was not an ordinary Indian citizen. Hence, it should have been understood by those who had set their spies on him that a man of his stature, with the reputation of being a most forward-looking and a progressive ruler, was bound to attract many people, in India as well as abroad, who were vying for an opportunity to meet him. Therefore, he should not have been faulted if these very same people came forward to claim acquaintance. However, he admitted to have helped Bipin Chandra Pal with £50 when the man had been facing abject poverty.

From the discussion on the rumours, Lord Crewe was left in no doubt that even if they were true, it could hardly be interpreted as an act of treason. A man in his position as the Maharaja could hardly be expected to not meet with various types of people when travelling abroad. It was finally decided that a stricter vigil should be kept on him and his movements. On his part, the Maharaja derived from the meeting with Lord Crewe that he would have to take greater care to not do or say anything that might be interpreted as disloyalty to the British government. In the meeting, Sayajirao III also made it plain that he had been deeply offended with the treatment meted out to him by Lord Curzon which was in the manner of dealing with a servant, and though he had nothing against the Prince of Wales, he had stayed away during his visit to India because of Lord Curzon. Indeed a plausible explanation on the face of it, but acceptable officially? No. But still the meeting had ended smoothly with assertions of mutual regard by both participants with each feeling he had done his duty. One fact stood out now which Sayajirao III was quick to see—there was no question of him staying away from the Delhi durbar for King George V. That would be professional hara-kiri.

Lord Crewe sent the entire transcript of his meeting with Sayajirao III to Viceroy Hardinge who was considerably miffed that the Maharaja had got off so easily. He felt that Lord Crewe should have extracted an apology from the king and a promise to mend his ways instead of which they had simply exchanged their views on the rumours and the Maharaja had actually blamed Lord Curzon for his absence from the durbar of the Prince of Wales. How could a native, even if he held the exalted position of a Maharaja, have a quarrel with a viceroy and actually boast about disregarding his edict? It was unthinkable. Viceroy Hardinge must have silently thought of a scheme to put the native king in his place. As of now, he could do nothing except content himself with a few pinpricks. One particular kind that offered was the request from the Baroda durbar asking for permission to use horses instead of bullock carts in their light field battery. To which Viceroy Hardinge replied that he was ill disposed to make any further concessions to the Baroda durbar at present. Considering the reports sent by Lord Crewe which indicated Sayajirao III's links with seditious people, it would be foolish to allow him to step up his military efficiency in any way.

Sayajirao III, for whom the meeting with the secretary of state had been an eye-opener, made up his mind to not give the watchdogs of the empire a chance to report anything on his part that could be misconstrued as being disloyal to the British government of India and that included not attending the coronation durbar.

37

The Coronation Durbar Incident

The royal family from England arrived in Delhi on 5 December and proceeded directly from the station to the 'chiefs' reception pavilion,' the same amphitheatre that had been the venue of the durbars held earlier in 1877 and 1902. It was now the winter of 1911, and with the weather being more than conducive for such an event, Viceroy Hardinge was determined that his durbar outshine all those durbars held in the past by Lord Curzon or Lord Minto and organized the event on a lavish scale. 'A city of tents had been commissioned, twenty-eight square miles of canvas roads had been laid,'[1] lawns manicured to perfection and seeds sown in advance to show a garden blooming with flowers. A polo match was organized and forty bands were playing for the entertainment of the guests.

The royal family from England was to receive homage from their Indian subjects at a ceremony to which more than a hundred thousand guests had been invited. The truth of the matter was that Indian princes and kings found in this form of paying obeisance a degree of self-abasement which went against their self-respect. It was more in the nature of a public acknowledgement of the British as their overlords. While most of the native rulers took it in their stride, it was galling to an intelligent man like Sayajirao III who felt that they had not been vanquished in a battle and the Britishers were not their conquerors; treaties had been signed with the East India Company as equal allies and had been paid for it. It was purely a business arrangement for which they had been paid either in cash or in territory in exchange for the Company's military help. Therefore, this did not make Indians the Company's subordinates or subjects; the treaties were pure business contracts and had no clause in them that demanded homage by Indian princes to any of the Company's dignitaries. Even accepting the fact that the unilateral taking over of the Company's business by the British government technically made Indians subjects of the British Crown, still, to acknowledge that subjecthood by obsequious homage to the monarch was unjustified and unwarranted. However, these dismal thoughts and the prospect of having to play a part in the 'pageant of the empire that was being prepared in Delhi' were overshadowed by two personal problems. One concerned Sayajirao's daughter Indira who was strongly objecting to getting her marriage arranged with the Maharaja of Gwalior, Madho Rao Scindia, and the other was himself being embroiled in a sex scandal.

Madho Rao Scindia was a very rich, powerful, but benevolent autocrat. He was steeped in tradition and convention, believing that women should be in purdah. For the Gaekwads, it was a perfect match as it would tie the two states politically, which would be beneficial to both. Madho Rao Scindia was thirty-six years old, sixteen years older than Indira and a die-hard conventionalist who did not believe in the emancipation of women and was already married—plural marriages being common in Gwalior and not uncommon even in British India. Indira, who had been brought up on the lines of a well-bred Englishwoman, was educated and a product of a finishing school in Eastbourne. She took objection to being a second wife and, above all, to his conservatism as she had an absolute horror of the purdah system. How could her parents ever think of getting her married to such a man as him? She argued, but in vain, for her parents did not relent and were set on the match. Her engagement was announced and preparations for her trousseau began in full swing. The Maharaja of Gwalior who was also in London for the coronation gave a lavish party in honour of the engagement.

The other problem was caused by a woman named Beatrice Statham who, along with her husband, Ernest Emmanuel Statham, had hatched a scheme to extort money from Sayajirao III by pretending to be in a relationship with him.

The husband, expressing false indignation, had demanded money from the Maharaja if he did not want his name to be cited during the divorce proceedings in the court or in the papers. Sayajirao III ignored the threat as advised by his lawyers and Statham filed for a divorce citing Sayajirao III as co-respondent.

Whether Sayajirao III had ever been involved with the woman remains a matter of doubt as there was no evidence to give credence to anything of that sort, but common sense dictates one to question how a woman with an infamous reputation, such as the one that Beatrice Statham possessed, could have dared to link her name with a person of Sayajirao III's stature.

Unless they had met a few times, probably at one of those social gatherings that London's 'high society' is famous for, and she had seen an opportunity to drag him into a sex scandal undoubtedly backed by someone among the higher-ups keen on getting the Maharaja deposed.

This unsavoury incident (recounted in detail in another chapter), a shot in the dark fired by the Stathams to extort money from the Maharaja, had left its mark on Sayajirao III and the government of India. They left London soon after—Sayajirao III for Scotland to stay with some friends and Chimnabai II for Germany to complete her cure—giving rise to rumours already doing the rounds that Sayajirao III had no intention of returning to India to attend the coronation durbar which was scheduled for mid-December.

Meanwhile, there was a change in the designation of the officials of the British government in India. The change was only in name and not in the powers of the representatives of the government. The designation of AGG in Baroda was now changed to Resident. Whatever the name, rank or status they were designated did not change their nature as for the most part they were an 'imperious abrasive lot not renowned for their deportment or charm'.[2]

The new Resident, Cobb, was a perfect example of these species. Cobb expected the English dewan Seddon to blindly support him in his battle against sedition. Seddon, who was finding it difficult to deal ruthlessly with the nationalists in the state, found himself facing harsh criticism from the other. Cobb's argument was that Seddon being a fellow Britisher and a member of the civil service should have lent his support wholeheartedly in dealing with seditionists. Seddon felt that as the dewan of the Baroda state, he had his responsibilities clearly etched out and was not obliged to serve as an assistant to the Resident. As a result, they were at loggerheads with each other and after a while Seddon withheld his arguments against the other's accusations about all Baroda's subjects being seditionists since there was no point in doing so with a person who saw 'sedition lurking round every street corner and behind every tree'.[3]

As the time for the durbar drew near, Cobbs became more aggressive and virulent. He went to the extent of insinuating to his superiors that Seddon was conniving with the seditionists when the latter refused to take action against two men in Baroda service. Both the men—Khaserao Jadhav and Keshavrao Deshpande—held appointments as subhas or district commissioners, Deshpande at Mehsana and Jadhav at Naosari. The allegations were that they had not cooperated satisfactorily in curbing anti-British activities in their districts. Seddon knew Jadhav and Deshpande to be honest, upright men and he held them in high regard; therefore, he was reluctant to follow Cobbs's wishes on flimsy evidence passed on by the Residency's informers. In 1911, Cobb gathered what he thought was enough evidence to show that the two men were involved in anti-British activities, but on examining the evidence Seddon found it to be insufficient. But since he was aware of what he was up against, he decided to wait for Sayajirao III's decision when he returned. Sayajirao III and Chimnabai II returned to Baroda on 10 November well in time for the coronation durbar, putting all contradictory rumours to rest.

A day or so after his return, he was apprised by Seddon of the case against Jadhav and Deshpande. Sayajirao III was well aware of this allegation but since it did not warrant dismissal, he had them transferred according to their merits. Deshpande was transferred from administrative to judicial duties and Jadhav to another less prestigious post. Deshpande promptly resigned and left Baroda, thus providing Sayajirao III the opportunity of doing what Cobb had wanted him to do; however, according to the Resident, both men had got off lightly and expressed as much in his report to the viceroy. The viceroy agreed with him wholeheartedly. Sayajirao III by now had realized that his earlier plan to boycott the durbar would have to be abandoned as he was well aware that the viceroy was on the warpath and it would be professional hara-kiri to do so.

The coronation durbar had been scheduled for mid-December. The day arrived and prior to Sayajirao III's departure for Delhi to attend the durbar, he did something that sparked off even further indignation among the British officials. Viceroy Hardinge had sent him a copy of the programme for the durbar in which all detailed instructions of what the participants were expected to do were clearly written. Sayajirao III, never content to be a man of the shadows, had sent a reply suggesting some alterations in the manner in which native rulers should be received by the king. Viceroy Hardinge was not one who would alter anything at the suggestion of a native king and duly ignored the suggestion. The suggestion served the sole purpose of a warning that Sayajirao III had no intention of observing the protocol laid down for him. The day before the durbar, a rehearsal was held so that everyone should know what part he had to play. Sayajirao III did not attend the rehearsal and sent his brother Sampatrao as proxy to observe the ritual. Sayajirao III's intention was to not conform to the prescribed ritual but to let it appear that any lapse on his part would be an unintentional slip. (The fact that he had deliberately missed the rehearsal in itself suggests this.) However, his violation of the prescribed ritual was not subtle at all and was noticed by all those present in the Durbar Hall. Sayajirao III had not bargained for the fact that he was being watched by all the officials and especially by those who would waste no time in putting their own construction on any breach in etiquette on his part. The ritual demanded that the native rulers wear formal court dresses according to their custom with all the British decorations, jewellery, medallions, and they should approach the raised platform where the king and queen sat. Then they were to make a formal Indian bow, first to the king and then to the queen, after which they were to walk backwards seven steps before exiting from the hall.

'Maharaja Sayajirao broke every rule. He wore the simplest of white garments and, contrary to everyone's concept of a formally attired Maharaja, wore absolutely no jewellery; he conveniently "forgot" to wear the sash of the order of the Star of India, which he should have been proud to wear "as it was one of the highest-ranked of the Empire's decorations; and in place of the sword that was compulsory he carried a gold topped cane". He approached the dais when his turn came after the Nizam, "stood before the king, made one cursory bow" then took a couple of steps backwards and making an abrupt turn with his back to the king and queen, he hurried from their presence.'[4]

The Durbar Hall was filled with people; among them there were those who noticed and did not think much of the lapse in protocol, but then there were some who had been looking out for something of this sort and made a point of it. The viceroy who had been expecting Sayajirao III to step out of line did not see anything amiss and was quite prepared to let the matter drop till Cobb poisoned his ears by stating that the Baroda state was 'honeycombed with sedition', which stirred a hornet's nest. Fully convinced that the insult to the royal couple had been deliberate and was linked to sedition in Baroda, the viceroy changed his mind about not making an issue of the durbar gaffe. All the charges that he had made against Sayajirao III in his report to the British government were now validated by his appearance at the durbar and it was time for a showdown.

Sayajirao III who had anticipated something to happen had not bargained for the kind of tempest that was unleashed which might end with the government demanding his abdication. The first sign of the storm was seen the same evening when he was denied entrance to the tent where Sir George Clarke, the governor of Bombay, was residing temporarily for the durbar. Sayajirao III was told that Sir George 'was not at home' when he asked to see him. He found his old friend G.K. Gokhale waiting for him when he returned to his own camp; Gokhale told him that he had infuriated the higher-ups in the governmental department by his behaviour at the durbar. A very worried Gokhale advised Sayajirao III to make amends immediately and on his advice the Maharaja dashed off a letter to the viceroy expressing his deepest affection and loyalty to Their Majesties and blamed his indiscretion on 'nervousness and confusion due to the presence of their Majesties'. It was not a very convincing explanation, but it helped to abate the fury that had been aroused. Sayajirao III had done what Gokhale had advised him to do but 'almost at the moribund point' because if deposed, he as well as the Baroda state stood to lose a lot by way of his progressive reforms coming to an abrupt halt; and, who knew what the fate of his people would be in the hands of the British.

But this thinking should have preceded his action for after all, it would have been better for him to follow the protocol as dictated by the viceroy and save himself the humiliation of rendering an abject apology. Whatever one might say in his defence the fact is that Sayajirao III was wrong. The British were the paramount power in India, a fact he should have borne in mind and been more cautious in his behaviour. There was nothing wrong in making the customary bows to Their Majesties and taking the seven steps backwards—the Nizam of Hyderabad had followed protocol, so why couldn't he? The cold hand of common sense should have prevailed at that time and it would have spared him all the misery he underwent because of his childish resentment towards the rules laid down by Viceroy Hardinge.

Whatever the reasons given by Sayajirao III for his misbehaviour at the durbar, the significance was not lost on the shrewd Britishers and on those it had been intended. No doubt, many Indians must have secretly applauded him for his chutzpah, particularly people from the Indian press and the nationalists who admired him. However, the gesture revealed his real feelings and it would not be long before the government of India would come down on him with axe in hand. 'Kiplings' India buzzed with anger and the Anglo-

Indian paparazzi for whom the mystique of the empire was food and drink were in an uproar.'⁵ To make things worse than it already was, there was a snippet of the Statham case in the following morning's papers mentioning Sayajirao III's name as co-respondent in the case where the husband was seeking a divorce from his wife. The slur on the Maharaja's character coupled with his behaviour at the durbar roused the anger of the public in London to a pitch. The jackals of the empire condemned the insult to their majesties and screamed for his deposition, 'he should be stripped off his rank and deported, his twenty-one gun salute reduced...They clawed at the history of the Baroda state.'⁶

Whether Sayajirao III had been involved with Beatrice is a matter for debate. That they had met at social gatherings was known to quite a few, and Ernest Emmanuel Statham in connivance with Beatrice had taken advantage of that fact to get him embroiled in the divorce proceedings.

However, on 22 December 1911, the judgement came in Sayajirao III's favour. It clearly stated, 'His Highness by international law is not capable of being made co-respondent in a suit for dissolution of marriage in the High Court in England, and his name must be struck out as co-respondent. I, however, give leave to the petitioner to proceed without making any co-respondent as to those paragraphs of the petition in which His Highness' name appears.'

After absolving the Maharaja, the judgement in the divorce proceedings was read as such:

> In the divorce division, before Justice Bargrave Deane, judgment was given yesterday on the motion of George Wellington Statham in a petition of divorce from his wife Beatrice Alice Statham. The motion asked for directions as to service of the petition by some method other than by personal service on His Highness Maharaja the Gaekwad of Baroda, who had been cited co-respondent. His Lordship also dealt with the summons which asked for the dismissal of His Highness from the suit on the ground that he was a reigning sovereign and not amenable to the jurisdiction of the court. His Lordship in giving the judgment, discussed the history of the House of Baroda, and drew from his examination of the authorities on the question of suzerainity the conclusion that His Highness had the status of a Sovereign Prince, and was not capable of being made a

co-respondent in a suit for dissolution of marriage in the High Court in England.

This status was accorded to the sovereigns of the Baroda state by the Treaty of Baroda in 1802 by which the British granted the Baroda state autonomy in exchange for acceding as an Indian princely state under the British Crown. Thus, in accordance with the treaty, the verdict was given on 22 December, after the coronation durbar, in which case whether the Stathams ever really got divorced or waited till they found another victim to try their wiles on is anybody's guess and Sayajirao III's absolvement from the case did not in any way reduce the intensity of fury of the British hierarchy. The real truth of the matter was that Sayajirao III was advised by his lawyers to pay a sum of 5,700 pounds to Statham to withdraw the case against his wife as the scandal was something that the Maharaja could ill afford then. Statham accordingly made a request to the court that since his wife and he had resolved their differences he undertook not to renew the charges made in the court against his wife. Whether or not Sayajirao III was involved with the woman is a debatable point, however he got off the hook and the matter was put behind him.

But Sayajirao III's troubles did not end here as Viceroy Hardinge, who was still on the warpath, smarting at the durbar insult, felt that Sayajirao III's letter of apology should be given fullest publicity as public fury over the insult to their king remained unabated. Aware of the Maharaja's reluctance to the publication of the letter, he issued an ultimatum—either the letter got published emphasizing that 'people *should* know how sorry you are... or consider yourself uninvited to the reception I am giving this evening in honour of His Majesty The King.'[7] Poor Sayajirao III must have bemoaned the fact that he had not paid enough attention to the advice of his old dewan Madhav Rao when he was first given the reins as an adolescent, 'Obey them for they are the paramount power...'

The letter was duly published and it ran thus:

Dear Lord Hardinge,

I hear the manner in which I paid homage to His Imperial Majesty the King-Emperor has been the subject of unfavourable comments. I take the earliest opportunity of writing to you to explain what actually occurred, and to assure you that the very last thing I intended, or could ever intend, was to do anything that could displease His Imperial Majesty, or lead him or anyone to doubt the reality of my loyalty and allegiance to his throne and person. To the British government, the Baroda state owes everything, and to that government, my state and I myself personally will always be truly grateful and loyal. When approaching and returning from the dais at the Durbar, I am said to have failed to observe that exact etiquette prescribed. If this was the case, it was due entirely to nervousness and confusion in the presence of their Majesties, and before that vast assembly. Only one chief, the Nizam, had made obeisance before me, and I had not had the opportunity of noticing others, and, in fact, in the confusion of the moment, I had hardly been able to note the details of what the Nizam did. After bowing, I receded a few steps and turned round to ask which way I was to go. I was under the impression that I actually descended by the proper passage, but I am told that I did not. Having turned to ask the way, I became confused, and continued to walk round. For this mistake I can only say how sincerely sorry I am...

All hell broke loose in London when *The Times* published Reuters telegram dated from the Durbar Camp, Delhi, on 16 December in which there was a summary of the letter to the viceroy. The article with the heading 'The Gaekwar and Indian Sedition' severely criticized Sayajirao III on his conduct from 1905 onwards. The paper blatantly, without validating its accusations with evidence, stated that the Baroda state and the palace where the Maharaja resided was home to many Indian extremists, who were given employment in the state and 'even in the Gaekwar's household'; that the press run by extremists did not include him in their scurrilous attacks on loyal Indian princes. Here, a reference was made to when His Highness and the maharani, 'an accomplished but exalted lady', had made the acquaintance of people like Krishna Varma and Madame Cama who were promoters of the assassination campaign in India. The article also said that a printing press in Baroda patronized by officials had been responsible for circulating seditious literature and when it was traced to this particular press, the cooperation from the state officials had been 'extremely lukewarm'. Again, the article brought the attention of the reader to the durbar incident and hoped 'that the humiliation that he had brought upon himself by his conduct at the Imperial Durbar would serve as an effective warning to him'. Further to this, the press in London and even the 'temps' in Paris published a message sent from Delhi, stating that 'Gaekwar had never made a secret of his hatred of the British rule'. *The Pioneer* had published the article on 18 December which had first made its appearance in *The Times*.

Sayajirao III, thinking that it was time to end these speculations, accompanied with false accusations, telegraphed to *The Times* that the article contained grossly exaggerated comments on his behaviour at Westminster Abbey and at the Delhi Durbar. He protested that since he had been present at the coronation at Westminster solely in the capacity of a spectator, it puts to rest any question of 'breach of etiquette' by him at the ceremony. As regards the Delhi Durbar, the circumstances had already been explained and apologized for. Pertaining to the allegations of his involvement with seditionists, he stated that he had not met Krishna Varma since he left England many years ago, and certainly did not meet him in 1910. Regarding seditious literature, he stated that the press was in no way connected to the state and assistance to the maximum had been given to the British authorities by the Baroda council for the investigations. Due to lack of legal evidence, the case had been dismissed, but he, the Maharaja, had confiscated the press and had banished the writer.

The durbar incident was still fresh in the minds of the British people and also among the native princes and the Indian people.

The editor of *The Indian Sociologist* in Paris published Krishnavarma's letter in *The Times* dated 27 December in which he pointed out that he had been introduced to Sayajirao III by Lord Northbrook at the end of 1884 and had met him elsewhere and also in India but had not set eyes on him ever since he left India and migrated to Paris in 1907; the letter further mentioned that he had not corresponded with Sayajirao III. In fact, he had strongly criticized the Maharaja for presiding over a luncheon in London, in honour of the KCSI title being bestowed on Sir K.G. Gupta on the occasion of the coronation.

Excerpts taken from the Delhi Durbar showing Sayajirao III's gaffe while paying homage to Their Majesties and published in the London illustrated papers added further sparks to the already smouldering stack. Matters were made worse when the durbar incident was shown on celluloid; the howls of the wolves were loud and they demanded that he be stripped of his rank and deported. A few days later, Keir Hardie, MP, fatuously remarked in his article in *The Pioneer* that the Maharaja's conduct at the durbar contrasted well with that of his fellow rulers who had been taught to grovel before the 'throne' thus complimenting Sayajirao III while also hinting that his intention had been deliberate. Matters were made worse for the Maharaja. Philip Sergeant in *The Ruler of Baroda* declares Keir Hardie's praise was more unjust in its effects than all the attacks of which the most scurrilous appeared in *The World* of 9 January, which touched the lowest depths of journalism. After the papers had done their worst, all the brouhaha over the durbar fiasco subsided for a while, but the respite from name-slandering was only a brief one. It was triggered into full swing when on 8 October, Viscount Hardinge, the brother of the viceroy, defended the Maharaja over the durbar incident in one of his lectures in London, declaring that it was grossly exaggerated, pointing out that 'since the Maharaja was a much travelled man and the most world travelled among Indian princes, he would never have been so senseless and bold to show disloyalty at a public ceremony with 3,000 loyal Europeans and a 100,000 loyal natives watching him.'[8]

Three weeks later, the following article dated 29 October 1912 appeared in the *Pall Mall Gazette* in London:

'DURBAR STORY'
By One Who Knows

After ten months of silence during which one of the ruling princes of India, one of the most loyal and certainly the most enlightened, has lain under an unjust suspicion of disloyalty and deliberate discourtesy at the Delhi Durbar, Lord Hardinge, brother of the viceroy of India, has raised his voice to clear Gaekwad of the charges levelled against him. Why this has not been done before is a mystery for the grave attack of certain leading journals and the insults of lesser papers have constituted a deplorable injustice and raised popular anger against a ruler who has deserved better at British hands. The few who are acquainted with the facts, especially with the antecedent circumstances, have been constrained to hold their peace knowing that no voice not official or exceptionally influential would be listened to in all the hubbub, and that no credence would have rewarded a plain statement of the truth when the charge had apparently the high authority of the press. At last, Viscount Hardinge has broken the silence. But, even he has not gone far as the facts justify. He, as an eyewitness, has 'no hesitation in saying that the whole thing has been grossly exaggerated'...and after testifying to the high status of the Maharaja he gives us to understand his entire disbelief in the charge of disloyalty, and for 'disloyalty', he rightly substitutes 'nerves'. If he, together with those who moved the public to indignation, and been more fully conversant with all the circumstances, he would, one may believe, have spoken sooner and dismissed in still more emphatic terms the whole fabric of the charge. Here then is the story of this absurdly magnified incident, of how a simple mistake in the excitement of a moving, epoch making, moment has been distorted into wilful rudeness, political gaucherie and disloyalty amounting almost to sympathy with sedition. All this even after his *amende honorable,* the Gaekwad, one of the most chivalrous and prudent of men, has had to suffer in silence for the best part of the year. For years those who have been admitted to the friendship of the Gaekwad have known his views on British rule in India. He has never hesitated to proclaim that rule to be not only beneficent, but absolutely necessary and essential, declaring that if it were once withdrawn the nation of India would be at each other's throats; and he holds it to be inconceivable that British rule could be exchanged for another.

At the same time, he is an enthusiastic educationist. It is known that his is the only state in Asia, and one of the few in the world with compulsory education and cannot see eye to eye with those who hold that education is the road to sedition. On the contrary, he concludes that enlightenment is the path to loyalty.

When the durbar preparations reached the point of dealing with the form in which the princes and the rulers were to do homage the Gaekwar as the most travelled of them, had ventured to offer his views to headquarters as to the manner or form that might be adopted. As the native princes were closely associated in the matter, it was not unreasonable that he should offer suggestions, suitably expressed, for consideration; for acceptance or for rejection. It appears that this action gave offence before the time for the durbar had arrived so that in one quarter at least, his subsequent actions were regarded with unmerited suspicion. The occasion soon arose, for when he presented himself at the durbar in a plain white garment, while all the princes had decked themselves in gorgeous costumes and dazzling jewels; the simplicity of his appearance was taken to signify a direct slight. This view was so far excusable perhaps that it is known that Gaekwad possesses the finest jewels in India. But, it was forgotten that in the coronation procession in London, His Highness had appeared with the same chaste simplicity and no one complained or remarked about it. It was forgotten too, that this is the costume worn by Gaekwad on ceremonious occasions. Moreover, having spent much time in England, he is aware that the note of good breeding is the opposite of ostentation, and if he applied the principle when appearing before the Emperor and Empress of India, he might be held lacking in judgement as to the fitness of things in the matter of dress. but to have charged him, as was done, with intentional disrespect was absurd, for such conduct would be worse than pointless—it could obviously only recoil upon himself and create an impression of a painful kind from which he would be the only sufferer. The crowning trouble was soon to come as the actual act of homage the Resident informed him, so he has positively affirmed only one bow was to be made. How the mistake arose has not been publicly explained but it seems impossible to hold Gaekwad responsible for it. One prince by right preceded Gaekwad who was too excited as he has practically admitted, to notice exactly what was done. What was the cause for this excitement? In the first place, His Highness is naturally shy and he feels his position in great public assembly. At the supreme moment of this tremendous occasion, unique in history, under the eyes of the Emperor and Empress, and of the brilliant attendance, before all the ruling princes and princesses of India and countless thousands beyond it is not surprising if a natural modesty and nervousness developed into what Viscount Hardinge calls 'nerves'. There was something else, which all the world knows of, but which has not been taken into account. Nor, so far as the writer knows, referred to by the Gaekwar himself. A charge was being advanced against him, which his advisors it is said, never for a moment believed would be openly brought. Yet, it was so brought and on the very day before the durbar. A few hours later it was flashed to India and would be the talk of the town the very morning when he was about to step before the Emperor to make his obeisance, without an opportunity of making a reply. The acute position of such a man at such a time and at such a place may be imagined! Exposed to such a charge within sight and hearing of the whole world. What wonder if he forgot, if he did actually forget, or ever knew the exact predetermined formula of the act of homage. But we have the exact predetermined formula of the act of homage had not been correctly imparted to him. He himself remarked, 'To make one bow only to the King struck me as strange' adding 'I am sufficiently chivalrous enough to bow to a lady, especially should I have wished to do so to the Queen. But one must not ask questions as to ceremony in the framing of which one had no choice.' There is good reason to believe that when all was over he was totally unaware that anything serious had happened and when the subject of complaint was brought to his notice, he believed that the incident was a pure accident of so trifling a character that it was hardly worth notice or would be taken notice of, but the unfavourable comment of witnesses reported to him by friends quickly disillusioned him and distressed him too exceedingly at the painful impression that he knew would be created in England. But he was not at that time prepared for the exaggerated severity of the newspaper reports from India; still less for the bitter hostility of newspaper comments on the despatches. So far, as I know, he remarked to a friend 'no mistake took place except that I turned back a little too soon. A few steps more and it would have been all right. But it was a sheer mistake. Yet some people for some reason or the other wish to make capital out of it. Someday the truth will be known. Well here it is!'[9]

A few days later, another article appeared in the *Pall Mall Gazette* (found in the files of the India Office Records, London): —'What Led to the Durbar Incident: Studied Insult! Inflated View of His Own Importance; The Full Story: By One Who Knows Better. The first paragraph alluded to the earlier article by 'One Who Knows' accusing the writer of giving rise to false impressions to the public. Then, it stated that Sayajirao III was the only ruler to disregard the official injunctions, with which he had been explicitly acquainted. He knew the injunctions quite well and had not hesitated to express his objections to them. Further the article by 'One Who Knows' defended Sayajirao III for appearing at the durbar in a 'plain white garment' and said that this was the costume worn by His Highness 'on ceremonious occasions'. The writer further stated 'that having spent so much time in England, Gaekwad is aware that the note of good breeding here is the opposite of ostentation'. If that is the case, said the writer of this article, 'one would have expected the King-Emperor to be too well bred to wear his crown!' The remark made in the earlier one that 'He often affects the same chaste simplicity' is countered with 'when it becomes his duty to attend any public ceremonial at which exalted British personages are present. But, in his own state, on occasions, he is wont to appear in much braver array. Those who wish to see a portrait of the Gaekwads as he presents himself at times to his own people, may be recommended to turn to the 'sketch' of 27 December 1911 and they will see Gaekwad in full uniform of his 'army', which is neither very simple nor very 'chaste'. They will see something else too. They will see Gaekwad wearing the aiguillettes of an aide-de-camp to the King-Emperor, an honour he does not possess. They will further see him wearing the Star of an 'order' of his own state above the 'Star of India' and every prince understands the slight implied. He wore this same 'order' in the presence of the King-Emperor at the investiture. But, perhaps the point about his costume is sufficiently disposed of when I say that at the 1903 durbar, Gaekwad wore a white satin robe edged with gold and the riband of the 'Star of India'. In 1911, he elected to do homage to the King-Emperor in cheap white cotton such as the clerks in his public offices elect to wear.

The mention of the orders brings one to the question of the decorations worn by Gaekwad at the Delhi Durbar. 'One Who Knows' asked us to believe that Gaekwad wore no jewels because he was not accustomed to do so. At the 1903 durbar, he wore a 'breastplate' of diamonds valued at a quarter of a million sterling, as was duly recorded at that time. At the state ball in 1903, he wore a chain of diamonds. The thing that damns the apologia of 'One Who Knows' is that Gaekwad actually arrived at the King-Emperor's durbar wearing jewels before the King-Emperor arrived, but for some reason, best known to him, he took them off. There are many who were present to testify to that statement. Moreover, the viceroy arrived twenty minutes before the

King-Emperor. The programme laid down was that everybody should rise when His Excellency drove into the arena and to remain standing until he had taken his seat under the Imperial Canopy. Everybody duly rose except one man. In that vast assemblage, one man remained defiantly seated. That one man was Gaekwad of Baroda. Just as the viceroy's carriage drew abreast to the spot where Gaekwad was sitting, the British Resident at Baroda was observed to bend down and say something to His Highness. Gaekwad jumped up as if he had been shot, but almost instantly resumed his seat before the viceroy had alighted from his carriage. A hundred thousand people including some of the greatest princes of India were standing at that moment. Again one asks whether Gaekwad's action was due to 'nerves'?

I come now to the act of homage. The Nizam of Hyderabad made obeisance first. Gaekwad came second. His Highness was carrying a stick. I know that one of his little affectations is to carry a stick, but would any member of the English royal family, any minister of state, any great noble, any of the numberless princes over whom King George is suzerain and sovereign lord, dare to appear before the monarch at a Levee in London with a stick in his hand? There is no oriental warranty for such an act, for everyone in India knows what the late Nizam would have done even if his heir had been audacious enough to appear before him in open durbar armed with a stick.

The use of a stick was an act of effrontery and so was the episode that followed. Instead of making the prescribed number of bows and backing to the edge of the dais, Gaekwad strolled up, nodding to His Majesty, took no notice of the Queen-Empress at all, turned his back on Their Majesties, an unpardonable insult in the East and West alike, walked off the dais and went away twirling his stick. There was no mistake about his intentions, nor need I emphasize these statements. Thousands saw the act and hundred thousands have seen it reproduced in cinematograph.

The facts are not disputed by Gaekwad himself. According to 'One Who Knows', His Highness says it was a 'sheer mistake', but when he tore off his jewels was that a mistake too?

Then, there is quite a vitriolic attack on the Maharaja and his administration, unfortunately linking it with sedition.

Another article in *The Times* dated 18 December 1911 with the heading 'Gaekwar And Indian Sedition' stated:

It is no secret that the behaviour of the Gaekwar at the King's Coronation at Westminster provoked a good deal of comment amongst those present who were familiar with Indian customs and etiquette.

At various periods since, on attaining his majority, the Gaekwar received his ruling powers in 1881, his Highness has shown a tendency to disregard the duties imposed upon him by the relations of the State of Baroda to the Supreme Government. But it is only since 1905 that his conduct has been open to very strict strictures. We have no wish to believe that his Highness has been guilty of anything worse than grave indiscretions.

But it could not escape notice in India that many Indian extremists come from Baroda, or found employment in the State and even in Gaekwar's household! That the Indian extremist Press always studiously excepted the Gaekwar from the scurrilous attacks to which Indian princes were persistently subjected on account of their loyalty; that advanced politicians engaged in an anti-British campaign were not excluded from the Gaekwar's generosity; and that neither His Highness nor the Maharani, an accomplished but exaltee [sic] lady, shrink when they were travelling in Europe in 1909, even from contact with such people as Krishna Varma and Madam Cama, who for some years past had been openly promoting from Paris a campaign of outrageous assassination in India. Within the last few months, an extensive circulation of seditious literature in the Bombay Presidency has been traced to a printing press in the State of Baroda, patronized by the officials of the State and the assistance rendered by the Baroda authorities to the British police investigation has been to say the least extremely lukewarm. Acts of disloyalty to the British Crown have hitherto been recognized in Baroda as offences punishable at law, but only acts of disloyalty to the ruler of the State, and it is only since his return a few weeks ago from England that his Highness has been induced to recognize the expediency of introducing legislation with regard to sedition which will bring the State of Baroda into line with other native States. The Gaekwar has acquired, especially in his country, the credit of liberal and progressive ideas, by the introduction into his State of free and compulsory education the merits of which it is perhaps too early to pass definite judgement, and he has made some admirable speeches in support of the movement for raising the 'depressed classes' of India. But his methods of governance remain as autocratic as in most native States and it may be noted that the land revenue raised in Baroda is, on the whole, considerably heavier than in the adjoining parts of British-India. He has, moreover of late lost a great deal of the credit he enjoyed with the most enlightened social reformers amongst his own fellow-countrymen by sanctioning the marriage of his daughter with the Maharajah Scindia of Gwalior, who is already married. No one blames the Maharajah Scindia who has never professed to be anything but an orthodox Hindu, for following such an ancient Hindu custom as that of taking a second wife if no heir has been born from the first marriage. But it is felt, and has been freely stated in influential native newspapers, that the Gaekwar by countenancing such an alliance and surrendering his lofty professions of principles to considerations of political expediency and family aggrandizement, has dealt a serious blow to the cause of social reform, of which he had constituted himself one of the most prominent champions. It is to be hoped that the humiliation which Gaekwar has now brought upon himself by having to publicly explain away his conduct at the Imperial Durbar will serve as an effective warning to His Highness, and that he will give much practical effect to his assurances of loyalty as to leave no doubt as to their sincerity.[10]

It was in this anti-Sayajirao III atmosphere that a film of the coronation was shown in the London cinemas, that provoked boos and catcalls from the audience who screamed their protests in words, 'Down with Gaekwad; depose the traitor and hang him'. When on 17 December 1911, Sayajirao III with his entourage left Delhi, the palaver caused by the durbar incident was at its height but on reaching home turf a further shock awaited him in the form of a telegram from Madho Rao Scindia asking, 'What does the princess mean by her letter?' Indira, who had been busy falling in love with the handsome, debonair Jitendra, younger brother of the then Maharaja of Cooch Behar who had also been present at the Delhi durbar, had sent a letter to Madho Rao Scindia breaking off her engagement to him, just as Sayajirao III's train left the Delhi railway station. The wedding preparations that had begun well in advance with decorations on roadsides and archways erected, the bridal trousseau was ready and invitations sent to hundreds of guests were halted midway and a public announcement was made that the wedding would not take place. This coming after the durbar fiasco had newspaper editors connecting the two and a couple of them hinted that the prospective bridegroom had felt humiliated and had called off the wedding.

The other fact was that the princess had not fancied herself as playing second wife to an already married man and to his extremely orthodox views was just too much for the young princess to have to tolerate for the rest of her life. For the durbar coronation, splendid camps had been set up for the participants and while everyone was busy, according to Miss Totenham, Indira 'went by herself too often to the Cooch Behar camp where she had a gay time dancing with one of the brothers, Jitendra, who had fallen in love with her'.[11]

The result was the broken engagement with Madho Rao Scindia. Her parents were, of course, very disappointed as Sayajirao III had hoped the alliance would strengthen the bond between Gwalior and Baroda.

The higher officials of the Raj had their eyes trained on the Baroda state looking for evidence that would nail Sayajirao III as a seditionist. A native king who had had the temerity to insult their monarch should not be allowed to go scot-free.

The truth of the matter was that Sayajirao III was too involved with his reform measures to get deeply involved in sedition which made the accusations from the pro-British press baseless at that particular point of time. In his own domain the common man who had his basic needs met was more than satisfied with Sayajirao III's rule. As a result, Baroda had come to acquire the reputation of a progressive state which did much to foster talent, support industries, introduce legislation to bring about social uplift which was much more than what the Raj did, and whatever they may have thought of him, the people of Baroda were happy with Sayajirao III's rule. However, the wheels of deposition with the intent to depose the Maharaja were set in motion and confidential reports from British Residents appointed for the Baroda state to the secretary of the government of India's foreign department flew in rapid haste to London in 1910-12. These reports, chiefly from Residents H.V. Cobb, L.A. Kinlaid, LT Colonel L. Impey Impey had pretty much insinuated that the Maharaja encouraged these seditious activities.

38

The Truth about Sedition

It was true that Sayajirao III was involved with seditionists and their revolutionary activities. He was fully aware of all the anti-British propaganda that was doing the rounds, and aided and abetted it. He did provide employment and refuge to revolutionaries in the Baroda state. This was in keeping with his true identity as Gopalrao, 'son of the soil' of India, and his 'conscience' that kept reminding him that these foreign predators should be ousted from the country where they had no right to be. The accusations from British officials though slightly exaggerated were nevertheless true as those illustrated in the letters quoted below.

A letter dated 29 September 1911 from L. A. Kinlaid to the secretary of the government of India's foreign department reads as follows:

> Since 1905, the British police carried out a partial investigation with regard to the source of a publication titled *VanaspatiDavao* (vegetable medicine), in which the murder of white Residents in India was advocated. The publication was circulated in Poona where the vernacular is not Gujarati. Enquiries led to the strong suspicion that the source was to be traced to the Baroda state. The reports also stated that 'an ex-convict Aba Saheb Ramchandra and another notorious character with a gang of kindred spirits Madhavrao had settled at Billamora, a short distance from Naosari. A surprise visit by the Bombay police to the latter's house resulted in the discovery of 500–600 copies of the said publication concealed in a well. A joint enquiry by the Baroda durbar and the Bombay government resulted in the discovery of the author being Narsinh Patel, a clerk in the employment of the Baroda durbar. The publication had been printed at the Shikshak press in Mehsana'. The previous proceedings were pointed out to the Baroda durbar in March 1909 and the Resident was informed in April that a prosecution would be instituted against

him by the state, but nothing has been done. Not an isolated case of the detection of a most seditious book written and published in Baroda. If the state had shown willingness to assist in the joint enquiry and if there were no other reasons to connect Baroda with movements directed towards subversion of British rule in India, the episode might be regarded as possessing only temporary importance, but these conditions have not been fulfilled. Mehsana case is only one out of a multitude of proofs of what has been going on consistently in the state of Baroda. In a native state the conduct of all affairs and the attitude of the people depend entirely on the character of the chief. In no state of India is this principle more conspicuously operative than in Baroda, where His Highness the Gaekwar holds the reign of government completely in his own hands and the tone of officials and people are derived from that Head. The Government of India are in possession of the facts which, whether taken individually or as a whole show... the attitude of Gaekwad has, for some time, been one of thinly veiled hostility to the British government. He has not hesitated to give countenance to persons of whose extremist views he must be well aware of. Even in Vancouver he accepted an address from Babu Taraknath Das, a violent agitator. In New York he received visits from Dr Bumpus a dismissed official of the American Natural official Museum, who has held meetings of disaffected Indians in his house. It may well be asked, what object a chief in his position of the Gaekwar can have in admitting such persons to his presence, and by what agency his contact with them is brought about. His visits to Sarvajanik Sabha of Poona has been the subject of communications from the government of Bombay, that he should publicly give his patronage to this extremist body in the capital of the Deccan illustrates his disregard to the obligations of ordinary courtesy to the government of India. His friendliness to Aurobindo Ghosh is well known and he has supplied funds to Bepin Chandra Pal who though outwardly cautious in his writings and utterances has been in association with the party of violence. Whether the Gaekwar visited Krishna Varma is uncertain but the Maharani has visited and been in association with Madam Cama. Neither the Maharani nor her second son attempt to disguise their violent hostility to British rule in India. The results of the attitude of the Gaekwar and his family are plainly visible. Extremists can find shelter in the state. At least two institutions inculcating sedition—the Ganganath School and professor Manekrao's Akara are known to exist. Further, no law to check the authorship of seditious literature or the performances of objectionable theatrical plays directed against the British government. No legislation controlling the collection of arms, the use of explosives and the manufacture of bombs. The loyal chiefs of India have not hesitated to enact legislation with these objects in view, but Baroda has stood significantly aloof. Gaekwar's powers are not brought into play but only under pressure and with great reluctance. The case of the *chabuk* and the *pudhari* are well known to the government of India. No effective action has been taken with regard to the *Baroda Gazette* which has been guilty of offensive publications V. D. Ganthra a member of the National Union of India who was prosecuted in connection with the Hind Swarajya and a library of seditious books was discovered in his house, but before proceedings could be taken he escaped into Baroda territory. The durbar in possession of this knowledge granted him permission to start a new publication.

Whatever grievances the Gaekwar may have, he has always been treated with the utmost consideration, kindness and suggested in the kindest manner that he should publicly express his disapproval of seditious movements in India. At the same time ample warning has been given to him of his unfriendly attitude of himself and his state towards the government of India to whom he owes the gadi and in the light of that should not forget it.

Apart from the effect in British India of seditious influences emanating freely from Baroda, I am to point out that the object lesson which the Gaekwar is providing for the protected princes of India generally cannot be ignored. They must and do observe his proceedings and note with amazement the consideration which he continues to receive. They are doubtless aware of more than has come to our notice. Continued tolerance of these proceedings would necessarily appear to them in the light of exceeding weakness on our part. It can hardly be denied that our position vis a vis to the native states of India depends wholly upon visible signs of strength. If such signs can no longer be discerned their allegiance which may be of vital importance to us before long will certainly be imperiled.

All these considerations have forced upon the governor in council the conviction that the present attitude of the Gaekwar must be changed and that decisive and immediate measures with this object are imperatively demanded. To pass forth with legislation dealing with the press and theatres, with arms and explosives in the form of the existing British Acts and providing equal penalties whether the offences are committed to the detriment of the British or of the Baroda government. He must be required to amend his penal code so as to make the class of offences dealt with in chp. vii of the Indian Penal Code punishable when committed against the British government as they are at present and when committed against his own government. Further since Law in a native state may become a dead letter unless enforced by the will of the chief, it seems essential that Baroda should accept British officers as chief judge and head of the police for a term of years. In conclusion, prompt and stern measures are advocated to put an end to all evils which are increasingly grave and mainly to bring Baroda administration directly under control of the Bombay government, Baroda was a part of the Bombay Presidency geographically it wasn't but by its proximity. The government in council is well aware that any action taken against the Gaekwar would trigger an outburst of protests in the state. By judicious employment of agents the impression has been created in England that Baroda is the most progressive state in many respects able to set an example to the British government. Special care has been taken to disseminate illusions on the Free and Compulsory Education in Baroda, and Mr Ramsay Mcdonald was apparently informed that the Gaekwar spent 60,00,000 pounds a year on education when his gross state revenue amounted to about one and a quarter million sterling only!

There is another possibility which should not be ignored. The Gaekwar may be riding for a fall, and there is some reason for such a supposition. In this case he would abdicate under strong protest and take up his residence in Europe with the object of arousing sympathy for his cause. Trouble might evidently be thus engendered, but it is the strong opinion of the government in council that this would be a far lesser danger to the public peace in India than the continuance on the part of the government to tolerate the situation as it now exists in the state of Baroda, and the markedly disloyal attitude of one of the leading Native Chiefs of India.

Prior to Kinlaid's letter to the government of India, Resident Cobb in a letter to the government of India, dated 21 September, explained in detail the seditious activities rampant in the Baroda state:

> Another seditious proscribed book like the *Yadukulno Ithihas*, etc., made their appearance in Bombay in August 1910; and several copies were sent to the police commissioner by an Indian gentleman to whom the book had been sent anonymously, 150 of these books were received for distribution around and in Bombay. The book *Yadukulno Ithihas* (history of Yadukulno) purports to be an account of the art of modern warfare with examples from the Boer War. More importantly it was duly proscribed under government notification no 5353 dtd. 21st September 1910 and vigilant enquiries were instituted to trace whence the book emanated. Following shortly upon this the Bombay Criminal Investigations Department received information that this objectionable book *YogMaya* was being distributed *gratis* to the subscribers of the 'Sayaji Vijaya' of Baroda. Again this book was proscribed under notification 6314 dtd. 7 November 1910. Vasanth Dayalji Gantra was responsible for its distribution in Surat and a search of his premises revealed a library of 245 books in Bengali out of which two books and seven inflammatory publications had been proscribed by the government of Bengal. Considerable attention had been paid to Gantra's activities in Surat and it is significant that this firebrand settled down in Baroda and became a contributor to the *Baroda Gazette*. The fact that seditious literature was being freely circulated suggested that the Baroda state appeared not to be doing its duty in connection with that offensive. Vanaspati Davao purported to have been printed at the Suryodaya Press in Bombay in

1905. Enquiries revealed the absence of any such press. Contents of the book were found highly objectionable.

Aba Sahib, a notorious swindler, was allowed to establish himself in Billamoria there to surround himself with a number of youths to become the agent of the *Jalashwar Balram* Lottery, to open a press and to have working under him boys from the *Ganganath Vidyalaya* of Baroda show an astounding laxity on the part of the Baroda state officials. What the methods of police investigation in the Baroda state are, it is difficult to say. During the time I [Cobb] worked there with these officials, I was struck by their apathetic indolence; by their incompetence and by their spirit of opposition and hostility...Highly seditious and inflammatory pamphlets forwarded to the police in February and March 1911 were received enclosed in envelopes which had printed labels affixed to the effect that this letter is extremely important and should be read with care. These envelopes were dropped into the Post Boxes of various shops apparently at night. The last pamphlet was received late in June 1911. Aba Sahib was found to be the originator who used to send his agents to distribute these envelopes at night. Every effort was made to capture the parties concerned with little success. The last pamphlet was received late in June 1911. Aba Sahib was found to be the origin of this distribution by sending his agents to distribute these envelopes at night. Under the preventive section of criminal penal code, four local members of Aba Sahib's gang were taken into custody and from that date no more pamphlets have come to light. There was further ground for believing that these various seditious publications emanated from the Baroda State and their distribution was certainly being engineered by the notorious criminal Aba Sahib. Further a box containing 150 books of Yadukulno Ithihas was sent to Bombay by Aba Sahib and distributed by a whole batch of criminals who had the eyes of the Bombay Criminal Investigation Department on them. Aba's gang consisted of over thirty people sworn to secrecy, among those was P. T. Vincharkar who was J.N. Thatta's accomplice in the manufacture of bombs at Sajjangad in the district of Satara. The police in Baroda could have laid their hands on the whole of this gang but they let the golden opportunity slip and contented themselves with arresting Aba Sahib and his chief lieutenant, Madhavrao alias Vinayak Gadgil. Proof obtained in the form of a railway receipt showed that the boxes came from Billamora, a place which since August 1910 [had] been suspected as the source of distribution; this takes the case one step nearer to the Baroda state and the necessity of making enquiries there. Bhimsen, an agent of Aba Sahib was questioned and after a lengthy examination, revealed a house in Naosari where the books came from. A move was made to Naosari only to be told that 500 of those books were lying at the bottom of a well. On wanting to examine the house pointed out by Bhimsen, Mr Chawan, the acting commissioner of police entered on a dissertation of the fact that the offence of the sedition was not applicable to Baroda, that in any case it was a non-cognizable offence and any search conducted would be illegal. However, it was pointed out by F. H. Vincent (police inspector sent from Bombay) that as Bhimsen had come with him to point out certain property entrusted to him with a view to discovering its real owner was surely permissible? Chawan gave way, but his acquiescence was clearly an indication of the attitude which was likely to be adopted by the Baroda state, an impression which subsequent events proved to be fully justified. However the search revealed 15 books of the Vanaspatini Davao. The books in the well were in good condition which proved they had been kept there for only a few hours, probably thrust there the previous night by Bhimsen's accomplices in Naosari. The Baroda Police have been indifferent to the case. The attitude of the Baroda police is the attitude of the Baroda official in other words of the state, and where this attitude is adopted in connection with a seditious movement clearly endemic in the state, it is a grave menace to the sovereign power. Finally, the investigation revealed that the consignment of books discovered in Naosari was received and brought to Naosari by Chunnilal (an agent of Aba Sahib) from somewhere up the line and kept in one Dr Dixit's (a doctor residing in Naosari) compound and removed by Chunnilal and Bhimsen to a house hired for the purpose by Aba sahib. Aba sahib, having undertaken to distribute them on behalf of Mohanlal Pandya, who is the superintendent of sericulture in the Baroda state. Investigations on these books and its distribution brought many persons involved to light. The books were obtainable through a pleader named Poonjabhai of Kaira (and one of the gang) and were probably printed at Mehsana. If true then it showed that the State workers were active participators in this seditious campaign and it also explained why every obstruction was placed in my way. It also explained Chunnilal's mysterious disappearance after the books had been recovered. Chunnilal having been spirited away, Poonjabhai's connection with the movement provoked attention. It was learnt that Poonjabhai was an out and out extremist whose age, position, education and influence make him doubly dangerous and that he had internal knowledge of the enquiry we had been conducting in Naosari even to the extent we had discovered the marks on the boxes.

Sub-inspector Patwardhan, who had been in the disguise of a student, was charged to communicate to, author of *Vanaspatini Davao*, Narsinghbhai Patel, inter alia a warning message, had been sent two days before and another the previous day that the Bombay police had traced the marks on the boxes and that every precaution should be adopted, even burning the books while retaining a few, 'as the boys had not yet got them'. Patwardhan met Narsingh in Mehsana and handed over Poonjabhai's letter as his credentials. Narsingh was very cautious but ultimately gave him a note on a blank postcard written thereon with his left hand, a guarded reply-note which was duly copied by Vincent. Narsingh met Poonjabhai and expressed his inability to accompany him to Mehsana and gave him a second note tearing off the lower part of the postcard for the purpose. This was again copied and photographs of these three documents are appended. Poonjabhai agreed to accompany Patwardhan to Mehsana. On the way to Mehsana one Jathabhai Hathibhai Patel, a Baroda state servant employed at Amreli in the Patel Boarding School, met while travelling.

Poonjabhai confided in him the object of his journey and from their conversation, it can be assumed that this man is also a dangerous extremist. He accompanied the party to Narsingh's house and Poonjabhai's presence at last reassured Narsingh who said with such regret that he had burnt the stock of books which were 800 in numbers retaining only a few with a friend. Narsingh handed over six books to the sub-inspector Patwardhan while retaining one as likely to be useful. Our agent patwardhan was unable to ask anything about the book but got an insight into Narsingh's character. Narsingh who calls himself a free thinker clearly became contaminated in the years 1901–1903 when he was with the Baroda Library, at the time when the Bengal element was strong in the state. In the latter year, Aurobindo Ghosh flourished there. Narsinghbhai Patel is a Baroda servant of many years standing, working under Kashirao Jadhav, the subha of Mehsana. Jadhav's hostile and open opposition to the British is in complete sympathy with Narsingh's activities. As Jadhav is a personal friend of His Highness—the factor of factors which crippled such half-hearted assistance as I might have obtained from Khan Bahadur Yusuf Ali (a senior police officer acting as British agent and working in the heart of the Baroda police headquarters)—the seriousness of the position is patent? Finally, with documentary evidence and Patwardhan's account, confronting Narsingh and Poonjabhai was possible. Poonjabhai was asked to furnish a security of Rs 10,000 with two sureties of Rs 5,000 each. As the accused refused to plead, the order was made final and he was remanded to jail till further orders. The books were traced to a shiksha press in Mehsana. Seddon, the dewan having heard the evidence of the compositor and binder, was convinced and wrote in his reply that he was morally convinced that the books had been printed in Mehsana and Baroda state should now accept full responsibility for it. Printing seditious literature is not a grave offence according to Baroda law which gives immunity to the offender which in British India might lead to transportation for life! This was probably the reason for indifference on the part of the Baroda police to act.

In the penal and procedure code of the state or durbar's penal or criminal procedure codes, there are no provisions of any sort either in the durbar's penal or criminal procedure codes that deals with sedition as directed against the King-Emperor or the government of India. As far as the durbar's substantive penal law is concerned, sedition can be carried on with absolute impunity! When His Highness's attention was called to this deficiency in May

1908, the Resident received a letter from His Highness's minister which practically declined to take action until the British Indian laws had been amended so as to provide for similar offences directed against the durbar of and [sic] when they were committed in India. The Prevention of Seditious Meetings Act—the durbar has no such enactment. The Explosive Substance Act—the state have no equivalent law. The Newspaper and the Indian Press Act—its provisions do not apply to the author or printer of seditious work and the enactment is so loosely worded and so carelessly enforced that when called to initiate procedures the prosecutions have invariably failed.

A new Press Law was drafted a year ago as a result of our remonstrances in the case of two seditious Baroda journals—*Pudhari* and *Chabuk*. The minister and the legal remembrancer pressed upon the Maharaja the crying necessity for passing it before he left for England last April, but His Highness refused. As in the case of the existing act, neither the author nor the printer of seditious publications can be touched. The responsibility for deficiencies in the legislative position in Baroda rests entirely with the durbar. They have alike declined to act *suo motu* while they have received the friendly advice we have offered them in a spirit of uncompromising hostility. In the rest of the native state in the seventeen years of experience, I can recall no parallel to this attitude. The alacrity with which other important native states, some thirty months ago, issued manifestos to their subjects against sedition and co-operated with us in introducing legislative enactments similar to our own is so well known to the government of India that I need not recall it. Baroda alone, as far as I am aware, has turned a deaf ear to our overtures. Baroda has become a veritable alsatia for the enemies of British rule. Many of the state's officials including some of the highest, are declared extremists and do not even hesitate, as Mr Vincent's report exemplifies to use their official position to our detriment... nor is disloyalty confined to the official classes. I have reason to believe it has spread to the unofficial classes as well and I believe that in no part of India, is the political outlook more menacing or the atmosphere more charged with dangerous electricity as it is here. When there is no law against sedition, when the government refuses its co-operation, and when above all, the attitude of the ruling chief and his family is openly hostile, it would indeed be astonishing if seditionists from British India did not regard Baroda as a city of refuge and utilize it accordingly. Mr Vincent's enquiry, important as the results are have only touched the fringe of the question. It has however served to focus on position and from what has actually come to light the government of India can draw their own conclusions as to what is going on beneath the surface. In my opinion, Baroda laws should be modelled on British-Indian lines...A cursory glance at the map shows how Baroda territory is interlaced on all sides by British districts and other native states that it is often difficult to see where one ends and the other begins! Continuity of law in the matter of sedition is therefore an absolute necessity. Equally and perhaps more essential is the continuity of policy and the right of the paramount power in its own interests to demand both. The mere passing of laws is only a means to an end and not the end itself. Though I see little hope as the police, the executive officers and indeed the government itself in Baroda take their cue from the Maharaja. The state's attitude is merely a reflection of the Maharaja's towards the British government...unless the attitude is reversed, I see no hope of real improvement in the situation. Indeed I consider that things can only go from bad to worse.

Your most humble, devoted servant, H.V. Cobb.

It is difficult to say why Cobb was determined to run down the princes and the kings to the best of his ability and for all intents and purposes; was it simply out of distrust of native rulers or was it born out of pure dislike for the Maharaja whose impeccable administration prevented the Resident from undue interference, is not clear. There is another letter dated November 1911 from him to the secretary of state, where he talked about his interview with Sayajirao III and the maharani:

> [D]uring the course of my remarks, I referred to Her Highness's admitted association with Madame Cama and I said that even His Highness's own name was not clear in this respect in consequence of the events which had occurred one evening in Paris just before

he left for India in 1910. On hearing of this, His Highness, who had throughout displayed some nervousness, showed his genuine alarm by the most unmistakable signs. His hands, wrists and arms, which he had close to his face at the moment visibly changed colour. Then without waiting for me to proceed, he volunteered the remark that he knew I was referring to the dinner in Paris which was given by an Indian banker and to which he had gone because he had been promised some Indian food. Proceeding, he said in a most incoherent manner that he did not know the names of the persons there, that he would not have recognized their faces the next day and that when he accepted the invitation, he had no reason to suppose he would be likely to meet revolutionaries. At one moment, he seemed to admit Madam Cama was there, while a moment later he said he thought she was not. In brief his condition of fright was so pronounced that I deemed it best to leave the subject and to pass on to other matters. He had, however, admitted quite enough to show that the information, received at the beginning of this year by the Criminal Intelligence Department, as to the 'soiree' at Paris and as to His Highness's presence thereat was substantially correct. And then I pointed out to the Maharaja the strange inconsistency of his having addressed an invitation to their Imperial Majesties to visit Baroda at or about the very time when he was believed to be associating with some of the most bitter enemies of the English Throne and Government. Subsequently I turned the conversation back upon the Coronation Durbar and elicited His Highness's admission of a fact which I have not hitherto reported, because I was not satisfied as to its truth. This is that shortly after arriving at the amphitheatre, the Maharaja divested himself of the jewellery he was wearing except his Star and medals, and handed them over to his son Dhairyashilrao who was seated just behind him. The significance of this action followed, as it was, by the subsequent incidents mentioned in my letter, dated the 14th instant which speaks for itself to anyone who is conversant with Indian ceremonials and durbar etiquette. It affords one more instance— and a very striking one—of the Maharaja's deliberate rudeness upon this the most public and ceremonial occasion which has occurred in India for centuries. And it helps to prove, should the government of India still entertain any doubts in the matter, how completely misleading is the so-called apology tendered by the Gaekwar with its fallacious suggestions of stage-fright and nervous confusion. ... Towards the close of the second interview, I again emphasized the gravity of the present situation and the obvious necessity for prompt and strong measures on His Highness's part to rehabilitate, as far as might be, the good name for himself and the state. Just before leaving me, the Maharaja assured me again he was ready and anxious to do all in his powers to put matters straight, and he thanked me repeatedly for having shown to him so clearly, though in so friendly a spirit, the danger of the present position. Several times over he shook my hand saying that...I had played the part of a true friend in awakening him alike to the imprudences which he had himself committed and to the existence of sedition in his state which he now accepted as a patent fact. The only question left in his mind, he said, was whether immediate action such as I had counseled, was advisable, or whether it would not be wiser to defer action for some time. When I enquired what he meant by this cryptic remark, he explained that if he took immediate action, people might say it was the result of fright, and thus the good results he hoped for might be discounted. I replied he ought not to mind what busy bodies think. He had an obvious duty to perform and ought to perform it fearlessly. Thus the second interview ended with many amiable protestations on His Highness's part of gratitude to and friendship for myself and of his desire to do the right thing and to retrieve his position. In brief, the Maharaja's eyes, hitherto blinded by flattery and his own vanity, are at last open to the real facts. He is amazed and terrified to realize how much we know about him, and probably imagines that we know more than we really do. I am inclined to think that advantage might be taken of his changed attitude. Were it possible for His Excellency to see Gaekwad at Bombay or Calcutta after the departure of their Imperial Majesties, I think it not unlikely he would make a clean breast of all his misdoings and would give definite and binding assurances of future good behaviour and reform. If, on the other hand, the opportunity is not made use of there is the fear that the Maharaja, Pharoah-like, will again harden his heart, and wrap himself up once more in his impenetrable mantle of egoism and self-conceit. Finally, I wish to make it quite clear that the Maharaja fully understands that the advice I have tendered to him is my own, and is not the voice of the government speaking through me. Your hands, therefore, are left free to pursue whatever policy may ultimately be decided upon. I can only trust that in these difficult circumstances I shall not be held to have exceeded my instructions, and that the government will be pleased to approve of what I have done.[1]

Following this, there was another letter from Cobbs to the secretary to the government of India dated 2 December 1911:

I have the honour to enclose for the information of the government of India an extract from the *Baroda Gazette* of today's date containing an order issued under the signature of His Highness banishing Narsinghbhai Ishwarbhai Patel from Baroda territory for five years and fining him 300 rupees and confiscating the Shiksha Press, and an order passed by the dewan forfeiting a long list of proscribed books under the provision of the New Press Act. Both these orders, if they are given effect to, should help improve the position in Baroda and to remove in some degree the stigma now lying upon His Highness and his government.

Cobbs couldn't resist adding, 'This is followed closely by the conversation I had with him in Delhi on the afternoon of 14 December...A notification was made public on 24 February 1912, signed by the Dewan B.L. Gupta. It stated that His Highness has been pleased to order that no library or school building which is under government's supervision shall be used for any political meeting or for any proceedings which are likely to create a feeling of disaffection towards the Government of His Highness or the British government or to offend the religious susceptibilities of any community; and that, in cases where any doubt arises, the decision shall be final.'

On 27 December, His Highness from his palace declared to the public:

The breath of political unrest which disturbed British India a short time ago will not be allowed to ruffle the tranquil bosom of this state. Laws have, therefore, had to be enacted which had heretofore been deemed unnecessary. And, however much I may deplore the circumstances which rendered such legislation necessary, I wish to declare my intention of vigorously enforcing such laws against all evil-minded persons who infringe their wholesome provisions. I therefore, enjoin all my officers, in places high or low, and my subjects of all classes and creeds, whose welfare and happiness is nearest to my heart, to cooperate with me loyally in stamping out every vestige of disaffection to the British government wherever found; in maintaining the relation of goodwill and sincere friendship between the British government and mine; and in regarding as an enemy to order and good government every misguided person who attempts to excite feelings of ill-will, hatred or contempt against the British government.

This declaration and Sayajirao III's willingness to amend the laws in accordance with the government of India's terms which, by the way, also protected the Baroda government from sedition, a clause that had been inserted upon the wishes of the Maharaja, and the public declaration put in abeyance any action to depose the ruler. But constant references to the durbar incident were made to give impetus to the accusations of his involvement with sedition. However, the storm that had broken over the durbar incident subsided and the dust that had settled with the lapse of time receded into the dim recesses of the people's minds, only to be picked up as a means for conversation. Never were these charges investigated into, it had been pure conjecture as probably the hierarchy in the government knew, and with no evidence to substantiate it, fell to disuse. However, the Maharaja was considerably upset as can be derived from his letters; referring to the one he wrote to Lord Lamington on 3 January 1912, he said, 'I deeply deplore the breach of etiquette for which I was responsible at Delhi. It was, however, quite unintentional, and due to unforeseen nervousness and confusion, which I do not think would have overtaken me if I had been in my usual health at that time... I think that the very fact that I went, of my own accord, to London to attend the coronation should give the lie to any charge of intentional disrespect on my part, either at Delhi or at Westminster.'

At this time, he was unaware that there was another charge of omitting to bow before the queen. Sayajirao III explained this in a letter to M.H. Spielman, 'I was asked to make one bow only, as the first few princes were, I learn, asked to do. I am chivalrous enough to bow before a lady, and to make one bow only to the king did strike me; but one dare not ask questions on ceremonies in the framing of which we had no choice.'

A man of conscience, he did as dictated by it and the magnificent diplomat that he was, doused the raging fire of belligerence with profuse apologies as seen in his letters. Whatever his thoughts were at that time, he displayed with a lot of chutzpah and got away with it! One is inclined to think that the durbar incident was at the prodding of Gopal, 'his other self', the keeper of his conscience, and the humble apology that came in the form of a letter was from Sayajirao III, the ruler of Baroda. It must have been tough to satisfy both the identities by turns. No wonder his health suffered in the bargain, though it would have been simpler to have listened to his old mentor Madhavrao and been politically correct. All the flak and humiliation he received at the end of it could well have been avoided. In truth, for Sayajirao III the durbar incident served to be the turning point of his life. Realization dawned upon him that it had not been worth sacrificing himself for a little show of defiance. He understood that all the good work he had done in the past thirty years of his rule would come to nought with just a flick of a finger or simply by a stroke of a pen by the people who ran the Raj and he simply could not afford it. There was still a lot of work to be done for his people before he could step down or run the risk of being made to. It was not in him to show open servility, but he was well versed in Western ways to appear friendly and cultivate a sort of bonhomie in his dealings with the ruling race. He changed his approach and henceforth became more amenable to their wishes. Instead of finding excuses to avoid viceregal visits, he encouraged them. Emulating his adoptive father, he began to entertain the ladies and gentlemen of the Residency and British officials camping in Baroda. He went a step further and severed all his connections with nationalists and studiously avoided them. He was very circumspect in his behaviour at social functions and gatherings fully aware that the watchdogs of the empire had their eyes trained on him. This change in his attitude brought on by compulsion served to make him withdraw more and more into himself. However, the guardians of the Raj were not taken in by this sudden change of attitude and those who were still burning under the smouldering stack that had been lit by the durbar incident found various ways and means to pile upon him little incidents bit by bit as acts of transgression to bring the ruler down to his knees. For example, that the Maharaja should appear at a dinner party wearing European evening dress but without his traditional Indian headgear! Or that he did not raise his glass to a toast and drink to the king's health was another point to discedit him—Sayajirao III remarked to a friend that being a teetotaller, his glass had not been filled with water and if he had raised an empty glass that would have been construed as a direct insult to their king!

The charges he faced for harbouring seditionists in the state were far more serious, and the Maharaja was deeply pained by it. In his letter to Lamington, he spoke of the injustice of the attack upon him by *The Times*. He also pointed out that he could not be held accountable for the happenings in his state during his absences. The case which was only one had been brought to him and he had banished the offender. Besides, though he did not mention it in his letter to Lamington, in 1910 and 1911 he had a dewan, N. C. Seddon (Seddon), who was a Britisher, which itself was proof enough that he wanted to rule his state according to the British standards or that during his absence the Resident had more powers to wield than when the ruler was present. Sayajirao III's policy in all matters and with all persons was governed strictly by fairness. He always wanted to be convinced with evidence before he took any drastic, irrevocable measures to dismiss anyone from Baroda service or for that matter any decision in his administration of the state. Complaints were made to him by the government of India that a certain K.G. Deshpande, the subha of Amreli, was implicated in *seditious* activities and demanded a dismissal of the said person from Baroda service. The proofs supplied were not good enough and the Maharaja was not satisfied. He was reluctant to dismiss him, but bearing in mind that he himself was under a cloud of suspicion after the recent attacks from the press, he let the man go but with a compensation of Rs 10,000.

His policy, he stated much later, was that arbitrary punishment without evidence was not his idea of right conduct of a ruler. But with definite, concrete evidence, he was ready to do the needful and issued a warning, the Huzur Order, at the end of February 1912, the moment he got to know that there was growth of dissenters against the paramount power in his state. In the order, he stated that a certain press in Naosari had been responsible for printing seditious books, and the press had been confiscated and the author had been suitably dealt with. He expressed shock and pain to know that some people in Baroda sympathized with the author and he was determined to banish any form of sedition in his state; anything that came to disrupt the order and good government in the state must be regarded as an enemy by all the people of Baroda. They must regard as their enemy 'every misguided person who attempted to excite ill-will, hatred, or contempt against the British government'.

Next, it became the turn of D.L. Purohit whose dismissal was demanded by the British government for his association with Aurobindo Ghosh who was now residing in Pondicherry, where he had retired to start an ashram in the picturesque French colony. Purohit was a professor of philosophy in the Baroda College and it was Sayajirao III who had sent him to England to study religious and social questions, administration of charities and other matters. He had let him travel across India to compare the ideas of the two countries on these subjects. Reaching Pondicherry, he was advised to meet Aurobindo Ghosh with whom he could have an enlightened discussion on the subjects. Aurobindo was from Bengal, educated at St Paul's School, and Cambridge, and later developed anti-British views and was regarded as an enemy of the paramount power. Aurobindo was the editor of the paper *Bande Mataram*. Purohit's visit to one regarded as an extremist and an enemy of the British did not go unobserved and his removal from service was demanded. Though the Maharaja had not paid any attention to Aurobindo's political views, he knew he had no choice but to comply with the demand, so, when Purohit gave in his resignation, he accepted it. The fact that these two persons had been in Baroda service caused the cloud of suspicion hanging over the state and its ruler to deepen further; there are always those who want to believe the worst and they certainly did, implicating the Maharaja's name with seditionists.

The durbar affair that had no doubt been blown out of proportion and impartially judged was not proof of the Maharaja's disloyalty to the British government in India. But, at the same time, it gave rise to the thought that the Maharaja should have been more careful since he was aware of what the consequences could be of such lapses. All this served to make him more taciturn, and he withdrew more and more into a shell. In actual truth of the matter, which Sayajirao III felt himself, was that he had been deliberately misunderstood and treated unjustly. An unintentional breach of etiquette is embarrassing no doubt, but is definitely not a yardstick by which one can measure one's loyalty to any person. Regarding the men who were in his employment with different political views, why should the Maharaja have been blamed for it? Hadn't he proved time and again by his words and actions that his loyalty to the Crown of England was unquestionable?

39

Chimnabai II Steps In

There was a curious incident when Chimnabai II rallied to Sayajirao III's support in a matter that could not have augured well for the Maharaja had the queen not used her presence of mind and saved the day for him. The governor general of India, Lord Minto and his wife along with their daughter had come to Baroda on 13 November 1909 for a four-day visit. In honour of their visit, special arrangements were made and a variety of entertainment was organized. Lord Minto's visit was with the distinct purpose of extracting an explanation from the Maharaja on his involvement in seditionist activities and ask questions, which rested in a note in his pocket, about the Maharaja's loyalty to the paramount power in England. Sayajirao III was not made the ruler of Baroda for nothing and was fully aware of the purpose of the governor general's visit. Strangely, the opportunity was never given to Lord Minto to draw out the note with questions from his pocket and tackle the Maharaja with it.

The first reason was that the dignitaries were honoured with lavish entertainment in the form of hunting expeditions, sports, dinners and balls especially organized for them; it was so pleasing that Lord Minto and his family were overwhelmed by the generous hospitality which itself spoke of the high regard the Maharaja had for the British peers. A cricket match had also been included in the four-day entertainment and was to be played by the college students of Baroda at 4 p.m. The students resented having being asked to play a match for the British dignitary's benefit and planned to show their objection by parading in the maidan dressed in black and carrying black flags! A blatant show of hostility of this kind would have had serious repercussions on the Maharaja. No amount of threats or cajoling could make these students change their minds and in desperation the dewan and other ministers went to the Maharaja for counsel, who hit upon a plan.

The foreign dignitaries were to attend a tea party in Chimnabai II's private chambers at three o'clock. The Maharaja sent a message to the maharani asking her to delay the party till well past six in the evening when it would be too late to witness the match in the cricket grounds. She proceeded to do so and, according to plan, engaged Lord and Lady Minto in such a delightful conversation that they were hardly aware of the time flying by and the maharani served tea when it was well past four! Exclaiming over the time, the dignitaries were prepared to leave saying they had to be at the cricket grounds by four o'clock for the match. Chimnabai II again forestalled them with persuasive remarks, 'A cricket match is just like any other, nothing remarkable about it and you see a lot of it in England, it would be more entertaining for Your Excellencies to witness our ladies here who specialize in the rare form of art, our special classical music which I am sure you have never heard before?' The excellencies capitulated and the performing artists were brought in. After a few minutes of music, they were so enthralled that the cricket match was completely obscured from their minds by the rich melody of the music so that by the time they left the queen's chambers, it was well past 6 in the evening! The crowd who had come to watch and the students who had come to the ground to display their hostility waited and waited in vain and finally they returned home after dark, dejected. Thus, the Maharaja's presence of mind saved the day!

Lord Minto was so charmed with his visit that he left the Baroda state with the note containing questions in his pocket unanswered! Well before the durbar incident it was becoming apparent to the Raj that Baroda was in some way involved with the national freedom movement which was slowly gaining momentum. Doubts whether Sayajirao III was hand in glove with the revolutionaries rose in the minds of those who ran the machinery of the Raj and it was fortunate that Sayajirao III chose to be away from his state during that time. The Maharaja had left India towards the end of March 1910 and had returned only on 16 December of the same year. After a brief stay of four months in Baroda, he and the maharani had left Indian shores for Europe as Chimnabai II needed her cure at Bad Nauheim and had returned to Baroda on 5 December in time for the durbar at Delhi. This was the period when sedition was rife in the Baroda state and it was his good fortune that he was away from the Baroda state. It was also fortunate that Seddon happened to be an Englishman borrowed from the Indian Civil Service which ran the affairs of British India. Had Sayajirao III remained in India, he would have been swept away by the force of the tide that unleashed itself. Viceroy

Hardinge and his officials could make what they liked of the Maharaja's cavalier behaviour at the durbar, but without proper evidence they could not connect him with what they had dug up as instances of sedition in the Baroda state. Seddon was peremptorily recalled from the Baroda service to avoid sedition being passed on to a British civil servant. Sayajirao III left no stone unturned to get the best person for the vacant post and he did not have to look far—he promoted his minister of justice, B.L. Gupta, to that post. Gupta had impeccable credentials and he too had belonged to the Indian Civil Service; he retired after having served as a judge of the Calcutta High Court and had been conferred the Order of the Companion of the Indian Empire by the British government for his services. He was the dewan for two years and became a close friend and confidant of the Maharaja. After he retired from the post he continued to serve Sayajirao III in an advisory capacity. It was on his advice that Sayajirao III conceded to the demand made by the government of India to amend the laws in the Baroda state. Being a cautious, prudent man he advised Sayajirao III to give in. The dewan's advice was followed and under the heading Huzur Order, a manifesto dated 28 February 1912 was publicly declared, which placated the runners of the Raj. It stated in no uncertain terms:

> I have recently had under my consideration the result of the enquiry held into the discovery of copies of a certain seditious book at Naosari. The author of the book has been dealt with by a separate order, and the Press in which it was printed has been confiscated. In connection with that enquiry, however, I have been painfully surprised to know that there have been within my territory certain persons who openly or secretly sympathized with the author, and a few others who were believed to entertain feelings of disaffection to the British Government. I, therefore, take this opportunity of expressing in the clearest terms my strong disapprobation of such writings and feelings, and my firm determination to punish and suppress sedition in any form wherever found within the limits of my State.
>
> The interests of the Native States are inseparably bound with those of British India, and all persons who conspire to subvert the Government in the one, offend equally against the other. The maintenance of the cherished relations of true friendship and

good understanding which have uniformly existed between the Baroda State and the British Government has unceasingly claimed my attention, and the preservation of peace and order and the advancement of the material, intellectual and moral well-being of my people, which has been the constant aim of my life, are dependent on the maintenance of these cordial relations; and any attempt within the limits of this State to disturb those relations will meet with my entire disapproval and will be suppressed with a firm hand.[1]

Prior to this manifesto there was a public notification on 24 February 1912, from B.L. Gupta: 'His Highness has been pleased to order that no library or school building which is under Government supervision shall be used for any political meeting or for any proceedings which are likely to create a feeling of disaffection towards the Government of His Highness or the British Government or to offend the religious susceptibilities of any community; and that in cases where any doubt arises, the decision of the Minister shall be final.'[2]

In keeping with this public declaration Sayajirao III agreed to the demand from the British government that he amend the laws in the state and a draft by the government of India with all the amendments to be incorporated with regard to the executive and legislative measures to be enforced in the state, were sent to him. The amendments curtailed the purchase of arms, ammunition and explosives by anyone unless he was authorized by a British officer for a valid reason. Amendment of the police regulations empowered the police to suppress the performance of dramatic plays likely to cause disaffection to the British government, the Baroda government or against any native states in India. The enactment of a New Press Act on the basis of the British Press Act, 1910 empowered district magistrates to take securities and suspend or close any press or any periodical with seditious literature and the government was to forfeit seditious books. By the amendment in the executive measures, power was delegated by the Maharaja to his minister to expel anarchists and political agitators from the territory of Baroda. Prohibition of the use of public buildings for political meetings and also forbidding public servants from joining any society or social institutions without the permission of government officials, and raising of subscriptions or taking part in organizing lotteries was enforced.

The Maharaja agreed to these amendments and a fresh version was drawn up and made public. Further, he also advised appointing a British officer as the head of the police in Baroda, about which Cobbs wrote, 'He agreed not spontaneously but under pressure from the results of Vincent's enquiry, and personal representations of Seddon and Gupta have, no doubt, played a part in influencing his decision.'[3]

The Maharaja had also written on 21 December 1911 from his Laxmi Villas Palace to Cobbs after their interview in Delhi: 'When you talked to me the other day at Delhi about sedition, I could not understand the seriousness of the position as your remarks were very general and little can be done till definite facts are stated...All steps are being taken. I heard that the Gangadhar Institute is to be closed, saves me the trouble of passing further orders.'[4]

In response, Cobb's letter dated 22 December 1911 said, 'It's a relief to hear from Your Highness. The matter we refer to has been receiving my almost undivided attention for a whole year and it has hitherto been impossible to bring home, to some of your officers, the full gravity and menace of the situation...I refer to the need of a definite lead on Your Highness's part so that your subjects and, still more your officers, mainly understand once and for all, that any action on their part, be it positive or negative, which is inimical to the paramount power, is hostile to yourself and to your state and will be visited with prompt, condign punishment...Therein lies the crux of the position and upon this point more than any other I look confidently for Your Highness's active co-operation.'[5]

Earlier in June of the same year, a letter from W.C. Hopkinson stated that the Maharaja donated a sum of money to assist Hindu students attending educational institutions in Washington and California. 'I am told that Dass has the exclusive handling of the money and that it was not used for the purpose it was given.'[6]

With charges of sedition mounting against him, it was leading to Sayajirao III's deposition as ruler of the Baroda state. Was history going to repeat itself? We shall see. On 2 November 1911, a letter from the government of India signed by C.J. Windham to the viceroy gave indications of it: 'It would surely be out of the question to allow Gaekwad to settle in Europe where, under the protection of international law, he would engage in anarchistic propaganda with impunity... If he wishes to abdicate, it would be permitted on one condition only that he resides out of India in some place like Ceylon where he can be closely watched and his movements controlled. His predecessor and family were deported to Madras...It does not seem that any useful purpose would be served by a public declaration of loyalty. He is just going to pay homage at the durbar!'[7]

This letter to the government of India was written just before the durbar incident! No wonder the incident took on such magnified proportions.

The government of India, wiser after the event, had since made amends to him for its share in the humiliation inflicted on him. But the real culprits have not or they would have come out in the open and admitted it.

40

Over to Scotland Yard

The storm, though it did cast a shadow, did not even dent the surface of a remarkably successful reign. There was one very unpleasant incident, however, that was to leave its mark on the ruler of Baroda. Towards the end of 1912, Viceroy Hardinge and his wife were making what one might call their state entry into Delhi when, during the procession, a bomb was thrown by an Indian nationalist at the elephant on which they were riding. Though the excellencies had a miraculous escape they were thoroughly shaken by the incident. The blame would in due course be put on the Baroda state for allowing the distribution of anti-British pamphlets and the ruler would come under their volley of fire. The Nizam of Hyderabad took the prudent step of organizing a silent procession—though it was conducted on the lines of stately grandeur—by driving all the locals out of the city of Hyderabad.

These unpleasant incidents disturbed Sayajirao III's mental peace but were not of such magnitude as to seriously disturb the well-being of the Baroda state. A couple of domestic problems mentioned earlier bothered him a great deal, such as his daughter Indira's marriage, which he didn't approve of. A worse blow was his son Shivajirao's untimely return from Oxford with his studies there still incomplete.

However, worse was the knowledge that Jaisinhgrao had been thrown off a horse and was suffering from concussion. Jaisinghrao had returned from America and had been put to work in the department of the administerial work in the state, but now it was all coming to nought.

All these events and happenings in his official and personal life left much to be desired and *exacerbated* his insomnia and nervous unrest. Being the dedicated ruler that he was, he did not allow it to come in the way of his efforts to improve the various systems in the administration, notably carrying out an increase of the popular element in the legislative council.

There were certain officials of the Raj who were still infuriated with the durbar incident and their indignation at the Maharaja's deliberate insult to the British majesties had not waned with time. These officials were busy making secret preparations to avenge the insult.

Sayajirao III had put the fiasco behind him and felt that the government had accepted his explanations and was ready to let the bugles blow truce. Miss Tottenham recalled that on a visit to Simla 'the viceroy and Lady Hardinge were extremely cordial during the stay of the Barodas'.[1] Nevertheless, the relations between those who ran the Raj and the Gaekwads were distinctly cool, which did not augur well for the royal Gaekwads.

When Jaisinghrao was well enough to get married, Sayajirao III became ill with gout and fever and had to attend his son's wedding, which took place in February 1913, in a wheelchair. He left India on 3 May1913 accompanied by the maharani and Indira (hoping she would get over her infatuation for the Cooch Behar prince) for Evians-les-Bains as advised by his doctors for a six-month cure there.

On the day of embarkation, Sayajirao III was handed a list with a curt order from the Resident, and told not to contact those people whose names were on that list; they were people who were believed to have contacted him on his earlier trips. As if to add insult to injury, the list was handed to him by the police chief of Baroda, Macrae, who, even though he had been appointed by the British, was a Baroda servant. The list included the names of those who had already established their reputations as nationalists, and who lived in exile, such as Madam Cama, Krishna Varma, R.S. Rana, Govind Amin and some others. Needless to say, Sayajirao III bristled with anger at the deliberate insult to his dignity and status as a ruler and dashed off his protest in a letter sent in the pilot launch (a motorboat with a pilot to carry messages) to the Resident. Miss Tottenham wrote that the maharani implored him to exercise caution and restraint. She 'challenged some of the sentences and wished the meaning to be expressed more tactfully'.[2]

Some years later, it became apparent that the strictures on protocol as dictated by the Residency through the list were only a ruse to get the Maharaja to step out of line, as it was a well-known fact that the Maharaja hated any curbs on his independence. Having given him the list of people he should avoid, all they had to do was to prove that he had broken the inviolable political department's commandments.

So far the political department had employed its usual informers with an ear to the ground for keeping a trained eye on the Maharaja's activities, but now they needed specialists for the job.

Sir Charles Cleveland, the head of India's Criminal Intelligence Department, decided to bring in Scotland Yard for the purpose of keeping a watch on the Maharaja and his family, including the servants, as this time there were to be no sketchy reports—they had to be packed with enough ammunition to depose the Maharaja who had got 'quite above himself' according to Viceroy Hardinge. Therefore, a strict surveillance was kept on not only Sayajirao III but also Chimnabai II, who was rumoured to be on quite intimate terms with Madame Cama. Both ladies were seen taking the cure together at Vichy.

Even the servants accompanying the Maharaja and the maharani were kept under strict surveillance. In the letters and reports from the informers, Sayajirao III was referred as Mr A. In France, they were able to find someone who could be relied upon to intercept the mail of the principal suspects and to make copies of all the letters. Strange that the India Office 'which did not see eye to eye with the arch imperialists of the viceroy's council also seemed to have become a party to these unsavoury proceedings.'[3] However, there was nothing substantial in these reports that indicated the Maharaja's involvement in any nefarious activities or any voluntary action on his part that implied sedition.

The file on the Maharaja's visit to Europe in 1913 is in two parts and available in the India Office Records in London. It provides 'some stark glimpses into the secret workings of the machinery of the Raj'.[4] The notes on Sayajirao III's visit to Europe mainly have information on his arrivals in and departures from various cities and towns of Europe, and the mode of his travels to these cities and towns and details of the hotels where the entourage resided. They also mention the names of his visitors and the duration of their visit, but say nothing about what happened during that time or what was discussed. For example, one note said, 'During the morning of 19/5 Anupchand H. Shah and Khimchand Banker (both Paris Indians) visited H.H. Mr Nimbalkar, H. H's secretary, came down to the hotel hall to receive them and conducted them upstairs to H.H. They remained half an hour with H. H. On the 20/5 at 10. 40 am, Hiralal Banker (of Paris) called and was shown up to the Gaekwad's apartments, where the Maharani interviewed him. H.H. was out with Dr Mayer his medical attendant. Both the Dr and the fair-haired governess with the Gaekwad appear to be Germans. On the

21/5, H. H. gave a dinner party at the Ritz Hotel, covers for 8 being laid. Besides the three members of H.H.'s family, H.H., Agha Khan, the Gaekwad's private secretary two European ladies were present.'[5]

Point no. 6 in the report indicates that Sayajirao III's Italian chauffeur seemed to play the role of a private detective. On 31 May, the maharani was noticed at Evion, having come directly from London; point no. 10 in the report indicates that H.H. was being whimsical, 'At 5 pm on 3/7, H.H. and the Maharani accompanied by Hiralal Banker went out in a motor (No. 1863) in the direction of the Grand Boulevards. H.H. is constantly making arrangements for travelling to various places and cancelling them at the shortest notice. One day, he is going to Marienbad, on another, to Contrexeville and so on; at a time, the tickets are even taken and the journey countermanded at the last moment.'[6]

The truth of the matter was that Sayajirao III suspected that the prince of Cooch Behar was following the party and wanted to shake him off!

Point no. 11 is a little more meaningful as it talks about the letter written by Madame Cama to a certain Mahadeo Rao but it does not clearly state who this person was; obviously, details of him are in a secret dossier in the political department. The letter was as follows: 'This is to remind you that you have not sent back yet "The Everyman" which you took from me in the train on Sunday last on the promise of returning it. If Messrs. Banker Freres have not given you something for me then please give Mr Khimchand this enclosed note and kindly bring me his reply.'[7] The enclosed note was in Gujarati and when translated read as follows, 'Well brother, this time Varma has paid up, and you brothers have not yet thought of me as you brothers told me on Sunday that you would give it to Rao; but as yet Rao has brought nothing, therefore I have to write this letter.' Whether this was a code language which actually said something else rather than its superficial contents is not known.

Then, there are some details of Sayajirao III's luggage being transported to the station by Mirza and D. Bhavsar and again the names of the people who visited his secretary Nimbalkar and that Gaekwad's luggage was consigned to their house (48 Av. Neully) and came there in an omnibus from the Gare de Lyon. A list of those of the Maharaja's staff is mentioned as also his movements, which does not say anything to arouse suspicion. As mentioned earlier, the Maharaja's constant change of plans was to shake off his daughter's unwanted suitor. His private life was so blemishless as to put a saint to shame and for this reason, the administrators of the British Empire found him an enigma.

Miss Tottenham's explanation of the matter resembled a romance seen often on the celluloid screen for she said how, when they were staying at a hotel in Evians-les-Bains, it was discovered that an old man with a beard used to visit Indira regularly. He was none other than her suitor Jitendra Narayan in disguise. Later enquiries revealed that the Cooch Behar party had been following the Gaekwads all over Europe, which explains the private detective, if there really was one, and the sudden change in travel plans. 'But,' Miss Tottenham said, 'Jitendra and the princess continued to meet and correspond. It was clear that she had something up her sleeve, telegrams and letters were being received, and her maid was obviously acting in collusion.'[8] Indira, by the look of things, was planning to elope with her paramour. In Miss Tottenham's words, 'Their Highnesses were at last persuaded of the necessity of yielding to the force against which they were really powerless.'[9]

In the end, the headstrong princess had her way and her parents, left with a Hobson's choice, gave their consent but made their disapproval clear by not attending the wedding. Miss Tottenham represented Chimnabai II and Sayajirao III's solicitor represented him. The wedding took place in London at the Buckingham Hotel, on 25 August according to Arya Samaj rites.

Sayajirao III and his queen had another setback when Shivajirao was sent back from Oxford. Shivajirao had been used as a scapegoat in a prank to invade the private rooms of the dons, a rag the students had indulged in after the Australian cricket match and had been expelled as a result of it.

The empire had their spies planted everywhere but most of what they reported was based on conjecture and seldom on facts. The Maharaja's physician 'Dr Mayer appeared to be a German' which, considering the impending war, was definitely alarming. Then, the reporter goes overboard in dubbing the 'fair-haired' governess as German. Among the staff accompanying His Highness, there were only two non-Indians, of which one was Mrs Burrows, the maharani's dressing maid, who any way was an Anglo-Indian, and the other was Miss Tottenham, a thoroughbred Englishwoman with unimpeachable conduct and impeccable credentials. Miss Tottenham was 'the niece of the Bishop of Calcutta who was well known to some of the senior most officials of the Raj'.

In point no. 12 of the report it was stated, 'he had telegrams from a gentleman named W. A. Borden asking for an interview'. From the sentence, Borden is made out to be some sinister character, but in reality he was an American expert on libraries whom the Maharaja had engaged to organize the state's libraries.

As far as the Banker brothers were concerned, they were jewellers dealing in precious stones so it should not have been surprising to anyone if Chimnabai II was seen visiting them at 56 Rue Lafayette where they had their shop.

All in all, the report did not make for spicy reading and the cannibals of the empire must have been sorely disappointed. Even if it had, there was absolutely no evidence of treasonable conduct. This must have put the viceroy and his advisers in a dilemma of how to solve this conundrum which had shown such promise. After all there was proof of Sayajirao III being visited by the Banker brothers and Anupchand Shah and what's more, he had allowed his secretary Nimbalkar to get friendly with them. It must be remembered that Nimbalkar did not know French and being unfamiliar with the French capital, had to resort to the Banker brothers to help him out. Sayajirao III never shut the door in anybody's face; he was kind and generous to a fault and if he allowed these people on the black list to meet him, so what? It did not mean he had to get involved in their activities, particularly if they had the government's disapprobation. But unfortunately the runners of the empire did not think so, they just felt he was playing a far more diabolic game and were waiting to catch him red-handed. Viceroy Hardinge with his hackles raised over the bomb incident was ready to believe that Sayajirao III was the devil incarnate, but he was unable to do anything except smoulder with rage and ask the political intelligence department to keep a stricter vigil on the Maharaja's activities. Nevertheless, he dashed off a telegram to King George V to refuse an audience to Sayajirao III when he paid his customary courtesy call on him. As far as King George V was concerned, he had dismissed the durbar breach of etiquette as of no consequence and it had receded to some obscure corner of his mind but, unlike his father who had been a jovial and broad-minded man fond of the good things in life like wine, women and sports, his son was simply different. King George V had neither a prepossessing appearance nor was he broad-minded. His sense of humour had probably been blighted at a young age for he displayed a bureaucratic insular mentality and believed that a viceroy's recommendation was one of the ten commandments and virtually inviolable. To disregard it was a serious breach of the principles of sovereignty. Therefore, he promptly did not answer Sayajirao III's obligatory courtesy call. Sayajirao III found, to his astonishment, that instead of the royal summons that he had anticipated and looked forward to with such pleasure, he got an urgent invitation from Lord Crewe asking him to come over to his house for a private talk. Lord Crewe too was different from the rest of the officials who ran the machinery of the Raj in that he did not have the imperialistic attitude that all Englishmen were of a superior race and the dark-skinned fellow men fit only to be their slaves. The meeting with Sayajirao III was handled by him with finesse and good humour. Keeping within the bounds of British propriety, he allowed Sayajirao III to unburden himself and heard his complaints against the men who made a habit of sniping at him.[10] Lord Crewe too in a no-holds-barred conversation let Sayajirao III know what the charges against him were and reminded him of their 11 July conversation of the previous year. Lord Crewe made no charges against him, but he told him that looking at reports from the Scotland Yard surveillance and from the foreign police, it was evident that a party of extremists was in close contact with some persons in his entourage and there was a great deal of communication between them. To this, Sayajirao III, not to be outdone in forthrightness, answered quite candidly that he was aware that Indian extremists living abroad were under surveillance and yes, it was possible that his staff had some friends among them. Since it was not his policy to enquire into the movements and doings of his people, he was unaware of it. Sayajirao III also complained about how he was asked to dismiss some of his officials and staff members without any evidence of disaffection. Lord Crewe neatly sidestepped this issue and pointed out to the Maharaja that while it was his duty to look after his people, it was also his duty to not remain silent, until the government was prepared to bring definite charges against them. Sayajirao III was not in the role of a recalcitrant ruler being chastised for his lapse in duty, nor was Lord Crewe in the role of the empire's imperialist admonishing a subject, but the message was clear that the Maharaja had better look out for himself or the consequences would be grave. He did concede that the rumours were no doubt exaggerated, and advised Sayajirao III not to press for interview with the king on this occasion. He also referred to Sayajirao III's grievance that there was excessive interference from the British officials, and said that he had heard nothing of that sort and the viceroy would certainly not approve or permit any unwarranted interference. He reminded the Maharaja that it seemed he had not kept his own people in Europe under better control, 'Sayajirao, chagrined at the accusation said, "he challenged that statement and that in any case he thought the reports were highly exaggerated". It augured well for His Highness that those words were spoken to Lord Crewe and not someone like Curzon who would have taken him to task for such "a show of recalcitrance". But, Lord Crewe took it in his stride and concluded the report with the words—after a little more conversation, the 'interview closed in quite a friendly manner'.[11] Lord Crewe sent his report to Viceroy Hardinge with the appendage, 'Is there any sort of colour for his assertion that at home he has been asked, or rather told, to dismiss officials against whom no definite charges were brought, merely a vague suspicion of disloyalty? I told him that no hint of any objection on his part, or of any protest, had ever come here.'[12] That it hadn't was not surprising as most of the time viceroys hardly paid any attention to a 'native ruler's grievances leave alone passing them on to the India Office, particularly viceroys like Curzon and Hardinge who acted like Mughal subhedars, absolute, and not answerable to either ministers or parliament'.

In the political circles of British India, eyebrows were raised and people asked each other why Viceroy Curzon had divulged the information that spies had been planted in Europe to spy on the Indians living there? They were not supposed to know, 'too much of the velvet glove and too little of the iron fist' had been the way Viceroy Curzon had handled the Maharaja. How could he be allowed to challenge a statement made by the functionaries of the empire? The viceroy and his councillors must have wondered if it had been worth spending money on having Sayajirao III and his coterie under Scotland Yard surveillance in Europe when it was not going to produce the expected results. Nevertheless, there was a glimmer of satisfaction in the fact that King George V had refused the Maharaja an audience.

The second part of the report deals with the period from 10 August to 30 October, which was the date on which Sayajirao III left for India. The reports again had nothing that one would call 'damning evidence' which would stand in a court of law and send the accused to prison; in fact, it contained very little information. The Banker brothers featured in most part of the report and the suggestion that Sayajirao III and Chimnabai II used them to keep in touch with undesirable Indians was played for all its worth. It insinuated that the maharani met them often on the pretext of buying jewellery or having her stones reset. It suggested that jewellery was some sort of code word. From the letters that were intercepted, they got to know that the 'Banker brothers subscribed to Madame Cama's revolutionary funds and have intimate dealings with her and Rana'.[13] Four photocopies of Madame Cama's letters again referred to sums of money which the Banker brothers had promised to pay, and a complaint about the *London Times* not being forwarded to a friend. There was a casual reference to Indira's wedding not being attended by her parents. This, in short, was the nature of parts 1 and 2 of the reports, both parts being bland with nothing in them to make the vampires of the empire sit up and take notice. This is not to say that the watch had been called off. No, it was to continue with renewed vigour and plans were already under way for surveillance of the Maharaja when he ventured on his next trip.

Sayajirao III returned to Baroda on 18 November. A starry-eyed Miss Tottenham recorded how 'when Maharani Chimnabai emerged from her carriage at the palace station, she was seen to have discarded the purdah. A new era seemed to have dawned after this European trip'.[14]

There were some changes in the Residency as well. Cobb, who had modelled himself on the standards of the earlier breed of Residents in Baroda, had left the services. His place was taken by Colonel Impey. Miss Tottenham credited the man with 'sound common sense'[15] though he was not much of an improvement on his predecessor.

Sayajirao III's complaints made to Lord Crewe earlier of interference and hectoring from the Residency was not unfounded, for immediately upon his return he was asked to dismiss D.L. Purohit from his position as professor of philosophy in the Baroda College. This was against Sayajirao III's principles and justice ethics, but there was little that he could do, since his reputation was still under a dark cloud. He was also aware that the eyes and ears of the imperial powers were trained on him. However, the problem was solved with Purohit tendering his resignation. Finding the climate of Baroda most insalubrious to his health, B.L. Gupta was anxious to retire. In his place, Sayajirao III's choice fell on V.P. Madhav Rao who had served in the administrations of Mysore and Travancore and was known for his efficiency and brilliance as an administrator. Sayajirao III must have thought of his old dewan every single day and realized how true his words of advice had been.

The significance of the reports from the central intelligence having fizzled out, it was recognized that no charges could be levelled against Sayajirao III, so Impey was instructed to subject Nimbalkar to a Spanish inquisition of his visits to the Bankers' establishment. Nimbalkar explained that his visits were merely in the course of his duty and besides, he adroitly pointed out that the Bankers' names had not been mentioned in the blacklist. He also said that the Baroda state had dealt with these jewellers for some years and always purchased stones or had them set or reset through them. With this plausible explanation, the Resident had to be content. The British government was now in an embarrassing position and was ready to sweep the entire mess under the carpet or pretend that they had nothing to do with the spying work abroad. This awkwardness was caused by Sayajirao III's pertinent point that he could not avoid meeting seditionists if he did not know who they were. The experts of the central intelligence put their heads together and let their fertile brains compile a list of the names of those who were the 'more dangerous' of seditionists which together comprised fifty in all. The list was handed over to the Maharaja by the Resident who called on him for the specific purpose. He also conveyed the message that before he called on anyone or allowed the visit of anyone he should first make sure that they were not friends of Madame Cama or any of the people mentioned on the list. With such a rigid curtailment of his social life, it prevented the Maharaja from calling on Lord Crewe, who himself was well disposed towards one person on the list—B. Dube!

That the list was the product of the most irrational people in the central intelligence set-up is evident in the fact that it was impossible to abide by the conditions. It was not possible to stare at every person on the street and check the list before responding to his greeting or run away from a social do because the person mentioned on the list *happened* to be there too, and besides, how was it possible to know all his friends' acquaintances and *their* friends? There was bound to be a link somewhere, for that matter there were probably one or two who were linked to the Residency itself. Cleveland's highly overrated opinion of the ruler of the state was well known as he was heard to remark to his senior colleagues, 'I do not trust him!' Can the Indians be blamed if their good intentions were blighted by such an attitude driving them into the arms of terrorists? The list as such was of no consequence as it was a repetition of the names mentioned in the earlier one with a few additions to it, but the description entered in the margin against each name was, and a few names which should not have shown up on the list were on it as well. The name Dube is clearly mentioned in four places with different initials—Dube Vishnu Prasad, Dube Sitaram and Dube Debendranath and Dube Bhagwandin whose address is given as Belsize Park, Hampstead, London and Chambers near the Middle Temple respectively. Any of the Dubes mentioned in the list could be the one Lord Crewe was well disposed to but from the initial B. and the London address, it was assumed that Bhagwandin Dube was well acquainted with Lord Crewe. Lord Crewe, when he received the list, was dismayed to read Cleveland's scurrilous remarks against some of the Indians in London and he stared at it in 'shocked disbelief!' For B. Dube, a barrister with a good practice before the Privy Council whom the secretary of state himself had appointed to the advisory committee for Indian students, to be clubbed with those who openly advocated assassinations showed a complete lack of discrimination in compiling the list. Sir Arthur Hersel, the secretary of the political department of London in his letter apprehended, 'If the list were to go astray it would be regarded as an official production.'[16] Some of these descriptions were marginally entered against certain names while some of them, Lord Crewe was advised, 'are defamatory... the mere divulgence of the list and descriptions would discredit the government and could not be defended in debate. It is unfortunately impossible to regard the risk of divulgation as negligible (because) the contents of the list are known to the staff of Gaekwad.'[17] Sir Arthur Hersel concluded his letter dated 15 May 1914 to J.B. Wood, blaming the Criminal Investigations Department for the slipshod way in which they had handled the surveillance and in compiling the list so indiscriminately as to 'bring its operations into disrepute and to make it difficult for the authorities here to justify the department to a public opinion which is rightly sensitive to such matters.'[18]

Given the nature of the list and the remarks on it, utmost care was taken to keep it a well-guarded secret. Nevertheless, made Lord Crewe and his colleagues in the cabinet uneasy minds and gave them sleepless nights as they pondered over the consequences if Sayajirao III in a fit of anger with the viceroy chose to leak the list to the press and then pretend he knew nothing about it. That monster reporter Kier Hardy would pounce on the opportunity to create such a scandal that would rock London and discredit the empire in the eyes of the world. What would happen if that irrepressible Kier Hardy was to know that an official document had described James Holten as a most 'objectionable renegade' or an Indian barrister with a Privy Council practice was described as a 'notorious extremist'? And think of the French press taking action for libel against the British government for referring to Madame Cadiou as being described as 'a jackal of Madam Cama'?'[19] Needless to say, Cleveland was on the dock for incompetence and was so severely reprimanded that he must have wished the ground below him would open and swallow him up. For a man whose opinions had never been challenged, his professional competence being questioned and becoming the target of such a battery of fire, he must have visibly recoiled from it. 'He had shown himself as wanting in a sense of proportion, had exposed the government to the risk of an indefensible libel action, and brought the operation of his own department into disrepute.'[20] In defence, Cleveland's letter was pathetic. For one, the excuses offered were flimsy and showed him as a dubious bureaucrat, trying to justify his careless handling of the job and his lack of discernment. The letter was in direct contrast to his earlier stance of a contemptuous superior overlord laying down the law that must be obeyed at any cost. His sentence in the letter, 'I do not think that the Gaekwad will expose the details of the list to be used against the government in India or abroad'[21] is so contradictory to his earlier 'I do not trust the Gaekwad' as to arouse laughter rather than anger.

Thus the petty display of authority and the sordid method devised by those in power to get rid of not only a great ruler but also a man known for his honesty, sacrifice and uprightness of character does not enhance the reputation of the British government in India. Suffice to say they came to their senses and the super secret file on Sayajirao III's visit to Europe in 1913 was closed. Again, it must not be assumed that the file was closed due to overactive consciences of those in the British hierarchy, but with the advent of the 'war of all wars' priorities shifted and the file was abruptly closed. Most importantly, someone who was seen as a potential seditionist was now seen as a valuable ally to be humoured. The first sign of this change in attitude came in the form of the welcoming smiles and gestures of courtesy from the who's who in London and the icing on the cake was King George granting him the long-overdue interview with grace.

41

Sayajirao III: A Patron of Arts

Sayajirao III had long cherished a desire to present a collection of European paintings in the picture gallery that he had built in the public park in Baroda in 1910. This park came to be named Sayaji Bagh later and in it stands a fine building which houses a magnificent exhibition of Indian art, unrivalled anywhere in the world.

The Maharaja was a great patron of art and the story goes that one day, the renowned Indian artist Raja Ravi Varma was painting in his studio and was absolutely absorbed in his work. The Maharaja wanted to visit the artist in his studio and look at his works of art that had already made waves in India. Ravi Varma, hearing of the Maharaja's desire, took out his paintings and set them up for display. The Maharaja soon arrived at the studio and was cordially welcomed by the artist. After the customary drink of coffee, the artist showed him his paintings on display. The paintings were scenes from the great epics Ramayana and Mahabharata, of Sage Vishwamitra and the celestial damsel Menaka; Ravi Verma had also drawn inspiration from the Puranas and painted many scenes from those stories. It seemed as if the figures that he had painted had come to life. The Maharaja was stunned to see such a display of divine art. Then, turning to the great artist, he exclaimed, 'On my travels to Europe, I have seen paintings of the great masters in which scenes from the Bible have been painted and I had expressed to Dewan Madhavrao that similar scenes from our epics too should be painted and displayed and he promptly referred your name to me. These paintings of such divine magnitude must be made available to the public for view!'

Raja Ravi Varma replied, 'Yes, Your Highness. It has always been my keen desire to paint scenes from our great epics and exhibit them to the world, therefore, please do not keep these paintings locked in the palace but these should find a place in a gallery where the public can go and view them.'[1]

'Indeed, they shall!' replied the Maharaja and the paintings were exhibited for a week in the Moti Baug Palace for public view, and thousands thronged the hall to view the paintings. Ravi Varma's work was appreciated and acknowledged as the finest work of art, the best among the best in the world. The Maharaja rewarded him with Rs 50,000 in appreciation of his work exclaiming while doing so, 'Ravi Varma! You are a prince among painters and a painter among princes!'[2]

Such was the Maharaja's reaction whenever he saw real talent he encouraged it to the best of his ability.

Alongside Ravi Varma's paintings is a fine collection of European art in the museum at Kamati Baug or Sayaji Baug as it is now called, a public park designed and built for public benefit. The war caused a delay in opening the Western collection to the public, and it was only in April 1921 that the gallery was opened.

In the picture gallery, the Maharaja has provided his people with two collections of pictures—one Eastern and one Western—which together go to make the institution truly unique. Perhaps in no picture gallery are the different schools of the East and the West represented in so balanced a manner. The rooms on the upper floor contain the Western collection, and the verandas contain sculptures. There is also a room devoted to medals and medallions. Mr Spielman, a leading art critic in London, was requested to select pictures for the collection, while E. R. Dibdin, formerly of the Walker Gallery, Liverpool, came to Baroda to superintend the hanging of the pictures. Altogether there are 188 pictures in the collection from the European school of art and six hundred pictures in the Eastern collection. Spielman did a wonderful job of building the collection from scratch. The collection consisted of rare masterpieces of paintings such as Titan, Bonifezzio and Durer which before the war had cost a thousand pounds each, a hundred years later they are priceless. The priceless collection of paintings includes almost every well-known school, Dutch, French, Italian, English, and German too. 'There are paintings by Rommerwall, Heric de Blaise, Raikchart, Daikmanns, Fragonard, Claude, as well as by a galaxy of Englishmen, Sir Joshua Reynolds, Sir Thomas Lawrence, Lord Frederic Leighton, Sir John *Millais*, Sir Edward Poynter, Rommney, Hoffner, Turner and Constable. Then there are Landseers, Morriesses, Archerdsons and Hamiltons, which are regarded as particularly fine examples of their work.'[3] The Baroda museum also displays beautiful specimens of art in silver, gold, brass, copper, bronze and other metals; plain and engraved, inlaid and encrusted pottery; inlaid marble; stoneware; Ming from China and so much more. A large collection of old arms and various kinds of textiles in the rich patola and paithani styles adorn the showcases. The Maharaja was keen to encourage talent and made provision for an art school so that Baroda should be able to train its own artists.

While war was being waged in Europe steps were being taken to safeguard the country from the enemy landing suddenly on Indian soil. In view of this, the police department had set up camps along the coastline of India. A letter dated 20 June 1915 from Mr Wormwood to the Baroda camp said:

I am instructed by the government of Bombay with a view to protect India and to stop all German propaganda from spreading and of mischief making. Local offices to be on guard and report anything suspicious observed on the coast. All revenue and police officials whose jurisdiction extends to the coast; rewards will be given for securing and imparting to the authorities concerned, information leading to the conviction of any subject of a hostile nature or any of its agents landing on the coast, let all this be generally known in the coastal villages of Naosari, Okhamandal and Kodinar. Instructions to be given confidentially to the Patels and the police so as to not cause alarm. Water police to be specially armed.[4]

The ominous dark clouds had rolled away but the sky was still grey for the ruler of Baroda. It must be remembered that the government of India had been poised to depose the Maharaja, but for the advent of the war. The list of charges against the Maharaja had not been completely buried in obscurity and still lurked in the minds of many in the hierarchy. To the charges of showing disrespect to King George, harbouring seditionists in the state and laying claims to sovereignty, there was one more that topped the list and amounted to treason—that was Sayajirao III's friendship with the German consul general Baron Von Rosen in Calcutta. They had corresponded with each other, and even though the letters were of a purely social nature, stray sentences could have been construed as being pro-German. The political department was inclined to view it as treason, for it was treason to keep up a friendship with a representative of the German government. Fortunately for Sayajirao III, it was not made much of as with the new change in the policy of the British government towards the princes of India, the allegation was never pressed. But the political department had their instructions to keep a strict watch over him and report all his movements to the government of India.

42

Abandonment of the Purdah and a Royal Escape

Baroda's royal couple was back in the state early in November 1913, but with their health not fully recovered; in the following year in spring they were once again on their way to Europe. Before their departure, two events of special significance took place. In February 1914, Chimnabai II 'signalized her abandonment of the purdah by sitting on the same sofa with the Maharaja at a prize distribution function held at Nyay Mandir'.[1] The other was the unveiling of the equestrian statue of the Maharaja by Maharaja Holkar of Indore. It was sculpted by Derwent Wood. The statue was erected to commemorate the silver jubilee of the reign of Sayajirao Gaekwad III.

The royal couple from Baroda was visiting Europe for health reasons only, but it was the wrong time to do so. With Europe a boiling pot of fury and indignation at the assassination of Austria's Emperor Franz Ferdinand, Austria-Hungary had declared war on Serbia. Germany and Italy also joined in for expanding their empires like Britain and France had done by establishing colonies almost all over the world. Germany, Austria-Hungary and Italy formed the Triple Alliance against the Triple Entente of France, Russia and Britain that feared that Germany was becoming too powerful and might take over the world. The assassination of Franz Ferdinand was the spark that lit the stack of hatred into a blazing fire and soon Europe was in the midst of the First World War in 1914.

Sayajirao III and his queen chose first to stop in the Riviera and North Italy. From there, they proceeded to Evian-les-Bains and after a brief halt in London, they proceeded to Vichy in France for cures. The maharani chose to spend time at Carlsbad which in those days was a highly fashionable spa in Austria. The frontiers were closed for normal travel. Trains were commandeered and roads reserved for troop movements. All foreigners were under suspicion and banks were closed for transactions and international communications were suspended. Even though Sayajirao III had been lucky enough to be in an India-friendly country, it was not without some manipulation on his part. With the help of the British consul he was able to get on a Paris train, generously sharing his first class carriage with a host of stranded Indians, and reached Paris on 16 August. A hop to London from there was easy and he made it.

On the other hand, Chimnabai II's escape from Austria has all the thrills and excitement seen in a thriller film.

Carlsbad is closer to Berlin than to Vienna and its nearest frontier is Germany. In Carlsbad, the maharani along with her retinue of maids, her companion Miss Tottenham and her secretary Ambegaonkar were residing at the Savoy Westend Hotel.

Even after war was declared, the maharani did not take it seriously. She didn't register it when she was on a shopping spree, when she noticed that shops were closing down and were selling their goods at sinfully low prices. Even after the actual fighting began, she made no move to leave the country. It was only when their hotel was invaded by mobs who drove away the French waiters and cooks that she woke up to the fact that there was a war going on and her life could be in danger.

The Americans on holiday there were evacuated by the American embassy in Vienna. Only after Britain had declared war on Austria did Chimnabai II get ready to leave with her coterie. She made arrangements to drive in hired cars all the way to Switzerland. She solicited the help of the Austrian foreign minister for the necessary papers to enable her to cross the borders. He offered her and her companions a safe route through Vienna to Switzerland, but since it was longer, she promptly turned it down. Then she told Baron Gerlach, who had brought the suggestion from the minister, that she preferred to go via south Germany to Switzerland as there was no trouble in Munich. Some credit must be given to the Baron for keeping his countenance composed while she suggested that route. Stranded in Austria which, along with Germany, was at war with England, and she was thinking of going to Germany! However, in a gentlemanly manner, he offered to accompany her as far as the frontiers of Germany. Meanwhile, Sayajirao III was in London, and as one more concrete proof of his allegiance to the Crown and the British, offered to render all possible help to the British in their war efforts.

On 21 August, they set out for the frontier of Eger. A few miles from the frontier, they halted for breakfast at Hotel Kaiser Wilhelm, while the Baron did a quick survey of the surroundings. He came back speedily and told her that the German guards at the frontier were on the lookout for her, and were making enquiries, 'India, they said was part of the British dominion therefore all Indians are British and as such enemies of Germany. Therefore, the Indian Maharani is also our enemy.'[2] The Baron, advising their return to the Savoy in Carlsbad, accompanied them back to the hotel. Needless to say, the manager, Aulich, was aghast to see them back as they would now be stranded there till the war came to its conclusive or inconclusive end! He offered to arrange their departure by road, via Linz and Innsbruck and from there to Zurich. The maharani agreed, but when he pointed out the restrictions for baggage, she was adamant that all her luggage should go with her. Aulich accustomed as he was to the whims of the rich agreed to send it on with his porter to Zurich from where she could have it collected.

Aulich proved to be not only a man of action but one with brains. He had bribed one of the officials in the passport office to describe Chimnabai II and her party as West Indians from South America and as such, members of a neutral country. He had all their luggage covered in thick sheets of brown paper. Joseph Wagner was the 'trusted courier' who was to accompany them on the journey being undertaken in two cars. The journey to the Swiss border took three days. During an overnight stop, they saw newspaper hoardings in black letters: '*Wau Nach Paris Frei, Hamur Gefallen* (The way to Paris is free; Hamur has fallen!)!'

The documents provided by Aulich proved to be their saviour. Barriers were opened and they passed through. Next morning, after an overnight's stop at Ragatz, they were in a train to Zurich and Lausanne. At Zurich station, Chimnabai II told Ambegaonkar to wait for her luggage which had not yet arrived. In Lausanne, the British consul told her to proceed to Paris as there was no other way she could go to London. After a three-day wait, they were able to get as far as Lyons where they again had to wait for a Paris connection. By now the war was fast becoming a reality to them, especially when they saw train loads of the wounded go by. In the Paris hotel, they were warned that the Germans might arrive there any moment. On the strength of a personal letter from the British ambassador to the secretary general of the railways, they got places on a train with a compartment to themselves.

Meanwhile, Chimnabai II's luggage had arrived, booked to London. She and her party left by a train bound for Paris and after arriving there they crossed the Channel in a 'hospital ship' and reached London with the song, 'It's a long way to Tiperrary' ringing in their ears. A week later, Sayajirao III and Chimnabai II left for Scotland and remained there till arrangements could be made for their safe return home.

43

Farzand-i-Khas-i-Inglish-Daulatia

The four years of the First World War that cemented the bond between the British Raj and India. It was India's honeymoon with the Raj as its stoic support during the war ended all speculation regarding the country's loyalty to the paramount power. At no time, ever since Queen Victoria took over the management of the East India Company in 1858, was the country so wholeheartedly supportive of British rulers. Whatever Britain was fighting for, India would fight on Britain's side for it too; British victory was India's victory and man to man, shoulder to shoulder, Indian troops under British command fought in the war alongside the Allies. British interests were India's interests; a British victory would be India's victory too. All the old feuds were forgotten and the new wave of nationalism was kept in abeyance. The British government in India could now look forward to a reign unhampered by political agitations.

Meanwhile, Sayajirao III's offer to the imperial government of all his troops and the resources of the state was publicized by the very journals and newspapers that had made him the victim of scurrilous attacks on his disloyalty to the British government, citing the durbar affair as an example. He was now lauded by the very same people and when he requested an audience with Their Majesties in London, almost immediately it was granted through an invitation to visit Buckingham Palace. It will be recalled that a similar request had been made earlier in May when he had been curtly told that the king was 'hard pressed for time'. This was certainly a reversal in the attitude of those in the corridors of the paramount power who had realized that it was better to cultivate the goodwill of Indians for their cooperation which was an invaluable asset during wartime. In particular, the ruler of Baroda who was not only popular in his own state but was looked upon by all enlightened Indians as a leader. Trivialities were to be brushed aside in view of the fact that the Maharaja had deigned to support them in the war.

A reception by Their Majesties, King George and his queen, followed in September where in the words of Sayajirao III, 'Their Majesties were gratifyingly amiable'.[1] Upon his return to Baroda on 4 December, he made it a point to inform Resident Bosanquet that while in London he had had a pleasant time with the king. He then sent his army to help the British in the war in keeping with his earlier promise to help them. Thus the four years of the First World War was India's honeymoon with the British.

With the Baroda coffers full due to his prudence, the Maharaja could afford to be generous.

To Lord Hardinge, the Maharaja donated Rs 5,00,000 for buying aeroplanes; to Lady Willingdon, wife of the governor of Bombay and the future vicereine, he sent a contribution of Rs 60,000 for her war relief fund; a sum of Rs 15,00,000 for Ford vans; Rs 2,10,000 to the Imperial Indian War Relief Fund; Rs 40,000 to the Red Cross; Rs 30,000 to the Prince of Wales's War Relief; and another Rs 4,000 for a separate fund started by Miss Impey, the Resident's daughter. His total contribution to the war fund amounted to Rs 40, 00, 000. Apart from all this, horses from the state cavalry and tents for hospitals' use in France were also offered. His residence in Bombay, Jaymahal Palace, was lent to be used as a hospital for officers wounded in war. Most importantly, the purchases of war loan bonds by the Maharaja amounted to Rs 1,00,00,000. The total purchase of bonds by the Baroda state amounted to Rs 11,22,04,000. After this, it would have been sacrilege to doubt Sayajirao III's loyalty to the British Empire or say that Baroda had not responded to the call of the war. Even Gandhiji had taken an active part in the official recruitment drive and had been awarded with a Kaiser-i-Hind medal. Sayajirao III was once again 'Farzand-i-Khas-i-Inglish-Daulatia', favourite son of the British Empire, and all was well once more between Sayajirao III and the paramount power in India and England.

However, it brought little change in the attitude of the British officials towards the Indian people over whom they ruled. They continued to wield a *de haut en bas* when dealing with Indians. The new policy ordained by British statesmen of soft-pedalling Indians may have not gone down too well with most of the British who believed in the superiority of their race, but as it must have been pointed out in numerous conferences and political meetings within the hierarchy that they could not go on treating Indians as their servants and expect them to come out and help by fighting on *their* side in the war. Thus, the British adjusted to the new policy and relations were on a more cordial footing. One can safely say that the days of Phayre, Biddulph, John and Curzon and later on, Hardinge too were now relegated to obscurity. Even social life underwent a change as the wives of Residents were more amiable and did not throw tantrums at some imagined slight, nor did their husbands try to pin sedition on a ruler or try to catch him in a minor breach of protocol. Moreover, the wives of top officials in the British service depended largely on the native rulers to donate generously to their war funds. You could not fault a Maharaja for failing to turn up at an official dinner without his 'traditional headdress if you knew his wife was depending upon you to underwrite her scheme for a new ward to a soldiers' hospital and (which you secretly hoped would bear her name); your wife could not pick a row with the Maharaja's wife over some lapse in the etiquette of paying formal calls when you knew that the next knitting party on the lawn of the Government House would be regarded as a fiasco if the maharani did not show up with her entourage.'[2]

The war years made it impossible to travel to distant places, so until peace reigned all over Europe, Sayajirao III had to restrict his travels to places within India. In the middle of May, with Baroda temperatures soaring, he fled to Ooty, his favourite hill station in the south, where he had his own house. The house named Woodstock stood on extensive grounds and overlooked the lake and after he had remodelled and refurbished it to suit his European tastes, it resembled a large English country house. In the monsoon months of June and July, he was off with the maharani on a long trip through south of India right up to Cape Comorin. En route, they paid state visits to the raja of Kollengode and the Maharaja of Travancore. On his return, Sayajirao III was also able to visit the ruins of the great Hindu city of Vijayanagar, which was destroyed by the Muslims in the sixteenth century. On 24 July 1915, he was in Bangalore (Bengaluru now) where he delivered a speech at the Sanskrit Academy and soon he was back at his desk in Baroda attending to the workload. Summer was not yet over (in Baroda, the humidity level can be very high in July and quite often summer stays in Baroda till August), but the steady orders were resumed and so was his habit of writing letters. All his letters were not related to business or instructions for reforms. He wrote to Clements, the district judge of Dharwar, in British India, inviting him to a meeting in Baroda since he had an interest in Indian music. There were letters written to art critics asking for advice on how best to display his paintings, letters to architects discussing plans and aspects of proposed buildings and to scholars and educationists agreeing to make donations. Innumerable little acts of kindness performed with a well-bred distaste to appear charitable. To Reverend Weeden, the author of the book *A Year with the Gaekwad*, he wrote offering to buy fifty copies of the book and also enclosed a cheque for £150, 'as a present which I hope you will accept'.[3] The Reverend Weeden not only accepted it but wrote back that he had expected fifty more, which was promptly sent to him.

To the members of his family, Sayajirao III wrote mostly to render advice—to spend less money, to work hard, to lead a less pointless life and so on.

While in England, at the beginning of the war, Sayajirao III badly wanted to do something for the family of his erstwhile tutor, Elliot, who passed away in 1910, but was unable to find the whereabouts of his wife. In his letter to Ella, Elliot's daughter, he wrote of his frustrated attempts, 'I attempted to send some money as a present to you and your mother but she was not to be found.'[4] Soon after, her whereabouts were discovered and the Maharaja arranged for money to be sent to her so that she and her daughter could set up the business they had in mind and live more comfortably.

Sayajirao III hated waste and his reminders to his staff both in the palace and office to cut down on unnecessary expenditure was a perennial task.

44

Sayajirao III: A Patron of Music

Sayajirao III was a passionate lover of classical art, be it a painting by Raphael or Ravi Varma; he enjoyed studying a painting to understand the mind of the artist and more often than not the work ended up in his collection. There are letters to art critics inviting their opinions on the paintings he wanted to buy, he also sought advice from connoisseurs of art on how best to display the priceless pearl carpets ordered and bought by his adoptive father the late Maharaja Khanderao Gaekwad. Architects of that time were invited to draw up plans for proposed buildings and for landscaping gardens. Scholars and educationalists too were encouraged and generous donations given for the publication of books in the Indian languages.

Similarly, he loved listening to pure classical music whether it was of Bach, Mozart or Moula Baksh from Baroda, enriching his taste with the purity of the art. Even classical dancers from Tanjore were invited to perform in the durbar on occasions. A music conference was held every year in the Laxmi Vilas Palace where renowned musicians and dancers performed in the palace durbar. The conference to which Sayajirao III had invited Clements and his wife began on 20 February 1916. It lasted for three days and included discussions on the various aspects of Indian music, and on the reviews by music critics of music as well as the performances of some of India's noteworthy musicians. Clements read a paper on 'The Notation System in Indian Music'. The fact that it had been the tradition of Indian rulers to invite classical musicians and dancers to perform in their palace durbars illustrates that the classical form of art that has survived over centuries has been mainly due to their encouragement. Tansen got his due as a musician, unrivalled in the history of north Indian classical music, by Emperor Aurangzeb who gave him a palace to live in so that he could listen to him whenever he wanted. Sayajirao III's predecessors Khanderao and Malharrao had virtually no time for the arts. Khanderao was absorbed in sports and festivities, while

Malharrao was preoccupied with overcoming all the intrigues in and outside of the palace. He had neither the time nor the inclination to devote to the arts. So much so that when Sayajirao III became the Maharaja he found that the School of Music in Baroda was in danger of becoming extinct and he set about to revive it.

Sayajirao III set up a department of music which was attached to his household. In 1898, he had sent Allaudin, the son of Moula Baksh, to Europe to study European classical music and try to imbue some aspects of their music into the Indian form. The discipline and complete dedication of the musicians of Western classical music must have been apparent to Allaudin. He was made head of the music department. By 1916, the number of artists in the music department had increased to forty-eight.

The music conference became an annual affair in Baroda and the duration increased as the years went by. All the famous artists in classical music and dance from all over India were invited to perform in the durbar of the Laxmi Vilas Palace. This was due to Chimnabai I who hailed from Tanjore. She was proficient in south Indian classical dance and Carnatic music and it was due to her patronage of the arts that the Baroda Music College got exposed to it. The queen brought her own dance troupe to Baroda after her marriage to Sayajirao III. The Tanjore quartet as it was known was absorbed into the Baroda University. She was instrumental in making Baroda a flourishing centre for classical arts. It was a pity that she died when just on the threshold of life; had she lived longer Baroda would have been the cultural centre for classical arts.

Music and dance aficionados thronged the hall of the durbar. Some of the renowned artists who performed in the festival of music regularly were Fakiruddin Khan from Udaipur, Muzaffar Khan from Alwar and Hussain Khan from Tonk.

Theatre too was encouraged by Sayajirao III and Baroda got to see Marathi and Gujarati plays being performed by veteran masters of theatre. Gandharva Natak Mandali, a theatre group from Bombay, was also encouraged by him; he even allowed the troupe to advertise itself as being 'Under the Patronage of Maharaja Sayajirao of Baroda'.

Maharaja Sayajirao Gaekwad III's investiture portrait by Raja Ravi Varma, 1881
Photograph courtesy: Royal Gaekwad Collection, Baroda

Maharaja Sayajirao Gaekwad III with Maharani Chimnabai Gaekwad II
Photograph courtesy: Royal Gaekwad Collection, Baroda

Maharaja Sayajirao Gaekwad III and Maharani Chimnabai II with their four sons Yuvraj Fatesinhrao, Prince Jaisinhrao, Prince Shiwajirao, Prince Dhairyashilrao and daughter Princess Indiraraje
Photograph courtesy: Royal Gaekwad Collection, Baroda

Maharaja Sayajirao Gaekwad III on his 52nd birthday in 1914
Photograph courtesy: Royal Gaekwad Collection, Baroda

Maharaja Sayajirao Gaekwad III in darbar dress with huzryas and attendants in 1910 wearing the famous triple-tiered Baroda diamond necklace
Photograph courtesy: Royal Gaekwad Collection, Baroda

Maharaja Pratapsinhrao Gaekwad of Baroda
Photograph courtesy: Royal Gaekwad Collection, Baroda

Maharani Shantadevi Gaekwad of Baroda
Photograph courtesy: Royal Gaekwad Collection, Baroda

Family photograph of the late Maharaja Ranjitsinh Gaekwad (Seated-Maharani Shubhanginiraje and Maharaja Ranjitsinh Gaekwad, Standing-Maharajkumari Alaukikaraje, Yuvraj Samarjitsinh and Maharajkumari Anjanaraje)
Photographed by Miyoshi, 1989. Photograph courtesy: Royal Gaekwad Collection, Baroda

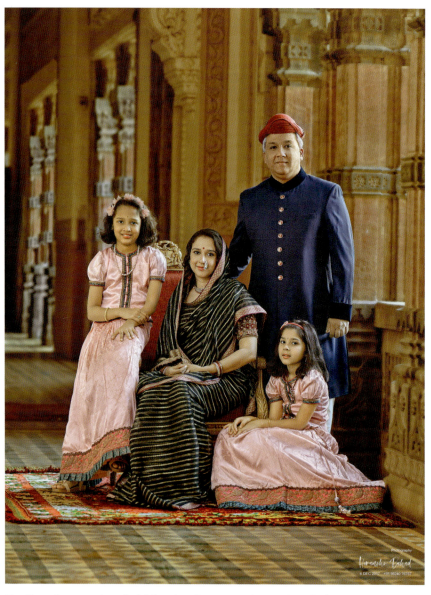

Family photograph of Maharaja Samarjitsinh Gaekwad (Standing-Maharaja Samarjitsinh, Seated-Maharani Radhikaraje, Maharajkumari Padmajaraje, Seated below-Maharajkumari Narayaniraje)

Photographed by Himanshu Pahad, 2017. Photograph courtesy: Royal Gaekwad Collection, Baroda

45

Aftermath of the First World War

Sayajirao III made his routine visit to Delhi early in 1916 and was gladdened by the news that Viceroy Hardinge was leaving for the shores of England, never to return as viceroy and that Lord Chelmsford had been appointed in his place. The Maharaja was so relieved by the tidings that he could have jumped with joy, thrown his headgear in the air and shouted hurray!

Viceroy Chelmsford seemed to be a fairly amiable person and displayed none of the traits that had been so predominant in his two predecessors, Viceroy Curzon and Viceroy Hardinge. As soon as Viceroy Chelmsford arrived in India, the Maharaja and the viceroy began to correspond with each other, the former having met him in London earlier.

Later in the year, the Maharaja was invited by Viceroy Chelmsford to spend a few days with him in Simla. Sayajirao III, as it was well known, was an introvert and took time to make friends. Viceroy Chelmsford too did not make friends easily. As far as the Maharaja was concerned, a viceroy was a viceroy and if he was the type who got along well with Indians all the better for it, but Viceroy Chelmsford who had probably heard all that had gone on before the war did not let it cloud his judgement and quietly assessed the man he had heard so much about. During their time together in Simla they were able to establish a fairly cordial relationship. Now there was a viceroy who had taken a neutral stand without any of those racial prejudices seen earlier in Residents and viceroys; this attitude was most heartening and moreover it was clearly reflected in the attitude of other British officials.' There were no more irritating provocations, no clever little traps set to establish that Gaekwad encouraged terrorism in his domain, above all no niggling restrictions placed in the way of his insatiable passion for travel. From now on, he could go and come as he liked. The Curzon Circular may never have been issued; the "incident" at Hardinge's durbar never taken place.'[1]

In the summer of the same year, Dewan V. P. Madhav Rao retired and

Manubhai Mehta became the dewan. Manubhai's work as a senior Baroda official had impressed the Maharaja to such an extent that on Madhav Rao's resignation, he immediately appointed him as the dewan. Manubhai had also been well groomed for the post as he had also acted as Sayajirao III's private secretary earlier and proved worthy of the choice. He remained in service for the next twelve years, retiring only in 1927.

In the month of May the following year, the Maharaja escaped the Baroda heat by going to Kashmir and stayed there till October. Sir Pratap Singh, who had earlier in March enjoyed his visit to Baroda, was anxious to reciprocate the hospitality he had received. As Srinagar was quite hot in May, they moved to Gulmarg. The Maharaja, captivated by the scenic beauty there, compared it to paradise, and mentioned the same in his letter to Sir John Watson dated 9 July 1916: 'The Persian poet calls this place a paradise.' [2] However, he enjoyed his time with his family and his infant grandson. Shivajirao too was with him in Kashmir though the Maharaja expressed his disapproval in his remark, 'the idea of change to a cold place for young men is being carried out too far in our family'. [3] He believed in giving his children the best in education and did so by sending them to England for it but did not believe in pampering them with physical comforts and spoiling them.

The Maharaja was always on the lookout to adopt new measures for improving the systems and even in Kashmir, he had the reins of the state of Baroda firmly in his hands. Communicating with Manubhai Mehta, he urged the necessity of pushing a new railway line in Kadi, the importance of careful inspections by subhas (district officers) and naib subhas (assistant district officers) of the work of their subordinates, the need for sending him reports from his officers when appointed to new posts, and other occasions. He also reminded the accounts department of its responsibilities and instructed that it should look into the work of the other departments and check for carelessness.

In August he was forced to abstain from work and rest, but at the end of the month he was writing to his dewan that the education department had opted to have informative and useful foreign books translated into the vernacular language, Gujarati. He instructed his dewan to ensure that at least 10 to 15 books were translated into simple and easy-to-comprehend Gujarati. This work was systematically carried out and because of the Maharaja's interest, a lot of Western knowledge was made available for the linguistically less accomplished of his subjects.

In early October, the Maharaja proceeded from Kashmir to Simla, where he was a guest of Viceroy Chelmsford. From Simla, he visited the ruler of Kapurthala at his invitation, who was also an old friend. Then he returned to Baroda but soon after left for Delhi to attend the conference of the Council of Princes. The Maharaja went with some reluctance since he did not see anything of importance in the agenda, and had no liking for ceremonies which did not end in discussions of important matters. The following year, when E. S. Montague visited India, he worked out a scheme to enlist the useful cooperation of the princes and the kings in the government of India. In his letter dated 7 November 1917 to the Maharaja of Nabha, Sayajirao III explained:

> I think that the formation of a separate council of the representatives of Indian princes, something after the model of the German Bundesrath, might meet the case... I had suggested a somewhat similar idea to the viceroy some years ago. I offer these suggestions with considerable hesitation, as I feel that this is a matter which lies more in the province of the scientific constitution framer...I have no doubt that if any matter which concerns the princes of India comes into discussion, the government of India will consult the princes before coming to any conclusion. There are, however, many questions of policy which it is essential for the princes to open up on their own initiative... It would be better for the princes to restrict their attention to the following matters—formation of a council of states and the formation of a properly representative court of appeal in matters of dispute arising between the government of India and Indian princes.... The princes should not lose sight of the fact that these reforms are only the means to an end. The end is the reduction, or even cessation, of interference in purely internal matters and the right to be consulted in matters which affect both the native states and British India equally. [4]

This letter illustrates his views as to the rightful position of the 'native' states within the empire which were by no means in concurrence with those of Indian nationalists and still less with archaic Anglo-Indian ideas. Sayajirao III also sent a letter to the Maharaja of Kolhapur in which he elaborated his views and proposed, among other things, that there should be in India, provincial and state autonomy. He also expressed that all questions relating to internal interest be dealt with by the provincial governments and the states respectively, and regarding imperial matters and internal affairs affecting British India and the states jointly, there should be established a House of Princes' representatives, to meet simultaneously with the imperial legislative assembly.

However, the proposed conference of princes in Delhi did not come off due to an epidemic of influenza, and had to be postponed to January in the following year. The new year's honours list of 1917 showed that Sayajirao III had been given the GCIE. After a lapse of more than a decade, this honour had come to him. His first British honour had come when he was twenty-four. Normally, the Raj dispensed such gifts to princes as a matter of routine; the fact that the Maharaja had been ignored was a sign of their strong disapprobation of him. Now that he was being honoured with such a title as this, it was a strong indication that he was once more being accorded the recognition of being a favourite son of the Raj.

Sayajirao III could not attend the conference of princes as he was obliged to tour the surrounding districts of the state which were suffering from the failure of the monsoons of 1917, causing a steep rise in prices of nearly all food commodities. Nor, again, did he consider the agenda of the conference sufficiently important for him to attend. However, he did recognize the fact that the conference of princes had performed some useful functions. He expressed his satisfaction in two of his letters to Viceroy Chelmsford in January and in October 1918 that in a resolution on minority administration in native states, the government of India had been guided mainly by the advice of princes at the conference held in 1916. Similarly, in his second letter, he noted with pleasure that a memorandum on the rights of succession in Indian states had accorded due consideration to the views of the princes of that conference.

In 1919, the Maharaja was bestowed the honour of the GCIE by King George of England, and in February, Lord Willingdon paid a couple of days visit to Baroda to offer his congratulations in person.

A letter from the government of India, the foreign and political department, to Edwin Montagu (King George's secretary of state for India) dated 8 January 1920 stated:

The relations between the government of India and His Highness have much improved in recent years and the attitude adopted by the durbar is now consistently friendly. It is evident that His Highness is anxious to cooperate with the government of India and that anti-British movements no longer receive encouragement. His Highness gave large sums for the prosecution of the war and was created a GCIE on 1 January 1919. We are disposed to think, therefore, that there is now no longer any need for the submission of half-yearly reports on current affairs in Baroda. The Resident at Baroda is in a position to keep the government of India fully informed of events as they occur and any unfavourable reports that may be made by him in future will be at once transmitted for the information of His Majesty's government. We accordingly recommend that the half-yearly report on Baroda affairs may be discontinued.[5]

By this time, as always during summer, the Maharaja was suffering from gout and he left for the cool hills of the south. He was in Ooty when the grave news reached him of his brother Anandrao's illness. Anandrao had been ill with pneumonia. Sayajirao left the hills for Baroda but was told in Bangalore that his brother had succumbed to the disease. Too ill to proceed further and attend the funeral, the Maharaja returned to Ooty. The loss of his brother affected him deeply as he wrote in his letter to Sampatrao: 'He was a good brother and a wise, sensible man of good common sense. He would have been fit for any big office, had he educated himself.'[6]

Plague was rampant that winter in Baroda, prompting Sayajirao III, who was still unwell, to travel to Simla spending four days there as a guest in the viceregal lodge. The cold winter months were consequently spent in Mysore and Bombay where he received a visit from Edwin Montagu in both the places. In his letter to the yuvraj of Mysore, he described Edwin Montagu as 'a very nice man.'[7] Further on his doctor's advice, he went to Devlali near Nasik for the rest of the winter.

The Maharaja was back in Baroda in April to attend the wedding of his granddaughter, Indumati (Fatehsinghrao III's daughter), to the eldest son of the Maharaja of Kolhapur.

The rest of 1918 was spent in the hill stations of India as influenza was still rife, claiming lives. In Dehradun, Sayajirao III and Chimnabai II were able to try electric treatment for their health complaints. Their return to Baroda was greeted with good tidings. The first World War had finally ended with

Germany signing the peace Treaty of Versailles and the Maharaja expressed his reaction in his letter of 8 December to Lord Reay as 'India is devoutly thankful,' adding, 'All the country has celebrated the triumph, and in Baroda we have spent three days in festivities and in feeding the poor'.[8] Funnily enough the Indians who fought in the war did not even know where Germany was and yet they were fighting along with the British against *their* enemy, but of course it was more for the rewards they hoped to gain in the form of political concessions.

Sayajirao III wrote in the same mood to General William Birdwood ten days later. In both letters, he alluded to the sufferings in India due to high prices, profiteering and shortage aggravated by the failure of the rains and by epidemics. Speaking of the war many years after, the Maharaja floated the idea that India had never wished for a British defeat. He admitted that some were willing to see early disasters as a corrective of the excessive pride with which they were unhappily familiar, in some British in India, but loyal support was given to the government nevertheless.

The Maharaja had been anxious to receive a visit from Viceroy Chelmsford in Baroda during the viceregal winter tour of 1918–19, and his wish was granted with the viceroy arriving in the capital on 24 March 1919.

A state banquet ended the two-day entertainment put up for the viceroy's benefit. At the banquet, Viceroy Chelmsford paid a well-deserved tribute to the Maharaja in his speech: 'The ruler who has for forty-three years devoted so much care and thought to the promotion of his people's welfare, the wise promoter of a system of political and social order aiming at the combination of all that is best in eastern and western civilization.'[9] Here with something like déjà vu, a scene repeated from 1909 after the viceregal visit, when a letter had been received by Sayajirao III from Lord Minto warning him of sedition. Now on 28 April 1919, after Viceroy Chelmsford's visit, we find the Maharaja was acknowledging the receipt of a letter with a copy of a resolution regarding the violent agitation against the passing of the Anarchical and Revolutionary Crimes Act. His reply was, 'I am glad to inform Your Excellency, that, so far as I am aware, the contagion has not spread to my territories. Your Excellency may certainly count upon my full support and cooperation in the suppression of outbursts of lawlessness.'[10]

The déjà vu ended with letters and though there were grave disturbances in British districts of Gujarat, these did not extend to the Baroda state, nor was there any attempt to implicate the hand of Baroda in them. This time history did not repeat itself.

Now that the war of all wars had ended, the Maharaja was free to do what he loved best. A passionate traveller, he began to contemplate another visit to Europe though the real motive behind this was that his second son Jaisinghrao was seriously ill and the doctors had advised a change of climate for him.

The Maharaja and his family were in Kashmir in the month of June 1919 but even there the heat proved unbearable and Sayajirao III was confined to bed with a severe attack of gout. The family returned to Baroda where they learnt that Prince Jaisinghrao's health was deteriorating and that facilitated another move. Jaisinghrao was sent to Europe, and on 22 September, his parents followed to see what best could be done. Shivajirao was left behind. Sayajirao III himself needed a rest cure and he was just preparing to go into a nursing home in London when the devastating news of the death of his son Shivajirao arrived on 24 November 1919.

Shivajirao had been only thirty but the spirit of daredevilry due to his his irrepressible school-boyish demeanour had induced him to bathe in cold water and drive out in the cold air when he was feeling feverish. The drive brought on pneumonia and he succumbed to it. The royal couple was numbed with shock. Shivajirao, handsome with a strong physique, debonair, full of fun and laughter and a zest for life, had been snuffed out like a candle flame in the wind; it was too much for the stoutest to take in his stride.

A rest cure of nine weeks in London was followed by a stopover in St Moritz and then at Montreux, 'which', he said in his letter to Viceroy Chelmsford, 'is like going from winter to spring. This has been my first experience of nursing homes and nursing, and although the cure was rather exacting, I am hoping for results which will make it quite worth the trouble and loss of time. I am still taking the after-cure, and have not yet regained my normal strength; but I think that Eastbourne will set me up.'[11]

The Maharaja stayed in Eastbourne until July. In August, he was in Scotland, after which he spent most of 1920 at Hartsbourne Manor, Bushley Heath. In another letter to Viceroy Chelmsford, he wrote about the reception of the maharani and himself by the royal majesties of England and his own reception by the Prince of Wales the following day. To the prince he expressed his desire that during his forthcoming trip to India, he would honour Baroda with a visit, a matter on which he had already written to the secretary of state for India.

By the end of the year, Jaisinghrao was shifted from London to Berlin, where his health seemed to improve. The Maharaja and the maharani followed him to Berlin. The royal couple finally left for Baroda and reached the state on 5 February 1921, after an absence from it of over a year and four months.

The Maharaja had fallen into a state of apathy, owing to the shock of losing Shivajirao and acute distress over his other son's illness.

Even amidst sorrow, he had something to be glad about as he received the news that Okhamandal was restored to the jurisdiction of the Baroda state.

46

Okhamandal's History

The Okhamandal taluka of Amreli has a curious history. At the beginning of the nineteenth century, it was independent of the rule of the Gaekwads of Baroda. The inhabitants of Okhamandal were the Vaghers who were a primitive, fierce lot of tribals. They were actually fishermen who had taken to piracy and armed robbery. In 1804, certain pirates among the tribe seized a Bombay vessel off their coast and threw all on board into the sea. The government of Bombay did not react immediately to this, but in 1807 Colonel Walker, who five years earlier had been appointed as the first Resident, was ordered to put matters right. Accompanied by the Baroda force, he marched into Dwarka, occupied it and imposed a fine of Rs 1,10,000. The Vaghers reluctantly agreed to pay the fine and promised to cause no further trouble. Their depredations began again, making another expedition necessary to put them down, but it was not until 1814 that one-third of the fine was recovered from them but they with their allied chieftains continued to cause trouble till at last the Bombay government took drastic steps to reduce them to subjection, which was achieved only in 1816. In view of the fact that Okhamandal was a holy place with shrines important to the Hindus like Dwarka and Beyt, the district was given as a gift to the Gaekwads of Baroda, who conceded certain privileges to the East India Company in return. Okhamandal was then incorporated into the territory of Gaekwad in Kathiawad, which was known as Amreli prant.

The administration of the place proved extremely difficult and trouble broke out in 1818 and 1819. It was only with the help of the British that order was restored in 1820. For some time peace reigned, but again in 1857 due to the Baroda administration not being able to exercise enough control, the Vaghers and other tribes were constantly raiding Kathiawad. Insurrections broke out in the two following years also and the British were forced to intervene yet again. Absolutely fed up with the problems in Okhamandal Khanderao Gaekwad expressed to the Resident that he would like to hand over the administration of the taluka to the British. The insurgents, believing a rumour that British rule in India was on the verge of a collapse, put up a strong resistance to the expeditionary force from Bombay, but after Dwarka was stormed and the tribesmen driven to the jungle, peace was restored by the end of 1859. By the change in the control of affairs in Okhamandal, Gaekwad still retained his sovereignty over the district, but a British political officer, appointed by the Bombay government and acting under the orders of the Resident, was stationed in Dwarka —he was in charge of affairs there and had exclusive control over the Vaghers and allied tribes. Matters continued this way for sixty long years. In 1909, the government of India decided that Baroda magistrates should exercise second-class powers over the Vaghers, reserving higher powers for the assistant Resident in Dwarka. Again in the year 1919, the government of India agreed to give complete control of the administration of Okhamandal to Baroda. In May the following year, Resident, Lt. Colonel C.J. Windham, went to Dwarka and in the presence of the dewan informed the Vagher chiefs of the transfer of power: 'In view of the altered habits of the Vaghers, and of the efficiency of the Baroda administration in which the government has every trust, the government of India now wish to relax the stringent control which has been exercised by the Resident, and to make over the charge of the Vaghers to the government of Baroda, whose subjects they are and [have] always been.'[1]

Along with the control of Okhamandal and its tribes, the Okha Battalion had been originally recruited from among the Vaghers alone, but in 1865 other Indian tribes began to join the battalion. This battalion remained with the Baroda army for a long time. Ever since then, the Vaghers settled down to a civilized life and routine and the earlier practice of issuing passes to a Vagher every time he wanted to go out of Okhamandal was abolished with the exception of those who had a really bad record.

Now the news that its jurisdiction had been restored to the Baroda state made His Highness extremely satisfied.

Education began by slow degrees to make itself felt. Also, the Boy Scout movement was initiated in January 1919. A specially engaged scout-master-in-chief organized a troop of one hundred boys selected from the schools in Baroda city to which Sayajirao III after his birthday durbar presented colours. The troop was known as 'His Highness the Maharaja Gaekwad's Own Boy Scouts, Baroda'. Mr Prasad was the chief and was doing an excellent job.

The Maharaja, with his ear to the ground, had heard a good account of it.

It was almost the end of Mr Prasad's term when early one morning His Highness, who was in the habit of walking around the city incognito to assess the level of efficiency of the state administration, found some boys going hurriedly past him at that unearthly hour. Surprised, he stopped them and asked them where they were bound. They answered, 'We are Boy Scouts and are going for the morning parade.'

'But today is Sunday! Is it not a holiday?' asked His Highness.

'Yes. But we also enjoy our Sundays there as old games are played and new ones taught.'

The Maharaja asked, 'Don't your parents object to this?'

The boys answered in unison, 'No sir, in fact they are happy about it and wake us up early so we are in time for the parade.'

His Highness, reluctant to let the boys out of his sight asked them, 'But why are you running?' One of them answered, 'Roll call bugle is at six o' clock and we have to be there.'[2]

His Highness queried, 'Who is your chief, and why does he bother you so much? I hear that he ill treats his students.'

The boys, taken aback, answered stiffly, 'Who says so? Our Boy Scout Commissioner is Mr Prasad and he is a very nice person. We have to take an oath to be truthful and be kind to the poor.'

The Maharaja remarked, 'I heard that he will be leaving soon, then you will be well rid of this tyrant!' The boys answered in chorus a trifle crossly, 'We will not let him leave!' The Maharaja retorted, 'And who are you to stop him?' Just then, a man in full military uniform stepped out from the shadows exclaiming, 'Maharaja! It is time to return! Shall we leave?'[3]

The stunned boys were left to gather their scattered wits as they realized they had been talking to the king himself! Sayajirao turned away smiling, satisfied he had derived an honest opinion of the boy scout commissioner's work. The following day he sent an order that Mr Prasad be given an extension in service.

With the reins of government now restored to Baroda, the district of Amreli was separated from Amreli prant, and was under a commissioner who exercised the powers of a subha and district judge.

The restoration of Okhamandal to the House of the Gaekwads in 1921 was extremely gratifying to Sayajirao III.

The Maharaja's return to Baroda in February was but for a short duration, for in seven weeks' time, they were again on their way to Europe. He stated in one of his letters to the Maharaja of Mysore, 'You must not think that I have given up my interest in India and am going to settle down in Europe... The importance of health is not wisely and fully recognized by our people, and for temporary convenience they often incur permanent loss in the way of ill health. I am trying to avoid this as much as I can.'[4]

In spite of his ill health and innumerable family problems, the Maharaja never stopped his vigil on his administration of his state. Testifying to this were the radio cables that were sent from him to his dewan with instructions: 'Please start and expedite earthworks, extension of Zakwa railways. Please study budget and management of the Khangi department in consultation of the Maharani's convenience and suggest definite improvements.'[5] Chimnabai II was the head of the department of the palace Khangi, meaning 'household'. The Maharaja who hated a profligate lifestyle wanted streamlined measures taken in the management of the palace household department. Miss Tottenham who knew of the goings-on in the palace household and outside it, wrote, 'The palace had two kitchens, both fully staffed, one for European food and the other for Indian food. The Indian kitchen was the responsibility of Maharani Chimnabai, but the European kitchen was supposed to be run by a department under the Maharaja's supervision.'[6]

According to Reverend Weeden, it provided the sort of food 'you would get at a first-class restaurant in London Prince's or Carlton...prepared by a French cook and served under the experienced eye of an English *maître de hotel*. Pluck a very imposing person in fine dark blue coat with a velvet collar and gold buttons with a ribbon in his buttonhole who was Lord Amphill's butler when he was the governor of Madras.'[7]

Miss Tottenham, who was also directed by Sayajirao III to serve as a member of the committee appointed by him to go over the expenses of the European kitchen, had this to say, 'Every day at four o'clock for three weeks, the commission sat. We examined accounts, we interviewed staff, we looked through stores and considered the capacity and ventilation of storerooms and larders...investigated the local bazaar supplies and those sent from Bombay.

'We arrived early to see how the supplies were delivered in the mornings, we visited local meat shops and fish market; we went over vegetable gardens at the jail and the public gardens both of which "fed" the palace.'[8]

The committee, after a thorough scrutiny of the accounts, was horrified to discover that the cost of providing European food per head came to Rs 19 per day, excluding expenses in 'entertainment, wines and smokes'.

Something was obviously wrong in the management of the European kitchen, but, try as they would, they could not find the source of the drainage to stem the flow and put an end to it without it affecting the quantity and quality of the food served. Henceforth, every expense had to be accounted for and signed requests were prerequisites for any purchase. Even the ADCs, when they reported for duty, had to sign a chit for their request for a cigarette, when earlier they had been accustomed to a fresh box of supplies being placed in their room every day. In spite of these economies, the cost of feeding the inmates of the palace was ten times more than the expense of a similar fare in a normal household.' The lesson being, you could not live in a palace and apply normal rules of management!'[9] The preponderance of the palace had to be taken into account and the inevitable wastage.

Regarding the Zakwa railway line, the Maharaja's idea was that in order to save time, the best and the most expensive parts of the construction of the Zakwa railway line should be immediately taken up as in the case of the earthworks company, and at a later period, when the line was completed and fully equipped, the state's finances would be able to manage with less strain on it.

Not one to forget his role as one bound to honour the British hierarchy when they chose to visit his state, he sent a letter, dated 28 March 1921, to the newly appointed viceroy, Lord Reading, from Evian-Les-Bains, 'Hearty Greetings! I must regret that I will not be in India to take part in welcoming you and I hope, Lady Reading and yourself will have an enjoyable stay in India crowned with the fulfilment of your high aspirations which have raised such great hopes in the hearts of the princes and people of India.'[10] The letter was signed by the Maharaja in his own hand. Viceroy Reading's response was equally cordial and endeavoured to meet the high expectations of his people. Other cables sent by the Maharaja pertained to transfer of officers to other departments, and sending some of them abroad for study and training so that they may on their return use their expertise for the benefit of the state. For example, in a letter dated 30 March, he instructed his minister Manubhai, 'Select two young men between the ages of 20–25 or below 30 years to study farming methods in America along with a young Indian well-versed in farming methods and with knowledge of the vernacular tongue, in order to interpret farming instructions to them and take down notes, pick up new ideas...'[11]

Letters and cables from Sayajirao III with instructions for sending reports and statements of accounts to him, and for giving a grant of Rs 10, 00, 000 for promoting Ayurvedic medicine and setting up dispensaries within a radius of five miles of any place within the state were posted and wired to the dewan, Manubhai Mehta.

The Maharaja always asked for estimates in facts and figures before embarking on or sanctioning any project. Selecting a site for building houses for the poor, instructions were given to the dewan on how all departments should function independent of each other and of outside control, were given to him. Further, officers who needed promotion and were diffident of approaching the Maharaja directly, resorted to currying favour with superior officers to get what they wanted, or put forward their claims through acting officers. Direct approach through tippans (requisition notes) was better and a circular was issued to this effect after receiving instructions from the Maharaja while in Paris.

Even his grandchildren had to send in tippans for their requests.

Regarding accounts statements from the Khangi Kharbari, instructions were given that these should be checked and verified by the assistant accounts general of the Khangi department. Different departments of the administration were to submit reports pertaining to the work of each. The progress in the education of his children too had to be mentioned in the State Annual Report!

The above is some of the monumental work that was administered by the Maharaja during his travels abroad. A telegraphic code was devised to keep important state as well as personal matters confidential.

Letters to the dewan insisting that regular reports from all departments be sent to him on a monthly basis also testified to his vigilance of the state's affairs; even from afar, he had the pulse of the administration and the knowledge of it on his fingertips. Even the European head of the department had to send in his monthly reports to the Maharaja when he was abroad. The Maharaja did not lapse in his duties as a ruler even while travelling to far-off places. From his first trip to Europe in 1889 till his last in 1939, his correspondence dealt with reforms, instructions with regard to administration, relief work and donations for famine and floods with its alternative occurrence in the state or improving the education system and sanitation and a lot more that it seemed like the Maharaja was governing the state with an invisible hand.

A confidential letter from the Maharaja to the dewan regarding reorganizing of the state forces' military department dated 23 December 1923, ran this way: 'The government of India has refused to grant the type of battery asked for by the state. The right to develop military power has been banned by the government of India or to manufacture arms. Therefore, to join in their scheme would not be satisfactory to us or to the British military authorities.'[12]

Their scheme stipulated the following terms:

1. Army should be reformed for internal security.
2. Refund of the expenses of the contingent and of the excess revenue of the districts assigned for the maintenance of the subsidiary force.
3. The government of India would not contribute unless the Baroda state spent more than 15 per cent of the gross revenue on *their* military forces.

This shows that the subsidiary force which was kept as guarantee for British protection and maintained by the Gaekwads (first introduced by Anandrao Gaekwad through the Arab sibandi and taken up by the British after the Arab sibandi had been disbanded) was still in existence and had not been done away with! The British contingent force was maintained by the Gaekwads in return for their protection.

Further in a letter written by the Maharaja on 5 February 1925, he reiterated his objection to joining the British scheme: 'Proposals made by the government of India will eventually lead to a position in which the state will be little more than the paymasters of the army without due control of the machine for which it is paying. If only the proposals would permit of a more complete independence of the state, while trusting to its loyalty in any time of crisis, as indeed is fully guaranteed in various treaty clauses, they would appear more acceptable. It is certainly not desirable to forfeit the advantages of modern arms, the training of officers and the rebate of Rs 3,00,000–3,25,000, but the possible danger to our independence must be duly and seriously considered.'

Interestingly, there was a cable from the Maharaja dated 1 October 1921 where he had instructed his minister that the foundation stone for the library in Baroda should be laid by the commissioner of education and give him the dewan's powers, as 'The government of India did not allow the Prince of Wales to lay the foundation stone for anything on his tour!'[13]

47

The Villiers Debacle

Sayajirao III wished to get an expert from the government of India to help in examining the accounts and organizing the financial systems of the finance and accounts departments. The unsatisfactory state of affairs of the Khangi, the Raj investments as well as the Villiers accounts had him worried.

From the time the reins of government had been handed to him, Sayajirao III's prudence in the financial management of his state had led to an annual surplus of cash in the state treasury. Sayajirao III allowed himself a privy purse of Rs 25,00,000 a year, out of which he was able to regularly save in some sound investments and very soon began to invest in some financially stable business concerns outside the state. His intention was that the profits would serve as a reserve to fall back on in the event of an emergency in the state or for him personally. In the early days of his reign he had personally supervised these investments but of late had left it to two financial experts. One of these was the accountant general, A. N. Datar, and the other was C. E. Randle, the manager of the Bank of Baroda. Without the approval of these two financial wizards, no investment was authorized by the dewan. Things ran along smoothly and by 1915 Baroda's investments had grown steadily over the years and it was at this point of time that a gentleman called Villiers arrived on the scene.

Impeccably dressed, Villiers appeared to belong to the upper class of Englishmen, had the right connections in the right places and also happened to be related to Viceroy Chelmsford the viceroy. Lord Sandwich, an aristocrat, was also related to him and he claimed a close friendship with Lord Chatwynd, also an aristocrat belonging to the high ranks of the British class of nobles. With such impeccable credentials it would have been rude to ask to examine the reports of the coal properties he owned or to enquire into his financial backing. Villiers seems to have convinced the dewan and the two financial experts of his financial credibility and they in turn did not bother to make enquiries about the status of coal in his coalfields nor did they bother to enquire who his financial backers were. Villiers' plan to siphon off as much money as he could from the Baroda treasury into his own pockets had got off to a good start. Sayajirao III, convinced by his three advisers, initially invested Rs 45,00,000 in Villiers' company, when in actual fact Villiers' coalfields were useless and the financial backers non-existent. But Villiers was a crook and he kept floating one company after another with promises of rich returns on investments till the Maharaja found that his coffers were practically empty. Within a matter of eight years, a sum of Rs 89,00,000 had been invested in Villiers and further, a sum of Rs 1,000,000 invested in the Tata Iron and Steel Company on the excellent security of valuable real estate in Bombay had been withdrawn and loaned to Villiers' company for a new steel mill which Villiers proposed to start. The new company was called Eastern Irons. All the funding for these fictitious ventures had been solely on Sayajirao III's side, but he received no interest on the loans. By this time the dewan, Manubhai, and the two financial experts must have realized the futility of the investments. They had either connived with Villiers to line their own pockets or been too afraid to let Sayajirao III know the truth till the bubble finally burst with the Eastern Irons going into voluntary liquidation.

At this stage Sayajirao III called in M/s Billimoria and Company, an auditing company to audit the books of Villiers twenty-odd enterprises. The auditors' report showed that Baroda state and the Maharaja personally had lost a staggering amount of seven million rupees in Villiers. Manubhai and the two wise men of finance were called to explain, which ended in the dewan blaming the other two. Manubhai left in disgrace to join the Maharaja of Bikaner where he could try afresh his talents in the new opening, while Ranade defended himself with his stand that he had genuinely believed the ventures would yield substantial profits. No firm action was taken against him but he was dismissed from his position as manager of the Bank of Baroda.

Sayajirao III was anxious to avoid a major scandal which would have shown the English gentleman, who was highly connected, as a crook. It could be that Viceroy Chelmsford may have never backed Villiers in his ventures but Villiers had used the relationship to his advantage and had swindled money from the Baroda treasury to line his pockets. Nothing could be done to regain what had been lost except to impose stricter vigilance in the finance department of the state and trust no one.

More than the financial loss, the fact that there were gaping holes in the fine fabric of his administration irked him deeply and made his insomnia worse. He withdrew more and more into his shell as he realized there was nobody he could really trust.

48

Sayajirao III as an Administrator

Regarding the machinery of administration, the Maharaja's assessment of the capabilities of officials and assigning to them work they were suited for; for instance, in a cable, he instructed the dewan, 'By Huzur order, Mr Shirgaonkar takes over the Khangi Kharbari post. Major Parab will revert as Naib Khangi Kharbari, on a salary of Rs 400+Rs 100 as allowance for accommodation. Major S. Pawar to be made to work for two months in the Khangi accounts department and pick up the work with Sardesai to guide him.'[1]

The Maharaja's policy exercised in his administration was to get people trained first in the department before appointing them into service as it ensured greater efficiency and expertise. He also believed that officers should not be allowed to remain in the same posts for more than three years, 'As they not only become inefficient but also become corrupt. All superintendents can be changed in rotation at intervals though, not all at the same time. There are always subordinates who can keep up the work and these subordinates should be able to work independently without having to run to their superiors for instructions.'[2] He also advised officers to take greater interest in the work of their juniors, 'They must teach them the principles of their work and must encourage imitativeness in order to develop pride in their work along with a keen desire to improve it. Any suggestion from a subordinate clerk, whoever, no matter how small, it should be welcome, and the practice of going over the same ground over and over again must be discouraged.' The Maharaja made it his policy to listen with a willing ear to complaints or suggestions for improvements in the infrastructure of the state from the common man by publishing the state budget in the newspapers, for criticism from the public.

There is an interesting story with regard to this—the famine in 1900 had caused death and devastation in the province of Gujarat. The farmers were badly hit by drought and prices soared sky-high. Sayajirao III, deeply disturbed by the plight of his people, particularly the farmers, appointed a committee to analyse the causes and chalk out proper relief and preventive measures to avoid such calamities in the future. For eleven years the committee toiled over the project assigned to them but could not come up with a substantial report. The main reason for this was frequent changes in the committee members due to incompetency. The little paperwork that had been done was just being rotated around all the departments with little effect. Manilalbhai Nanavati, who had joined the Baroda service in 1904, had been observing the fate of the project. Eager to prove his versatility, he sent a tippan to the Maharaja asking that he be given an opportunity to make the desired report. The message was sent through Dewan Seddon who upon reading it, said to himself, 'This man seems too sure of himself; when an entire committee could not complete the project in eleven years, how will he solitarily be able to complete it?' Summoning Manilalbhai, he demanded to know that when the super-efficient British officials had not been able to come up with adequate solutions to the problem, how did Manilalbhai imagine that he would be able to? Manilalbhai replied without losing confidence, 'Yes, I am fully aware that many have tried but, let one more person make an attempt.' Seddon, defeated in the face of logic, agreed and ordered the staff of the investigation department to hand over all the papers connected with the famine relief measures to Manilalbhai. The Maharaja was extremely pleased with Manilalbhai's sincerity when he got to hear about it. The fact that the committee had taken eleven years over the job impelled him to call up Manilalbhai often to know how he was progressing on the given project. Manilalbhai's attitude was different from the rest; he worked with full involvement in the project. He toiled over it night and day and after four months came up with a splendid report on the different types of problems that farmers had to put up with most of the time. Manilalbhai had run from pillar to post to get accurate information directly from the farmers themselves. Meanwhile, Seddon had left and B. L. Gupta had been appointed in his place as dewan. Manilalbhai submitted his report to the dewan, who was astounded that Manilal had completed the task in just four months! Gupta also saw that there was a lot of truth in the analysis and asked Manilalbhai to leave the report on his desk and collect it the following morning. The following morning, the moment the doors of the administrative department opened, Manilalbhai walked into the dewan's office. The dewan rose from his chair and came forward to greet him.

Manilalbhai got tense and thought all his work of the past four months had come to nought, and he barely registered the fact that the dewan was actually pressing him to sit down opposite him. When he did, the dewan said, 'My dear Manilal! I congratulate you on your report. Your work is astounding. Last night, I read your entire report at home. From the report, quite a bit of information I have noted for the records and accordingly you bring it to light but you have also criticized the agricultural system as laid down by Sayajirao III who will not take kindly to it, so I suggest you delete it from your report or you may lose your job.' Gupta added after a minute, 'Don't get me wrong, your report is the best of all that has come to my table so far!' Manilalbhai was in a dilemma for honesty was second nature to him, but before he could decide whether to follow the dewan's advice, he got summons from the Maharaja's office to go over there with the report.

With a lot of trepidation, Manilalbhai went and submitted the report to His Highness who studied it thoroughly. After about two hours, the Maharaja said, 'Manilal, I do not agree with everything you say in the report but you go ahead and publish it without further delay.' Manilal stammered his protest, 'B-but Your Highness those points on which you...' His Highness cut him short, 'It is not necessary to delete those points. Without any hesitation, just publish the report as it is.' Manilalbhai who was thankful that he still had his job left.[3]

The above is just one of those examples that showed that Sayajirao III never allowed his ego to come in the face of constructive criticism.

Budgets were fixed for all departments of the administration and any excesses had to be properly accounted for. There was a prize of Rs 500 for presenting the best budget to the Maharaja.

All transfers of staff from one department to another had to sanctioned by the Maharaja in order to avoid confusion and khatpat! In his absence, permission had to be obtained from the council. Promotions were to be given on merit and not because a man had foreign qualifications. Even those who did had to start at the bottom rung of the ladder and gradually by diligence and through result-oriented performance reach the top. This order was passed on 10 December 1922 by the Maharaja sitting in Hyde Park, London.

Extremely conscious that the finances for running the state came from public funds in the form of revenue and taxes, he exercised caution and avoided wastage. For instance, regarding machines for the railway department, he said in a letter that they 'should be properly inspected in consultation with the chief engineer periodically and the public works department should evaluate the machines after wear and tear and compare it with the cost of the machine as on date of purchase and the value of it after deducting depreciation.'[4] Reports on the standard of maintenance of machines in the railway department had to be submitted in a condensed form to the Maharaja and records kept for future use.

Before introducing any scheme into the administration irrespective of which department it was railways, education, agriculture, etc., he advocated a thorough study of its history before implementing it. If the scheme had been successful earlier, fine, and if not, the reason for its failure was to be analysed and proper remedial methods were to be devised to ensure its success. Any constructive step beneficial to the public taken by the government in Western countries was quickly adapted by him. For example, while in London he read complaints from the British public in the newspapers about bad sanitation and unhygienic food being served in public schools' boarding houses, affecting the health of children. The Maharaja immediately cabled his dewan to organize periodic inspections in boarding schools and hostels by the health and sanitation authorities in Baroda. 'School inspectors, district medical officers and the sanitary and educational commissioners should examine the sanitation of these schools when they go on inspection work,'[5] he said in his cable. After that, reports were submitted on the progress of the hygienic standard in schools and hostels and regular inspections took place.

Sayajirao III's thoughts centred on the well-being and happiness of his subjects. His administration was open to the public for criticism. 'The public is invited to point out defects and inconveniences in the administration in his absence and suggest definite practical remedies to improve them within three weeks of this notification.'[6] This was stated in a cable dated 2 November 1925 when he was due to sail from Paris for India on the 6th of the same month.

Sayajirao III was as fastidious in his investments as he was in engaging employees in the service of the state. But, in spite of it, he lost heavily in some of his investments like Villiers' company. A letter from S. C. Ghosh, the manager of Bird & Company in Calcutta to Sayajirao III advising investment in the coal-bearing land in the Karanpura coalfield which, the letter stated, 'contains large areas of excellent coal. Bird & Company offer to be agents and also handle His Highness's funds for safe investments, in return for a commission and power of attorney to act on His Highness's behalf.'[7] The Maharaja, in response, said he would consent after his auditors Lovelock & Lewis had assessed the financial soundness of the company and of the investment suggested.

Bird & Company of Calcutta was not a small or insignificant firm. It controlled the biggest group of jute mills and collieries in the provinces of Bengal, Orissa (Odisha now) and Bihar. But, in spite of that the Maharaja stipulated that all terms should be open and no secret commissions would be paid. He also cleverly suggested opening a branch of the company in the state as they were agents for a lot of manufacturing companies in India. This testifies to his prudence and cautiousness in investments; after all, he had learnt his lesson with the Villiers debacle. He wanted that all reports on investments and important matters to be sent to the councillor in charge of particular portfolios, with the intention to centralize the work and information in one place where it would be easily available. 'All diaries and reports should come through the accountant general, to the higher officers who will scrutinize it several times and check on the directors and officers to do their duties properly and defects are rectified in time.' Overworking was not recommended by the Maharaja 'as it affected one's health and resulted in carelessness and inefficiency, therefore he advocated assistance to ensure better performance.'[8]

When it came to improvements in town planning, the plots were measured for their size before any steps were taken and the work was entrusted to the Maharaja's brother Sampatrao Gaekwad to supervise 'in the hope that desirable facilities and conveniences are secured. It is also necessary not only for saving office routine work but also for the public whose time and worry must be saved.'[9]

All departmental heads had to send monthly statements of expenses as well as reports on the work entrusted to them and completed. He also desired that officers, when taking orders, should not omit any material point in matters that required his consideration.

His oft-repeated advice to higher officers in the administration was that 'it's not in numbers that one can guarantee efficiency, one good worker can do better the work of three men by a proper increase in his wages.'[10] He also believed that the heads of departments should be given as much importance as possible by increasing their powers 'as the welfare of the department rests more with them than on ministers or councils. A dictionary for legal terms was to be prepared. For preparing departmental rules, one more assistant should be given to the nyay mantra (minister of justice) whose duty was to complete all the rules and regulations and issue a circular to all departmental heads in the administration of the state.'[11]

Among his many feats was organizing the police force where he advocated a novel way of ensuring trained personnel in the police force by recruiting men from the military who were first subjected to the necessary exams before being selected for the post. Sayajirao III was extremely fastidious about employing the right people for specific jobs in the state. Not one who believed in half measures, he always made a thorough study of a project before undertaking it. For instance, regarding boring wells to solve the perennial problem of water scarcity in the state, he instructed in his letters, 'For boring wells, experts are required for the job so that adequate water can be supplied for irrigation purposes in the districts of Kadi and other parts of Baroda. Expense no bar!'[12] The Maharaja firmly believed that water was of paramount importance and was ready to spend thousands on the experiment: 'The Public Works Department and the Railway Department who may be bestowing wells in Dwarka, their help is solicited.'

Sayajirao III was anxious that the work of all departments should run smoothly in his absence and not give cause for British interference.

In his correspondence with his dewan, Sayajirao III gave directions for transfer of staff, investments, oil and gas operations, reconstruction of the Gujarat province after the floods, relief measures in the famine-affected areas as both calamities followed one after the other. It's heartening to read a cable from Sayajirao III instructing the dewan to engage his son Prince Dhairyashilrao and his granddaughter Princess Indumati in relief work during the famine in Baroda. In spite of their royal status they were made to work like any other person. Instructions were shared to set up relief camps and houses with proper sanitation. In a cable dated 26 September 1927, he asked his dewan for a report on the relief measures taken by him for villages hit by the Baroda floods and also to request the Bombay sanitary commissioner to visit Baroda and advise regarding sanitation in the state after the floods. He granted a donation of Rs 10,00,000 for the flood relief fund and awarded the gold medal of the Rajaratna Mandal to Gajanan Yeshwant Mantrao 'for his rescue work at a considerable risk to himself.'[13]

The Maharaja, concerned about those rendered homeless on account of the floods, considered rebuilding houses for them which would also temporarily solve the unemployment situation in the state and sent a letter was sent to his dewan to that effect. Every aspect of the after-effects of the calamity had to be considered and resolved.

The Maharaja had instructions for the education department too. In a letter, he asked for Hindi instructors to be appointed in schools. His cable of 14 September to Rao Bahadur Hargovandas Kantawala noted, 'In recognition and in appreciation of your notable achievement in literature and your contribution thereby to the honour of my state, I hereby name you the first recipient of my newly established order of distinction and I appoint you to the highest grade—Designated Companion of the Said Order.'[14]

And so on and so forth—it's no small wonder the man suffered from insomnia!

Sayajirao III's thirteenth European trip (in 1921) was for seven months as he wanted to be back in Baroda to receive the Prince of Wales as the prince had included Baroda, upon the Maharaja's invitation, in his itinerary. He was back in Baroda on 11 November and twelve days later the Prince of Wales arrived.

The Prince of Wales got a rousing welcome from the crowd of people who had thronged the streets of Baroda to greet him. According to *The Times* correspondent, the arrangements made for his entertainment were admirable. In the royal tradition, the prince was shown the crown jewels at the Nazar Baug Palace the estimated value of which was over Rs 3,00,00,000. It's unimaginable to estimate its value today, in the new millennium!

At the state banquet given in his honour at the Laxmi Vilas Palace, the prince expressed his gratification with his reception: 'I shall retain the most pleasant impressions of Baroda, the first Indian state which I have visited during the course of my tour and of the wonderful sights which I have seen here. I have but one regret, that my stay with Your Highness must necessarily be so short. But, short as it is, it has enabled me to strengthen and tighten the ties which bind your House and mine; and the most pleasant of my Baroda memories will be the pleasure which I have experienced in making the closer acquaintance of Your Highness.'

49

Declining Health of Sayajirao III

Sayajirao III and Chimnabai II remained in Baroda for the next four months spending the Indian winter and spring at home. In April 1922, they had begun their journey to Europe. This was to be a long absence, in fact his longest from the state of his entire reign.

Apart from their ill health, they were grief-stricken over the loss of their son Jaisinghrao who had passed away on 27 August 1923. The Maharaja had lost three of his sons while the maharani had lost two. All three had died in the height of their youth and that's what made the tragedies harder to bear. Dharyashilrao, the youngest of the princes, remained the only surviving heir to the throne.

Much earlier in 1901, the Maharaja had stated in one of his speeches at a prize distribution function at the Bombay Medical College, 'It would be a mistake to think that Indians have less wish to live than Europeans. I believe they are as much in love with life and if they do not take much care to preserve it, it is partly due to poverty, but still more to their ignorance to [sic] the laws of health.'[1]

Unfortunately for the princes who ought to have imbibed healthcare knowledge from their exposure to the West had been influenced only by those insidious elements in Western culture which require an exceptionally strong character to resist. The trauma of losing three of his sons within a short span of time played havoc with Sayajirao III's health and his old problem of gout returned to plague him with renewed vigour. In the course of five months from his landing in Bombay in November 1923, he was unwell for three weeks at a time.

As chancellor of Hindu University, Benares, he had promised to read a paper at the annual convocation. By the middle of January 1924, his health took a turn for the worse and on his way to Benares, he was seriously indisposed. Unable to meet his commitment to the university, he returned to Baroda with influenza complications and was bedridden for a month. The doctors recommended a visit to Matheran, followed by a trip to Europe. The Maharaja's health improved after a fortnight's stay in Matheran but he still had to be carried in a wheelchair to board the *S. S. Macedonia*. He finally left for Europe on 26 April and the large party saw him off with serious misgivings. The maharani accompanied him along with his personal physician, Dr V. Y. Modak, a nurse and a small staff of four comprising two ADCs, a secretary and an assistant secretary—a radical change from his first European trip. The refreshing sea air and the change in the environment probably did what the doctors couldn't and soon the Maharaja began to recover speedily on board the ship and even before they reached Aden his mind turned to the administrative affairs of his state. They landed at Marseilles and after a short stay of eleven days in Paris, on 3 June they crossed over to England to reside in the Maharaja's new house, 'Russels' in Watford.

With his improved health and not one to let the grass grow under his feet, Sayajirao III was as busy as a beaver. He made six visits to the Wembley Exhibition to imbibe whatever he could for implicating into Baroda state. Another attack of gout confined him to bed, forcing him to miss not only Henley and Ascot, but also the Royal Garden Party at Buckingham Palace. A cure at Evian was suggested where therapeutic water flowed directly from the Alps and was considered excellent for health. The last three weeks of July were spent there. The maharani was already in Bagnoles-de-l'Orne and the Maharaja joined her there after testing the waters at Chamonix and Aix-les-Bains. The Indian royal couple was to return to their home town in early November but on receiving the sudden news of Prince Dhairyashil's illness the maharani took the first available ship for Bombay, leaving Genoa on 13 September.

The nature of the illness was not that grave for the Maharaja to abandon his cure and return to India and as he still needed his rest in the winter months in Europe, as advised by his doctors, he proceeded to Switzerland after spending a few days in Paris. One of the sights which interested him most was the colony for railway servants, established at Tergnier by the Compagnie du Nord, which he visited on 5 October. Testifying to this is the large railway quarters at Goya Gate, 'one of the institutions on which His Highness prides himself and with good reason.'

In Switzerland, he participated in winter sports, thoroughly enjoying the exhilarating experience of exercise in the bracing weather. A man who tolerated the European winter better than he did the Indian summer, he stayed on at Gstaad and in early February 1925, he left for Nice where he stayed for a couple of months, continuing his physical activities in the form of regular exercises. As a result, at the end of his European trip his health was reported to be excellent. Now that he was rid of most of his health issues, his mind, as it always did, turned to work. The Maharaja, during the winter, had completed negotiations for the purchase of a house in Paris-6, Avenue Van Dyck, close to the Parc Monceau and took up residence there on 8 April, ostensibly to work in peace and quiet. The return of his secretary enabled him to clear his backlog in three or four days, which would normally have taken months.

Among the arrivals in Paris was his old friend—Sir Madho Rao Scindia, the Maharaja of Gwalior, in a critical condition, which led to his death on 5 June. Sayajirao III left for England after the cremation.

The Maharaja spent about a fortnight in London staying in his house 'Russels' and was kept busy with various visits for a week. He called on Viceroy Reading who was on leave at Lowndes Square on 13 June. The following day, he entertained the mayor of Watford and about two hundred local residents at a garden party at his residence, and in the course of the afternoon, also received Lord Birkenhead (the first Earl of Birkenhead) and his elder daughter. The same evening, he accompanied the secretary of state for India to an open-air meeting of representatives of conservatives club in the Watford division. When he was prevailed upon to address the audience, he alluded to himself as a 'colleague of the Empire' and insisted on the community of ultimate aim between England and India. The next couple of days, 24 and 25 June were taken up with entertaining Lord Birkenhead at dinner at the Carlton and attending a luncheon given for Lord Reading by the British Indian Union. Finally, he attented at the reception given by King George V at Buckingham Palace, but of course, only after a private audience with the king had been granted.

Sayajirao III went to Paris where he spent ten days followed by a fortnight's stay in Evian and a visit to Lausanne, but by then this prodigious activity brought back his gout and he had to return to Paris, and to his wheelchair. After he recovered, he spent the last days of August in Biarritz, interspersed with visits to San Sebastian and the Pyrenees region in south-western France. A night and day was spent in Lourdes, where the annual festival was on and the sight of the pilgrims brought back to him similar scenes at famous shrines in India.

His fifteenth trip abroad was now drawing to an end and on 1 September, Sayajirao III returned to England and spent a month there, mostly at his home, while many business affairs, including the sale of that house were attended to. A luncheon party at the Carlton for the members of the India Council at the Carlton served to divert him from the monotony of business affairs and after spending a month in Paris, he sailed from Marseille on the *Rampura*. The Maharaja spent his time constructively abroad and since the affairs of the state were running smoothly, he could also afford to give his health the attention it deserved. Besides, Sayajirao III's doctors had cautioned that Baroda summers could be deleterious to his health as well as life if he chose to brave the heat by staying on.

The Maharaja landed in Bombay to the salute of twenty-one guns and the same night left Bombay from the Grant Road Station in his newly built saloon car, reaching Baroda the following morning at 9 a.m. He was welcomed by the assistant Resident and his own ministers while a British guard of honour was drawn up as he alighted on to the platform; outside the station, another guard of honour from the state army was drawn up for him. After inspecting both guards of honour, the Maharaja drove directly to the Laxmi Vilas Palace, with a cavalcade of cavalry, elephants and so on along the streets thronged by people who stood, waved and greeted him as he drove by, glad to have their ruler back in their midst. The same evening at five, a durbar took place in which civilians as well as the military were present. The durbar lasted an hour and a half, and it says a lot for the Maharaja's conscientiousness and energy that once the durbar was over he went directly to the guest house to see whether the new quarters that had just been completed for the reception of state guests were comfortable.

The following day was declared a public holiday to celebrate his return and the news of Queen Alexandra's death the day after, impelled the closing of all offices and shops in the state.

The golden jubilee celebrations were fixed for January 1926 which gave the Maharaja some time to catch up with the administrative affairs of the state and, true to his nature, he was back at his desk in no time with his ministers attending to issues that had risen in his absence and also planning for the future.

On 11 December, the Maharaja made his first public appearance, at Kareli Baug, where he opened the Arya Kumar Ashrama.

On 13 December, he left for Dabhoi, a historic town about twenty miles away from Baroda city. He took along with him his grandson Prince Pratapsinghrao, his heir apparent, and a couple of guests. He visited the neighbouring provinces as far as the frontier from there to the south, and east, and problems on irrigation were discussed. Amid cheering crowds they rode on elephants around the town the following day, accompanied by cavalry and took the opportunity to visit the famous temple of Kalika Mata and to see the fine gateways that had not been entirely destroyed by the Muslim raiders at the end of the thirteenth century. Before he left Dabhoi, the Maharaja formally opened a new boarding house for boys at the local high school, built by public subscription and was a guest at a garden party of a club recently founded in the town.

The seventh annual Vijaya Gymkhana, a sporting event, was held from 23 to 26 December, opposite the gates of the Laxmi Vilas Palace on the Gymkhana grounds. The prize distribution was on the last day and the entire royal family was present for it.

On 30 December, wrestling and elephant fights were held outside the Pani Gate of Baroda for public entertainment. Not only the Maharaja's party and guests filled the Grand Stand, but every seat was overflowing. The year and month ended with a New Year's Eve State Banquet at the Durbar Hall of the palace to which the guests were restricted to eighty, due to the absence of many English officers and the prevalence of an illness in Baroda.

The days between 11 and 13 January were set aside for the golden jubilee celebrations in Baroda; hence the Maharaja decided to tour the Kadi prant with his coterie in the first week of January. He travelled changing at Ahmedabad station from broad gauge to meter gauge railway, the latter being the gauge all over Kadi. In Kalolon, on the way to Kadi, he stayed in a guest house that he had built outside the town, and tents were put up for the rest of the party. A durbar was held the following morning for people to meet him and present their problems and in the evening when he rode around town, he was cheered most enthusiastically by the people who had thronged the streets. The dust for which Kadi is famous, rose in clouds as the children pursued the procession through the streets. During Sayajirao III's stay in Kadi, he devoted his attention to the shortage of water supply and the cotton ginning industry which showed great promise, provided water could be procured. On 5 January, he continued his journey to Becharji, crossing an intervening strip of British territory. Becharji is the name of the goddess whose temples gives the locality its name. The tank outside the temple contains water which is supposed to be holy and pilgrims make it a point of bathing in it, but with so many people dipping into it the waters must have been anything but inviting!

The Maharaja, of course, was interested in an alternative water source, and an artesian well being sunk to supply the area with sweet water thereby solving the very pressing need for water. On 7 January, he was back in Baroda after touring the agricultural centre of the surrounding districts in time for the jubilee celebrations being held to honour fifty years of his successful rule.

50

The Golden Jubilee of Sayajirao III's Rule

There was much rejoicing and fanfare among the public in the state of Baroda on the occasion of the fiftieth anniversary of Sayajirao III's rule. The festivities began with a public reception on 11 January which was held in the marquee especially erected in the Waroshia field in the north of the city. Sayajirao III made a spectacular entry riding in a gold ambary mounted on an elephant and escorted by troops. In the marquee, he took his place on the gaddi placed on a raised platform with the maharani at his side while gold and silver chairs were placed for various members of his family, including the widowed maharani of Cooch Behar (Indira), who had come especially for the jubilee functions. At the reception, the Maharaja was presented with addresses by all the communities which comprised the entire state of Baroda, including the antyajas (the depressed classes). These congratulatory addresses were read out in different languages—Gujarati, Marathi, English, Hindi, Arabic and Persian—as though to drive home the point of what a diverse nation we are. The Maharaja replied in English. He laid importance on being self-reliant and the need to develop a national consciousness.

'A citizen must learn to do things for himself instead of looking to the state to do things for him. India was not a land of serfs except in so far as the Indians themselves chose to make it so, by hugging the fetters of their own ignorance and prejudices,'[1] was the keynote of his address. There had been criticisms from certain quarters of the educated that the Maharaja had lost his zeal for making the legislative assembly or Dhara Sabha more independent and since 1907 it had remained purely an advisory body. The criticisms were true but even though Sayajirao III had drafted a new constitution for Baroda which would have two Houses instead of one, it could not take a concrete form as it was not practical for a princely state to function within the framework of the British empire. Apart from the practical side, the Maharaja firmly believed in people having a representative who could voice their wishes and needs and refer the matter to him after which he would address their wants to the best of his ability—a sort of a paternalistic government was what the state of Baroda needed. However, he answered his critics by saying that he had in the past, 'of his own accord... introduced constitutional reforms, and that he would continue to do so in the future whenever the time was ripe', and he also advised them that, 'when differences arose, to accept his verdict without question'.[2]

The reception and the Maharaja's response to the addresses by the various communities was the chief function of the jubilee; in the rest of the week there were other functions such as a review of the army, distribution of food and clothes to thousands of poor people, a garden party, a display of fireworks, a children's party, plays in Gujarati and Marathi, musical evenings and classical dancing, an open air dance by a troupe of Bhil men and women, etc.

More important were the concessions made by the Maharaja to his people on the occasion of the golden jubilee, which were published on 14 January in the *Gazette Extraordinary*. These concessions included remissions in the arrears of land revenues, a suspension of the collection of cotton excise duty, the release of a number of convicts serving prison sentences, the establishment of a new science college, the setting up of a project of linking the main towns in the state by telephones and laying the foundation for the Kirti Mandir or the Temple of Fame (inspired by the Pantheon in Paris or the Westminster Abbey in London). The Kirti Mandir's spectacularly beautiful building seeks to honour many great men as well as the Maharaja's ancestors. While laying the foundation stone, he made a memorable speech in which he defined true greatness lay in a person 'who stands unbroken and undaunted in the face of physical misfortunes'. The Maharaja then laid the foundation stone and performed the ceremonies as per Hindu rituals, raising a chhatri (canopy) in honour of his predecessors on the throne, at which shraddhas or offerings may be made whenever due. Shraddhas, the Maharaja explained should 'enshrine the best of filial virtue, of reverence for virtue and to be an inspiration to faithfulness to one's kith and kin.'[3] He ended his speech with the words, 'Their bodies are buried in peace, but their names liveth for evermore.'[4]

The opening of the Pilaji Ananthashram, a home for the destitute and the aged, was a special contribution by the Maharaja on the occasion. It was made clear that the home was not for any particular class or community but open to all and this was demonstrated by reading passages from not only the Hindu scriptures but also from the sacred texts of other religions. Here, he made a speech in Marathi and emphasized that charity should not be imposed as a religious duty and should not be given to the able-bodied but only to the crippled or those who were unable to earn their living because of the infirmities of old age. 'Dharma is no doubt important,' he stated and quoted a Sanskrit couplet which translated into English meant, 'The real ornament of a hand is not the bangle but the act of giving.' The Maharaja then concluded his speech by citing another quotation on the duties of a ruler, 'Be as a father to the fatherless, so shalt thou be as the son of the most high, and he shall love thee more than thy mother.' It must be said here that Sayajirao III was a man of exemplar noble qualities.

It was during one of the ceremonies that an eagle-eyed Resident noticed that the Maharaja was wearing a headdress studded with jewels and with the arches it closely resembled the crown worn by the imperial majesties of Britain. This was tantamount to desecrating the sacred symbol which was the sole prerogative of British monarchs, and he reported the offence to the viceroy. The viceroy in turn reported the matter to the India Office in London. It is a matter of great significance that the India Office wrote back saying that the matter 'should not be broached till after the demise of Maharaja Sayajirao'—a direct pointer to the immense personal prestige with the British that Sayajirao III had acquired at this stage in his life.

After the inauguration of the Pilaji Ananthashram, the Maharaja along with the maharani and other family members were guests of the club which was founded by his officers and named Sayaji Vihar. Originally instituted as a club for heads of departments only, in 1909, with the Maharaja's cordial approval, Sayaji Vihar was thrown open to junior officials also. Later, non-officials too were admitted and even Europeans. On 11 February 1926, it was resolved to permit ladies, hitherto only allowed to come as guests on exceptional occasions, to join as members. This was indeed a revolution in club life! Sayaji Vihar had all the facilities to encourage sports as recreation for the members.

51

Visit of Their Excellencies, the Readings

Viceroy Reading, accompanied by Countess Reading and a party of about 340, of which 260 were Welsh Fusiliers, paid their promised visit to Baroda on 21 January 1921. The Readings were lodged in the Makarpura Palace and the rest of the party was lodged in tents on the palace's vast grounds.

The Indian princes did not look forward to viceregal visits which were nerve-wracking formalities, strict protocols and an incredible waste of not only time but also energy and money. These visits served no other purpose but to drive home the fact that the host was an especially favoured person whose loyalty to the Raj had been adjudged to be of the requisite purity. Considering it was nearing the middle of the twentieth century, it bordered on the ludicrous. Perhaps some of the British officers thought so themselves.

'Rarely,' writes Sayajirao III's great-grandson in his book *The Prince and the Man*, 'did a visit pass off without incident.'[1]

The princes, unused to the ways of the West, tried hard to please, but there was always *that* something that could go wrong, 'like a panicky waiter spilling soup on an ADCs dazzling uniform, or still worse, a chauffeur misunderstanding a memsahib's kitchen-Hindi instructions and driving her through the red-light area could cause tempers to flare.'[2] Most princes came up with the solution of stunning their guests with food and drink regardless of expenses. Baroda's answer was to rehearse every item on the programme several times and reduce it to a drill.

Lord Reading's visit, however, went off without a hitch; in fact, it was a resounding success with everything going like clockwork right from the ceremonial reception, procession throughout the town, durbar, state banquet, informal dinner, display of fireworks and gymnastics to other special amusements of Baroda such as elephant fights, buffalo fights and tricks performed by trained parrots. Nonetheless, the tense and overwrought officials of Baroda must have given an audible sigh of relief when the viceroy's cream and gold viceregal special pulled out of the Baroda railway station. They could have patted themselves on the back that a viceregal's visit had passed without any untoward incident. Something unheard of! The success of the visit was evidenced by the lengthy telegram that followed soon after, with the words, 'Her Excellency and I carry away most pleasant memories of our visit and of the kindness and hospitality of Your Highness and Her Highness, the Maharani.'[3]

Sir Stanley Rice in *Life of Sayajirao* wrote, 'The sky was clear; the dark clouds of Curzon's time had rolled away, and the war as one of its blessings had drawn the states closer to the paramount power.' But what really contributed to improved relations and what must have really impressed the viceroy was the toast proposed by Sayajirao III at the state banquet in the Durbar Hall in which he paid a handsome tribute to the viceroy's work in India. He also alluded to Baroda's unswerving loyalty to its obligations during nearly a century and a quarter of the British connection, to his own efforts for fifty years to follow out his ideal of a modern state and to his hope that, though much remained to be done, he could claim for Baroda an honoured place in the Indian empire. And more importantly, he spoke of the deep interest with which the Indian states had watched the progress of British India from stage to stage of self-rule, and of his own earnest wish that the claims of the Indian states should not be forgotten. Further to this, he quietly put his oar in with the words:

In the new era, the Indian states now claim a place in the sun, and believing that their ancient rights and dignities will be fully revived. For my own state, it is only natural in me to hope that its original sovereignty will be restored. Over a hundred years ago, the British government then elected to mediate between my House and its tributaries... to collect the tribute on our behalf free of charge. It was a sacred trust then undertaken. A hundred years of British peace, progress and order have now ensued. In the interests of efficient government, and with the utmost solicitude for the good of the Empire, I suggest to the British government that the ancient privileges be now fully restored to their friends and allies of old. [4]

The allusion here by Sayajirao III was to his ambition that his house should be once more not only the fiscal, but also the political overlord of Kathiawad. In short, Kathiawad should be restored completely.

In conclusion, he expressed his pleasure that Lady Reading who had been ill earlier had recovered enough to come to Baroda and assured her of an abiding place in the affections of the Indian people, due to the splendid manner in which she had fulfilled the exalted functions of her post. The viceroy reciprocated by heaping praise on Baroda's 'long and glorious record of loyalty'.

In an expansive mood, he continued, 'I need not dwell in detail on the earlier history of the connections of the Baroda state with the government of India. Suffice to say that more than a hundred years have passed since it began, and that from the outset to the present day loyalty to the British connection has been revered as a sacred obligation to the state. On those occasions when there has been opportunity to put that obligation into practice, the rulers of the state have not hesitated to demonstrate their fidelity to that tradition.

'In the days of the mutiny, the Gaekwads of Baroda openly supported the British cause and took all possible measures to preserve peace in Gujarat. In the crisis of the Great War, Your Highness, true to the same tradition, exerted yourself to the utmost to help the cause of the Empire. I need not enumerate all the services rendered at that time by Your Highness and your state but I may note that besides recruitment of combatants and non-combatants for our forces, Your Highness lent your palace in Bombay for use as a war hospital and made contributions amounting to approximately Rs 60 lakh for war purposes. Not less well known are the administrative and social measures with which Your Highness's name will always be associated and to which you have alluded, with such marked modesty, in your speech. Your Highness's rule has been characterized by the deep thought you have given to these problems and the personal attention you have devoted to securing that there should be progress and that progress should be along sane lines. Your Highness has wisely concluded that no worthy superstructure can be raised unless the foundations have been well-laid and constructed from sound materials. You have conceived that the first essential for the well-being of your state are the establishment of law and order and the provision of an efficient administrative machine and you have successfully laboured to provide these requirements. You have rightly decided that general progress must rest on a broad basis of better social and economic conditions and wider facilities for education among your subjects, and you have given effect to your convictions by arrangements for free and compulsory primary education and extensive facilities for higher education and by your measures to promote the social and economic welfare of the people. In all these measures, Your Highness has displayed the greatest consideration for the interest of your subjects and the wisest forethought in equipping your state to meet any changing conditions which the future may hold in store. It is not vouchsafed to all men to reap where they sow or to see the results for which they have laboured. The work of many men brings happiness and profit only to those who follow after them. In your case however, Your Highness has not only provided for the satisfaction of your successor, for the welfare of your state and for the happiness of your people in the near future, but you have also been rewarded by seeing many great and beneficent changes, for which you laboured, coming to pass in your own state, in your own time. Your Highness may indeed look back on the fifty years during which you have been the ruling prince of this state, with a sense of duty well done. Your Highness has alluded to the position occupied by the Indian states side by side with the gradual development of self-governing institutions in British India, the position of the ruling princes and the Indian states was most carefully and scrupulously considered; and the sanctity of the treaties and the intention to preserve and maintain the rights and privileges of the Indian princes was specially and solemnly reaffirmed by His Majesty in a royal proclamation. At the same time, without prejudice to the relations subsisting between the paramount power and each individual state, the ruling princes as a body by the institution of the Chamber of Princes, were given an opportunity of taking a wider part in the destinies of India and the Empire by offering counsel in questions affecting the states as a whole or the states in British India and by association in the discussion of certain questions of Imperial concern.

'I can assure Your Highness that you need have no apprehensions that, when any future enquiry is held regarding constitutional advance in British India, the position of the states and the privileges of the princes will run any risk of being ignored or injuriously affected. I am convinced that their interests will be most carefully borne in mind and considered.

'British India is still in the first stage of her journey towards responsible self-government. At this moment, I shall not speculate on the precise position the states may occupy when a final stage of development has been reached, but of this I am certain that at all times, whatever changes may be under consideration, the claims of the states will continue to receive the attention to which their position and importance in India and the Empire justly entitle them.

'Your Highness has referred to special representations which you have made regarding your own state. I cannot discuss them tonight, for these representations are still under examination. Your Highness may, however, rest assured that when the examination is completed, they will receive the most careful and impartial consideration at the hands of myself and my government.

'Let me thank Your Highness once more for your cordial welcome and the hospitality you have extended to Her Excellency and myself. Your Highness has been most thoughtful in providing all that could interest and charm us during our visit. We shall carry away the most pleasant recollections of our visit to Baroda and of the friendly feelings of Your Highness and Her Highness the Maharani towards us. Permit me to add that I greatly esteemed the privilege of meeting Her Highness.'[5]

From the above reciprocal speech of the viceroy, one can sense the regard and esteem he had for Sayajirao III, a sentiment that was shared by quite a few of his peers.

Prior to his departure from Baroda, Lord Reading laid the foundation stone for a new science institute in the grounds of the Baroda College. There was a large gathering of Baroda personalities and British guests to witness the ceremony.

Dewan Manubhai Mehta opened the proceedings with a speech in which he spoke of the proposal of adding a Faculty of Law and ultimately providing a university not only for Baroda but for the whole of Gujarat. After this, in response to the Maharaja's invitation, Lord Reading, in a graceful tribute to the intellectual activities of Baroda, laid the first foundation stone.

52

Port Rights in Okhamandal

After all the excitement of the jubilee celebrations died down, Sayajirao III set out for Kathiawad peninsula on 10 February. His main purpose was the formal opening of the pier which he had got constructed by the firm of Meik and Buchanan in the western-most part of his territories, Okhamandal lying on the Arabian Sea and the Gulf of Kutch. The Maharaja also desired to participate in certain religious ceremonies, including the opening of the Shardha Mathin Dwarka, the holiest place for all Hindus as the birthplace of Lord Krishna and a place the Maharaja had not visited for five years. It took the Maharaja nearly twenty-six hours to reach Dwarka, Okhamandal's principal town. Earlier, one had to get there on horseback so a train was definitely many steps forward in travel, especially since the railway track had now been extended right up to the pier at Okhamandal port. The railway and port had come up only after the territory had come under Baroda's jurisdiction, thus realizing one of the Maharajas several dreams—Baroda now had its own access to the sea.

Here, one needs to explain to the reader the dilemma of port controls the rulers of Baroda were subjected to under British rule. The Gujarat province had six ports, all opening out onto the Arabian Sea and offering excellent opportunities for overseas trade. However, over a period of time, due to the weaknesses of the past rajas, these ports fell under British control; for example, going back to the Treaty of Sawantwadi dated 1819, which was concluded with the joint regents Savitribai and Narbadabai with the British for British protection. The terms of the treaty stipulated that the British would protect the state of Sawantwadi from invaders for which the regency acknowledged British supremacy and agreed to abstain from political intercourse with other states and deliver those guilty of offence in British territory to the British; to cede the entire coastline from the Karli River to the boundaries of Goa which was under the Portuguese and to receive British troops into Sawantwadi. Savitribai and Narbadabai were the two surviving widows of Raja Khemsawant III. Now the ceded territory yielded a revenue of net Rs 30,000 and was restored the following year when the regency was terminated in 1822 and Raja Khemsawant IV was entrusted with the administration of the state. However, there was rebellion and disorder in the state and the British troops had to be called in to suppress it. It could not be completely suppressed and the sardars became independent of the raja's authority. The British government assumed control over the state and the raja gave them the right to levy tax and customs duties in Sawantwadi in exchange for an annual income of a sum equal to the average amount realized in the three preceding years. In this way, the British got full control of Sawantwadi port.

Another port was the well-known Vengurla. The East India Company was given the right to levy tax and sea customs duty. The port had access to the sea via the creek of Tiracol. The Company had the right to appoint posts at customs on the British frontier as well as the port of Banda on the creek of Tiracol. Compensation to the raja was fixed at Rs 13,443 of which Rs 1,700 appears to be on account of the abolition of land customs. The Sawantwadi durbar readily cooperated with the British government and ceded the port of Banda and the right of establishing customs posts on the frontier on the terms stated in the Davidson committee's report.

This arrangement deprived Sawantwadi of a good amount of revenue and plunged it into economic instability. It was a scheme designed to protect British revenue and the compensation was inadequate and did not justify the cessation of revenue rights. A state that had ceded its maritime rights to the British was not only deprived of its customs revenue but also had to pay tax and customs duty to the British posts there. Thus, it incurred a treble burden on itself not borne by a simple maritime state in India.

The state was under the management of political agents from 1838 to 1924.

It was only years later that it came to some concrete understanding when V. T. Krishnamachari became the dewan of the Baroda state and asked for full compensation rights and full maritime rights in Sawantwadi in a letter dated 15 December 1935. There was correspondence to this effect between the dewan of Baroda and Shirgaonkar, the dewan of Sawantwadi, but the issue was not resolved in Sayajirao's lifetime.

The main object of the British government in 1838 was to secure an effective frontier line against Portuguese territory in Goa in the interest of British revenue. The Sawantwadi state adjoined Goa and marched with it on the southern side. North of Sawantwadi lay a continuous block of Indian states and territories. The shortest and most effective and indeed most practical was a frontier line along the southern boundary of Sawantwadi taking in the creek and the fort of Tiracol and the land on the frontier.

There were other grievances apart from those stated above. Developing the port of Aronda would have brought in an income of Rs 15,000 or more to the people of Sawantwadi. The British had no interest whatsoever in developing this port as it meant extra expenditure by way of staff and the raja, by signing away maritime rights, had also through ignorance, signed away customs duties and excise duty on salt to the British, who taking full advantage of the raja's ignorance walked away with the customs and salt excise duties in their pockets. When a protest was made, the British argued that the waive of transit duties was compensation enough but the transit duties had been included in the Rs 11,000 compensation while the salt tax amounted to several thousand!

53

Busy Days

On his voyage from Aden to Europe in 1927, Sayajirao III instructed his secretary to write to the dewan and ask him to give due encouragement to Haji Ismail who had salt works in Aden and Kapilram H. Vakil of the Tata Company in their scheme to develop the salt trade in Okhamandal, so that the salt trade would have a successful future. Vakil, the managing agent of the Okha Salt Works Company, had got an eminent partner with a reputation for a successful salt trade to cooperate and finance the scheme. The dewan wrote to Kapilram: 'His Highness trusts that you will make the salt scheme a great scientific and commercial success by remaining personally associated with and responsible for the working of the scheme with your well-known qualifications as an industrial chemist and will not transfer your rights merely for profits to any financial house.'[1]

In the late 1920s, Vakil, a chemical engineer educated in England, saw the possibility of developing salt works in Okhamandal. He approached Sayajirao III, always keen on developing his princely state, gave his assent. In 1927, Vakil independently set up salt works in Okha and V. T. Krishnamachari laid the foundation stone for it.

There were further instructions to keep up confidential negotiations with the Tata Iron and Steel Company and to use the Okha harbour for importing coal and pig iron from Calcutta and exporting salt in exchange to Calcutta.

'His Highness,' the letter said further, 'would gladly help in the development of the harbour and in any agreement, not less than ten years' binding. Erect extensive glass houses on modern lines instead of covering dumps of salt with earthen tiles, and also use vacuum pans for producing part of the salt of Liverpool and Cheshire quality like Bengal does. From steam, develop electric power and establish an overhead trolley line from your works to the harbour and the state department of Baroda would be most cooperative in the matter. His Highness requires a report on the chemical works scheme in Kathiawar.'[2] The above instructions were given once Okhamandal came under the Baroda administration.

For the next three days of his visit, Sayajirao III stayed in the white-washed bungalow facing the sea that had once housed the Assistant Resident during the British administration of Okhamandal, while the rest of the party were accommodated in other buildings or in tents on the picturesque cliffs overlooking the Arabian Sea, and within walking distance of the Dwarkanath temple.

On 14 February, he went by train over the last few miles to the pier that had been constructed at Adatara, where a cargo steamer of 6,000 tonnes was waiting to be loaded to coincide with the inaugural function of the port. After the symbolic cutting of the ribbon by the Maharaja, there followed a distribution of poshaks (robes of honour) to the three people who had contributed most towards the development of Okha port within the stipulated time limit; interestingly the men were an Englishman, an Indian and a Chinese. A photograph taken a year later shows the pier at Okhamandal with a crane dangling some large barrels over the hold of a ship while a railway engine spews smoke on the adjoining track. The picture must have found pride of place among the Maharaja's possessions as testimony to one whose efforts had finally borne fruit.

Sayajirao III left Dwarka on 15 February now that his plans for this barren tract had been fully realized.

Being the kind of ruler he was, the Maharaja was already turning over in his mind the next plan for developing Baroda's own seaport—Okha was already drawing off an ever-increasing proportion of the traffic from the overcrowded harbours of Bombay and Karachi and even becoming a regular port of call for passenger ships.

The Maharaja's thinking was much ahead of his times and it was not until after his death that Okha was to come into its own as one of the busiest of India's ports.

A few days after his return from Dwarka, seized with a strong urge to visit the village of his birth and childhood, Sayajirao III went to Kavlana. Childhood impressions vary a great deal when viewed from the eyes of an adult and he found that 'everything was small compared with what he remembered of it. The bridge, the river that he had waded in as a child with brothers and cousins...which now was being used for irrigation purposes, the high road from Manmad which was only a stone's throw earlier seemed a good distance away.'³ Everything seemed to have diminished in size. The only recognizable landmarks were the village temple and the hills in the distance. He remembered with nostalgia the times when he would go in a bullock cart beyond the hills to the famed Ellora caves, a journey that had taken four days and had been the happiest days of his Kavlana years. He ventured to the Ellora Caves again this time and was absolutely bowled over as 'nothing had shrunk'; the caves still made him gasp with wonderment. He visited Ajanta for the first time, not knowing what to expect, and was so astonished that he exclaimed, 'What a wealth of Indian art, really Indians cannot be too proud of it!'⁴

Nawab Mehdi Nawaz Jung, a young nobleman who was deputed by the Nizam of Hyderabad to play host to the Maharaja as both caves were in the princely state of Hyderabad, was impressed with the Maharaja. Talking about the impact of the meeting later, he said, 'I really drew inspiration from His Highness's perfect manners, punctuality, national aspiration, fearlessness, learning and knowledge. I was a young man and regarded him as a hero.'

The Maharaja was back in his state in the first week of March where a few public appearances occupied him for a couple of weeks before he sailed in the *Rawalpindi* on 12 March for his sixteenth trip to Europe, leaving the administration of the Baroda state in the capable hands of Dewan Manubhai Mehta. He reached Marseilles on 26 April.

Sayajirao III perhaps saw in himself an ideal ruler striving hard to provide ideal governance. If one were to look back upon the years, one would realize that the purpose of bringing him to Baroda had sunk and embedded itself so deeply in his mind that he felt he had been brought to Baroda for the sole purpose of working for the people and only for the people, nothing else mattered. His inherent virtue, conscientiousness, had enabled him to take up the responsibility that had been entrusted to him with the utmost seriousness. Needless to say, he was also influenced by the brilliance and efficiency of his old dewan T. Madhavrao's system of working and had followed along those lines after his assumption of full powers.

Sayajirao III, however, insisted on thinking out matters for himself and personally working on the details of every scheme as desirable for Baroda. Intensely observant by nature, there was nothing that escaped his eye, nothing that did not prompt him to enquire about it. Particularly on his European tours, in his eagerness to learn, he was avidly curious about the workings in the West and its impressive infrastructure that facilitated efficiency and speed in the various organizations. He was keen to adopt it in the Baroda state. His thinking must have run along these lines, 'If this can be done here, why not in our country and in the Baroda state?' Wherever he travelled, he tried to glean new ideas and concepts that were constructive towards the improvement of his state. Even when suggestions were made by any of his ministers or the dewan, he never brushed them aside as inconsequential but was receptive to them.

Particular mention must be made on the occasion of his visit to Europe in 1923, when he was already sixty years of age. That summer he spent a month in Berlin where he worked from 9. 30 a. m. till 6 p. m. every day. He inspected research and educational institutions, dye works and factories manufacturing wireless sets as well as gave interviews with a lot of people. In the same year, he manifested a great interest in agricultural banks and cabled his ministers in Baroda to enquire whether a land mortgage bank could not be established there on the lines of the Crédit Foncier and the Egyptian Agricultural Bank. While in Rome, he collected all available documents concerning the International Institute of Agriculture. Earlier, on his visit to the United States, as mentioned before, he wanted to implement its system of education and the subjects of industrial development, agriculture and labour unionism was what occupied his mind when touring the country. Nothing was too trivial for him that could be put to use, his life rotated and revolved around observing, learning and adapting and cared for nothing else. Even if visiting a poultry show in England meant improving the egg-laying qualities of fowls in India, he went.

While returning from Europe in 1925, he was struck by the system of ventilating the cabins with 'punkah louvres' and immediately ordered enquiries as to whether they could be introduced in buildings in Baroda. The Maharaja's gift of keen observation, the mastery of detail must be added too—necessary traits for a reformer ruler in India. His prodigious talent and diligence combined with shrewdness had been the governing factors throughout his reign. He knew his state thoroughly from one end of the province to the other since he insisted on doing his own work. His mind could swing like a pendulum from one subject to another without confusion, a rare trait not seen among most human beings. Right from the time the Maharaja ascended the gaddi, he would lie awake unable to relax as ideas flitted across his mind urging him to implement them. It was a common saying among his ministers, 'When the Maharaja sleeps well, his officers are happy!' His insomnia was a result of over anxiety and his zeal for reforming the state so it could get to the level of the Western countries. Sayajirao III was a thorough optimist and for him nothing was impossible if there was a will to attain it. A ruler who even as a callow youth could stand up to his ministers when he encountered opposition would make no concession or compromise to gain an end which seemed right. At the same time, if he was faced with a will equal to his own, then he showed remarkable patience and waited for years to find the right person to put reform through.

54

Sayajirao III's 'Split Personality'

Sayajirao III had two personalities—the idealist and the realist. The idealist was the ruler while the realist was the farmer's son from Kavlana. This dichotomy resulted in frequent conflicts, especially when ideology was argued with realism. The argument probably went this way, with the realist Gopal asking the idealist Sayajirao, 'Arrey Gopal, do you really think that our people will ever accept widow remarriage?' and the idealist must have replied, 'Why not? We can at least educate them on the evils of barring a young widow from marriage!' and so on and so forth. Even though he had assumed the royal throne and the robes of a prince he never forgot his true identity. It was also said that the clothes in which he had first arrived as a child of thirteen to Baroda were kept in a special place in his wardrobe till the end of his life. It was there to remind him of who he really was! This aspect of his dual personality has been brought out in a Gujarati play titled *Gopal ane Sayaji* (Gopal and Sayaji) by playwright Makarand Musale and the play ran to a full house in Baroda for several weeks.

A man of simple tastes and habits, Sayajirao III was not enamoured by or greedy for the rich food that was brought to his table and longed for home-cooked bajra roti and buttermilk that he had been fed with before he was brought to Baroda. Once while touring the districts of Gujarat, he stopped at a farmer's house for lunch. The hosts had been expecting him and cooked up a lavish meal but when it was set before him, the Maharaja said, 'No bajra roti? I came here thinking bajra roti would be served for my lunch and I was eagerly looking forward to it.' The farmer hastily sent one of his boys to procure the flour and in no time at all the farmer's wife made the rotis after which the Maharaja sat down to eat, enjoying his meal with relish especially after he had drunk his glass of buttermilk. He had thrust aside the rich dishes in favour of the bajra rotis, that's how simple he was.[1]

Sayajirao III had all the material comforts to give him contentment. Practically everyone in the state too was contented; even though less fortunate, they did not really lack in the basic comforts and were happy. In spite of it all, Sayajirao III was lonely and expressed his loneliness to some of his close friends. Whenever he spotted a boyhood friend from the village of Kavlana, he would wave out to him, overjoyed and would get emotional. In this context, Ramachandra Mane Patil (ADC to Sayajirao III) wrote in his own words,

> Once when I was residing with His Highness at his residence in London, I heard from a friend that the famous Gujarati snack, bakharvadi, and some other savouries had been brought to London by some common friend. As I was aware of Sayajirao's penchant for bakharvadi and other Gujarati savouries, I took some bakharvadi and went to offer it to His Highness at his residence. He was absolutely overjoyed at the sight of his favourite snack and exclaimed happily 'Mane, you have brought this bakharvadi for me for which I am really thankful! People address me as Your Highness but stay far away from me so, whenever I am met with homely behaviour by anyone it makes me very happy and deeply contented. This is true happiness and real contentment. Our tragedy is that we do not enjoy the happiness of ordinary mortals. Nobody really understands that a ruler can also have problems of his own. ' Then, he rambled on, "Today, I am reminded of my mother; whenever she visited Kavlana, our village, she used to send me puranpoli and other savouries for Diwali; the sweetness of those puranpolis have become a distant memory." Sayajirao's mother Umabai was an expert in cooking and whenever any relative of theirs would travel to Baroda from Kavlana, she would send freshly-made, soaked in ghee puranpolis for her son along with some of his other favourites. His Highness would then sit down to enjoy these along with the person who had brought them and his brothers while reviving old memories.[2]

Perhaps it was because of this internal conflict between his real identity and the one he had been made to wear, that he introduced reforms with the necessary prudence. He was always Gopal, which was his real identity and he was never separated from that true self. When he funded the Indian national movement, he was being true to that identity which dictated that as the son of the soil he should support the cause of India's freedom because that was justice, that was truth, and therefore, that was right, but when he donned the mantle of the Maharaja where the protection of his state and his people meant it was necessary to keep diplomatic relations with the British, he became Sayajirao and was politically correct. Again, when he refused to follow the ritual at the coronation durbar he was being true to his real identity that of Gopal, in other words to his 'conscience', which dictated that the India belonged to Indians. On the other hand, when he heaped lavish praises on the British in his speeches at the Guild Hall in London, or when he gave banquets in honour of viceroys, or lectures before the East India Association in London, he was Sayajirao III, the Maharaja of Baroda, strengthening diplomatic ties between the paramount power and the Baroda state because it was imperative for the safety of his state and his people.

This internal battle that was being waged between the two identities must have sapped his energy and worn him out. Not that he had any grave misgivings about the correctness of carrying out reforms, but of its application. As a result, he never forced the pace. In the early years of his reign, he followed the three W's—watch, wait and work! 'Never be afraid of being late in an undertaking, so long as you have it in view,' he said in a letter dated April 1888, to the Khangi Kharbari when he was only twenty-six years old![3] This attitude is well manifested in the history of reforms such as the setting up of a system of compulsory education and allowing his people a share in the government of the state. His prudence is again evident in the delay in introducing progressive measures that could offend the sensibilities of the caste system and the conventions of the Hindu community. He insisted that no religious reforms, such as inter-caste marriage, the remarriage of widows or the cessation of child marriage, could be carried out in India through compulsion because if enforced, these reform measures would not last. Persuasion and not force was a better way. Needless to say, even if Sayajirao III had wanted to impose imprisonment instead of a light fine in the case of child marriage, he could not have done so with the ever-watchful paramount power in India. 'Don't stir up a revolution' was the British attitude and Sayajirao III had no choice but to follow this, though not letting the ambition of carrying out reforms vary his policy of *festina lente* (make haste slowly).

Ironically, the Maharaja was criticized in the later years of his reign for being too slow and that perhaps he had developed an apathy towards progress, meaning that he had not introduced 'popular government' to its full capacity. In 1926, an article appeared in *The Servant of India* which said that 'with all his desire to model his state on Western lines, he had never been known to favour popular government.' The article did give credit to the fact that Baroda, thanks to Sayajirao III, was among the first to admit its people into consultation on legislative and administrative bodies, though these were still in the same rudimentary state as they were at the start, while other states like Travancore and Mysore had overtaken Baroda with respect to popular government. It was hoped that the Maharaja would take the opportunity of the jubilee occasion to introduce substantial constitutional reforms but these hopes have come in the way of disappointment rather than fulfilment.

Earlier, when the Maharaja was away in Europe there had been a debate in the Baroda state assembly for an enlargement of the assembly, for two-thirds of its members to be elected and for it to be given more responsibilities and powers rather than being a mere advisory body. The Maharaja, after his return to India, in his speech at the state durbar said that unasked by the people he had of his own accord introduced constitutional reforms and bestowed privileges and would continue to do so in the future at the proper time, and until then they should accept his opinions ungrudgingly whenever a difference arose. This was said in modulated tones but nevertheless it was a warning to those who wished to speed up democracy. He was of the firm opinion that his work had to be consolidated and the machinery of the government made more efficient, instead of introducing new measures.

'If my people are really progressive,' he said on one occasion in a private conversation, 'they have now in Baroda all the facilities necessary for progress. But, they must themselves prove that they are progressive.'[4] In the reforms introduced to the state, which had been advantageous to them and free of cost except the land tax and the income tax introduced between 1897 and 1905, they should show that they were deserving of it and be willing to contribute towards the cost of the benefits they enjoyed. This, though reasonable, caused slight discontent among his people. The Maharaja was not unduly troubled by it and remarked, 'My people are good people and when they have sufficient work to occupy their minds, very loyal.'[5] This is testified to by the adulation he received on his district tours; it was only the think tanks in big towns who felt a slight dissatisfaction. The Maharaja's pragmatic view on this was that he stood 'in a gap between two civilizations,

Western progress and Indian tradition.'[6] Given the thinking of the times, it must have been difficult to comprehend that the Maharaja wanted to keep what was good in the traditional life of India, and at the same time, where the methods of the West were better, to adapt them in the East. To see eye to eye with him, the people of the state they needed to get educated; therefore until that time, for the good of Baroda, he would be at the helm of affairs.

Sayajirao III's standards were high and justly so, as Professor J.M. Mehta has said of the great Maharaja:

> No ruler of an Indian state can it be more truly said that he subordinated his own interests to the welfare and prosperity of the state than of His Highness, Maharaja Sayajirao of Baroda. Ever since his accession to the gaddi, he has been the soul of the administration. There has been a succession of efficient ministers with high degree of intelligence who have advised him on important problems of policy but almost all important measures taken in the state have been initiated and finally shaped by him. The whole administration of Baroda largely bears the imprint of his personality. Like Frederick the Great, it can be said of him that he was first a servant of the state.

55

Sayajirao III's Address to Professors and Students

On 16 December 1926, Sayajirao III was invited to address the staff and students at Professor Manikrao's Physical Culture Institute, Baroda. After a lecture by Principal G. C. Bhateon, titled 'Cardinal Newman's Ideal of a University', the Maharaja began his speech. He started by stressing on the importance of the subject which was explained by the principal and said, 'Judgement cannot be passed on it in a moment, and careful study is essential...a discussion of this subject can be best carried out by experts.'[1]

The important part of his speech was very illuminative as extracts from it reveal, 'Before adumbrating any new reform or launching any new scheme, it is absolutely necessary that one should exactly assess the readiness of society and the response likely to be given by the masses. One has to study the environments, the history of the past, the events of the present and the possibilities of the future. A comprehensive survey of these three periods is a necessary step. They are, so to speak, the connected links of grandfather, father and son, and this must be kept in mind when the scheme is taking shape... I want to emphasize that you should not be in any hurry, or jump to any conclusions not warranted by experience. You must realize the great difference between Europe and India.

'In Europe, there is plenty of money; in India, there is abject poverty. Therefore, we have to make a start and work from the very beginning.

'We have to think of the exploited labourers sweating in the mills and factories, and of the oppressed untouchables denied all amenities in life. It is all very well to talk of knowledge for the sake of knowledge, but the vital question is that of food...The order of precedence should be first, food, that is, the necessities of life, and second, knowledge to acquire it, and then the rest.

'My predecessors used to spend a lot of money in giving dakshinas to Brahmins in the month of Shravana and used to freely distribute food grains in the form of kichari, but realizing that this form of charity was being abused, I had to divert the greater part of the funds to other and better purposes. The baneful idea of Brahmin superiority and the stigma attached to untouchability is ruinous to Hinduism and such narrow beliefs and customs will have to be thrown overboard. We must extend the range of love to humanity. The present concept of society calls for a radical change. It must become liberal and broad. Here in India, we have to think of removing the absurd discrimination between Brahmins and depressed classes and scrutinize the evil effects of it.

'Again, we want a common language for our country. The multiplicity of tongues and dialects is an impediment. It does not allow us to understand our next door neighbours besides causing a number of other problems.

'Take, for instance, Baroda, where I have to run Gujarati, Marathi and Urdu schools side by side. Had we but one language much money would be saved.

'Even in matters of education, we need revolutionary changes, taking into account our needs and the altered and rapidly altering times. Baroda tries its best in honestly trying to achieve what is feasible in this direction today, but we can still see many fashionable fads. The necessity has arisen for putting a stop to all these fads and fancies and devise altogether a new scheme of education.

56
Sayajirao III: The Reformer

Sayajirao III had no formal education, so he very early in his reign realized the value and importance of education. He knew that the only way to lift people from the morass of ignorance and superstition was to educate them.

In one of his speeches, the Maharaja said, 'I have no hesitation in saying that we cannot do better than educate all our subjects. This is absolutely necessary for the realization of my ambitions and wishes for the future of my people.' Again, in his speech at the Aligarh College in 1901, he said, 'Education is the basis of all reforms and is the only salvation from our present condition.'[1] This thinking prompted him to introduce free and compulsory education in his state long before it was introduced in British India.

It was not only primary education that absorbed his interest but quite early in his life he had understood the significance of higher education. On 8 January 1923, while laying the foundation stone for the Baroda College, the Maharaja remarked:

> Education is all-important to India. It is the lever by which this vast country can be extricated from that stationary condition in which it has remained through incalculable ages. It is therefore the duty of everyone to promote education. But higher education even though is of a smaller number, is still more important in the present condition and circumstances of India. I feel that one Indian to whom higher education has been imparted at the cost of Rs 1,000 contributes infinitely more towards the general progress of society than those 333 Indians who are only superficially or slightly educated at the cost of Rs 3 per head. The truth is that a certain force is required to break the iron chains of intellectual bondage and merely elementary education fails to generate the required force. Hence, the foundation of the building, which will indeed, at first, accommodate our high

school but which has been really designed to answer the more extensive requirements of a college is fairly in prospect under the able and zealous directions of Mr Tait, the principal.

The Maharaja realized the usefulness of having educated, intelligent officers in his administration, which the college in course of time would be able to provide. This thought was given expression by Dewan T. Madhavrao who said that he hoped that long before a single hair on his head assumed a silvery hue, the Maharaja would enjoy the proudest satisfaction of seeing himself surrounded by numbers of his countrymen of high intellectual training, of unsurpassed probity and principles, of abundant practical ability to assist him in the good governance of his kingdom, all gratefully owning themselves to be graduates of the Baroda College. It was then a dream but that dream has been fulfilled.

The Baroda College was affiliated to Bombay University in 1881 and received recognition from the university for the purpose of accepting students and preparing them for what was then called the previous examination. The college actually commenced work in 1882 with a class of thirty students. In 1887, the college embarked on teaching science. In 1890, the college was recognized for its arts and science courses leading up to BA and BSc degrees. The Arts College grew with every year and by 1931 there were 911 students. In 1925, thirteen lady students enrolled in the college and by 1931, this number had increased to thirty-five with adequate numbers of professors, lecturers, demonstrators and librarians and was considered to be among the best colleges in India.

The idea of a separate university for Baroda had germinated in the mind of the Maharaja as early as 1909 and he had directed Principal Clarke to enquire into the possibility of the foundation of a university in Gujarat and Kathiawad to which the colleges of Baroda, Ahmedabad, Bhavnagar and Junagad would be affiliated. Enquiries were made but the result was not encouraging and the educationist inspector remarked, 'I am afraid we must relinquish this very attractive idea...'[3]

But 'this very attractive idea' had captured the mind of the Maharaja and Professor Seshadri of Benaras University was asked to submit a scheme for the purpose. A regular commission was appointed under Professor Widgery, who taught comparative religion in the Baroda College) and after all the pros and cons were outlined, the scheme was dropped for the time being.

The Maharaja remarked in his speech at the golden jubilee function that he had not abandoned it but had set it aside as the time was not quite propitious for the venture. His standard of education was where practical training could be combined with abilities as mere theoretical knowledge was not enough. For real progress in the country, technical education was essential and this thinking led him to open Kala Bhavan in 1890, which brought fame to Baroda and still draws students from across India. The firm conviction in the value of scientific education prompted him to build the Institute of Science adjacent to the Arts College.

Before his accession to the gaddi in 1875, there had been only one high school in Baroda (established in 1871), but by1931, the number of high schools had risen to fifteen, and of state-aided high schools to nine, and later, under the auspices of the Maharaja, high schools sprang up in each of the districts of the Baroda state. School education was a great success with more than 60 per cent of students passing in the matriculation exams.

Sayajirao III was extremely keen on the education of women. His memorandum published in 1885, which addressed the subject, said, 'I would particularly emphasize the importance of educating girls. It is the unremitting watchfulness and conciliatory supervision of intelligent and educated mothers which form powerful factors in giving the right tone to infant minds and which are the best agents for the eradication of crooked ways. Women regulate the social life of people where men and women rise or fall together. To fit the girls for their function in our social life, I would give my special attention to the opening of Girls Schools.'[4]

In 1905, for the first time, English classes were opened in the Female Training College. In 1910, there were 171 girls learning English in these classes, out of which 23 were from the high school where Miss Wiltshire was the principal, and 148 were from the Lower school. In 1917, the school got a separate building of its own. Chimnabai II who had always evinced considerable interest in the cause of female education donated a generous amount of money to the Mahila Pathshala (Women's College) and the following year the college received a substantial grant from the government.

Closely connected, or rather intertwined, with educational reforms was the act of making reading possible to all and in this connection the Maharaja, an avid bibliophile, opened an extensive library at Sankhetwada in the heart of the city which housed 1,24,000 books.

In his speech at the opening of the library, he said, 'The people must rise superior to their circumstances and realize that more knowledge is their greatest need. They must be brought up to love books and regard it as part and parcel of their lives. Libraries will then not be regarded as mere luxury, but a necessity of existence.'[5]

At the Marathi Granth Sangrahalaya in Bombay, he said in his inaugural speech, 'A library must be built up as men are built slowly and carefully and with due consideration of the work to be performed. This is an institution that should never die, an institution, the work of which in the future may help or mar the man by whose hands that future will be formed, and we must look well into our handiwork that generations to come may be benefited, so that we may be honoured in the thoughts of our children.'[6]

Sayajirao III of Baroda stands pre-eminent amongst the makers of modern India. His name is intimately associated with every aspect of social, economic, administrative and educational reforms. Baroda by 1940 was indeed almost entirely the work of its enlightened ruler. Nearly all the numerous agencies for social upliftment of the people, economic improvements, general culture and education in the Raj owed their origin or inspiration to the Maharaja. The citizens of Baroda in the mid-twentieth century took great pride in the fact that their state claimed a high rank in India in terms of literacy. This was the result of free and compulsory education, aided by the operation of a rural library system which had been in force for twenty-one years. Sayajirao III was the pioneer of free and compulsory education in India and his answer to a question on what he considered was the most successful reform among the many he had introduced, he had unwaveringly replied, 'free and compulsory education'. In spite of this achievement in education, the Maharaja was not completely satisfied. He felt that many children from the rural areas tended to lapse into illiteracy after leaving school. Worried over this, in a letter to his dewan from Paris dated 2 June 1927, he advised, 'Restrict expenditure on schools where full advantage of compulsory education is not taken, lasting only up to two years, and concentrate on those where proper advantage of the education offered is taken, and the staff are competent enough in the discharge of their duties, properly manned by properly trained teachers.'[7] However, a solution to this problem was found in the establishment of the free country library system.' The school and the library,' remarked an

American educationlist, 'are the two legs upon which the body politic stands. One exists to start education and the other to continue it; but more importantly, to teach children what to read as much as it is how to read.'[8] From this we can deduce that the foundation of the Baroda library system was not an impulsive act of generosity but a concept that evolved and took shape in the Maharaja's mind ever since he took control of the administration.

57
Establishing the Library System in Baroda

During Sayajirao III's first visit to America, under his instructions, liberal provision was made for the establishment of circulating libraries. The library department comprised two sections—the Central Library and the country section. The former included a free and open access lending library, a reference section, a newspaper reading room as well as a ladies' library and reading room. A children's playroom was also provided, which was one of the most original and interesting features of the library. It comprised a large hall, well-ventilated, furnished and provided with English and vernacular books and papers together with a variety of indoor games to keep children occupied constructively. It was adorned with a series of murals executed by art students from the Kalabhavan Technical Institute. The Central Library circulated more books than any other library in India. There was also a travelling library which circulated books in boxes, which were strong enough to stand hard wear-and-tear, and each box had a capacity to hold thirty books. The book boxes were dispatched free of charge to other institutions and schools in the state with the freight expenses also being borne by the department. During the monsoons, library classes were held in Baroda and people learnt to take a genuine interest in the local library, which often became the centre of social and cultural activity for the village or town. In villages where women did not visit the library, books were sent to them through the school teacher. Separate ladies' and children's libraries were established apart from ladies' reading rooms and children's reading rooms.

A lot of work was done to propagate the value of reading as the Maharaja was so convinced of the cultural and educational value of these institutions. The associated libraries established a State Library Association which held very successful conferences at various centres and the organizers invited educational officials and social workers from outside Baroda to these meetings. Exhibitions of books, pictures, charts and posters were an integral part of these conferences where the value and importance of public libraries were emphasized. Another novel idea in propaganda was in instituting a Library Day throughout the state on which special efforts were made to collect funds from the affluent public along the same lines as Hospital Sunday in England. The Baroda Library Association established a cooperative society for the wholesale purchase of books, periodicals and supplies. Publishing work too was undertaken by this society. The Baroda Library Department was represented by a collection of exhibits in the British Empire Exhibition held in Wembley in 1924. A small selection of books, photographs and coloured charts were forwarded to the library exhibition held in connection with the World Conference of Librarians convened in Rome in June 1929.

Another step forward was to give professional training to librarians sent by other states and libraries.

The launching of the Gaekwad's Oriental Series in 1915 was such a remarkable success that it gave birth to the Oriental Institute of Baroda which was established to develop the work and take charge of the valuable collection of Sanskrit books and manuscripts that had been acquired by the Central Library. The director of the Institute was Dr B. Bhattacharya, a celebrated Sanskrit scholar.

The Central Library had been honoured with visits by no less than five viceroys. The countess of Willingdon recorded her impressions of the visit in the following gracious terms, 'I did so much enjoy my second visit to the library which is doing such great work in the state.'[1]

The viceroy, Lord Willingdon, in his banquet speech while addressing Sayajirao III, said, 'Your picture gallery and your Central Library with its remarkable system of travelling rural libraries are famous far beyond the boundaries of Baroda and I am glad to learn that this great scheme of yours for educational study to reach even the most remote village is progressing extremely well!'[2]

His predecessor Lord Irwin had described the Central Library as a valuable asset to the educational system of the state. The visitors' book in the Central Library contained similar words of appreciation from renowned scholars, celebrities and the elite. To cite Sir Govind Madagaonkar who was president of the Royal Societies of Bombay, 'In my varied capacities as a student, as Resident of the Royal Society, Bombay, and as an old admirer of His Highness, the library fills me with pleasure and pride. If not this generation, its successors will do justice to the work of His Highness Maharaja Sayajirao to whom they owe so much!'³ A library assistant from London remarked, 'His Highness must be one of the most remarkable men of his time and the library system which exists today is the permanent and incontestable record of his benevolent enthusiasm for literary culture and wise government which would put to shame that of many European countries!'⁴ Similarly, the *Publisher's Circular London,* said, 'The system which His Highness had done much to foster is one of the best organized in the world!' Dr E.A. Baker, D.Litt., director of the School of Librarianship, University of London, remarked, 'The Baroda Library system is a most admirable organization as we in England are well aware. We envy your numerous fine buildings which are so admirably adapted to Indian conditions and which are evidently doing first-rate work!'⁵ Similar praise was found in an annual entitled the 'Years' work in librarianship' in the British Museum. More significant is a thirteen-page article entitled 'Les Bibliotheques de Lietat de Baroda in La Revuedes Bibliotheques Parids', written by M. Pierre Le Livere, a French librarian of note. It is in the main a review and digest of Mr Dutt's book, *Baroda and its Libraries,* which describes the Maharaja's library scheme as worthy of imitation by officials in the French colonies. It was reprinted as a pamphlet and distributed to members of the French Chamber of Deputies and to many colonial administrators and educationists. Likewise, articles by another writer appeared in *La Quinzaine Coloniale* the organ of La Unida Coloniale Francaise. These articles came to the notice of the government of French Indo-China which write to the Baroda Library Department for further information about its work. Now, the French were, and still are, a high-minded proud nation, who claimed to be the leaders in European art and culture; thus, for them to learn that Baroda should be held up by their own publicists as a state whose educational and cultural work was worthy of imitation is significant proof of the high regard in which the Maharaja was held abroad as a long-sighted, progressive statesman and educationlist. In other parts of India, this scheme was being emulated with great success.

The library scheme's success was wholly due to the public spirit and enlightened policy of Sayajirao III who conceived the idea, founded the organizations, liberally supplied them with funds, assisted and guided the staff with well-meant criticism and constructive suggestions. He continued to watch over the destiny of the libraries with the solicitude of a loving parent.

58
Social Reforms and General Administration

Sayajirao Gaekwad III received high praise for his activities in the field of education, social reform and general administration from Viceroy Lord Willingdon, who characterized his rule as the golden age in the history of Baroda at the State Banquet on 12 December 1932. That this praise was not well-deserved cannot be said, even by the Maharaja's most sceptical critics. Such a ruler, and more importantly the kind of person that he was, could not be expected to sit quietly with folded hands when he perceived the grave defects that were undermining the solidarity and happiness of the Hindu society. Brought up in an environment steeped in convention and tradition, the Maharaja was well aware of the sensibilities and susceptibilities of the people at large and, therefore, introduced his reforms cautiously, feeling his way, coaxing with suggestions whenever he sensed resistance, gradually leading the way to his object. He was opposed to radical methods of reform and preferred convincing rather than forcing, allowing people to evolve, believing in evolution rather than revolution.

For Sayajirao III, education was the panacea for all the shortcomings in the country's progress. On his travels abroad, the Maharaja imbibed a great deal of the constructive measures that the West had adopted and sought to imbue these in the minds of his people without letting caste prejudices and religious superstitions come in the way. His modern rationalistic outlook influenced his reform measures and benefitted his people for more than half a century. He was a man with a wide vision and was passionate about consolidating Hindu society and building a strong nation, able to hold its own against any predatory nation.

The Maharaja hated caste prejudices, which is still a dominant feature of the Hindu tradition and culture. As a lad, he had been a witness to innumerable rituals and religious ceremonies in the palace which were performed more out of fear and superstition than actual faith or love for God. He had also seen Brahmin priests being pampered with money and lavish gifts for performing these rituals. He insisted that these priests should have a thorough knowledge of the Vedas and the ancient scriptures and should explain the rituals at ceremonies in the vernacular to the parties concerned. He also established a Sanskrit Mahavidyalaya for training priests and threw open the doors to all Hindus irrespective of their caste. He considered the profession of a priest similar to other professions which could be followed by anyone with the necessary qualifications. The Maharaja believed in the religion of humanity, in which the chief principles were social service, equality, liberty, fraternity and the perfect harmony of the human race as a whole. He believed that the Almighty did not require flattery but adherence to the principles and ethics of religion, chiefly service to humanity in all spheres of life. He was a hater of caste prejudices, particularly priestcraft in all ages. He insisted on the vedokta ritual being performed for the royal house of Baroda, as a sign of the recognition of the Marathas as Kshatriyas, by the Brahmin priests, who were prepared to do so, thus tacitly acknowledging the Kshatriyahood of the royal house of Baroda. As most so-called priests did not comprehend rituals and ceremonies, the Maharaja told Shankar Moro Ranade (a Sanskrit scholar in Baroda) to compile an account of all the religious ceremonies performed in the royal family with the help of the shastris.

The Purohit Act which he introduced in 1915 ensured qualified priests would perform religious ceremonies and also insisted that they explained the meaning in the vernacular to the host or hostess or in the case of weddings to the bride and bridegroom. If he failed to do so, he was penalized with a fine. This way he ensured that priests were not paid under false pretences, and innocent people were not exploited under superstitious fear. The Maharaja caused to publish an authorized translation of the Sanskrit ritual of marriage in the *State Gazette*.

The Religious Freedom Act was passed in 1902 by the Maharaja which gave an individual the right to change their religion without any loss of property or other lawful rights. Excommunication from caste also did not warrant forfeiting of any of these rights. This is a fine example of the Maharaja's cosmopolitan outlook and his broad-mindedness.

Among the Jains, it was laid down by the committee that no person below sixteen years of age be given deeksha (consecration for a religious ceremony). Also, if a person above the age limit was given deeksha and he was married, then he had to ensure that his wife and children were well provided for before taking deekshahood. This law was laid down for all communities, but particularly for the Jains.

As mentioned earlier, Sayajirao III considered the caste system prevalent among the Hindus a monstrosity, and in a lucid expression of his views at the eighteenth Indian National Social Conference held in 1904, he said:

> It hampers the life of an individual with a vast number of petty rules and observances which have no significance. It cripples his relations with his family in his marriage and in his education of his children. It weakens the economic position by attempting to confine him to a particular trade, by cutting him off from education in the West, and by giving him an exaggerated view of his own importance. In crippling his professional life with distrust, it prevents him from free use of his abilities, making him exclusive, thus ruining not only his social life but also aborts his intellectual development.

In short, the Maharaja's indictment of the caste system was based on the fact that it destroyed all hope of national unity and acted as a barrier towards real progress. Without the caste system, its prejudices and differences, all Indian people could unite and avail themselves of opportunities and be charitable and generous to those in need. This way a remarkable improvement could be brought about not only in society but also in the country which would then rise to similar standards as Europe.

'Caste,' said the Maharaja, 'is the enemy of reform. Every reformer in the past who has endeavoured to secure the advancement of our society has been driven out by the operations of caste! By its rigidity, it preserves ignorant superstition, clings to the past, and does nothing to bring about those changes that Nature is ever pressing upon us.'[1]

A more eloquent indictment of the caste system cannot be found in the literature of social reforms than the one quoted above. It speaks highly of the great ruler as a person. The Maharaja's first step towards putting words into practice was in introducing the Baroda Special (Civil) Marriage Act in order to promote inter-caste marriages. This enabled those belonging to different religions to marry without requiring the parties to make a declaration to the effect that they did not belong to any religion as was done elsewhere. This reform was slow to take effect but by the middle of the century quite a few inter-caste marriages were taking place. A provision was further added to the existing law which declared that all caste customs that were against public policy, or were immoral or interfered with material progress or advancement of the caste such as prohibiting inter-caste marriages between different castes or geographical groups, ordaining ruinous expenses and putting unnecessary restraints on foreign travel should not be binding on the civil courts of the state.

The Maharaja was happy to see at Sayaji Vihar Club, Brahmins and non-Brahmins, Hindus and non-Hindus, touchables and untouchables sitting in close proximity at a dinner given in his honour.

Further steps taken in this reform was opening Antyaja schools and hostels for all irrespective of caste or creed to allow them access to free education. Scholarships were given, free secondary college education was provided and Arya Samajist teachers were engaged to impart instruction. All public offices and courts doors were thrown open to untouchables and officers were ordered to mete out equal and fair treatment to them, as given to others. Dr Ambedkar who worked and devoted his entire life to the cause of the removal of untouchability was first inspired by Sayajirao III to do so. The Maharaja was extremely generous in promoting the cause of education and a number of donations and scholarships were offered to deserving students.

One evening, while Sayajirao III was spending some time in Bombay, Damodar Savlaram Yande, the owner of the Induprakash Press, who had also published books for the Baroda durbar, went to see the Maharaja to seek help for a boy from the Malhar clan. The help he sought was in education—the boy had done brilliantly at school and was desperate to obtain higher education by going to college. Damodar decided to take the boy along for an interview with the Maharaja who was staying at Jayamahal Palace. Damodar knew that it was the habit of the Maharaja to grant interviews to people in the afternoons. Damodar and the boy arrived at the gates of the palace but when Damodar asked the boy to come with him to meet the Maharaja, the boy refused on the plea that since he was a Malhar the Maharaja might not want him inside the palace. Shrugging his shoulders, Damodar went inside and was shown to the veranda where the Maharaja was sitting. After listening to what Damodar had to say, the Maharaja said, 'You said you have brought him, so where is he?'

Damodar replied, 'He is waiting outside.'

Sayajirao III then asked him, 'But why didn't you bring him with you?'

When Damodar stated the reason, Sayajirao III was so distressed that he immediately sent for the boy, and when the boy appeared before him, the Maharaja said, 'Well, my boy, now you are here tell me what you intend to do after you finish your studies.'

The boy replied, 'Whatever Your Highness directs.'

The Maharaja, meanwhile, had been closely observing the lad standing before him in shabby clothes but with his discerning eye noted the sincerity in the boy's answer and also that he had an honest face. Impressed, the Maharaja replied, 'Do not worry about the expense for your studies abroad, it will be taken care of by me but on one condition. After you complete your education, you will devote your energies towards the upliftment of the downtrodden, work for the cause of promoting education and for the removal of untouchability from our society.'[2]

Then, summoning his secretary, he gave instructions for a telegram to be sent to Baroda to provide a scholarship of Rs 50 every month for the boy. 'Study hard and if you do well I shall fund your education even further,' he said thereby making the greatest contribution to the cause of removal of untouchability. After that, the Maharaja left for his customary afternoon drive, not realizing that by his little act of kindness he had kindled a spark that flared into a zealous fervour. Later the boy devoted his entire life towards the removal of untouchability. He was none other than Dr Bhimrao Ramji Ambedkar! He worked till the end of his life for spreading education and the removal of untouchability.

Owing to a welcome change in public opinion later, the time was thought to be propitious for admitting girls into the Antyaja schools. All students sat together and the practice of their segregation in separate Antyaja schools was done away with and separate schools were abolished. The Maharaja was awarded the title of 'Sanctifier of the Fallen' by the Arya Samaj for his unflinching devotion to the cause of uplifting the depressed classes.

The Maharaja believed that widespread education coupled with freedom of access to the trades and profession would raise the standard of economic efficiency of the whole people and enable some of them to achieve outstanding positions.

His order to throw open all state temples to Harijans was appreciated by Mahatma Gandhi who also professed to be a champion of the backward classes. This expression of the Maharaja in the cause of humanity culminated in all the touchables and untouchables being led by high-caste leaders in a procession to the Vithal Mandir, and sitting together in the temple singing bhajans. It was an epoch-making day in the history of Hinduism.

Untouchables were employed in public offices and local self-governing bodies like district boards and municipalities. The Harijans considered Sayajirao III as their greatest saviour. The Maharaja was especially fond of children and always treated them to sweets whenever he found them on his palace grounds. He was extremely fond of his grandchildren and sought to spend some time during the day with them. His third son, Shivajirao, was residing in the Chimanbaug bungalow, and he had two adorable sons Udaysinghrao and Khanderao. The Maharaja would visit them every evening. The gardener whose name was Anandrao reminisced, 'I remember when I was a little boy, 7–8 years of age, my sister Kashibai used to work in the help service of the Khangi Kharbari and lived close by. Quite often, I was sent to live with my sister and whenever she was called to help in the bungalow, she took me with her. There, I enjoyed playing with both the princes as they were of the same age as I. One such evening, His Highness dropped in to visit his grandsons, who were playing with me downstairs. The princes left the game and running up to the Maharaja, their grandfather, went upstairs and I was left alone to fend for myself. It was quite late in the evening and I was tired after playing games. My eyes fell on the driver standing close to His Highness's car. I took the liberty to open the car door and creep into the back seat of the car. The driver who was absorbed in conversation with a driver of another car parked close by did not notice my entry into the car. After a while, I felt sleepy and unable to control myself I stretched out on the seat and immediately fell asleep! I was told later that His Highness returned from his session with the princes and walked to the car with his ADC. Opening the car door, he espied me asleep on the back seat. Turning to the driver, he barraged him with questions, "Who is this child? How did he get in? How come he is here in my car?" The driver was stunned as he realized his gross carelessness as he had been absorbed in idle talk with another driver. When the driver was about to wake me, His Highness stopped him from doing so with the words, "Do not wake the sleeping child, let the poor child sleep. If you know where the child lives, we will first drop him home and hand him over safely to his parents and after that you can drive us home. " The driver explained that the child was the gardener Laxmanrao's child and related the circumstances. "All right, it does not matter, let us see the child home first," instructed Sayajirao, getting into his car. The following morning, the gardener Laxmanrao sought an audience with His Highness to apologize profusely over the incident. His Highness brushed it aside with the admonition that "No matter what, never wake up a sleeping child".

The above incident drives home his special compassion towards children and shows the Maharaja as a human being, having seen him as a ruler and a reformist earlier.

Sayajirao III was attached to the people who had served the state well and for whom he had high regard for their honesty and uprightness. We have seen earlier how reluctant he was to let go of his counsellor, friend and teacher F. A. H. Elliot; now the other person he was deeply attached to was G. S. Sardesai who was the most trustworthy person serving in the Baroda state. When Sardesai turned sixty and expressed his desire to retire from service, the Maharaja replied in response to his wish, 'Sardesai, I need you here—you cannot leave me and go elsewhere. Your place is here, you will work and live here in the palace till the end of your days!'[3] But, Sardesai was adamant and after he repeatedly put forward his wish to be relieved from service, the Maharaja had no choice but to let him go, which he did with utmost reluctance. The Maharaja was deeply hurt by Sardesai's retirement and it is said that a lapse of fifteen years did not diminish the hurt.

After Sardesai retired from Baroda service, he moved to Poona to the Peshwa's office where he received financial aid from the Bombay government to write the history of the Marathas. Interestingly, the famous historian Jadunath Sarkar was also involved in the project. After a good initial start, for some inexplicable reason, the financial aid was stopped and the historians could not progress further in their work. Both Sardesai and Sarkar tried their level best to persuade the Bombay government to continue with the aid to enable them to complete their work, but the attempt proved futile as the government staunchly refused to do so. The Bombay government was very sympathetic but advised them to get the funding from the rulers of states or from estate owners, like the Scindias, Holkars and Gaekwads of whom Sayajirao III was the most generous and popular ruler! Ironically, the task of approaching Sayajirao III was given to Sardesai, who shrank from the responsibility the moment it was given as he was well aware of the Maharaja's displeasure on his retirement. Besides, the Maharaja was at that time travelling in Europe, but Sarkar advised him to approach the ruler by letter and said, 'If he responds positively, our problem is solved, if not we can always try elsewhere.' [4] With this advice, Sardesai went ahead and wrote a long letter explaining the purpose and their predicament and also the high value of the historical work. The amount needed was a sum of Rs 3,000 and the balance of Rs 9,000 he would try to obtain from the rest of the rulers of the other states. Sardesai did not expect a favourable reply in view of what had gone before, but the Maharaja being a man of procedure, asked his dewan to check the bona fide of the request and report to him. The dewan had to leave for Bombay on official work and asked Sardesai to meet him there. The dewan met him and was satisfied by the genuineness of the request. By cable, he sent his opinion to the Maharaja who by return cable instructed that the sum of Rs 3,000 be immediately handed over to Sardesai. This manifestation of the Maharaja's magnanimity leaves one speechless.

59

A Portrait of Chimnabai II

Sayajirao III and Chimnabai II took great interest in uplifting the status of women. The maharani's book on the *Status of Women in India* is a monument of her industry, sympathy and intelligence in the cause of women.

The practice of infant marriage acted as an impediment to female education as well as the health of women. The Maharaja had raised the age of marriage for girls to sixteen but public resistance compelled him to lower it to twelve for girls and sixteen for boys. The object was to prevent marriage of children an age when they were ignorant of its significance and also to bring down the rate of premature motherhood resulting in deaths and unhealthy babies as a result of premature births.

The Hindu Widow Remarriage Act was another social reform that the Maharaja undertook, which gave protection to widows if they chose to remarry. As a Hindu marriage was considered sacrosanct, it was indissoluble, but educated women in Baroda clamoured for divorce. Women abused by their spouses wanted release from such bonds. Polygamy was legal but women were not at liberty to marry another man even if she was unhappy in her marriage. Because of this disparity in circumstances, the men were not in need of divorce, but for a Hindu woman there was no way out, hence divorce was necessary to free these women from bonds of slavery and also to put a stop to burning of daughters-in-law for dowry and to reduce cases of suicide. Thus, the Hindu Divorce Act was passed by the Maharaja in response to educated public opinion and as a result Hindu marriages are now dissoluble.

Hindu women had limited property rights and their rights to succession and inheritance were also restricted. As economic independence is a *sine qua non* in raising the status of women, a committee was appointed by the Maharaja to investigate into the question of property and inheritance rights. The aim was to give equal rights to women as wives, mothers, widows and daughters such as their more fortunate sisters in the West enjoyed. Chimnabai II too had benefitted a great deal from her travels to Western countries and had observed the liberty and equality that existed between the sexes. She wished that Indian women too be given the same treatment as those in European countries. As a manifestation of this thought, at a prize-distribution function held in Baroda, the maharani took a bold step and sat on the same sofa as Sayajirao III, an open declaration of her doing away with the purdah tradition altogether! It did cause raised eyebrows among the British officials and disapproval among diehard conventionalists, but she scored a point, as the purdah system, over a period of time, had become an obscure thing of the past.

It must be emphasized that the royal couple translated their thoughts into actions and was always putting what they advocated into practice. For example, however disappointed they may have been over Indira's marriage to the prince of Cooch Behar, who was a non-Maratha, they agreed to it, exemplifying inter-caste marriage in her person.

Chimnabai II was a progressive woman, a passionate advocate of women's education, disapproved of child marriages and also the purdah system, even though she practised it while at home in the palace in Baroda. In recognition of her efforts in this direction she became the president of the All India Women's Conference in 1927.

Described as a spirited and adventurous lady, along with her progressive ideas the maharani was also known for her passion for jewels and gems. Even though her husband was more abstemious by nature, she allegedly bought jewellery that had earlier belonged to Russian grand dukes after the revolution, mostly large emeralds. She was particularly adept at outsmarting top European jewellers with her expertise in diamonds, a skill which amazed even her husband. Chimnabai II, without any inhibitions, wandered around Europe and visited jewellers of repute, particularly the ateliers of Cartier whom she invited to Baroda in 1911. Intelligent and talented, she was also very thorough and was careful to keep an Indian craftsman with her at all times. The court jeweller accompanied her too in order to advise her on purchases from European firms.

Sayajirao III was extremely fond of her as she was intelligent, well-read and beautiful. During his visit to Baroda, Reverend Weeden described her as a woman of exquisite taste and good looks. He said, 'The Maharani is of middle height, but carries her head so proudly and yet so gracefully that she appears taller than she really is. Her carefully kept abundant hair is hidden by a white sari shot with gold, which falls over the perfect outline of her exquisite figure and is gathered between the knees, showing the ankles circled with pearls and the small bare feet which are as beautifully kept as her hands. She has two features that distinguish her beyond all other women, her magnificent teeth revealed within a firm mouth by her rare and charming smile and her arms are the most comely in the world. It was not till I had been with her for sometime that I noticed the collar of emeralds as large as pigeons' eggs round her neck and the chain of priceless pearls that falls from her shoulders to her waist.'[1] Chimnabai II was a great asset to her husband and gave him unstinting support in his reforms with regard to the upliftment of women.

60

Transforming Baroda

A benevolent ruler had several advantages in matters of social legislation as compared with the British government. He was the custodian of the rights of the people. Chanakya, the master in statecraft in the Mauryan administration, had proclaimed the sovereign authority as the fountainhead of laws and rules for the benefit of society including the order of priests. Manu had covered him with a halo of divinity, which probably inspired Henry VIII to declare the 'divine right of kings'—for selfish reasons, of course! But according to Manu, 'The acts of God are for the benefit of mankind, so the activities of a benevolent ruler are always to be taken as having been good for the welfare of his subjects.'[1]

Whatever was wholesome in the legislation of British India was adapted and assimilated by the Baroda state without unnecessary delay.

In 1904, the work of legislation was transferred to the newly created Legal Remembrancer's Department. The legal remembrancer as the consulting lawyer of government, in addition to the work of legislation, advised all its departments on legal questions connected with administration of public affairs, and on legal proceedings in which it was concerned or interested. He also acted as the conveyancing lawyer of the government and was always consulted for drawing up important deeds on behalf of or for the government.

One of the standing orders of Sayajirao III was that the legal remembrancer of the state should always keep himself in touch with the progress of legislation in British India as well as in the Western countries, and submit a report to the government of the Maharaja at the close of every official year. The landmarks in the history of social legislation were also in the state of Baroda.

The Indian Social Conference came into existence along with the Congress in about 1886. It passed resolutions, disapproving infant marriages and advising people to encourage marriages between grown-ups. This awakened the people to certain social evils. It was only when the government of the Maharaja took the bold step and passed the Infant Marriage Prevention Act in 1904 that infant marriage was banned.

Just as Rome was not built in a day, it was after some years of mature deliberation and thoughtful consultation with the leaders of the people that the legislation was passed and came into force. However, in the year 1927, the Maharaja appointed a committee of eminent scholars to consider the actual working of the act and suggest modifications. The report of the committee was advertised as information to the public and their suggestions were considered and subsequently, amendments were made in accordance with the people's wishes.

The act penalized marriage of minors defined by age, below eighteen for boys and below sixteen for girls. Such marriages, if performed, were declared null and void. Any violation of this act attracted a penalty of one month of imprisonment or a fine of Rs 500 or sometimes both. This shows that the Baroda state was far more advanced in legislation than British India. All marriages had to be compulsorily registered. The importance of the act lies in the preamble which runs as follows, 'It is expedient to prevent infant marriage with a view to concentrate public opinion on physical culture which would increase the vitality and longevity of the future generation.' This preamble embodies the intense feelings and sentiments which the Maharaja had always entertained on this subject. Regarding disparity in caste, the Baroda civil procedure court was empowered to entertain suits pertaining to caste questions.

In 1911, the Maharaja felt that the jury in the civil courts were not exercising their powers in the right direction, as the panchayats were often the strongholds of orthodoxy and perpetuated some evil customs in a rigid way. Some rules were framed to bring the panchayats under the control of his government, and certain amendments were carried out in the Local Civil Procedure Code. Unfortunately, the social stigma attached to the lower castes could not be obliterated by law, nor could the law interfere with the wishes of a high-caste person wanting to exclude a lower-caste person from ceremonies or dinners given by the high caste persons. It was further provided that those customs that were detrimental to the well-being of the community should not be binding on anyone. This legislation was intended to allow liberty of conscience to those social reformers who had the moral courage to differ from the orthodoxists on questions of social reforms. The courts too were instructed not to recognize those customs that impeded progress, whether it was moral or aimed at the prosperity of the community.

Similarly, the Hindu Divorce Act introduced by the Maharaja enabled a Hindu wife to obtain divorce on the following grounds: impotency on the part of the husband; his imbecility, if he was suffering from ulcerous leprosy; proof of cruelty; and in the case of both spouses, disappearance for seven years; on becoming a recluse, conversion to another religion, desertion of either party without reasonable cause for more than three years after cohabitation, addiction to alcohol or drugs; and adultery. Similarly, if a man married another woman while his wife was alive then the marriage was nullified or gave grounds for judicial separation with alimony and a separate residence for the wife. If a woman was pregnant at the time of her marriage and the fact was not known to her husband, he could obtain a divorce or get the marriage annulled. However, there was one salutary provision in the act that enabled a wife to seek separate residence without presenting a suit for judicial separation. This provision that offered relief and protection to the wife also enabled the parties to settle their differences and resume their marital relationship. This was remarkable progress.

In order to reduce the high mortality rate among pregnant women, infants and to prevent the use of untrained midwives, the Dai Act was passed in 1920.

Further steps were taken in social reforms such as the Hindu Purohit Act, passed in 1915 that prevented Hindu priests from exploiting Hindus in the name of religion. This act was meant to improve the moral and intellectual calibre of the priests who officiated at different religious ceremonies. A law was passed regarding joining sanyasihood. No person below the age of sixteen could renounce the world and become a sanyasi. A married man had to obtain permission from his wife to do so and even that after making adequate provisions for her and their children's maintenance. Further, a declaration form had to be filled out and registered. It was declared a violation of the law if sadhus consecrated people to this order in contravention of the provisions of this law and also an offence for a man to join, against the principles of this law. This law protected minors as well as wives.

The sum total of all the legislative activities of Sayajirao III was sufficient to mark him out as one of the greatest legislators of India.

But that is not all, there was phenomenal work done by him in other spheres that were imperative to improve the infrastructure and bring about prosperity in a most constructive way.

Matubhai Kantavala, a student in the Law College in Ahmedabad, who was later called upon by the Maharaja to serve on many committees that had a direct bearing on commerce, admitted that he was first inspired by the Maharaja's speech at the opening of the National Industrial Exhibition in Ahmedabad, which was a landmark in the industrial progress of India. He was inspired to work in a factory rather than practise law, if he wanted to join the rank of industrialists and be of service in the industrial growth of his country. He migrated from Ahmedabad to Baroda and had a very satisfying career.

During the fifty years of Sayajirao III's rule in the Baroda state, commerce and industry developed to such an extent as to render the state and the people of Baroda twice as prosperous as British India. Back in 1887, when Sayajirao III first visited Europe, he was very impressed with the infrastructure he saw there and when he met Dadabhai Naoroji, the brilliant statesman, he was admonished with the words, 'Don't you ever talk or brag that India trades with China, Japan, Sri Lanka, Iran, Arab countries, Cambodia, Egypt, Africa, Italy and Mexico as they will remind you of your bondage to the British. You must take up the challenge, you have the authority and will to industrialize Baroda, so go ahead and do it!'[2] He took up the challenge and how!

There was an increase in the growth of industries, railways, trade, roads, literacy, schools, waterworks and municipalities.

The Baroda state was dependent on the neighbouring territory with its inordinately long frontier and no comprehensive scheme of economic welfare could be applied without being immediately marred by neighbouring influences or contact with a region where there had been no attempt at improving the conditions of the people. In face of this handicap, it was no small achievement on the part of the Maharaja to have brought the state to the forefront despite its lack of important mineral resources or large forest produce.

Abolition of octroi was the first step towards speeding up commerce as it enabled free movement of traffic along highways. This was further accelerated by the provision of railways. One of the greatest successes of the Maharaja's administration of Baroda was the provision of the railway system connecting all the towns and principal villages of the state. An initial step was taken towards this by Ganpatrao who shortly before his death ceded a strip of land for the construction of the Bombay–Baroda and Central Indian Railways on condition that he should be compensated for any transit dues. But as it was a British enterprise and had British sovereignty, they had full jurisdiction of the British strip. The first train left Baroda station in 1860. Ganpatrao's brother Khanderao took the credit for starting the first line of any kind for Baroda. Towards the end of his reign, he resolved to build a light railway from Karjan on the Bombay-Baroda and Central Indian railways to the important trading centre of Dabhoi which was twenty miles to the east; for the same and also for the purpose of having carriages and trucks built in India, three light engines were imported from England. Old rails were used and in 1869, a narrow gauge line of 2 feet 6 inches was opened at a cost of Rs 50,000. The attempt was not a qualified financial success and Khanderao consented to a thorough overhauling of the line and handed the project over to the Bombay-Baroda and the Central Indian Railways. It was reopened for regular traffic on 8 April 1873 during the reign of Malharrao, and was the first native-owned railway to be seen in any Indian state.

Thus, at the beginning of his minority, Sayajirao III's territory had twenty miles of light railway, in addition to the British-owned main line running across the state from south to north. Madhavrao in 1876-77 had urged the need for more railways. Proposals were floated to connect Dabhoi, north-westward with Baroda city, eastward with Bahadapur and southward with Chandod. The last two sections of the line were opened in 1879, the first was named in 1880, while in January 1881, a two-mile extension in the immediate neighbourhood of Baroda (Goya Gate to Viswamitri) was added. Thus, when the Maharaja took over the administration, there was fifty-nine miles of state-owned light railway in working order. His study of the question of communications in his state soon made him an ardent advocate of railways, and his work in this direction may be judged by the fact that by 1925, Baroda had 642 miles of railway lines. During his fifty-seven years of reign, he gave the state 674 miles of open lines in all the three systems—broad gauge, meter gauge and narrow gauge—constructed at a total cost of Rs 5, 00,00, 000 from the state's savings. He took over the management of the Bombay—Baroda and Central Indian Railways into his own hands and reduced the expenditure by half.

Sayajirao III's genuine, personal interest in the development of railway lines was due to the fact that it was a way to develop the country as it facilitated the transport of produce. The development of the village Mehsana into a town is an eloquent testimony of his vision. Mehsana was made into a town by the rail connections and was often cited as an example of a constructive use of the Maharaja's railway policy. Okhamandal too was an example of his far-sighted vision. People loved the railways as a means of transport. One, it brought them to their destination sooner and two, it was very convenient to carry large sizes or large numbers of produce without having to worry about the fate of the animals forced to draw bullock carts. Above all, it was safe from dacoity on the highways. The number of passengers increased and the railway venture became a profitable one. There was one mile of railway to every ten square miles of the total area of the state—an intense development of the railway connections not to be found elsewhere! Baroda was the first Indian state to build railways on an extended scale; even while travelling abroad, there was correspondence to this effect; for example, the Maharaja wrote from abroad in a letter dated 2 December 1927, 'To adopt British experiences, rules and regulations pertaining to railway administration, the chief engineers of railways and communications should work together for the development of roads as that would be necessary in connection with railways.'[3]

Mention must also be made of the workshops at Goya Gate, two miles to the south of Baroda old city, where European visitors may well be surprised at the up-to-date character of the concern. In the workshops, everything connected with the railways was turned out, except wheels, axles and springs; and repairs, particularly of boilers, were a speciality. There was a power station manned entirely by Indians, with the exception of the engineer-in-chief. The power station had two electric engines, with floor space for more units, and supplied the needs not only of the railways but also of private consumers of Baroda city. The electrical department, once a separate concern and housed in the grounds of the Laxmi Vilas Palace, was amalgamated with the railway administration under one control, all at Goya Gate, which it had long been the Maharaja's intention to make the industrial quarter of Baroda. The story of the Maharaja as a railway builder is one of the most instructive chapters in the annals of his administration.

Side by side, expansion of roads was embarked upon, but the roads did not come into their own until the advent of the motor car. The motorcar offered stiff competition to the railways with its investment of Rs 5,00,00,000.

The Gujarat province with its six ports made overseas trade attractive and lucrative. With this in mind, harbour improvements were commenced and completed by 1925. The opening ceremony of the pier at Adatara in Okhamandal by the Maharaja took place on 14 February 1926. In the course of his sixteenth European trip, the Maharaja had the satisfaction of arranging for the institution of a regular service of steamers to Adatara or Okhamandal port. In August 1926, and subsequently, conferences were held in London with Sir John Ellerman, as a result of which the Ellerman Company agreed to run a monthly service to Okhamandal port, without guarantee or subsidy, but on the condition that if there was no cargo for the outward voyage the company may cancel the sailing. Further, an associated American line agreed to run steamers from America to Okhamandal port. Okhamandal was developed into a fine modern port of which the Maharaja and the official engineers may well be proud! Okhamandal yielded a lot of salt naturally obtained from the sea, and could have been a major source of revenue to the state if export of it had been allowed apart from being a saving to the people if it could be derived from the domestic market. However, since this was detrimental to British interests, the sale of salt was banned outside Okhamandal though manufacture of salt was permitted. Madhavrao as the dewan of Baroda had recklessly agreed to the British demands that no salt or collection of earth salt should be carried on in the prants of Baroda, Kadi and Naosari but as Kathiawad existed outside the 'salt line', Okhamandal was permitted to manufacture the white ingredient so vital to cooking. In consequence, while Okhamandal salt merchants could export salt to Zanzibar, the inhabitants of eastern Baroda had to pay thrice as much for purchase of salt than their western counterparts.

Regarding the plight of agriculturists who were worst hit in times of famine and floods, much was done to safeguard their interests during calamities inflicted by nature. Wells were dug and new methods of irrigation for agricultural purposes were introduced. Implements and tools for farming were sold to them at subsidized prices and a serious attempt was made to deal with the division and subdivision of land. Three agricultural banks were opened at the instigation of the Maharaja—two in Naosari and one in Kadi—with liberal funding from the state. Credit cooperative societies were legalized in Baroda, by an act of 1905, and by 1921, there were over five hundred of them, out of which 461 were agricultural. As these societies offered only short-time loans, it was proposed to establish a Land Mortgage Bank to offer loans for a longer period and thus prevent farmers from getting into debt by borrowing for that extra sum from moneylenders. Some eighty-four acres of land situated about a mile from the Baroda railway station was used for experimenting in farming. It was started as a practical training ground for students in 1892 when Sir Thomas Middleton was professor of agriculture in the Baroda College. Experiments in growing different types of crops, fruits, oilseeds and tobacco were conducted here. Instruction classes were held at the farm for ten weeks where students from the College of Agriculture learnt the use of agricultural implements which were labour-saving devices, and latest farming methods imbibed from abroad, and use of tractors to test the soil were taught to aspiring agriculturalist. This was called the model farm. The education of agriculturalists by demonstrations and general propaganda work made great strides and even though the classes were attended with reluctance by the educated who were seeking greener pastures for a living, progress was made.

The labour for the model farm was drawn from good conduct convicts who lived on the farm while on parole and derived an opportunity to earn a fair sum of money by the end of their sentences. This was an example of the Maharaja's general reformatory policy with regard to prisoners. He believed in giving people a chance to learn from their mistakes instead of depriving them of their livelihood; for example in the Khangi Kharbari there was a man by the name of Kharshetji who looked after the royal stables and had committed a serious lapse in duty in his job. But when the complaint was brought to the Maharaja for the ultimate decision, he replied, 'Have the man transferred to the elephant stables instead, to look after the elephants.' Kharshetji was relieved and happy that he had not been dismissed and in this frame of mind looked after the elephants with all the enthusiasm brought on by gratitude. The Maharaja was very happy and patting the man on the back thanked him profusely. His Highness's policy? 'When you look only for faults in people, it is only your own hands that get black!'

Regarding water, the scarcity of it from above the ground drove the Maharaja to seek it underground! Plans were drawn up for drilling agricultural bore wells in places where water was scarce due to scanty rainfall and wells being dry. This project was under the charge of the agricultural engineering department. The work initially began with developing the already existing wells, instead of boring new ones. In 1911, a superintendent from Nadiad, a village near Baroda, demonstrated the operation of a boring machine in the Model Farm. The purchase of these machines was sanctioned and a student was sent to Nadiad to get trained in boring well operations. The scheme was successful and out of the 1,247 attempts made in fourteen years, 971 were successful boring operations which brought about an increase in the quantity of water to about 4,37,500 gallons an hour! The state did the work for a cultivator who applied for it, charging him for the cost of bringing the machine and other items but where the operation was unsuccessful, the state wrote off the labour charges.

Philip Sergeant in his book *The Ruler of Baroda* draws a realistic picture: 'The visitor who travels through the villages and fields of Baroda state, especially in the early hours before the sun has begun to assume his full powers, there is a primitive, idyllic charm about it, touched to quaintness by the proximity of railways and telegraph poles, and occasional advertisements of English goods. In a time of peace, happiness did not seem far, were there only more water and less dust!'

As mentioned earlier, the Maharaja was not only interested in the upliftment of agriculture for economic development, he had other irons in the fire and between the years 1891 and 1906 much was attempted by him to industrialize the state. A glass factory, a stone quarry, sericulture, pearl-fishing, wax production, a castor oil factory, flour mills, a paper mill and other factories were established. But these enterprises met with little success and he admitted as much in his speech at the opening of the Ahmedabad Industrial Exhibition in 1902: 'I am sorry to say the results have been disappointing... I found that the managers were not sufficiently interested in the scheme, and not impartial in the working of it. I am convinced, however, that the fault lay not with the industries themselves, but in the fact that they were state enterprises.'[4]

Never one to say die, the Maharaja set out to appoint a director of commerce and industry and in 1909, the department of commerce and industry was separated from the revenue department, which until then had also been supervising commerce and industrial development in the state. Further, the Maharaja founded the Bank of Baroda in 1908 which has been considered as the most successful of his remarkable achievements in his economic development of the state as it was a flourishing bank from which loans could be obtained at low interest.

Private enterprises were encouraged and in a notification dated 23 March 1920 it was stated on what terms a person or company desirous of starting a new industry in Baroda might receive state aid. The director of Commerce and Industry, after looking into the bona fide of the applicant, made an enquiry into the prospects of the venture and if the venture was found worthwhile, made an estimated cost of the enquiry for which the government shared half the cost and the applicant the other. If the venture was profitable, then the applicant bore the entire cost, if not, then the government would refund the applicant's entire deposit. This system of 'cooperative investigation of industries' was reinforced by financial assistance from the state in the form of debentures and a generous portion was laid aside for that. Instead of state enterprises, it was replaced with state-aided enterprises. The reason for this was stated in Huzur's orders: 'Private enterprises are preferable to state enterprises, as government interference can then be obviated.' It was an incentive for entrepreneurs to be completely involved in their enterprises. Investigations were carried out by the state at government expense of the possibility of manufacturing of glass, cement and oil, calico printing, handloom weaving, and so on. Their immense value in the development of the state has been proved by the establishment of a cement works which was successful. Hand-printed calico was revived in Baroda and the oil pressing industry too gained momentum. Many miscellaneous industries sprang up due to the policy of concessions granted to these industries. Cotton mills and other mills, Alembic Chemical Works, a hundred ginning, pressing and other factories were subject to control under the State Factory Act and nearly a hundred joint stock companies with a total subscribed capital of over Rs 4,00,00,000 were established. Beginning with efforts made in 1911 till the changes in the industrial policies in 1920, and from 1921 to 1931, Baroda expanded with its industries and was industrialized almost to its full capacity, but there were limitations. For instance, they could not fix railway tariffs, locate ports or give adequate protection to agriculture and industries by a judicial system of tariffs.

Building of roads, both metal and kunker, had not been neglected by the Maharaja. Under the Maharaja, the Public Works Department, laid more than nine hundred miles of such roads for an expense of Rs 75,00,000.

Sayajirao III's work in providing proper medical facilities and medical relief to his people not only in the city of Baroda but also in the rural areas was a remarkable feat, which no other ruler in the past was able to achieve. A healthy mind in a healthy body is an old aphorism but nevertheless true and who knew it better than the royal personage in Baroda, who practised what he preached. The Maharaja and his dewan T. Madhavrao realized at an early stage of the Maharaja's rule that if the administration was to succeed and not end in ruin, they must take measures to ensure the good health and lives of the people of the Baroda state. With this thought in mind, Sayajirao III laid the foundation for a strong and active medical department in his programme of reforms which he launched at the beginning of his benign reign. With characteristic efficiency, Sayajirao III set about to work with due caution and forbearance. The problem was more with the attitude and the mentality of the people, who were reluctant to take advantage of the facilities offered by the government to fight diseases and pestilence. They were living in a morass of ignorance and superstition which made them suspicious of doctors and nurses and of their treatments. These people preferred their Ayurvedic quacks who meted out potions based on superstition rather than medical diagnosis. These men who practised witchcraft professed to have control over spirits and could thus get diseases cured by rattling off some mumbo-jumbo were infinitely preferred by the common people on the street to allopathic medical experts. To lift the general public from this quagmire of ignorance was a long-drawn-out battle which, to a great extent, was overcome with tact and patience. When the Maharaja ascended the gaddi, there was only one hospital in Baroda called the State Hospital built in 1833 during the reign of Ganpatrao, and one dispensary in Amreli dating back to Malharrao's time. These two were attached to the divisions of the army stationed in Dwarka and Dhari. In 1876, care was taken to restructure the hospital and dispensary by equipping them with the best qualified medical staff. Extensions of the hospital were projected and new ones opened. Malharrao's dispensary was converted into a hospital in 1877. The same year, Sayajirao III opened a new hospital named after Jamnabai in the heart of Baroda city. To the State Hospital, new additions were constructed in 1886, 1898, 1899, 1907, 1914 and 1918. The 1898 and 1914 additions were of special significance as in 1898 the Victoria Jubilee Ward was added for women patients in honour of Queen Victoria, and in 1914 was added the Seth Himmatlal Shivalal ward, named after a rich businessman who had donated twelve beds to the hospital's maternity ward. The districts and villages of the Baroda state were not ignored and got their due medical privileges. In the more populous towns and district towns, first-class hospitals were provided. Many of these owed their origin to the generous donations by the public who recognized the importance of adequate medical care. While the bigger towns acquired hospitals and dispensaries, the villages were served by a network of dispensaries scattered all over the territories. As is but natural with the main city, the State Hospital was the recipient of all the latest amenities in the field of medicine and surgery. It was one of the best staffed and equipped hospitals in India. The hospital was known not only for the care of patients but also as a training centre for nurses and midwives, a scheme that received enthusiastic approbation from the public.

Along with caring for the sick, there was also the thought of how to avoid sickness by the practice of proper hygiene, and the Maharaja took the necessary steps to propagate it.

In talking about the reforms introduced by the Maharaja during his reign, another step forward to ensure justice to all on proper judicial grounds was also taken by Sayajirao Gaekwad III.

61

Revamping the Judiciary and Other Systems

Until 1802, owing to internal feuds, the state of affairs was most unsettled in Baroda. The ruler's attention was directed more on the collection of tributes and the levy of exactions than on the administration of justice. People generally resorted to primitive methods of violence as retributive justice based on the adage of an eye for an eye and a tooth for a tooth in the absence of proper legislation. State interference came much later along with progress in civilization.

Sir T. Madhavrao as the dewan, while purifying the administration of justice in Baroda, took away from vahivatdars (revenue heads) their power to try civil cases which was then given to munsiffs or subjudges. Revenue officers were left, however, with powers in criminal cases.

When Sayajirao III took the reins of the government in his hands, his travel around the districts showed him that the vahivatdars were overworked in their dual capacity of executives and judicial officers; it also impressed upon him the impropriety of one man being simultaneously the prosecutor and the judge. He did away with this system though moving cautiously and after due deliberation, Sayajirao III decided to separate the two. A revenue officer could not assume magisterial powers and the munsiffs or judicial officers could only try civil and criminal cases without playing any part in the revenue affairs of the state. Munsiff courts were set up in all the talukas—this way proper discernment of cases was ensured as well as better efficiency in the revenue and judicial departments. After this system was introduced, a definite procedure was followed in civil and criminal courts. Judges and the general public were aware of the penal laws and hence brought about better law and order in the state of Baroda.

From this we gather that the separation of the two departments of law—the judiciary and the legislative—was brought about. In 1892, Sayajirao III entrusted the task of drafting the civil and criminal codes to two eminent legal experts, J.S. Gadgil and J.R. Naylor, respectively. Later, a legal remembrancer was appointed. The codification of laws and the separation of the judiciary from the legislative functions, as expressed in the words of Lord Minto, 'had elicited the warm interest of the government of India'.[1]

Adequately qualified prosecutors were appointed by the legal remembrancer for better discernment of a case before its acquittal, thus saving a person from being prosecuted through the lack of proper judgement.

Petty crimes and major offences in civil courts and criminal courts reduced considerably and with proper law and order enforcement, a safe and secure environment was established. In a letter from the dewan to the Maharaja dated August 1925, the dewan spoke highly of Rao Bahadur Ghatge who was successful in completely suppressing dacoity in the Baroda, Kadi and Amreli districts and deserved a reward for it. Apart from maintaining law and order within the state by keeping it free of crimes, the Maharaja was equally keen on reorganizing the army and a letter from him, while abroad in Europe, to his dewan dated 5 February 1925 spoke of his views on the proposals made by the government of India which have been enumerated earlier. The Maharaja wrote in his letter:

> Proposals made by the government of India will eventually lead to a position in which the state will be reduced to being very little more than the paymasters of the army, without due control of the machine for which it is paying. If only the proposals would permit of a more complete independence of the state, while trusting to its loyalty in any time of crisis as indeed is fully guaranteed in various treaty clauses, they would appear more acceptable. It is certainly not desirable to forfeit the advantages of modern arms and the small arms factory in Nepal with the help of Krupps, the steel giant of Germany.[2]

This was done under the guise of making tiles, but British spies smelt a rat and the revolutionist's efforts for an armed revolution was nipped in the bud.

The Maharaja also advised in response to Kelkar's (he was the vice-president of the Sarvajanik Sabha in Poona) speeches sent to him by the dewan by letter, dated 19 February1925:

> We should not always be copying British methods but only adapt those that suit our environment. How many of us Indians, except by asking the government for this or that power, do anything towards cleaning up the difficulties which lie within our own power and

in our own households? Are we doing anything towards removing inequalities, evils of the caste system, feeding the poor and needy, educating women and children, improving the sanitary conditions at home, preventing the iniquitous practice of marriage contracts? Let us achieve what lies closer to our hands, it may be a cry in the wilderness but numbers alone are not always right, it is as bad to run too quickly as it is to run too slowly. I am ready to remove the existing evils but slow in taking measures which are needed only in imagination. See that justice is done, listen patiently to those that are wronged and suggest solid and wise improvements. Let the honest thrive in peace and the evil feel fear enough to cease from their evil practices. If you have achieved this, a lot would have been done.[3]

While in London, he was always Sayajirao III the diplomat and made it a point to visit British officials and peers of the paramount hierarchy apart from what 'Rule Britannica' imposed. For instance, we see from the dewan's letter to the minister that the king of England held court on 18 June 1925 in Buckingham Palace which the Maharaja attended. The king gave Sayajirao III a private audience just before holding court. The Maharaja also called on his good friend Lord Reading earlier in the week and had a half-hour interview with him. 'His Highness was to give a "Garden Party" to the local gentry next Saturday when 200 people will attend and be entertained.'[4]

Whatever may be said regarding relations between Indian princes and the British Crown, the Gaekwads stand out for cementing the bond between the British Crown and themselves; somehow, they seemed to have a particular affinity for the majesties of England!

The first and most striking fact is that Sayajirao III's reign presented a pleasing contrast from the reigns of the past rulers of Baroda. Internal feuds, external wars and dissensions, the greed and avarice for wealth and territory and the total apathy for the prosperity and good of the public—it all belonged to a nightmare of the past. From 28 December 1881, when the Maharaja ascended the throne, the people of Baroda got fifty years of excellent administration.

Let us begin with T. Madhavrao the dewan who was a brilliant statesman himself and set the mode for the future progress of the state. The dewan and his assistants had laid the foundations and sketched out a programme for a systematic and civilized government. But to make the administrative machinery effective, to grapple with difficulties in questions of internal reforms and to trajectorize the state on to the path of progress was a task which the young Maharaja found reserved for him alone. Sayajirao III was not a genius in the Madhavrao mould nor was he a brilliant statesman like Dadabhai Naoroji with whom he kept in touch to seek his opinion on various subjects, but what the ruler had was a profound interest in delivering the goods. This interest prompted him to seek the advice of his mentors and in the main his observance of British methods in administrative matters helped him to incorporate the same into his administration and make it very successful.

Another of his constructive reforms was the levy of income tax throughout the state on a uniform level, which earlier used to be levied mostly on the poorer class of people. Now, with the new income tax reform, the poor were exempted from taxation, while the wealthy class bore with a proportionate burden, which they had earlier avoided. It also imposed on bureaucrats a fair share of tax which they had avoided before; there was no discrimination in taxes between villages and towns or between different classes of the subjects. The tax was moderate—a levy of 1 per cent of the income, allowing all his subjects, right down to those who earned Rs 300 a year to pay the tax. This tax reform was brought into effect from the commencement of official year 1904–05.

Another feather in the cap of the Maharaja was establishing a teachers' training college for men and later for women as well. There is an interesting story behind this too. One summer, while Sayajirao III was spending his time in the cool resort of Mahabaleshwar, he had with him as his companion A. K. Trivedi, a professor of philosopy at Baroda College. The Maharaja was in the habit of being read to by Professor Trivedi who sometimes accompanied His Highness on holidays for this express purpose. The usual time fixed for the reading session was 4. 30 p. m. One afternoon, Trivedi had gone out for a walk, promising to return in time for their reading session, but was late. When the Maharaja questioned him about the reason for his delay, the professor replied that while he was walking he had bumped into Professor Balakrishnan who was the principal of Rajaram College in Kolhapur and he had invited him to his bungalow nearby to have tea.

'What if you did?' quizzed Sayajirao III.

Trivedi replied, 'We got talking and Balakrishnan told me that he was thinking of starting a teachers' training college in Kolhapur.'

The Maharaja looked up, his impatience forgotten, and asked, 'Where is our teachers' training college in Baroda?'

'Your Highness, we do not have a teachers' training college in Baroda,' Trivedi answered.

'What! We do not have one? If Kolhapur can have a college for training teachers, why don't we? Send a telegram to the dewan with the order: "Immediately send proposals for starting a teachers' training college in Baroda"!'[5]

That was how Baroda got its first teachers' training college and later many more for men as well as women sprang up.

Under a wise and thoughtful system of developing the resources of the state and of controlling expenditure, the financial position of the Baroda state was getting stronger every year and in the seventieth year of his reign, it stood at Rs 10,00,00,000, of which over Rs 2,00,00,000 was invested as liquid assets in securities as a safeguard against a lean year in the future. For this reason, the Maharaja wisely insisted upon the maintenance of a reserve, at least to the extent of one year's revenue. He considered the preparation of the annual budget of income and expenditure as very essential to the financial success of the administration. Therefore, he insisted that all the necessary papers in this connection be prepared and laid before him within a reasonable period, before the commencement of the year to which the budget referred. In order to not militate against the principles of making a budget, he insisted that as a general rule sanctions over and above the budget should not be asked for, barring in extenuating, unforeseen circumstances.

The state budget was to be made public inviting criticism from the people of the state so that improvements and expenditures could be made with the people in mind.

Money, which earlier had been spent lavishly on priestcraft and ceremonies based on superstition, was now channelized to funding scholarships and education. Whenever a department required funds to meet an increase in expenditure, the department had to also point out where there had been any wastage that could have met the increase. All the departments were strictly advised to curtail unnecessary expenditure and not pay undue prices for the purchase of articles. With regard to this, an auction committee was appointed which consisted of one naib dewan as the president and as the head of the department; there were others too who were appointed by the Maharaja as members.

A public service committee was appointed to scrutinize appointments and make recommendations for posts not filled in by promotions and to advise the Maharaja's government on problems relating to conditions of service. A training school for clerks was opened to train new entrants in office procedures and clerical work, before they were allowed to join service. The head of departments had to fill up vacancies from among these trained clerks.

A special secretariat library aimed at collecting blue books and other publications of interest was started with a view to keep the officers' knowledge of administration up to date.

Properly trained and qualified people were appointed into state service as per the requirement of the state. Promotions were given according to the tenure of service and proof of capacity. Advancement in rank or pay was the general rule but was applied in a rigid manner, not on seniority. Complete involvement in the service was expected by the Maharaja.

The key to Sayajirao III's success as an administrator lay in his interest in being well-informed of the comings and goings of his servants and their performances. He was as generous in praising laudable work as he was stern in punishing defaulters. It was the duty of departmental heads to bring to the notice of the Maharaja subordinates who had done exceptional work, for them to be rewarded for it. The Maharaja also received, from all departmental heads, a periodic statement of those who had been punished and the reasons for it. If the punishment was adequate, the order was revised or reversed, if necessary, no matter from whom it originated. This vigilance kept everyone on their toes! Repetition of rules and regulations was not encouraged as that was a waste of time. His policy was to adopt in the state such laws enacted in British India that could be useful to the state of Baroda. This was done with regard to commercial laws where uniformity between laws in the state and those in British India was necessary in the interest of the public.

The Maharaja favoured direct contact with the common people of the state and encouraged his officials to tour around and get authentic information as to the problems and wants of the people. He desired that his officials be totally involved in their work and not perform perfunctorily just to keep their jobs! Interaction between departments and perfect harmony in their working relationships was the order of the day; he was intolerant of petty bickering among his staff. Friction, he believed, was detrimental to the smooth running of the government and should be avoided at all costs. Interdepartmental conferences were held under the chairmanship of the minister to identify difficulties and sort them out without waste of time and effort. Criticism was welcome for growth, but the critic had to be knowledgeable to criticize. If the work was unsatisfactory, then the fault lay with the individual and not with the system—the Maharaja made sure of that. Strict and intelligent control was exercised by the heads of departments and above them was the minister.

Executives had to set a high standard in punctuality and dedication to their work for their subordinates to follow their example and bring the standard to the desired level of perfection. The Maharaja was often heard to remark that efficiency did not lie in numbers but in the capacity and sincerity of the few. In one of his orders in 1899, he said, 'The administration of the state really suffers often from there being too many hands rather than there being too few! One good worker can do better than three lazy ones.'[6]

In his letter to his minister he opined, 'I have noted that a good deal of work turned out by our officers is stamped with a want of completeness about which I want you particularly to see and find out the underlying causes and how best to remove them... The lack of finish, if I may put it that way, is due to want of coordination in our services. The evil is accentuated, I think, by the lack of interest which the superior officer should really take in the training and preparation of his subordinates.' This is a perfect illustration of the standards from a man who worked round the clock![7]

Sayajirao III firmly believed in decentralization of powers. He believed that if the work and responsibilities were distributed along with power to subordinates of the minister and departmental heads, then the lower officials would have the freedom to take decisions and delays could be avoided. They would also be in a better position to advise the Maharaja when matters came up for consideration, as this way they would be more cognizant of the local conditions. Only matters of vital importance were to be brought to the Maharaja for consideration, which also put an end to the time when he was consulted on purchases of mats and door handles! The policy of decentralization, however, was tempered with caution, and was confined to reasonable limits.

While Sayajirao III deprecated unnecessary delay, he also cautioned against undue haste. In one of his orders, he stated, 'How many officers and men try to pass on correspondence or depose questions with no other view than to save their own skin and promote their own selfish interests by appearing to be fast dispatchers of business, while only pretending to lay claim to it!' Proper analysis and discernment was required when going into delays or where there was undue haste.[8]

While abroad, he expressed that he was disturbed by the difference between Indians and Europeans in one of his letters to his dewan.

'Our people lack common sense,' he said, 'they need detailed instructions...they go by the word of directives rather than the spirit behind the orders.'

In another, he lamented, 'When will Indians learn to shoulder responsibility? They just like to obey orders.'[9] What he really meant was that Indians lacked initiative.

'For development, the common man will have to be trained and his level must be raised.'[10]

Sayajirao III was in this frame of mind while on a tour to oversee the drought-hit area of the state. He arrived in one of the villages late in the afternoon, tired and thirsty, as it was unbearably hot. Sitting down on a charpoy, he asked for some water to drink. The attendant brought him warm water which did not quench his thirst. When he demanded for some ice to cool the water, he was told that there was no ice. His lieutenant exclaimed impatiently, 'Maharaja, so many people are dying of hunger and here you are worried about a glass of cold water!'

Sayajirao III replied calmly, 'It is not a question of whether I get cold water to drink or not on an insufferably hot day but it's about administration. If a man cannot look after his ruler how can he look after his subjects?'[11]

Never one to claim superiority in knowledge, Sayajirao III always considered himself a student and insisted on others doing the same. Originality and innovation always met with his approbation and he encouraged it. It did not matter to him who was giving a suggestion; whether it was a clerk or an officer of high rank, he lent a willing ear, considered the proposal and implemented it if he found it worthy of implementation. The Maharaja advocated perfection in conduct and efficiency to all heads of departments and that they act as role models for their subordinates to follow—this way he made sure that the standard of efficiency was raised to a high level. No wonder, Sayajirao III has been called the 'Maker of Modern India'.

The tippan system devised by Sayajirao III was a speciality of the Baroda administration. It was a report that encapsulated all the facts of the case and was submitted to the authorities for them to act upon it. Oral instructions were apt to be misunderstood or, worse, misrepresented. A tippan left no room for ambiguity. This was so successful in decision-making that the Maharaja insisted on tippans even from his grandsons whenever they wanted favours! That 'brevity is the soul of wisdom' is well illustrated in the device of tippans. All orders from the Maharaja were written and initialled by him, leaving no room for doubt. All suggestions made by the officer-in-charge were carefully looked into by the legal remembrancer and modified or corrected, if required to do so. All appeals had to be first sent to the immediate officer before Sayajirao III. Direct appeals to the Maharaja only served to swell up his post bag!

Sayajirao III was a pioneer of social reforms, as stated earlier, but the most remarkable one was the ordering of the codification of Hindu laws as early as 1904. This was successfully carried out so it was no longer necessary for people to wade through complicated textbooks, all the essential principles having been embodied in a few simple rules.

Another profound step the Maharaja took (in the year 1928) was the issue of currency notes in the Baroda state. A letter from the Maharaja addressed to solicitors Horn and Burkett, London, expressed his desire to issue paper currency in the state: 'Paper currency is a technical branch of political economy and His Highness would like to consult a good expert in England. Please suggest names and approximate fees for consultation.'[12]

The suggestion was refused by the British government of India on the following grounds: the issue would have to be against a gold reserve with the result that the gold would be claimed and probably hoarded or converted to jewellery. Directly the gold reserve was insufficient to cover the issuing of currency notes, depreciation would result! Ali Beg, a minister (treasurer) in the Nizam's court of Hyderabad thought that arrangements could be made under which the state would not be bound to pay gold against the note currency. In Hyderabad, it had been successful because they had their own currency and had refused to enter into the arrangement for British currency. Therefore, there would be two concurrent currencies—as Baroda's currency depreciated in value, British currency would decrease in circulation, and would incite people to get rid of it before it depreciated further. It was unlikely that the British Indian government would supply a British currency to support a Baroda one.

Hurst gave his full approbation and support to the Maharaja's scheme for a separate Baroda currency. A letter from Ali Beg spoke of the advantages of the scheme: 'First, it would have net profits to the tune of Rs 2 lakh a year based on the dewan's calculations. Secondly, it would have large indirect advantage to trade. Thirdly, it would encourage entrepreneurship. Fourthly, the banking aspect of the scheme ought to prove a beneficial enterprise of great utility and of considerable profit.'[13] Ali Baig expressed his wish to Chandrashekar, a financial expert, in a letter dated 2 October 1928 that he should join in the service of the Baroda state in collaboration with Horn and Burkett in connection with the financial aspects and hammer out a scheme and examine further the agreement of 1900–01 to see if 'a radical change in the metallic currency was possible.'

The entire basis of the agreement of 1900–01 was silver coinage; 'the basis has been changed without the Maharaja's assent by the substitution of what the government of India call the "gold bullion" standard.'[14] The gold bullion scheme which, when interpreted into the Currency Act of 1927, was one shilling six pence had everything to do with the internal as well as external exchange. The standard of currency in India in 1927 was gold. It was something like forty tolas of fine gold received in exchange for twenty-one to twenty-three annas and ten paise per tola or offer of four hundred ounces of silver and demand its equivalent in 1,065 tolas of fine gold.

In view of the fact that the Indian currency was not a silver standard currency but a paper currency at a fixed rate to sterling and that sterling is itself a gold standard currency, therefore any issue of paper currency by Baroda should be linked with gold. A scheme for gold currency sanctioned by the British government was to convert the currency not merely into foreign exchange but into metallic gold. 'An obligation that is absolute and unlimited.'[15] This statutory obligation was for internal purposes at the stabilized exchange rate of one pound and six shillings with a view to put gold coin into circulation as soon as sufficient gold was available. The essence of the system was 'a fixed gold parity of the rupee at one pound six shillings for internal purposes'.

The proposed note was to be issued by the Bank of Baroda on its own responsibility, under the guarantee of the state. 'This will give the scheme a purely business and non-political aspect for the utilization of the credit for His Highness and his subjects.'[16]

Under the terms of the agreement made with the government of India in 1900–01, the Maharaja had a right to issue a paper currency. At that time (after the closing of the British Indian mints to the free coinage of silver rupee) the British government in order to eliminate exchange problems agreed to substitute British Indian rupee for the Baroda or the babushai (silver coin) rupee and to supply such circulation for a term of fifty years, while the Baroda government agreed that the babushai silver currency should cease for the said term to be legal tender in the state. As a false impression existed among some of the Maharaja's advisers that the British Indian currency was still (as it was before the closing of the mints) a silver standard currency, it was explained by Mr Hurst from Horn and Burkett a firm of solicitors that it was not so. He explained in his letter to the dewan that 'The Indian silver one-rupee coin is now a token coin only, which the British government in India was endeavouring to maintain on an exchange basis of one shilling and six pence in relation to sterling.'[17]

A great deal of effort was also made to enhance the beauty of the Baroda state. William Doring, an expert gardener, was assigned to create gardens around the palaces and in the city of Kamati Baug. Fountains too were installed all over the city, so much so that Baroda came to be known as a city with parks, fountains and luminaries.

Sayajirao III's penchant for art and art works is well known and the Baroda Museum is a standing testimony to it. He also was a proud possessor of some rare pieces of art. A man with profound wisdom and intellect, the Maharaja was also a voracious reader and his tastes were fastidious as ever. His vast collection included literary English classics like Dickens's *Nicholas Nickleby*, Clay on political economy, *The Cambridge History of Mughal Art*, Shaw's *Pygmalion*, Geike on geology, Spengler's *Monumental Philosophy*, the histories of Germany and England and Bentham's *Theory of Legislation*.

The workings of his mind are discernible in all his speeches. For example, in a banquet given by him at the Laxmi Vilas Palace in honour of Lord and

Lady Reading, he concluded his speech with:

> For my own state [Baroda], it is only natural for me to hope that its original sovereignty will be restored. Over a hundred years ago, the British government elected to mediate between my house and its tributaries, which were then temporarily handed over to them [the British government] for the collection of tribute—they elected to collect the tribute on our behalf free of charge. It was a sacred trust then undertaken... In the interest of efficient government, and with the utmost solicitude for the good of the Empire, I am prompted to suggest to the British government that the ancient privileges be now fully restored to their friends and allies of old. For it is only as true allies and partners in a commonwealth of states that our Indian states can really become pillars of the Empire. [18]

This is what he was convinced of though, he did not advocate democracy as he felt that until India had resolved its caste, religion and communal differences, a democratic government was not the answer to the country's problems. A country under a benevolent ruler was the need of the hour or England and India share the responsibility of governing the British India empire as equal partners but that again was utopian thinking on his part!

The history of Baroda under the Gaekwads cannot be concluded without a proper explanation of their tumultuous relationship with the British government created a raucous chord particularly during the reign of Sayajirao III when conflicts between the two governments reached a crescendo bringing the ruler to the brink of deposition.

On a deeper analysis British relationship with the Gaekwads began with Fatehsinghrao I and gained momentum with Anandrao Gaekwad signing off all his powers to the British in the treaty of 1805. Due to this if the relationship between Sayajirao II and the British peers was a long drawn-out battle with one trying to subdue the other, with Khanderao it was one long honeymoon! We have seen how the tides of fortune turned against Malharrao ending in his deposition, but with Sayajirao III it was a battle of wits at every stage! At the investiture, Lord Northbrook had pointed out in his speech that Sayajirao III owed his lofty status to their good offices and it would do him well to remember that and never break the golden rule of implicit obedience. The AGG's condemning reports, the Durbar incident, Lord Curzon whose intense dislike for the Maharaja stemmed not only from the fact that Sayajirao III spoke out his mind but from the fact that he had a mind at all! Strangely this seesaw relationship of his with the British did not tilt him over and he retained his balance. Perhaps it was because he had been appointed by *them*, and the fact that her late majesty Queen Victoria had thrown her mantle of protection in bestowing the title of favourite son of the British empire that had a lot to do with it. For it must be remembered that he was the only indigenous ruler who was accorded a 21-gun salute while the Nizam of Hyderabad was accorded only 19!

Apart from the incidents cited earlier, there was the matter of revenues of which the Baroda state was unjustly deprived. To begin with, on the assurance Sayajirao gave of extending his wholehearted cooperation to the British Empire during emergencies and for the defence of the empire he was prepared to place at the disposal of the British all his resources including the railway and telegraph for their use. To be fair the British also recognized the Maharaja's generous contributions in funds and men during the World War I and during the South African war and Afghan uprisings. On the other hand, the Baroda government demanded full liberty to improve and extend all means of transport and communication so vital for an organized life during war and peace times. But what really happened was that by one fiat the Government of India raised the postal rates and telegraph charges, and the receipts from these were not handed over to the states for the benefit of the people who suffered the effects of this taxation. The British government acknowledged the claim of Indian states to a share in these receipts, but the people of the Indian states had no voice in the regulation of those service charges. The Baroda government demanded that the people of Baroda should have an equal say along with the British subjects on the matter. Similarly, railway fares were enhanced at the people's cost but did not enhance the amount in the state treasury. Likewise Indian industries were paralysed with unnecessary freight rates and surcharges. The Baroda government felt that the state's subjects should have a say in the matter of freight which could ruin their industries and curtail its development. Apart from this, the state of Baroda was deprived of considerable revenue from its ports in the form of excise and customs tariffs. Worse still was the prohibition to develop the ports for trading as it interfered with British interests, for how could they allow a native state to develop similarly along British lines and in the long run be a threat to them? The ban on salt manufacture was dealt with by Sayajirao III as Okhamandal manufactured salt that was superior to any in the country. He pointed out that as Okhamandal came entirely under his jurisdiction the manufacture of salt there should be allowed to continue but it was pointed out to him that it could not be traded outside Okhamandal. The ban on opium was not frowned upon by the Baroda government as it did more harm than good, though it brought in rich revenue to the state. Though the Indian states had been assured complete internal autonomy, they were denied jurisdiction over European British subjects and other non-Asiatic foreigners. In some cases, the government of India interfered even on behalf of British subjects or British servants and thus impaired the autonomy of the states. Internal autonomy was only partially recognized and unnecessary interference hampered the smooth running of the administration of the states. Indian states were denied the privilege of coinage and were induced to close down their mints and were not admitted to the benefit of Seinorage. To sum up, as per the policy of the British government, as the de facto power in India, wherever their interests were at stake due to competition from a native state, the latter had to withdraw in their favour whether they wanted to or not. Regarding justice, the 'British standards were basically different when applied to the English people from those applied to the people of the colonies and the former Indian Empire. In their dealing with the native States they had only two guiding principles one of political expediency and the other convenience.'[19] However, from all past actions of the British and the political relationship between two governments, the British and the native, one factor reveals itself in a startling manner. The political officers of the British government who were responsible for the day-to-day dealings with the Baroda government gives us a good look into the quality of the British character and their method of governing the people. The fact that reveals itself is that the British from such a tiny island like the British isle could establish and own a vast empire extending throughout the surface of this planet. That brings us to the question of what were the characteristics of this empire building quality? First and foremost, they were shrewd negotiators, they knew with whom they were negotiating and for what they were negotiating. Secondly, they played upon the ignorance of the native rulers particularly their ignorance of the language in which the treaties were drawn, and thirdly the interpretation of these treaties which was interpreted with *their* main policy in mind which was to take over. The British were shrewd enough to disguise this ambition by pronouncements of fair play, justice, equity, all on paper, and in their speeches the state durbar, banquets would invariably be used for the purpose. Detailed explanations for the grounds on which their decisions were arrived at were never given either in words or in their correspondence. The British were proficient in the art of administration. Sayajirao III himself adopted their methods in the administration of his state. The huge civil structure which existed in India was greatly augmented by them. They outwitted all the foreign powers on the soil of India in this art. 'These characteristics, over and above many others were chiefly responsible for the carving out a large empire for themselves thus giving them a place of prominence in the comity of nations.'[20] Nevertheless, there were quite a few in the British hierarchy who were different and were not only able to see the native prince's point of view but also, like Lord Irwin, tried to get the state provincial autonomy, and certain other viceroys who saw eye to eye with Sayajirao III like Lord Reading and Lord Minto with whom Sayajirao III was able to form a steady friendship.

All the offences mentioned earlier resulted in the formation of the Chamber or Council of Princes with the object as Sayajirao III observed 'should emphasise the importance of adding to the internal autonomy of the states and removing unnecessary interference with free intercourse with their brother princes in the Chamber and outside, that reference to the Judicial Tribunal should ordinarily be the usual practice, that disputes with estates under any guarantee or protection should also be referred to the Tribunal, the Government of India being deemed a party to them, that there should be a commission of enquiries even when a ruler is unduly kept back from exercising his full rights; the position of a Resident should resemble that of a diplomatic agent with little or no power of interference.'[21] The Council of Princes did not prove effective but by then Sayajirao III due to the factors related above realized it would not be long before the people of India would find their voice in those spearheading the Indian national movement and he too by the year 1920 was deeply involved in it though from afar. Sayajirao III knew the only solution to the pressing problems was education and unity and unless these two could be achieved a dominant power would always dominate us hence he made it a point to refer to these two pressing needs in all his speeches.

This is what he was convinced of though, he did not advocate democracy as he felt until India had resolved her caste and communal differences, a democratic government was not the answer to the country's problems. A country under a benevolent ruler was the need of the hour but that again was utopian thinking on his part.

At the annual prize distribution function of the Maharani High School for Girls, Baroda, on 11 December 1935, he said, 'Women's education is not given here merely in imitation of Western civilization. In our Indian homes, women in the olden days were as well-educated as the men. In ancient India, women also used to be trained to take a leading part in public activities and even in philosophical discussions. There is no reason therefore why you of the present generation should not take your opportunities, why you should not be able to hold your own, working steadily in literature and other activities in the same way as men. Let not your spirit be marred by jealousy. Aim at healthy competition which is always good for everyone. Your ideals should be mutual help, mutual welfare and mutual progress. You should never seek to benefit at the expense of others but should seek to rise by your own merit and through your own efforts. It is my earnest desire that you should rise to the best of your ability and I hope that you will be actuated in your efforts by the highest motives.

'Men and women are not enemies. They are indispensable to each other, and for the progress of the world and humanity, it is essential that they should advance together and help each other to achieve the great objective of life, namely the happiness of the home. Unless this is done, education will fail in its aim.'[22]

At a dinner given by the alumni of Baroda College on 12 January 1936, he said, 'An able and progressive administrator, in my opinion, must study the past, carefully observe the present and look ahead to the future. I am convinced that the people of our country are in no sense inferior to any others in the world, and yet our progress is slow.'[23]

The Maharaja's speeches on different occasions display that his thoughts and ideas were far advanced for those times and left an indelible imprint on the minds of his listeners.

Sayajirao III was not involved in seditious activities at the time he was accused of them as he was more focused on giving the state of Baroda good governance and that occupied all his thoughts and time which left him scarcely any moments for his family leave alone for seditious activities. But that is not to say that he was completely unaware of what was going on and secretly championed the cause. As the years rolled on, the winds of democracy swept over the Indian terrain with such ferocity as to render the British government of India helpless in their wake. From 1922 onwards, Sayajirao III chose to be away from India and spend most of his time in Europe and other places abroad, the ostensible reason being he did not want to be the 'whipping boy' for the British political department at a time when India was being blatant about its desire for 'home rule'. The Maharaja was well aware that the reconciliation between him and the paramount power rested on flimsy grounds and any word or action that was likely to be misconstrued would bring the whole edifice of his kingdom, so carefully consolidated by his ancestors, tumbling down. Henceforward, adopting a more *c'est la vie* attitude, he silently made his plans to travel abroad and spend less time in his state. It was better, he must have reasoned to himself, to be thought of as an absentee playboy rather than a seditionist which could end in his deposition and also the end of his reforms. He returned to India every year during winter to maintain contact with his people and also to ensure his progressive reforms were being carried out.

Sayajirao III had now turned sixty and his health was no better, though the cool climate of Europe suited him and in the main provided him with a justifiable excuse to remain there. The year 1922 saw two auspicious events in the family—in spring that year, his son Dhairyashilrao was married to a girl from the family of the Maharaja of Dhar, and a month later, Sayajirao III's granddaughter Lakshmidevi, daughter of Fatehsinghrao III, was married to Bapusaheb Khemsawant, the raja of Sawantwadi.

Though away from his state, Sayajirao III's heart had been left behind and everything concerning Baroda's affairs was reported to him and noted by him. He funded the Indian National Congress and surreptitiously aided the freedom movement in India. Great freedom fighters like Lokmanya Tilak, Aurobindo Ghosh, and some other prominent figures like Barrister Keshavrao Deshpande, Khasherao Jadhav, who were deeply immersed in anti-British activities were silently supported by the Maharaja. Therefore, it's not surprising that Ganganath Vidyalaya and Manikrao Akhada became the centres for revolutionary activities in Baroda.

While in London and Paris, the Maharaja's association with Krishna Varma and Madame Cama is well known. Mahatma Gandhi and Sardar Vallabhbhai Patel too were well acquainted with him. Even though the Maharaja could not take a stand without the risk of exposing himself, his support to the cause strengthened and he had a private meeting with Gandhi after they had both attended the Round Table Conference and the latter had paid the Maharaja a visit in his hotel in London. The Maharaja assured his support to Gandhi, it must be surmised, because after that Gandhi did not consider Sayajirao III as one from the adversary camp. He, probably like the other prominent Gandhi family, had an innate distrust of the royals of India!

In 1929, Gandhi was going to march with his followers from his ashram in Sabarmati to Dandi near the sea to protest the ban by the British on the manufacture of salt in Gujarat. He was to openly collect water from the sea and manufacture salt from it in defiance of the British law. The territory that Gandhi was treading on to reach Dandi was interspersed with Baroda territory and the British were diffident about arresting one who was gaining popularity in India by the minute, so, they put subtle indirect pressure on the Baroda administration to do the job. Nadkarni, the subha of Naosari district, was told by Graham, the collector of the neighbouring British district of Surat, that if he arrested Gandhi in Baroda territory, Graham would get him the position of Rai Bahadur. But Sayajirao III, anticipating this, sent a message secretly to Nadkarni not to disgrace the fair name of Baroda and resign immediately from his post as subha of Naosari district. Gandhi too was told through a secret messenger that he was not to hold meetings and give speeches on his Dandi March. This way, he was able to avoid arrest, for when questioned by the British officials, the Maharaja had replied, 'How can I arrest a person who came into the state quietly and left quietly without disturbing the peace?'[24]

Along the banks of the Narbada, a long line of dharamshalas and temples for pilgrims were built on the pretext of providing resting places, but they were actually meeting places for the revolutionary activities funded by Sayajirao III.

In 1936, it was declared that the Olympics would be held in Berlin. The

Maharaja expressed his desire to witness the world-famous sports event where Dhyan Chand, the veteran hockey player, would be representing India in the hockey match against Germany. Sayajirao III was an avid sportsperson and no one except the British doubted his reason for going to Berlin. To a great extent, the British were right because under the pretext of witnessing the Olympics, Sayajirao III wanted to meet Adolph Hitler and enlist his support to supply arms to India to fight against the British. Sayajirao III believed 'an enemy's enemy is our friend'. Vishnu Nene, who was the personal assistant to the Maharaja at that time, was sent to Germany in advance to arrange the meeting with the Führer. The Maharaja must have told the British Resident that Vishnu Nene was being sent to ensure that the Maharaja and his assistant got good seats at the Olympics.

Sayajirao III left for the Olympics and was given an audience with Adolph Hitler and, according to Vishnu Nene and retold by his son Dr Damodar Nene in his book *Shrimant Sayajirao*, the Maharaja had a two-hour meeting with the Führer where the Maharaja promised Hitler the support of all Hindu princes in case of a war in Europe. It was agreed that Hindu princes would back Hitler during World War II if Hitler supported India in its struggle for freedom. Hitler agreed to it and to also supply arms and ammunition from his Krupps factory in Berlin.

Thus, the famous Baroda–Berlin Pact was signed by both dignitaries. Sayajirao III as chancellor of the Chamber of Princes was confident that all the members would support him. At the opening ceremony of the Berlin Olympics, 'his box was right under Hitler's' reported Dr Nene in his book.

Dr Damodar Nene, the biographer of Sayajirao III, recounts how the Indian hockey team in Berlin were very nervous when it came to the finals at the Olympics match against Germany. The Berlin team had beaten them in the semi-finals and now they were afraid that they would be beaten at the finals too resulting in India's defeat in the match. When the final match started, Dhyan Chand and his team seemed out of sorts and barely managed to score one goal against their opponent in the first half of the game. Sayajirao III was genuinely surprised at the poor performance of the Indian players. It was then that Vasantrao Kaptan, the chief of the Gujarat Krida Mandal and a confidant of the Maharaja, who was accompanying the king, requested Sayajirao III to speak to the players as they needed someone to boost their confidence. Sayajirao III met Dhyan Chand during the break and asked him why he should put up such a poor performance at the prestigious Olympics. Dhyan Chand, after a moment's hesitation, replied that he was used to playing barefoot and the shoes were proving to be an impediment to his movements on the field. Sayajirao III asked him to remove his shoes and play barefeet. He then proceeded to inspire the rest of the players by saying that they should win the match for the country and if they did, they would be well rewarded. Dhyan Chand, with his shoes off, gave his best performance and scored three goals in the second half and won the match for India. Hitler, who had been watching Dhyan Chand's performance with avid interest, invited him for a chat in his private office. At the meeting, he offered Dhyan Chand the rank of a colonel if he agreed to change sides and play for Germany instead, but Dhyan Chand refused the offer saying he was committed to playing for his own country.

As mentioned before, Sayajirao III was a great lover of sports; it was probably a legacy passed down from his ancestors. The traditional slaying of a buffalo with one stroke on Dusshera day speaks volumes for the vigour that had flowed in the veins of the earlier Gaekwads. Thanks to the refined outlook on the part of Sayajirao III, this barbaric sport of proving one's physical prowess had been stopped. The sathmarai (elephant fights and buffalo fights) testifies to Sayajirao III's interest in it, for every time the viceroys or the Prince of Wales visited Baroda, they were treated to a feat of this kind of sport which afforded them a novel experience and they enjoyed it thoroughly. He loved cricket too and in one of his letters, he admitted, 'I myself have never played the game but I have had it taught to all my sons by professional Parsi cricketers.'

His efforts in this direction were amply lauded when Shivajirao showed great promise by being chosen to play in the Oxford cricket team. In fact, after the match between England and Australia, he was hoping to become an 'Oxford Blue' when he died tragically. Shivajirao had made his mark as a good batsman in India too, when he played on the side of the Hindus in the famous Quadrangular Tournament. In the Freshman's match of 1911 he had scored 10 and 51 and in the subsequent trial, 4 and 61 which had secured him a place in four of the university fixtures. In seven completed innings he made 97 (including 51 not out versus Kent) with an average of 16.16. Following year, he scored 92 in the seniors match and 31 in the trial, he played against S. Africans and Australians (it was the year of the Triangle

Tournament) making 62&0 versus the former and 17 and 12 versus the latter. The Maharaja's favourite sport was tennis and he loved indulging in the game but for his gout which kept him away from it. It was due to his patronage that Baroda had the honour of holding the first All India Tennis Tournament where the best players in India and England competed. Sayajirao III's early training from his illustrious mentors Madhavrao and Elliot who had stressed the importance of physical activity was greatly responsible for his love for a good game. He was a good shot and a very good rider, and his daily routine included a walk before dawn. He patronized the Hind Vijay Gymkhana and under his patronage, the institute held an All India Athletic Sports Meet every year in which a number of athletes from all over India took part and competed with each other in different types of games.

Sayajirao III, as well as his entire family, graced the sports event with their presence and evinced keen interest in it. He distributed trophies to the winners and also donated generously every year to the institute. It was also his ambition to turn the tournaments to the Grand Olympics of India.

The work accomplishment by Sayajirao III requires volumes for it to be written about. But suffice to say, he was the greatest ruler the country was fortunate to have.

62

Family Affairs

Sayajirao III was perceptive and sensitive to the needs of others especially his subjects but somehow lacked the ability to comprehend his children. It bothered him greatly that he had failed in his parental duty to rear them the way they should have been reared, and even if they had not risen entirely to his high expectations, they could have led a normal, decent life and in doing so lived several years longer.

Fatehsinghrao, his eldest, had gone downhill and had reached a point of no return with his addiction to alcohol. He had fallen into bad company of 'friends' who flattered him and got him to spend lavishly on them. People who were aware of his wealthy background steadily led him on the path of destruction. The college authorities at Cambridge where Fatehsinghrao III was a student and his tutor had been warned several times that Fatehsinghrao III should not be treated like royalty or addressed as 'Prince' as it was his father's wish that he be treated as a student like the rest. Even 'Gaekwad' was to be omitted from his name so that any connection with the royal family of Baroda could be avoided. However, it was not enough to grant stability and bring in the awareness that he needed to keep his feet planted firmly on terra firma. Perhaps the loss of his mother at a young age and being thrust into the hands of a not-too-kind stepmother, as rumours indicate, must have been the root cause of the trouble. From the correspondence shared between Lt Col. M.J. Meade to Sir Louis Dane, secretary to the government of India, it is learnt that Sayajirao III wanted to bring his son back to Baroda from Deolali to cure him of his alcohol addiction but the letter confirms, 'A talk with the Maharani she said she did not want Fatehsinghrao III to live with them as he was such a bad example to her own children. She added that her elder sons had to be kept away from Baroda as she was afraid that Fatehsinghrao III would lead them astray and she was most anxious to avoid any further troubles of this sort. Therefore she begged me to urge the Sayajirao to keep his eldest son in Deolali.' This more or less confirms the rumours.

For all her forward thinking, Chimnabai II did not practise it at home, which was a pity as it affected her relationship with her husband. Further, the Maharaja's refusal to have him admitted into the cadet corps must have aggravated his frustrations. No doubt the temptations in London must have lured him to a life of dissipation.

From the correspondence of Sir Wyllie, assistant secretary in the political department, India Office, to Sir L.W. Dane, secretary to the government of India foreign department, it seems the prince was heavily in debt to the tune of £5,000 to £6,000, and his creditors were jewellers and dealers in precious stones in London, Henry Lewis and Lewis Dornur, to whom Fatehsinghrao III had given promissory notes which, as per the letter, 'his father will have to redeem'. The letter further stated, 'While posing at Cambridge as a reformed character and gaining the good opinion of Mr Jackson, his college tutor, Fatehsingh indulged freely in dissipation in London. It seems difficult to understand that Mr Spooner, the private tutor, should not have had an inkling of his proceedings, but Mr Spooner assures me that he was completely deceived.'[1]

However, Mr Jackson in his letter to Wyllie was very supportive of the young prince:

> Regarding the debts he contracts in London, this more than anything else, shows the curious lack of judgment of his father. As you probably know, Fatehsingh had a large allowance while in Baroda amounting to several thousands a year. Now, His Highness suddenly reduces this to zero in order as he imagines will reform him of his extravagant habits. So, during the last six months, Fatehsingh had to actually ask Spooner for every single shilling which has been doled out to him. Is it therefore a wonder that he contracts debts or borrows money? I feel sure if he had an allowance somewhat compatible to his position, we should hear little of his debts.[2]

Whatever may have been Jackson's summing up of the situation, it was clear that there was no hope for Fatehsinghrao III unless he took it upon himself to discard his undesirable associates and venture on the straight path.

The Maharaja suffered bitter disillusionment when Fatehsinghrao III was 'sent down' from Balliol. His formal education ended at nineteen. Sayajirao III posted his son to a regiment in Baroda in the hope that he would learn about military operations and conform to army discipline, but here too his hopes were blighted as Fatehsinghrao III only showed an interest in alcohol and self-indulgence. Chimnabai II refused to look after him and have him near her children lest they too should acquire his bad habits.

In 1908, Fatehsinghrao III's wife Padmavati gave birth to a son who was named Pratapsinghrao, who turned out to be the heir apparent and created a history of another sort as was seen years later. The birth was celebrated with the customary fanfare, a little watered down, as the infant's father was seriously ill. An illness acquired from dissipation.

Fatehsinghrao III died on 14 November 1908 at the height of his youth. He was only twenty-five and his death plunged Sayajirao III into grief. 'Everything had gone wrong.'[3] As a father he had done his best for his son but perhaps that's what had been wrong—giving him too much.

In the year 1912, his second son, Jaisingh, had been thrown off a horse and had been brought home unconscious. Miss Tottenham, who probably kept an eye on the young prince, wrote that Jaisingh was unconscious for two days and there seemed no danger to his life except that he was in the grip of fearful headaches and he found his neck 'strangely difficult to turn'.

As if this anxiety was not enough, Sayajirao III learnt from England of his other son's accident. Shivajirao, who was at Oxford and had made a name for himself by excelling in cricket, had suffered a severe head injury, the result of a 'rag' in which he had been the main participant. Egged on by friends, he had broken into the private quarters of the Don in Oxford. It could be that he had been struck on the head with a heavy object and the hard blow had resulted in an injury. This had taken place on the night of the cricket match against the Australians and Shivajirao was hoping to get his cricket blue after that.

Jaisingh gave his parents some hope six months later by making a full recovery and 'in glaring contrast to his sister Indira who was hell bent on marrying the prince of Cooch Behar, he married a girl of his parents' choice even though she was only thirteen and did not know the English alphabet!'[4]

However, the reprieve was only temporary as Jaisingh too went down steadily on the path with no hope of redemption. In 1919, Sayajirao III had to hurry back from Kashmir to Jaisingh's bedside because he had taken ill. In all probability, Jaisingh had not really recovered from his fall off the horse and his condition had worsened due to his heavy indulgence in alcohol. Doctors in Bombay and Baroda had done their best, but despairing of the young prince not getting any better, had advised a prolonged course of treatment in a well-known clinic in Europe.

Sayajirao III's health too was not good as the trying heat of an August summer in Baroda had brought on an attack of gout, but his unhappiness over his sons' misdemeanours was the real cause of it. He continuously agonized over the weaknesses of his three surviving sons as all three had shown a marked preference to the beverage that was deleterious to health. All three drank to excess, showed no inclination to work and easily got away with outrageous behaviour owing to their birth and status. The Maharaja did his utmost to instil discipline into them and even went to the extent of terminating their allowances but that only drove them to further excesses.

Sayajirao III's beautiful but wilful daughter who had managed to get her way and become the maharani of Cooch Behar was chosen by her brothers to act as the intermediary on their behalf. She was fond of her brothers and must have done so, but she did not realize that their father always preferred a direct approach. There was a letter to Sayajirao III where Jaisinghrao complained that he treated his grown-up sons as if they were still small children. Sayajirao III's reply was, 'Your views don't differ from mine'[5] and then he asked his son, admitting there were mistakes, to enumerate them and to feel free to discuss it with him and set things right. When his youngest son, Dhairyashilrao, sent a letter to him written by his sister Indira, the father's hurt and anger was roused to such a pitch that he answered with some belligerence, 'I cannot understand why Dhairyashil is behaving as he is. Beyond self-indulgence and idleness, he has no idea of duty to self, to family...' An ordinary man would have stopped here but Sayajirao III, being a dedicated ruler for whom the country came first above all else, went on to add 'country or humanity... in what way can we be more kind to him when he himself is selfish and egoistic and has no ideas of his duties? But I bear him no ill will.'[6]

The gap between Sayajirao III and his children widened considerably with time. Perhaps they found him too serious and resented his sermons on duties and education; among other things, the durbar was full of sycophants who must have flattered them with words like 'you are a prince you don't need to work' which must have gone to their heads.

Sayajirao III's initial upbringing and the discipline that had been instilled in him, the rigorous training, education under such capable hands like Elliot and Madhavrao had succeeded in sharpening his intellect and moulding his character. Their job had been easy as these qualities were already inherent in him. But for Sayajirao III the father, it was not so. His sons were headstrong, who had been spoilt with fine living, pampered as children and as grown young men, and further spoilt with too much money. Expensive schools in England had only served to expose them to the wrong side of Western culture, and temptations of the Western world. Words like duty, self-discipline and responsibility were alien to them and when they were subjected to talks from him on them, they drifted further away from him. His marathon efforts to bring them in line proved futile.

'Hard work *and* study?' was the horrified reaction from Dhairyashil when Sayajirao III suggested that he do so when his son had returned to Baroda. Sayajirao III had wanted him to divide his time between government, work and study. Dhairyashilrao's preference for a *dolce vita* existence was apparent and there were constant complaints from his superiors when he was put to work; Dhairyashilrao himself grumbled that he had no wish to work in a 'native state'. His father's reaction, can be summed up as despairing, was manifested in the reply, 'I tried in my small way to introduce better organization in my family; but the expectations have failed.'[7] He knew the reason for his son's aversion to work was that he was hankering for the temptations of the West as well.

Sayajirao III wrote to Viceroy Chelmsford to try and get Dhairyashilrao a commission in the cadet corps that the British were about to raise in India to placate Indians, who complained that in spite of the numbers of Indians who had served in the war, they were the minimum commissioned officers. Sayajirao III's influence worked and Dhairyashil was duly granted a commission in the cavalry. His father was so delighted that he ordered a horse that would 'serve as a charger for my son... who will be in an Indian cavalry regiment from 1 February 1920.'[8]

Jaisingh too had his share of criticism—he had returned from Harvard and to the horror of his father had become shockingly Americanized in his thoughts and speech too! Jaisingh had been employed in the highest cadre in the state's service but was often absent from work. Sayajirao III instructed his dewan to curtail his 'leave' and be more strict with him. To Jaisingh's protests that he was not given the privileges that the other state employees enjoyed, his father replied, 'You are your own worst enemy...'[9]

A truer statement could not have expressed the boy's character more clearly. Jaisingh by the age of thirty-four had become an incurable alcoholic, making his parents miserable. In the year 1919, Jaisingh was not responding to treatment; he had earlier been removed to a clinic at Charlottenburg in Germany, but it was becoming apparent that there was no hope of recovery for him. The same year, Sayajirao III's daughter-in-law Padmavati died of cancer. But, as if that was not enough, two weeks later, Shivajirao was dead too.

Shivajirao, the most athletic, high-spirited and lovable son of the family had his life snuffed out at the height of his youth. This was a severe blow to the Maharaja who had looked upon Shivajirao as one who showed most promise. In a letter from Dewan Manubhai dated 6 June 1918, 'Prince Shivajirao secured the post of one of the secretaries to Maharaja Holkar of Indore and is likely to leave next month. Has an idea of working in an honorary capacity and was anxious to send up his tippan without the intervention of the council.' His request was sent directly to Sayajirao III with the opinion of his guardian, 'His behaviour so far has been correct for the present.' The Maharaja's reply to this was: 'Since he should be allowed a fair start in his career, his allowance is to be adjusted and should be deferred for six months, and if he does not relapse into his bad habits and does honest work, then do not handicap him with any shortage in his nemnook (allowance), and let him not leave with any rancour in his mind.'[10]

But this was the briefest interlude in the boy's indulgences. Correspondence between the dewan and the Maharaja dealt only with medical treatments and doctors' reports of which one clearly stated, 'Prince Shivajirao is weak-willed, an alcoholic with a tendency towards depression.'[11]

Handsome and debonair, Shivajirao had been his mother's favourite and Sayajirao III had pinned all his hopes on him as the only one who could fulfil his hopes. The realization that Shivajirao would come to no good must have shocked and numbed Sayajirao III's senses, and that had serious effects on his health. He developed an apathy towards the affairs of the state as his thoughts centred on his family and the tragedies that surrounded it. He was tormented by guilt and a feeling of inadequacy that he had let things slide. He invited his widowed daughter-in-law Kamaladevi and her three children to live with him as well as Pratapsinghrao who had also suffered bereavement at the loss of his mother. In need of a large house for the purpose, he bought two houses—the house on the Russel estate near Watford and Lord Tennyson's house in Surrey called Aldsworth. This only gave him a brief respite from his gloomy thoughts but once the purchases were over, he lost interest in it and sank into the grief and pain.

When Sayajirao III sailed home conscious that he and the maharani were leaving Jaisingh to die alone in a foreign land, the journey made him so ill that when the ship docked at Bombay, he had to be in a wheelchair.

In the spring of 1922, there were two weddings in the family that brought some cheer. One was the wedding of Dhairyashil and the other, the wedding of granddaughter, Lakshmidevi, the daughter of his eldest son Fatehsinghrao III.

Sayajirao III and Chimnabai II left for Berlin where Jaisingh was a patient in a clinic since 1919. They were told that there was hardly any chance of a full recovery for him. They stayed on hoping for a miraculous recovery or for a specialist to suggest a cure that would enable it, but it was in vain.

Sayajirao III spent an interesting time trying to assess how the Germans were reacting to their defeat in the war and was pleasantly surprised to see them hard at work in their fields with their crops ready to be harvested. He admired the Germans' ability to look forward instead of backwards and wondered if Indians would have done the same in a similar situation and whether they would realize that being subjected to subservience was most humiliating.

At that precise moment in Indian history, Mahatma Gandhi was bringing about a wave of nationalism, which Sayajirao III watched with keen interest. Meanwhile, he and the maharani were told by the doctors that there was nothing in the way of a cure that could be done for Jaisingh. The royal couple left for Brussels with a heavy heart, and upon their arrival there, they received a cable from London informing them that their son-in-law, the Maharaja of Cooch Behar, was dying. In spite of the fact that they had strongly disapproved of their daughter Indira's marriage to him, they rushed to London to comfort their daughter; however, they reached London in time to hear the news of his death.

Repeated tragedies inflicted on a mortal being can turn the most soft-hearted to stone and Sayajirao III was plunged into depression. Fate had cruelly snatched from him his two sons while one lay dying, and now his daughter too had not been spared; her life was also marred with the loss of her husband, though it was rumoured that the marriage had not worked out and Indira was taking consolation in alcohol. A man reticent by nature taciturn to the extreme withdrew completely into a shell. Perhaps if his old friend Elliot had been alive Sayajirao III could have confided in him, but it is doubtful, for the agonizing pain caused by the irretrievable loss of a loved one is understood by only the one who has had to suffer the loss. He lost all interest in world affairs and spent nearly all of his time travelling around Europe where he could silently grieve, avoiding a return to Baroda where social graces and his status demanded that he keep up appearances.

In a letter to his dewan Sayajirao III said, 'I regret that my sons have turned out to be wasters due to a lack of discipline. Remedies should be found, so that fewer mistakes are committed in parental guidance and society benefits.'[12]

The year 1923 did not bring Sayajirao III any cheer either by way of hope of Jaisingh's recovery or financial recovery from the Villiers' disaster. But as if to take his mind off his immediate problems, in the summer of the same year, while in Rome, he got to meet the king of Italy, Victor Emmanuel and Benito Mussolini, the Italian dictator. Mussolini had not yet struck fear in the minds of the British and it was a British ambassador, David Graham, who had actually arranged the meeting. Perhaps the reason was that people did not fear Fascism the way they regarded and feared Communism.

Rome the fragment remains of a once powerful empire that influenced the civilizations of the world... The Greek and Roman civilizations have exerted great influence in moulding the destinies of the world, especially Europe. The remains of art and literature, one so fine, that makes one wonder at the sight of them.'[13]

Sayajirao III had an interesting conversation with the Italian dictator and came away very impressed by the 'rapid strides Italy had made under his leadership to win a place for itself among the nations.'[14] A man like Sayajirao III, who valued the infrastructural development of a country, was immensely appreciative at the tangible achievements of the dictator, in the fine buildings, stadiums and parks. He later even described his meeting with Mussolini, who had impressed him, and referred to him as 'a good man'!

Sayajirao III reached his favourite haunt, St Moritz, after his tryst with Rome and Mussolini only to receive the devastating news of Jaisinghrao's death on 27 August. In Stanley Rice's words, 'Jaisinghrao's body was conveyed to Paris where a kindly Indian Resident gave it shelter, and in his house it lay in state, covered with the ochre flag of the Gaekwad state... A cortege of the whole Indian colony and the personal staff of [the Maharaja] followed the coffin to the historic cemetery of Pere La Chaise.'[15]

The funeral was not attended by Sayajirao III who was beside himself with grief.

The following morning on 28 August a sense of impending doom blanketed his mind when, to his shock, he read his own obituary in the newspapers, the reason being the confusion in the name Gaekwad. Jaisinghrao's death had been reported in the Reuters newsflash and the newspapers had reported accordingly without bothering to check which Gaekwad it was. The English newspapers, while referring to the Maharaja as a great reformer, did not hesitate to allude to his little fracas with the British government and the coronation durbar incident. The Indian newspapers were, of course, very laudatory and spoke of his achievements. The moment he landed in Baroda, he was greeted by his people with tears in their eyes and people thronged from all over Gujarat to get a glimpse of their favourite ruler.

A deputation of the Kaliparaj tribe awaited him to make some demands. Sayajirao III as far back as 1884 had done much to make life easier for the tribe. A commission had been set up to study their problems and eradicate many of those that were caused by their traditional practices. He had abolished veth (free labour), a custom by which landowners made these tribal people work in their fields without paying them. Schools had been opened, wells dug, dispensaries for the sick had been set up and land had been set aside in their villages for which they were given special occupancy rights by the passing of a special Act. These primitive people, a carefree, ignorant lot with a devil-may-care attitude, were exploited by the traders and landowners in the village. Ever since the Kaliparaj tribe had obtained government support, they had resorted to violence to wreak vengeance on those landlords and merchants who had earlier exploited them. The position of these people was now reversed as they were the ones to be feared by the affluent members of the community. Besides, the Kaliparaj outnumbered the upper class by 1,50,000, whereas the landlords and merchants populating the villages were a scanty 500. With violence increasing every day it was a situation that could have been easily set right by calling out the army or even with armed policemen, but then there was an unexpected turn for the worse. A group of religious fanatics calling themselves Gaulis intruded into their midst. These people came from Baglan, which is in the district of Nasik, and allegedly were on a mission to reform the tribe and convert them to orthodox Hinduism. The true intent of the Gaulis was to instil fear into these animists through their own gods and subjugate them. These intruders who were just as primitive as the Kaliparaj tribe, in the name of religion wanted the tribe to give up their addiction to alcohol and become vegetarians. In order to convince them, they demonstrated through ceremonies to the Kaliparaj how infinitely more powerful their own gods were. The ceremonies were more in the nature of witchcraft with the Gauli head priest in the role of a witchdoctor mumbling some mumbo-jumbo meant to be incantations to drive away the old gods and goddesses whom the Kapilaraj had worshipped. Red banners which were supposed to contain the writings of the Mata were banished. Amidst cries of 'there runs Devlibai and Sailibai', the old deities were removed from their places of worship and the new deity goddess Bhavani was installed. Bhavani is the fearsome form of the goddess Parvati, Lord Shiva's consort. The Kapilaraj with their childlike innocence were thoroughly convinced when they were strictly told that the cult involved complete abstinence from alcohol and meat. The new converts immediately sold their poultry and sheep at throwaway prices, by which the Muslims and Parsis reaped a rich harvest! However, it did not take long for the Kapilaraj tribe to discover the hypocrisy of these evangelists who were consuming alcohol and meat on the quiet. Thoroughly disillusioned by what they saw and aroused to anger, they took the law into their own hands and attacked those who had bought their poultry and deprived them of their livelihood. They also vented their anger on the Gaulis who had taken them for a ride, by breaking up their camps and driving them out of their villages. As matters were getting out of hand, the authorities intervened and brought the situation under control. The Kapilaraj had every right to be angry, but they had no right to molest their fellow citizens. With the law cracking down on them they turned their wrath on the government which it seemed was actually on the side of their age-old enemies, the landlords and merchants and decided to revolt against the government.

But before that, they decided to wait for the Maharaja to return, knowing that he was a fair man and would see they got justice. The Maharaja after listening to their complaints sympathized with their predicament but pointed out that they had lost their poultry through their own foolishness and not under any compulsion. The delegates were severely rebuked and were bluntly told that some of the privileges granted to them by his government would be curtailed unless they reformed and gave evidence of good behaviour.

Thoroughly chastised, they took the scolding meekly and accepted his verdict. They left shamefaced and also with increased respect for the ruler who had chastised them. Sayajirao III, with his keen sense of perception, had known how to deal with these people who looked at softness as a sign of weakness. Philip Sergeant commented, 'The whole of the trouble which had threatened to develop into a class war... had subsided unexpectedly soon.'[16]

After his return, he gave a speech in Baroda in response to an address of welcome and his listeners were surprised to hear the Maharaja extol Gandhi's efforts to remove untouchability. At this time, the mere mention of Gandhi's name would have provoked a British police officer to land his stick on the back of the offending individual; some years later, John Revett-Carnac, a police officer, boasted of this feat to a BBC interviewer. And here was Gaekwad, who had already been on the 'rack' earlier with his name being linked to sedition, boldly praising the ace revolutionist who was thinking of winding up the Raj!

Sayajirao III had no qualms in referring to the 'messiah' of the Indian people in glowing terms in connection with the man's efforts to remove untouchability. Sayajirao III who believed in being true to himself and being the kind of person that he was—passionately devoted to the cause of the depressed classes—saw no reason why he should not be voluble about it. The Britishers saw it as a ruse to slip in Gandhi's name and made a silent note of it in their records. The fact that no derogatory reference was made to it was due to the fact that the freedom movement had advanced by leaps and bounds. Any open attack on the ruler of his stature would have triggered a widespread protest! It was not that Sayajirao III was being provocative, he was simply being himself. Gandhi's efforts for the cause of removing untouchability was a subject that was closest to Sayajirao III's heart and he felt it should not go unnoticed. It was as simple as that. Sayajirao III was a much travelled man and highly educated; even the most biased and cantankerous of British officials would not have failed to notice how he had evolved over the years and how his horizons had widened. His credibility with his people was above reproach, making his credentials unassailable. He saw himself more as a spectator watching the scene objectively. Sayajirao III, if truth be told, had become indifferent. He knew that driving the British out was only going to bring on more complications which would not be obliterated or effaced from the country by any one single person unless the country came together as a whole.

In the same speech, he said, 'I am getting old. I have reached the age of sixty.' That was his state of mind. In India then, sixty was looked upon by Indians as the time to retire and reflect on life, and watch the world go by. Perhaps the sentence reflected Sayajirao III's intentions of doing just that.

Soon after that, he gave a nostalgic speech to the students of the Baroda College, when he recalled the time he had laid the foundation stone for the college at the age of sixteen. 'The laying of the foundation stone of this building was one of the first public acts of my life. I was then but a boy of sixteen, full of the joy of life at is dawn, free from any cares other than those of a schoolboy. To visit an institution of which I have laid the foundation stone when I was a youth at a time when I have reached the present age touches chords within me which vibrate powerfully.' [17]

Soon after that, he was laid up in bed with an acute attack of gout. He had been made the vice chancellor of Banaras Hindu University and was due to go there to deliver the convocation address sometime in January the following year. In view of this important engagement, he had cancelled all others. By mid-January, he was well enough to travel but had a relapse on the train so that his speech which had been painstakingly prepared by him had to be read by his dewan. At the time of the convocation, the Maharaja fell very ill and could not leave Benares for a month and a half. Afterwards, he went to Delhi when he was still far from well. Compelled to spend another fortnight in the capital, he returned to Baroda in March. The weather was just beginning to get warmer and his health problems continued to plague him as he went down again with influenza and other complications. With the weather not being conducive for his recovery, he opted to move to Matheran, the hill station in the south of Bombay. The illness had ravaged him to such an extent that he had to be carried on a stretcher from the Laxmi Vilas Palace to Baroda station to board the train. He recouped a little in the cool hills of Matheran, and later left for Bombay by a special train. However, he was still too weak to walk and had to be carried on board the S. S. *Macedonia* in a wheelchair.

The summer of 1924 saw the Maharaja on his way to Europe accompanied by a medical team including his official coterie. It is difficult to identify the exact nature of his illness, but gout was the chief problem. There seemed no permanent cure, only palliatives which offered him temporary respite from his pain. In the final analysis it was thought that insufficient sleep had taken a toll on his stamina, leading to a number of health issues. Sayajirao III realized the vital importance of good health and never missed an opportunity to advocate a healthy lifestyle to people.

At the garden party given in his honour by the Baroda Municipality on 15 December 1937, Sayajirao III began his speech with, 'I am glad to have this opportunity of meeting you all this evening. When I accepted your kind invitation, I had no intention of making a speech, but after hearing what your president has to say on the progress of municipal activities and your aspirations, I am tempted to say a few words:

> It is indeed most gratifying to know that the city municipality is making slow but steady progress. Nevertheless it must be admitted that we are lagging far behind other nations. Progress depends upon the political, social and economic conditions of the day and there is no end to it. You would indeed be surprised if you could see what is being achieved in the outside world. That a lively curiosity in this respect has risen in Baroda, is a matter of great satisfaction. A healthy mind in a healthy body that is a proverb well known to you all. Health depends mainly upon sanitation and in turn, sanitation depends mainly upon doing your duty to yourself and to your neighbours. At all times you should have every consideration for others and not allow your outlook to be warped by petty-minded narrowness. Seek to make your surroundings clean and beautiful and you will help to create a healthy life for yourself and those around you. As I have already remarked, what you have done so far is but a tithe [one-tenth] of what is being done elsewhere. Education and perseverance are two remedies which will remove most municipal ills. Cultivate them sedulously and, in the fullness of time, the results will rebound to your honour and glory. The world is changing rapidly and we are apt to imitate everything new. But you must avoid slavish imitation.

Consult your own heart, study your own surroundings, see what is good and what is bad for you, rejecting the latter and retaining only the best. Such should be the great determining factor in the adoption of new methods or new equipment. A ruler and his administrators, those entrusted with office, are but part and parcel of society. They alone cannot carry society forward and there are obvious limits to progress unless the governed cooperate whole-heartedly with them. Success cannot be achieved single-handed. There must be genuine support and assistance from all.... You should be aware of what is published in the newspapers. Do not accept blindly or be misled by what others say, but subject everything to the test of reason. After all, man is endowed with a brain, he must use it to reason with, to worry out the solution of his own problems, and thus keep himself abreast of times. I started my public life with such ideals and I hit upon education as the only solution for all civic ills. Let me urge you all to educate yourselves for a healthy civic life and to remember that your duty lies in creating a vigorous atmosphere for such a life, and insistently claiming it. It is easy to clamour for power and to ask for a share in the administration, without any such training. It is much more difficult, but very much more fruitful, to offer proper and efficient cooperation in carrying on a government for the good of the people. I congratulate you on having this magnificent building as your headquarters. I doubt if any municipality in India has one more imposing and I trust that it may constantly stimulate you to imposing efforts and achievements. I congratulate you also upon the progress you have so far achieved in civic welfare and I trust that the economic welfare of my people will increase in no less measure.[18]

He had in one of his speeches advocated physical exercise to be healthy. 'A healthy mind is a healthy body', yet, he was plagued with anxieties, official and personal. From the time he had ascended the gaddi, sleep had walked out of the window; he never knew the luxury of a good night's sleep. The Maharaja's close friend G.S. Sardesai recalled his time with Sayajirao III and said, 'He would have me read to him every night. By dawn, his eyes would be closed and thinking that sleep had finally overtaken him, I would close the book and be ready to leave when without opening his eyes, he would point out to exactly where I had stopped and ask me to continue reading.'[19]

Either it was the sea air or the fact that he was 'away from it all', but his health perked up on the voyage and in Aden he was able to discard the wheelchair!

He spent spring at his new house in Watford, from which he derived a great deal of pleasure. Summer saw him in Paris to try the cure first at Evian and later at Bagnolo del'Horno. For a time, he felt better with the waters and the change of scene, but this was only a temporary respite as the treatment did not do lasting good.

In Paris, he thought it was time he learnt French since most of his time in Europe was spent in France and thus he engaged a tutor, Mademoiselle Lux, to teach him the language after he bought a house on No. 6, Avenue Van-Dyck.

Whenever in Europe, Sayajirao III made it a point to visit London as frequently as he could and this trip was no exception. He had many friends there whose company he enjoyed. At the end of May 1925, when he was back again in Paris to continue with his French lessons, he heard at a luncheon that his old friend Madhavrao Scindia of Gwalior had fallen seriously ill on board the ship and had been brought to Paris for treatment. Sayajirao III, greatly disturbed at the news, did his best to see that his friend was comfortable and had good medical treatment. However, the best did not do for him and Madhavrao Scindia, not responding to the treatment, died on 5 June 1925. The man who had nearly become his son-in-law was now no more and it was with a heavy heart that he attended his funeral and left for London. He shunted between Paris and London till November when he left for Baroda looking forward to being there in the year of his golden jubilee.

By 1926, the relationship between Sayajirao III and Chimnabai II had become decidedly strained. She managed the Khangi Karbari and Sayajirao III, who was frugal by nature, felt that she was overspending and not keeping proper accounts. Requests were sent through letters through the dewan and in reply to one where Chimnabai II had requested for a gold tea service and the rate of interest on her Dharmadaya savings (invested by her), the Maharaja had exclaimed, 'Is this family divided or a joint one? Both of you are working on a wrong principal... Why does she jump into commercial affairs that bring her losses? She has been well provided for and should be satisfied. I need knowledge of her private money...'[20]

Relations were also strained because of the unhappiness over the loss of their sons and now Dhairyashil was proving to be no better than his brothers as he too led a dissipated life. There was no earthly reason for Dhairyashil to take refuge in alcohol; in fact, he had every reason to want to live. As the only surviving son, he was reckoned to be the heir apparent to the throne—then, what was the cause? The Maharaja's grandson Pratapsinghrao was being groomed for the job as was made obvious to all and more so to Dhairyashil who must have felt thwarted watching, with frustrated eyes, the moulding and grooming that was going on for his nephew for obvious purposes. Chimnabai II too must have been resentful of this.

Pratapsinghrao had been brought to live in the Laxmi Vilas Palace with his grandparents after his mother Padmavati had died in 1919. The maharani gave the same stepmotherly treatment to Pratapsinghrao. Sayajirao III, shrewd and observant by nature, was aware of his wife's behaviour towards her step-grandson, so he had him watched as he suspected his life was in danger. Dhairyashil was the only surviving son of Chimnabai II and she would want to have him seated on the throne of Baroda hence Sayajirao III felt uneasy about the state of affairs. He instructed his loyal servant Kashirao Jadhav, 'Treat Pratapsinghrao as your own son. If anyone gives him anything to eat and drink, test it first, wait awhile, then give it to him. Do you understand the implications of what I am saying?' Kashirao kept his promise and in the process of testing the boy's food, the loyal friend and servant lost his life. This incident was recounted by Subhadrabai, Kashirao's daughter. After this incident, the marital relationship of the Maharaja and maharani was one of mutual discord.[21]

Dhairyashil's health was taking a turn for the worse. In a letter the dewan reported to Sayajirao III, 'Prince Dhairyashil's liver is enlarged due to alcoholic indulgences, his heart is weak and he has kidney disorders. His habits must improve. Her Highness is proceeding to Poona to bring him back to Baroda.'[22]

The Maharaja, perturbed over the reports, felt that Chimnabai II and the dewan were not looking after Dhairyashil the way they should, for in his letter of 16 September 1926 to the dewan he complained, 'A domestic matter like this ought to be properly and effectively arranged by our own people and not ask for intervention of the British government. A little firmness and knowledge of daily life seems to be lacking in which these things are managed... Children have been allowed to get out of hand and now it is too late!'[23]

This guilt was so firmly entrenched in Sayajirao's mind that he decided to raise his grandsons very differently. Pratapsinghrao, being the eldest of his grandsons, underwent rigorous discipline. He was instructed by the Maharaja in a letter from Paris, 'I want you to join Baroda College and if possible learn Survey and Accounts out of college hours.' Further, in a letter to the dewan in July 1926, he instructed, 'Let Pratapsingh follow the usual college curriculum... I think a little more education in Algebra and Trigonometry will certainly not do him any harm, but will help to develop his mental and reasoning powers which are of much importance. I only wish that these subjects could be taught in an intelligent manner and not crammed. All young men of the rich, especially children, have to be pointed out the importance of education and how at a certain stage it is necessary to take trouble to acquire it. Still, if they show disinclination to learn then it will be their own concern and if any losses accrue from it, it will be their own fault.'[24]

Sayajirao III was very anxious that Pratapsinghrao remain in Baroda under his watchful eye. When it was suggested that he should go to Poona for his college studies, Sayajirao III insisted that he should go through the entire curriculum, and take the full college course in Baroda. He opined, 'With regard to Pratapsingh, education is more important for a prince than for ordinary men.'[25] Not only did he lay down strictures in education but also in wasteful expenditure. There is an interesting story in connection with this:

Once Pratapsinghrao, as a young lad in Baroda College, brought four friends to the palace with him and they stayed for dinner. The Maharaja too was present at dinner though he occupied a separate table to let the young men have their privacy. After dinner, the boys spent some time chatting in the prince's room and then left for the night. Sayajirao III, after making sure that they had left the palace, had Pratapsinghrao summoned by one of the staff. Pratapsinghrao duly arrived and stood before his grandfather. Sayajirao III asked him, 'Pratap, did you inform the household staff that you would be bringing your friends home to dinner?'

Pratapsinghrao said, after some hesitation, 'No, Baba, I did not.'

Sayajirao III then had the chief chef and the server summoned.

Sayajirao III asked, 'Did you know that Pratapsingh would be bringing guests for dinner?'

The kitchen staff knew there was no point in trying to protect the prince with a lie as his grandfather would definitely catch him out, so playing safe, the chef said, 'No, Maharaj.'

Sayajirao III asked, 'Can you give me an estimate of the cost of each boy's dinner based on how much he consumed?'

After a few minutes, they came up with a figure.

The Maharaja thanked them and they left.

Sayajirao III then said to Pratapsingh, 'The amount will be deducted from your allowance and in future without prior information to the kitchen department do not invite your friends for a meal here.'

Pratapsinghrao, who knew better than to argue with his grandfather, apologized for his thoughtlessness and left.[26]

Pratapsinghrao was not in any way upset at being chastised by the old patriarch as much as he was annoyed with himself for having stepped out of line in his grandfather's eyes. Years later when he ascended the throne of Baroda in 1939, he paid the finest tribute to his grandfather when the credit for Baroda's progress was given to V.T. Krishnamachari. In the young prince's words, 'The credit for having made modern Baroda cannot be claimed by any of his ministers. Baroda owes its good name and repute as an advanced and efficient state to the genius and strenuous efforts of my illustrious grandfather. In this stupendous work, Maharaja Sayajirao was the chief architect and skilful organizer; he was ably assisted by a galaxy of great dewans who left no room for any interposition of the authority by the paramount power. The dewans risen from local service and the dewans imported from outside all faithfully helped their great ruler in carrying out his master plans—they included within their rank statesmen like Sir T. Madhav Rao, Bahadur Srinivas Iyengar, R. C. Dutt, B. L. Gupta and some others.

'The last twenty years of my revered grandfather's life were sadly embittered by the unfortunate bereavements in the family and the dewans, but even during this trying period, Sir Manubhai Mehta and Sir V.T. Krishnamachari only followed the lines of the policy so wisely chalked out by him. Baroda for its sagacious policy in the matter of compulsory education, libraries and local self-government was held up by even the British House of Commons as a model of enlightened administration for British India to emulate!'[27]

Pratapsinghrao accompanied Sayajirao III on his tours around the districts of the Gujarat province and was exposed to administrative problems and the politics of the state at a young age, which stood him in good stead as he was able to fulfil his grandfather's aspirations for Baroda to a certain extent.

In fact, there are instructions from Sayajirao III in Paris by cable to Dewan Manubhai Mehta, 'Pratapsingh should attend the council and sign as extra member whenever matters of public work are discussed enabling him to learn the workings of the council, but it should not interfere with his other studies.'[28] Reports on the young prince mentioned that he was above average in his studies, had an excellent memory and was fond of riding, swimming, polo, and also played a good game of tennis. He was keen on his work—a point which must have pleased his grandfather no end and also the fact that he hated English food! The other two grandsons too were given the benefit of good education. Udaysinghrao and Khanderao were the sons of Shivajirao. After Shivajirao's death, both the sons were first sent to Rajkot College and then later to Cambridge. Both Udaysinghrao and Khanderao had a strict upbringing and had to make do with the small allowance given to them. Interestingly, to testify to this there is a letter from Udaysinghrao to his grandfather dated 26 October 1937 when he found himself broke:

My dear Baba,

I was delighted to learn you are coming to Cambridge and look forward to meeting you on Thursday the 28th.

I am extremely worried by the recent orders which you have passed regarding our finances which as they are already none too lavish and I request you earnestly to reconsider the matter favourably. I feel there is great injustice done to us, penalized for no fault of ours but for the shortcomings of others which may have annoyed you. We have always tried our best in carrying out our filial duties towards you, our beloved grandfather, and shall ever continue to do so, for which we never expect a reward as it is after all our duty to do so. But do hope at least to be treated fairly and kindly.

I hope dear Baba, you will realize such shocks cause great mental distress which has a very undermining effect on one's health.

Signed:

Yours,
Most Affectionately,[29]

The Maharaja must have been sorely tempted to concede to the request made by his young grandson but the thought of what excesses can do to a young man's life must have prevented him from capitulating. After all, he had lost his sons that way. His reply was contrary to the grandson's expectations and his letter ended with the words, 'If I had begun with some of the cuts when the allowances began, there would have been no cause for complaint...'[30]

His other grandson, Khanderao, while thanking his grandfather for the £85 sent to him, requested an additional sum to meet his coaching fees, to which the Maharaja replied, 'To give young men more money than is really needed is to give them a chance to get spoilt. It is with this object that I have fixed the sum. All the money is to come from your income. Your wants must not exceed the amount allowed.'[31]

The Maharaja saw to it that his widowed daughter-in-law and her three children were well provided for in shares and securities, which were put in a trust for Udaysinghrao and Khanderao with their mother as the trustee who enjoyed a substantial income for the rest of her life.

Sayajirao III made his daughters-in law Kamaladevi (Shivajirao's wife) and Shakuntalaraje (Jaisinghrao's wife) attend office and learn to work there so as to make them conversant with the procedures and all the ramifications of administration. This was also done to make them independent and manage their affairs efficiently and properly and not become tools in the hands of officers and intermediaries.

The year 1926, after his golden jubilee, saw the Maharaja spend hardly any time in India. But he returned in November during the winter since Manubhai Mehta (who had been knighted by the British) was leaving the service of the Baroda state after having served it for so long. Sayajirao III now had to find a replacement and his discerning eye fell on a veteran Madras civil servant, V.T. Krishnamachari. Sayajirao III discovered to his delight that he had made an 'inspired choice' for VTK was not only capable of handling the day-to-day administration of the state entirely on his own but could deal with any crisis without the intervention of the British or the Maharaja. By the end of the year, he had won the confidence of Sayajirao III to such an extent that the Maharaja began to depend solely on him for all matters—that the tables were so swiftly turned speaks volumes for the dewan's capabilities! V.T.K served the Baroda state for seventeen years.

By 1927, the boy, who had come from the village Kavlana and had become a prince, had seen it all and done it all, but his not-yet-jaded eyes thirsted for more and he was granted this for he was among the first Indians to experience air travel provided by the London–Paris service of the early 1920s. He was also among the thousands of spectators to watch and gasp with wonder at the first aircraft 'breaking through the clouds over LeBourget aerodrome near Paris. Charles Lindenberg had crossed the Atlantic. The flying age had finally arrived!'[32]

Sayajirao III and Chimnabai II left for Geneva where he learnt from the newspapers that Baroda was being ravaged by floods. Frantic cables to VTK did not solicit a response for the simple reason that all communications had been cut off! He learnt in the course of a few days that the monsoon had made a late arrival and had been heavy but the pre-monsoon rain had also been so heavy that the Vishwamitri River overflowed its banks, flooding the areas in many places. The Vishwamitri flows through the city, hence the danger of floods. But this was not an isolated case, as floods happened every year. On 24 July there was such a downpour that by nightfall the river had divided the city into small islands, making it necessary to cross by boat. Part of the railway track too had been submerged in water with the continuous fall of rain for four days. People were marooned on trees or on top of their houses as the interiors were flooded with water. The floods claimed lives and cattle not to mention the high numbers of people who were stranded, homeless. The wild animals and exotic birds in the Baroda Zoo died in their cages. VTK was a pillar of strength in the crisis and handled it with exemplary initiative, strength, calmness and fortitude. He organized rescue operations, distributed food, blankets and water to the needy and established temporary camps for displaced people to stay in till the waters receded. After the crisis was over, resettlement operations were on in full swing. Loans and free building material for those who had lost their homes were given without undue delays.

When Sayajirao III returned to Baroda expecting to see a devastated state, he was pleasantly surprised to see a city restored, though there was still unmistakable evidence of extensive damage. It was also obvious to him that a lot of work had gone into bringing about some semblance of normalcy after the floods. It heartened him to know that the more affluent among his subjects had donated generously towards relief work that was still on. He was even more heartened to know that help had arrived from the neighbouring districts and even from Bombay. He must have blessed the day he had chosen VTK, with his phenomenal organizing abilities and energy, to be the dewan of Baroda!

The Simon Commission was to visit India in 1928. Now, this commission was a group of seven British members of parliament under the chairmanship of Sir John Allsebrook Simon. The commission arrived in India to study constitutional reforms in British's most important colonial dependency and suggest new reforms. One of the members was Clement Atlee who became committed to Indian independence in 1934 and achieved that goal much later. Now, the Indians were enraged that the Simon Commission had not included a single Indian member.

The Simon Commission left England in January and arrived in Bombay on 3 February. Almost immediately on arrival, its members were confronted by throngs of protesters, even though there were some supporters in the crowd who saw it as the next step on the road to self-government. A strike began and many people turned out to greet the commission with black flags.

This occurred in every city the seven members of the commission chose to visit. In Lahore, a similar protest was staged and Lala Lajpat Rai, who had moved a resolution against the commission in the legislative assembly of Punjab, was among the protesters. In order to make way for the commission, the local police got violent and Lajpat Rai was beaten. He died two weeks later in a hospital.

The outcome of the commission was the Government of India Act, 1935, wherein the British government stated that Indian opinion would henceforth be taken into account and that the natural outcome of the constitutional process would be dominion status for India. Despite the protests, the Simon Commission went about doing its business of fact-finding to decide in to what extent to grant political concessions to India.

The Indian princes, who were commonly divided among themselves, were expected to make a common representation to the commission. Sayajirao III with a view to offer his opinion privately to the princes planned a tour of some of the major central Indian states such as Gwalior, Bhopal, Dewas and Kotah (Kota now). He also went to Sanchi to see its famous Buddhist relics. By the end of February he was back in Baroda to hold a public durbar to bestow rewards and honours upon those of his officials who had done commendable work during the floods and to those who had donated generously to the flood relief fund. Ever since he had lost his sons, he had become detached from worldly affairs and now at the age of sixty he withdrew from being too actively involved with the administration of the state. He had a most capable man as his dewan and left most of the governance to him.

To be sure, wherever he was abroad, he wrote and issued instructions to his dewan which were mostly of a general nature and invariably hedged with provisos. He did not seek consolation in the social life of Europe; he had become a sort of a loner though not a recluse. Whenever he felt well and got a brief respite from his wheelchair, he became active and attended many public and social engagements. In the 'interludes of good health and in the mood for novelties,' [33] he began to take lessons in skiing at the age of sixty. Five years later, persuaded by Indira, whose relationship with her father had changed after she had lost her husband, he went hunting with some of the most famous packs in England. In England, he led the life of an English country squire of his age with enough resources to indulge in expensive sports, hobnobbing with the right sort and spending as much time in the open air as possible. He had worked like a horse and to the best of his ability, had achieved a lot, fulfilled the task that had been entrusted to him by his adoptive mother Jamnabai and now he had no regrets.

The wave of nationalism sweeping the country was to bring along with it the winds of change that would not only sweep away the Raj, but also the princes and, what he had termed as 'rubbishy states' would disappear. It was inevitable—the old order must goeth and the new order must cometh. Sayajirao III's pragmatism made him accept the fact that what he had prophesized some years ago came true, but logically when that did happen, he wanted to be spared the mental adjustments that would be demanded of him. Now, in his twilight years, it was time to stop playing the principal role in the drama of life!

In the beginning of winter in 1929, he was in Baroda to witness the wedding of his grandson and heir apparent, Pratapsinghrao, which took place on 4 January 1929. Pratapsinghrao, who was only twenty-one, was married to Shantadevi, the daughter of Sardar Mansinghrao Ghorpade of Kolhapur. According to the tradition of that era, the bride was chosen by Sayajirao III, no doubt assisted in the task by the Gaekwad ladies. But, as the grand old patriarch of the family had imbibed something of the broad-mindedness of the West in the course of his travels, Pratapsinghrao too had been consulted in the matter.

Soon after the wedding, the bride was made to sit down for her English lessons with her tutor, no doubt at the behest of Sayajirao III whose passion was education! Apart from the wedding of his grandson, Sayajirao III had the visit of the new viceroy, Lord Irwin, to look forward too, though it also caused him a little anxiety because of the volatile political climate in India at that time.

Viceroy Irwin was not Viceroy Hardinge nor did he have the mentality of Viceroy Curzon who had displayed a derisive patronizing attitude of a thoroughbred Englishman looking down on a 'native' prince or commoner, with the view that these natives were all the same. Lord Irwin was a reasonable, compassionate, wise man who had done much to bring calmness to the smouldering haystack of resentment that was the dominant feature in the politics of India. He was not an Englishman prejudiced by racial differences and perceived matters in its truth and practicality. He had probably remarked to his closest friends that if Indians wanted their country to be restored to them, then it should be! This thinking led him to make his celebrated pact with Gandhi at the risk of jeopardizing his own career!

Lord Irwin's visit to Baroda, though expected and watched with some trepidation, passed very well. The visit had been meaningful with more than an exchange of polite platitudes. There were veiled references to the political situation in India and the impending changes that would be brought about by the recommendations of the Simon Commission. It was referred to obliquely by Sayajirao III at the durbar held in honour of Viceroy Irwin, 'We are on the edge of an approaching crisis...'[34] If the recommendations made in the Simon Commission's report were rejected by the Congress leaders, the peace in the country would be shattered and with the nation up in arms over it, there was no saying what would happen. Even though people were to a great extent, as Gandhi's followers, following the path of non-violence, still anything could trigger it off on a mass scale and destroy the political stability of India. It was only recently that a bomb had been thrown in the legislative assembly while Sir John Simon and some other members were in the House; and an attempt had also been made to blow up the train that the viceroy had been travelling in. However, contrary to Sayajirao III's fears, the viceroy's three-day visit to Baroda passed without a hitch. By now, it was clear to both the viceroy and the Maharaja as well as to the shaky paramount power in England that unless the Congress leaders accepted the Simon Commission's programme, the Raj would not have any force. Since the terms of the Simon Commission had been decided solely by the British and could only be advantageous to them, it was doubtful if the Congress party, which had complete sway in India, would agree to it. The Raj wielding its baton over the native princes and the Indian populace were drawing to a close. The bigwigs of the Raj were gently being elbowed out of the Indian political scenario.

After Lord Irwin's visit, Sayajirao III took time off to open a new reservoir which was to be an additional source and supply of water to the denizens of the Baroda state and was named Pratapsagar Sarovar.

63

Rebellion in the Air

The Roundtable Conferences did nothing much except cause a skirmish among Indians themselves and among Indian representatives fighting with each other wanting to have a say and play a more important part in the making of laws for the benefit of their communities. The Third Roundtable Conference was sparsely attended; even Sayajirao III was not present and a month later he was on his way to India.

Between 1930 and 1932, there was a rush of correspondence between the secretaries of the government of India and the Resident in Baroda regarding problems arising from seditious activities and other crimes being committed by those residing in territories owned by the British as also those residing in the Baroda territory and evading capture by the police by escaping to different areas in the Gujarat province.

As mentioned earlier, British territories were interlaced with Baroda territories, so much so that it was impossible to decipher which was British territory and which was the Baroda state. Further adding to this complex situation was those people who belonged to the part of Gujarat controlled by the British and were termed as British subjects while those residing in the territories owned by Sayajirao III were likewise termed Baroda subjects. Now towards 1930, sedition was rife—rebellion was breaking out in almost all parts of India. On the face of it, thanks to the capabilities of Dewan V. T. Krishnamachari, Baroda was spared the blame. In this case, history did not repeat itself.

A letter dated 16 December 1930 to Sir Charles Watson, political secretary to the government of India, from Resident C. G. Crosswaite stated, 'A note on the informal meeting between the commissioner, of the northern division, the dewan of Baroda state and myself, held at the Residency on 15 December 1930 to discuss the situation prevalent on the borders of the Baroda and British districts of Kaira, Broach and Surat. Baroda territory is extensively used not only as a refuge for colonies of migrated British subjects seeking to evade payment of revenue dues, but also partly as a result of the latest Ordinance IX as centres for agitation, meetings, and propaganda by both British and Baroda subjects. The dewan admitted the existence of the colonies of immigrant cultivators, but explained the difficulty he found in taking any legal action to turn them out. He explained that all his local officers had instructions to do their utmost to persuade these unwelcome guests to return to their homes, but the result had not been encouraging. Baroda revenue code was practically identical with the Bombay land revenue code.

'As centres for meetings and propaganda, the dewan was ready to hand over, under extradition procedures, any undesirable person the British authorities might name. In connection with this, there was a police enquiry to trace parcels containing Congress patrikas from the Baroda railway station and Mr C.N. Amin's house was searched on suspicion on 1 April 1930. A duplicating machine and other articles were found which were duly handed over to the British police.

'His Highness's government proposed to take proceedings against Amin under the security sections of the local criminal procedure code. But he is absconding and is believed to be hiding either in Ahmedabad, Ujjain or Nadiad.

'There are complaints from the district magistrates that the printing of Congress pamphlets was taking place in Baroda territory. While not denying these allegations, the Baroda authorities pointed out to the Kaira District Police of the existence of a cyclostyle printer used for printing these pamphlets in the British village called Ras and the cyclostyle printer was subsequently seized with a number of the Congress propaganda pamphlets. It was also stated that Congress refugees were taking shelter in the Baroda state and are conducting their propaganda from the border villages, frequently crossing over when the opportunity arises. These reports have been brought to the notice of the dewan.'[1]

Both the British authorities and the Baroda government caught in the welter of democracy had to deal with the Gujarati populace who now chose to chant the mantra 'Gujarat for Gujaratis', making the Maratha officials take an anti-Congress stand! The report further stated:

> Congress influence in the Baroda city during the past two weeks appears to have been concentrated on attacks against the post office, savings bank and government currency note issues. The Bank of

Baroda has been called on to encash government currency notes to a very large amount and efforts have been made by Congress to frighten people as to their value. Then, there was the perplexing problem of how to deal with British subjects who had committed offences in British Indian territory, under the ordinances recently promulgated and who had fled to Baroda territory and likewise Baroda subjects who had committed similar offences in British Indian territory and who had thereafter returned to Baroda.

The dewan of Baroda wanted to know what policy the government of India wished him to adopt apropos the Hijrat movement into the Baroda state during the Civil Disobedience movement.

The dewan assures that Baroda state border is being closely watched.

The report is signed by C. G. Crosswaite.

Crosswaite also wrote a letter to Watson, the Resident at Baroda:

My Dear Watson,

Sub: Financial assistance to the Civil Disobedience Movement.

From a hint or two I have received from a certain quarter, I have reasons to believe that such Congress funds may be deposited in the Bank of Baroda either at headquarters here or in their branches such as Naosari.

I mentioned my suspicions to Dewan Krishnamachari who gave me to understand that there were no reasons for my suspicions. The Bank of Baroda under the managership of Mr Randle who as a banker is unable to give me any information that is more than worthwhile. If the CID could give special attention to the possibility of the following:

Have there been any recent transfers of suspicious sums from the Bombay Bank or Bank of Baroda's branch in Bombay or any branch of any bank in any state into the Bank of Baroda in the Baroda state?[2]

Watson's reply to Crosswaite was:

Baroda durbars gladly agreed to take action and extradite British subjects who commit offences in British India under the ordinance recently promulgated and take refuge in Baroda territory.

They also note with satisfaction that the Baroda durbar is prepared to extradite Baroda subjects who commit similar offences in British India and return to Baroda.

His Highness's co-operation is welcome in the matter of preventing Congress leaders and supporters from taking refuge in Baroda territory, and if so, to take action in Baroda itself, against demonstrations in favour of Congress or activities in pursuance of the Congress programme.

The government of India considers it most important that such action should be taken immediately in order that Congress may not be able to establish a centre for further activity in Baroda territory.

Enquiries into Congress funds being deposited in Baroda, you will be informed immediately of the result of those enquiries.[3]

Thus, the Indian national movement gained considerable momentum between 1930 and 1947 with the civil disobedience movement, the boycott of British goods, satyagraha and other protests leaving the British with their senses reeling and India in a worse state of confusion.

Within a few days of Sayajirao III's return to Baroda, adulatory reference to Gandhi as the 'messiah' of the Indian people did not go unnoticed by the British officials who made a careful note of it in their records. Sayajirao III, always true to the person he really was, had no qualms in extolling Gandhi's virtues in connection with untouchability.

Perhaps the fact that the freedom movement had reached a stage at which it was too late for the paramount power to object strongly to a ruler of Sayajirao III's stature praising the nationalist without causing a massive revolution not only in the province of Gujarat but in most parts of India, they chose to remain silent spectators.

In 1930, an event that brought joy into Sayajirao III's life was the birth of his great-grandson. On 2 April, Shantadevi gave birth to a son who was named Fatehsingh. The event was celebrated state-wide and the day was declared a public holiday in the Baroda state. The Maharaja was happy and secure in the knowledge that fate had been kind to him in providing a successor to the gaddi. In high spirits, he left for Paris. His earlier attack of gout in the summer of Baroda had gone untreated and now in Paris, with treatment, he was better but it did not bring him much relief.

Dominion status for India that Lord Irwin had supported, and which was finally granted after the Simon Commission had completed its report, was contrary to the Indian people's expectations. It was a moderate form of provincial autonomy with the real powers still in the hands of the British.

There had been no formal transfer of power to India.

Many Indians protested. The princes who had earlier formed a part of the Chamber of Princes which had been set up nearly a decade ago but with the big states like Hyderabad, Mysore and Baroda showing pallid interest in it, the Chamber of Princes had dissolved with nothing solved. When the Roundtable Conference was to take place, Lord Irwin had these princes invited to be the Indian representatives in the conference. Sayajirao III who was indisposed, suddenly perked up as the conference drew near and decided to attend it himself instead of sending his dewan who was to deputize for him in case he couldn't make it.

For the first time in his life, Sayajirao III gave a speech in the House of Lords where he said he hoped that all efforts by all present would ensure the success of the conference. But despite 'all efforts', the Roundtable Conference was a disaster in view of the fact that Gandhi and the Indian National Congress boycotted its proceedings. It was believed that the Indian representatives had played false and did not have the Indians' interests at heart, particularly the princes. Finally, the Raja of Bikaner, Sir Ganga Singh, being the princes' spokesperson, said that they too would like a federal form of government even if it meant losing some of their powers. Later, they must have regretted their decision because when India eventually got its independence, the first thing that the Indian government did was wind up the princely states.

Sayajirao III did not believe in a democratic form of government for India, but that is not to say that he believed in an autocratic one. He simply felt that India as a nation was not ready for democracy, but what it needed was a strong ruler who would govern the nation with wisdom and bring the people together to unite as one whole—only then would there be real progress. Yes, it was important to drive the aliens out of India's soil but that was not going to resolve the multitudinous problems that the country would face after independence—the divisions in caste, community, religion would forever be stumbling blocks to the nation's real progress. He was right. The buck was passed down to ministers and their subordinates so that by the time the source was detected the problem was forgotten as other worse ones cropped up and the state or country remained in a welter of confusion. Probably that was why the Maharaja preferred to be away from the scene and chose to be *non persona grata* in the nationalist movement, which was so predominant in the political environment of the country that time.

In the first week of November 1932, the new viceroy, Lord Willingdon, and his wife paid a visit to the city of Baroda as the Maharaja was in the state and had not left for his travels abroad. The Willingdons and Sayajirao III were very well acquainted and their friendship had lasted for twenty years.

The Baroda College also celebrated its golden jubilee on 25 December 1932. In spite of it being the festival of Christmas, the hall was packed with the faculty, students of the university and guests. Fifty long years had gone by and the Maharaja, who had laid its foundation stone, began his speech with nostalgia:'A crowd of memories comes surging into my mind when I look back in thought through the dim corridors of the past and connect today's festivity with an event which was one of the first public acts of my reign—the laying of the foundation stone of this College, which has just completed its first half century. When I look back on this early event, I think of the men who were around me and associated with me in this task; when I find that I am the only one of them left to be present here today; when I survey the hopes, fears, expectations, the devotion and labour of all those who tried to make a success of the cause of the spread of education in my state, I would not be human if the memory of all this had not stirred up the deepest and tenderest thoughts in me. At the same time, my heart swells with very natural joy and pride when I cross over, as it were, in mind from the dusty plain, the lines of excavation, the heaps of mortar and bricks, a trowel and a stone on that cool evening in January nearly fifty-four years ago, to the ordered paths and drives and green lawns; the magnificent pile surmounted by a wonderful dome and, what is even more, to the large and joyful foregathering of those who have received and those who are being nurtured in the ambience of these buildings.

'My earliest convictions, as far as I can recall them, were concerned with the promotion of education among people. I had begun to realize that it was the lever by which our country and our people could be moved from the inertia of ages that had weighed them down.

'The Baroda College was founded under my aegis in 1879, when I was quite a boy. There was then widespread interest in higher education and it was hoped that the seed planted would grow into a strong and vigorous tree.

'Those hopes and expectations have been realized, for we have met today under the shade of the wide spreading branches of that tree, bearing the promise of a very fruitful future. We therefore owe it to ourselves to think on this occasion with a grateful and reverent memory of all those who, with clear vision and foresight, prepared the ground, took much thought to nurse this growing sapling, watered it with the sweat of their brow and breathed into it the passionate breath of their souls...

'I have always looked upon education as an essential thing to instill the spirit of progress of the people at large. Being aware of the importance of education and desiring that all my people should enjoy in some measure the advantages of education, I inaugurated a policy of compulsory education throughout my state.

'In the minds of the present generation, science has come to dominate the field of education. There can be no doubt that the study of any branch of natural science opens possibilities of discovering new truths. There is scarcely a branch of Physics or Chemistry or of Biology or Natural History in which the student may not hope to extend the boundaries of knowledge.

'This is what makes or should make the study of science so attractive.

'One is occupied with what is permanent, one is in quest of reality...

'The value of knowledge depends on the use we make of it; if we use it for selfish objects or ignoble purposes we had better be without it. Those high and noble faculties of mind and will which is not the exclusive inheritance of any race or country have been given to us not that we may employ them for our own benefit alone, or cultivate them merely for their own sake, but that by developing them to the utmost we may apply them to the welfare of our fellow men, whether they be rich or poor. Realization of this truth makes for the correct spirit of democracy. This is an ideal worthy of our most constant effort. We must not be content with the measure of success we have already achieved. I know that it is much easier to criticize than to construct, and I would not have you think that I am unmindful of the good points of our higher educational system. But I am conscious of the defects and I hope you are too because it should be your aim so to perfect the system, so that those who come after you may receive even greater benefits than you are receiving. It is the task of the youth, which has had the benefit of education, to show the world what true democracy is. There will be real democracy when every man, woman and child in a state is filled with an irrepressible desire to do everything possible to make that community better, stronger and freer. This ideal cannot be achieved without educated people—educated not only in letters but educated in those deep, and moral truths which are implied in the phrase "the service of the community".

'Students of the Baroda College, let me ask you to realize that your position as men and women of higher education and your influence among your fellow citizens is great—it must be great and must increase. Resolve each one of you that you will give your best thought, your best work, not only to furthering your own individual interest which is of course natural, but also to the great community of which you are a unit. This is the surest way to achieve that fundamental unity which is the greatest and the most crying need of our country. Remember too that what is also needed in a democratic country is that we should not only level the mass upwards as far as it is capable of rising, not only make the highroads of learning wide and make them free to all who can walk, but also that we should not impede the progress of those who wish to motor or fly...

'I do trust that you will find the time, for there certainly is the opportunity, to give thought to, and lend a helping hand in, this work of such tremendous moment to the fair name and prestige of this great land.'[4]

64
Birthday Celebrations

In the year 1933, the grand doyen of reforms was turning seventy. It was a very special year, not only for him and his family but also for the people of Baroda who revered him and loved him deeply, so much so, that even eighty years later, after he left the throne vacant for his descendants, people eulogize him. For a man of his stature, with a life full of achievements to his credit, his seventieth birthday was a landmark of special significance and justified the celebration that followed.

The celebrations in Baroda were held in advance, prior to his birthday, which was actually on 17 March, and were over by mid-March to enable him to go to Maharashtra to attend the celebrations organized for his birthday in Bombay and Poona. When his train halted at Bombay Central station, there was a vociferous greeting from the crowd that had gathered there to welcome him. The Royal Opera House, Bombay's most elegant theatre, was hired to hold the main function of felicitating Sayajirao III and was attended by the most elite of Bombay's who's who. Renowned barrister M.R. Jayakar read out the address and the Maharaja was congratulated and garlanded by the presidents of various institutions of the city—about 150 were present for the ceremony. From Bombay, the following evening, he arrived in Poona and was met with a standing ovation from the crowd who had gathered at the station to meet him. In Poona, there were a number of institutions engaged in historical research, promoting the ancient language of India—Sanskrit—and also the Ahilya Ashram, an institute for untouchables that Sayajirao III had supported and encouraged. He visited these institutions in the three days that he was there.

A public reception was given in his honour on 21 March and Kelkar, Tilak's close associate, and editor of Tilak's paper *Kesari,* whose name had been taboo a decade ago for his anti-British activities and propaganda, read out the address. The officials of the Raj were passive onlookers and no objection was raised for inviting a 'notorious extremist and agitator' to the reception. It was a sign that India had moved away from the Raj and was gradually carving its own destiny. The adulation that the Maharaja received from the public in Poona—where he was garlanded by representatives of several public institutions and a garden party was given in his honour—was not showered on any other prince. No other prince in India had been given such adulation, reverence and genuine affection by the people of India. The newspapers were full of it and referred to him as one of India's most enlightened princes in their editorial columns. Even the *Times of India* which had been his worst critic over the durbar incident and had been very pro-British in criticizing the Maharaja and linking him with sedition, now, after a decade, chose to conclude its paean on the Maharaja with a quotation from India's gifted writer, poet and winner of the Nobel Laureate, Rabindranath Tagore: 'It is a rare power of uniting, in his vision, the undying traditions of Indian thought and culture with the spirit of the modern age, which I believe, especially distinguishes His Highness as a ruler.'

Tired but gratified that he had made his people happy, who in turn had, in some small measure, assuaged the disappointments and grief caused by his sons' weaknesses, leading to their untimely deaths, he left India on 22 April, satisfied in the knowledge that he did not live his life in vain.

Just before his ship left the shores of Bombay, he was handed a book beautifully bound in purple velvet and with its title embroidered in gold thread which read *Shri Sayaji Gourva-Granth* (In Praise of Shri Sayaji), brought out by the Birthday Celebration Committee formed by the citizens of Baroda and which contained quotes and extracts from eminent luminaries of the intellectual world.

In the middle of the year, he was invited to preside at the World Religious Conference to be held in Chicago. After an interval of forty years, the session was being held, which made it all the more prestigious. Delighted, Sayajirao III accepted with alacrity and when he arrived at the station on 26 August he was met by an impressive reception committee and a guard of honour. It was a huge affair with eleven world religions being represented at the gathering and a congregation comprising some 26,000 people. Sayajirao III's speech clearly conveyed his thoughts on religion that basically all of them were the same, only divided by different names! His speech was heard in spellbound silence by the entire crowd of 26,000!

On his return to Baroda from Chicago, he was asked to inaugurate the seventh annual meeting of the Oriental Conference. The Maharaja, with no idea of what the conference was about, subjected Dr B. Bhattacharya, the head of the Gaekwad's Oriental Series, to a Spanish inquisition, who assured him that it was not a 'stunt' to feast his friends at the state's expense, but was a serious conference with delegates attending it from all over India and abroad. What Dr Bhattacharya remembered of the meeting was that after the questioning the Maharaja whispered in his ear, 'You will be the Maharaja of Baroda for these three days and all will obey your orders.'[1]

The three-day session began with the Maharaja's inaugural address where he spoke about the problems that research scholars had to put up with, how it was a most unrewarding task and the difficulties they had to contend with. He also pointed out that out of the five hundred copies that were brought out by the Gaekwad's Oriental Series, 125 copies were given away to libraries and educational institutions and the remaining were sold at nominal prices, but even then it took twenty years to sell the balance 375 copies. He spoke with feeling about the hardships that academic research scholars faced and he had a lot of respect for them and understood their problems because he was himself an 'eager student'! The Maharaja was kept busy granting interviews to most of the delegates, gave a party for them, visited different camps and, more importantly, attended several sectional meetings where he could interact with intellectuals and satiate himself with discussions and readings.

In the month of December, when the air was nippy and the time conducive for open air exercises and sports under a benign sun, the Gujarat intercollegiate sports meet was organized in Baroda on the 15th. After distributing prizes to the winners, the Maharaja expressed his views on the display he had witnessed and stressed the importance of physical exercise. Reminding the students and professors assembled of the famous English proverb, 'All work and no play makes Jack a dull boy', he said that the students who only bury themselves in their books and do not participate in any games invariably lack enterprise and enthusiasm. 'Every young man must try to be healthy and strong. Without health and strength, you will not be able to face with resolution the difficulties with which the path of life is strewn and in the end, no matter what your walk of life, defeat or disappointment may well await you.' Since the faculty members of the colleges too were present, he also included them in his speech: 'I consider it essential that you should spare some portion of your time each day to be devoted to manly exercises, and that in your curriculum, provision should be made for games and recreation. It gives me great pleasure that the university authorities are alive to this need and that to meet it, they have organized these intercollegiate sports. Besides improving your health, they bring you into closer contact with students of other colleges and thus create in you a spirit of brotherhood and goodwill. As you study further and gain worldly experience, you will discover that it is not only futile but harmful to differentiate between man and man on the grounds that A is Gujarati, B is a Kathiawari and C is a Deccani. Our ignorance is responsible for this warped judgement. As you come in close contact with one another, you will realize that you are all branches from the same tree with the same, identical interest. It is, therefore, my earnest desire that you should take a greater part in these activities, both to improve your health and cultivate the spirit of brotherhood and sportsmanship.

'I congratulate those students who have been successful in these competitions and have won prizes. Not all can win, but the spirit of striving in the losers also merits praise. To them, I would like to say instead of being discouraged they should strive all the more to achieve success on the next sports occasion.'

This speech has been cited because it is another manifestation of Sayajirao III's desire to promote unity among his people and what better way than students coming together through sports? His perennial worry that dogged him to the end of his days was the differences in the caste and religious systems prevailing in India.

Again, a week later, at the unveiling of the statue of the late Maharaja Shrimant Khanderao Gaekwad on 23 December, he emphasized the importance of health and physical exercise for a healthier outlook, 'Though nearly seventy years have passed since the rule of Shrimant Khanderao Maharaj, he is still fresh in our memory. His life's motto was that "Physical well-being is the first means to Dharma". He had a great love for exercise and used to perform wonderful feats of strength. A man blessed with a conciliatory nature and liberal temper, his charity knew no bounds, and it was above all considerations of caste and creed. Bhavbhut's famous adage "Harder than a thunderbolt, softer than a flower" could be most appropriately applied to him. He had a deep love for his subjects, and when, in 1857, at the very beginning of his reign, the mutiny broke out, it was to prove a severe test of his merits. How he emerged triumphant from the ordeal and how it benefited the state, is well known to all of you. Among the outstanding achievements of his reign were the construction of the Dabhoi–Miyagaon railway, the introduction of the British-Indian model of a system to collect revenue and to survey and classify the land, the scheme of water supply to Baroda city from the Narbada River, the enactment of certain beneficial laws, the establishment of judicial courts and of banks, and an increase in well-trained military forces.

'It is difficult for us nowadays to visualize the mental strain upon Maharaja Khanderao caused by family feuds and the presence of a minister like Bhau Shinde. The Marathi proverb well illustrates this predicament, "One can know the difficulties of a situation only by personally experiencing them" is indeed true. It is really remarkable that despite all his troubles and worries he achieved so much during the brief span of fourteen years' rule. Even the most superficial observer's eye would agree that by introducing social and economic reforms, Shrimant Khanderao Maharaj laid the foundations for good government in the state of Baroda.

'And it is in recognition of his great achievements and as a token of our gratitude that it is our duty today to unveil his statue.'[2]

Sayajirao III was by this time an erudite scholar, and had read several books on religion and the importance of worshipping ancestors who had departed from the world. He then proceeded to talk about how deities like Yama and Indra who were invoked in order that the departed might attain heaven and those left behind might be suitably left with longevity, prosperity and progeny as given in the ancient Hindu religious text, the Rig Veda. He also talked about the practice of worshipping the dead existing in all religions; for example, Barsi among Muslims, Dosla among the Parsis, Masses among the Roman Catholics and Shinto among the Chinese and Japanese. 'The best form of non-manifest worship is to study and understand the good qualities of our ancestors and to carry on the good work initiated by them...' The Maharaja described the statue and complimented the sculptor Karmakar with the words, 'I am confident it will add to his fame!' Describing the building of Khanderao Market, where the statue was unveiled, he said, 'This imposing and handsome building follows what is known in architecture as the Indo-Aryan style, which is characterized by a happy blend of symmetry and proportion—qualities of outstanding importance in our everyday life.

This style reached its zenith in the reign of King Siddharaj of the Solanki lineage and again in King Vishaldeo's time. Temples, palaces and waterworks constructed in those times can be seen in the Baroda state even today at Dabhoi, Patan, Sidhpur and elsewhere. The central arch in this market building recalls the Hirabhagol at Dabhoi. The background of this statue of Shrimant Khanderao is decorated by the dome on the arch, and by the tall turrets, and spacious and attractive roofs which flank it. To complete the setting, there is the proportionate foreground of the Mandi or Market Building, and eventually there will be a beautiful garden which is at present under construction.

'May the constant reminder of a great king make the minds of our people like unto his mind—liberal, fearless and strong—and their bodies also like unto his—healthy and vigorous.'

He continued to remain in Baroda as his gout was in limbo and he was feeling quite healthy. He loved the Baroda state and nobody, not even his family, realized how much. He took this opportunity to enjoy the 'feeling well' phase while it lasted to tour the districts and in his letters to his dewan he seemed to have a renewed interest in his surroundings. His letters talked a lot about the importance of physical training in schools; about marriage laws and Hindu rituals. In a letter to his granddaughter-in-law who was holidaying in France, he advised her to not neglect her studies, and do exercise every day. He also invited the Maharaja of Kolhapur for a holiday when they could go pig-sticking.

Sayajirao III himself was fond of exercising and never lost an opportunity to do so. One day, he invited Dr Bhattacharya to walk with him round the parade grounds near the Makarpura Palace. While they walked together, the Maharaja as was his habit kept the man mentally occupied with a volley of questions which, that particular afternoon, were distinctly morbid—what happens after death and questions about afterlife. Perhaps he was beginning to feel his age and was wondering how long it would be for his turn. Whatever the reason for this strange premonition, it certainly had the most injurious effects on his companion's feet. Round and round they went on the parade grounds till Dr Bhattacharya was exhausted with a parched throat that cried for water and needed a dressing for his blistered, bleeding feet.' The Maharaja walked so fast that it was difficult to keep pace with him,'[3] he was said to have remarked later.

Another example of Sayajirao III's sympathy and offering help to those in a genuine predicament through no fault of theirs is well illustrated in the following story:

It was in early 1934 that Sayajirao III unveiled the statue of Sir Dadabhai Naoroji at Naosari where the great man and 'India's political grandfather' had been born. Dadabhai Naoroji had a long association with the Gaekwads of Baroda since Malharrao's days after which, with Sayajirao III's help, he had been able to further his political career in England. The Maharaja also unveiled a magnificent statue of another extremely able Maratha warrior, Chhatrapati Shivaji Maharaj, the founder of the Maratha Empire. This statue stands in Sayaji Baug in Baroda, but was meant to grace the Shivaji Memorial Park in Poona. The sculptor was Ganpatrao Kashinath Mhatre from Bombay. When he finished sculpting it in Poona, there were serious differences of opinion between the committee and Mhatre over the resemblance of the statue to the great Maratha warrior which resulted in the committee in charge of the memorial rejecting the man's work and ordering another. Mhatre had spent two years labouring over it and a good deal of money too, which the sculptor could ill afford. He was in a pitiable predicament since no one would buy the life-size statue in an equestrian position. Mhatre was a very good sculptor and an artist of no mean calibre so when the Maharaja got to hear of his predicament, he sent for him and offered to buy it for the same price agreed upon by the Poona committee and to give it a suitable place in the centre of Sayaji Baug garden in Baroda. Sayajirao III was always ready to help the deserving in difficulties, which brings out another agreeable trait in his character.

65

Niggling Doubts and Anxieties

Baroda's old, outstanding disputes with the paramount power had to be resolved and there was an urgency to do that because the political climate was uncertain and no one knew what changes the advent of the new Federation might bring. It was imperative to have all pending matters sorted out as quickly as possible between Baroda and the central government, before a new form of central government came in. Sayajirao III was more familiar with these cases than anyone else. He had them written down, printed and sent to the government and he himself kept pursuing Viceroy Willingdon for a speedy decision.

First on the list of priorities was the question of Baroda being allowed to manufacture salt and to sell it within its own territory without having to pay the Indian government port dues. Second, the aberrant situation of the East India Company acting as revenue collector in the province of Gujarat and Kathiawad had severed the traditional bond that had existed between the Gaekwad and these tributaries. The feudal lords of these tributaries had always looked up to the Gaekwads as their rightful masters since it had been the Gaekwads who had freed them from Muslim domination and tyranny. This action had resulted in creating a multiplicity of jurisdictions with small areas of princely states. The situation was further complicated with British territories that peppered the Gujarat province of the Baroda state, which was a boon for lawbreakers and a veritable curse for those who wished to remain on the right side of the law.

Third, from the territories that had been ceded to the East India Company in Bombay the British the right to collect revenue from these areas, but on the clear understanding that it was to go towards the upkeep of their contingent force stationed in Baroda. When the subsidiary force had been dismantled and removed from the Baroda state, the deal had become invalid so the British authorities should have handed back to the Baroda state the territories ceded to them earlier. This was not done, but if the matter had to be resolved in a court of justice, the verdict would have been in favour of His Highness as factual evidence dictated that it should. But this was a matter Sayajirao III knew would only be resolved with no advantage to either side for once India gained its independence all the territories would come under the jurisdiction of the new government. Until then, there was no way this particular problem would ever get resolved; what had gone on for a hundred years had given it a validity that was difficult to invalidate unless the government changed. Till then, it posed something of a cliff-hanger ending to the situation.

As mentioned earlier, the Maharaja had taken to spending less time in Baroda and more on travels abroad to the West. His remarkably efficient dewan was left with the administration completely in his capable hands. Correspondence was still as brisk as ever between the Maharaja and the dewan but pertained more to generalities and there was a curious air of detachment that revealed the state of mind of the Maharaja as if somehow nothing really mattered any more'. However, his letters were very profound and constructive in their content. He said in one, 'Real patriotism, sense of justice and fairness to all is the foundation on which alone a good government can be built.'[1]

Dhairyashilrao continued to cause him some anxiety; as a result of the earlier tragedies, he saw his son had reached a point of no return and hence adopted a *c'est la vie* of the inevitable. He did write from Paris towards the end of 1934 as a last attempt to save his only surviving son's life and expressed his concern, 'I am frightened about the state of your health. You have been getting fits...something must be done immediately to save you... but you must put yourself under medical care in a good nursing home.' He had already suffered an acute loss earlier in the autumn when he was living in Aldsworth, his house in England. He was planning to return to India later in the year when the news reached him of his brother Sampatrao's death. Sampatrao, it will be recalled, had been one of the contestants for the gaddi sixty years ago when he had accompanied Sayajirao III to Baroda. Sayajirao III had been very fond of his brother and had done a lot for him and now that he was dead, he felt the loss acutely. So many losses of his near and dear ones had numbed him. Reluctant now to return to India, he shelved his plans and sailed for America instead. He wandered around museums in New York and Washington, always looking for some feature to implement in his own museum in Baroda.

There is much to be said for the stature of Sayajirao III. He was probably the only Indian ruler to be received by President Franklin Delano Roosevelt in Washington. As the Maharaja had seen all he wanted, he made the voyage from New York to Europe on 3 November.

Unfortunately, he suffered an attack of fever which was diagnosed as rheumatic, probably due to his exposure to the cold in New York and Washington. However, he was taken off the ship in an unconscious state in Cherbourg and rushed to Paris for immediate treatment early the following morning. He recovered to some extent with the treatment but was forbidden by his doctors to travel to India for some months. He must have been very depressed, the loss of his brother coming on top of the loss of his dearly loved sons, while one was on his way to the burning ghats. To add to it all was his illness.

His only hope now was his grandson Pratapsinghrao, who had shown a willingness to learn the business according to the standards and timetable drawn up by Sayajirao III. More than anything else, Pratapsinghrao had not shown any inclination for the strong beverage so favoured by his uncles in the past—this endeared him to his grandfather more than anything he could have done or would ever do! Pratapsinghrao was with his grandfather during his illness in Paris and he was proving to be the steady, dutiful and obedient young man that his grandfather had wanted him to be. Before their return to India, Sayajirao III wrote to Dewan V. T. Krishnamachari, 'I have certain views about his training which I will discuss with you in due time. He has many good qualities and his value will increase if he reads more and knows the history of Baroda and of other states.'[2]

66

The Diamond Jubilee and Thereafter

The year 1936 was again a very special year for the Maharaja and for Barodians as it was the diamond jubilee of his reign. As Fatehsinghrao IV, his great-grandson remarks in his book *Sayajirao of Baroda*, 'The astrologers who had settled upon 27 May 1875 as being auspicious for Sayajirao's succession to the gaddi of the Gaekwads must have read his stars amazingly well.'[1] Their predictions had been accurate, in that he had fulfilled the hopes and aspirations of not only his adoptive mother, but also those of Madhavrao, Elliot, and the people of the Baroda state. It is not every prince who gets the good fortune of celebrating any jubilee of his reign and here he was, celebrating sixty years of his rule, in the diamond jubilee year of 1936. It was decided to hold the celebrations till January 1936 when the Maharaja would be back in Baroda. While all the preparations were on in the state, on the actual day of the jubilee, the Maharaja was in London receiving congratulatory messages and good wishes from the Emperor King George V, the secretary of state for India, Sir Samuel Hoare and a multitude of friends and acquaintances. The people of Baroda, however, wanted their king in their midst for the celebrations and clamoured for his return, resulting in the postponement of the celebrations till the day he returned.

After considerable debates with various committees, it was decided to hold the celebrations for ten days, a week being insufficient to fit in all the functions organized by various public and private institutions to felicitate Sayajirao III on the grand occasion. The celebrations were to begin on 1 January 1936 and last till 10 January. Lord Willingdon and his wife were to grace the occasion with their presence, an unusual feature for a viceroy to pay a visit to a princely state for the second time during his tenure of office, which speaks of the high regard they must have held for the ruler of Baroda.

The Maharaja was back in his state in the first week of November and was swept into a whirlwind of activity in connection with the celebrations. There were statues to be unveiled, buildings and parks to be opened, hundreds of people to be met who had travelled from afar to the state to felicitate him. Similarly, as in the golden jubilee, there were grand processions, military parades, fireworks, and entertainment for the public by way of sports, plays by theatre companies, and music and dance performances. Besides all this, there was revocation of revenue arrears, remission of prisoners' sentences in the state jails, generous amounts given as donations and gifts distributed to the poor.

The ten-day diamond jubilee celebration got wide press coverage and even the *Times of India* condescended from its habitual hauteur to 'echo the official approbation signified by the viceroy's presence.'

'While promoting the lot of his subjects, the Gaekwad has, on occasions, spiritedly defended his position from encroachments by the political department of the government of India. Some of his differences with the authorities in Delhi were due to misunderstandings and the proof that no bitterness was left behind is to be seen in the tributes which successive viceroys have paid him.'

With this, as the bulwark of prejudices came crumbling down to merge with the dust, one could almost hear the loud whisper of 'et tu Brutus' from the lips of Biddulph, Curzon and Hardinge! The sixty years of nurturing a state and bringing it to the progressive level it was at, in the year 1936, was reiterated several times by the mayor, and several other dignitaries in their laudatory addresses. The zillion things he had done to make life comfortable for his subjects; the old Baroda and the new modern one that had been created by him, one who had made the impossible possible. Could any 'untouchable' from the Antyajas draw water from the village well in the old Baroda? But in the new one, he surely could and send up a prayer to bless the man who had made this transition possible! All his constructive work for the state and his reforms have been talked about in the earlier chapters, but the miracle was the introduction of electricity in the bigger towns, telegraphs and telephones as a boon to the people of Baroda, and what's more, people could turn the taps on and get pure drinking water from the lakes and reservoirs constructed by him. Among others the most significant were the Divorce Act, the Widow Remarriage Act and the Caste Intermarriages Act, which gave women a new identity.

The Pioneer, an Allahabad newspaper, hit the right note: 'The most remarkable thing about Baroda is that she is much in advance of British

India in the matter of social legislation.' The other cities that boasted of finer buildings and more advanced amenities had achieved very little in matters of education and saving girls and boys from being married off while still in their cradles. The Prevention of Infant Marriage Act had saved the lives of many toddlers and had allowed them a chance for a healthier life. A widow's life was not over with widowhood, she could marry again and live her life without hassles. A king who had given all this and much more to his people, and cared for them like a parent, deserved all the accolades showered on him by thankful and appreciative people who had come to the main function held on 3 January, in a huge stadium specially built for the purpose.

Two days earlier, on 1 January, the message from Maharaja Sayajirao Gaekwad, Sena Khas Khel, Shamsher Bahadur, Farzand-i-Khas-i-Inglish-Daulatia, GCSI, GCIE, LL. D, to his beloved subjects on the auspicious occasion of the Diamond Jubilee of his accession to the gaddi was read out to the public. The message said:

> Creation of the Diamond Jubilee Trust: On this occasion when my people all over the state are celebrating the diamond jubilee of my accession, I desire to announce that I have decided, in commemoration of this happy event, to set apart a fund for Rs 1 crore to be called the Diamond Jubilee Trust, the income of which will be devoted to improving the conditions of life of the rural population, especially those of the poor and of the depressed classes, supplementing the amounts which will be progressively devoted to such purposes in the regular budgets of the state.
>
> My ideal in improving village life: As you well know, for over fifty-two years, I have laboured assiduously in the cause of rural development. Indeed no cause has been dearer to my heart. My ideal is to improve village life—all sides of it. I wish to develop in my people a keen desire for a higher standard of living—a will to live better—and a capacity for self-help and self-reliance. I earnestly desire to make village life interesting and farming a career, the rewards in which will satisfy the most enterprising among the villagers. You all know the main lines in the policy I have followed, but I may state them as simply as I can.
>
> Compulsory mass education: (i) First, there is compulsory mass education. This indeed is at the root of all progress. Introduced first

in Amreli in 1893, education has been compulsory for boys and girls in the state for many years. Today, we have in the state over 6,500 teachers engaged in imparting literacy to people. Efforts are made to give a 'rural bias' to primary education; the object being to stop the 'drift' to towns. It is also my aim that the teacher should take his legitimate share in the life of the village. With this in view, the training college gives instructions in the elements of village problems. (ii) There is further a network of village libraries to supply the people with knowledge of the kind needed by them to prevent the evil of lapse into illiteracy.

Village panchayats: One of my earliest measures was the setting up of village panchayats. Every village in the state is under a panchayat. This has separate resources of its own, and its function is to improve village life. The funds of the village panchayats should be judiciously employed on works of permanent utility.

Prant panchayats and their duties: I have always insisted that prant panchayats should bear in mind prominently the needs of the rural areas. I shall refer here only to the programme.

For feeder roads, (ii) for wells, and (iii) subartesian borings which are being carried out by these bodies at considerable cost.

Technical departments and their work: I have set up technical departments for dealing with the economic problems facing the agriculturists—

a. The agricultural department teaches what crops to grow, how to select seeds, how to treat plant diseases, etc.
b. The care of cattle is the business of the veterinary department.
c. The cooperative movement finds capital on reasonable terms to agriculturists and assists them in buying what they need and in the sale of their crops.
d. The industries department teaches industries suitable to agriculturists for their spare hours and for the months in which farming is not possible.
e. Then there is the public health department which tackles questions connected with rural sanitation, pure water supply and allied services.

Social legislation: I should refer to the legislation passed for the abolition of harmful social customs like

i) Early marriages which are against nature and biological laws,
ii) Caste tyranny, and
iii) Untouchability which is against laws of social justice.

Untouchability: It is difficult to speak of this subject with restraint. It is repugnant to our common humanity that those who should be regarded as our brothers and sisters are branded with this unnatural stigma. In my eyes and in the eyes of my government, there is no difference between man and man. Moral decay is the inevitable fate of those higher classes who deprive millions of their fellow creatures of all self-respect and all hope of betterment.

Results: Now, I am far from claiming that all these measures have had their full effect and have produced all the results I desired. The ideal I have placed before myself is a high one and I remind myself that the inertia of centuries is not easily overcome and that the superstitions of ages are not removed in a decade.

Object of the fund: I desire now to give a further stimulus to the movement I began fifty-five years ago. It is with this object that I am constituting this special fund. From the income of this, grants will be made for useful schemes like extensions of gamthans to relieve overcrowding, village water supplies, communications, educative work of all kinds, etc. Special preference will be given (i) to the poorer areas which probably have been neglected in the past and (ii) to the needs of the backward communities like the Raniparaj, the Antyajas, the Thakardas, the Rabaries, etc.

As I have already said this will be over and above the usual state expenditure which I trust will increase with the expansion of our revenues. If circumstances change and if the government thinks it necessary hereafter, this fund will be utilized for other beneficial objects.

Hope: It is my earnest hope that, by this action of mine, the happiness of my people may be increased and they may be led to a higher and better manner of living. Should even a part of this ambition be realized, I shall feel myself amply rewarded for a lifetime dedicated to the well-being of my subjects.

Valedictory: In conclusion, I wish to tell you one thing—if you understand correctly the great laws of truth and apply them rationally to the practicalities of life, you are sure to derive happiness from it. I send my loving greetings to all my people and pray that they may be blessed with long life, happiness and prosperity.

The affection and sincerity of the message from their beloved ruler must have brought tears of gratitude and joy to the people of Baroda.

At the banquet given in honour of Lord and Lady Willingdon, at Laxmi Vilas Palace, on 5 January1936, Sayajirao III raised a toast followed by a speech: 'I have enjoyed their friendship for many years, and while it is always a privilege to welcome to my capital the representative in India of His Majesty, the king Emperor, the presence of old friends on the occasion of the Diamond Jubilee of my accession enhances that privilege and gives me particular pleasure...Lord Willingdon arrived in Bombay on the eve of the Great War which changed India as it changed the world. India was united in loyalty, but nationalism could not but grow when the greater part of the world was thinking in terms of home rule and self-determination. Lord Willingdon realized that the surge of national sentiments and constitutional ambition was inevitable, and the home government found Lord Willingdon convinced of the necessity of conceding to India a liberal measure of responsible self-government.

'It was thus fitting that Lord Willingdon should be chosen to inaugurate the Montague-Chelmsford reforms in Madras. Once again, he strove to anticipate the march of events, refusing to allow diarchy to function to the detriment of joint and increasing responsibility. When he left Madras, the hope was generally expressed that he would return to India in a still greater position. Happily for India, that hope was fulfilled five years ago as the best minds of both countries were engaged in the task of carrying the Montague-Chelmsford reforms one step further to their logical outcome—the Dominion status for India. Again his personal influence was all on the side of a generous and impressive measure of advance, and, as he has himself informed us, he sought in precept and in practice to become India's first constitutional governor general. Lord Willingdon has indeed been a great servant and a true friend of India...Sixty years have passed since I was first called upon to begin my life's work in Baroda; fifty years since I first had the pleasure of welcoming the representative of the queen Empress to my capital. I am proud that my alliance with the crown is 150 years old, still prouder that during all these years, it has been steadily upheld and maintained.

'Of all that has passed through my mind, it is impossible to speak, and I must confine myself to certain reflections which seem appropriate to this occasion. The occasion shall be my excuse for speaking first of my state and of a lifetime spent in pursuit of an ideal...the feeling uppermost in my mind is how much remains to be done...Every passing year confirms my belief that education for the humblest member of society is the only sure foundation on which to build. Every effort has been worthwhile.

'India has changed greatly during my lifetime and in no respect more profoundly than in the constitutional status...For many years, I have thought the federation to be the best and most hopeful line of advance, and I am sure that the decision to build on such a stable foundation is a wise one. In an All-India Federation with British India and the states as equal partners working for the common good, the states have a great part to play...In order, however, that the states may play that part to the greatest advantage, they are entitled to invite consideration of certain essentials which are inseparable from their distinctive traditions and proud histories. Enterprise and individuality will be destroyed if any attempt is made to force them into a uniform mould, and a wealth of varied political and administrative experience will be lost to the new India. In all matters, outside the federal sphere, the states should have unfettered autonomy and they should be freed from restrictions and limitations imposed upon them jointly or severally in the circumstances which have now ceased to exist. Only then will the states be able to develop naturally and fruitfully as virile responsible entities, equipped for the manifold duties of good government and determined to bring such qualities to the best service of India. I am gratified to know that these matters, especially questions like retrocession of jurisdiction on railways are receiving attention... I may refer to a question which concerns my own state, its relations with tributary states and estates. Over a hundred years ago, the British government elected to mediate between my house and the tributaries. Conditions have changed greatly since, and the policy of these early days needs a new orientation. I have proposed a scheme for the readjustment of these relations. In preparing this, I have kept two principles in view. The first is that the powers of these states and estates should on no account be reduced; but that on the other hand, their financial position should be strengthened by the abolition of the tributes which were not fixed on a logical basis and are unequal in their incidence. Secondly, the interests of good government and economic development in this part of India should be furthered.

'I venture to express the hope that this scheme will be accepted and that the new order of things will soon be established.

'In Baroda, we are doing what we can in terms of education, abolition of irksome restrictions on rights of women, the encouragement of child welfare and allied activities, to enable woman to take her rightful place in society.

'Ladies and gentlemen, let us drink to the toast...'

One can conclude how meaningful and purposeful his speech was on the evening of the banquet.

Lord Willingdon reciprocated: 'It is a real pleasure to renew my friendship with Your Highness, and I consider myself fortunate indeed that the auspicious occasion of Your Highness's diamond jubilee of accession should have taken place during my viceroyalty and that I have been able to come to Baroda and extend to you in person my warmest and most heartfelt congratulations. Your Highness, it is my pleasant duty now to read out a message which His Majesty the king Emperor has been graciously pleased to entrust me to convey to Your Highness:

"It gives me much pleasure to convey to Your Highness my sincere congratulations on celebration of the diamond jubilee of your accession to the gaddi of Baroda.

"To a few Princes, is it granted to rule for so long a period of time and to look back with satisfaction upon sixty years of continued material and moral progress in the lives of their subjects. I trust Your Highness may be spared to your state for many years to come and that prosperity and happiness may increasingly attend your rule.

"The year 1875 when Your Highness succeeded to the gaddi, marked the beginning of a new era of material and steady progress in the state. Under Your Highness's enlightened guidance, Baroda has never looked back. At the outset, Your Highness set high ideals, some of which have already been attained. Others you steadfastly pursue, and I can truly say that you have devoted your life to the interests of your state and the welfare of your subjects. The fruits of your labours are in evidence on all sides. The administration of the state is on a high level, but what is perhaps more important, it is built upon sure foundations.

"It has afforded me much gratification to see the announcement which Your Highness had made that in commemoration of your diamond jubilee you have created a trust with a capital of Rs 1 crore, the income from which is to be devoted to the improvement of rural conditions in your state. I can imagine no more fitting manner in which the memory of this historic occasion could be perpetuated.

"The people of Baroda are fortunate indeed that Your Highness has been spared for so long a period of service for their common good, and I am confident that your name will be emblazoned in gold upon the annals of your state and will be long remembered by your people with gratitude and affection...As I stated when I visited you three years ago, my firm conviction is that an All India Federation with necessary safeguards will be to the advantage and in the interests of the states and British India alike. Since the time that the Government of India Act has been placed upon the Statute Book, and I am glad to know that this measure has the support of broad-minded and experienced rulers like Your Highness. The future of India is now placed in her own hands. In that future, the states will be called upon to bear an ever-increasing share in the problems which beset every government and Baroda, by reason of its high standard of efficiency in education and administration, will be expected to play a role of great importance.

"I have been greatly interested in Your Highness's reference to the scheme which you have put forward with a view to the readjustment of the relations existing between the Baroda state and certain of her tributaries. Under this scheme, while you have sought to effect an improvement in economic and administrative conditions and to provide for financial relief to the states and estates concerned, you have wisely taken care to leave their powers and privileges unimpaired. I sincerely trust that the feudatories to whom Your Highness has referred will give your proposals their full and careful consideration, for they will certainly be well advised to do so...I ask you all ladies and gentlemen, to join with me in offering to His Highness our warmest congratulations upon the happy occasion of his diamond jubilee and to drink to the long life and happiness of Their Highnesses and prosperity to the Baroda state. '"

The national dailies had sent their reporters to cover the event and gave the proceedings the widest coverage: The *Times of India* commented:'While promoting the lot of his subjects, the Gaekwar has, on occasions, spiritedly defended his position from encroachments by the Politcal Department of the Government of India. Some of his differences with the authorities in Delhi were due to misunderstandings and the proof that no bitterness was left behind is to be seen in the tributes which successive viceroys have paid him.

It was as though the last bastion had crumbled.'

Sayajirao III in his speech to the Dhara Sabha (legislative council) at Laxmi Vilas Palace on 9 January 1936 said, 'Gentlemen of the Dhara Sabha, I have received your address with great pleasure and interest and I have noted the chief points that are mentioned in it. They are not beyond my comprehension or beyond my knowledge, and are always in my mind.

'Since the inception of the Dhara Sabha, I have been closely watching its work... Nothing in this world is permanent. The world is always changing, and in conformity with the needs of the times, changes have been made and will continue to be made in the constitution of the Dhara Sabha. We have however to proceed cautiously in the attainment of our goals. Let us not be carried away by mere fashion or show. We must strengthen our body corporate, seek unity, and facilitate mutual trust, confidence and cooperation among ourselves, while giving as much liberty as is consistent.

'Remember you are part of my people—the subjects and the officers. Matters cannot proceed smoothly if these two refuse to cooperate. I am glad to learn that good relations and cooperation exist between you and my officers. If we refer to the past history of Baroda, we shall find many defects from which lessons can be drawn. You have much to learn from such lessons and you cannot afford to ignore or forget them. Do not commit the same mistakes. Pursue higher ideals in promoting the happiness of the people and to increase our prosperity. You should always remember that the path of sacrifice in service leads to more noble, more healthy ideas. If these are followed, the benefits will still be greater. Sacrifice first and then the higher ideals, thus shall we enrich our mutual interests.

'With these words may I thank you once again for the cordial reception you have given me this evening.'

The diamond jubilee celebrations were over formally on 10 January, but felicitations from different cadres and branches of associations, universities continued unabated. That their Maharaja was still in their midst and had not yet left the shores of India was itself a reason for jubilation and rightly enough the almuni from the Baroda College hosted a dinner in his honour on 12 January 1936. Thanking them for their felicitations he recalled, 'Laying the foundation stone of Baroda College was one of the very first acts of my rule, and since then, over half a century later, a number of pictures crowd into my mind. I wish I had the art of Mr Munshi who can so ably produce pen pictures of important events of the memorable past. I wish too that I deserved the many good things he has said of me.

'It is only a fortunate few who can witness the fruition of their labours within a limited span of life, and especially of labours in the administrative field. An administrator can be better judged some fifty years after his death when both friends and enemies are no more. The effects of his rule, good or bad, will bear fruit in time and by such results he will then stand to be judged impartially.

'An able and progressive administrator, in my opinion, must study the past, carefully observe the present, and look ahead to the future. I am convinced that the people of our country are in no sense inferior to any others in the world and yet our progress is slow.

'In the early days of my rule, I felt that the social evils and superstitions surrounding the people were the main handicaps to evolution, growth and progress. As a ruler, it was my duty not to attempt to overthrow the existing social order, but to modify it as to make individual evolution widely spread amongst my people to achieve that purpose, and to utilize legislation if necessary. Next it was my intention to cut the bonds which social evils provide and thus help individuality to grow. There followed a series of legislative measures destined to achieve that end, but they were undertaken only after educating and gathering public opinion. My administrative measures were neither conceived nor put into operation in great hurry, and sufficient time was always allowed for social adjustments. The operations so begun have not ceased yet. It is my duty to strive more and more in that direction with both caution and determination. I have, in fact, tried to help my people to free themselves from the social evils with which I saw them struggling desperately and from which they were eager to be freed. Throughout my more than sixty years of rule, I have consistently kept in mind what can be achieved and what cannot, what is good and what is not good for my people, keeping in main causes of progress in other countries which I have visited over and over again for the purposes of study and of health.

'Turning to the idea of a University of Baroda, let me assure my friend Mr Munshi and all of you here, that it is still under my consideration and is never out of my mind. A small state like Baroda must carefully consider whether it could shoulder the heavy financial burden involved before any decision is reached.

'I am anxious to see the expansion of this college and other institutions; I am anxious to improve the lot of my agricultural population and go ahead vigorously with village upliftment work. I am also anxious to do much that yet remains to be done in the direction of social regeneration. All these demand close attention and adequate finance. Again I emphasize that nothing should be done in a hurry or without a clear idea of future commitments, if it is to be done thoroughly and well.

'Mr Munshi has referred to my attempts to improve the joint family system and to eradicate the evils which prevent growth and progress of individuals. Let me assure all of you that I have never caused, neither would I permit, necessary legislation to be undertaken, unless and until I felt that public opinion was sufficiently vocal and the people ready for it.

'Whatever the limitations to which I, as a human being like yourselves, am subject, I can assure you that every motive has been for the good of my people. I want you to judge me by the motives which guide me rather than by the results achieved. What I am always anxious for is thorough cooperation of my people. You as graduates of this college and as the intelligentsia, can help me a great deal by advising the government from time to time of needs that arise and thus help us to accomplish much more than we have been able to do so far...

Before we depart, let me add that I feel assured of your active and sincere help in all that I have yet to do for the good of my people and of future generations.'

The following summer in 1936, the Maharaja was watching the Olympics after he had made the secret Berlin pact. He wrote to Pratapsinghrao from Berlin, 'A very enjoyable fortnight, watching the Olympic Games.' He described the event in detail to his grandson, being impressed with the stadium and the parade of the athletes but most of all he mentioned the spirit of the tournament. He wrote, 'If the Olympic spirit of good-natured rivalry, friendliness and comradeship, so very marked among these young men and women, could be infused into our national and international affairs, there would be far less misery and misunderstandings, while many of our problems would disappear altogether.'[2] He was absolutely thrilled when India won in the hockey match against Germany in the Olympics after a poor start, and the fact they did win in the finals was due to him, the details of which have already been related earlier in the book.

After the Berlin Olympics, Sayajirao III left for London, and his mind, never free of the innumerable social problems that wind themselves around the lives of the Indian people, he wrote to Lord Willingdon who had just completed his term as viceroy asking him for his opinion on the joint family system prevailing in most families in India and suggesting a meeting with him to discuss the evils and benefits of it. 'Should it be encouraged or discouraged either by legislation or by any other means?' The Maharaja probably wanted an objective opinion from a rank outsider so as to be able to rightly assess the value of the system and whether it should be advocated at all. The fact that Lord Willingdon in his tenure of office in India had ample opportunity to witness for himself the good and evils of the system, hence the question. (There is no indication from any of his correspondence whether Lord Willingdon replied to that question—from this it is understood that he was chary of voicing a frank opinion on Indian customs and culture.)

The Maharaja was preoccupied with religion and was curious to learn the tenets of other religions. In connection with this he asked the Maharaja of Patiala, Bhupinder Singh to send him someone who could explain the fundamental principles of Sikhism.

As the ruler, he had funded innumerable scholarships to graduates and talked about funding deserving students who might take up the study of comparative religions. He wrote to his dewan about it. His declining health and mental state at this time can be well gauged from his correspondence to friends and his dewan. At the end of 1936, he was back in Baroda.

As the days went by, Sayajirao III's morbid mood got the better of him. He began to ponder on life after death and the journey of the soul once it left the body, and often after sunset when he had Dr Bhattacharya for company, he voiced these thoughts to his companion. Often they had discussions, and both of them enjoyed sparring on a variety of subjects, especially religion and philosophy.

One evening, Dr Bhattacharya recalled that he came to the palace and found Sayajirao III reclining on a chair in the vast open terrace of the palace, reading. The terrace was bathed in moonlight and the air had a curiously surreal quality about it. When he was ushered in, he was met with the question, 'Have you not noticed how excessive parasitism is eating into the vitals of our society and paving the way for our ruin?' Dr Bhattacharya was reduced to silence, wondering what the question was leading up to. Then, the Maharaja expressed his distress on the plight of 'poor kheduts (farmers) who have to sweat and toil for a living... and these kheduts also pay land revenue to support the government servants who are themselves parasites... who live on the sweat of labourers.'

Now these opinions voiced in public would have labelled him a communist and his enemies would have accused him of being secretly in league with communist countries. Dr Bhattacharya was further put into an embarrassing plight with the Maharaja's next remark, 'All officers of the state including yourself are parasites,' but his next sentence reduced the other's embarrassment when he called himself a 'giant parasite'. Dr Bhattacharya, deciding it was time to refute the other's opinion, defended his own viewpoint that even a government servant and a city dweller had a rightful place in society. But the Maharaja was not to be led by such an argument and after a while he pointed out 'that for this sin we will have to perform prayaschitta, that is, penance for this sin.'[3] Dr Bhattacharya left soon afterwards, a little disturbed by Sayajirao III's state of mind, wondering what had brought on this communist way of thinking and whether the book he had been reading when he came in was one of Karl Marx's.

Sayajirao III was now assailed with a longing to get away from it all and visit places that had none of the palace comforts or the luxuries of the western hotels. Introspection had made him decide to be harsh on himself. He had no right to live a life of luxury while others toiled and could barely eke out a living to keep body and soul together—this thought that plagued him, and in this restless mood he left for Egypt. He spent time in the ancient pyramids and monuments, examined the tombs of the long-dead pharaohs at Luxor, tried to interpret the ancient scrolls and scripts at Alexandria and always eager to look at how others met flood disasters and scarcity of water, he visited the famous dam at Aswan and from there made his way to Khartoum. As a footloose and fancy-free globetrotter, he satiated his curiosity and something else, a *je ne sais quoi* quality that had him touring around places. Then Africa, that until recently had been thought of as the 'dark continent', beckoned him in his mood for prayaschitta. He flew to Uganda, toured the Belgian Congo and traversed the terrain less travelled by mortals and ended his tour driving all the way through Kenya and Nairobi. The Maharaja with his spirits uplifted by all that he had seen, wrote to his daughter-in-law and some of that buoyancy is evident in his letter as he related that he had a 'most interesting tour of 20,000 miles'![4] He was absolutely awestruck by the dense jungles of wild Africa and captivated by its exotic beauty.

The radical change in comfort from lush carpets, satin quilted beds to temporary sheds made of grass with the sky overhead to gaze upon, must have assuaged some of the guilt and was responsible for his cheerful mood, which made him resolve to go there again.

This was in 1937 and he was going over the same terrain that another traveller bitten by the same wanderlust bug had trod earlier. Had Sayajirao III made his way to this part of the continent a few months earlier, he could have enjoyed the experience with Ernest Hemingway. Considering Sayajirao III was now in his seventies, this was an amazing feat. All the nagging aches and pains had been left behind and being exposed to open air, most of the time, had cured his insomnia to a great degree. His health had improved and he was in fine fettle. An intrepid voyager, he vied with Homer in travelling 'with a hungry heart' for new impressions and experiences, sorting them out and weighing them all in the light of what, by adaptation, could contribute to the progress of Baroda and the happiness of his people. He was now enjoying the experience which air travel provided him. Still hankering for remote spots from the equatorial climate of Africa, he went to the other extreme and the middle of August found him exploring the Arctic regions. In an old but comfortable ship, *Reliance,* he made his way to Iceland. He voyaged miles in the *Reliance* taking in whatever he could make of the scenery with most of the ice-bound places being enveloped in fog, reaching a point 530 miles from North Pole. If Sayajirao III had been allowed his way, he would have gone to the North Pole and been the first Indian to plant a flag in the snow!

Sayajirao III was back in London in October and was due to return to

India and to practicalities for the winter. His letter to V.T. Krishnamachari expressed his unhappiness over Dhairyashil's behaviour. He had still not learnt his lesson from watching his brothers go to waste and bad habits had become so deeply entrenched in him that it was useless to lament over it. The other letter was to his granddaughter Laxmidevi consoling her on the death of her husband, Raja Khemsawant of Sawantwadi.

On the homeward journey, he met with Subramaniyam Iyer, a professor in the University of Mysore. Iyer had been to Europe to lecture on Indian philosophy and was now returning home. The Maharaja struck up a friendship with him and refreshed himself with the other's knowledge and views. Deeply impressed with the man, he wrote to the Maharaja of Mysore, his old friend, asking him if he could loan Professor Iyer for a month or two, beginning his letter with, 'if it would not cause inconvenience.'[5] In April, he was back in London, having flown by KLM Royal Dutch airlines.

He wrote to Colonel E.J.D. Colvin who had replaced Colonel R.L. Weir (as Resident), 'KLM has definitely reached a stage for high-speed passenger liners, for they spoke quite confidently of flying from Europe to India in one day at no very distant date.'[6] He loved flying and would have loved the jet age.

On 14 May 1937, he attended the opening of the Imperial Conference at St James's Palace, London. The Maharaja's address to the prime minister and members of the conference ran along these lines: 'It is my privilege to address the Imperial Conference on behalf of India on this historic occasion, when the conference follows closely upon the coronation of the sovereign to whom the great communities here represented all acknowledge allegiance.

'The splendid and moving ceremony of two days ago, the vast crowds gathered together in order and freedom at the centre of the British Commonwealth, the presence here today of men representing different communities in widely-separated parts of the world—all remind us that the crown remains as it has been for generations. It is still surrounded and sustained by the reverence and affections of millions; it is still the visible symbol of the Empire's unity and the centre of loyalties.

'We are confident that His present Majesty, with his gracious consort by his side, will show himself a worthy heir of the highest traditions of the British monarchy; and as spokesman today of the government, princes and people of India, I tender to Their Majesties respectful greetings and our assurances of unswerving devotion and attachment.

'The internal affairs of India are not before this conference, but you will not expect that, speaking for India today, I should pass them over in silence. For sixty years, I have been closely concerned with public affairs in my own state and outside it. During that long stretch of time, I have striven to watch events and, what is more, to interpret them with detachment—to divine those unseen currents of ideas, emotions, aspirations, which ultimately determine the course of history. Nowhere do those currents flow more strongly than in India today. The great cities of India ferment with social and industrial vigour. But much more far-reaching is the fact that the traditional life of the peasant, the very foundation of India, is being touched, I will not say shaken, by many influences—it is awakening from a long quiescence. It is not too much to say that the whole of India pulsates with life. And this vast energy which is now being realized—to what goal is it to lead her many millions? I answer, politically—towards the attainment of her full stature as an autonomous unit of the British Commonwealth of Nations; socially—towards the attainment of the ideal inseparably bound up with that Commonwealth; freedom perfected by order, order perfected by freedom.

'In that attainment, India will have no mean contribution of her own to make to the Commonwealth. No two nations, no two races, interpret and realize those words "order" and "freedom" in precisely the same way; but their realization may be none the less true and rich if they are transmuted by the genius of individual people. If India has received and will continue to receive much from the Commonwealth, she has equally much to give. I should wish to conclude these few remarks by expressing our gratitude to you, Sir, for the welcome which you have just given to us in such cordial terms, and by offering to His Majesty's government our sincere thanks for the abundant and gracious hospitality extended to us.'[7]

The above speech is important for its subtle inference to India attaining her freedom. At the Oxford Raleigh Club, he had the unique experience of sharing the platform with the renowned orator Winston Churchill on 22 May of the same year. Speaking for the first time at Oxford, he described it as 'renowned as the home of liberal thought which has given so many great men to India, I am to respond on behalf of India to the toast of the British Commonwealth.

'The British Commonwealth is based upon one fundamental conception—freedom. Within each nation of the British Commonwealth, the individual has or at least we desire him to have, that freedom; each nation is free within the Commonwealth—free to develop according to its own genius and to determine its own destiny.

'The Commonwealth stands before the world as a British League of Nations and as such is a factor of ever growing importance in preserving the world's peace.

'The ideal underlying our present understanding of the Commonwealth may not always have been there but happily the Commonwealth is alive. It can and does constantly adapt itself, though sometimes tardily, to changing conditions. Looking to the future, I can see a still greater destiny for the Commonwealth along the lines which I will attempt to indicate briefly. It is not merely the western races that can achieve their destiny within the Commonwealth. There is a definite place for other races which have grown up with other civilizations and other conceptions of life. As in Greece so in India, with her ancient traditions and civilization, the underlying principles of the Commonwealth were known and practised many years ago, though the modern electoral system is new to us. And nowadays, a new and vigorous spirit is to be detected everywhere. I feel that if broadminded statesmanship demonstrates that there is room for India and all that India stands for, within my conception of Commonwealth ideals, then only will the Commonwealth achieve its highest mission...

'It is not an uncommon suggestion that an eventual clash between Europe and Asia is inevitable. But with India as a free autonomous unit in the Commonwealth such a clash cannot occur and is indeed inconceivable.

'To my mind, it is only along these lines that future development can lie, if we are true to our ideals. Anyone who talks in this strain may be called an idealist but great empires cannot be built without idealism. ... India as a contented member of the British Commonwealth will be an effective safeguard against any clash between East and West, and I am confident that statesmanship in England and India will work steadily to secure that contentment. If impatience is deemed to be injurious, the retarding of an inevitable development would not be in accordance with the ideals of the great Commonwealth to the toast of which I have the honour to respond on behalf of India.'

It was a hint that there was no stopping India from obtaining her independence.

A couple of days later, Sayajirao III was at Grosvenor House replying to Baldwyn's toast to the British Commonwealth, Empire Day Dinner:

'Your Royal Highness, My Lord Chairman, Prime Minister, Lords, Ladies and Gentlemen, it is indeed an honour to be asked to answer the toast proposed tonight by Mr Baldwyn. He has held for years the high office of Prime Minister of the United Kingdom. We all know that he is now to relinquish that office. It has been held in the past by many great men but none I believe in whom the Empire has felt more undivided confidence. He takes with him from the conflicts of the House of Commons, the affection and esteem of the many millions who constitute the people of the British Commonwealth.

'That Commonwealth is no mechanical aggregation of races; it is a living organism, changing and developing as does everything in life. At heart of its being are the two moving principles of liberty and of order; and if it to be true to itself, those two principles will always govern the changes and development which are the unfolding of its innermost nature. Such changes are the necessary accompaniment of human development and the necessary condition of human happiness among the great peoples whom they directly touch.

'The happiness of the people is the test by which ultimately all forms of government, all constitutions come to be judged. Will posterity hereafter be able to point to the new Constitution of India, and say, "With all its complexities, with all the imperfections inherent in such a work of human minds, this was, on the whole, a successful attempt to promote human dignity, brotherhood and happiness in a vast population over a vast area of the earth's surface?" This new constitution is admittedly a welcome step towards our goal of a free and autonomous unit within the Commonwealth, though more rapid and extensive progress would have been preferred by my countrymen. So, we may cherish the hope that India's political development will win from posterity a verdict to that effect. I am certain that those words may already be used concerning the great organization of which India is a part—the British Commonwealth of Nations. It is that hope and that certainty which are the source of the deep pleasure I feel in responding to this toast.'[8]

Two weeks later, on 11 June, he was making a speech at the East India Association's reception to Indian delegates to the Imperial Conference, Grosvenor House. Here in his speech, he talked of changing times and the fast-approaching changes in the eastern part of the world: 'The East is said never to move, but the East is changing fast. We are imitating some of your best things and with the adoption of such manners and customs I think it will be much easier to mix than it has been hitherto.'[9]

Whenever the occasion arose and the time was ripe to talk of universal brotherhood he grasped it with both hands and emphasized the need to unite, whether in India or abroad or London at the prestigious Grosvenor House.

At Edwin Haward's lecture given before the East India Association on 'India and the Far Eastern Crisis' at Caxton Hall, London, on 11 April 1938, the Maharaja was asked to say a few words on the subject. He began by admitting that the subject was new to him, very controversial and of great importance, 'So far as India and China are concerned, there is no doubt that it is very old. Many ideas, superstitions and even matters of taste are common to us. For example, the garments worn by ladies in India closely resemble those worn in China... If you want to change a nation or a race, you must go to the village, to the family, and to each individual member of the family. Educate them in the right way, give them an outlook on life and above all, serve their economic needs. Then probably you can expect greater independence, greater interest and a greater striving for better conditions than they have at present. To improve economic conditions a fundamental problem in India, we must come in contact with the rest of the world, see the march of progress and study what may be profitably introduced into India, so that in the end we may be able to serve other nations.

'People who were originally divided by caste are now divided by nationality. Each nationality tries to make itself as complete and self-contained as possible, and thus the law of division ever continues. If there were a little more sympathy, a little more kindness and cooperation, more sustained effort to benefit humanity as a whole, there are important problems in which, without restriction of caste and creed, we might combine and increase the happiness of mankind. For that purpose, nations which are oppressed or which have only partial liberty, should be given greater freedom, as the British government is doing in India... India needs freedom and that freedom should be wisely, properly and quickly given.'[10]

As usual, he shunted between London and Paris, but his health was beginning to let him down again and he faulted the weather as being 'very trying'. In early August, he was bedridden but recovered soon enough to go to Lausanne where he chose to spend the rest of the summer and returned to India for the winter season in Baroda. Reaching Bombay, however, he was very ill, with a uremic condition which made him unconscious. Chimnabai II had to be summoned from London to be at his bedside. After this bout of illness, he recovered well enough to make plans for leaving Bombay and returning to his home and palace in Baroda. It had been months since he had been away and now he was longing to be back, but it was not to be. He suffered a setback in the end of November. With treatment, he recovered sufficiently after a week to sit up in bed, only to die on 6 February 1939.

The Maharaja's mortal remains were brought to Baroda by a special train that very night and were cremated according to Hindu rites the following day. His ashes were immersed in the holy waters at the confluence of the Ganga and Yamuna rivers.

With that last act, nothing remained of the great phenomenal ruler except what he had left behind, along with memories. A man who had come to Baroda because he was born to rule had left behind the fruits of his labour that for generations to come the people of Baroda would enjoy.

His actions had always been guided by the policy which Shakespeare's words sum up:

'Let all the ends thou aimest at be thy country's,

Thy God's and Truth's'

With his passing, the golden era ended and the curtain was rung down forever on the most glorious reign of one of the greatest rulers who had ever lived.

The war and its aftermath plunged the world into darkness with cataclysmic consequences.

The sweeping tide of independence washed away the old glory that had once clothed the country with a shining mantle of grandeur. The Raj too had wound up, and the new government did not take long to put Sayajirao III's prophecy into practice, for it wound up the princely states too, but 'that chiselled pile' a testimony of a glorious past still stands today in the town of Baroda.

Epilogue

Much has been said and written about Maharaja Sayajirao Gaekwad III and yet there remains a lot more to be said. I have transcribed some of the great ruler's speeches, which are important as a manifestation of his character that was exemplary to the point of causing incredibility in those who did not know him for he had none of the normal human failings that govern those in power. To transcribe all his speeches would require a few volumes. Hence only a few of them can be read in the book.

We have seen earlier that since he had lost three of his sons and one lay dying with no hope of recovery, the Maharaja chose to groom his grandson Pratapsinghrao for the most responsible position in the state once he had vacated it. Pratapsinghrao Gaekwad carried out his grandfather's wishes and made his dream come true. He was instrumental in expanding the University of Baroda, which was initially founded by his grandfather and named it most appropriately as Maharaja Sayajirao University.

The Faculty of Arts building has not changed in its exteriors since the previous century. It continues to command attention with its imposing façade. Built in the Indo-Saracenic style of architecture, it is a fusion of the Indian and Byzantine styles in its arches and domes built in brick and polychrome stone. Seen at sunset, the building glows in a mélange of russet and gold—a sight that stops you in your tracks as you walk on the pavement outside. It certainly is a proud reminder of the achievements of the Gaekwads. Pratapsinghrao aided and abetted the advance of education just the way his grandfather would have wished him to do. He also settled the Sayajirao Diamond Jubilee Memorial Trust which exists till date catering to the educational and other needs of the people of the former Baroda state and has its origin in the Baroda Science College established in 1881. The tradition to uphold education and use it in the service of mankind, as laid down by Sayajirao III, continues to be carried on by his descendants.

Pratapsingrao's eldest son, Fatehsinghrao IV succeeded to the throne after his father was deposed in 1951 by the government of India. Pratapsinghrao had committed bigamy by marrying Sitadevi who was the daughter of the

Maharaja of Pitapuram. She was already married to Apparao Bahadur, a zamindar of Vuyuru in modern-day Telangana and was a mother of three children. Sitadevi had set her cap at Pratapsinghrao who was reputed to be the eighth richest man in the world with the sole object of becoming the queen of Baroda and enjoying all that copious wealth. They met at the Madras races in 1943 and Pratapsinghrao fell in love with her. Pratapsinghrao was a much married man with eight children. His wife Shantadevi was the daughter of Sardar Hanskar Mansinghrao Subbarao of Hasur. She was married to Pratapsinghrao in January 1929. Shantadevi was well read and articulate and was the president of the Kamatibaug Women's Club in Baroda.

After consulting her legal advisers, Sitadevi obtained a divorce from her husband by adopting Islam. Once she obtained her divorce, she reconverted to Hinduism in order to marry the king. The viceroy strongly objected to the marriage on grounds of the anti-bigamy law that had been passed earlier by the British government in India. But objections were overruled with Pratapsinghrao claiming that the anti-bigamy law did not apply to Maharajas who in the past had had more than one wife. His dewan, V.T. Krishnamachari, a staunch conservative and other state officials strongly advised Pratapsinghrao that both for public opinion and administrative reasons he should not contract a marriage with Sitadevi. The dewan even went to the extent of threatening to resign from his post if the Maharaja brought Sitadevi into the palace. Pratapsinghrao ignored their advice and threats and went ahead. They were married and in 1946 they left to reside in Europe. Krishnamachari resigned from his dewanship and other officials too showed their disapproval by following in his footsteps.

When India got its independence Pratapsinghrao and his wife returned to India and demanded of the new government that Indian kings should be allowed to rule their respective states, independent of the central government. As matters were getting out of hand, the government of India deposed him in 1951, and his son Fatehsinghrao IV was declared the Maharaja of Baroda. Sitadevi, known as the Indian Wallis Simpson, obtained vast sums of money and jewellery, including some from the famed Gaekwad collection. She auctioned the Gaekwads' valuable paintings in Paris and made a fortune out of it for herself. She left Pratapsinghrao once he was stripped of the title of Maharaja, leaving him alone to live out his days as an embittered soul in Paris. The entire episode had the family of the Gaekwads in the throes of unspeakable misery, apart from arousing anger in the city of Baroda and giving rise to agitations in some areas where the orthodox community lived. The episode unfortunately obliterated all the constructive work done by the king prior to the scandal. Pratapsinghrao died in 1968.

Fatehsinghrao IV was the chancellor of the university till 1988. A keen sportsperson, he was well known for his involvement in the cricket test matches. He dabbled in politics with panache and secured a membership in the Rajya Sabha. That he had inherited his great-grandfather's genes is evident from the success he obtained in all his ventures. His younger brother Ranjit Singh took over the mantle of responsibility as the Maharaja of Baroda in 1988 following Fatehsinghrao IV's death. He too followed the family tradition by encouraging music, art and talent. He died in 2012. His wife Her Highness Maharani Shubhangini Raje is as dynamic and versatile. An honours graduate in English literature with history and economics as minor subjects from Loreto College, Lucknow, she does constructive work as the chancellor of the Maharaja Sayajirao University. She stood twice in the general elections—as an independent candidate in 1996 and again in 2004 as a Bharatiya Janata Party (BJP) candidate—from Kheda district. An articulate person, a chat with her, which I was able to cadge, was a charming experience. When I asked her opinion on British rule in India, she had this to say, 'British rule in India at that point of time was good because it helped the country to develop, though they did wield power in a way that was not in accordance with one's self-respect and dignity, still in many ways they helped us to progress.'

What was Her Highness's opinion on the durbar incident?

'Oh, that was deliberate on his part!' she exclaimed. 'You just have to watch the film showing the royals of India at the Royal Albert Hall in London and the proof is there for all to see.'

After a while, she explained, 'The British were the paramount power in India and you had no choice in matters of paying obeisance to the emperor, I mean King George *was* the emperor ruling India and that was it.'

As to what Shubhangini Raje would like to change in Baroda, the Rajmata pointed out that she would like to bring a more organized system of planning in the layout of the city.

And anything in the history of the Gaekwads that she would like to change?

'Yes! One can't change the past but I would like to erase the Sitadevi episode in my father-in-law's life which had cast such a gloom in the environment of the palace. My father-in-law carried on the good work from 1939 after his grandfather left the state in his capable hands, and would have done much more if he had not been made to abdicate the throne in 1951.'

Pratapsinghrao had all the capabilities and qualities required for developing a state and bringing in progress by leaps and bounds. Unfortunately, people remember the Sitadevi episode which seems to have erased from their minds all the good work Pratapsinghrao did for the people of Baroda. His work in education, particularly with regard to the university, is remarkable. Sayajirao III founded the Baroda College but the credit for founding the university and making it one of the most prestigious ones in India must be given to his grandson Pratapsinghrao.

Regarding her position as the chancellor of the university, Shubhangini Raje is kept busy with hardly any time for leisure though the university has been in the hands of the Gujarat government. 'The government has five representatives in the senate, the vice chancellor has two, and I do not have *even* one to represent me in the senate!' She laments over it but has not allowed it to deter her from carrying on the Gaekwad royal family tradition of working for the cause of education.

Samarjitsingh Gaekwad is the present Maharaja of Baroda. The only son of the late Ranjit Singh and Shubhangini Raje, he is the seventeenth ruler to ascend the gaddi in the Gaekwad dynasty. Early schooling in Doon School provided him with the necessary discipline and exposure. He joined the Maharaja Sayajirao University of Baroda and is a graduate in marketing. With a good physique, Samarjitsingh Gaekwad was a former Ranji Trophy player and is a keen sportsman. He is the president of the Baroda Cricket Association. For the past ten years, Samarjitsingh Gaekwad has been a member on various committees, including the important working and technical committees of the Board of Control for Cricket in India. In addition to this, he also represents three important local clubs as their patron, which cater to over 5,000 children across different age groups. He is credited with building the first private championship golf course in Gujarat. He is also president of the Gaekwad Baroda Golf Club.

In the year 2017, Samarjitsingh Gaekwad became the first member from Gujarat to be elected council member of the Indian Golf Union, the government-approved body for golf in India.

Samarjitsingh Gaekwad is now founder president of the recently formed Gujarat Heritage Hotels Association to promote heritage properties in Gujarat. Most importantly, he is very involved with the Maharaja Sayajirao University as a senate member. Keen on following the path laid down by his erstwhile ancestor—Sayajirao III—he wishes to get more deeply involved with education in the university.

In my interview with Samarjitsingh Gaekwad, when he was asked who according to him should get the credit for bringing Sayajirao III to the throne as ruler of Baroda, his quick reply was, 'Jamnabai, of course. She managed to pull it off!'

This corroborates the story of the part she played in conniving with Phayre to depose Malharrao in 1877.

As a trustee of the Maharaja Sayajirao Diamond Jubilee Trust, Samarjitsingh actively participates in the various rural development programmes undertaken by the trust—making check dams to digging bore wells, helping bright children in the villages get access to advanced education in Baroda or Ahmedabad colleges and providing them subsidized accommodation in hostels in both the cities of Gujarat.

Radhika Raje, daughter-in-law of Shubhangini Raje, is also very involved in the upliftment of the downtrodden. She is young with none of the 'airs' that one would normally associate with a queen and is very sympathetic towards the plight of destitute women. She has arranged for many of them to receive vocational training where they are taught needlework, embroidery, fabric painting, block printing, bookbinding, etc., so that they can be engaged as skilled labourers in private industries and eke out a living for themselves and educate their children. She feels strongly that the children of these poor women should obtain the necessary tools for improving their living standards and live well. She is also very actively involved with NGOs.

The descendants of Sayajirao Gaekwad III have certainly done him proud! By 'Huzur Order!'

Acknowledgements

My grateful thanks to Shubhangini Raje Gaekwad, the Rajmata and chancellor of the Maharaja Sayajirao University, Baroda, for her encouragement in writing this book and for facilitating research through the assistance of her staff in the university.

My grateful thanks to Samarjitsingh Gaekwad for the interview with him in Baroda.

My grateful thanks to Radhika Raje for the interview with her.

My grateful thanks to Ujwala Raje Gaekwad Shah for initiating the process and for her kind hospitality shown to me over the years in Baroda.

My grateful thanks to the government of Gujarat for their kind permission to research their archives and incorporate the information in this book.

My grateful thanks to Professor Parimal Vyas, vice chancellor of the M. S. University, for his valuable guidance.

My grateful thanks to Miss Adhya Saxena, head of the History Department of the M. S. University for her valuable guidance on the books for reference.

My grateful thanks to Bansilal Sharma for the anecdotes on Sayajirao Gaekwad III.

My grateful thanks to Dr D. V. Nene for sharing with me information from the book in Marathi authored by him.

My grateful thanks to M. R. Adwanikar for translating some of the information from Dr Nene's book.

My grateful thanks to Manda Hingurao, curator of the Maharaja Fatehsingh Museum for all her help in photocopying F. A. H. Elliot's book *Rulers of Baroda*.

My grateful thanks to Dr Sweta Prajapati, director of the Oriental Institute, for all her help.

My grateful thanks to Dr N. Pushpa Patel for extending her kind hospitality to me in Baroda.

My grateful thanks to the librarian of the Oriental Institute, Digambar Kashikar for all his help.

My grateful thanks to Selina, the librarian in the Hansa Mehta Hall Library.

My grateful thanks to the staff of the Sarkarwada Library, Palace Library for their assistance in locating the books and for photocopying.

My grateful thanks to Miss Kejal for all her help.

My grateful thanks to the Archeological Department of Gujarat.

My grateful thanks to Mrs Ranu Mukherjee Vanikar for her guidance.

My grateful thanks to Makarand Musale for some valuable information on Sayajirao Gaekwad III.

My grateful thanks to Chandrashekhar Patil, professor in the Faculty of Fine Arts, Baroda for some valuable information on Sayajirao Gaekwad III.

My grateful thanks to the British Library, The Department of Asian Manuscripts and India Office Records, for letting me source information from their files on 'Baroda Affairs'.

Endnotes

CHAPTER 1

1. Fatehsinghrao Gaekwad, *Sayajirao of Baroda: The Prince and the Man* (Bombay: Popular Prakashan, 1989), p. 9.

CHAPTER 4

1. F.A.H. Elliot, *Rulers of Baroda* (London: Education Society, Oxford University Press, 1897), p. 48.
2. Ibid., p. 50.

CHAPTER 5

1. Elliot, *Rulers of Baroda*, p. 55.

CHAPTER 6

1. Elliot, *Rulers of Baroda*, p. 59.
2. Ibid., p. 73.

CHAPTER 8

1. Elliot, *Rulers of Baroda*, p. 125.
2. Ibid., p. 160.
3. Ibid., p.160.
4. Ibid., p. 160.
5. Ibid., p. 161.
6. Ibid., p. 138.
7. Ibid., p. 142.
8. Ibid., p. 143.
9. Ibid., p. 149.
10. Ibid., p. 154.
11. Ibid., p. 151.
12. Ibid., p. 155.
13. Ibid., p. 158.
14. Ibid.

CHAPTER 9

1. Elliot, *Rulers of Baroda*.
2. Ibid., p. 176.
3. Ibid., pp. 177, 178.

CHAPTER 10

1. Elliot, *Rulers of Baroda*, p. 184.
2. Ibid.
3. Ibid.
4. Gaekwad, *Sayajirao of Baroda*, p. 29.
5. Elliot, *Rulers of Baroda*, p. 191.
6. Ibid., p. 198.
7. Ibid.
8. Ibid., p. 182.

CHAPTER 11

1. Elliot, *Rulers of Baroda*, p. 160.
2. Ibid.
3. Ibid.
4. Ibid., p. 161.
5. Ibid., p. 207.
6. Gaekwad, *Sayajirao of Baroda*.
7. Ibid., pp. 29, 30.

CHAPTER 12

1. India Office Records on Baroda Affairs, British Library, London. File EURF/126/95. Period 1875.
2. Gaekwad, *Sayajirao of Baroda*.
3. Ibid., p. 34.
4. Ibid., p. 35.
5. Ibid., p. 37.
6. India Office Records on Baroda Affairs, British Library, London. File EURF126/95.

CHAPTER 13

1. Gaekwad, *Sayajirao of Baroda*, p. 48.

CHAPTER 14

1. Gaekwad, *Sayajirao of Baroda*, p. 51.
2. Ibid.

CHAPTER 15

1. Sergeant, *The Ruler of Baroda*, p. 32.
2. Ibid.
3. Sergeant, *The Ruler of Baroda*, p. 36.
4. Gaekwad, *Sayajirao of Baroda*, p. 59.
5. Sergeant, *The Ruler of Baroda*, p. 37.
6. Ibid., p. 40.
7. Gaekwad, *Sayajirao of Baroda*, p. 70.

CHAPTER 17

1. Gaekwad, *Sayajirao of Baroda*, p. 86.
2. Charles D. Hazen, *Modern Europe up to 1945* (New Delhi: S. Chand, 1963), p. 189.
3. Gaekwad, *Sayajirao of Baroda*, p. 85.
4. Ibid., p. 82.
5. Ibid., p. 86.

CHAPTER 19

1. Gujarat state archives, Baroda.
2. Sergeant, *The Ruler of Baroda*, p. 61.
3. Ibid.

CHAPTER 20

1. Gaekwad, *Sayajirao of Baroda*, pp. 82.

CHAPTER 21

1. Gaekwad, *Sayajirao of Baroda*, p. 95.
2. Ibid., p. 96.
3. Sharma, Bansilal, *Lok Smruthi Mein Sayajirao*. Delhi: Lokvani Prakashan, 2006.
4. Gaekwad, *Sayajirao of Baroda*, p. 98.
5. Sergeant, *The Ruler of Baroda*, p. 62.
6. *Speeches and Addresses of Sayajirao-III (1877-1927)*, p. 29. London: MacMillan & Co, 1928.

CHAPTER 22

1. Gaekwad, *Sayajirao of Baroda*, p. 105.
2. Nene, D.V., *Shrimant Sayajirao Gaekwad*. Pune: Ved Gandharva, 2010. Translated from Marathi into English by M.R. Advanikar.

CHAPTER 23

1. Sergeant, *The Ruler of Baroda*, p. 77.
2. Ibid., p. 78.
3. Ibid., p. 79.
4. Ibid.

CHAPTER. 25

1. Sergeant, *The Ruler of Baroda*, p. 82.
2. Ibid.
3. Ibid., p. 83.

CHAPTER 26

1. Gaekwad, *Sayajirao of Baroda*, p. 120.

2. Ibid., p. 121.
3. Ibid., p. 125.
4. Ibid., p. 137.
5. Ibid., p. 78.
6. Ibid., p. 79.

CHAPTER 27

1. Gaekwad, *Sayajirao of Baroda,* p. 129.
2. Ibid., p. 129.
3. *Speeches & Addresses of Sayajirao Gaekwad III (1877-1927)*. London: MacMillan & Co, 1928.

CHAPTER 28

1. Gaekwad, *Sayajirao of Baroda,* p. 146.
2. Sergeant, *The Ruler of Baroda,* p. 87.

CHAPTER 29

1. Gaekwad, *Sayajirao of Baroda,* p. 152.
2. Ibid., p. 152.
3. India Office Records on Baroda Affairs, British Library, London. File IOR/126.
4. Ibid.
5. Ibid.
6. Gaekwad, *Sayajirao of Baroda,* p. 159.

CHAPTER 30

1. Gaekwad, *Sayajirao of Baroda,* p. 162.
2. Ibid., p. 171.
3. Sergeant, *The Ruler of Baroda,* p. 97.
4. Ibid., p. 98.

CHAPTER 31

1. *Speeches & Addresses of Sayajirao Gaekwad III (1877-1927)*. London: MacMillan & Co, 1928.
2. Ibid.

CHAPTER 32

1. Sergeant, *The Ruler of Baroda,* p. 102.
2. Ibid.
3. Gaekwad, *Sayajirao of Baroda,* p. 181.
4. Ibid., p. 182.
5. Ibid.
6. Sergeant, *The Ruler of Baroda,* p. 103.
7. Ibid., p. 105.

8. Gaekwad, *Sayajirao of Baroda*, p. 185.
9. Sergeant, *The Ruler of Baroda*, p. 106.
10. Ibid., p. 107.
11. Gaekwad, *Sayajirao of Baroda*, p. 194.
12. Ibid., p. 195.
13. Sergeant, *The Ruler of Baroda*, 110.
14. Ibid.
15. Ibid., p. 110.
16. Ibid., p. 197.
17. Sergeant, *The Ruler of Baroda*, p. 112.
18. Sergeant, *The Ruler of Baroda*, p. 113.
19. Ibid., p. 114.

CHAPTER 34

1. *Speeches & Addresses of Sayajirao Gaekwad III* (1877-1927). London: MacMillan & Co, 1928. pp. 117, 118.
2. Ibid., pp. 122, 123.
3. An anecdote as told to the author by Prof. Patil-Faculty of Fine Arts-Baroda.
4. Sergeant, *The Ruler of Baroda*, p. 116.
5. *Speeches & Addresses of Sayajirao Gaekwad III* (1877-1927), pp. 75, 76.
6. Ibid., p. 77.
7. Ibid., p. 78.
8. Ibid., pp. 79, 80.
9. Sharma, *Lok Smruthi Mein Sayajirao*.
10. Gaekwad, *Sayajirao of Baroda*, p. 205.
11. Sergeant, *The Ruler of Baroda*, p. 120.

CHAPTER 35

1. *Speeches & Addresses of Sayajirao Gaekwad III* (1877-1927). London: MacMillan & Co., 1928.
2. Rice, Stanley. *Life of Sayajirao-III, Maharaja of Baroda*. London: H. Milford, 1931, p. 5.
3. Ibid., p. 6.
4. Ibid.
5. Sharma, *Lok Smruthi Mein Sayajirao*.
6. Ibid.
7. Sergeant, *The Ruler of Baroda*, p. 123.
8. Ibid., p. 124.
9. Ibid.
10. Ibid.

CHAPTER 36

1. Rice, *Life of Sayajirao-III*, p. 6.
2. Ibid., p. 6.

3. Sergeant, *The Ruler of Baroda*, pp. 127, 128.
4. D.S. Damodar Savlaram Yande, ed., *Sayaji Gaurav Granth*. Baroda: Vadhadivas Mandal, 1933.
5. Gaekwad, *Sayajirao of Baroda*, p. 227.

CHAPTER 37

1. Gaekwad, *Sayajirao of Baroda*, p. 224.
2. Ibid., p. 232.
3. Ibid., p. 233.
4. Ibid., p. 237, 238.
5. Ibid. pg 239.
6. Gaekwad, *Sayajirao of Baroda*, p. 239.
7. Ibid., p. 240.
8. India Office Records, London.
9. Ibid.
10. Ibid.
11. Gaekwad, *Sayajirao of Baroda*, p. 240.

CHAPTER 38

1. India Office Records on Baroda Affairs, British Library, London.

CHAPTER 39

1. India Office Records, London.
2. Ibid.
3. Ibid.
4. Ibid.
5. Ibid.
6. Ibid.

CHAPTER 40

1. Gaekwad, *Sayajirao of Baroda*, p. 251.
2. Ibid.
3. Ibid., p. 252.
4. Ibid.
5. Ibid., p. 253.
6. Ibid., p. 254.
7. Ibid., p. 254.
8. Ibid., p. 256.
9. Ibid., p. 256.
10. Ibid., p. 264.
11. Ibid., p. 265.
12. Ibid., p. 266.
13. Ibid., p. 268.
14. Ibid.

15. Ibid., p. 268.
16. Ibid., p. 276.
17. Ibid., p. 277.
18. Ibid.
19. Ibid.
20. Ibid
21. Ibid., p. 278.

CHAPTER 41

1. Sharma, *Lok Smruthi Mein Sayajirao*.
2. Ibid.
3. Gaekwad, *Sayajirao of Baroda*, p. 331.
4. India Office Records on Baroda Affairs, British Library, London. IOR I/1/169, L/PS/10/264/2.

CHAPTER 42

1. Sergeant, *The Ruler of Baroda* , p. 145.
2. Gaekwad, *Sayajirao of Baroda*, pp. 280-81.

CHAPTER 43

1. Gaekwad, *Sayajirao of Baroda*, p. 283.
2. Ibid., p. 286.
3. Ibid., p. 288.
4. Ibid., p. 289.

CHAPTER 45

1. Gaekwad, *Sayajirao of Baroda*, p. 293.
2. Sergeant, *The Ruler of Baroda*, p. 148.
3. Ibid., p. 149.
4. Gaekwad, *Sayajirao of Baroda*, p. 297.
5. India Office Records on Baroda Affairs, British Library, London. IOR 2/531/294.
6. Sergeant, *The Ruler of Baroda*, p. 153.
7. Ibid.
8. Ibid., p. 153.
9. Ibid., p. 154.
10. Ibid., p.155.
11. Ibid., p. 157.

CHAPTER 46

1. Sergeant, *The Ruler of Baroda*, p. 160.
2. Nene, *Shrimant Sayajirao Gaekwad*.
3. Ibid.
4. Sergeant, *The Ruler of Baroda*, p. 161.

5. Gujarat State Archives, Baroda.
6. Fatehsinghrao Gaekwad, *Sayajirao of Baroda*, p. 289.
7. Ibid.
8. Ibid., p. 290.
9. Gujarat State Archives, Baroda.
10. Ibid.
11. Ibid.
12. Ibid.
13. Ibid.

CHAPTER 48

1. Gujarat State Archives, Baroda.
2. Ibid.
3. Sharma, *Lok Smruthi Mein Sayajirao*.
4. Gujarat State Archives, Baroda.
5. Ibid.
6. Ibid.
7. Ibid.
8. Ibid.
9. Ibid.
10. Ibid.
11. Ibid.
12. Ibid.
13. Ibid.
14. Ibid.

CHAPTER 49

1. Sergeant, *The Ruler of Baroda*, p. 164.

CHAPTER 50

1. Gaekwad, *Sayajirao of Baroda*, p. 346.
2. Ibid., p. 347.
3. Ibid., p. 348.
4. Sergeant, *The Ruler of Baroda*, p. 179.

CHAPTER 51

1. Gaekwad, *Sayajirao of Baroda*, p. 349.
2. Ibid., pp. 349-351.
3. Sergeant, *The Ruler of Baroda*, pp. 181-82.
4. *Sayajirao Gaekwad III, Speeches and Addresses, 1927-1938*, pp. 727–728.
5. Ibid., p. 723.

CHAPTER 53

1. Gujarat State Archives, Baroda.
2. Ibid.
3. Gaekwad, *Sayajirao of Baroda*, p. 352.
4. Ibid., p. 353.

CHAPTER 54

1. Sharma, *Lok Smruthi Mein Sayajirao*.
2. Ibid.
3. Gujarat State Archives, Baroda.
4. Sergeant, *The Ruler of Baroda*, p. 195.
5. Ibid., p. 196.
6. Ibid.

CHAPTER 55

1. Sayajirao Gaekwad III, Maharaja of Baroda. *Speeches and Addresses, 1927-1938*. Cambridge: Privately printed at the University Press, vol. 4, 1938, p. 729.

CHAPTER 56

1. Yande, *Sayaji Gaurav Granth*, pp. 115.
2. Ibid.
3. Ibid., p. 124.
4. Ibid., p. 127.
5. Ibid., p. 201.
6. Ibid., p. 201.
7. Baroda Archives.

CHAPTER 57

1. Yande, ed. Vadhadivas Mandal, *Sayaji Gaurav Granth*.
2. Ibid.
3. Ibid.
4. Ibid.
5. Ibid.

CHAPTER 58

1. Yande, ed. Vadhadivas Mandal, *Sayaji Gaurav Granth*.
2. Nene, *Shrimant Sayajirao Gaekwad*.
3. Ibid.
4. Ibid.

CHAPTER 59

1. Wikipedia.

CHAPTER 60

1. Yande, ed., *Sayaji Gaurav Granth.*
2. Nene *Shrimant Sayajirao Gaekwad.*
3. Gujarat State Archives, Baroda.
4. Yande, ed. Vadhadivas Mandal, *Sayaji Gaurav Granth.*

CHAPTER 61

1. Sergeant, *The Ruler of Baroda*, p. 125.
2. Gujarat State Archives, Baroda.
3. Ibid.
4. Ibid.
5. Sharma, *Lok Smruthi Mein Sayajirao.*
6. Gujarat State Archives, Baroda.
7. Ibid.
8. Ibid.
9. Ibid.
10. Ibid.
11. Sharma, *Lok Smruthi Mein Sayajirao.*
12. Gujarat State Archives, Baroda.
13. Ibid.
14. India Office Records on Baroda Affairs, British Library, London.
15. Ibid.
16. Ibid.
17. Ibid.
18. *Speeches & Addresses of Sayajirao Gaekwad III (1877-1927)*, p. 723.
19. V.K. Chavda, *Gaekwads and the British 1878-1920*, p. 173.
20. Ibid., p. 177.
21. Ibid.
22. Ibid., p. 775.
23. Ibid., p. 820.
24. Nene, *Shrimanth Sayajirao Gaekwad.*

CHAPTER 62

1. India Office Records on Baroda Affairs, British Library, London. IOR 2/531/294.
2. Ibid IOR 126/88-83.
3. Gaekwad, *Sayajirao of Baroda*, p. 213.
4. Ibid. p. 250.
5. Nene, *Shrimant Sayajirao Gaekwad.*
6. Ibid.
7. Ibid.
8. Gujarat State Archives, Baroda.
9. Ibid.
10. Ibid.
11. Ibid.

12. Ibid.
13. Ibid.
14. Gaekwad, *Sayajirao of Baroda*, p. 341.
15. Ibid., p. 343.
16. Sergeant, *The Ruler of Baroda*, p. 271.
17. Gaekwad, *Sayairao of Baroda*, p. 343.
18. *Speeches & Addresses of Sayajirao Gaekwad III (1934-1938)*, pp. 864-866.
19. Nene, *Shrimant Sayajirao Gaekwad.*
20. Gujarat State Archives, Baroda.
21. Nene, *Shrimanth Sayajirao Gaekwad.*
22. Gujarat State Archives.
23. Ibid.
24. Ibid.
25. Ibid.
26. As told to the author by Prof Patil, Faculty of Fine Arts, Baroda.
27. India Office Records on Baroda Affairs, British Library, London. IOR 4092.
28. Gujarat State Archives, Baroda.
29. Ibid.
30. Ibid.
31. Ibid.
32. Gaekwad, *Sayajirao of Baroda*, p.355.
33. Ibid., p. 359.
34. Gaekwad, *Sayajirao of Baroda*, p. 360.

CHAPTER 63

1. India Office Records on Baroda Affairs, British Library, London. IOR 2/531/294
2. Ibid.
3. Sayajirao Gaekwad III, Maharaja of Baroda. *Speeches and Addresses, 1934-1938*. Cambridge: Privately printed at the University Press, vol. 4, 1938, pp. 740, 741.
4. Ibid.

CHAPTER 64

1. Gaekwad, *Sayajirao of Baroda*, p. 369.
2. Sayajirao Gaekwad III, Maharaja of Baroda. *Speeches and Addresses, 1934-1938*. Cambridge: Privately printed at the University Press, vol. 4, 1938, pp. 781-785.
3. Gaekwad, *Sayajirao of Baroda*, p. 370.

CHAPTER 65

1. Gaekwad, *Sayajirao of Baroda*, p. 373/374.
2. Gujarat State Archives, Baroda.

CHAPTER 66

1. Gaekwad, *Sayajirao of Baroda*, p. 376.
2. Gaekwad, *Sayajirao of Baroda*, p. 379.

3. Ibid., p. 381.
4. Ibid., p. 382.
5. Ibid., p. 384.
6. Ibid.
7. *Speeches and Addresses of HH Sayajirao-III*, p. 858.
8. Ibid., p. 861.
9. Ibid., p. 862.
10. Ibid., p. 889.

Bibliography

Chavda, V.K. *Gaekwad and the British*. Baroda: M.C. Kothari, 1962.

Desai, Govindbhai (ed.) *Gazetteer of the Baroda State*, Vols. I & II. Baroda: G.H. Desai, 1923.

Elliot, F.A.H. *Rulers of Baroda*. London: Education Society-Oxford University Press, 1897.

Gaekwad, Fatehsinghrao. *Sayajirao of Baroda: The Prince and the Man*. Bombay: Popular Prakashan, 1989.

Gense, J.H. and D.R. Banaji (eds). *The Gaekwads of Baroda*. Bombay: D.B. Taraporevala & Sons, 1937.

Hazen, D. Charles. *Modern Europe up to 1945*. New Delhi: S. Chand (third edition), 1963.

Nene, D.V. *Shrimant Sayajirao*. Pune: Ved Gandharva, 2010. Translated from Marathi into English by M.R. Advanikar.

Rice, Stanley. *Life of Sayajirao-III, Maharaja of Baroda*. London: H. Milford, 1931.

Sayajirao Gaekwad III, *Maharaja of Baroda. Speeches and Addresses, 1927-1938*. Cambridge: Privately printed at the University Press, vol. 4, 1938.

Sayajirao Gaekwad III, *Maharaja of Baroda. Speeches and Addresses during 1877-1927*. London: MacMillan & Co, 1928.

Sergeant, W. Philip. *The Ruler of Baroda*. London: John Murray, 1928.

Sharma, Bansilal. *Lok Smruthi Mein Sayajirao*. Delhi: Lokvani Prakashan, 2006.

Yande, D.S. Damodar Savlaram (ed.), *Sayaji Gaurav Granth*. Baroda: Vadhadivas Mandal, 1933.

Archives

Gujarat State Archives, Baroda. Letters in original and copies from registers and files from 1885-1938.

India Office Records on Baroda Affairs, British Library, London.